Introduction to Security

Eighth Edition

Robert J. Fischer, Edward Halibozek, and Gion Green

ELSEVIER

AMSTERDAM • BOSTON • HEIDELBERG • LONDON
NEW YORK • OXFORD • PARIS • SAN DIEGO
SAN FRANCISCO • SINGAPORE • SYDNEY • TOKYO

Butterworth-Heinemann is an imprint of Elsevier

Acquisitions Editor: Pamela Chester
Marketing Manager: Marissa Hederson
Project Manager: Melinda Ritchie
Cover Design: Joanne Blank
Cover Images (clockwise): © FEMA Photo/Leif Skoogfors, US Department of Defense
Photo Archive/PA1 Chuck Kalnbach, Marvin Nauman/FEMA Photo
Composition: Charon Tec Ltd. (A Macmillan Company)
Printer/Binder: Sheridan Books

Butterworth-Heinemann is an imprint of Elsevier
30 Corporate Drive, Suite 400, Burlington, MA 01803, USA
Linacre House, Jordan Hill, Oxford OX2 8DP, UK

Library of Congress Cataloging-in-Publication Data
Application submitted

British Library Cataloguing-in-Publication Data
A catalogue record for this book is available from the British Library.

ISBN: 978-0-7506-8432-3

For information on all Butterworth-Heinemann
visit our Web site at www.books.elsevier.com

Printed in the United States of America
  09 10 11 12 10 9 8 7 6 5 4 3

Table of Contents

Preface

Although it has been only four years since the release of the seventh edition of this book, many changes have occurred since that writing, with more to come. As we write this eighth edition, a complete revolution in the security industry is occurring. The aftermath of the September 11, 2001, attacks on the World Trade Center in New York and the Pentagon in Washington, D.C., has shaken the security industry, whether private or governmental. Government involvement in the security business has become a must, as evidenced by the Airport Security Act of 2002. Additional legislation at the federal level, for example, indicates major changes in the U.S. government's involvement in the security industry since World War II. Whether this involvement is entirely positive or is heavy-handed, as exemplified by the suggestion of a national identification system, is yet to be seen.

Coupled with the security industry's response to the growing threat of world terrorism is the need to keep up with an ever so rapidly changing technology used both in the industry and against it by criminals. Protection of information, traditionally handled by placing it in vaults and marking it PROPRIETARY or TOP SECRET, has become ever more complex. Computer systems that now contain all types of information, from personal identification to inventory records, are making life both easier and more complex. Information exchange occurs in the click of a computer key. This exchange of information relies on the Internet, and there are plenty of examples that show that the computer network that is connected to the Internet is subject to attack by outside hackers and other criminals.

The seventh edition of this text sought to maintain the basic concepts of the first edition, covering the total picture and giving the reader a glimpse of diverse components that make up the security function. However, much of the security industry has undergone tremendous changes since the publication of the sixth edition in 1998. The World Trade Center has been bombed twice, and the Murrah Federal Building in Oklahoma City was victimized by American domestic terrorism. These attacks and President George W. Bush's call for an international coalition to wage war against world terrorism put the world's citizens on alert. The world of security changed on September 11, 2001. This eighth edition continues to utilize the same basic concepts that have made this text a basic primer in the security field. However, the success of the seventh edition and hopefully this eighth effort lies in the focus on current problems within the basic framework of security theory.

This new, thoroughly updated edition has three fewer chapters but not less material. Two chapters are still devoted entirely to the security issues created by the growing presence of world terrorism. In addition, new topics related to securing information, identity theft, transportation, contingency planning, and new forms of piracy are discussed.

Even as we put the final touches on this 2008 edition, the reality of the quickly changing times makes some of the materials outdated. However, we maintain the belief that the basic principles of loss prevention and security remain. The tools that allow us to apply the principles have become more sophisticated and are constantly changing. We still lock up our valuables. Some use traditional locks and keys, others have sophisticated electronic tools that operate electronic locks, while still other information is locked into databases using information technology security, including encryption and passwords.

Acknowledgments

We want to thank the individuals who took time to complete surveys distributed by the publisher; their responses provided us with suggestions for updating the book for this eighth edition. These individuals include Ken O'Keefe, Governors State University; Corey Tinsman, University of North Texas; and Skip Grubb, Columbia State Community College.

In particular, special thanks to the content experts who reviewed and at times made substantial updates to materials contained in various chapters. These experts include Professor Gayle Carper, Law Enforcement and Justice Administration Department at Western Illinois University, who has reviewed the legal chapter for every edition since the fourth, and Professor Don Bytner, Macomb Fire Department Chief, retired, who thoroughly reviewed the chapter on fire, bringing it up to date. Professor John Chuvala reviewed and commented on chapters dealing with careers in security and in his primary area of concern, training, licensing, and regulation.

Thanks to staff from the Department of Community Health and Health Services Management at Western Illinois University: Dr. Jamie Johnson, who reviewed the information on drugs in the workplace, updating the chapter originally prepared by Dr. Kathy Fischer, and Dr. Pam Terry, who made suggestions on updating Dave Walters's materials on workplace violence.

I am particularly indebted to Dr. Vladimir Sergevnin, Colonel, Russian National Police and Senior Researcher, Illinois Law Enforcement Training and Standards Board's Executive Institute, and my old student and friend Colonel Fred Burger, retired, who helped tackle the initial problem of creating a chapter on terrorism that both answers some of the questions about the nature of the tool as well as challenging the reader to consider what actions are appropriate in dealing with the problem. Dr. Sergevnin has done an outstanding job bringing this new chapter up to date.

We also thank Bob's longtime friend and coauthor on *Loss Prevention and Security Procedures*, Richard Janoski, corporate security investigator at Deere and Company. Many of the updates to this edition were reactions to Dick's challenge to "reengineer" our thinking about security. Dick also reviewed and revised chapters on the origins of security, security's role in the organization, and security management/organization.

We also thank Pam Chester, acquisitions editor at Elsevier-Butterworth-Heinemann, for her encouragement to update this classic text. Pam's understanding of the changing security climate inspired Bob to tackle an eighth edition and add Ed as a coauthor.

Finally, we thank our dear wives Kathy and Phillis, who have always been understanding of the time needed to complete this project.

Introduction

The chapters in Part I provide an overview of security and loss prevention. Chapter 1 introduces the reader to the Department of Homeland Security and the related homeland security issues in the private sector. Chapter 2 gives an historic overview of how security developed in Europe and America, ending with a report on the status of the profession in the 21st century. Chapter 3 presents an overview of security functions and roles, delineating the various categories of loss prevention. The materials also provide an overview of the differences between contract and proprietary security operations and their offspring, the hybrid operation. Chapter 4 presents an overview of the proprietary structure commonly used within security operations. Chapter 5 covers career options, and Chapter 6 presents a discussion of the development of security as a profession. The materials follow the development of security training, education, certification, and regulation.

As noted in the Preface, the events of September 11, 2001, changed the face of security operations worldwide. Security has become a common theme considered by almost every person in our country. However, as security professionals already know, the basic concepts and theories of security and loss prevention are not changed by a single event. Antiterrorist professionals had been predicting much of what happened on 9/11 in general terms for the past several decades. What is important is that we learn the lessons that are present in the development of security operations, apply those that pertain to our present situation, modify those that have potential to assist us in our efforts, and discard outdated and outmoded ideas and technology.

The information presented in Part I, along with the recommendations just presented, will serve as a basis for understanding and applying the materials presented in Parts II and III.

Homeland Security: What Has Happened to Security Since 9/11?

1 Introduction

Few events create a truly lasting impression. However, no one of cognizant age will likely forget where he or she was on the morning of September 11, 2001. This was a day that changed life in the United States and throughout the world. Security as we had come to know it began an evolution that will continue for many years. President George W. Bush made a commitment to the American people and others in the world community to fight a war on terrorism. More will be said about terrorism later in this text. But the most telling change in the United States was the eventual creation of the Department of Homeland Security.

On January 24, 2003, Tom Ridge was sworn in as the first Secretary of the Department of Homeland Security. The cabinet-level department merged 22 federal agencies with over 170,000 people. To put this landmark move into perspective, the department's establishment represented the largest reorganization of the U.S. federal government since the creation of the Department of Defense in 1947. President Bush remarked at the swearing-in ceremony that this "begins a vital mission in the defense of our country." While it appears that the Department is here to stay, ongoing problems with the administration of this vast bureaucracy are apparent. Disappointment with the Federal Emergency Management Agency (FEMA), administered by the Department of Homeland Security, is just one symptom of a larger problem of handling such a large and complex organization.

> The security field continues to undergo the most significant changes it has seen since World War II!

The significance of this move cannot be overstated. The security industry, which for the most part operated independently of federal control, has undergone dramatic changes. For example, the federal government, with the creation of the Transportation Security Administration (TSA), has taken over the security of U.S. airports, traditionally patrolled by private contract and proprietary services. The hand of federal involvement is also visible in other transportation fields such as maritime activities and trucking.

The American people are also experiencing greater federal involvement in establishing and maintaining the nation's security. The Department also created the Homeland Security Advisory System, designed to provide the American public with an ongoing indication of the level of potential terrorist threat in the nation in the form of color-coded warnings. In February 2003, the federal government raised the terrorism alert to orange, the second highest level of concern. Many distressed citizens purchased plastic and duct tape to prepare their homes for a possible biological or chemical attack by terrorists. As this text goes to print, this advisory system seems to have outlived its usefulness, or it might never have been truly useful.

Public law enforcement continues to wonder what role it will play along with private enterprise in maintaining public safety in the face of terrorism. Although the Department of Homeland Security initially dispersed billions of dollars in grants to states and local law enforcement agencies to assist them in preparation of terrorists' incidents, the Department recently changed strategies to target only the major cities for significant funding over the next few years. Many public safety departments can boast of hazardous materials training and equipment, but few are pleased with the level of information exchange and intelligence cooperation that currently exists with the federal government.

1.1 Global Security

The focus of this chapter is on the United States and its Homeland Security Initiative, but it would be foolish to believe that the destruction of the World Trade Center has not impacted other countries. President Bush's declaration of war on terrorism resulted in a worldwide coalition in this battle. It was estimated that governments around the world spent an estimated $550 billion on homeland security each year. The figures reached $572 billion by 2005. For comparison purposes, the United States spends nearly $56 billion annually.[1] In February 2007 the Pentagon Comptroller reported that the war on terrorism had cost Americans $545 billion to date. From the $56 billion figure from 2003, the cost for 2008 escalated to an estimated $141.7 billion.[2]

2   Private Enterprise Response

The response in the private sector has been varied. Although it is clear from some of the following examples that private response is often prompted by federal regulations, private industry has also initiated many security enhancements on its own. The American Society for Industrial Security (ASIS) International worked closely with the U.S. government in an attempt to pass industry standards such as the Private Security Guard Act of 2002. Ultimately, this effort resulted in portions of the 2002 Act being included in the Intelligence Reform Act signed by the President in December 2005. As a result, the Department of Justice (DoJ) now allows employers in all 50 states to receive FBI criminal background checks on people applying for or holding jobs as private security officers.[3] In addition, ASIS has initiated an effort to establish industrywide standards for security operations and new certification programs for security professionals, such as the Professional Certified Investigator (PCI) and Physical Security Professional (PSP).

In addition, ASIS has been a leader in sponsoring seminars on terrorism issues. A check of the ASIS Website reflects the society's commitment to providing timely and accurate information. ASIS also continues to sponsor programs such as an international program on world terrorism in Prague, Czechoslovakia, as well as a program on bioterrorism.

> ASIS International proposed uniform standards for the security industry.

Executives have mixed reactions to the impact that terrorism has had on security operations. In a poll by Booz Allen Hamilton conducted in late 2002, a year after the bombing of the Trade Center, 80 percent of the CEOs of 72 firms with more than $1 billion in annual revenues believe that security is more important now than prior to 9/11, but 33 percent expected no increase in security spending. Other surveys indicate that security concerns and spending will be directed at limited areas of security responsibility, such as mailrooms and corporate travel.[4]

2.1   Transit Security

According to the General Accounting Office (GAO), transit agencies have taken many steps to improve security. These include traditional security vulnerability assessments, revising emergency plans, and training employees. However, the GAO indicates that many challenges remain to be addressed. Chief among these is funding. In an effort to reduce this barrier, the Federal Transit Administration (FTA) is working to get increased funding for transportation security. They have been successful in gaining attention for airport, maritime cargo, and some land transportation systems. Still, the real problem is endemic to the system itself. The transportation network must be open and accessible if it is to remain a viable means of public transport and a healthy sector of our economy.

2.1.1   Airport Security

Airport security was dramatically impacted by the 9/11 hijackings. The TSA reported that it confiscated over 4.8 million prohibited items at airport passenger security checkpoints between February 2002 and February 2003. Although passengers attempting to board planes with prohibited items has decreased, an additional 2.7 million items were confiscated between February 2003 and December 2006. The total confiscated items now tops 7.5 million. Among these items were:

- 1,437 firearms
- 2.3 million knives

- More than 2.4 million sharp objects (scissors, 49,331 box cutters)
- 125,273 incendiary/flammable objects
- 15,666 clubs[5]

Airport security is discussed in greater detail in Chapter 14, "Transportation and Cargo Security."

2.1.2   Bus Security

The bus transportation system, represented by the American Bus Association, has established an Antiterrorism Action Plan designed to improve safety and security for bus operations. The four goals of this plan are:

- To promote security vigilance among operators through training and partnerships with law enforcement agencies
- To assist companies in developing plans
- To preserve the bus industry as a strategic transportation reserve
- To protect the transportation infrastructure[6]

2.1.3   Port and Shipping Security

In the arena of port security and the shipping industry, security leaders are encouraging the U.S. government to extend the nation's boundaries to foreign ports. That would put much of the emphasis on security at loading points in foreign ports. One plan, the Container Security Initiative (CSI), first proposed in early 2002 by the U.S. Customs Office, has major international components. The CSI calls for international security criteria to identify high-risk cargo containers. These containers would be pre-screened at their point of shipment. Of course, such security measures might be difficult to implement, considering the need for international cooperation and additional security personnel. By mid-2004, however, 20 of the world's largest seaports had become CSI partners with the United States.[7]

Still, a study by BDP International found that 30 percent of shippers are factoring in additional time to comply with the Advanced Manifest System, which went into effect in February 2003. This Department of Homeland security rule requires the filing of complete import manifest documentation at least 24 hours before U.S.-bound ships are loaded at foreign ports.[8]

The maritime shipping industry will have more federal involvement as the Coast Guard increases patrols at U.S. ports and waterways. Sea marshals from the Coast Guard are assigned to "high-interest" vessels arriving and departing from U.S. ports. The Coast Guard is also providing increased protection around the nation's critical petrochemical facilities.[9]

One possible model, which already works, is the Federal Aviation Administration (FAA) foreign airport security assessment program. Following this model, U.S. Customs would identify ports that fail to meet standards set by the United Nations' International Maritime Organization. What has hindered this approach is a general lack of direction.[10]

Still, the International Maritime Organization, composed of more than 100 governments, agreed to a security plan that would impose significant regulations on ports and seagoing vessels. The International Ship and Port Facility Security Code took effect in July 2004. The code will eventually require ship operators to develop security plans, appoint ship and company security officers, and maintain a minimum level of on-board security. Port officials will be required to develop similar plans and hire a port facility security officer. The code allows the state controlling ports to deny access to ships that do not meet security standards.[11]

This code is certainly a paper victory, but the reality of cooperation often has a blanketing effect on agreements. In recent testimony from the GAO before the Subcommittee on National Security, Veterans Affairs, and International Relations of the House Committee on Government Reform, the Director of Physical Infrastructure Issues testified that U.S. efforts to widen security to exporting countries is often slowed by lack of follow-through by foreign governments. In one case, Estonia delayed installing detection equipment for seven months while finalizing an agreement, and monitors sat for two years while Lithuanians argued over the correct power supply.[12]

2.1.4 Rail Security

In the area of rail transit, the sheer number of travelers and products transported around this country makes extensive security measures almost impossible. However, Amtrak and regional metropolitan systems have increased security, in some cases requiring rail staff to check tickets prior to train boarding. In large rail terminals, taxi stands have been moved to the street from their previous underground near-rail locations. States and

FIGURE 1.1 Members of a U.S. Coast Guard security unit patrol the harbor near a vehicle cargo ship. (DoD photo by PA1 Chuck Kalnbach)

local governments have been asked to provide either police or National Guard protection for selected rail bridges. The rail companies have been asked to increase security at major facilities and key rail hubs. At the request of the Department of Transportation (DoT), railroads will monitor shipments of hazardous material as well as increase security measures on trains carrying such materials.

There are approximately 140,000 miles of rail in the United States. On average, the system carries approximately two million loads of hazardous materials and chemicals each year. Although the United States rail system has yet to be a victim of any large-scale attack, systems in other countries such as England, Spain, and India have been targeted over the past five years.

Even though the TSA is responsible for transportation security and ranks an attack against chemicals in transit and stored as among the most serious risks facing the United States, budget allocations for rail and other surface transportation methods pale in comparison to the budget for aviation.[13]

2.1.5 Over-the-Road Security

Over-the-road security is without a doubt the most difficult area to regulate, with over 4 million miles of interstate, national, and other roads in use by the trucking industry.[14] Still, the government and trucking industry are working to monitor hazardous materials carriers. Companies are suggesting increased security to include:

- Employee identification checks
- Communication plans including increased use of Global Positioning Systems
- Operator awareness training

The recently formed Freight Transportation Security Consortium, including businesses in asset tracking, vehicle monitoring, and the freight industry, is suggesting expanded use of geographical positioning satellites (GPS). In particular, the group would like to see all hazardous materials carriers monitored so that vehicles moving from their predetermined routes will be spotted early and law enforcement alerted to a possible problem. However, the cost associated with the proposal has drawn criticism.

In 2003 the TSA announced plans to randomly search vehicles outside airport terminals during orange or red alerts established by the Department of Homeland Security.[15] Although they cite Supreme Court and other legal precedents in establishing their authority for the random searches, it is likely that such warrantless random searches will be challenged in the courts.

2.2 Electrical Grid Issues

In 2002 the Pacific Northwest Economic Region (PNWER), a group of electric power companies, conducted a simulated terrorist attack on the region's power grid. The result showed clearly that the region was not prepared to handle such an attack. To deal with the lack of security, both private and government organizations have developed guidelines for protecting electric facilities and distribution systems. On the private side, the Edison Electric Institute (EEI) developed guidelines that have been passed on to the North American Electric Reliability Council (NERC), the U.S. Department of Energy's coordinator for the U.S. electrical infrastructure. Among other things, the guidelines cover:

- Vulnerability/risk analysis
- Threat response
- Emergency planning
- Business continuity
- Communications
- Physical security
- Cyber issues
- Intrusion detection
- Backgrounding/screening

It should be clear that these are traditional security concerns. However, until the impetus from the 9/11 events, most power companies had not taken them as serious issues. Some companies do have model security programs, but the majority of regional power firms have lagged behind. This is to be expected, since previously the threat did not seem probable.

According to Michael Gips in an article for *Security Management,* "Most experts ... said that their utilities were either well on their way to meeting all the recommendations or were well beyond them."[16]

While the NERC guidelines are being considered, the Federal Energy Regulatory Commission (FERC) has also developed security standards for electric utilities. In developing standards, FERC sought the assistance of the NERC. The final result is an amalgam of NERC recommendations and FERC standards. The standards are designed to prevent anyone from disrupting the electrical market and to ensure the reliability of the electrical grid. The proposed rules took effect January 1, 2004.

2.3 Nuclear Facilities

In the meantime, the Nuclear Regulatory Commission (NRC) is requiring additional security within its already relatively significant control measures to protect radioactive materials. Currently, 104 nuclear reactors are operating at 65 sites in 31 U.S. states. Oversight of emergency preparedness is shared by the NRC and FEMA. Although the NRC has issued orders to increase standards, it was of concern that following September 11, 2001, the NRC did not know how many foreign nationals were employed at nuclear reactors and that background checks were generally not adequate. According to a report by Representative Edward J. Markey (D-MA), the only reactor that was designed to withstand ramming by a large airliner is at Three Mile Island in Pennsylvania. Markey's report also expresses concerns over the handling of spent nuclear fuels. The NRC has taken Markey's report seriously and has been involved in a complete security review since 9/11, issuing over 30 directives since that date, including orders to increase guard presence, construct barriers, and increased surveillance. Contractors at nuclear facilities are being scrutinized for possible security risks. While the NRC works on security upgrades, many of the plans require cooperation with other federal agencies such as the FAA, FBI, and DoD. Funding limits have also slowed the NRC's progress in meeting its own deadlines.[17]

For additional information, see the NRC Website at www.nrc.gov/about-nrc/emerg-preparedness.html.

FIGURE 1.2 A nuclear power facility.

2.4   Oil and Gas Facilities

The United States has more than 2.2 million miles of gas, oil, and hazardous material pipelines. Security of the lines is, of course, only part of the issue because refineries and oil/gas fields are also potential targets. Prior to 9/11 there were minimum standards for this morass of pipelines. Recently the DOT's Office of Pipeline Safety (OPS) began looking at risks associated with pipeline safety and security. The OPS has required that pipeline operators identify and address risks in areas where a rupture would have the greatest impact on populations or the ecological system.

Although this is a step in the right direction, the GAO indicated that the inspection program associated with the risk analysis would not be completed before 2006. That means that many of the security/safety measures were not even contemplated until the risk analysis was completed.[18]

One of the most promising tools for dealing with pipeline monitoring and other oil and gas security challenges may rest in the application of unmanned aerial vehicles (UAVs). Since 2003 UAVs have been monitoring offshore oil fields, checking for thieves and oil leaks. Infrared technology works well in detecting oil and gas leaks.[19]

Protection of U.S. distribution and manufacturing facilities is important, but terrorists recognize the potential for disrupting the American economy by attacking other suppliers. The Arabian Peninsula's e-magazine *Sawt al-Jihad* (*Voice of Holy War*) posted a notice that Venezuela and Mexico are big oil suppliers for the U.S. market. In addition, Canada, which exports over half its daily production of 2.5 million barrels of oil to the United States via pipeline, was targeted by al Qaeda in Web postings in 2007.[20]

2.5   Water Utilities

The DoJ has notified water utilities that the enforcement of the Safe Drinking Water Act security provisions is a top federal government priority. The American Water Works Association's (AWWA) executive director reports that the industry has been active in trying to meet federal security deadlines.[21] According to Jack Hoffbuhr, "Water utilities throughout the nation have spent hundreds of millions of dollars in infrastructure costs, including water monitoring, physical security systems, and emergency training and planning to protect American's water supplies from terrorism." The Public Security and Bioterrorism Act mandated that water systems serving more than 100,000 persons must meet vulnerability assessments by March 31, 2003. The EPA reported to Congress on these assessments. It concluded that $276.8 billion is needed in infrastructure improvement over the next 20 years to comply with current regulations. Of this amount, $1 billion is needed for security-related needs.

Most of the covered water utilities were in compliance by the March 31 deadline, but most water systems serve populations under 100,000. The AWWA estimates that it would cost over $450 million to bring these smaller systems into compliance with the Public Security and Bioterrorism Act. Communities of between 50,000 and 100,000 had until December 31, 2003, to meet standards, whereas small communities (3,300 to 50,000) had until June 2004.

The Act authorized $160 million in funding for FY 2002 and funds as needed through 2005. Supplemental funding provided $90 million for assessing vulnerabilities and security planning. The EPA provided $53 million in 2002 funds to assist the largest water suppliers in meeting the March 31, 2003 deadline.

In 2005, President Bush requested $5 million for state water security grants and $44 million for a new water security initiative, Water Sentinel. Water Sentinel is designed to establish early warning systems in several pilot cities through water monitoring and surveillance for chemical and biological contaminants. The House Appropriations Committee urged the EPA to clear up goals and provide better justification for the request in its FY 2007 budget. The EPA requested $41.7 million for Water Sentinel for FY 2007.[22]

In 2006 Congress allocated $837.5 million to help communities finance projects needed to comply with drinking water standards.[23]

2.6 Retail Facilities

With the federal government sending messages that the next major attack by terrorists might be against retail mall facilities, mall security operations have come under scrutiny. Many stores retain their proprietary security forces to catch shoplifters and internal thieves, but those located in malls also rely on mall security personnel to provide protection to shoppers in the mall commons and parking areas. The mall owners often contract these services. In response to concerns over targeting of mall properties, there was a brief interest in bringing out horse patrols. Although the malls have not taken this direction, the entertainment business has increased security through the use of horse patrols. Horse patrols provide good mobility and a high observation point in crowd conditions. Their lack of use in the retail environment is blamed on the poor economy and weak consumer spending.[24]

In the aftermath of 9/11 a number of malls began training security personnel in how to spot suicide bombers. They are receiving training that was at one time reserved for Israeli police and the U.S. military. Training to spot possible terrorists is important. The International Council of Shopping Centers has held antiterrorism classes since 2004. According to a spokesman for the Council, everyone, from mall managers to engineers and maintenance people, has a role in the effort.

Are malls good targets for terrorist attacks? According to antiterrorism instructors it is nearly twice as likely that a commercial establishment will be targeted over a government building or military installation.[25]

Yet even with good intentions, questions remain regarding the quality of mall security personnel. On February 14, 2007, six people were killed in Trolley Square, a major mall in Salt Lake City. A single armed gunman committed the murders and was eventually killed by the local SWAT team. Where were the mall's security personnel? According to a DoJ report, *An Assessment of the Preparedness of Large Retail Malls to Prevent and Respond to Terrorist Attacks*, 60.2 percent of the 120 mall directors surveyed reported that training for security staff had not improved since 9/11, and 94 percent indicated that there had been no change in hiring requirements.[26]

2.7 City Centers

The concern that a terrorist organization might attack public gatherings focused interest on security measures at civic and cultural city centers. However, it was clear that many centers had been considering security an important issue long before 9/11. A prime example of what security can accomplish is the Town Centre Improvement District (TCID) just outside Houston, Texas. The Center covers 1.5 square miles, employs approximately 15,000 people, and draws over 15 million visitors each year. Security measures include the use of mounted patrols and contract services with local law enforcement departments. The visible presence of security has made employees and shoppers feel safe, an issue of great importance following 9/11.[27]

A 2006 Rand study identified 39 security measures that can substantially reduce the risk of terrorist attacks at enclosed shopping centers. Among these are the following:

- Public information campaigns encouraging people to report suspicious packages
- Placing vehicle barriers at pedestrian entrances to block suicide car bombers
- Searching kiosks for bombs and weapons
- Clearly labelling exits so shoppers can quickly find their way out in an emergency
- Searching all bags and requiring everyone entering shopping centers to remove their coats to check for explosives and weapons[28]

2.7.1 *Public Events and Cultural Centers*

2.7.1.1 **Sports Arenas**   Sharpshooters, fighter jets, bomb-sniffing dogs, and 1,500 police officers secure Yankee Stadium!

Immediately following the 9/11 bombing of the World Trade Center, the World Series was being conducted at Yankee Stadium. How do you protect thousands of fans? The Yankee management decided to have 1,500 police officers on alert in and around the facility. However, they also used sharpshooters and fighter jets. Bomb-sniffing dogs were employed to sniff the area. All flights over the stadium were banned. All this was probably a wise move, considering predictions of additional terrorist attacks, but such measures are extreme and no one expects that level of security when attending public functions.

According to a *Security Management* survey of 150 (of a total of 752) U.S. and Canadian sports facilities, all but one of the 47 respondents have increased security since 9/11. In most cases these increased security measures have tightened restrictions on fans carrying in bags, coolers, and other items. Patrons are carefully inspected at the gates, whereas over 90 percent of the organizations lock down the facilities between events. Also included in security upgrades is greater credentialing of staff. Almost 80 percent of the organizations also monitor air intakes, but only 33 percent monitor water systems. Furthermore, 66 percent have increased electronic surveillance.[29]

The increase in security for arenas is also the result of the eventual rise in the U.S. sports hooligan. Facility managers are being proactive in attempting to assure the public of a safe, secure, and enjoyable experience at their chosen arena event.

2.7.1.2 **Conference Sites and Hotels** But what is reasonable? What expectations should the public have when attending a play, meeting with colleagues at a convention, visiting museums, or staying at hotels? These are real concerns of companies planning conventions. Some firms in the aftermath of 9/11 avoided New York City in favor of other locations such as Tampa, Florida. Security, which was often invisible, is now expected to be seen to quell perceptions of danger by visitors.

At a minimum, security managers for hotels and resorts report that they have been requested to review disaster and crisis management plans and in some cases conduct drills for employees. Employees have been trained to watch for abandoned luggage, and there are ongoing discussions about screening hotel guests' baggage. Of course, subterranean parking facilities are considered potential targets, but there has been little change in most self-park hotel operations.

> One conference planner discovered that nine applicants to attend the conference were using credit cards that were not their own.

Conference planners are also concerned about the potential of foreign students and professors, who could be working for their government or a terrorist organization, to try to infiltrate seminars in larger numbers as the Department of Homeland Security's SEVIS computer begins to deny student visas to many of these individuals. One conference planner that initiated increased background checks of attendees in 2002 discovered nine applications out of 350 attendees who were listed as university students but were using credit card numbers listed to other people. The firm became suspicious since their programs had never drawn attendees from Nigeria or Ghana. An FBI inquiry confirmed the firm's concerns.[30]

2.7.1.3 **Museums** Museums appear to have reacted to the potential terrorist threat by increasing access control measures. This includes stronger package-checking standards. In some cases better identification systems have been implemented. In addition, Steve Keller, museum security consultant, indicates that some properties have increased security staffing or requested greater police presence.[31]

2.8   Construction Industry

The construction industry has also become involved in security concerns. In 2002 the Construction Specifications Institute announced plans to revise its MasterFormat system to include more on security. The format includes recommendations for contractors on such things as construction requirements, products, and activities. According to Dennis Hall, chair of the CSI's MasterFormat task team, "We're not opposed to creating a strict security division if the industry (security) comes back and says we need a security division."[32] According to architect and author Barbara Nadal, architects and building planners are even considering threats such as chemical and biological weapons in their designs and retrofits. Structural engineers are considering "progressive collapse design," where only the impacted area of a building collapses while the remainder of the structure stays intact.[33]

2.9   Agriculture

Although most Americans were not aware of the $50 million loss to the beef industry in 2001, concerns over perceived agroterrorism have resulted in tighter security over investigations conducted by federal agriculture inspectors. Experts agree that infecting cattle, pigs, sheep, or other animals with disease would likely erode public confidence in U.S. food supplies. Source diseases are common, and with the predominant use of feedlots and confinement farming, disease can infect thousands of animals at a time. The regular trading of animals at auctions and fairs would also move the disease rapidly from a source site to other areas of the country.

With the creation of the Department of Homeland Security, the U.S. Department of Agriculture's (USDA) department of Animal and Plant Health Inspection Service-Veterinary Services (APHIS-VS) has received support for expanded services to monitor borders.[34]

In another agro area, the concerns of the American Psychopathological Society (APS) focus on two broad areas: prevention and preparedness. Prevention efforts focus on traditional issues of security, border protection, and secrecy. Preparedness is concerned with early detection of threats, rapid diagnosis, and response/recovery. The private sector is concerned that the federal government seems to be focusing its efforts only on security, as shown by legislative initiatives during 2002. For example, the USDA has already created a list of plant pathogens considered high risks for terrorist use against U.S. crops.

There are those who believe that the key element in the battle against potential agroterrorism has been overlooked. The farmer must learn about the potential of attack and what to look for. According to a recent study of farmers by the Extension Disaster Education Network, over 66 percent of the farming respondents said that they either lacked access to materials about agroterrorism or were unaware of whether they even had access to such materials. Seventy-five percent said they had not made investments to make their farms biosecure.

The American Farm Bureau Federation reports that it has been encouraging its members to track who is on their property and develop ties with local law enforcement agencies.

2.10   Hospitals

Although hospitals have been sensitive to security issues for decades, the aftermath of 9/11 brought a renewed emphasis on security issues. Many hospitals have been working to increase access control as a primary means of mitigating problems such as theft, terrorism, vandalism, narcotics problems, and handling the mentally ill and disgruntled.

In terms of increased access control, modern state-of-the-art controls are being used. While applying traditional access control theory, closed-circuit TV (CCTV), identification systems, access control cards, metal detectors, and other devices are being used and evaluated in an environment that requires public access to many areas of the hospital complex.

Parking facilities are being carefully monitored using CCTV and cashier-monitoring stations. Security officers are also employed to patrol the facilities. Many facilities have also installed emergency call boxes.

High-risk areas such as the emergency room, obstetrics/pediatrics, psychiatric wards, cash handling, pharmacy, research, operating rooms, and locker rooms are controlled with increased access controls that include alarmed doors, detectors, card readers, and CCTV.[35]

Still, according to Jeff Aldridge, a nationally known expert on hospital security, "Even today, many hospitals still have the same open-door policy they have practiced for decades." The concept of "public access" is taken literally so that any person may enter the hospital to seek treatment or to visit someone. They have the right to come and go as they please. Aldridge suggests that the open-door policy is no longer safe. Everyone who enters the hospital must be identified through controlled access. Old and misunderstood fire codes and outdated open building designs contribute to problems of restricting access. However, access can and must be controlled. Aldridge suggests that all hospitals must conduct a security assessment or audit.[36] You can read more about managing such security risks in Chapter 8.

3   Federal Response in the United States

3.1   Department of Homeland Security

The most significant federal move following 9/11 was the eventual creation of the new Department of Homeland Security (DHS). As noted in the introduction, this new department folds 22 law enforcement, security, and intelligence agencies into one organization. The primary task of the DHS in 2003 was integrating these independent agencies into an effective conglomerate agency. During 2003 the department attempted to fill 460 inspector positions at land ports of entry, 615 inspectors for airport security, and 85 inspectors for seaports. In total, the agency's plan for 2003 included hiring 1,700 new inspectors and 570 new border patrol agents.[37]

> The most significant federal move following 9/11 was the eventual creation of the new Department of Homeland Security (DHS).

DHS's primary concerns are:

- Preventing terrorist attacks within the United States
- Reducing U.S. vulnerability to terrorism
- Minimizing damage and recovering from attacks that do occur

While Congress sought to have a new organization with its own intelligence-gathering operation, the DHS suggested that intelligence operations are best left with the existing agencies within the new department. The DHS set up a Terrorist Threat Integration Center staffed by analysts from the CIA, FBI, NSA, Pentagon, and new employees of Homeland Security. Congressional leaders still worry that such an arrangement does not improve on the intelligence situation that existed prior to 9/11.[38] In 2007, President Bush created a new position to oversee intelligence coordination as Congressional fears regarding organizational failures and interagency competition proved to be all too true.

The DHS has been the leader in creating the Homeland Security Advisory System (HSAS) mentioned in the introduction. President Bush signed the system into law in March 2002. The system was designed to improve coordination and cooperation among all levels of government and the public. It was intended to offer a common vocabulary to help people understand the threat of terrorism. Of perhaps more significance and less controversy is the Ready Champaign (www.ready.gov), designed to educate the public on potential threats and steps in proper planning. The site is still active and provides good information on a variety of topics, but the color-coded warning system developed by DHS has for the most part not been effective.

The interest in protecting the United States from further terrorist attacks reflects several issues discussed at great length in the security business. First, what are the respective roles of the state and private enterprise? In the preceding section, the private response was discussed. In the following section, the response by the U.S. federal government and other government units is discussed. The federal government seems to be exploring efforts to control segments of American life that have not previously been subject to government scrutiny. Whether such efforts will be successful—or perhaps more important, accepted—is yet to be seen.

3.2 Computer Protection

The USA PATRIOT Act was perhaps the first major tool developed to investigate and fight world terrorism. The PATRIOT Act increased the reach of the federal government in investigating computer crimes. The Computer Fraud and Abuse Act was the base, but the PATRIOT Act allows the United States to reach out to foreign computer users who pass information through a server in the United States.

A new PATRIOT Act II, first proposed by then Attorney General John Ashcroft, received such a negative reaction when leaked to the public that it was disassembled and parts inserted into other legislation. For example, the Intelligence Authorization Act was signed into law by President Bush on December 13, 2003. The new act increases the use of surveillance measures in the war against terrorism. The original PATRIOT Act had given the FBI authority to obtain client records from banks by requesting the records using a "National Security Letter." There was no need to appear before a judge or show probable cause. The Letter also directed the institutions to be silent regarding the release of information. This included the client whose records were being sought. The new legislation expands the FBI power to include stockbrokers, car dealerships, casinos, credit card companies, insurance agencies, jewelers, airlines, the U.S. Post Office, and any other business "whose case transactions have a high degree of usefulness in criminal, tax, or regulatory matters."

Opposition to the Act is plentiful. To many, the Act violates judicial oversight and the Fourth Amendment protections that prohibit unreasonable search and seizure.[39]

One effort initiated by the Office of Homeland Security is the securing of the nation's computer networks. The most significant suggestion is the development of a private, compartmentalized federal network for government agencies and private sector experts to share information during major events. The system would be part of the newly created Cyber Warning Information Network (CWIN), which includes federal offices responsible for the security of the federal computer systems as well as private sector interests.

CWIN's supporters note that this is not a government regulation effort with government mandates but rather an industry-led activity to find solutions. According to Harris Miller, president of the Information Technology Association of America, this is important because between 85 and 90 percent of the infrastructure used by government and industry is owned by private industry.

However, there are those who feel that the approach, although worthy, lacks teeth. There is no system to enforce guidelines, since they are "only guidelines."[40]

3.3 Operation Liberty Shield

An additional effort by the federal government, perhaps as a result of the growing concern over the U.S. coalition's Iraq War, is Operation Liberty Shield. Announced prior to the Iraq War in March 2003, the national plan is designed to make U.S. citizens and the country's infrastructure secure while maintaining life with minimal disruption of the economy. The program is a cooperative effort that includes:

- Increased border security
- More protection of transportation systems
- Ongoing efforts to disrupt threats against the United States
- Protection of critical infrastructure and key assets
- Increased public health preparedness
- Better availability of federal resources

The FBI will continue monitoring individuals suspected of terrorist links. In particular, the Bureau, along with the DoJ and DHS, is working to identify organizations and individuals who facilitate terrorism through fundraising, logistical support, and recruitment.

The Department of Health and Human Services (HHS) has put local health departments, hospitals, and medical care providers on alert to report any unusual disease patterns. The department also has enhanced its inspection of imported foods.

In addition, the HHS, in cooperation with the Centers for Disease Control and Prevention, issued regulations for procedures in laboratories handling certain toxins or pathogens. The regulations limit the handling of these agents to certain people. Each facility must develop and implement a plan to ensure security of designated agents. The plan must include inventory control, security training for nonsecurity personnel, methods for reporting suspicious persons, loss of agents, and alteration of inventory documents. Access controls must be established for all employees and visitors. Visitors and employees who are with housekeeping or maintenance in areas of laboratory or security operations must be escorted and monitored at all times. Designated agents must be secure at all times.

The health care industry, while reacting to the needs for security, is also impacted by President Bush's decision to have military personnel, health services workers, and other first responders vaccinated against smallpox. In December 2002, President Bush ordered smallpox vaccinations for 500,000 soldiers. Many health officials ponder whether the risk of death associated with the vaccinations is worth the preventive value. Once again, only time will tell whether this program was overprotective.[41]

The USDA has alerted food and agriculture community workers to monitor feedlots, stockyards, and import and storage areas. The USDA has also stepped up its efforts to provide resources to protect the $140 billion agriculture industry. In 2006 the USDA published it Pre-Harvest Security Guidelines and Checklist 2006. The document provides farmers with guidelines for risk assessment, checklists of things to do to protect various types of agricultural activities, and a list of Websites for various agricultural resources.[42]

FEMA developed the publication *Are You Ready? A Guide to Citizen Preparedness.* This comprehensive guide to disasters provides a step-by-step outline of how to prepare for a disaster. The guidelines include information on disaster supply kits, emergency planning, how to locate and evacuate to a shelter, and more. A full copy is available online at www.fema.gov/areyouready.

Following the problems associated with the lack of appropriate response from FEMA to the New Orleans Hurricane Katrina disaster of 2005, the DHS established a National Advisory Council. The Council will advise FEMA on all aspects of emergency management in an effort to ensure close coordination with all involved.[43]

The Bureau of Immigration and Customs Enforcement has proposed more detailed information about people who enter or leave the United States by boat or plane. Even U.S. citizens may be required to fill out forms detailing their travel. With this request is a proposed system that will allow for quicker cross-checking of databases and matching records of arrivals and departures.

The proposed rules would not impact buses, trains, or private transportation, but they target commercial airlines (passengers and crews), cruise ships, cargo flights, and vessels. Canadian officials who believe the system would bog down in the border areas between Canada and the United States have voiced concerns over the program.[44]

In May 2002, The Enhanced Border Security and Visa Entry Reform Act was signed into law. The act requires that foreign nationals who want to enter the United States must have a tamper-proof, machine-readable visa with biometric identifiers. The Act implementation deadline was October 26, 2004.[45] Beginning in January 2008, all persons entering the United States must have a legal passport. This includes U.S. citizens who routinely cross the borders to Mexico and Canada.

3.4   US-VISIT

According to the Department of Homeland Security, the US-VISIT Program is a top priority because it:

- Enhances the security of citizens and visitors
- Facilitates legitimate travel and trade
- Ensures the integrity of the immigration system
- Protects the privacy of visitors[49]

3.5   The Student Exchange Visitor Information System

In the area of tracking potential terrorists, the DHS initiated a $36 million computer tracking system to monitor student and exchange visitors at universities. The Student and Exchange Visitor Program (SEVP) was designed to track approximately 500,000 foreign students who come to the United States each year to attend school. Two of the terrorists involved in the 9/11 attacks were approved for student visas six months after the attacks.

The Student and Exchange Visitor Information System (SEVIS) links approximately 70,000 schools admitting foreign students to the Bureau of Immigration and Customs Enforcement, the agency that replaced Immigration and Naturalization Services in 2002. The rollout of the SEVIS system in March 2003 resulted in a multitude of problems. Forms were not available on the SEVIS Website; printed information designated for one school might turn up on a printer thousands of miles away at another school. Foreign students and professors were held up for days, and active students were listed in the system as "dropped out."

Although the intent of the system is a good one, the zero tolerance built into the system is oppressive. As one university official said, "You can't fight terrorism by terrorizing students."[46]

Despite early problems, the program has continued to grow. As of April 2007 there were 951,654 active nonimmigrant student exchange visitors (counting dependents) in the United States. The SEVIS database includes more than 2.5 million entries. The largest populations of students are in the states of California, New York, Texas, Massachusetts, and Illinois.[47]

3.6   Federal Identification Cards

Federal identification cards, a hot button topic for many Americans, have been discussed at some length since the destruction of the World Trade Center. The federal government continues to discuss options that would allow for higher levels of trust in identification systems currently controlled by most states. These include driver's licenses, birth certificates, and death certificates. Such a coordinated system would require agreement and cooperation among all 50 states. An effort to develop a federal identification card failed to receive support in the version presented in the PATRIOT Act II.

3.7   Homeland Security Presidential Directive/HSPD-12 (HSPD-12)

On August 27, 2004, President Bush released the Homeland Security Presidential Directive 12, commonly referred to as HSPD-12. To establish a policy for a common identification standard for federal employees and contractors, the directive established a mandatory governmentwide standard for a secure and reliable form of identification issued by the federal government to employees, contractors, and contract employees. "Secure and reliable" means identification that:

- Is issued based on sound criteria for verifying an individual's identity
- Is strongly resistant to identity fraud, tampering, counterfeiting, and terrorist exploitation
- Can be rapidly authenticated electronically
- Is issued only by providers whose reliability has been established by an official accreditation process

The system includes criteria for a graded security system.[48]

3.8   Total Information Awareness Program

The Defense Advanced Research Projects Agency (DARPA), in conjunction with the DoD, is working to develop, among many other projects, what it calls the Information Awareness Program (IAP) in supporting the DoD war on terrorism. The program would utilize new surveillance and information analysis systems aimed at protecting U.S. citizens. When completed, the system would provide a computerized record of an individual's private life, supplying a paper trail of the person's entire life, including vital statistics, medical, financial, e-mail, Internet, phone, and travel records. More information on this program may be found at www.darpa.mil/DARPATech2002/presentation.html.[50]

There are many questions about this initiative, including issues involving privacy safeguards, limitations on access, and protection of records already protected by existing legislation.

DARPA activities continue as the engine for radical innovation in the DoD. DARPA's mission is to prevent technological surprise for us *and* to create technological surprise for our adversaries. Stealth is one example of how DARPA creates technological surprise. DARPA delivered its updated Strategic Plan to Congress in February 2007.

The following is a list of ongoing DARPA research that promises major benefits to DoD and which may become icons of significant technical achievement by themselves. (The Strategic Plan may be downloaded from DARPA's website, www.darpa.mil):

- Networks. Self-forming, robust, self-defending networks at the strategic and tactical level are the key to network-centric warfare.
- Chip-scale atomic clock. Miniaturizing an atomic clock to fit on a chip to provide very accurate time as required, for example, in assured network communications.
- Global war on terrorism. Technologies to identify and defeat terrorist activities such as the manufacture and deployment of improvised explosive devices and other asymmetric activities.
- Air vehicles. Manned and unmanned air vehicles that quickly arrive at their mission station and can loiter there for very long periods.
- Space. The U.S. military's ability to use space is one of its major strategic advantages. DARPA is working to ensure that the United States maintains that defense advantage.
- High-productivity computing systems. Supercomputers are fundamental to a variety of military operations, from weather forecasting to cryptography and the design of new weapons. DARPA is working to maintain the U.S. global lead in this technology.
- Real-time accurate language translation. Real-time machine language translation of structured and unstructured text and speech with near-expert human translation accuracy.
- Biological warfare defense. Technologies to dramatically accelerate the development and production of vaccines and other medical therapeutics from 12 years to only 12 weeks.
- Prosthetics. Developing prosthetics that can be controlled and perceived by the brain, just as with a natural limb.
- Quantum information science. Exploiting quantum phenomena in the fields of computing, cryptography, and communications, with the promise of opening new frontiers in each area.
- Newton's Laws for Biology. DARPA's Fundamental Laws of Biology Program is working to bring deeper mathematical understanding and accompanying predictive ability to the field of biology, with the goal of discovering fundamental laws of biology that extend across all size scales.
- Low-cost titanium. A completely revolutionary technology for extracting titanium from ore and fabricating it promises to dramatically reduce the cost of military-grade titanium alloy, making it practical for many more applications.

FIGURE 1.3 The MQ-9 Reaper drone, a small unmanned aircraft system. (U.S. Air Force photo by Senior Airman Larry E. Reid Jr.)

- Alternative energy. Technologies to help reduce the military's reliance on petroleum.
- High energy liquid laser area defense system. Novel, compact, high-power lasers making practical small-size and low-weight speed-of-light weapons for tactical mobile air and ground vehicles.

3.9 DARPA's Eight Strategic Thrusts

DARPA's strategy for accomplishing its mission is embodied in strategic thrusts. Over time, as national security threats and technical opportunities change, DARPA's strategic thrusts change. The eight strategic research thrusts that DARPA is emphasizing today are:

- Robust, secure, self-forming networks
- Detection, precision ID, tracking, and destruction of elusive targets
- Urban area operations
- Advanced manned and unmanned systems
- Detection, characterization, and assessment of underground structures
- Space
- Increasing the tooth-to-tail ratio
- Biorevolution[51]

3.10   Federal Building Security Initiatives

Even with federal efforts, there have been problems. In the aftermath of the 1995 Oklahoma City bombing of the Murrah Federal Building, the DoJ moved security at federal buildings to the top of its priority list. Following 9/11 the GAO was asked to consider how well the concerns voiced after the Murrah bombing had been addressed. Auditors found that only 50 percent of the agencies had completed security assessments. Security appears to be easy to discuss but more difficult to implement. The GAO continues to monitor progress on security recommendations.

3.11   Protection of Chemical Manufacturing Sites

As this book goes to press, the DHS is spearheading efforts to set federal standards for the chemical manufacturing sector. The agency's rules will be designed to provide safeguards to prevent sabotage and require enhanced perimeter security at chemical plants. Some states—for example, New Jersey—although not opposed to legislation, do not want it to set a standard that the states cannot exceed. In the case of New Jersey, the state already has standards in place that exceed those expected to be implemented by the federal government.[52]

3.12   Antibioterrorism

DHS BioWatch program was established in 2003 in approximately 30 cities to monitor the air for possible biological attack. Equipment was installed quickly, but there was no detailed plan on how to respond in the event of positive alarms. The impact was felt in Houston in October 2003 when the alarms showed positive for tularaemia, a naturally occurring pathogen. Too often well-intentioned plans are not tied to the reality of response by actual cities and their responders.[53]

4   State and Local Response

All areas of the country are seeing local response to the potential threat of terrorism. In Alaska, the Anchorage Fire Department has rekeyed its facilities. In Arizona, the Gilbert Police Department has assigned extra officers to schools, power plants, and water supply operations. Rockford, Illinois, has added a bomb-sniffing dog to its ranks. Orange County, Florida, sheriff's deputies were among the first county law enforcement officials to receive smallpox vaccinations. Such added security measures are costly.

4.1   The Costs

In an example of cost associated with heightened security for the protection of the United States, the governor of Illinois reported that the orange alert terror status costs the state about $20,000 a day. Such costs can be devastating to state and local governments without some type of federal support.[54]

In its most recent survey of community spending on security, the U.S. Conference of Mayors found that cities were spending $70 million a week on homeland security costs.

At the 2002 U.S. Conference of Mayors, leaders of 192 cities with populations of over 30,000 were polled. The pollster reported that it is estimated that municipalities would spend approximately $2.1 billion on equipment in 2002. A 2003 study of cities of over 30,000 (1,185 in the United States) found that this group of communities was spending $70 million a week on security. New York topped the list, spending an extra $5 million each week. San Francisco, Los Angeles, and Atlanta were spending just over $2 million per week, followed by Fresno at $1.5 million. Other cities report little added expense due to homeland security, including Rockford, Illinois; Winston-Salem, North Carolina; and Fort Collins, Colorado. San Antonio, Texas, reported an increase of only $15,000 per week.[55]

This is a drop in the bucket compared to the $525 million spent between September 11, 2001, and January 1, 2002.[56] The significance of the need for local support in the federal government's battle against terrorism is exemplified by where the government is spending money. In March 2003, the DHS released approximately $600 million to the states for local first responders, out of an annual federal allocation of roughly $38 billion. The funds are designated for equipment, planning, and training exercises. The problem, as with many federal initiatives, is that the money did not begin flowing until July. In addition, the department provided another $750 million for firefighters.[57]

A quick check of the math will show that although the funding is welcome, it is only a small portion of what local and state governments have already invested in the federal government's war on terrorism.

Still, President Bush continues promising to increase funding to states for security, education, and health care associated with homeland security by 9 percent, or $400 billion. In 2003, $3.5 billion was promised to states for security operations. But again, the money flows slowly: Only $600 million of the allocated funds were released for use. A 2003 effort by state governors to have funding released for immediate relief of incurred costs was set aside on a straight party-line vote.

In 2007, funds have been spent on first responder equipment and training, but many state officials, particularly those in law enforcement, complain that there has been too little effort placed on improving communication of vital intelligence information and not enough emphasis on local intelligence operations. The total FY budget for homeland security was estimated at $54.3 billion.[58]

4.2   School Safety

The DHS has encouraged local school districts to implement or review crisis/emergency planning. In cooperation with the Department of Education, the two agencies have designed a "one-stop" shop to help local school districts plan for any emergency, including usual natural disasters, violence, and of course, terrorism.

In addition, the Department of Education announced that it would make $30 million available to help schools improve emergency response and crisis management plans. An additional $30 million was included in the FY 04 budget plan. More information may be found at www.ed.gov/emergencyplan.[59]

4.3   Emergency Response Plans

Many cities have or are working on or reevaluating emergency response plans. The plans not only fill a need in case of a terrorist attack, they are also useful in case of natural disasters. Existing plans in Washington, D.C. and Dallas/Fort Worth are cited as examples of how having plans can reduce confusion and get the city back to its business, although, in after-event analysis, both plans were found lacking in the areas of coordination of specific communication.

What is evident in most of these plans is the multijurisdictional nature of the response and the need to coordinate and communicate actions taken by various team members. In addition, these plans have been developed utilizing a variety of sources, including FEMA and the Critical Incident Protocol developed by the School of Criminal Justice at Michigan State University.[60]

4.4 Examples of Specific State Responses

Mississippi has enacted a law making it illegal to possess or release harmful biological substances. The law also prohibits false claims of exposure. The punishment established by the law is a fine up to $100,000 and 20 years of prison.

Illinois mandated that all municipalities with population over 1 million adopt an ordinance mandating emergency procedures for high-rise buildings by January 1, 2004. Plans include procedures for evacuating people with disabilities, the roles of building personnel, contact information, and instructions for conducting drills at least once per year.[61]

In Colorado the Denver Department of Public Health set out to monitor early symptoms of a bioterror attack. The program, called Syndromic Surveillance, looks to identify changes in health patterns early, so that a bioterror attack may be identified before too many people fall ill. The program was featured on the Homeland Security Website.

In December 2002, Western governors agreed to work together to develop common standards for emergency communications systems and procedures for use in responding to terrorist attacks or other emergencies. Such systems require cooperation between state and local governments as well as private companies.[62]

The Port Authority of New York and New Jersey has spent approximately $2.7 billion on security-related costs since the 9/11 attacks. Expenses are primarily for security personnel at cargo facilities located at Newark Liberty, Kennedy, LaGuardia, and Teterboro airports. It is estimated that the Authority spends approximately $2.3 million weekly to protect these air cargo facilities. In 2007 the Authority will spend $394 million for police and emergency salaries, up from $180 million in 2000. The Authority will also spend $18 million on black-box tracking technology used in all shipping containers, which can then be monitored by satellite.[63]

The Chicago Transit Authority (CTA), working with the Chicago Police Department, made it possible for Chicago police cars to watch live views from inside buses. The CTA is outfitting buses with radio equipment with signals that can be picked up by nearby police cars. The city is studying a proposal by AT&T and EarthLink to create a Wi-Fi system to monitor the entire city.[64]

5 Public/Private Joint Initiatives

The importance of cooperation between public law enforcement and private security has never been greater. Yet the difficulties in establishing effective cooperation between the two areas, particularly in the area of emergency planning and response, remain a major obstacle to effective responses. According to Penelope Turnbull, director of crisis management and business continuity for Marriott International and vice chair of the ASIS International Disaster Management Council, "I do believe that there is a growing realization that greater cooperation between and within the two sectors is required."[65] According to Turnbull, initiatives will need to overcome traditional issues of trust, jargon, and objectives.

A good example of how public and private cooperation can work was seen in the aftermath of the crash of American Airlines Flight 77 into the Pentagon on 9/11. Through preplanned cooperation of local law enforcement and commercial communications companies, communication problems usually associated with increased telephone and radio traffic were minimized. The Public Safety Wireless Network (PSWN), a joint initiative between the Departments of Treasury and Justice, reported that the response showed true interoperability, despite the fact that many departments operate on different frequencies. Cooperation with the Arlington County dispatch center and commercial companies Nextel, Cingular, and Verizon made the effort work. However, although the response worked well, there were still lessons to be learned. Most of these had to do with information sharing prior to an event that would make all known resources available to the users.[66]

The National Institute of Justice also took a "let's work together" approach. The Institute published flowcharts, diagrams, matrices, and other help aids for businesses in the chemical industry interested in analysing their security systems.

The Austin, Texas, public transportation system increased its security by purchasing wireless digital cameras that are located both inside and outside city buses. The funding for this program is from the federal government and could reach over $0.5 million. Although the general public has often seen "Big Brother" in such projects, the Austin community seems to have accepted the cameras. The Austin Police Department also played a significant role in specifying the camera system and establishing chain of custody in the event the cameras record criminal activities.

According to the DHS, companies, universities, and government agencies are reporting cyber attack crimes to the U.S. Computer Emergency Readiness Team (US-CERT) in increasing numbers. In 2005, 5,000 incidents were reported. In 2006, 23,000 incidents were reported, an almost five-fold increase. In the first quarter of 2007 more than 19,000 incidents were reported.[67]

In an effort to assist local and state law enforcement agencies faced with possible attack using nuclear or dirty bombs, the U.S. National Nuclear Security Administration has been working on "Render Safe" devices that could be used to disarm such weapons. The Render Safe program is in response to concerns that in the event of a terrorist threat involving nuclear or dirty bomb technology, the Nevada-based Nuclear Emergency Search Team (NEST) would not be able to get to the scene of the attack in time.[68]

The DHS promotes investment in the Render Safe system, but others criticize it as an extraordinarily costly program that will provide few security gains. Costs must certainly be a concern as New York officials are haggling over the burden of maintaining and operating a network of detection machines that the Domestic Nuclear Detection Office of the DHS is planning to install in New York City.[69]

6 Concerns

No one should minimize the loss of 3,000 lives to a single terrorist attack or ignore significant attacks by terrorists throughout the world, but it is equally important to consider the impact of overreaction on the health of the world, both mentally and economically. In the big picture, most businesses and institutions do not represent viable targets for terrorist attacks. The emphasis on protection from terrorism may be diverting attention and funding away from other, more significant and real threats. This is something that risk analysis through vulnerability/probability studies may be able to shed light on.

"Just how much protection do we need and at what cost?"

At the same level of thinking, it is worth noting that the U.S. government has established the largest new cabinet-level department since World War II around homeland security. Within the operations of this superdepartment are government plans to play larger roles in protecting the American public. The questions that need to be in everyone's mind are, "Just how much protection do we need and at what cost?"

Some believe that al Qaeda may have achieved a portion of its goal in the establishment of the DHS. The impact of the terrorist attack may have caused government and industry to overspend on security. This argument is countered by a look at the percentage of the gross domestic product (GDP) that goes toward homeland defense. The Federal Reserve Bank reports that although expenditures on security have tripled, the total allocated to this area in 2003 ($38 billion) represents only 0.35 percent of the GDP. Even when added to the DoD budget of $379 billion, the total still is less than 3.8 percent of the GDP. The Federal Reserve also indicates that the amount being spent by state and local governments is less than 1/1,000 of state and local budgets.[70] Estimates in a recent study indicate that the Fed figures were still accurate through 2005.[71]

Still, state and local governments are complaining that expenses are in addition to already allocated funds. Fiscal health remains an important issue in many states where deficit spending continues to be a major problem.

On another level, tension has arisen between the need to monitor and evaluate people entering this country and those already here. Security needs appear to be great. To accommodate those needs government agencies are asking for unprecedented access to personal information. On the other side is what many Americans consider a given right to privacy. The right to privacy requires that steps are taken to protect personal information. Recent legislation has increased the security of personal information, whereas legislation following 9/11 has also increased the government's ability to monitor and control personal behavior in public places. The public opinion immediately following 9/11 was in favor of increased security, but there seems to be a shift back to privacy as time passes. This shift is best exemplified in the change in public opinion concerning the use of federal identification cards with biometric identifiers. Polls conducted by Harris, Pew Research Center, and the *Washington Post* found that support for the national ID system ranged from a low of 44 percent to 70 percent. In a poll by Gartner Group (March 2002), only 26 percent of the respondents viewed the system as positive.[72]

Departing House Majority Leader Dick Armey warned in 2002 that the nation should be careful in sacrificing freedom for safety in the fight against terrorism. American Civil Liberties Union (ACLU) cyber chief Barry Steinhardt has said, "The surveillance monster is growing, but the legal chains to these monsters are weakened even when we should be strengthening them."[73] He refers to projects that call for high-tech security cameras to instantly match people with names and information in databases.

Although the establishment of the DHS was touted as a progressive move, bringing together the intelligence and response capabilities of various and often competitive federal agencies, the truth is that the transition to a "superagency" has not been smooth. Competitive egos are deep rooted and difficult to root out. The post-Katrina failure of FEMA reflects poorly on its supervising unit. In a recent GAO bulletin, the DHS is criticized for failure to provide adequate support to its mission components. In particular, DHS has problems in acquiring goods and services and providing proper oversight of this function.[74]

In addition, some legislation passed soon after the 9/11 attacks, though well intentioned, has failed to achieve any meaningful objectives. For example, the 2002 Federal Information Security Management Act (FISMA) mandated security planning for agencies, requiring a risk analysis of IT systems and certification and accreditation of the systems. The act is appropriately written, but there is no way under the current legislation to measure whether the plan actually improves security. According to Bruce Brody, vice president of information assurance at CACI International Inc., "Federal systems and networks are like Swiss cheese. FISMA over five years has not helped us to be appreciably more secure."[75]

Perhaps the most telling assessment of the new Department is the February 7, 2007 report by the GAO. Though DHS is just over six years old, the importance of its stated mission requires that any problems associated with the consolidation of over 22 agencies into a cohesive unit must be overcome. As of the February 2007 report, the GAO notes that DHS continues to face programmatic and partnering challenges. To help ensure that its missions are achieved, DHS must overcome continued challenges related to cargo, transportation, and border security; systematic visitor tracking; efforts to combat the employment of illegal aliens; and outdated Coast Guard asset capabilities.[76]

For additional information on many of the programs discussed in this chapter, see Appendix B, "World Wide Web Resources for Security Response."

□ □ □ ▬▬▬▬▬▬▬▬▬▬▬▬▬▬▬▬▬▬▬▬▬▬▬▬▬▬▬▬

Critical Thinking

What are the potential liabilities associated with limiting individual rights? Are the potential protections afforded by greater government scrutiny worth the reduction in individual freedom?

▬▬▬▬▬▬▬▬▬▬▬▬▬▬▬▬▬▬▬▬▬▬▬▬▬▬▬▬ □ □ □

Review Questions

1. What new initiatives are under way through the American Society for Industrial Security International?
2. What impact have federal regulations, rules, and guidelines had on private business in the United States?
3. Summarize what you know about the Department of Homeland Security.
4. What measures, if any, have been taken to secure world ports and the shipping industry?
5. Discuss the problems associated with electrical power security.

References

1. "Homeland Security Spending to Continue to Rise," *Security Beat*, March 11, 2003, downloaded 3/11/2003, www.securitysolutions.com.

2. Garamone, Jim, "Top DoD Budget Official Outlines War on Terror Costs," American Forces Information Services, www.defenselink.mil/news/NewsArticle.aspx?ID=2949.

3. ASIS press release, "Workplace Security Legislation Supported by ASIS International Implemented by Department of Justice," February 7, 2006.

4. Anderson, Teresa, "A Year of Reassessment," *Security Management*, January 2003, 61+.

5. Longley, Robert, "Airport Screener Raking in Hidden Weapons," About.com: U.S. Gov Info/Resources, http://usgovinfo.about.com/cs/waronterror/a/aaseized.htm?p=1.

6. The American Motorcoach Industry's Anti-Terrorism Bus Association, 2002.

7. "Cargo Security Initiative Established at World's 20 Largest Seaports," Current Issues, USINFO, July 27, 2004.

8. "Security Rules Adding Time to Shipments," *Security Beat*, March 18, 2003, downloaded 3/18/2003, www.securitysolutions.com.

9. "Ports Vow to Run a Tight Ship," *Security Management*, May 2002, 16–7.

10. Ibid.

11. "Maritime Security", *Security Management*, March 2003, 142.

12. "Container Security," *Security Management*, February 2003, 21.

13. White, Charles H., Jr., "Guest Viewpoint: Developing Railroad Security," Institute for Supply Management, Tempe, AZ.

14. Ibid.

15. "TSA Cites Authority to Search Vehicles; Gets Passing Grade from GAO," *Security Beat*, February 25, 2003, downloaded 2/25/2003, www.securitysolutions.com.

16. Gips, Michael A., "They Secure the Body Electric," *Security Management*, November 2002, 77–81.

17. "NRC Struggling to Address Reactor Shortcomings," *Security Management*, June 2002, 17.

18. "New Regulations in the Pipeline," *Security Management*, February 2003.

19. www.aeronautics-sys.com/Index.asp?CategoryIC=116&ArticleID=276&Page=1, June 20, 2007.

20. Jones, Jeffrey, "Canada oil sector takes al Qaeda threat seriously," Reuters, www.reuters.com/articleId=USN11433721020070214.

21. "Water Utilities Scramble to Meet Federal Deadlines," *Security Beat*, March 18, 2003, downloaded 3/18/2003, www.securitysolutions.com.

22. Tieman, Mary, "Safe Drinking Water Act: Implementation and Issues, Congressional Research Service for Congress," May 3, 2006.

23. Ibid.

24. Premo, Rita, "City Center Solutions," *Security Management*, April 2002, 85–92.

25. Apuzzo, Matt, "Mall Security Guards Get Anti-terrorism Training," *Daily Texan*, December 3, 2004.

26. "Mall Shooting Spree Raises Security Questions," *Retail Traffic*, February 14, 2007.

27. Premo.

28. "Study Identifies 39 Ways for Malls to Combat Terrorism," *Access Control & Security Systems*, www.securitysolutions.com/news/mall-terrorism-study/index.html, February 13, 2007.

29. "Survey Assesses Sports Facility Security," *Security Management*, February 2003, 14.

30. "When Attendees May Be Terrorists,"*Security Management*, March 2003, 16–18.

31. Gips, Michael A., "Open Spaces in a Tight Spot," *Security Management*, January 2002, 47–54.

32. "Security Can Cement Construction Role,"*Security Management*, March 2003, 22.

33. "Building Security Starts with Planning and Design,"*Security Beat*, February 25, 2003, downloaded 2/25/2003, www.securitysolutions.com.

34. Gips, Michael A., "The First Link in the Food Chain," *Security Management*, February 2003, 41–47.

35. Leahy, Robert F., and Michelman, Bonnie S., "Healing Access Control Woes," *Security Management*, March 2003, 88–96.

36. Aldridge, Jeff, "Hospital Security: The Past, the Present, and the Future," SecurityInfoWatch.com, August 31, 2005.

37. "DHS Details Funding Plans," *Security Beat*, March 11, 2003, downloaded 3/11/2003, www.securitysolutions.com.

38. "Using the Same Old Eyes," *Newsweek*, March 10, 2003, 7.

39. Martin, David, "With a Whisper, Not a Bang," *San Antonio Current*, December 24, 2003.

40. "Cyberspace Protection Plans Get Mixed Reviews,"*Security Management*, November 2002, 42.

41. "Widespread Smallpox Vaccination Too Dangerous for U.S. Population,"*Security Products*, March 2003, 54.

42. Pre-Harvest Security Guidelines and Checklist 2006, USDA.

43. "Homeland Security Establishing A National Advisory Council," FEMA release HQ-07-014, February 7, 2007, www.fema.gov/news/newsrelease.fema?id=33888.

44. "Government Wants Detailed Information About Guests," *Security Products*, March 2003, 52.

45. "Green Link: Can a Financial Institution Really Know Its Customers?" *Security Products*, March 2003, 56–59.

46. Becker, Robert, "Glitches Riddle Database to Track Foreign Students," *Chicago Tribune*, Monday, March 17, 2003, 1.

47. Student and Exchange Visitor Information System: General Summary Quarterly Review, April 24, 2007.

48. Homeland Security Presidential Directive/HSPD-12, August 27, 2004 press release, www.whitehouse.gov/news/releases/2004/08/print20010827 8.html.

49. www.dhs.gov/xtrvlscc/programs/content_multi_image_0006shtm.

50. Lasky, Steven, "TIA: Big Brother or Bogeyman?" *Security Technology & Design*, January 2003, 6.

51. Tether, Tony, "Statement by the Director, Defense Advanced Research Projects Agency, submitted to the Subcommittee on Terrorism, Unconventional Threats and Capabilities House Armed Services Committee, United States House of Representatives," March 21, 2007.

52. Marsico, Ron, "An Appeal on Chemical Plant Safety," *The Star-Ledger*, February 9, 2007.

53. Lipton, Eric, "New York to Test Ways to Guard Against Nuclear Terror," *New York Times*, February 9, 2007.

54. "Governor Outlines More Security Preparations," *The Macomb Journal*, Thursday, March 20, 2003, 2A.

55. "Cities Spending Extra $70 Million a Week on Security, Survey Says," CNN.com, March 27, 2003, downloaded 4/4/2003, http://cnn.allppolitics.printthis.clickability.com/pt/cpt?action=cpt&expire=-1&urlID=583092.

56. "Municipal Security,"*Security Management*, April 2002, 19.

57. Sarkar, Dibya, "Hometown Security Gets Funding Boost," *Federal Computer Week*, March 17, 2003, downloaded 3/18/2003, www.fcw.com/fcw/articles/2003/0317.

58. Hobijn, Bart and Sager, Erick, "What Has Homeland Security Cost? An Assessment: 2001–2005," *Current Issues in Economics and Finance*, Vol. 13, No. 2, February 2007.

59. "Paige, Ridge Unveil New Web Resources to Help Schools Plan for Emergencies," U.S. Department of Education, downloaded 3/18/2003, www.ed.gov/PressReleases/03-2003/03072003.html.

60. "What It Took,"*Security Management*, March 2003, 68.

61. "U.S. State Legislation–Illinois," *Security Management*, February 2003, 93.

62. "Western Governors Agree to Work Together for Common Emergency Communications," *Security Products*, February 2003, 34.

63. "Port Authority Spending Its Own Funds on Security,"*Access Control & Security Systems*, January 23, 2007, www.securitysolutions.com/news/port-authority-security/index.html.

64. Van, Jon, "In Chicago, Police to See Live Surveillance from Buses," SecurityInfoWatch.com, June 21, 2007.

65. "Public-Private Emergency Planning,"*Security Management*, November 2002, 39.

66. "Wireless Works for First Responders,"*Security Management*, April 2002, 33.

67. Lemos, Robert, "Companies Increasingly Reporting Attacks," www.securityfocus.com/brief/430.

68. Davidson, Keay, "Devices Could Disable Terror Bombs," *San Francisco Gate*, February 7, 2007, A-3.

69. Lipton, Eric, "New York to Test Ways to Guard Against Nuclear Terror," *The New York Times*, February 9, 2007.

70. "Homeland Security Costs,"*Security Management*, February 2003, 20.

71. Hobijn and Sager, 2007.

72. "Green Link: The Threat of Terrorism and the Role of Financial Institutions,"*Security Products*, February 2003, 38–41.

73. "ACLU Cyberchief Worried About Privacy,"CNN.com, March 30, 2003, downloaded 4/4/2003, http://www.cnn.technology.printthis.clickability.com/pt/cpt?actions=cpt&expire,04%2F29%2F20.

74. "Observation on the Department of Homeland Security's Acquisition Organization and on the Coast Guard's Deepwater Program," GAO Highlights, GAO-07-453T, February 8, 2007.

75. Jackson, William, "Experts: It's time to fix FISMA," GCN, www.gcn.com/online/vol1_no1/43103-1.html.

76. "Management and Programmatic Challenges Facing the Department of Homeland Security," GAO Highlights, February 2, 2007, GAO-07 452T. The security field continues to undergo the most significant changes it has seen since World War II!

2

Origins and Development of Security

OBJECTIVES

The study of this chapter will enable you to:

1. Know the history of development in security beginning in England
2. Outline the historical development of security in America
3. Understand the role of professional associations and organizations in the development of a professional security industry

1 Introduction

Security implies a stable, relatively predictable environment in which an individual or group may pursue its ends without disruption or harm and without fear of disturbance or injury. The concept of security in an organizational sense has evolved gradually throughout the history of Western civilization, shaped by a wide variety of institutional and cultural patterns.

In examining the origins and development of security, we should note that security holds a mirror up, not to nature, but to society and its institutions. Thus in medieval England there were programs to clear brush and other concealment on either side of the king's roads as a precaution against robbers, and there were night watchmen to protect citizens from night thieves. In the United States in modern times, these rudimentary security measures find their counterparts in the cleared areas adjoining perimeter fences and buildings, in security patrols, and in intrusion alarms. Throughout history it is possible to trace the emerging concept of security as a response to, and a reflection of, a changing society, mirroring not only its social structure but also its economic conditions, its perception of law and crime, and its morality. Thus security remains a field of both tradition and dramatic change. The introduction of high-tech systems and computers has changed the nature of the job of the 21st-century security professional. Security today must be directed toward modern problems, including computer crime and world terrorism. Yet we cannot forget the basic foundations on which the field developed.

2   Security in England

2.1   Feudalism and Security

In early England, feudalism provided a very high degree of security for both the individual and the group. The Anglo-Saxons brought with them to England a predisposition to accept mutual responsibility for civil and military protection of individuals. They also brought a strong affinity for the feudal contract, whereby an overlord guaranteed the safety of persons and property and provided arms and treasures to vassals who administered the work of the serfs bound to the land.

In a world of constant warfare between men of power, security could be found in no other way. Stability lay in the system and in the power and cleverness of the lord. Group security lay in group solidarity. The formal systems of security that developed over the years of the Middle Ages were largely confirmations of those systems toward which the people of this society had gravitated naturally.

2.2   Post-Norman Reforms

Post-Norman England, beginning with King John, saw the introduction of concepts declaring the supremacy of law over the arbitrary edict, thus developing a base of confidence in the continuity of the system and its institutions. Above all, there was a formal declaration of the individual's rights and of responsibilities between the state and its subjects and among subjects themselves.

Judicial reforms during this era saw the emergence of local juries, circuit judges, coroners to restrain the power of local sheriffs, and justices of the peace appointed to hear and determine criminal cases. The movement also began that would eventually see the complete separation of courts and the exercise of the rule of law from the whims and power of the king.

Concurrently, there were measures specifically aimed at the enforcement of public order. The Statute of Winchester (also known as the Statute of Westminster) in 1285 revived and reorganized the old institutions of national police and national defense. It described the "duty of watch and ward," which enjoined every man to pursue and bring to justice felons whenever "hue and cry" was raised.

Every district was made responsible for crimes committed within its bounds; the gates of all towns were required to be closed at nightfall, and all strangers were required to give an account of themselves to the magistrates. Interestingly, one "security" practice already mentioned required brushwood and other concealments to be cleared for a space of 200 feet on either side of the king's highways to protect travelers against attack by robbers.

Attempts were made to control vice and crime at the local level, and boroughs enacted their own ordinances to that end. Since organized agencies for the enforcement of such laws were virtually nonexistent, however, these efforts had limited success. Privately established night watches and patrols were often the citizens' only protection against direct assault.

2.3   Exploration and Change

The development of systems of protection and enforcement appeared to come with greater rapidity and sophistication from the 14th through the 18th centuries. Seeds for this development were planted during the social revolution that heralded the end of the remaining elements of the feudal structure in the latter half of the 13th century.

Security was one thing in a largely rural society controlled by kings and feudal barons; it was another thing entirely in a world swept by enormous changes. The voyages of exploration, which opened new markets and trade routes, created a new and increasingly important merchant class whose activities came to dominate the port cities and trading centers. Concurrently, acts of enclosure and consolidation drove displaced small tenants off the land, and they migrated to the cities in great numbers.

By 1700 the social patterns of the Middle Ages were breaking down. Increased urbanization of the population had created conditions of considerable hardship. Poverty and crime increased rapidly. No public law enforcement agencies existed that could restrain the mounting wave of crime and violence, and no agencies existed that could alleviate the causes of the problem.

Different kinds of police agencies were privately formed. Individual merchants hired men to guard their property. Merchant associations also created the merchant police to guard shops and warehouses. Night watchmen were employed to make their rounds. Agents were engaged to recover stolen property, and the people of various parishes into which the major cities were divided hired parochial police.

Attention then turned to the reaffirmation of laws to protect the common good. Although the Court of Star Chamber, which gave the English monarchy all control over decisions of law, had been abolished in 1641, its practices were not officially proscribed until 1689, when Parliament agreed to crown William and Mary if they would reaffirm the ancient rights and privileges of the people. They agreed, and Parliament ratified the Bill of Rights, which for all time limited the power of the king as well as affirming and protecting the inalienable rights of the individual.

2.4   The 18th Century

As we study this history into the 18th century, it is possible to discern both the shape of efforts toward communal security and the kinds of problems that would continue to plague an increasingly urban society for the next 200 years.

In 1737, for instance, a new aspect of individual rights came to be acknowledged. For the first time, tax revenues were used for the payment of a night watch. This was a significant development in security practice because it was a precedent-setting step that established for the first time the use of tax revenues for common security purposes.

Eight years later, Parliament authorized a special committee to study security problems. The study resulted in a program employing various existing private security forces to extend the scope of their protection. The resulting heterogeneous group, however, was too much at odds. It proved ineffective in providing any satisfactory level of protection.

In 1748 Henry Fielding, magistrate and author (most notably of the unforgettable *Tom Jones*), proposed a permanent, professional, and adequately paid security force. His invaluable contributions included a foot patrol to make the streets safe, a mounted patrol for the highways, the famous Bow Street Amateur Volunteer Force of special investigators, and police courts. Fielding is credited with conceiving the idea of preventing crime instead of seeking to control it.

It is interesting to note that Fielding also wrote an ironic novel called *Jonathan Wild: The Story of a Great Man*. Its hero, Jonathan Wild, was a real person in 18th-century

London, perhaps the most notorious fence, thief, and master criminal of modern times. He was so real, in fact, that an account of his activities occupies eight pages of a staff report prepared in 1972 for the Select Committee on Small Business of the U.S. Senate, more than 200 years after Wild was hanged at Tyburn.

How is it that the specter of Jonathan Wild still haunts today's bodies charged with finding means to minimize crime? In many ways, Wild's career typified the problems of security—or more specifically, theft control—in the 18th century. For many centuries, English common law almost totally ignored the receiver of stolen goods. As the Senate committee report observes, "Because Jonathan Wild was such an extraordinary criminal, it is easy to lose sight of the fact that first he was at best a receiver and that second his whole organization was geared to facilitate that primary enterprise."[1] But mere receiving of stolen goods, even with knowledge, did not make the receiver an accessory in the eyes of the law.

Perhaps this attitude of common law can be explained in part by the relative unimportance of dealings in stolen property in the early stages of the development of criminal law. Until the 17th century, the amount of movable property available for theft was probably limited, and opportunities to dispose of this property, other than by personal consumption, were rather restricted. Lacking a professional police force, the attention of the community, and the law, was primarily directed toward apprehending offenders rather than tracing and recovering stolen property. The victims of property crimes were left to rely on their own ingenuity, bolstered by several shaky legal remedies, to secure the return of their plundered goods and chattels.

It was not until the late 17th century that Parliament moved for the first time to combat the problem of the receiver of stolen goods. In 1691, under a statute enacted during the reign of William and Mary, the receiver was made subject to prosecution, but only as an accessory after the fact. The tradition remained throughout the 18th and early 19th centuries that the receiver was an accessory rather than a principal to the crime. The weakness of the law in its attitude toward property crimes as much as the lack of effective law enforcement combined to make possible Jonathan Wild's legendary career.

2.5   The Impact of Industrial Expansion

The Industrial Revolution began to gather momentum in the latter half of the 18th century. By 1801 the poet William Blake, of apocalyptic vision, was writing disapprovingly of "these dark, Satanic mills." Like the migrations off the land 200 years earlier, people again flocked to the cities—not pushed this time, as they had been earlier, by enclosure and dispossession but rather lured by promises of work and wages.

The already crowded cities were choked with this new influx of wealth seekers. What they found were long hours, crippling work, and miserly wages. Men and women—even very young children—worked in unsafe factories. Disease periodically swept the crowded quarters. Family life, heretofore the root of all stability, was virtually destroyed in this environment. Thievery, crimes of violence, and juvenile delinquency were the order of the day. All the ills of such a structure, as we see in analogous situations today, overtook the emerging industrial centers.

Little was done to alleviate the growing problems. Indeed, the prevailing philosophy of the time argued against doing anything. In 1776 Adam Smith gained a large and appreciative audience with his *Wealth of Nations*. In it, he contended that labor was the source of wealth and that it was by freedom of labor, by allowing the worker to pursue his own interest in his own way, that the public wealth would best be promoted. Any attempt to force labor into artificial channels, to shape by laws the course of commerce, or to promote special branches of industry in particular counties would be not only wrong to the worker and merchant but also harmful to the wealth of the state.

In this new age in which such statements of *laissez faire* were generally accepted, industrial centers became the spawning grounds for crimes of all kinds. At one time, counterfeiting was so common that it was estimated that more counterfeit than government-issued money was in circulation. More than 50 false mints were found in London alone.

The backlash to such a high crime rate was inevitable and predictable. Penalties were increased to deter potential criminals. At one time, more than 150 capital offenses existed, ranging from picking pockets to serious crimes of violence. Yet no visible decline in crime resulted. It was a "society that lacked any effective means of enforcing the criminal laws in general. A Draconian code of penalties that proscribed the death penalty for a host of crimes failed to balance the absence of efficient enforcement machinery."[2]

Private citizens resorted to carrying arms for protection, and they continued to band together to hire special police to protect their homes and businesses.

2.6   Sir Robert Peel and the "Bobbies"

In 1822 Sir Robert Peel became home secretary. He had an abiding interest in creating a strong, unified, professional police force. This interest had emerged earlier when, as secretary for Irish affairs, he had reformed the Irish constabulary—members of which were thereafter referred to as "Peelers." As home secretary, Peel initiated the criminal law reform bill and reorganized the metropolitan police force, also referred to as "Peelers," or more commonly, "Bobbies." He also attempted to decentralize police efforts and to develop the responsibility of each community for its own security.

Unfortunately, not all of Sir Robert's efforts met with success. Neither the Police Act of 1835, establishing city and borough police forces; the County Act of 1839, setting up county police; nor various other acts passed in midcentury created adequate police operations. Private guard forces continued to be used to recover stolen property and to provide protection for private persons and businesses.

Nevertheless, based on Peel's thoroughgoing reforms and revisions, the metropolitan police force became a model for law enforcement agencies in years to come, not only in England but also in the United States. Modern policing, it is often said, was born with the "Bobby."

3   Security in the United States

Security practices in the early days of colonial America followed the patterns that colonists had been familiar with in England. The need for mutual protection in a new and alien land drew them together in groups much like those of earlier centuries.

As the settlers moved west in Massachusetts, along the Mohawk Valley in New York, and into central Pennsylvania and Virginia, the need for protection against hostile Indians and other colonists—both French and Spanish—was their principal security interest. Settlements generally consisted of a central fort or stockade surrounded by the settlers' farms. If hostilities threatened, an alarm was sounded and the members of the community left their homes for the protection of the fort, where all able-bodied persons were involved in its defense. In such circumstances, a semimilitary flavor often characterized security measures, which included guard posts and occasional patrols.

Protection of people and property in established towns again followed English traditions. Sheriffs were elected as chief security officers in colonial Virginia and Georgia; constables were appointed in New England. Watchmen were hired to patrol the streets at night. As *Private Security: Report of the Task Force on Private Security* notes, "These watchmen remained familiar figures and constituted the primary security measures until the establishment of full-time police forces in the mid-1800s."[3]

Such watchmen, it should be pointed out, were without training, had no legal authority, were either volunteer or else paid a pittance, and were generally held in low regard—circumstances that bear a remarkable similarity to observations in the RAND report on private security in 1971.[4]

3.1 Development of Private Security

The development of police and security forces seemed to follow no predictable pattern other than that such development was traditionally in response to public pressure for action.

Outside the establishment of night watch patrols in the 17th century, little effort to establish formal security agencies was made until the beginnings of a police department were established in New York City in 1783. Detroit followed in 1801 and Cincinnati in 1803. Chicago established a police department in 1837; San Francisco in 1846; Los Angeles in 1850; Philadelphia in 1855; and Dallas in 1856.

New York, influenced by the recent success of the police reforms of Sir Robert Peel, adopted his general principles in 1833. By and large, however, police methods in departments across the country were rudimentary. Most American police departments of the early 19th century, as a whole, were inefficient, ill trained, and corrupt.

In addition, the slow development of public law enforcement agencies, both state and federal, combined with the steady escalation of crime in an increasingly urban and industrialized society, created security needs that were met by what might be called the first professional private security responses in the second half of the 19th century.

In the 1850s Allan Pinkerton (see Figure 2.1), a "copper" (police officers who were identified by the copper badges they wore) from Scotland and the Chicago Police Department's first detective, established what was to become one of the oldest and largest private security operations in the United States, the Pinkerton agency. Pinkerton's North West Police Agency, formed in 1855, provided security and conducted investigations of crimes for various railroads. Two years later the Pinkerton Protection Patrol began to offer a private watchman service for railroad yards and industrial concerns. President Lincoln recognized Pinkerton's organizational skills and hired the agency to perform intelligence duties during the Civil War. Pinkerton is also credited with hiring the first woman to become a detective in this country, well before the women's suffrage movement had realized its aims.[5]

In 1850 Henry Wells and William Fargo were partners in the American Express Company, chartered to operate a freight service east of the Mississippi River; by 1852 they had expanded their operating charter westward as Wells Fargo and Company. Freight transportation was a dangerous business, and these early companies usually had their own detectives and security personnel, known as "shotgun riders."

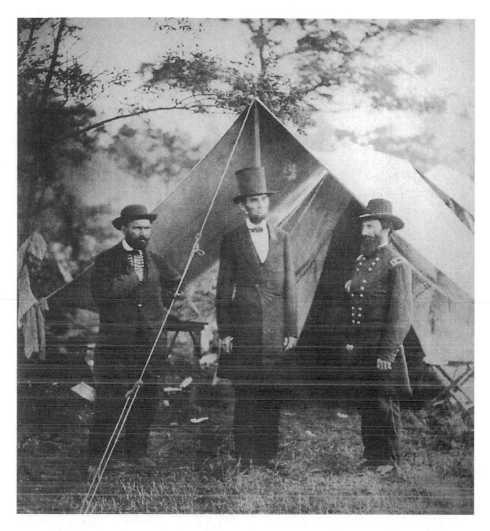

FIGURE 2.1 Allan Pinkerton, President Lincoln, and Major General John McClellan. (Photographed October 1862, Antietam, Md.; courtesy of the National Archives.)

Washington Perry Brink in Chicago founded Brinks, Inc., in 1859 as a freight and package delivery service. More than 30 years later, in 1891, he transported his first payroll—the beginning of armored car and courier service. By 1900 Brinks had a fleet of 85 wagons in the field.[6] Brinks, Wells Fargo, and Adams Express were the first major firms to offer security for the transportation of valuables and money.

William J. Burns, a former Secret Service investigator and head of the Bureau of Investigation, forerunner of the Federal Bureau of Investigation (FBI), started the William J. Burns Detective Agency in 1909. It became the sole investigating agency for the American Bankers' Association and grew to become the second largest (after Pinkerton) contract guard and investigative service in the United States.[7] For all intents and purposes, Pinkerton and Burns were the only national investigative bodies concerned with nonspecialized crimes in the country until the advent of the FBI.

Another 19th-century pioneer in this field was Edwin Holmes, who offered the first burglar alarm service in the country in 1858. Holmes purchased an alarm system designed by Augustus Pope. Following Holmes, American District Telegraph (ADT) was founded in 1874. Both companies installed alarms and provided response to alarm situations as well as maintaining their own equipment. Baker Industries initiated a fire control and detection equipment business in 1909.

From the 1870s into the 20th century, only private agencies had provided contract security services to industrial facilities across the country. In many cases, particularly around the end of the 19th century and during the Great Depression of the 1930s, the services were, to say the least, controversial. Both the Battle of Homestead in 1892, during which workers striking that plant were shot and beaten by security forces, and the strikes in the automobile industry in the middle 1930s are examples of excesses from overzealous security operatives in relatively recent history. With few exceptions, proprietary, or in-house, security forces hardly existed before the defense-related "plant protection" boom of the early 1940s. The impetus for modern private security effectively began in that decade with the creation of the federal Industrial Security Program (today named the Defense Industrial Security Program [DISP]), a subordinate command within the DoD. The National Industrial Security Program (NISP) is the nominal authority in the United States for managing the needs of private industry to access classified information. The NISP Operating Manual (NISPOM/DoD 5220;.l22m) today consists of 11 chapters and three appendices. The most recent 2006 revisions include the Intelligence Reform and Terrorism Prevention Act of 2004 and other changes taking effect since 9/11.[8]

By 1955 security took a major leap forward with the formation of the American Society for Industrial Security (ASIS). Today the organization is the American Society for Industrial Security International, reflecting the global emphasis on security operations. For most practitioners, 1955 signifies the beginning of the modern age of security. Before 1955 there were no professional organizations of note, no certifications, no college programs, and no cohesive body to advance the interests of the field.

Today's changed climate for increased security services came as businesses undertook expanded operations that in turn needed more protection. Retail establishments, hotels, restaurants, theaters, warehouses, trucking companies, industrial companies, hospitals, and other institutional and service functions were all growing and facing a serious need to protect their property and personnel. Security officers were the first line of defense, but it was not long before that important function was being overchallenged by the increasing complexity of fraud, arson, burglary, and other areas in which more sophisticated criminal practices began to prevail. Security consulting agencies and private investigation firms were founded in increasing numbers to handle these special types of cases. From among these, another large contractor was to emerge and join the field alongside Pinkerton, Burns, Globe, and Brinks. In 1954 George R. Wackenhut formed the Wackenhut Corporation in company with three other former FBI agents. Today these giants are joined by firms such as Baker Industries and Guardsmark, along with many regional firms such as the Midwest firm Per Mar Security. The largest such firm in the 21st century is now Securitas.

The private sector entered the security field in another form during the 1960s and 1970s. Common businesses and industries created central repositories of security information deemed important to all their common interests nationwide and made it available in various ways to their separate groups. Their purpose was to decrease loss by networking information that would prevent criminals from victimizing members of the group once anything was known that could be used to alert them.

Variously called "alliances," "bureaus," or security or loss prevention "institutes," these groups became deeply entrenched as providers of valuable information and services. Their methods of dissemination vary with what is appropriate to the business for which they were founded but include circulating "hot" lists, newsletters with "wanted" pictures and descriptions of characteristic modes of operation, telephone chain calling to alert merchants within an area, and so on. Nationally available repositories of other types of industry-specific data are usually maintained also and can be accessed by members. Not only do these groups serve the private sector in its effort to survive against crime—they also make their collected intelligence available to law enforcement.

Some currently existing groups are the National Insurance Crime Bureau (NICB) (www.nicb.org), the International Association of Arson Investigators (IAAI), the Property Loss Research Bureau (PLRB), and the Jewelers Security Alliance (JSA) (www.jewelersecurity.org). Still other groups serve similar functions by collecting records of insurance claims and spotting fraud, issuing periodic records of defaulted or dubious credit cards, and so on. The measures taken by these and other business associations to limit their losses and protect their members have spread to other areas in which there is today an increasing concern about excessive risk. Some of these areas include computer and other high-tech industries and antiterrorism and executive protection alliances. The need for information for employment background checks has also led to the creation of information bureaus. The Internet has added its own twist in providing fast service for those looking for information ranging from criminal histories to credit checks. A number of Websites sell information for fees ranging as low as $15 to more than $100 for each search request.

Expenditures in private security exceeded $100 billion annually in 2000 (ILJ.org, 2000), up from $66 billion in 1998.[9] The expenditures continued to grow, especially following the 9/11 attacks. Even as the anti-Vietnam War protest created a demand for additional security services during the 1970s, the threat of terrorism against U.S. business throughout the world, various extremist groups' kidnapping of executives assigned outside the United States, and drugs and violence in the workplace create a demand for the 21st century. With this dynamic growth have come profits, problems, and increasing professionalism. Each is a significant part of the picture of security today.[10]

3.2   Crime Trends and Security

During the 25 years roughly spanning the mid-1950s to the late 1970s, the United States became the victim of what the Task Force on Private Security of the National Advisory Committee on Criminal Justice Standards and Goals has called "a crime epidemic." The FBI's annual Uniform Crime Report Program (UCRP) documented the continuing steady increase in crimes of all types until 1981. Then, for the first time, the UCR Program reflected a modest overall decrease that has continued through the beginning of the 21st century.

In 2005, however, 14,094,186 arrests occurred nationwide for all offenses (except for traffic violations), of which 603,503 were for violent crimes and 1,609,327 for property crimes. Although the number of arrests in 2005 increased only a slight 0.2 percent from the 2004 figure, arrests for murder rose 7.3 percent. An examination of the 2- and 10-year trends shows that the estimated number of property crimes in 2005 decreased 1.5 percent from the 2004 estimate and declined 13.9 percent compared with the estimate for 1996. Preliminary figures for 2006 show a continuing trend, with violent crime up 1.3 percent over 2005 and property crime down 2.9 percent over the previous year.[11]

Gallup polls taken each year indicate that the fear of crime is an even greater problem than the crime rate itself would indicate. The consistency of survey results indicating that crime touched 25 percent of all American households during the year preceding each survey led Gallup to conclude that "the actual crime situation in this country is more serious than official governmental figures indicate." The most recent National Crime Victimization Survey (NCVS) data (for 2005) continue to show a 25-year decline in crime. Since 1994, violent crime rates have declined, reaching the lowest level ever in 2005. Property crime rates also continue to decrease to their lowest levels since 1973. Of the 13 million completed thefts of property in 2005, there were 4.1 million property thefts of less than $50, 4.7 million between $50 and $249, and 3.2 million of $250 or more.[12]

Although the NCVS indicates a decline in the number of offenses, the cost of business crime continues to be a major concern. The estimated figures on the extent of crime against business, ranging from $67 billion to $320 billion, have not been adequately studied since the mid-1980s and dramatize the absence of consistent hard data indicating the exact size of the problem today. Variations of billions of dollars in estimates are the result of educated guessing, interpolation, and adjustment for inflation. Still, some progress has been made in the last decade.

According to a 2002 Brookings Institute report, the Enron and WorldCom scandals alone cost the U.S. economy approximately $37 billion to $42 billion off the GDP during the first year.[13] A 2002 joint conference of the National White Collar Crime Center and the Coalition for the Prevention of Economic Crime identified the following as the most serious of economic crime problems:

- Money laundering
- Identity fraud
- E-commerce crime
- Insurance crime
- Victim services
- Terrorism

The conclusion of the conference was that the amount of "dirty money" worldwide tops $3 trillion.[14]

Obviously figures vary, principally because satisfactory means of measuring many crimes against business and industry have not yet been found but also because much internal crime in particular is never reported to the police, either because internal disciplinary action has already been taken or to avoid bad publicity and management embarrassment that could result from exposing to the public the business's lack of security controls. Nevertheless, such questions as may exist concern only the degree, not the fact, of the dramatic escalation of crimes against business in our society. Security concerns remain constant for employee theft, property crime, and issues related to life safety. The newest problems revolve around fraud, computer crime, workplace violence, and terrorism.

As this brief history of security has indicated, there is always an intimate link between cultural and social change and crime, just as there is between crime and the security measures adopted to combat the threat. A bewildering variety of causes, both social and economic, are cited for rising crime in this era. Among them are an erosion of family and religious restraints, the trend toward permissiveness, the increasing anonymity of business at every level of commerce, the decline in feelings of worker loyalty toward the company, and a general decline in morality accompanied by the pervasive attitude that there is no such thing as right and wrong but rather only what feels good.

In addition, the rapidly changing technology of business and personal lives is often far ahead of security measures used to protect personal and business intellectual property. The dominance of the computer and related technology in business has improved worldwide business efficiency, but not without a price. The Internet, while providing the path for information transfer, has also provided unheard of opportunities to steal or manipulate intellectual property. Who had heard of a computer virus in the 1970s?

These changes in attitudes, personal values, and technology have created a new problem for security managers. In 1990 McDonnell Douglas Corporation fired 150 employees who allegedly used interest-free company loans intended for the purchase of computers to buy stereo equipment and other luxury items. A data-processing employee reportedly processed the $4,000 loans by printing phony invoices for computers.[15] These problems are dwarfed by the problems created with accounting practices at Arthur Andersen, WorldCom, and Enron.

In the wake of the Enron scandal, the government passed the Sarbanes-Oxley Act of 2002 to combat corruption in public companies. This regulation has aided the corporate chief security officer (CSO) by minimizing scandal and requiring greater financial disclosures, better scrutiny by corporate boards and their audit committees, and tighter overall accounting controls. Oversight by Securities and Exchange Commission (SEC) regulators, coupled with stronger internal control mechanisms, clearly define white col lar crimes as being prevalent and a security challenge that cannot be overlooked.

It is far beyond the scope of this book to attempt to analyze or even to catalog all the factors involved in the trend toward increasing crime, even were we to restrict such a study to crimes against business and industry. What is important here is to make clear note of the fact of such increases—and of their impact on society's attempts to protect itself.

Most significant is the realization that "the sheer magnitude of crime in our society prevents the criminal justice system by itself from adequately controlling or preventing crime."[16] In spite of their steady growth, both in costs and in numbers of personnel, public law enforcement agencies have increasingly been compelled to be reactive and to concentrate more of their activities on the maintenance of public order and the apprehension of criminals. Even community-oriented policing rests on the need for a cooperative approach to law enforcement. The approximately 500,000 local law enforcement personnel in this country cannot possibly provide protection for all those who need it.[17]

3.3   Growth of Private Security

Society has in recent times relied almost exclusively on the police and other arms of the criminal justice system to prevent and control crime. But today the sheer volume of crime and its cost, along with budget cutbacks in the public sector, have overstrained public law enforcement agencies. Private security must play a greater role in the prevention and control of crime than ever before. The Institute for Law and Justice, authors of the 1990 *Hallcrest II* report, indicated that by 2000 there would be more than 1.9 million people employed in private security, with total expenditures for private security products and services estimated at $100 billion.[18] This compares with police protection expenditures for federal, state, and local governments of only $45 billion. However, it must be noted that this gap will undoubtedly narrow as government agencies respond to

1285	1641	1737	1748	1783	1822	1835	1837	1850
Statute of Winchester	Court of Star Chamber abolished	Tax $ used to support watches	Fielding proposes paid sec. force	NYCPD founded	Peel Home Secretary	Police Act	Chicago PD founded	Pinkerton founded

1852	1859	1874	1892	1909	1954	1955	1968	1976
Wells Fargo founded	Brinks founded	ADT founded	Battle of Homestead	Burns founded	Wackenhut founded	ASIS founded	Omnibus Crime Control Act	Task Force Private Sec.

1985	1990	1995	2001	2002	2002	2005	2005
Hallcrest Report	Hallcrest II Report	Murrah Bldg. bombed	World Trade Center and Pentagon attacked	Airport Security Act	ASIS Suggested Guidelines	NCIC checks available to employers of security officers	Hurricane Katrina forces reevaluation of DHS

FIGURE 2.2 Significant historical timeline.

the events of 9/11. The Bureau of Labor Statistics reported that there were 1.2 million protective services employees in 2005 compared to public police officers, who numbered 16,000.[19]

3.4   Growing Pains and Government Involvement

Inevitably, the explosive growth of the security industry in the second half of the 20th century was not without its problems, leading to rising concern for the quality of selection, training, and performance of security personnel. The hijackings that led to the destruction of the World Trade Center in 2001 were blamed on poorly trained contract security screeners at U.S. airports and governmental intelligence agencies. Whether the blame is fair may be debatable, because screeners were not looking for box cutters or other implements used by the hijackers. Within months the U.S. government had established federal control over this segment of security. Even within the industry itself, there is increasing pressure for improved standards, higher pay, and greater professionalism. The American Society for Industrial Security International has developed industry standards that are regularly being discussed by representatives in the security industry and federal government.

Considering the importance of private security personnel in the anticrime effort and their quasi-law enforcement functions, it is ironic that they receive so little training in comparison to their public sector contemporaries. According to a 2005 study by Associated Criminal Justice and Security Consultants, the median number of hours of basic police training is 720 prior to licensing or certification by state police training boards. The same study found that many security officers, on average, receive less than eight hours of pre-job training.[20] To complicate these figures, often this training is completed through an orientation video. Still, there are contract and proprietary security operations that provide very good training programs. Some contract security companies such as Wackenhut, for example, have established client contracts that provide from 40 to 120 hours of pre- and post-assignment training requirements, dependent on the designated officer's position. This does not include OJT. In addition, a specified 16-hour annualized training requirement to refresh officers and avoid complacency can also be established. Security managers must not overlook the values of maximizing training opportunities and requirements.

This situation was debated during the 1990s. The Gore Bill, introduced in 1991 by then Senator Al Gore (D-TN), recommended minimum training for all security personnel without setting a minimum standard. The Sundquist Bill, introduced in 1993 by Representative Don Sundquist (R-TN), spelled out specific training requirements, adding to the 1991 Senate bill. The Sundquist Bill recommended 16 hours of training for unarmed officers and 40 hours for armed personnel. Also in 1993, Representative Matthew Martinez (D-CA) reintroduced a bill mandating 12 hours of training for unarmed security personnel and 27 hours for armed officers. What is obvious is that the federal government has started to take an active interest in setting minimum standards for the security profession. (For a discussion of these bills, see "Why Is Security Officer Training Legislation Needed?" by John Chuvala III, CPP, and Robert J. Fischer, *Security Management*, April 1994.) Still, it is important to note that *no* federal legislation regulating private security had been passed until 2002, following the World Trade Center disaster. With the support of ASIS, the Private Security Officer Employment Standards Act of 2002 was passed, allowing all security employers access to federal employment background checks through the National Crime Information Center.

3.5   Professionalism

Today private security has moved toward a new professionalism. In defining the desired professionalism, most authorities often cite the need for a code of ethics and for credentials that include education and training, experience, and membership in a professional society.

This continuing thrust toward professionalism is observable in the proliferation of active private security professional organizations and associations. It is promoted by such organizations as the ASIS (which has a membership of more than 30,000 security managers), the Academy of Security Educators and Trainers (ASET), the International Association for Healthcare Security and Safety (IAHSS), the National Association of School Security Safety and Law Enforcement Officers (NASSLEO), and the Security Industry Association (SIA). It finds its voice in the library of professional security literature—magazines, Internet sites, and books. And it looks to its future in the continued development of college-level courses and degree programs in security.

ASIS has adhered to a professional code of ethics, one mark of a true profession, since its inception. The group established the Certified Protection Professional (CPP) program, which requires security managers desiring certification to be nominated by a CPP member and to complete a rigorous test. This program and others are discussed in more detail in Chapter 6.

Despite the many efforts to professionalize the field of private security, there are still many who feel that major obstacles need to be overcome. The most persistent one has to do with the training and education of the contract security officer. (A distinction between contract and proprietary officers needs to be made. Proprietary officers—those hired directly by a company—are generally better trained and better paid than are their contract counterparts.) Many officers—no matter whether they are contract or proprietary—are underpaid, undertrained, undersupervised, and unregulated. Minimal standards do exist in some places, but there is still a reluctance to train, educate, and adequately compensate the security force. Business considerations in making a product for profit can make it difficult for companies to see the need to pay for costly security programs. Thus they often opt for the lowest-priced solution, no matter whether it affords real protection. Fortunately this kind of thinking is undergoing a change as industry realizes that the adage "You get what you pay for" very definitely applies to the quality of security. This realization should in turn add pressure on industry to upgrade the position of the security officer. Current standards, codes of ethics, and educational courses need to be supported by industry participation.

One development in the evolution of training for line security staff is the the Certified Protection Officer (CPO) program, established in 1986 by the International Foundation for Protection Officers, a nonprofit organization. The CPO program is being offered at a number of colleges in the United States and Canada. Additional information on this program is presented in Chapter 6.

"A systems approach to security is appropriate today, as more and more businesses are giving the responsibility for protecting assets to the security and loss prevention department."[21] In that insightful comment, Dr. Kenneth Fauth, former director of security and loss prevention at Spiegel, Inc., suggests clearly that security and loss prevention has evolved well beyond the officer at the gate. Though that post is still vital, today's business assets comprise an almost infinite variety of protection needs. Moreover, security increasingly includes protection against contingencies that might prevent normal company operation from continuing and from making a profit. And as the concept of risk management is further integrated into a comprehensive loss-prevention program, the security function focuses less and less on enforcement and more on anticipating and preventing loss through proactive programming. Such challenges indisputably require high-level security management and an increasingly well-credentialed group of security professionals.

The systems approach, as outlined by C. West Churchman in 1968, is the process of focusing on central objectives rather than on attempting to solve individual problems within an organization. By concentrating on the central objectives, the management team can address specific problems that will lead to the accomplishment of the central objective. As noted earlier, these central objectives for the 21st century include protection from terrorism and control of economic crimes as well as continuing to combat traditional security problems. Today, we talk about integrated security systems.

These problems must be approached from a team perspective. Public law enforcement at local, state, and federal levels, along with security interaction and operations, must work together, sharing intelligence to control these problems and reestablish a sense of security for the world's citizens. Security, therefore, is the safety of reassurance.

The establishment of joint councils within ASIS and the International Association of Chiefs of Police (IACP) has increased communication between the public and private sectors. In addition, the National Sheriffs' Association (NSA) has its Private Security Industry Committee. These groups have developed numerous cooperative programs, of which only a few will be mentioned. In the aftermath of September 11, 2001, cooperation among various law enforcement agencies—local, state, and federal as well as private security organizations—has been enhanced. With the establishment of the Department of Homeland Security, the federal government has attempted to increase the interoperability of all areas of the criminal justice system in an effort to eradicate terrorism in this country.

Summary

Although modern security focuses on technology, the basic theory of protection has changed little over the past centuries. Only the tools to implement the theory have changed. Where moats were once used, we have high-tech sensors and fences. Where warded locks once protected buildings and rooms, we see state-of-the-art, computer-controlled, electronic locking mechanisms. Where watchmen walked the beat, we find sophisticated camera systems.

Still, not every security measure has kept pace with the development of technology. Old techniques and technology are still commonplace in many operations. The one thing that has changed as we enter the 21st century is the need to consider terrorism as a major threat to our country and its businesses. The events discussed in the Preface and Chapter 1 have made it all too clear that our government and public businesses are now targets of individuals who choose to use terrorist tools to make their positions known. The potential has always been present, as noted by many security experts. However, the use of terrorist tools was not seen as likely given the ability of most individuals to find other means to express their positions.

We have entered a new era where the security professional must give full consideration to potential terrorist threats, just as they would to theft of intellectual property, burglary, robbery, shoplifting, fire, and other loss risks commonly associated with security/loss-prevention strategies.

□ □ □ ▬▬▬▬▬▬▬▬▬▬▬▬▬▬▬▬▬▬▬▬▬▬▬▬▬▬▬

Critical thinking

Why should a security professional have any interest in the historical development of the discipline?

▬▬▬▬▬▬▬▬▬▬▬▬▬▬▬▬▬▬▬▬▬▬▬▬▬▬▬ □ □ □

Review Questions

1. What events in medieval England brought about the creation and use of private night watches and patrols?
2. What factors or conditions of the times made it possible for Jonathan Wild to become so extraordinarily successful?
3. Who was responsible for developing the concept of crime prevention?
4. How did World War II affect the growth of modern private security?
5. How do you believe the events of September 11, 2001, impacted the changes occurring in the private security/law enforcement relationship?
6. Discuss the extent of security's growth in this country. What are some of the reasons for the professionalization of the field of private security?

References

1. An Analysis of Criminal Redistribution Systems and Their Economic Impact on Small Business (Washington, D.C.: U.S. Department of Justice, Oct. 26, 1972), pp. 21–29.

2. Ibid., p. 25.

3. Van Meter, Clifford, Executive Director, Private Security: Report of the Task Force on Private Security (Washington, D.C.: National Advisory Committee on Criminal Justice Standards and Goals, 1976), p. 30.

4. Kakalik, James S., and Wildhorn, Sorrell, *Private Police in the United States: Findings and Recommendations* (RAND Report R-869-DOJ) (Santa Monica, CA: The RAND Corporation, 1971).

5. Levine, S.A., *Allan Pinkerton: America's First Private Eye* (New York: Dodd, Mead, 1963), p. 33.

6. Kakalik and Wildhorn, *Private Police*, pp. 94-95.

7. Cunningham, William; Strauchs, John J; and Van Meter, Clifford W., *The Hallcrest Report II: Private Security Trends 1970–2000* (Boston: Butterworth-Heinemann, 1990), p. 295.

8. www.fas.org/sgp/library/nispom.htm.

9. Fischer, Robert and Green, Gion, *Introduction to Security*, 6th ed. (Boston: Butterworth-Heinemann, 1998).

10. Cunningham et al., p. 175.

11. Federal Bureau of Investigation, U.S. Department of Justice, Uniform Crime Reporting Program (Washington, D.C.: Government Printing Office), www.fbi.gov/ucr/06prelim/index.html.

12. Crime and the Nation's Households, 2005, U.S. Department of Justice, Office of Justice Programs, Bureau of Justice Statistics, www.ojp.usdoj.gov/bjs/abstract/cnh05.htm.

13. Brookings Institute, "Brookings Study Details Economic Cost of Recent Corporate Crises," www.brookings.edu/comm/news/20020725graham.htm.

14. "Funny Money," The Economist Global Agenda (May 3, 2002), www.economist.com/agenda/displayStory.cfm?story_id+1116239.

15. "150 Scheming Employees Fired," *Peoria Journal Star* (May 27, 1990).

16. Van Meter, p. 18.

17. Ibid.

18. Cunningham et al., p. 298.

19. U.S. Department of Labor, Bureau of Labor Statistics (2001, 2005, 2006).

20. Associated Criminal Justice & Security Consultants, PLACE Project, Kaplan University, Evaluation of Basic Training Programs in Law Enforcement, Security and Corrections for Academic Credit, June 2005.

21. Fauth, Kenneth G., as quoted in Bottom, Norman R., and Kostanoski, John, *Security and Loss Control* (New York: Macmillan, 1983), p. vii.

Defining Security's Role

OBJECTIVES

The study of this chapter will enable you to:

1. Define the concept of private security.
2. List various services offered by private security operations.
3. Understand the differences among proprietary, contract, and hybrid security operations.
4. Discuss the issues that contribute to continued relations conflicts between private security operations and public law enforcement.

1   Introduction

During the 19th and 20th centuries, public police operated on only a local basis. They had neither the resources nor the authority to extend their investigations or pursue criminals beyond the sharply circumscribed boundaries in which they performed their duties. When the need arose to reach beyond these boundaries or to cut through several of these jurisdictions, law enforcement was undertaken by such private security forces as the Pinkerton Agency, railway police, or the Burns Detective Agency.

As the police sciences developed, public agencies began to assume a more significant role in investigating crime and, through increased cooperation among government agencies, pursuing suspected criminals. Concurrent with this evolution of public law enforcement, private agencies shifted their emphases away from investigation and toward crime prevention. This led to an increasing use of security services to protect property and to maintain order. Today, in terms of numbers, surety forces are by far the predominant element in private security.

But what other protective measures are available? Who provides them? Who is responsible for planning and executing these procedures? Where do the roles of private and public police overlap, and where do they diverge? What are the particular hazards for which private security is now held responsible, and how is it determined that threats are sufficient to justify the adoption of protective procedures? To answer these questions, it is necessary to define private security and its role more exactly.

2   What is Private Security?

Although the term *private security* has been used in previous pages without question, there is no universal agreement on a definition or even on the suitability of the term itself. Cogent arguments have been made, for example, for substituting the term *loss prevention* for security.

The RAND report defines private security to include all protective and loss-prevention activities not performed by law enforcement agencies. Specifically:

> *the terms private police and private security forces and security personnel are used generically in this report to include all types of private organizations and individuals providing all security-related services, including investigation, staffing key posts, patrol, executive protection, alarm monitoring and response, and armored transportation.*[1]

The Task Force on Private Security takes exception to this definition on several grounds. The task force argues that "quasi-public police" should be excluded from consideration on the grounds that they are paid out of public funds even though they may be performing what are essentially private security functions. The task force also makes the distinction that private security personnel must be employees of a "for-profit" organization or firm as opposed to a nonprofit or governmental agency. The complete task force definition states:

> *Private security includes those self-employed individuals and privately funded business entities and organizations providing security-related services to specific clientele for a fee, for the individual or entity that retains or employs them, or for themselves, in order to protect their persons, private property, or interests from varied hazards.*[2]

The task force argues that the profit motive and the source of profits are basic elements of private security. Though this definition might be suitable for the specific purposes of the report, it hardly seems acceptable as a general definition. Many hospitals and schools, to name only two types of institutions, employ private security forces without for-profit orientation. Yet it would be difficult to contend that, for example, the members of the International Association for Healthcare Security and Safety (IAHSS) are not private security personnel.

The Hallcrest reports never formally defined the terms *security* or *loss prevention* but relied on the earlier definitions of these terms. These reports consider, however, the security or loss-prevention field in its broadest application and thus avoid getting bogged down in discussions of profit motive or specific tasks. The reports focus on the functional aspects of security, recognizing that the functions of security and loss prevention are performed by both the public law enforcement sector and private agencies.

Thus neither the profit nature of the organization being protected nor even the source of funds by which personnel are paid holds up as a useful distinction. A night watchman at a public school is engaged to protect a nonprofit institution and is paid out of public funds. His function, however, is clearly different from that of a public law enforcement officer. He is—and is universally accepted as—a private security officer. How then should private security be defined for the purpose of this text?

The opening lines of Chapter 2 suggest that "security implies a stable, relatively predictable environment in which an individual or group may pursue its ends without disruption or harm and without fear of disturbance or injury." Such security can be effected by military forces, by public law enforcement agencies, by the individual or organization concerned, or by organized private enterprises. Where the protective services are provided by personnel who are not only paid out of public funds but also charged with the *general* responsibility for the public welfare, their function is that of public police. Where the services are provided for the protection of *specific* individuals or organizations, they normally fall into the area of private security.

2.1 Protection of Life and Property

The hazards against which private security seeks to provide protection are commonly divided into manmade and natural. Natural hazards may include fire, tornado, flood, earthquake, hurricane, and other acts of nature that could result in building collapse, equipment failure, accidents, and safety hazards. It should be noted that fire is also quite often manmade, intentionally or unintentionally.

Manmade hazards may include crimes against a person (for example, robbery or rape) or crimes against property (theft and pilferage, fraud and embezzlement). In addition, man also creates problems through domestic terrorism, espionage and sabotage, civil disturbances, bomb threats, fire (as noted above), and accidents.

The degree of exposure to specific hazards will vary for different facilities. The threat of fire or explosion is greatest in a chemical plant; the potential loss from shoplifting or internal theft is greatest in a retail store. Each organization or facility must ideally be protected against a full range of hazards, but in practice, a particular protection system will emphasize some hazards more than others.

In some organizations, the area of accident prevention and safety has taken on such importance, primarily because of state and federal occupational safety and health legislation, that this responsibility has become a full-time objective in itself, in the charge of a director of safety. Security can then devote its energies to other areas of loss. Similarly, some large industrial facilities have full fire brigades. In most situations, however, fire, accident prevention and disaster preparedness, and business recovery are part of the responsibility of the security department.

2.2 Security Functions

Security practices and procedures cover a broad spectrum of activities designed to eliminate or reduce the full range of potential hazards (loss, damage, or injury). These protection measures may include but are by no means limited to the following:

1. Building and perimeter protection by means of barriers, fences, walls, and gates; protected openings; lighting; and surveillance (security officers)
2. Intrusion and access control by means of door and window security, locks and keys, security containers (files, safes, and vaults), visitor and employee identification programs, package controls, parking security and traffic controls, inspections, and security posts and patrols
3. Alarm and surveillance systems
4. Fire prevention and control, including evacuation and fire response programs, extinguishing systems, and alarm systems
5. Emergency and disaster planning
6. Protection of intellectual property or data

7. Prevention of theft and pilferage by means of personnel screening, background investigations, procedural controls, and polygraph and psychological stress evaluator (PSE) investigations
8. Accident prevention and safety
9. Enforcement of occupational crime- or loss-related rules, regulations, and policies
10. Prevention of workplace violence

In addition to these basic loss-prevention functions, security services in some situations might also provide armored car and armed courier service, bodyguard protection, management consulting, security consulting, and other specific types of protection.

These services may be *proprietary,* or in-house, in which case the security force is hired and controlled directly by the protected organization, or they may be *contract* security services, in which case the company contracts with a specialized firm to provide designated security services for a fee. Contract security employees are actually employees of the contract security firm. Most security functions may be provided by either proprietary or contract forces or services, and in practice, it is common to find a combination of such services used. This combination of proprietary and contract security is referred to as a *hybrid system.*

3   Security Services

Security services employed more than 1.1 million officers in 2000.[3] *Security* reported that after the September 11, 2001, attacks on the World Trade Center, 13 percent of respondents to the magazine's annual security survey indicated they would be adding in-house staff or hiring more security officers through an outside contract service.[4] These predictions might have come true. According to the Bureau of Labor Statistics, there were 1.2 million protective service officers in 2001, reflecting at least a 10 percent increase over the 2000 figures. However, by 2005, there were still 1.2 million protective service officers.[5]

Security services in 1990 totaled approximately 107,000 companies doing an estimated $51 billion in business, primarily providing guard, investigative, central station alarm, and armored car and courier services. It has been said that six large, publicly owned firms dominate the industry, accounting for approximately half of all revenues generated by contract security services.[6] In 2000 *Security Services Report* indicated that 14 firms totaled more than $1.5 billion in corporate sales.[7]

In 1999 Securitas Group entered the contract security business in the United States with its purchase of Pinkerton's, Inc. By 2003 the Group had purchased other major guard firms, including Burns International, to become Securitas Security Services USA, Inc. Securitas provides security services to 80 percent of the Fortune 1000 companies, producing annual revenues of over $2.5 billion. In 2007 Securitas is by far the largest contract security firm operating in the United States.[8]

Many firms, particularly the smaller ones, specialize in specific types of services offered to a client. The larger the firm, the more likely it is to provide a full range of security services. The major categories of these services are security forces, patrols, consulting services, investigative services, alarm response, and armored car delivery and courier services.

According to various sources, security officer services, whether proprietary or contract, are still in demand today despite the growth in the use of technology. People and companies turn to officers because psychologically they feel that technology or hardware might not be enough. *Security*'s reported prediction that the 1990s would be marked by diminishing in-house staff, redistribution of security decision making inside and outside, and an increased reliance on equipment[9] is only partially true. As noted previously, in the aftermath of the 9/11 terrorist attacks, security staffs increased by at least 10 percent. Although some proprietary firms are relying more on technology to reduce security cost overhead, three basic trends are apparent.

First, as the number of legal problems associated with inappropriate actions of officers increases, public outrage may eventually force states to regulate training and standards. However, as noted in Chapter 2, based on the June 2005 report by Associated Criminal Justice and Security Consultants, standards for security have not changed much since 2001. There have been several federal attempts to pass legislation mandating minimum standards for security personnel. In 2002 federal legislation to allow private security access to FBI records for backgrounding of private security personnel was passed with the help of ASIS. Second, as the field grows, it will continue to attract better qualified individuals. Of the 2,205 individuals responding to the *2005 Annual Salary Survey* conducted by ASIS, 63 percent held at least an undergraduate degree. Almost a quarter had a masters or higher degree.[10] Third, there will be a trend to disarm security personnel. This trend was true until the destruction of the World Trade Center. The presence of armed security personnel in some venues appears to be increasing.

4 Contract Versus Proprietary Services

Before we begin a discussion of contract and proprietary services, it is important to make a clear distinction between the two types of operations. *Proprietary security operations* are those that are "in-house," or controlled entirely by the company establishing security for its operations. The company—for example, Jones Distributing—hires a chief security officer (CSO) and all the necessary support personnel and equipment to operate a security department. *Contract security services,* on the other hand, are those operations provided by a professional security company that contracts its services to a company. In this case, Jones Distributing would contract with Fischer Security Services for specific security services. In most cases there would not be a CSO employed directly by Jones. Rather, the contract manager would work for Fischer Security Services. As we shall note later, the latest trend is to have a combination of proprietary and contract operations.

Early researchers perceived more rapid growth in contract security services than in proprietary security. Although today many firms are considering contract services, some existing proprietary security operations are converting to hybrids with proprietary management and contractual line services. *Security* reported that the trend would be toward increased use of contract employees, products, and services, causing the employee numbers in the contract area to double by 2000.[11] This prediction was at least partially accurate as we entered the new millennium. Several of the largest firms adopted contract security services to replace their proprietary systems. However, the change has not been a clear departure from company control to contract. Three Fortune 500 companies have made the move to hybrid systems utilizing proprietary oversight, contract officers, and increased reliance on electronic advancements to replace outdated equipment and guards.

Since the various contract functions described in the preceding pages can be undertaken as proprietary (in-house) activities, how is the choice to be made between the two types of services? The subject of contract services versus proprietary security has been debated in most of the major security periodicals for 20 years or more. Some of the conclusions are reflected in the following discussion of the relative merits of the two approaches to security services. The question of which is the most sensible approach, however, is best answered by the manager of the firm or organization contemplating security services. His or her decision will rest on the particular characteristics of the company. These characteristics will include the location to be protected, the size of the force required, its mission, the length of time the officers will be needed, and the quality of personnel required.

4.1 Advantages of Contract Services

4.1.1 Cost

Few experts disagree that contract officers are less expensive than is a proprietary unit. In-house officers typically earn more because of the general wage rate of the facility employing them. In many cases, that wage level has been established through collective bargaining.

Contract officers generally receive fewer fringe benefits, and their services can be provided more economically by large contract firms by virtue of savings in terms of costs of hiring, training, and insurance due to volume. Short-term security service on a proprietary basis can create such large start-up costs that the effort is impractical.

Liability insurance, payroll taxes, uniforms and equipment, and the time involved in training, sick leave, and vacations are all extra cost factors that must be considered in deciding on whether to establish a proprietary force.

4.1.2 Administration

Establishing an in-house security service requires the development and administration of a recruitment program, personnel screening procedures, and training programs. It will also involve the direct supervision of all security personnel. Hiring contract officers solves the administrative problems of scheduling and substituting manpower when someone is sick or terminates employment.

There is little question that the administrative workload is substantially decreased when a contract service is employed. At the same time, the contracting customer is obliged to continually check the supplier's performance of contracted services, including personnel screening procedures, on an ongoing basis. The customer must also insist on a satisfactory level of quality at all times. To this extent, the customer is not totally relieved of administrative responsibilities in terms of management.

4.1.3 Staffing

During periods when the need for officers changes in any way, it might be necessary to lay off existing officers or take on additional staff. Such changes can come about fairly suddenly or unexpectedly.

In-house forces rarely have this flexibility in staffing. If they have extra people available for emergency use, such staff are an unnecessary expense when they are idle. Similarly, if there were a temporary decrease in the need for officers, it would hardly be efficient to dismiss extra people only to rehire additional officers a short time later when the situation changed again.

4.1.4　Unions

Employers in favor of nonunion security officers support their position by arguing that such officers are not likely to go out on strike, are less apt to sympathize with or support striking employees, and can be paid less because they receive few if any fringe benefits.

Since most unionized officers are proprietary personnel, anyone subscribing to the arguments listed here would clearly favor hiring contract officers. Only a fraction, if any, of the officers employed by contract security agencies such as Securitas, Wackenhut, and Guardsmark are unionized. Although efforts to unionize contract security services remain, the relationship between contractors and unions is mixed. According to Stuart Deans, a veteran security officer and staff representative for the United Steelworkers union, the entire security industry may be about to take a huge step backward. It appears that security firms are pushing for an unregulated climate.[12] Contract firms make their profits on providing security services; because wages and other labor costs account for most of a company's expenses, having workers with high salaries makes bidding on new contracts difficult.

4.1.5　Impartiality

It is often suggested that contract officers can more readily and more effectively enforce regulations than can in-house personnel. The rationale is that contract officers are paid by a different employer and because of their relatively low seniority have few opportunities to form close associations with other employees of the client. If properly managed, this situation produces a more consistently impartial performance of duty.

4.1.6　Expertise

When clients hire a security service, they also hire the management of that service to guide them in their overall security program. This can prove valuable even to a firm that is already sophisticated in security administration. A different view from a competitive supplier trying to create goodwill with a client can always be illuminating.

4.2　Advantages of Proprietary Officers

4.2.1　Quality of Personnel

Proponents of proprietary security systems argue that the higher pay and fringe benefits offered by employers, as well as the higher status of in-house officers, attracts higher-quality personnel. Such employees have been more carefully screened and show a lower rate of turnover.

4.2.2　Control

Many managers feel that they have a much greater degree of control over personnel when they are directly on the firm's payroll. The presence of contract supervisors between officers and client management can interfere with the rapid, accurate flow of information either up or down the chain of command.

An in-house force can be trained to suit the specific needs of the facility, and the progress and effectiveness of training can be better observed in this context. The individual performance of each member of the force can also be evaluated more readily.

4.2.3　Loyalty

In-house officers are reported to develop a keener sense of loyalty to the firm they are protecting than do contract officers. The latter, who may be shifted from one client to another and who have a high turnover rate, simply do not have the opportunity to generate any sense of loyalty to the specified, often temporary, client-employer.

4.2.4 Prestige

Many managers simply prefer to have their own people on the job. They feel that the firm gains prestige by building its own security force to its own specifications rather than by renting one from the outside.

Obviously, in weighing the various factors on either side of this debate, prudent managers will carefully study the quality and performance of the security firms available to service their facility. They will make sure of the standards of personnel, training, and supervision in the security firm. They will also carefully analyze the comparative costs for proprietary and contract services and will estimate both services' relative effectiveness in a particular application.

In situations where the demand for officers fluctuates considerably, a contract service is probably indicated. If a fairly large, stable security force is required, an in-house organization might be favored. However, as noted earlier, the trend of the future is toward hybrid systems, with proprietary supervision and contract officers.

4.3 Deciding on a Contract Security Firm

Seven of 10 security directors from America's largest firms report that one of their top security concerns is "finding and retaining a really quality-driven contract security agency."[13] A variety of issues must be considered when a company or organization decides to hire a contract security firm. According to Minot Dodson, vice president of operations and training at California Plant Protection, Inc., the following areas should be analyzed:

- The scope of the work
- Personnel selection procedures
- Training programs
- Supervision
- Wages
- Licensing and insurance
- Benefits
- Operating procedures
- Contractor data
- Terms and conditions[14]

The analysis of the scope of the work should include, at a minimum, locations, hours of coverage, patrol checkpoints, and duties. The security firm should be aware of, and prepared to enforce, all applicable corporate security policies—particularly those dealing with access control, personnel identification, documentation procedures for removal of materials from the facility, handling customers and employees, and emergency procedures. Proprietary security objectives and priorities should be stated clearly. The employing (client) firm should also include references to expansion plans and determine how the security firm will handle the expansion. The client firm should also spell out expectations for security goals (for example, a 20 percent reduction of shrinkage) and determine how the security firm plans to meet these goals. Client performance criteria should be spelled out to include such things as what and when to report.

The organization choosing a contract service should also be able to set standards for the employees who will be protecting their facility. Standards for general appearance, rules of conduct, age, licenses needed, physical condition, educational levels, reporting skills, background, and language ability are certainly worth listing. According to Dodson, "You should check the personnel file on each prospective officer. Look for pre-employment background and police record checks, and verify application information."[15] The client firm should check training records and test scores as well as psychological test results (that is, pen and pencil tests, when they are available). It is even advisable in some operations not only to interview the security company but also to interview the prospective officer. The security company should agree to remove any officer for reasonable cause (that is, violating regulations).

In 1975 the Task Force on Private Security set the minimum recommended level of training for security officers at 120 hours.[16] Lobbying efforts on the part of cost-conscious CSOs, however, have reduced the generally recommended time to only 40 hours. Despite this recommendation, many security companies still maintain only an eight-hour indoctrination period. Client firms should review the security service's training procedures to make sure they meet specific company requirements. Some areas to consider are patrol techniques, first aid, liability and powers, firefighting, public relations, and report writing. Client firms also have the right to request additional special requirements. Whether the decision is to contract or not to contract, the firm will generally get what it pays for.

Supervision of the contract is another concern. Employing firms should understand the entire organizational structure in the security company. Supervisors from the contract service should maintain regular contact with officers (including alternate sites) and make random checks on all shifts and workdays. The response time of supervisors can be critical, and radio or telephone contact should be possible at all times. Direct contact with a supervisor, however, should also be available within no more than one hour.

Wages are tremendously important. The quality of personnel is often directly related to the wage level. The client company, not the security service, should establish the minimum wage to be paid to security employees. What is a good minimum wage? The Bureau of Labor Statistics reported that 50 percent of all guards made between $14,930 ($7.80/hour) and $21,950 ($11.43/hour) in 2002.[17] The *2005 ASIS Security Survey* reported that the range for 2005 was $10 to a high of $22.50 per hour.[18] Although these are better than the 2002 levels, some officers are still making less than a survival wage. One implication of this situation is that underpaid officers might take advantage of their employment and steal from the contracting firm. At a minimum, officers should be paid at least what semi-skilled labor in the area is earning.

Although fringe benefits offered by security firms might not seem an area of much concern to the employing companies, they should be. In a field where the turnover rate of some security services is 200 percent annually, fringe benefits become very important in retaining quality personnel. Benefits might include cash bonus plans, sick leave, health insurance, and overtime pay. Other perks might be life insurance, pension funds, and paid education and training. Perhaps the best fringe benefit for many contract officers is paid uniforms and equipment. Although the cost of these perks is usually reflected in the cost to the buyer, it should not be taken out of the officer's already meager wages.

The preceding discussion is just one way of viewing a security service; other factors can also be considered. Howard M. Schwartz, former vice president of the mid-Atlantic division of Securitas International Security Services, Inc., suggests evaluating the following:

1. The security agency's understanding of the psychological factors that influence security's effect on business and industrial environments and the firm's ability to incorporate these tactical measures into its services
2. The agency's understanding of the essential difference between security and law enforcement
3. The agency's ability to apply creative solutions to security problems
4. The agency's ability to involve all of the client firm's employees in a positive effort supporting the overall security program
5. The agency's willingness and ability to be flexible and modify tactical approaches to meet changing needs[19]

For one suggested format, consider the security firm evaluation analysis presented in Table 3.1.

Table 3.1 Security Firm Evaluation Analysis

Consideration	Score
1. Bid package	
a. All requested information provided in proposal	–
b. Quality of proposal presentation	–
c. Timelines of submission of proposal	–
Subtotal	–
2. Personnel	
a. Past employment checks (pre-employment)	–
b. Reference checks (pre-employment)	–
c. Psychological testing (pre-employment)	–
d. Polygraph testing (pre-employment)	–
e. Prehire evaluation of personnel	–
f. Prehire evaluation of personnel files	–
g. Basic qualifications	–
h. Security aptitude testing (pre-employment)	–
i. Management quality (top level)	–
j. Management quality (midlevel)	–
k. Supervision (first line)	–
l. EEO Program	–
m. Average length of employee service	–
Subtotal	–
3. Training	
a. Prehire classroom training (8 hours minimum)	–
b. Prehire classroom training testing	–
c. Training manual	–

(Continued)

Table 3.1 Continued

Consideration	Score
e. Training film usage	–
f. Training film testing	–
g. Training facilities	–
h. On-the-job training program	–
i. On-the-job training tests	–
j. Continuing training program	–
k. Continuing training tests	–
l. Advanced training program	–
m. Advanced training tests	–
n. State-certified training school	–
o. College-certified training/trainers	–
Subtotal	–
4. Supervision	
a. Selection	–
b. Training and testing	–
c. Site supervision	–
d. Field supervision	–
e. Visits and assistance	–
f. Employee evaluation reports	–
g. Response capabilities	–
Subtotal	
5. Employee wages and benefits	
a. Wage distribution by grade and scale	–
b. Longevity rewarded	–
c. Merit pay proposed	–
d. Health insurance	–
e. Life insurance	–
f. Holidays	–
g. Vacation	–
h. Sick pay	–
i. Bereavement pay	–
Subtotal	–
6. Insurance	
a. General liability	–
b. Care, custody, and control	–
c. Errors and omissions	–
d. Employee dishonesty	–
e. Excess liability (umbrella form)	–
f. Workmen's compensation	–
g. Automobile liability	–
h. Policy exclusions	–
i. Policy availability	–
j. Cancellation notification	–
k. Self-insured on any portion of insurance	–
Subtotal	–

(Continued)

Table 3.1 Continued

Consideration	Score
7. Operational considerations	
a. 24-hour, 365-day operations department	–
b. Management response	–
c. Additional services ability	–
d. Uniforms provided	–
e. Uniform cleaning and maintenance provided	–
f. Emergency response capabilities	–
g. Post orders	–
h. Client control of operations	–
i. Financial stability	–
j. Standard of performance for guards	–
k. Service agreement	–
l. Periodic polygraph testing	–
Subtotal	–
8. Cost of service	
a. Cost factor detail	–
b. Standard time fee	–
c. Overtime fees	–
d. Holiday fees	–
e. Effective rate	–
f. Equipment fee	–
g. Billing periods	–
Subtotal	–
9. Other considerations	
a.	
b.	–
c.	–
Subtotal	–
Grand Total	–

Source: "How to Select a Guard Company," *Security World* (November 1983): 39. Copyright 1983. A Cahners Publication. *Instructions:* Rate each proposal topic and other observation as follows: high = +1; average = 0; low = −1. Add all +1s and subtract all −1s in each section to obtain subtotals. Then add and subtract subtotals to obtain the overall rating. Ratings can be ranked as follows: 50 to 77, excellent; 25 to 49, above average; 0 to 24, average; −1 to −34, below average; and −35 to −77, poor. Retain this rating sheet to verify that you have done everything possible to select a competent security company.

5 Hybrid Systems

If the relationship between the client company and the contractor, whether a straight security provision contract or a hybrid program incorporating both proprietary and contract security services, is to be successful, all parties to the contract must be willing to communicate openly with each other. This means that both the contractor and the client must be willing to share in successes and mishaps. The in-house CSO has the power to optimize a contract.

A good hybrid security operation consists of four components:

- An engaged corporate liaison
- Consistent contract management support
- Periodic reviews
- Accurate quality measurements

5.1 Engaged Liaison

The right person for this job is someone who already knows and understands the basics of loss prevention and security. The company should not assume that the contract security firm would run itself. The liaison should monitor, but not micromanage, the security contract. The liaison should review security logs and follow-ups daily. The liaison should also be available to the contract manager to discuss any incidents or issues that need immediate attention.

5.2 Support

The contractor is also obliged to provide a responsive and interested manager. The manager must be able to juggle personnel, provide adequate training, satisfy customers, and still return a profit for the security company. The three keys to a successful contract are accessibility, meetings, and proper resource management.

5.3 Reviews

It is essential that a periodic review of services is conducted to determine whether the contract is being fulfilled. Officers assigned to the contract should continue to meet the expectations set forth in the contract. A company should periodically audit the contractor's records for compliance.

5.4 Measurement

Attainable and realistic activities should be expected. The contractor should make sure that officers know these expectations and comply. The liaison should expect compliance and when it is not forthcoming, action plans should be developed to remedy the situation.[20]

The growth in the hybrid security operation, though forecasted by the *Hallcrest II* report, is expanding at a rate greater than had been anticipated. According to Bill Cunningham, president of Hallcrest Systems, Inc., "the reduction in proprietary officers (was) dropping at 2 percent [per] annum compounded."[21] There are currently no available statistics on whether this trend continues.

6   Private Security and Public Law Enforcement

It should be noted that public and private police might, in certain circumstances, perform the same functions for the same individuals or organizations. For example, a law enforcement officer might in some circumstances be assigned to protect a threatened individual;

a private bodyguard frequently is hired to perform the same protective function. Public police commonly perform patrol functions, which include checking the external premises of stores or manufacturing facilities. But patrol is also one of the major activities of private security. The activity itself then is not always a differentiating factor. Private security functions are essentially client-oriented; public law enforcement functions are society- or community-oriented.

Another key distinction is the possession and exercise of police powers—that is, the power of arrest. The vast majority of private security personnel have no police powers; they act as private citizens. In some jurisdictions, "special officer" status is granted, in most cases by statute or ordinance, which includes limited power of arrest in specified areas or premises. The limitations on the exercise of special police powers and the fact that their activities are client-oriented and client-controlled (as opposed to being directed primarily by public law enforcement agencies) make it reasonable to include such personnel as part of the private security industry. (This discussion omits the situation of the law enforcement officer who is moonlighting as a part-time private security officer, because police powers in that situation derive from the public rather than the private role.)

As early as 1975 the Task Force on Private Security stated that "public law enforcement and private security agencies should work closely together, because their respective roles are complementary in the effort to control crime. Indeed, the magnitude of the nation's crime problem should preclude any form of competition between the two."[22] As noted in the previous section, however, even though the roles of the two groups are similar (in fact, overlapping in many areas), they are not identical. The roles should be complementary, but in reality the two groups interrelate and interact. Most contact between public and private agencies is spontaneous and cooperative, but far too often the contact is negative, to the detriment of both groups.

According to experts in the field, the relationship between the two groups continues to be strained (although personal contacts may be warm) because of several key issues:

1. Lack of mutual respect
2. Lack of communication
3. Lack of law enforcement knowledge of private security
4. Perceived competition
5. Lack of standards for private security personnel
6. Perceived corruption of police
7. Jurisdictional conflict, especially when private problems (that is, corporate theft, arson) are involved
8. Confusion of identity and the issues flowing from it, such as arming and training of private police
9. Mutual image and communications problems
10. Provision of services in borderline or overlapping areas of responsibility and interest (that is, provision of security during strikes, traffic control, shared use of municipal and private firefighting personnel)
11. Moonlighting policies for public police and issues stemming from these policies

12. Difference in legal powers, which can lead to concerns about abuse of power, and so on (that is, police officers working off duty may now be private citizens subject to rules of citizen's arrest)

13. False alarm rates (police resent responding to false alarms), which in some communities are more than 90 percent

Historically, public police have often accused the private sector of mishandling cases, breaking the law to make cases, being poorly trained, and generally being composed of those who could not meet the standards to be police officers. The private security sector often views the public sector as being self-centered and arrogant. Moreover, public law enforcement officers often moonlight, thereby taking work away from the private security sector. Even today public police still consider the private sector only somewhat effective in reducing direct-dollar crime loss, and its contributions to reducing the volume of crime, apprehending criminal suspects, and maintaining order are judged ineffective. Public law enforcement has given private security low ratings in 10 areas, including quality of personnel, training, and knowledge of legal authority. The feelings about the lack of training may be justified; only 50 percent of the states currently have mandated provisions for training security officers, although regulation through licensing has been the norm in most states.[23]

On the other hand, the employment of police officers as private security personnel during their off-duty hours has also caused much criticism. Some say that moonlighting police are only "hired guns" and that such police officers take jobs away from security firms. Other problems include the question of who is liable for the officer's actions. Is the employer of the off-duty officer liable, or does the liability stay with the police department that trained the officer?

Another source of conflict is the high rate of false alarms. Improved technology has reduced the number of false alarms, but there are still problems associated with the human element, "critter infringement," and the occasional electronic failure. When an alarm sounds, an alarm company employee may respond, or the police department may be called. In some jurisdictions, police report that 10 to 12 percent of all calls for police service are false alarms. Many experts believe that 95 to 99 percent of all alarms are false. Some police departments have reacted to this high rate by fining alarm companies or businesses and even delaying their response pending internal confirmation of an actual intrusion.

Yet much of the conflict between private and public agencies is the result of misconception. There is a general misunderstanding of the roles played by the respective agencies. Perhaps this is understandable because even within their own areas, police and private security officers often fail to understand the common goals of other agencies.

6.1 Complementary Roles

Despite the misconception that working together for a common goal is difficult to achieve, police departments and private security agencies are beginning to work together, at times unknowingly. The idea that only the public police protect public property is another misconception. The federal government has more than 10,000 contract security officers patrolling federal offices and buildings. In many cities, police departments have turned to private agencies to protect courthouses, city buildings, airports, and museums. In other areas, it is generally accepted that the protection of private property is the responsibility of the owner. When a crime occurs, however, it is the local police who are usually called.

A third misconception is that the private security sector is primarily concerned with crime prevention and deterrence rather than with investigation and apprehension. In reality, store detectives in many major cities make more arrests each year than do local police officers. In addition, certain types of crime are no longer investigated by local police departments but have instead become the job of private security personnel; these include credit card fraud, single bogus checks, and some thefts. The growing problems of drugs and violence in the workplace have also added to security's role in law enforcement. Cooperation between security and public law enforcement is vital in dealing with both these problems and the threat of terrorism.

Obviously some degree of complementary activity already exists. What can be done to improve the perceptions of two areas toward each other and to foster cooperative efforts? A variety of methods could improve cooperation between the two areas. The formation of joint private and public sector task forces to study responses to terrorism and major crime issues and to recommend strategies is crucial. Data files from both sectors should be more freely exchanged. Private security personnel are often not allowed access to information on criminal cases, even as a follow-up on data originally entered by them. Third, joint seminars on terrorism and business crime have been developed to help the two areas better understand their respective roles.

It appears that the private sector will become increasingly involved in crime prevention; public law enforcement will then be free to concentrate more heavily on violent crimes and crime response. Most CSOs are willing to accept more responsibility for minor criminal acts within their jurisdictions. The new activities most likely include intrusion alarm response, investigation of misdemeanors, and many preliminary investigations of other criminal offenses. The public sector is also willing to give up some areas of responsibility because it is "potentially more cost-effectively performed by private security."[24] Some areas—for example, building security—will need to be shared if we are to be successful in our war on terrorism.

However, other areas of conflict remain that may take some time to resolve. Often CSOs do not report many criminal offenses. This is a source of concern for many police managers. CSOs may fail to report crimes for any of the following reasons: lax charging policies of prosecutors, administrative delays in prosecution, court proceedings that might reveal more about their organizations than management wants known, and a perception that courts are unsympathetic to business losses.

Just how effective private security can be depends to a large degree on whether public law enforcement and private sector professionals are able to form a close partnership. *Hallcrest II* recommended:

1. Upgrading private security; statewide regulatory statutes are needed for background checks, training, codes of ethics, and licensing
2. Increasing police knowledge of private security
3. Expanding interaction; joint task forces are needed, and both groups should share investigative information and specialized equipment
4. Experimenting with the transfer of police functions[25]

Progress continues to be made in all these areas. Nationally recognized law enforcement/private security partnerships include the NYPD-Shield (Area Police/Private Security Liaison) and the Nassau County PD-SPIN.[26]

7   Relationships After September 11, 2001

The events of 9/11 brought private security operations and public enforcement closer. In the United States, cooperation between public law enforcement and private security was evident during the anthrax scare that followed the attacks on the World Trade Center. A study of the cooperation between the two areas was presented in Chapter 1.

The events of 9/11 have helped build private security/public policing partnerships to prevent and respond to terrorism and public disorder. This was demonstrated by the 2004 National Policy Summit project supported by the DoJ Office of Community Oriented Policing Services (COPS). This joint partnering effort involved the International Association of Chiefs of Police and the Security Industry Association (SIA), ASIS International, the National Association of Security Companies (NASC), and the International Security Management Association (ISMA).

Through their working groups, summit participants made five recommendations. The first four are national-level, long-term efforts. The fifth recommendation relates to local and regional efforts that could begin immediately:

1. Leaders of the major law enforcement and private security organizations should make a formal commitment to cooperation.
2. The DHS and/or DoJ should fund research and training on relevant legislation, private security, and law enforcement-private security cooperation.
3. The DHS and/or DoJ should create an advisory council composed of nationally prominent law enforcement and private security professionals to oversee day-to-day implementation issues of law enforcement-private security partnerships.
4. The DHS and/or DoJ, along with relevant membership organizations, should convene key practitioners to move this agenda forward.
5. Local partnerships should set priorities and address key problems as identified by the summit:
   - Improve joint response to critical incidents
   - Coordinate infrastructure protection
   - Improve communications and data interoperability
   - Bolster information and intelligence sharing
   - Prevent and investigate high-tech crime
   - Devise responses to workplace violence

Execution of these recommendations should benefit all concerned:

- Law enforcement agencies will be better able to carry out their traditional crime-fighting duties and their additional homeland security duties by using the many private security resources in the community. Public-private cooperation is an important aspect—indeed, a potent technique—of community policing.
- Private security organizations will be better able to carry out their mission of protecting their companies' or clients' people, property, and information while at the same time serving the homeland security objectives of their communities.

The nation as a whole will benefit from the heightened effectiveness of law enforcement agencies and private security organizations.[27]

Summary

Security/loss-prevention functions, while diverse, have a common goal. As we noted, the definition of security has been debated, but the bottom line is clear. Security services protect both private and public places. Law enforcement protects both public and private property. The difference is found in their primary goals. Law enforcement agencies are charged with the protection of government interests, representing the people. Private security is charged with protecting a specific interest, whether public or private.

The old distinction between public law enforcement and private security will continue to exist. However, the story is different when considering the relationship between contract and proprietary security. As business continues to evolve, it appears that the hybrid systems will become a dominant organizational scheme for many businesses establishing security operations.

Finally, all people concerned with security, whether federal government agencies, state law enforcement organizations, local law enforcement, or private security, will need to learn to work together to focus resources needed to successfully combat threats created by the potential of terrorist attacks and cyber crimes.

□ □ □ ▬▬▬▬▬▬▬▬▬▬▬▬▬▬▬▬▬▬▬▬▬▬▬▬▬▬▬▬▬▬▬▬

Critical Thinking

If you were to develop a security operation within a major company—for example, Rockwell International—would you favor a contract, proprietary, or hybrid security organization?

▬▬▬▬▬▬▬▬▬▬▬▬▬▬▬▬▬▬▬▬▬▬▬▬▬▬▬▬▬▬▬▬ □ □ □

Review Questions

1. What does the term *private security* mean?
2. What are the differences between proprietary and contractual security services?
3. What are the basic services typically performed by contractual security personnel?
4. What are the advantages and disadvantages of using contractual security services?
5. What are the advantages and disadvantages of using proprietary security services?
6. What factors should be considered when deciding on a security firm?
7. Describe the relationship between public law enforcement and private security. What are the major problems?

References

1. Kakalik, James S., and Wildhorn, Sorrell, *Private Police in the United States: Findings and Recommendations* (RAND Report R-869-DOJ) (Santa Monica, CA: The RAND Corporation, 1971), p. 3.
2. Van Meter, Clifford, Executive Director, *Private Security: Report of the Task Force on Private Security* (Washington, D.C.: National Advisory Committee on Criminal Justice Standards and Goals, 1976), p. 4.

3. *Protective Service Occupations*, U.S. Department of Labor, Bureau of Labor Statistics, February 2002, Bulletin 2540-11.

4. Zalud, Bill, "2002 Industry Forecast Study Security Yin-Yang: Terror Push, Recession," *Security* (January 2002).

5. U.S. Department of Labor, Bureau of Labor Statistics (2001, 2005, 2006a).

6. Siatt, Wayne, and Matteson, Sally, "Special Report: Trends in Security," *Security World* (January 1982): 25.

7. *Security Services-Private Companies Report*, Freedonia (October 2000), www.ecnext.com.

8. "Who We Are,"www.securitasinc.com/www/secus/uswebsite.nsf/dummyview2/1EA1E10210 C7C20C1256D100...

9. Zalud, Bill, "What's Happening to Security," *Security* (September 1990): 42.

10. *2005 ASIS Survey of U.S. Security Salaries*, ASIS International, 2005.

11. Zalud, Bill, p. 44.

12. Lyons, Tom, "Labour Looks Out for Security Guards: The Private-Security Industry Rolls Back Union Gains of the '90s,"www.eye.net/eye/issue/issue 03.02.00/news/guards.html.

13. Dalton D., "Looking for the Quality-Oriented Contractor," *Security Technology & Design* (September 1994): 6.

14. Serb, Thomas J, "How to Select a Guard Company," *Security World* (November 1983): 33.

15. Ibid.

16. Cunningham et al., p. 156.

17. *Protective Service Occupations*.

18. *2005 ASIS Salary Survey*.

19. Serb, p. 33.

20. Harne, Eric G., "Partnering with Security Providers," *Security Management* (March 1996): 36–39.

21. "Hybrid Staffing Grows as Contract Replaces Proprietary," *Security* (April 1996): 86.

22. Van Meter, p. 19.

23. ACJSC.

24. Cunningham, William; Strauchs, John J.; and Van Meter Clifford W., *The Hallcrest Report II: Private Security Trends 1970–2000* (Boston: Butterworth-Heinemann, 1990), p. 290.

25. Cunningham, William and Taylor, Todd H, *Private Security and Police in America: The Hallcrest Report* (Portland, OR: Chancellor Press, 1985), p. 275.

26. Security-Police Information Network, "Study of Law Enforcement-Private Security Partnerships," COPS Office funded project, 2007.

27. National Policy Summit: *Private Security/Public Policing*, (Olhausen Research, Inc., 2004): 3-4.

The Proprietary Security Organization

1   Introduction

Security problems become apparent in virtually every area of a given company's activities. The need to deal forcefully and systematically with these problems has become increasingly evident to the industrial and commercial community, and steps have been taken by greater and greater numbers of these organizations to create a security effort as an organic element of the corporate structure rather than turning to outside (contract) security services or to minimal efforts at physical security. The trend is toward security operations that are controlled by an in-house staff, with specific services provided by technology, contract security operations, and security consultants, referred to as hybrid systems as discussed in the previous chapter.

Where and how the in-house or proprietary security department operates within the organizational framework and the way this relates to the total security system of individual concerns depends on the needs of that organization. General principles will apply throughout much of the business community, but specific applications must be tailored to the problems faced by each enterprise. Our concern here, then, is with those considerations that have broad application in the organization of the security function.

2   Determining the Need

In evaluating the need to install or expand the company security function, the immediate urgency for increased security must be considered along with the status, growth, and prior performance of the current security effort, if any. The peculiarities of the company in the context of intracompany relationships, whether by design or natural evolution, must be a factor. The potential for growth of the company and the attendant growth of staff activities should also be considered.

Ultimately management will have to determine the costs and the projected effectiveness of the security function. The growing trend is for management to make this determination with the assistance and guidance of a professional consultant. This trend has caused growth in the number of security consultants, particularly independent consultants who do not have a vested interest in the outcome of their recommendations. Determining costs and effectiveness is only the first step, however. Management then must face the important question of whether security can be truly and totally integrated into the organization. If on analysis it is found that the existing structure would in some way suffer from the addition of new organizational functions, alternatives to the integrated proprietary security department must be sought.

These alternatives usually consist of the application and supervision of physical security measures. This inevitably results in the fragmentation of protective systems in the areas requiring security. These alternatives are sometimes effective, however, especially in those firms whose overall risk and vulnerability are low. But as crime against business continues to climb and as criminal methods of attack and the underground network of distribution continue to become more sophisticated, anything less than total integration will become increasingly inadequate.

Once management has recognized that existing problems—real or potential—make the introduction or enlargement of security a necessity for continued effective operation, it will be obliged to make every effort to create an atmosphere in which security can exert its full efforts to accomplish stated company objectives. Any equivocation by management at this point can only serve to weaken or to ultimately undermine the security effectiveness that might be obtained by a clearer statement of total support and by directives resulting in intracompany cooperation with security efforts.

Understanding the proper relationships among departments is critical during this period of rapidly changing technology, where security professionals are often asked to play a role in security operations and where security professionals are asked to monitor and control access to computer systems and the information stored in them. Companies seem to be struggling with issues of defining responsibilities assigned to the chief security officer (CSO), the chief information officer (CIO), or the information security systems officer (ISSO).

2.1   Security's Place in the Organization

The degree and nature of the authority vested in the CSO become matters of the greatest importance when such a function is fully integrated into the organization. Any evaluation of the scope of authority required by security to perform effectively must consider a variety of factors—both formal and informal—that exist in the structure. Figures 4.1 and 4.2 are organization charts showing security's position in two hypothetical corporations.

There seems to be a trend toward consolidating a number of related responsibilities under one broader department. Industry trends suggest growing linkages among security, risk management, facilities management, safety, operations administration, human resources, and internal audit.[1] One way of consolidating various related security functions is to create an assets protection department that can include the functions of

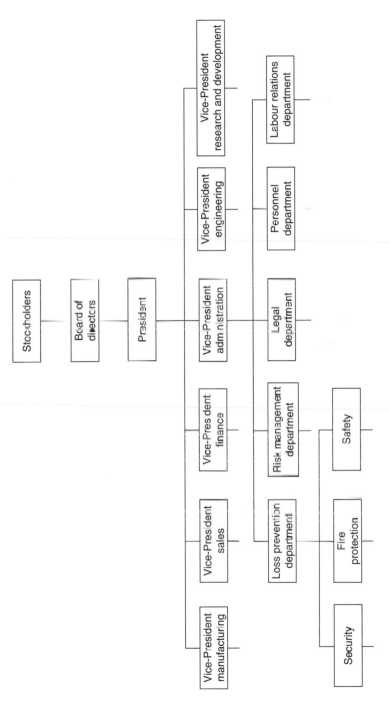

FIGURE 4.1 Functional departmentalization for a manufacturing corporation. (From Philip P. Purpura, *Modern Security and Loss Prevention Management*, 2nd ed. [Boston: Butterworth-Heinemann, 1989].)

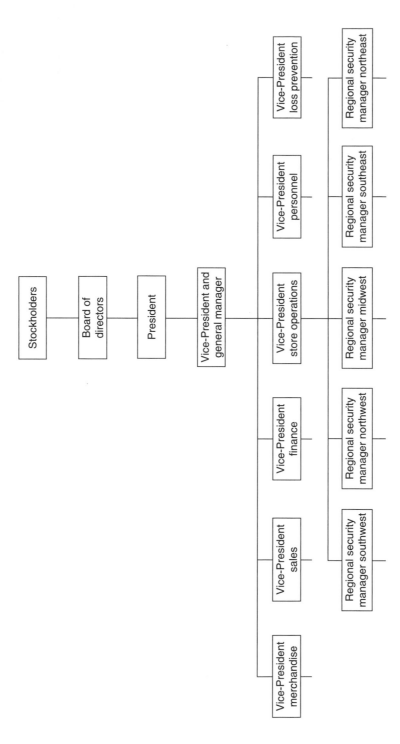

FIGURE 4.2 Geographic departmentalization for a retail corporation. (From Philip P. Purpura, *Modern Security and Loss Prevention Management,* 2nd ed. [Boston: Butterworth-Heinemann, 1989].)

security, information management (CIO), internal audit (chief financial officer, or CFO; chief fraud examiner, or CFE), and risk management.

However the security/assets protection department is constructed, certain distinguishing features should characterize it. It should:

- Champion asset protection
- Solve more complex issues with less staff
- Identify risk for the company
- Develop programs to manage risk
- Quantify results to the bottom line
- Develop pilot asset protection programs
- Provide business solutions to security problems
- Reduce insurance premiums
- Use shared resources to manage costs
- Establish common objectives with risk management, internal audit, and information management[2]

2.2   Definition of Authority

It is management's responsibility to establish the level of authority at which security may operate in order to accomplish its mission. It must have authority to deal with the establishment of security systems, be able to conduct performance inspections in many areas of the company, and be in a position to evaluate performance and risk throughout the company.

All such authority relationships, of course, should be clearly established to facilitate the transmission of directives and the necessary responses to them. Note, however, that these relationships take many forms in any company, not infrequently including the assumption of a role by a member of the organization who becomes accepted as a designated executive simply by past compliance and by custom. In such cases, where management does not move to curtail or redefine this authority, the executive continues in such a posture indefinitely, regardless of formal status. It is management's responsibility to reassess the chains of authority continually in the interest of efficient operation.

Organizational structure generally distinguishes between line and staff relationships. *Line executives* are those who are delegated authority in the direct chain of command to accomplish specific organizational objectives. *Staff personnel* generally provide an advisory or service function to a line executive.

In general, the CSOs can be considered to serve a staff function. Traditionally this means that, as heads of specialized operations, they are either responsible to a senior executive or (in the fully integrated organization) to the president of the company. Their role is that of advisor. Theoretically it is the president who implements the activities suggested by advisors.

But this is not always the practice. By the very nature of their expertise, CSOs have authority delegated by the senior executive to whom they report. In effect, they are granted a part of the authority of their line superior. This is known as *functional authority*.

Such authority appears on a table of organization, but it is often delegated and can be modified or withdrawn by a superior. In the case of security, this functional authority may consist of advising operating personnel on security matters, or it may (and should) develop into more complete functional responsibility to formulate policies and issue directives prescribing procedures to be followed in any area affecting company security.

Most department managers readily cooperate with security directives because they lack the specialized knowledge required of upper-echelon security personnel and are generally unfamiliar with the requirements of effective supervision of security systems and procedures. It is nonetheless important that the CSO operate with the utmost tact and diplomacy in matters that may have an effect, however small, on the conduct of personnel or procedures in other departments. Every effort should be made to consult with the executive in charge of any such affected department before issuing instructions that implement security procedures.

The best approach to complicated security issues associated with increased reliance on technology, especially computers, is a team effort. Often the only way to gather all the needed expertise to combat specific problems—for example, identity theft—involves the expertise of human resources, technical support, and security professionals.

2.3   Levels of Authority

Obviously there are many levels of authority at which CSOs operate. Their functional authority may encompass a relatively limited area, prescribed by broad outlines of basic company policy.

In matters of investigation, they may be limited to staff functions in which they may advise and recommend or even assist in conducting the investigation, but they might not have direct control or command over the routines of employees.

It is customary for CSOs to exercise line authority over preventive activities of the company. In this situation, they command the security officers, who in turn command the employees in all matters over which CSOs have jurisdiction. CSOs will, of course, have full line authority over the conduct of their own departments, within which they will have staff personnel as well as those to whom they have delegated functional authority.

2.4   Reduced Losses and Net Profit

Although security is a staff function, it could be viewed as a line operation—and one day might be. By reducing losses, an effective security program, intelligently managed, can maximize profits as surely as can a merchandising or a production function. In the 21st-century environment, security has achieved a renewed level of interest not seen since World War II. No CEO can afford to ignore the implications of 9/11.

With increasing crime rates from inventory shrinkage, employee theft, shoplifting, vendor fraud, and administrative error costing retail businesses approximately $41.6 billion in 2006, based on a joint study by the National Retail Federation and the University of Florida, every business is targeted for losses.[3] And all these losses detract from the net profit. Many managers, particularly those in retail establishments, push as hard as possible for new records in gross sales. They frequently brush aside words of caution about inventory loss from internal and external theft. Unfortunately, there are companies that generate millions of dollars in gross sales that have filed for bankruptcy. It is the net profit that keeps business and industry alive. The gross income may be a splashy figure, and it may provide some excitement for the proud manager. But the net profit is the bottom line: Anything that eats away at that lifeline seriously endangers the organization.

An effective security operation could cut losses by as much as 75 percent. The savings between the investment in security and the additional earnings realized from reduced losses are net profit. In this light, security can be seen as a vital contributor to the profit of any company. Any security operation that can minimize losses and maximize net profits should clearly take its place as an independent organizational function, reporting to the highest level of executive authority.

2.5 Nonintegrated Structures

In spite of the obvious advantages of integrating security into the organization as an organic function (an independent, basic unit of the firm, like accounting or engineering), many firms continue to relegate this operation to a reporting activity of some totally unrelated department (for example, engineering). Since in many cases the operation grew out of a security need that arose in a particular area, that area tends to assume administrative control over security and to maintain that control long after security has begun to extend its operational activities beyond departmental lines into other spheres of the company.

In this way, security was traditionally attached to the financial function of the organization because financial control was usually the most urgent need in a company otherwise unprepared to provide internal security. The disadvantages of such an arrangement are severe enough to endanger the effectiveness of security's efforts.

Functional authority cannot be delegated beyond the authority of the delegator. What this means is that when the CSO gets authority from the comptroller, the authority cannot extend past the comptroller's area of responsibility. If the comptroller can extend the role of security by dispensation of the chief executive, the line of authority becomes clouded and cumbersome.

Most business experts agree that functional authority should not be used to direct the activities of anyone more than one level down from the delegator, to preserve the integrity of line functions. Clearly the assignment of security under the financial officer is a clumsy arrangement representing bad management practices.

2.6 Relation to Other Departments

Every effort should be made to incorporate security into the organizational functions It must be recognized, however, that by so doing management creates a new function that, like personnel and finance, among others, cuts across departmental lines and enters into every activity of the company.

Security considerations should ideally be as much a presence as cost decisions in every decision at every level. This will not mean that security factors will always take precedence over matters of production or merchandising, for example, any more than that specific price factors will always take precedence over other decisions in these same areas. But security should always be considered. If its recommendations are overridden from time to time—sometimes a wise decision when the cost of disruption involved in overcoming certain risks is greater than the risk itself—this will be done with full knowledge of the risks involved.

Obviously the management of the security function and its goals must be compatible with the organization's aims. This means that security must provide for continued protection of the organization without significant interference with its essential activities. Security must preserve the atmosphere in which the company's activities are carried on by developing programs that will protect those activities as much as possible in their existing condition, rather than attempting to alter them to conform to certain abstract standards of security. When the overall objectives of any organization are bent and shaped to accommodate the efforts of any particular functions designed to help achieve those aims, the total corporate effort inevitably becomes distorted and suffers accordingly.

Organizationally, the relationship between security and other departments should present no difficulty. The interface serves to solve potentially disruptive or damaging problems shared by the two functions. The company's goals are achieved by the mitigation or elimination of all such problems. In practice, however, this harmony is not always found. Resentment and a sense of loss of authority can interfere with the cooperative intradepartmental relationships that are so vital to a company's progress. Such conflicts will be minimized where security's authority is clearly defined and understood.

2.7   The CSO's Role

Directing our attention to the generalization of the security operation and the manager's role in it, we can find many common elements that are significant. In its organizational functions, security encompasses four basic activities with varying degrees of emphasis:

1. *Managerial,* which includes those classic management functions common to managers of all departments within any organization. Among these are planning, organizing, employing, leading, supervising, and innovating.

2. *Administrative,* which involves budget and fiscal supervision, office administration, establishment of policies governing security matters and development of systems and procedures, development of training programs for security personnel and security education of all other employees, and provisions of communication and liaison between departments in security-related matters.

3. *Preventive,* which includes supervision of security officers; patrols; fire and safety personnel; inspections of restricted areas; regular audits of performance, appearance, understanding, and competence of security personnel; control of traffic; and condition of all security equipment, such as access controls and surveillance systems, computers, alarms, lights, fences, doors, windows, locks, barriers, safes, and communications equipment.

4. *Investigative,* which involves security clearances, investigation of all losses or violations of company regulations, inspections, audits, liaison with public police and fire agencies, classified documents, and any fraud or forensic investigation involving law enforcement and outside specialists.

It is important to remember that the last three functions must be carried out to further the organizational needs of security. It follows that to perform effectively, the CSO must be thoroughly conversant with all the techniques and technologies inherent in such functions. But to achieve the stated goals or the projected ends of the organization, the CSO must be sufficiently skilled in managerial duties to effectively plan, guide, and control the performance of the department.

The CSO cannot remain, as has been true so often in the past, merely a "security expert," a technician with a high enough degree of empirical or pragmatic information to qualify for certain basic preventive or investigative tasks. The more this manager is personally involved in such jobs, the more he or she will neglect the managerial functions. Security's role in the operation will suffer accordingly.

The company that recognizes the need for, and the efficiency of, incorporating security as an organic part of its enterprise has begun creating a new organizational function. Along with such traditional functions as marketing, production, finance, and personnel, security will play a significant role in the daily life as well as the projected destiny of the company.

In this light, it is clear that the CSO is an indispensable member of the staff with a role that extends far beyond the limited, time-honored position of principal in charge of intrusion alarms and package inspections. This is not to suggest that there is any trend toward establishing a power base for security management, but rather that many enlightened, modern company managers have assigned a higher priority to integrated security systems in an effort to encourage the growth of this essential element of the firm's survival.

Ron D. Davis, Davis Security Group Ltd., says:

> *A successful manager will need to develop certain skills. Among these are planning, motivation techniques, public speaking, personnel management, and budgeting. These areas will not only help in preparing the manager for the future but also make them more effective in their current employment.*[1]

3 Organizing the Security Function

Although the organization and administration of the security department is a subject in itself beyond the scope of this general introduction to security, it is nevertheless important to get an overview of the security organization by looking briefly at both its function and at the staff required to implement it. From a management point of view, organizing the security effort involves:

1. Planning and goal setting
2. Establishing controls
3. Organizing the security department
4. Hiring personnel
5. Training
6. Supervising
7. Implementing security and related loss prevention functions
8. Departmental reviewing and evaluating
9. Acting as security or loss prevention advisor to top management

3.1 Planning

An extraordinarily common mistake in security planning is to put the cart before the horse—that is, to create a department, hire personnel, and then look for something for the department to do on the premise that crime is rising, losses almost certainly exist, and therefore something must be done.

In reality, need comes first. A hazard must exist before it becomes practical to establish an organized effort to prevent or minimize it. The first step in security planning is a detailed analysis of potential areas of loss, their probability, and their gravity in terms of business impact should a loss occur that affects corporate goals and assets. Only then can the specific objectives of the security function be defined.

This relationship of corporate goals to security planning is suggested in Figure 4.3. To express this relationship in a simplified way, if a company's goal is higher profits and if the widespread prevalence of employee theft is eating away those profits, a primary objective of the security function should be to reduce employee theft and thus to contribute to the corporate goal of increased profits.

Analyzing risk is discussed in detail in Chapter 8. In addition to threat assessment, planning involves establishing objectives, allocating resources within prescribed or authorized budgetary limitations, and determining what should be done, how it should be done, and how soon it should be set into operation.

3.2   Establishing Controls

Security planning, including threat assessment, will result in determining the degree of security required in all areas of a company. Decisions must also be made as to the means by which such security can be most efficiently, effectively, and economically achieved. New policies and procedures may be formulated, physical aids to security ordered, and the number and deployment of security personnel determined. All these factors must be balanced when one is considering the protection of the facility to arrive at a formula that provides the most protection at the least expense.

Controls must be established over procedures such as shipping, receiving, warehousing, inventory, cash handling, computer protocol, auditing, and accounting. The most effective and efficient method of implementing such controls is to present a control or accountability system to the relevant department managers and allow them to express their views and make counter suggestions. In this way, a totally satisfactory control procedure can be mutually agreed on. With the use of computers for most of these operations, the ability to audit is enhanced. Along with benefits, however, the computer offers additional security challenges. Only when established controls break down or prove to be inadequate should the CSO or the deputy step in to handle the matter directly.

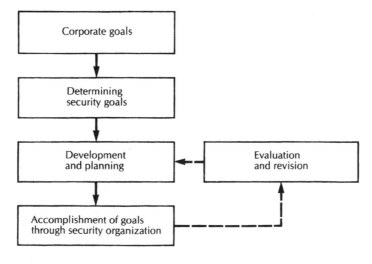

FIGURE 4.3 Establishing objectives in security planning.

As will be discussed in later chapters, loss prevention controls also cover all physical protection devices, including interior and exterior barriers, alarm and surveillance systems, and communications systems. Loss prevention also incorporates the principles of risk management that are discussed in Chapter 8. Identification and traffic flow patterns are other necessary controls. Identification implies the recognition of authorized versus unauthorized personnel, visitors, vehicles, goods, and materials.

3.3 Organizing the Security Department

An organization, as such, is people, so in considering the organizational structure of a security department, we are referring to the assignment of duties and responsibilities to people in a command relationship, to achieve defined goals.

It is necessary first to identify tasks and then to develop the organization required to discharge them. To put this another way, the department's goals or objectives are divided into practical work units, and within those units specific jobs are defined.

A simplified table of organization for a small industrial security department of 20 persons might take the form charted in Figure 4.4. Even such a small organization requires a careful description of specific duties and responsibilities, from the manager down to the security officer on patrol, with a clearly defined report command. In this example, the CSO would have more extensive line duties than would be the case in a larger department. He would be more directly involved in day-to-day operations (such as investigations), whereas in a larger department he might be occupied entirely with planning, advising, communications, public relations, and other administrative duties, leaving operations to subordinates.

The security organization, like any other organizational structure, must be designed to meet particular needs. For this reason, it is impossible to suggest a model organization for an individual security department even within the same type of enterprise (such as manufacturing or retail). The specific risks, the size of the company, the physical environment, and the budget all affect and to a great extent dictate the nature of the security response and thus of the organization needed to carry it out. One company's ideal organizational structure will not fit another's except by chance.

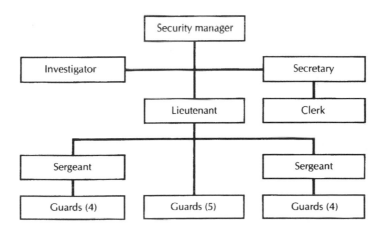

FIGURE 4.4 The organization of a small industrial security department.

This does not mean that the individual manager cannot benefit from the practices of others; he should not try to adopt any other security package, however. Instead he must adapt standard practices to suit the particular situation. Some common matters of concern in any organizational structure are delegation of authority, span of control, and the question of how many employees are required.

Delegation of authority is necessary in any organization containing more than a handful of people. Delegation separates the ultimate and the operating responsibility. In Figure 4.4, the CSO delegates responsibility for supervising security force operations to the lieutenant, who in turn delegates the operating responsibility to the sergeants on the first and third shifts because the lieutenant obviously cannot work three full shifts.

For delegation of authority to work, the responsibility must be truly delegated: It cannot be given and then routinely overridden. Once the manager in the example has determined that the lieutenant is capable of supervising the security function, he should allow the lieutenant to exercise that responsibility. And at each stage of the organizational ladder, the subordinate to whom authority is delegated must accept that responsibility; otherwise the entire command structure breaks down.

The degree to which a manager or supervisor is able to delegate responsibility rather than trying to do everything personally is a good measure of managerial ability. Conversely it has been said that the single most common management failing—in all organizations, not just security—is the inability or unwillingness to delegate responsibility and the authority required to carry out necessary tasks. The result is inevitably a bottleneck at the managerial level where one person must do or approve everything. The corollary result is a weakening of the entire chain of command below the managerial level.

Span of control refers to the number of employees over which any individual can exercise direct supervision effectively. In the small security department illustrated in Figure 4.4, there is a sergeant over four officers on both the first and third shifts. The lieutenant supervises the five officers on the second shift. Many would regard this as a relatively ideal situation. Giving a supervisor too little to do, however, can sometimes be as damaging as giving him too much. The effective span of control for a given situation will depend on the complexity of duties, the number of problems, the geographical area, and many other factors. In some situations, especially where duties are routine and of a similar nature, it would be satisfactory to have one supervisor over 10 or 12 officers. Beyond that number, however, the span of control becomes so wide as to be seriously questioned. Figure 4.5 shows a narrow span of control versus a wide span of control situation.

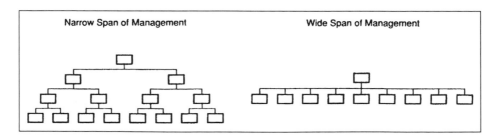

FIGURE 4.5 Span of control. (From Philip P. Purpura, *Modern Security and Loss Prevention Management,* 2nd ed. [Boston: Butterworth-Heinemann, 1989].)

The number of security personnel required is generally proportional to the size of the facility, expressed both in terms of square footage or acreage and the number of employees involved. Small businesses of 20 or 30 employees rarely require and even more rarely can afford the luxury of a security service of any size. At some point, however, as we consider larger and larger facilities, there is a need for such personnel. This can only be determined by the individual needs of a particular firm as demonstrated by a survey and as permitted by the funds available.

Where the security needs of a firm indicate the use of security personnel, they can be the single most important element in the security program. Since they are also the largest single item of expense, they must be used with the greatest efficiency possible. Only careful individual analysis of the needs of each facility will determine the optimum number and use of security personnel. For example, premises with inadequate perimeter barriers need a larger security force than do those with effective barriers. In determining security needs, therefore, it is important that all protective elements be considered as a supportive whole.

One rule of thumb that deserves mention concerns the number of personnel required to cover a single post around the clock, providing coverage for three eight-hour shifts. The number is not three but rather four and a half or five people, to allow for vacation time, sick leave, termination, and/or training. In a larger organization there is greater flexibility in the deployment of manpower, and four and a half persons might provide sufficient coverage. In a small organization, five officers would be needed at a minimum to cover that single post 24 hours a day on an ongoing basis.

3.4   Hiring Security Personnel

The selection of security personnel must be preceded by a careful analysis of personnel needs to implement plans previously drawn. Job descriptions must be developed, and labor markets must be explored.

Whatever specifications are determined, it is important that security personnel be emotionally mature and stable people who can, in addition to their other skills and training, relate to people under many conditions, including stress. It is also important to look for people with the potential to advance into the managerial ranks.

In considering the selection of personnel, it is useful to briefly examine the kinds of responsibilities they may be expected to assume. As noted in Chapter 3, in the discussions of proprietary and contract security, there are a number of tangible factors to consider in selecting security personnel.

3.5   Duties of Security Personnel

The duties of security officers are many and varied, but among them are common elements that can serve as a guide to every CSO:

1. They protect the buildings and grounds to which they are assigned, including their contents, occupants, and visitors.
2. They suggest and enforce rules and regulations governing the facility.
3. They direct traffic—both foot and vehicular.
4. They maintain order on their posts and help people who require assistance or information.

5. They develop and familiarize themselves with all special and general orders and carry them out to the letter.

6. They develop, supervise, and enforce applicable systems of identifying personnel and vehicles, conduct package and vehicle inspections, and apprehend people entering or leaving the facility without the required authorization.

7. They develop and conduct periodic prescribed inspections of all areas at designated times to ascertain their security and safety.

8. They act for management in maintaining order and report any incidents that disrupt such order.

9. They investigate and report incidents of employees engaged in horseplay, loitering, or violation of clearly stated policies.

10. They determine, monitor, and instantly sound the alarm and respond to intrusions and fires.

11. They log and turn in lost or unclaimed property. In the event that any property is reported stolen, they check the recovered property log before proceeding in the matter.

12. They make full reports to supervisors on all unusual circumstances.

13. They coordinate emergency planning with police and other first responders.

14. They protect intellectual property by working with information technology (IT) professionals.

Because of the growing number of lawsuits filed against firms for negligent security, the selection and training of security personnel have become critical issues for CSOs. Issues surrounding training are discussed in detail in Chapter 6, and liability issues are presented in Chapter 7.

3.6   Posts and Patrols

Although much of the security operation has been automated in recent years, making good use of surveillance technology, cameras have not in most cases completely replaced personnel. Security personnel may be assigned to a variety of posts, but these fall into just a few categories. Personnel may be assigned to a fixed post, to a patrol detail, or to reserve.

Fixed posts can be gatehouses, building lobbies, or any particularly sensitive or dangerous location. *Patrol duty* involves walking or riding a given route to observe the condition of the facility. The perimeter is an important patrol, as are warehouse areas and open yard storage areas. *Reserves* are people standing by in the event that assistance is needed by security personnel on fixed posts or patrol duty. The scope of their special orders varies from company to company, but a list of the things that might be required will give the flavor of the tour of duty in an industrial facility.

Security personnel on patrol will make their tours on routes or in areas assigned by the supervisor in charge. They must be fully aware of all policies and procedures governing their tour as well as those that govern the area patrolled. Duties include:

1. Make sure that the area is secure from intrusion and that all gates and other entrances are closed and locked as prescribed. In interior spaces, check to see that all doors, windows, skylights, and vents are locked and secure against intrusion as well as possible damage from the weather as prescribed.

2. Turn off lights, fans, heaters, and other electrical equipment when their operation is not indicated.

3. Check for unusual conditions, including accumulation of trash or refuse, blocking of fire exits, and lack of access to firefighting equipment. Any such conditions, if not immediately correctable, must be reported immediately.

4. Check for unusual sounds and investigate their source. Such sounds might indicate an attempted entry, the movement of unauthorized personnel, the malfunctioning of machinery, or any other potentially disruptive problem.

5. Check any unusual odors and report them immediately if the source is not readily discovered. Such odors frequently indicate leakage or fire.

6. Check for damage to doors, tracks, or weight guards. In cases where doors have been held open by wedges, tiebacks, or other devices, these should be removed and their presence reported at the end of the tour of duty.

7. Check for running water in all areas, including washrooms.

8. Check that all firefighting equipment is in its proper place and that access to it is in no way obstructed.

9. Check whether all processes in the area of the patrol are operating as prescribed.

10. Check the storage of all highly flammable substances, such as gasoline, kerosene, and volatile cleaning fluids, to ensure that they are properly covered and secured against ignition.

11. Check for cigar or cigarette butts. Report the presence of such butts in no smoking areas.

12. Report the discovery of damage or any hazardous conditions, no matter whether they can be corrected.

13. Exercise responsible control over patrol routes and fire-alarm keys as well as keys to those spaces that might have been issued.

14. Report all conditions that are the result of violations of security or safety policy. Repeated violations of such policies will require investigation and correction.

To carry out such assignments, it is essential that security personnel meet high standards of character and loyalty. They must be in good enough physical condition to undergo arduous exertion in the performance of their duties. They must have adequate eyesight and hearing and have full and effective use of their limbs. In some circumstances exceptions may be made, but these would be for assignments to posts requiring little or no physical exertion or dexterity. They must be of stable character and should be capable of good judgment and resourcefulness.

All applicants for such positions must be carefully investigated. Because they will frequently handle confidential material as well as items of value and because they will in general occupy positions of great trust, they must be of the highest character. Applicants should be fingerprinted and checked through local and federal agencies where legally permissible. Background investigations of the applicants' habits and associates should also be conducted. Signs of instability or patterns of irresponsibility should disqualify them.

All of these recommendations set high standards for the security officer, but nothing less will satisfy the emerging professionalism of the security function.

3.7 Supervision

In addition to planning, establishing controls, organizing a department, hiring personnel, and training, the CSO's responsibilities include supervision of security. It is in the handling of this function that the entire security program will prove either effective or inadequate.

CSOs must maintain close supervision over communications within their own departmental structures. It is essential that they communicate downward in expressing departmental directives and policies. It is equally important that they receive regular communication up the organizational ladder from their subordinates. They must regularly study and analyze the channels of communication to be certain that the input they receive is accurate, relevant, timely, concise, and informative.

In addition, CSOs must set up a system of supervision of all departmental personnel to establish means for reviewing performance and instituting corrective action when necessary. Above all, they must lead. Their qualities of leadership in and of themselves will ultimately prove to be the most effective supervisory strengths.

Security personnel are in many respects the most effective security devices available. They rarely turn in false alarms. They can react to irregular occurrences. They can follow and arrest a thief. They can detect and respond. They can prevent accidents and put out fires. In short, they are human and can perform as no machine can. But as humans they are subject to human failure. Security personnel must be adequately supervised in the performance of their duties. It is important to be sure that policy is followed, that each member of the security force is thoroughly familiar with policy, and that the training and indoctrination program is adequate to communicate all the necessary information to each member of the security staff. Guards must be disciplined for violations of policy and at the same time management must see to it that violators are made aware of the policy that was violated.

All these elements must be regularly reviewed. It must be remembered that well-trained, well-supervised security personnel may be the best possible protection available, but badly selected, badly supervised guards are not an asset at all and, worse, could themselves be a danger to security. They can, after all, succumb to temptation like any other individual. Their opportunities for theft are far greater than those of the average employee.

Issuance and use of keys to stockrooms, security storage, and other repositories of valuable merchandise or materials must be limited and their use strictly accounted for. Fire protection not otherwise covered by sensors or sprinkler systems is not often a major problem in such spaces, and in the event a fire were to threaten, the door could be broken or a guardhouse key could be used to enter the endangered area.

Although, theoretically, all security personnel are subjected to thorough background investigation before assignment and are closely observed during the early period of employment, they may still yield to the heavy pressure of temptation and opportunity when they have free and unlimited access to all of the firm's goods. Although it is not sound personnel practice to show distrust or lack of faith in the sincerity of security personnel, it is risky to fail to adequately supervise them. After all, we are all human! We are all subject to temptation and may succumb to anger. Such problems can be dealt with only through enlightened leadership and supervision.

3.8 Leadership

A CSO is expected to be a leader and an expert on security issues within the organization. Leadership is difficult for even the experts to define, and in this limited space, little can be said about this vital trait. Leadership, however, is more easily understood in comparison to "followership." The person who has the most influence in a group and carries out most of the leadership functions is designated a leader. Though leadership is difficult to define, it is easier to identify skills necessary to be a successful leader. The most widely accepted classification of skills was proposed by Katz[5] and later by Mann.[6] The skills are depicted in Figure 4.6. Just as skills for leaders have been identified in broad categories, so have roles. Mintzberg[7] identified 10 roles:

1. Figurehead
2. Leader
3. Liaison
4. Monitor
5. Disseminator
6. Spokesperson
7. Entrepreneur
8. Disturbance handler
9. Resource allocator
10. Negotiator

3.9 Manager

There is no doubt that in today's environment the CSO must be a manager. Though 20 years ago many retired law enforcement and military personnel were hired as security

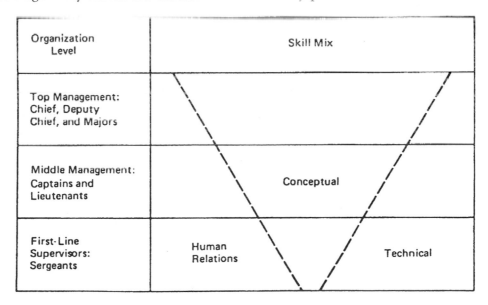

FIGURE 4.6 Skill mix: conceptual, human relations, and technical. (From Gary A. Yukl, *Leadership in Organizations* [Englewood Cliffs, NJ: Prentice-Hall, 1981], pp. 85–86.)

executives, the focus today is on management knowledge and experience. Managing people and maximizing personnel resources have become major parts of the CSO job.

Management incorporates many of the areas discussed in the preceding paragraphs. But it also implies an ability to see beyond supervision, leadership, or planning. It implies an ability to organize all these important components of executive work.

3.10   Implementation of Security

The next element with which the CSO must deal is the image or representation of the security function. For security to be effective in any organization, it must have the implied approval and confidence of that organization. Every time a guard is overbearing or a cumbersome and inefficient system is installed, security's image suffers.

It is the task of the CSO to undertake a regular program of indoctrination to clearly define the role of security and of security personnel within the organization. Since employee participation and cooperation are essential to the success of any security effort, it is extremely important that a thorough indoctrination program eliminate any tendency to alienate these important allies by overbearing or bullying attitudes on the part of security personnel. Such a program must also impress on all security people the importance of their roles in public relations, both as employees of the company and as members of the security department.

No matter how well the department is organized, it cannot be effective without the full support of the people in the organization it serves. To achieve this support, the department must be educated in attitudes, duties, and demeanor, and proper supervision must ensure that these attitudes are maintained. The very fact that security personnel are controlling the movement and conduct of other members of their community suggests that they must themselves be carefully controlled to avoid giving rise to feelings of resentment and hostility. The entire organization can suffer great harm as a result of general animosity directed at only one member of the security department who has acted improperly or unwisely.

3.11   Departmental Evaluation

Regular departmental evaluations should try to determine whether security policies and procedures are being properly followed and whether such existing policies and procedures are still desirable in their present form or should be modified to better achieve predetermined goals. These evaluations should also review all manpower and equipment needs and the efficiency of their current use in the conduct of the security program.

Since security concerns itself with prevention of damage, disruption, or loss, its effectiveness is never easy to evaluate. The absence of events is not in itself revealing unless there are accurate accounts of actual crimes against the organization during some prior, analogous period to provide a standard of measurement.

Even such a comparison is of dubious value as the basis for a thorough, ongoing, objective analysis of security effectiveness. Circumstances change; personnel terminate; motivating elements alter or disappear. And there is always the haunting uneasiness created by the possibility that security procedures might be so ineffective that crimes against the company have gone virtually undetected, in which case the reduction or absence of detected crime presents a totally misleading picture of the company's position.

3.12   Personnel Review

In reviewing departmental performance, all records of individual personnel performance should be examined. The degree of familiarity of employees with their duties, the extent of their authority, and their departmental and organizational goals should be examined. Corrective training programs should be required as indicated. The health, appearance, and general morale of each staff member should be noted. Of course, the most significant factor is performance. Work performance objectives and goals should be established with each employee, along with criteria to determine how results will be measured.

3.13   Equipment Review

The state of all security equipment should be reviewed regularly with an eye to its current condition and the possible need for replacement, repair, or substitution. This review should cover all space assigned for use by security personnel on or off duty, uniforms, arms (if any), and communication, alarm, and surveillance equipment; vehicles; keys and access control devices; data terminals; security programs; and databases. Carelessness or inadequate maintenance of such equipment should be corrected immediately.

3.14   Procedures Review

A review of security department procedures is essential to the continued efficacy of the department. All personnel should be examined periodically for their compliance with directives governing their areas of responsibility. Familiarity with department policies should be evaluated and corrective action taken where it proves necessary. At the same time, the very usefulness of prescribed procedures should be reviewed, and changes should be initiated where they are deemed advisable.

Training programs designed to remedy problems or covering new equipment or procedures should also be reviewed to determine whether they achieved the stated objectives.

Summary

Although the trend toward hybrid security operations continues, clearly understanding the role of security within an organization is a must. Hybrid operations may include only a proprietary CSO working with a contract manager, or they may include a full-blown security operation with contracts for only a few security services. Regardless, the CSO must understand long-held management principles as well as keeping current on new theories of leadership and development of personnel and programs.

☐ ☐ ☐ ━━━━━━━━━━━━━━━━━━━━━━━━━━━━━━━━

Critical thinking

What do you believe are the consequences of security management's failure to become integrated into a company organization?

━━━━━━━━━━━━━━━━━━━━━━━━━━━━━━━━ ☐ ☐ ☐

Review Questions

1. Discuss the following statement: In general, the CSO can be considered to be serving a staff function.
2. Why is functional authority important to the CSO?
3. What categories of concern should be reviewed during a security department evaluation?
4. What are the key tasks involved in organizing the security function? Explain the importance of each.
5. Describe the duties of the security officer on patrol.

References

1. Zalud, Bill, "Vanishing Jobs Mark Security Mid-Life Crisis," *The Zalud Report* (November 1990): 3.
2. Flynn, Edward J., "Revolutionary Call for Asset Protection Management," *Security* (May 1991): 25.
3. Grannis, Kathy, "Retail Losses Hit $41.6 Billion Last Year, According to National Retail Security Survey," National Retail Federation, www.nrf.com/modules.php?name=News&sp_id=318&op.
4. Davis, Ronald, "The Importance of Management Skills in the Security Profession," in John Chuvala III and Robert Fischer, eds., *Suggested Preparation for Careers in Security/Loss Prevention* (Dubuque, IA: Kendall Hunt, 1991), p. 51.
5. Katz, R.L., "Skills of an Effective Administrator," *Harvard Business Review* (January/February 1955): 33–42.
6. Mann, F.C., "Toward an Understanding of the Leadership Role in Foreman Organization," in R. Dubin, G.C. Homans, F.C. Mann, and D.C. Miller, eds., *Leadership and Productivity* (San Francisco: Chandler, 1965).
7. Mintzberg, H., *The Nature of Managerial Work* (New York: Harper & Row, 1973), 120.

5

Career Opportunities in Loss Prevention

OBJECTIVES

The study of this chapter will enable you to:

1. Discuss factors that affect the security job market.
2. Know the various job and career paths open to individuals pursuing careers in security.

1 Introduction

Today security is a major management function in businesses worldwide. Where they were almost unheard of 30 years ago, there are now vice presidents of loss prevention (chief security officers, or CSOs) reporting directly to the presidents of many companies and having the same impact on management decisions as, for example, the vice presidents of operations or distribution. As noted in Chapter 1, the impact of the events of September 11, 2001, has brought security back into the spotlight.

Career opportunities in areas of business, industry, and government security vary; the perceived need for an integral and integrated security function in the management of the widest variety of enterprises can be anticipated as becoming the norm in the near future.

1.1 Factors Increasing Security Opportunities

Among the factors that tend to create inviting career paths in security, none is more significant than the explosive growth of the protection function, as briefly described in Chapter 2. The events of 9/11 have also added to the already healthy growth of the security industry. *Security*, in its 2002 annual report on the status of the field, indicated that three factors were at work, providing mixed messages for security managers. First is the aftermath of 9/11, which forced organizations to reevaluate protection efforts and spurred spending on electronic security and hiring of additional security personnel. Second, the cost of insurance continued to spiral upward. This trend forced companies to shift more emphasis to security or accept uninsured losses. Third, the recession economy put pressure on security executives to cut costs.[1] In 2007 the economy was improved and the cost of insurance was once again under control, so companies were investing in the protection of company assets and hiring "professional" security staff.

Other positive considerations for the future of not only jobs in security, but also the changes and requirements for individual advancement or growth within the career field, include the following:

- The increasing professionalism of security is reflected in higher standards of educational criteria and experience, and correspondingly higher salaries, especially at management levels.

- The rapid growth of the loss prevention function has created a shortage of qualified personnel who have management potential, meaning less competition and greater opportunities for advancement for those who are qualified.

- The shift in emphasis to programs of prevention and service rather than of control or law enforcement has broadened the security function within the typical organization.

- The presence of both two- and four-year degree programs, as well as master's-level study in criminal justice and/or security at the college level, is creating a new awareness of a rising generation of trained security personnel at the corporate management level. Many companies, especially larger corporations, are actively emphasizing the degree approach in their hiring.

- The demographics of an aging police and security force at the management level create opportunities for advancement.

2   The Security and Loss Prevention Occupation

No matter whether you recognize the protection function by titles such as loss prevention, security administration, or industrial security, the basic function of modern security remains the same. Security helps prevent losses. As noted in Chapter 2, losses from crime are once again on the upturn after years of decline. For every product manufactured, someone is waiting to make an illegal profit by stealing or manipulating processes and records. For every security device installed, someone is determined to find a method to defeat it. As the events of 9/11 made clear, for every business and political entity, there is now a potential for attacks based on political and philosophical reasons.

Much like law enforcement, security is basically a recession-proof occupation, particularly at line (guard) levels. The need for educated and trained security officers and administrators is increasing with the need to counteract terrorism, computer crime, embezzlement, employee theft, drugs and violence in the workplace, fraud, and shoplifting. The U.S. Department of Labor indicates that employment in security is expected to grow faster than the average for all occupations through 2010 as concerns about crime, vandalism, and terrorism continue to increase the need for security.[2] *Security* reported that The Freedonia Group, Inc., projects that contract security services will increase at a rate of 7.3 percent annually through 2010.[3]

Security professionals are hired by almost all kinds of organizations at all levels—line; lower, middle, and upper management; corporate; and so on. Among organizations that have security operations are banks, colleges, government agencies, hospitals, public utilities, restaurants, hotels, retail stores, insurance companies, museums, mining firms, oil companies, supermarkets, telecommunications companies, transportation companies, and office buildings. Within each of these broad areas, security personnel perform many different functions, including personnel protection, computer security, coupon security, disaster management, crime prevention, proprietary information security (intellectual property), white-collar crime investigations, counterterrorism, guard force management, investigations, physical security, crisis management, plant security, privacy and information management, fire prevention and safety, and drug abuse prevention and control.

The American Society for Industrial Security International (ASIS) Committee on Academic Programs has suggested that students seeking careers in security should pursue course work in security, computer science, electronics, business management, law, police science, personnel, and information management.[4] This suggestion is supported by security educators and practitioners in *Suggested Preparation for Careers in Security/Loss Prevention*.[5] Building on the ASIS committee statements, the editors developed a book of readings that have a common thread: the need for security and loss prevention personnel to have a broad understanding of various disciplines and specific skills for certain specialties. The editors suggest that specific skills are needed for all students of security—communication, management, and law. Other subject areas, such as fire and computer security, will depend on students' interests.

2.1 Security Managers

Salaries of security directors (CSOs) with policymaking authority average $117,000 per year, according to a 2007 ASIS salary survey.[6] This a dramatic increase over the $72,000 figure reported by Langer and Associates in 2001. The average 2001 security executive had 10 or more years of experience and at least a bachelor's degree.[7] Over 70 percent of the 2007 managers have at least an undergraduate degree and more than 25 percent hold a master's.[8] The 2001 figures indicated less experience and education than the 1995 executives reported, supporting earlier comments about the exodus of more experienced executives through retirement. However, the 2007 data indicates the value that companies are placing on education; the author reports that many of these executives are young with experience in areas other than security. One possible answer to this shift is the principle of convergence in the evolving role of security professionals. Although the average salary is $117,000, many security directors make more than $250,000 per year.

2.2 Personal Security

With the danger of kidnapping and threats from other areas, including disgruntled employees, the demand for executive protection specialists, or bodyguards, is increasing.

According to the Professional Bodyguard Association, today's bodyguard can be anyone who has the desire to complete the appropriate training. The professional bodyguard is not just the "tough guy" portrayed in Hollywood movies. The bodyguard of the 21st century must be well trained and professional. Training includes familiarity with new technology, including threats of electronic bugging. However, the PBA also notes that traditional self-defense skills and firearms proficiency are still stressed.[9]

What they need is common sense, the ability to pay attention to detail, and patience. Bodyguards should also know about laws and customs in various places (countries, states, cities) where they might be living or traveling with their principals. In a field once dominated by men, women are becoming more prominent as protection specialists.

Most employers of executive protection specialists want a person who can fit into the executive's work and play schedule.

Bodyguard schools are now becoming prominent, and many of the students are former law enforcement or military personnel. Skills taught include use of weapons and hand-to-hand combat. In addition, schools might prepare the specialists with skills in protocol, dress, and specialized knowledge of alarm systems and closed-circuit TV (CCTV). The salaries and benefits are generally excellent, but burnout is high. Long hours and time spent away from friends and family eventually take their toll.

2.3   Private Investigators

The private investigator (PI) is a gatherer of facts—in essence, a researcher who spends the greatest portion of his or her time collecting background information for pre-employment checks on personnel, doing background checks of applicants for insurance or credit, and investigating insurance claims. Much of this work is not crime related, although it may involve either part- or full-time undercover investigations of employee theft or detection of shoplifting.

Investigations in divorce-related matters are declining as divorce laws become more liberal. Investigations of "significant others," however, are increasing as people become more interested in what their love interests do with their spare time. Tracing missing persons or investigating criminal matters on behalf of the accused is a very small part of a typical investigator's work.

Although there are situations in which private investigators are called on to supplement the work of public police, such as the long-term relationship between the American Bankers' Association and the Burns Agency, the great majority of private investigative work is complementary to the public law enforcement effort.

A growing number of investigators are engaged in litigation investigations—that is, gathering data for defense and plaintiff law firms preparing for trial in civil court. In general, PIs are involved in locating missing persons, obtaining confidential information, and solving crimes. Many PIs work for businesses and lawyers, whereas others work independently. Independent offices may be only one-person operations or may employ several operatives or contract work to part-time investigators. These independent investigators charge from $35 to more than $150 per hour. Long days and seven-day work-weeks are the norm when a PI is on a case.

Good PIs develop skills that include the ability to conduct good surveillance and background checks. Some cases involve undercover investigations and require a complete understanding of a sometimes dangerous assignment, including developing a cover and dealing with people who must not know who you are. The private investigation business requires the investigator to learn the law as well as interviewing and investigative techniques. The best PIs also possess good verbal and written skills as well as analytical skills. Attendance at or membership in the National Association of Legal Investigators is an excellent aid to improving basic skills. Generally speaking, the outlook for jobs in this area is good. According to the Bureau of Labor Statistics, the market is stable and good in all states, with an estimated 40,000 private investigators in the United States.

A person interested in this field should consult individual state laws, which vary greatly, to determine what criteria must be met for licensing. Criteria vary from virtu-ally none to extensive experience, completion of a written and/or oral examination, and interview by a state board. Various certifications are available for those wishing to specialize. For example, the Certified Fraud Examiner (CFE), the Professional Certified Investigator (PCI), or the Physical Security Professional (PSP) certifications may add credibility and value to services offered by investigators. More will be said about certification in Chapter 6.

2.4   Consultants

Many firms that seek professional assistance in determining their vulnerabilities and risks look not to the police but to those in the private security sector who are professionally trained to assess security needs and make appropriate recommendations. As with any profession, some people emerge as experts who then sell their expertise for a fee. These people are commonly referred to as *consultants* because they are paid for their professional opinions.

Security consultants are the specialists of the field. They generally operate as sole proprietors of a business that sells specific security expertise. Some security consultants charge more than $100 per hour and bill more than $200,000 annually. Security consultants provide advice for a fee. They do not work for specific equipment companies or firms. Advice commonly purchased from the consultant consists of information from three general areas:

1. Number, quantity, and use of security personnel
2. Direction and content of security policies and procedures
3. Alternatives in security hardware

Consultants also offer training seminars on specific problem areas—for example, executive protection, computer security, and disaster planning. Technical consultants generally recommend and in some cases install security systems. Security managers often rely on these technically experienced individuals to recommend CCTV/monitoring systems, biometric or other access controls, alarm systems, or software for a variety of purposes, including systems integration. Security consultants are generally people who have paid their dues working in investigation or security management. Many have published articles and books. Today the completion of a Ph.D. is helpful, since the title "Doctor" carries added weight if the consultant is called to testify in court. As civil litigation increases, the demand for security experts who can testify as credible witnesses also increases. It takes years of experience to achieve the levels of knowledge to operate in this arena.

2.5   Opportunities in Sales

With the tremendous growth in the use of technology, the opportunities to sell all types of security products are evident. For the person with the personality for sales, the opportunities to represent major security product manufacturers and distributors are excellent. Visit any major trade show, such as ASIS or the America's Security Expo (ASC), to get an idea of the number of well-versed sales representatives in the field.

2.6   Opportunities in Industry

Typically the greatest opportunities in industrial security exist in larger companies that employ proprietary security forces. Many firms actively recruit the career-oriented person with a certificate or degree in a recognized security or criminal justice program.

However, the trend toward hybrid security operations has reduced the demand for proprietary security officers in many companies. The largest employers, such as General Motors, John Deere, and Caterpillar, have made a transition to a system of contract officers with proprietary oversight. In addition, these industrial giants have been actively installing state-of-the-art technology that has changed the need for security officers.

Despite this reduction in demand, the security director at one major manufacturing facility with a highly progressive security program reports being interested in hiring only those applicants with at least a bachelor of science degree in security from a recognized security or criminal justice program.

2.7   Opportunities in Retail

The retail field provides a diversity of job opportunities in security, from the entry-level position of the uniformed security officer (or blazer-jacketed "host") to the internal theft investigator. Positions are available both with retail stores and chains and with security service companies, which provide such services as undercover and shopping investigations. There are many openings for those without experience but with the education, ambition, and aptitude that might make them successful in retail security. Many companies today provide their own training for shoppers and other investigators, even though the employees have no investigative experience. Alertness, resourcefulness, courage, and self-assurance are often more important than specific experience.

There are many different types of operations in the retail industry. Security has had its impact on virtually every operation—from the discount store to the department store to the supermarket. The recognition of the importance of inventory shrinkage to the company's profit picture and the necessity for loss prevention are, or soon will be, almost universal. Companies that do not accept this necessity, in the words of one ranking retail executive, simply will not remain in business.

The entry-level position in one company includes many students recruited from criminal justice and security programs as well as sales personnel crossing over to security. Many of these employees work part-time while they are going to school.

It will be interesting to follow this career field as traditional retail stores continue to see their markets diminished by Internet marketing. Although traditional retail security jobs may decline, this change in sales opportunities opens new jobs for persons interested in the security field.

2.8   Opportunities in Health Care

Hospital security officers make up the vast majority of persons employed in health care security. According to Russell Colling, a nationally known health care security authority and author of *Hospital Security* (4th edition), the officer who prepares for advancement (through a combination of education beyond high school and hands-on field experience) can look to numerous supervisory, investigative, training, fire prevention, and safety positions in the field.[10]

Hospital security officers generally earn more than their counterparts in other industries because of the variety of duties requiring a higher-than-average amount of training. The officer must also be able to interact effectively with the medical community as well as with patients and visitors under conditions of frequent stress. Salaries, however, do vary by location.

Security director positions generally require at least four years of college preparation and considerable field experience. Like so many other areas of security, as Colling observes, hospital security is just coming into its own.

2.9   Airport and Airline Security and Sky Marshals

As a result of the events of 9/11, airport and airline security has undergone tremendous scrutiny. The verdict was clear: Old ways of handling airport security measures were not adequate. Something needed to be done. With the passage of the Airport Security Federalization Act of 2001, airport security in the United States has changed forever. What had been the domain of contract and proprietary security organizations is now under the control of the federal government. To become a baggage screener, for example, the following criteria must be met:

- High school diploma or a combination of education and experience
  determined to have equipped the individual to perform the duties of the screening position
- Basic aptitudes and physical abilities, including color perception, visual and aural acuity, physical coordination, and motor skills
- Command of the English language
- Be a citizen of the United States

Preference will be given to individuals who are former members of the armed forces or former employees of an air carrier whose employment was terminated as a result of a reduction in workforce.

An older federal program, the Federal Air Marshals, was given new life following 9/11. The number of air marshals deployed on select passenger flights was increased significantly.[11] Standards are high, as is the rigor of the training program. The mystique of this position often clouds the fact that the job requires long periods of travel and much boredom. The number of marshals is classified, but estimates are that the current number falls between 2,500 and 4,000, up from the 23 agents employed in the program prior to 9/11. The average salary is approximately $62,000 annually. Though the position is prestigious, marshals often complain of fatigue and boredom. There are few chances for promotion. Over the past five years sky marshals have made only 51 arrests, none related to terrorism.[12]

In addition to airport security operations, now controlled by the federal government, there are opportunities with major airlines. However, most major airlines still prefer to hire former federal agents in managerial positions. This situation is not unique to airlines, of course. Former Federal Bureau of Investigation (FBI) agents can be found in a great many corporate security jobs in business and industry around the globe. Both the experience and qualifications required by many federal law enforcement jobs have generally been highly regarded in the private sector. The ambitious career-minded security aspirant could do far worse than consider a period of service with a federal law enforcement agency as a springboard to a promising position in industry, including airline security.

Qualifications are high. Almost all employees in this field have college degrees. Many have law degrees and five or more years of federal experience.

2.10   Hotel Security

The hotel and motel industry has been characterized in the past by serious neglect of many security responsibilities, an attitude that has only slowly been changing in spite of a number of very large awards by the courts in recent years against hotels or motels charged with negligent security, particularly in the area of protecting guests. This negligence, however, coupled with court-mandated responsibility, has created opportunity for security professionals.

In addition, as travelers express safety concerns regarding potential terrorist attacks, hotel security managers will need to find ways to assure interested travelers that their facilities have ample protection against such attacks.

Opportunities in the hotel industry exist in great numbers for both on-site positions and at the corporate home office level. Except at the corporate level or the management level in large hotels, however, the salary range is relatively low in relation to the security industry as a whole. On the other side of the coin, the entry level for the person with any combination of hotel experience and security education or experience can be quite good, with clear opportunities for advancement.

In a related area, the future of security in high-rise apartment buildings and housing complexes offers great potential for the security professional because of the growing emphasis on the concept of total environmental protection and the threat of civil suits by residents or guests who are victimized on building property.

2.11   Campus Security

The rapid progress of campus security during the past 25 years has created excellent opportunities for career positions in the field. Openings in many progressive and professional campus departments provide challenge, but also good salaries and fringe benefits as well as chances for advancement. Such departments are looking for the young, career-minded individual, with particular interest in those enrolled in, or graduates of, a criminal justice degree program. Interestingly, unlike many areas of modern security, campus security has generally evolved from a low-visibility operation to a highly visible, police-oriented image in response to rising crime problems on campuses.

A good-sized department will include line officers, field supervisors, shift commanders, a coordinator of line operations, and a director. Many departments also have specialized positions such as investigator and training officer. Salaries vary from department to department and from one area of the country to another.

2.12   Banking Security

Banks must comply with minimum federal regulations on security, as promulgated in the Bank Protection Act of 1968. The act mandates that there must be a security manager. Banks comply with this requirement in a variety of ways. Small operations often delegate security responsibilities to a senior bank officer. Larger banks, however, hire security managers who often are former FBI agents with an understanding of federal regulations regarding currency and fraud. There is a heavy reliance on electronic technology and physical security rather than on large staffs.

The bank guard may become a casualty of technological advances because many banks are finding it more cost-effective to eliminate guards in favor of physical security improvements.

2.13   Security Services

In general, security personnel at the lower operational levels earn less in contract security organizations than they do in proprietary guard forces. This is not necessarily true for investigators and other personnel at higher levels.

Young people should seek opportunities in security service organizations since the growth of security services has been meteoric and there is no leveling off in sight. The demand for good executives is insatiable.

Because the good loss prevention or security executive is much less a police officer than a systems expert, auditor, and teacher, security experts recommend broad-based education and experience in such areas as accounting, industrial engineering, management, personnel, law, statistics, labor relations, and report writing.

On another level, there is a demand for technically qualified individuals capable of providing specialized security services ranging from alarm sales, installation, and service of alarm systems. Continuing changes in the application of security hardware and systems will bring an increasing demand for the services of those who can advise users on their selection and implementation.

2.14   Guard Services

Guard supply represents the major service provided in the industry today. The majority of guards work for contract security agencies, but many firms hire their own security staff (proprietary security). Only part of the guard's job is crime-related. Whenever it is possible or necessary, guards are required to prevent major crimes and to report those that have been committed. But their major roles may be to direct traffic, to screen persons desiring access to a facility, and generally to enforce company rules. In many modern applications, the role is more helpful rather then regulatory. They may direct or escort persons to their destination within a facility, act as receptionists or sources of information, or be primarily concerned with safety.

Since many guards are concerned for only a small percentage of their time with crime-related activity, there is some effort in various quarters to adjust the guards' appearance to fit their roles by outfitting them in blazers and slacks rather than in a uniform with its police or coercive connotation.

A guard is, however, a guard. Even if, in a particular assignment, he or she is never confronted with criminal activity, the guard is still charged with certain responsibilities in that area and is responsible in addition for protecting the interests of his or her employer on the employer's property.

According to the Bureau of Labor Statistics, guard salaries range between $10.00 and $16.00 per hour.

Private guards differ from public police, both in their legal status and in that they perform in areas where the public police cannot legally or practically operate. The public police have no authority to enforce private regulations, nor have they the obligation to investigate the unsubstantiated possibility of crime (such as employee theft) on private property. The job of the private guard is to provide specific services under the direction and control of a private employer who wants to exercise controls or supervision over the company's property or goods, or to provide additional services that the public police as a practical matter simply cannot provide.

2.15   Patrol Services

Private patrol services offer a periodic inspection of various premises by one or more patrols operating either on foot or in patrol cars. The tour of such patrols may cover several locations of a single client or include several establishments owned by different clients within a limited neighborhood. Inspections of patrolled premises may be visual perusal from the outside or they may require entering the premises for a more thorough inspection. Typically the arrangement made with a client specifies that a certain number of inspections will be made within a given period of time or with specified frequency.

The patrol differs from the guard by operating through a tour covering various locations, whereas the guard stands at a fixed post or walks a limited area. The patrol service is more economical because the guard maintains a post for the full period during which a danger exists. But the patrol has the possible disadvantage of being circumvented by an intruder who knows that there will be some period of time between inspections of a given premises.

2.16   Armored Delivery Services

Armored delivery services provide for the safe transfer of money, valuables, or any goods the employer wants to move from one location to another. By far the widest use of this service is to transport cash and negotiables from a receiving point to a bank or other depository. Payrolls, cash receipts, or cash supplies for daily business are the principal traffic of the armored delivery service.

Personnel employed by such services are not concerned with the general security of the premises they serve; their responsibility is confined to the safe transport of sensitive items as directed by the customer. Courier services perform a similar function in the safe transport of valuables. They are distinguished from armored car services principally by using means other than special armored vehicles.

2.17   Locksmithing

This is a classic profession requiring a lengthy apprenticeship. Locksmiths in the United States sell, install, and repair locking devices, safes, and vaults. Some also sell and install various alarm and electronic access control systems. Positions are available in shops, where apprentice locksmiths spend their time learning the trade under a master craftsperson. Much of the work is done on an emergency basis; thus the hours are often long and irregular. The best jobs involve keying new facilities or rekeying older structures such as office buildings and motels.

2.18   Alarm Response Services and Technology Experts

Central station alarm systems consist essentially of alarm sensors located in the protected premises and a communication line from the sensors to a privately owned central station alarm board that is monitored and responded to by private security personnel (see Figure 5.1). Many city codes require that alarm systems be tied into a central station operation.

In some cases, central station systems do not dispatch personnel to respond to an alarm but rather relay the alarm received to public police headquarters. But in most such systems, the alarm is relayed and someone is also sent to the scene.

FIGURE 5.1 A security guard walks through an emergency housing site set up for hurricane victims. (FEMA photo by Leif Skoogfors.)

Alarms connected to a central station are usually designed to detect intrusion, but they can also be used to monitor industrial processes or conditions.

Certainly, central station coverage of a facility is cheaper than full-time security employees performing essentially the same function. A drawback is that the false alarm rates for many intrusion systems are still very high, resulting in resistance to the use of direct connection systems to police headquarters. Central station operators have some flexibility in checking the validity of an alarm before notifying the police, so they may to some degree reduce the incidence of false alarms demanding police response.

In cases where central station personnel actively investigate the intrusion and even take steps to apprehend a suspect before the arrival of the police, they supplement the public police effort.

With a dominant use of electronics in security, the demand for professionals who understand the applications of alarm technology, CCTV, and other high-tech applications within security continues to grow (Figure 5.2). Alarm installation is an excellent skill to learn. While most positions in this business are through distributors and contract security services, there is a trend toward proprietary positions. Certification for this area of study is available through the National Alarm Association of America (NAAA).[13]

2.19   Computer and Intellectual Property Security

This is an important example of the new frontiers opening in the loss prevention field in response to social and technological changes. Computer security executives and

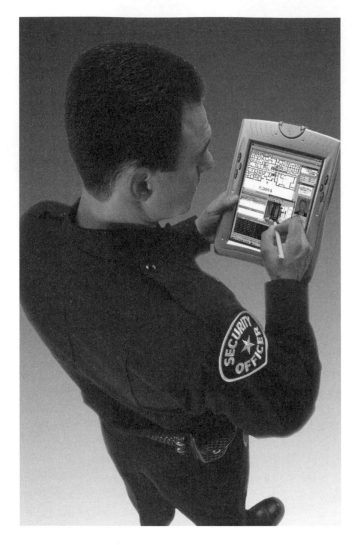

FIGURE 5.2 Security officer on foot patrol with handheld device. (Permission of Hirsch Velocity.)

investigators call for a blend of education and experience in computer science and security. Today virtually all organizations have computers that need protection.

Although the first response was to protect the computer and related hardware from attack, it soon became clear that of greater importance was protecting the information stored in the computers. With the advent of information transfer through intranet and Internet systems, the problems associated with the protection of company and private information being transferred among various locations has become an even bigger security concern. In today's e-commerce world many firms generate information (customer lists, research projects, and so on) that has become a major target of identity thieves, New Age bank frauds, credit thefts, and other scams.

A person with an interest in and aptitude for computer software, computer technology, and related industries could do well to consider using these talents to protect computer information and information transfer.

2.20   Government Service

Most people who study the loss prevention and security field are contemplating work in the private sector, but there are opportunities with public law enforcement and the military. Individuals with technical training or education in crime prevention are valuable additions to government organizations that are combating both traditional criminal activities (burglary, robbery, computer crimes) and acts of terrorism. Given the growing cooperative nature of the war on terrorism, opportunities for specialists appear to be good.

2.21   Other Services

In addition to the areas we've described, private security firms also provide such services as crowd control, canine patrol, polygraph examination, psychological stress evaluation, drug testing, honesty testing, employee assistance services, and other related loss prevention assistance to business and industry. Various firms have entered the area of drug testing to meet the demand for a drug free work environment. Consultants are also providing programs on how to deal with workplace violence. Still other firms are specializing in electronic sweeps because espionage activities have increased. And as would be expected, there are now many experts who offer advice on protection from terrorist attacks.

Summary

Although salary scales and security applications vary in different parts of the world as well as within the different areas of business and industry—or even within the same type of business or industry—it is nevertheless possible to perceive the coming of age of security throughout the 21st century.

Still, more universally accepted standards of training and applicant screening and higher wage scales are needed. The opportunity for vertical movement within the security structure must be both present and perceived. But even in these areas there are encouraging signs.

The use of outside investigators and security consultants will increase as security functions become more specialized. The current trend in hiring security executives is to find someone with a broad background because convergence is one of the key factors in the changing role of security executives.

□ □ □ ▬▬▬▬▬▬▬▬▬▬▬▬▬▬▬▬▬▬▬▬▬▬▬▬▬▬▬▬▬▬▬

Critical Thinking

If you were giving advice to someone contemplating a career path in security or loss prevention, would you guide them to a program in criminal justice or some other field such as computer science? Does the educational path have any impact on the type of positions that are available?

▬▬▬▬▬▬▬▬▬▬▬▬▬▬▬▬▬▬▬▬▬▬▬▬▬▬▬▬▬▬▬ □ □ □

Review Questions

1. What factors are increasing career opportunities in security?
2. Pick one area of security that interests you and discuss the career opportunities that exist today.
3. How important is a college education in obtaining a position as a security manager?

References

1. Zalud, Bill, "2002 Industry Forecast Study Security Yin-Yang: Terror Push, Recession Drag," *Security* (January 2002).
2. Protective Service Occupations, *Occupational Outlook Handbook*, 2002–2003 edition, U.S. Department of Labor, Bureau of Labor Statistics, February 2002, Bulletin 2540-11, pp. 14–17.
3. "Global Security Service Revenues to Exceed $160 Billion in 2010,"*www.security* magazine. com/copyright/BNP_GUID_9-592006, posted 3/1/2007.
4. *Career Opportunities in Security and Loss Prevention* (Washington, D.C.: ASIS Foundation), p. 1.
5. Chuvala, John III, and Fischer, Robert James, eds., *Suggested Preparation for Careers in Security/Loss Prevention* (Dubuque, IA: Kendall/Hunt, 1991), p. iii.
6. Moran, Mike, "What Are You Worth?" *Security Management* (August 2007), pp. 67–73.
7. *Compensation in the Security/Loss Prevention Field*, 13th ed., Abbot Langer & Associates, Inc., December 2001.
8. Moran.
9. Professional Bodyguard Association, downloaded from *http://myersmith.tripod.com/home. html*, 8/15/2007.
10. Colling, Russell L., *Hospital Security*, 4th ed. (Boston: Butterworth-Heinemann, 1992).
11. Airport Federalization Act of 2001, November 6, 2001, Sections 104, 105.
12. Meckler, Laura, and Carey, Sus, "U.S. Air Marshal Service Navigates Turbulent Times,"*Wall Street Journal* (02/09/07), p. A1.
13. Keller, Steven R., "Technology: Unlocking the Future for Security Practitioners," in John Chuvala III and Robert James Fischer, eds., *Suggested Preparation for Careers in Security/ Loss Prevention* (Dubuque, IA: Kendall/Hunt, 1991), p. 102.

6

Security Education, Training, Certification, and Regulation

OBJECTIVES

The study of this chapter will enable you to:

1. Understand the past and present situation regarding the training of security personnel.
2. Identify the key professional organizations and their efforts to provide professional guidance and certification programs.
3. Trace the efforts of the federal government to create legislation mandating security screening and training standards.
4. Discuss the role of higher education in providing a foundation for professional security.
5. Identify the professional and academic journals available to security practitioners.

1 Introduction

Until the last two decades, few security officers in the United States received adequate pre-job or on-the-job training to perform the tasks so often assigned to them. A few companies provided good pay, benefits, and training, but they were the exceptions. In addition, the industry leaders did little to establish criteria for the business through professional certification. Some industries did develop certification, such as the Certified Protection Professional (CPP) designation developed by the American Society for Industrial Security International (ASIS) and the Certified Protection Officer (CPO) program developed by the International Foundation for Protection Officers, based in Alberta, Canada. Otherwise little was done for the line security officer.

As noted in Chapter 2, concerns over the quality and regulation of training were first recognized at the federal level. In 1991, then Senator Al Gore introduced the first of several pieces of legislation aimed at setting minimum standards for the security profession. The other key legislative leaders were Representative Matthew Martinez (D-CA) and Representative Don Sundquist (R-TN).

Though progress has been made, the events of September 11, 2001, brought the issue of training and credentials for security personnel to the forefront. In the aftermath of 9/11, airport security procedures, security personnel, and training were called into question. As a result of the government and public focus on airport security, the federal government took over security at the nation's airports in an attempt to assure the public that high-quality, highly trained people are staffing our airport security operations.

As we enter the 21st century it appears that security may undergo major changes in the areas of training, regulation, and certification. These efforts are being led by the federal government and ASIS.

2   Adequacy of Private Security Training

The status of private security training has traditionally been low. A study conducted by the Private Security Advisory Council (PSAC) in 1978 indicated that, although security training programs were being offered by law enforcement agencies, educational institutions, training facilities, and contract or proprietary security firms, the quality varied widely. The variety in the programs was simply explained by the fact that there were no uniform standards for courses in terms of content, length, method of presentation, instructor qualifications, or student testing.[1] The report of the Task Force on Private Security found the same lack of quality programs and for the first time made specific recommendations.[2] Unfortunately, almost 30 years later, many of these recommendations have yet to be implemented, although progress has been made.

To further stress the need for private security training, the 1985 *Hallcrest II* report noted that the typical security guard received only four to six hours of preassignment training. The primary concern voiced by those surveyed at the International Security Conference (ISC)-East in August 1989 was lack of adequate security training. Although the ISC was 18 years ago, there has been little change since then. Security authorities correctly report that security training will not receive any attention until the cost of the training is less than the cost of litigation for failure to train.[3] Although government studies both past and present have called for attention to training issues and some standardization of training, training continues to be regulated by individual states, each with its own standards.

A 2003 review of state licensing information supported a 1990 study showing that only 50 percent of the states had any imposed training standards.[4] Just two years later, a 2005 review of state regulation and training found that 43 states now license or regulate the security industry. This is an impressive change from the earlier study, but mandated training occurs in only 13 states and the variation in hours ranges from four to over just over 40.[5]

It thus appears that training for private security personnel is less than adequate. This could be one reason that the public law enforcement sector, mandating a median basic training program of 720 hours, has for many years held a poor opinion of the private security profession. The occupation must be professionalized. You can find a listing of licensing and training requirements for security officers in the United States through the International Association of Security Investigative Regulators at www.iasir.org/Security.htm.

3   Proposed Federal Regulation

The first effort by the federal government to pass legislation to regulate the private sector was introduced by former Vice President Al Gore, then a senator from Tennessee. The bill proposed minimum standardized training for essentially all security personnel, although it would only be mandatory for those involved in government security operations either directly or as contractors. The Gore Bill proposed training in the following areas:

- Fire protection and fire prevention
- First aid
- Legal information relevant to providing security services
- Investigation and detention procedures
- Building safety
- Methods of handling crisis situations
- Methods of crowd control
- Use of equipment needed in providing security services
- Technical writing for reports

The bill mandated examination and commensurate certification procedures to ensure the quality of the basic training, but specifics were not spelled out.

The second initiative was made in 1992 under the direction of Representative Matthew Martinez (D-CA). The initial Martinez package was much more specific than the Gore bill. The Martinez proposal provided for a minimum of eight hours of basic classroom instruction and successful completion of a written examination, plus a minimum of four hours of on-the-job training. Individual states would set standards for individuals or entities conducting the classroom instruction.

The bill also stated that the classroom portion of the training must include, but may be expanded beyond (at the discretion of the instructor or state licensing agency), the following:

- Legal powers and limitations of a security officer, including laws of arrest, search, seizure, and use of force
- Safety and fire detection and reporting
- Instructions on when and how to notify public authorities
- Employers' policy, including reporting incidents and preparing an incident report
- Fundamentals of patrolling
- Deportment and ethics
- General information, including specific assignments and equipment use

In 1993 House Bill 2656 was introduced by Representative Don Sundquist (R-TN). This bill was similar to the Gore bill, mandating that states have screening, training, and other requirements and procedures for issuing licenses to security personnel. The Sundquist bill also stipulated that security employees would need to pass a drug screening test that met the guidelines of the National Institute on Drug Abuse, as well as physical and psychological fitness tests. The bill also required a check of records with the National Crime Information Center.

A major difference in the Sundquist bill was that it required a minimum of 16 hours of initial training, of which eight must be preassignment, with the balance occurring as on-the-job training. Armed personnel would need to complete a mandatory 24 hour program above and beyond the 16 hours already stipulated. In perhaps the most dramatic departure, Sundquist's bill also mandated annual training requirements, including a four-hour refresher course. Armed personnel would have to complete additional hours of refresher courses on firearms and requalify in the use of their duty weapon.[6]

Although these bills showed movement in the right direction, they would not have led to uniform federal standards. The United States, always sensitive to states' rights, is suggesting a minimum standard that states will be free to enhance. The most current effort is SB2238, the Private Security Officer Employment Standards Act of 2002. The key provision of this bill requires all security employees (contract and proprietary) to undergo a criminal history check.[7] This legislation is now law, allowing security employers access to criminal history records.

3.1   The Role of Higher Education

In November 1978 a seminar entitled "Meeting the Changing Needs of Private Security Education and Training" was held at the University of Cincinnati as a follow-up to the report of the Task Force on Private Security and the first National Conference on Private Security. The majority of participants were academics. The interest of the academic world in security education at first increased and then leveled off. However, the interest is certainly not new. The demand for improved training and education in the field of security has existed since 1957.[8]

With the 21st century renewed interest in security, brought on by increasing problems with security in our new technologically changing world as well as the threat of terrorism, has come a renewed emphasis on security education. Security programs will likely get a new "lease on life" as educational institutions find their place in the 21st-century struggles against world terrorism and techno-crimes.

As more and more private security managers receive their degrees, the overall quality of private security employees will increase because college-educated people will do their best to see that the private security occupation becomes worthy of the term *professional*. Perhaps of greater importance is the recognition that many of the new global security jobs require more education.

The problem for many colleges and universities continues to be defining security education. Most of the programs developed in the 1970s and '80s were shaped by law enforcement education, where these new programs were housed. From a review of the literature, it is apparent that educators are not of like minds on the placement of security curricula in colleges and universities. One view shows preference for equal status with law enforcement programs because the fields are very interrelated. A second view is that security should be a completely independent major with alliances to departments of business. Yet a third view indicates that the placement of the program is not as important as an interdisciplinary approach to the curriculum. The degree designation is of little importance.[9]

What is evident is that there are well-established security education programs at respected colleges and universities. Fischer and Chuvala presented information on security education at the 1993 ASIS annual meeting in Washington, D.C. They reported that in 1993, 60 programs had been identified as offering baccalaureate or higher levels of security education. In surveying this identified group, Fischer and Chuvala determined that only 21 institutions were actually offering security degrees. As Chuvala noted in his presentation, most of the other programs offered criminal justice degrees with security courses.[10]

Though the field has increased to more than 75 programs at the baccalaureate or higher level, many of these programs offer related degrees that have an emphasis on loss prevention and security.[11] Although only a third of the institutions of varying size and administrative organization were identified as offering degrees in security, we can make certain generalizations about security education at the baccalaureate level. In general, programs are small and are staffed by faculty who have more experience in public law enforcement than in security. Despite the small size of programs, most institutions express support for them.

It must be remembered that security education is still a relatively young discipline. The final determinant of program success or failure is a program's ability to deliver a product that is attractive to the security industry. If the graduates of a program are not of adequate quality, the program will fail. Though criticisms are many, there are programs that have been able to identify problems and develop successful degree plans. A close look at the demographics of one of the successful programs reveals a continuing development of security offerings and program direction. Responses from graduates of the program indicate that a large proportion of its majors entering the security field eventually achieve high-paying administrative or supervisory positions in security. The future of security education is excellent when one considers the growth evident in the field.

The involvement of the ASIS Foundation in sponsoring a master's program indicates the growing interest of professional security managers in providing graduate education in loss prevention and security for its membership.

Today ASIS tries to fill the role of a security institute. Over the past few years, the ASIS Foundation has made tremendous advances in providing innovation within the security profession. Perhaps the most visible success of the ASIS Foundation has been the establishment of *Security Journal*. The Foundation also offers scholarship funds to students interested in pursuing an education in security.[12]

In addition to the work through the ASIS Foundation, ASIS has also been actively involved with Webster University in preparing a graduate certification program in security management. The program is designed for individuals who are seeking additional education beyond the bachelor's degree but who don't want a master's degree.[13] ASIS, in cooperation with Wharton University of Pennsylvania, also offers a two-week program on basic business principles for security executives. Also to be considered is the availability of online courses. The World Wide Web has allowed for the distribution of many different types of information on the Internet.

Following the events of 9/11, and with the support of the federal government, a number of programs offering certification and various degrees in homeland security or emergency management have been developed. Whether these programs are simply "kneejerk" reactions to the terrorist threat or viable and sustainable programs is yet to be seen.

3.2 Training

Development and training of security personnel must be a continuing concern of management. Indeed, the lack of adequate training in the past has been the major criticism leveled against private security, both within the industry and outside it. Today wages for contract guards are still generally low and training has not improved substantially.[14]

Even though the majority of all guards (both proprietary and contract) receive some preassignment training, in the contract area 40 percent of the guards have completed only on-the-job training. In general, it is apparent that proprietary security personnel report more training than do contractual personnel. The Private Security Task

Force (Standard 2.5) recommended that contract security personnel complete a minimum of eight hours of formal preassignment training as well as a basic training course of at least 32 hours within three months of assignment,[15] but this recommendation has not been implemented. Even the recent federal initiatives through the Gore, Martinez, and Sundquist bills have not resulted in any substantive changes to date.

It is clear that adequate training can and must be an important aspect of security planning in the proprietary organization. The need is as great in contract security services, of course, where the problem is compounded by the competitive pressures of the marketplace. The onus for low training standards must be borne by employers whose overriding consideration in selecting security services is the lowest bid. Proficiency in security is largely a product of the combination of experience and a thorough training program designed to improve the officers' skills and knowledge and to keep them current with the field. The recommendations of the Task Force on Private Security included the following:

1. A minimum of eight hours of formal preassignment training
2. Basic training of a minimum of 32 hours within three months of assignment, of which a maximum of 16 hours can be supervised on-the-job training[16]

The merits of training will be reflected in the security officer's attitude and performance, improved morale, and increased incentive. Training also provides greater opportunities for promotion and officers' better understanding of their relationship to management and the objectives of the job.

It should not be presumed that former law enforcement officers require no training. They do. To be successful in security, they must develop new skills and—not incidentally—forget some of their previous training.

A training program should cover a wide variety of subjects and procedures, some of them varying according to the nature of the organization being served. Among them might be:

- Company orientation and indoctrination
- Company and security department policies, systems, and procedures
- Operation of each department
- Background in applicable law (citizen's arrest, search and seizure, individual rights, rules of evidence, and so forth)
- Report writing
- General and special orders
- Discipline
- Self-defense
- First aid
- Pass and identification systems
- Package and vehicle search
- Communications procedures
- Techniques of observation
- Operation of equipment
- Professional standards, including attitudes toward employees

At least one contract firm has also recognized changes in the field brought about by the technology revolution. Barton Protective Services has developed several technology training programs. The program relies on computer-based e-learning. The firm is also installing "Tech-Knowledge-y" labs in branch offices, affording an opportunity for all officers to participate in the e-learning process.[17]

As mentioned earlier, the Private Security Officer Employment Standards Act of 2002 was to be the beginning step in the federal government imposing uniform standards on the security industry. However, the version of the Act that actually passed did not address training standards. Rather, the Act focused on employment standards by allowing security employers access to criminal histories of prospective employees.

Appendix C provides a listing of all regulatory agencies with responsibility for certification, training, and monitoring of security personnel in each state.

3.3 Certification and Regulation

An area closely tied to training issues, and thus limited, is regulations and certification. The authors applaud ASIS for the development of its CPP program and its new initiatives for specialized certification. Given the current efforts by the federal government and ASIS, it is likely that a balanced approach between industry-imposed standards and pre-emptive state legislation will be the model for the United States in the 21st century. Industry-imposed standards can be successful, as noted by the success of the British Security Industry Association (BSIA). BSIA industry-imposed standards reportedly cover 90 percent of Britain's security industry. The BSIA has adopted standards pertaining to personnel screening, wage levels, supervision, training, liability insurance, and physical facilities.[18]

In 2003 ASIS International ventured into the area of industry regulation, creating an ASIS Commission on Guidelines. The goal of this commission is to "advance the practice of security through the development of risk mitigation guidelines." The Commission has written a set of General Security Risk Assessment Guidelines (see www. asisonline.org).[19]

3.4 Regulation

Considering the importance of private security personnel in the anticrime effort and their quasi-law-enforcement functions, it is ironic that they receive so little training in comparison to their public sector counterparts: zero to just over 40 hours, compared to a median of 720 hours for police officers. Though this difference is ironic, the reason is obvious. Legislation mandates training for public law enforcement personnel, whereas this is not the case for security personnel. A look at licensing standards for private security companies reveals that little has changed with regard to regulation of this already huge and still growing industry. Considering the lack of progress in establishing uniform training standards, it is difficult to support a contention that the "best regulator" is the marketplace. Still, the 2003 ASIS initiatives offer hope that the United States will have some success with industry-led standards, as in Great Britain. Federal and industry leadership is essential because it is doubtful that the states will provide any guidance.

In the states that do have legislation, the keywords that might be used to describe the composite package of legislation are "lack of uniformity." Terminology is not uniform, but more important, there is no consensus on the degree to which the state should regulate training, licensing, and education/experience.

It is also interesting to note that, of those states that do attempt to regulate security, only a few include proprietary security forces in their regulatory statutes. This has established a double standard for in-house and contract employees who are performing essentially the same functions.

In 2008 there is still a need for the following:

1. *Standards, codes of ethics, and model licensing.* The efforts of the Task Force on Private Security and the PSAC have stood the test of time, and both groups were well represented by law enforcement, business, and all facets of the security field. Statewide licensing should be required for guard and patrol, private investigation, and alarm firms. The profound effects of upgrading private security relationships with law enforcement will occur as a result of the cooperative action of the security industry, law enforcement, and state governments in implementing the measures encompassed by the Task Force on Private Security and PSAC efforts.

2. *Statewide preemptive legislation.* Although law enforcement agencies seek closer local control over private security, a proliferation of local licensing ordinances deters adoption of minimum standards and imposes an unnecessary financial burden on contract security firms with redundant licensing paperwork and fees. Some latitude might be granted local law enforcement agencies to impose tighter control on some aspects of private security operation, but the controls should not be unduly restrictive and should withstand tests and measures of cost-effectiveness.

3. *Interstate licensing agency reciprocity.* Interstate operation of contract security can be unnecessarily hampered by having the same personnel comply with different personnel licensing requirements in adjacent states—and sometimes in cities and counties. The same standards of state-level licensing and regulation in all states and reciprocity (e.g., recognition of other states' regulatory provisions) would facilitate more efficient delivery of security services and decrease state regulatory costs.[20]

HR 2092, the Martinez/Barr compromise bill, would have made it easier to determine whether a security candidate had a criminal record.[21] The new Private Security Officer Employment Standards Act of 2002 achieved what Martinez/Barr set out to accomplish.

3.5   Certification

Various certification programs were mentioned in Chapter 2. The growth of programs leading to certification is an indication of the professionalization of the security field. Today it is possible to receive several certification designations, each of which has its special appeal. An indication of the level of heightened interest in the broad-based security professional can be seen in the results of the diligent efforts of ASIS International. This society has long been interested and involved in creating standards of competence and professionalism to identify those security practitioners who have shown a willingness to devote their attention to achieving higher goals of education and training in their chosen career. As was noted earlier, the security profession has, in the past, been characterized by the transitory nature of much of its personnel. Training standards have frequently been low, and even many executives in the field were generalists without either specific work-related experience or specific training in security. Many factors have been brought to bear on this problem, and changes have been and are being made.

One ASIS program is designed to upgrade those career security persons who are willing and able to qualify for certification as CPPs. The certification board for this program was organized in 1977 and since that time has provided sufficient evidence of professional performance capability through certification to stress the importance of the CPP. "Positions available" announcements in the *Wall Street Journal*, the *Chronicle of Higher Education*, and other publications have included requirements that state "Certification as a Protection Professional by the ASIS [is] desirable," or the candidate "must have certification as a CPP." This trend will continue as employers and the public become more aware of the CPP program.

Certification in this program is far from pro forma. Both educational and work experiences are required before a candidate can be considered. If candidates meet the basic standards, they must then take an examination on both mandatory and optional subjects. It is through this program and those given by colleges and universities across the country that the goal of professionalism in the practice of security will be achieved.

Beginning in 2003 ASIS International began offering two technical certifications: Professional Certified Investigator (PCI) and Physical Security Professional (PSP). The PCI is for those whose primary responsibility is to conduct investigations, whereas the PSP is designed for individuals whose primary responsibility is to conduct threat surveys and design integrated security systems or for those who install, operate, and maintain security systems.[22]

Similar efforts have been made to improve the professional image of the security officer through the Certified Protection Officer (CPO) program referred to in Chapter 2. The program was founded in 1986 by the International Foundation for Protection Officers (IFPO). The first CPOs were granted in 1986, and that certification is now available through several colleges in the United States and Canada. The program is "designed to provide theoretical educational information to complement the field experience of Security Officers."[23] Topics of study include:

- Introduction to security
- Officer and the job
- Physical security
- Legal aspects
- Human relations
- Security as a career
- First aid and CPR
- Preventive security

Candidates must complete an application, obtain nominations from two security or police professionals, and complete the training program before certification is granted.

With the growth of integrated systems and the need to protect intellectual property, at least three certifications are available for security/information systems specialists. These are the Certified Information Security Auditor (CISA) offered by the Information Systems Audit and Control Association, the Certified Information Systems Security Professional (CISSP) from the International Information Systems Security Certification Consortium, and the Globally Certified Intrusion Analyst (GCIA) from the SANS Institute.

Other certifications are available in specific fields. The International Association for Healthcare Security and Safety (IAHSS) offers the Certified Health Care Protection

Administrator (CHCPA) designation; the United Security Professionals Association (USPA), Inc., offers the Certified Financial Security Officer (CFSO) designation; and the Academy of Security Educators and Trainers (ASET) offers the Certified Security Trainer (CST) program. With the increase in computer-based fraud, the Association of Certified Fraud Examiners was established in 1996 with its own certification program (CFE). As mentioned earlier, the events of 9/11 fostered the development of certification in homeland security. Of course, other groups have also developed various programs to identify competence in specific areas.

4   Magazines and Periodicals

Any discipline that claims to be a profession must have its own mechanism for distribution of information. In most disciplines or professions, information is distributed through professional publications. Security and loss prevention publications have changed dramatically in the last 20 years as a reflection of the growing professionalization of the field. At one time *Industrial Security* (now *Security Management*) and *Security World* (now *Security*) magazines were practically the only publications in the security field. Today the number has grown substantially.

Studies conducted over the years indicate that *Security Management* and *Security* dominate the field but that other publications are also being more widely read.[24] Other often mentioned publications include *Professional Protection, International Review, Levista Securidad, Pinkerton Focus, Campus Security, Hospital Security, Security Journal*, and *Journal of Security Administration* (now defunct). With the growing need to understand the electronic age, magazines like *Info Security* and *Beyond Computing* offer security professionals up-to-date information on the latest computer security technology and problems. *Access Control and Security Systems Integration*, along with *Security Technology and Design (ST&D)*, offers the latest in security technology advances. Appendix A lists the major publications in security.

With the advent of the technology age, a focus on publications cannot ignore the growing use of the World Wide Web. ASIS has developed its own information-sharing Web presence as ASIS Online and ASISNET. *Security* magazine has also developed its own Website. As the use of technology associated with the computer continues to improve, it is more than likely that other publications will join the trend toward Web dissemination. Many corporations and government units already make extensive use of the computer and its power to distribute information via the Internet. Appendix B provides a list of useful Internet sites.

Summary

Security education has undeniably undergone tremendous growth in the last 25 years. Academic programs in security, with a few exceptions, are young relative to traditional subject areas. Most were established within the last 35 to 40 years. In general, most have been reasonably successful as the demand for college-educated security managers has continued to grow. Leaders in the field, both academics and practitioners, indicate that security should seek recognition as its own distinct area of study. Although some believe that the programs can find this autonomy within the criminal justice field, others believe that the field would be better off based in colleges of business. The concept of convergence of fields for security managers may push this argument in favor of a broad education rather than a specialized focused degree.

Security education is here to stay, whether it is housed in criminal justice programs, colleges of business, or independent programs. In 1994 the World Institute for Security Enhancement (WISE, www.worldinstitute.org/wise/nav_left.html) was established. WISE offers training, consulting, research and development, and "think tank" services.[25] A good deal of research on various security topics is currently being produced at colleges and universities. Much of this research is academic in orientation, however, and perhaps of little value to practitioners. In this respect an institute much like the ASIS Foundation that would support practical research is certainly desirable.

The status of education in security is good news, but the same cannot be said for training. It is truly unfortunate that until 2003 the federal government had not taken an active part in establishing minimum requirements for security personnel, who often perform the same duties as police officers. Even the states that now regulate the security industry in reality pay little attention to it. Considering the fact that the private police outnumber the public sector by more than a two-to-one margin and that the field is growing at a rate of approximately 12 percent each year, it is time for the federal government to take an active role in requiring states to develop adequate legislation for security training or provide an impetus for a British model in the United States. This industry model may become reality as ASIS continues to develop industry standards.

The National Association of Private Security Industries (NAPSI), Inc., reports that 61 percent of all guard companies surveyed conduct continuing education courses for their guards and are continually looking for new training materials.[26] Let's take a lesson from the issue of police training. It was not until the establishment of the Law Enforcement Assistance Administration and federal legislation that the states began to require adequate training for police officers. Today they receive a median of 720 hours of basic training. In addition, most states also have an ongoing training program once the basic course has been completed. Given the improved quality of police education and training after federal involvement, it is likely that similar results would occur in the private sector, should the federal government decide to become involved in the regulation of training and education. Even though the Gore, Sundquist, Martinez, and Barr initiatives indicated a growing interest in federal regulation, more needs to be done to get similar bills out of committee and onto the floors of the House of Representatives and Senate.

On the bright side, the recent ASIS International efforts at establishing industry-based guidelines for security and the introduction of Senate Bill 2238, the Private Security Officer Employment Standards Act of 2002, which was signed into law, are evidence that perhaps we are beginning to understand the need for professional security services.

□ □ □ ▬▬▬▬▬▬▬▬▬▬▬▬▬▬▬▬▬▬▬▬▬

Critical Thinking

What are the future implications for regulating the training and certification of security personnel through federal mandates?

▬▬▬▬▬▬▬▬▬▬▬▬▬▬▬▬▬▬▬▬▬ □ □ □

Review Questions

1. How does the presence of college degree programs in security enhance the field?
2. What is your view of regulation in the security field? Should the government play a role, or should the industry regulate itself?
3. How do the levels of training and regulation for security personnel compare with those of the police?
4. Do you observe any differences in the level of professionalization between security management and line security officers? If so, what are they?

References

1. *Hallcrest Report: Model Security Guard Training Curricula*, Private Security Advisory Council to LEAA, U.S. Department of Justice (McLean, VA: Hallcrest Press, 1978), p. 1.
2. Van Meter, Clifford, executive director, *Private Security: Report of the Task Force on Private Security* (Washington, D.C.: National Advisory Committee on Criminal Justice Standards and Goals, 1976), pp. 88–89.
3. Cunningham, William, Strauchs, John J., and Van Meter, Clifford W., *The Hallcrest Report II: Private Security Trends 1970–2000* (Boston: Butterworth-Heinemann, 1990), pp. 150–155.
4. National Association of Security and Investigative Regulators, State Licensing Information, downloaded 12/3/02, www.iasir.org/Security.htm.
5. Associated Criminal Justice and Security Consultants, LLC., "Evaluation of Basic Training Programs in Law Enforcement, Security and Corrections . . .," June 2005.
6. Chuvala, John III, and Fischer, Robert J., "The Role of Regulation,"*Security Management* (March 1993): 61–63; and Chuvala, John III, and Fischer, Robert J., "Why Is Security Officer Training Legislation Needed?,"*Security Management* (April 1994): 101–102.
7. ASIS International, "ASIS Efforts Result in Change to Security Guard Screening Bill," downloaded 11/14/02, www.asisonline.org/newsroom/newsreleases/100802guard.html.
8. Wathen, Thomas W., "Careers in Security-One Professional's View," *Security Management* (July 1997): 45–48.
9. Cunningham, William, and Taylor, Todd H., *Private Security and Police in America: The Hallcrest Report* (Portland, OR: Chancellor Press, 1985), p. 264.
10. Fischer, Robert J., and Chuvala, John III, "Security Education: An Update," a paper presented at the Annual Meeting of ASIS, September 1993, Washington, D.C.
11. "Academic Institutions Offering Degrees and/or Courses in Security," ASIS International IRC, July 2007.
12. "Working for Security," *ASIS Dynamics* (January/February 1991): 8–9.
13. "Webster Offers Graduate Certificate in Security Management," *Security Management* (July 1996): 119.
14. Cunningham et al., pp. 141–156.
15. Cunningham and Taylor, p. 264.
16. Van Meter, pp. 99–106.
17. Cunningham and Taylor, pp. 263–264.
18. Ibid., pp. 152–153.
19. ASIS International, "ASIS International Develops Framework for Creating Security Guidelines and Standards," downloaded 1/12/03, www.asisonline.org/newsroom/newsreleases/010803guidelines.html.

20. Cunningham and Taylor, p. 265.
21. *Security Management* (January 1996): 114.
22. ASIS International, "ASIS International Launches Two Additional Professional Certification Programs," downloaded 1/12/03, www.asisonline.org/newsroom/newsreleases/120902certs.html.
23. *The Protection Officer: Training Manual* (Cochrane, Canada: The Protection Officer Publications, 1986).
24. Bottom, Norman R., "Periodical Literature in Security and Loss Control," *Journal of Security Administration* (June 1985): 9; Palmiotto, Michael J., and Travis, Lawrence F. III, "Faculty Readership of Security Periodicals: Use of the Literature in a New Discipline," *Journal of Security Administration* (June 1985): 30; Fischer, Robert J., "The Development of Baccalaureate Degree Programs in Private Security 1957–1980," unpublished dissertation, University Microfilms, Ann Arbor, MI.
25. Bottom, Norman, "Editorial: A Security Institute Is Born," *Journal of Security Administration* (December 1994): ii–iv.
26. "Guard Companies Specify Officer Training Needs," *Security* (January 1991): 9.

Basics of Defense

In this section, the basic tools used in security and loss prevention are discussed. These range from a theoretical understanding of law, honesty, risk analysis, and surveys to applied technology in locks, alarms, barriers, and procedures. Other tools include an understanding of contingency planning insurance, fire protection, and safety. These elements make up the foundation on which any good security program is based.

These are foundational tools, but it is important for security experts to realize that the applications of these tools can and do change with time. Technology, especially computing, has made the lock a modern security device. Old "insurance thinking" has been replaced by more cautious thinking in the 21st century. Case law continues to evolve, especially in the areas of liability.

Security and the Law

1 Introduction

Although in the United States public police and protection services derive their authority to act from a variety of statutes, ordinances, and orders enacted at various levels of government, members of private police function essentially as private citizens. Their authority to so function is no more than the exercise of the right of all citizens to protect their own property. Every citizen has common-law and statutory powers that include arrest, search, and seizure. The security officer has these same rights, both as a citizen and as an extension of an employee's right to protect his or her employer's property. Similarly, this common-law recognition of the right of defense of self and property is the legal underpinning for the right of every citizen to employ the services of others to protect property against any kind of incursion by others.

The broad statement of such rights, however, in no way suggests the full legal complexities that surround the question. In common law, case law, and state statutes as well as in the basic authority of the U.S. Constitution, privileges and restrictions further defining these rights abound. The body of law covering the complex question of individual rights of defense of person and property contains many apparent contradictions and much ambiguity. In their efforts to create a perfect balance between the rights of individuals and the needs of society, the courts and the legislatures have had to walk a narrow path. As the perception of society's needs changed or as the need for the protection of the individual became more prominent, a swing in the attitudes of the courts and the legislatures became apparent. This led to some confusion, especially among those with little or no knowledge of the law.

It is of enormous value, therefore, for everyone engaged in the security field to pursue the study of both civil and criminal law. Such a study is aimed neither at acquiring a law degree nor, certainly, at developing the skills to practice law. It is directed toward developing a background in those principles and rules that will be useful in the performance of the complex job of security.

Without some knowledge of the law, security officers frequently cannot serve their clients' interests. They may subject themselves or their employers to ruinous lawsuits through well-meaning but misguided conduct. In cases that must eventually go to court, handling of evidence, reports, and interrogations may be critical to the case; without security officers who have an understanding of legal processes and how they operate, the cases could be lost.

In short, the pursuit of security itself involves contact with others. In each such contact, there is a delicate consideration of conflicting rights. Without an appreciation of the elements involved, the security officer cannot perform properly.

Because for the purposes of this book we are primarily interested in civil and criminal law—both of which have major implications for the security officer and for the industry—it is useful to distinguish between them. Criminal law deals with offenses against society (corporations are of course part of society and can be either criminals or victims). Every state has its criminal code that classifies and defines criminal offenses. Criminal law is the result of a jurisdiction either using common law, which was adopted from English traditions, or passing specific legislation called *statutory law.* (In some jurisdictions both are used.) When criminal offenses are brought into court, the state takes an active part, considering itself to be the offended party.

Civil law, on the other hand, has more to do with the personal relations and conflicts between individuals, corporations, and government agencies. Broken agreements, sales that leave a customer dissatisfied, outstanding debts, disputes with a government agency, accidental injuries, and marital breakup all fall under the purview of civil law. In these cases, private citizens, companies, or government agencies are the offended parties, and the party found at fault is required to directly compensate the other party.

This chapter is intended as a guide to some of the intricacies of criminal and civil law, with primary emphasis on civil actions. Its aim is to describe those subjects with which a security officer would most likely be confronted. It deals with *substantive law* (statutes and codes), or that portion of the law that concerns the rights, duties, and penalties of individuals in their relationships with each other. *Procedural law,* the other of the two divisions of the law, deals with the rules of court procedure and the mechanisms of the legal machine.

2   Security, Public Police, and the U.S. Constitution

The framers of the U.S. Constitution, with their grievances against England uppermost in mind when they were creating a new government, were primarily concerned with the manner in which the powerless citizen was or could be abused by the enormous power of government. The document they created was concerned, therefore, not with the rights of citizens against each other but rather with those rights with respect to federal or state action.

Breaking and entering by one citizen against another may be criminal and subject to tort action (a civil wrong not involving a breach of contract), but it is not a violation of any constitutional right. However, similar action by public police is a clear violation of Fourth Amendment rights and, as such, is expressly forbidden by the Constitution.

The public police have substantially greater powers than do security personnel to arrest, detain, search, and interrogate. Whereas security people are, as a rule, limited to the premises of their employer, public police operate in a much wider jurisdiction. At the same time, public police are limited by various restrictions imposed by the Constitution. With some exceptions, private police are not as a rule touched by these same restrictions.

Public police are limited by the Constitution, which prohibits officials from denying others their constitutional rights. The Fourth and Fourteenth Amendments are most frequently invoked as the cornerstones of citizen protection against arbitrary police action. The exclusion of evidence from criminal proceedings is one penalty public police pay for violation of the Fourth Amendment's search provision. For the most part, private police are not affected by these restrictions.

3   Sources of Law

All law, whether civil or criminal, has its source in constitutional law, common law (also referred to as *case law*), or statutory law. The following discussion can be applied to either civil or criminal law as it has developed over the past century. Although today's criminal law is primarily statutory, civil law, particularly tort law, is essentially judge-made and created in response to changing social conditions.

3.1   Common Law

At one time, the principal source of law in the United States was English common law. Although common law may also refer to judge-made (as opposed to legislature-made) law, to law that originated in England and grew from ever-changing custom, or to written Christian law, the term is most commonly used to refer to the English common law that has been changed to reflect specific U.S. customs.

Some states have preserved the status of common-law offenses for their criminal codes; others have abolished common law and written most of the common-law principles into statutes. Some states are still using both common and statutory law.

3.2   Case Law

When a case goes to court, the outcome is usually governed by prior court opinions of similar nature. Those preceding cases have usually been resolved in such a way as to put to rest any doubts as to the meaning of the governing statutes or common-law principles as well as to clarify the attitude of the courts regarding the legal issue involved. The court opinions have established precedent that will guide other courts in subsequent cases based on the same essential facts. Because the facts in any two cases are rarely precisely the same, opposing attorneys cite preceding cases whose facts more readily conform to their own theory or argument in the case at hand. They, too, build their cases on precedents, or case law already established. It is up to the court to choose one of the two sides or to establish its own theory. This is a very significant source of our law essentially becoming common law.

Because society is in a constant state of change, it is essential that the law adapt to these changes. At the same time, there must be stability in the law if it is to guide behavior. People must know that the law as it appears today will be the same tomorrow, that they will not be punished tomorrow for behavior that was permitted today. They need to know that each decision represents a settled statement of the law and that they can conduct their affairs accordingly. So the published decisions of the appellate courts become guides to the meaning of the law and in effect become the law itself. Their judgments flesh out legislative enactments to give them clear outlines. Such interpretations based on precedents are never regarded lightly and in legal terms are *stare decisis*, which means "let the decision stand."

This does not mean that each decided case locks the courts forever into automatic compliance. Conditions that created the climate of the earlier decision may have changed, rendering the precedent invalid. And there are cases decided in such a narrow way that they cannot be applied beyond that case. Further, there is nothing that prevents review of a decision at the time of a later case. If the reviewing court agrees that the earlier case was in error, it may not be bound by the earlier precedent.

So we can see that case law is an important source of the law; it provides a climate of legal stability without closing the law to responsiveness to changing needs.

3.3   Statutory Law

Federal and state legislatures are empowered to enact laws that describe crimes. The authority to do so emanates from the U.S. Constitution and from the individual state constitutions. These constitutions do not specifically establish a body of criminal law. In general, they are more concerned with setting forth the limitations of governmental power over the rights of individuals. But they do provide both for the authority of legislative action in establishing criminal law and for a court system to handle these as well as civil matters.

Much criminal law is, in fact, the creation of the legislatures. The legislatures are exclusively responsible for making and defining statutes. The courts may find some laws unconstitutional or vague and thus set them aside, but they may not create statutes. Only the legislatures are empowered to do that.

3.4   The Power of Security Personnel

Security personnel are generally limited to the exercise of powers possessed by every citizen. There is no legal area where the position of a security officer as such confers any greater rights, powers, or privileges than those possessed by every other citizen. A few states go contrary to this norm and confer additional arrest powers for security personnel after the completion of a designated number of hours of training.[1] As a practical matter, if officers are uniformed they will very likely find that in most cases people will comply with their requests. Many people are aware neither of their own rights nor of the limitations of a security officer's powers. Thus security officers can obtain compliance to directives that, if not illegal, may be beyond their power to command. In cases where security officers have unwisely taken liberties with their authority, the officers and their employers may be subject to the penalties of civil action. The litigation involved in suing security officers and their employers for a tort is slow and expensive, which may make such recourse impossible for the poor and for those unfamiliar with their rights. But the judgments that have been awarded have had a generally sobering effect on security professionals and have probably served to reduce the number of such incidents. Criminal law also regulates security activities. Major crimes such as battery, manslaughter, kidnapping, and breaking and entering—any one of which might be encountered in the course of security activities—are substantially deterred by criminal sanctions.

Further limitations may be imposed on the authority of a security force by licensing laws, administrative regulations, and specific statutes directed at security activities. Operating contracts between employers and security firms also specify limits on the activities of the contracted personnel.

3.5   Classes of Crimes

Crime has been defined as a voluntary and intentional violation by a legally competent person of a legal duty that commands or prohibits an act for the protection of society.[2]

Since such a definition encompasses violations from the most trivial to the most disruptive and repugnant, efforts have long been made to classify crimes in some way. In common law, crimes are classified according to seriousness, from treason (the most serious) to misdemeanors (the least serious). Most states do not list treason separately and deal with felonies as the most serious crimes and misdemeanors as the next in seriousness, with different approaches to the least serious crimes (those known as *infractions* in some jurisdictions, *less than misdemeanors* in others, and *petty offenses* in still others). It will become apparent why security specialists should understand the nature of a given crime and its classification, because such considerations will be important in determining:

- Power to arrest
- The need to use force in making the arrest
- Whether and what to search
- Various other considerations that must be determined under possibly difficult circumstances and without delay

Serious crimes such as murder, rape, arson, armed robbery, and aggravated assault are felonies. Misdemeanors include charges such as disorderly conduct and criminal damage to property.

3.6   Felonies and Misdemeanors

From the time of Henry II of England there has been a general understanding that felonies comprise the more serious crimes. This is true in modern U.S. law as far as it goes, but clearly the definition of felony must be pinned down more precisely if it is to be used as a classification of crime and if courts are to respond differently to felons than they would to another type of lawbreaker. The definition of a felony is by no means standard throughout the United States. In some jurisdictions, there is no distinction between felonies and misdemeanors.

The federal definition of a *felony* is an offense punishable by death or by imprisonment for a term exceeding one year. The test, then, for a felony is the length of time that punishment is imposed on the convicted person.

A number of states follow the federal definition. In those states, a felony is a crime punishable by more than a year's imprisonment. The act remains a felony whatever the ultimate sentence may actually be. Other states provide that "[a] felony is a crime punishable with death or by imprisonment in the state prison." This definition hinges on the place of confinement rather than, as in the federal description, the length of confinement.

Some states bestow broad discretionary powers on a judge by providing that certain acts may be considered either felonies or misdemeanors, depending on the sentence. The penalty clauses in the statutes thus involved specifically state that if the judge should sentence the defendant to a state prison, the act for which he was convicted shall be a felony (under the state definition of a felony), but if the sentence be less than such confinement, the crime shall be a misdemeanor.

The distinction can be very important. In states where arrest by private citizens (for example, security personnel) is covered by statute, an arrest may be made only where the offense is committed in the presence of the arrester. In the case of arrest for a felony, the felony must in fact have been committed (though not necessarily in the presence of the arrester), and there must be reasonable grounds to believe the person arrested committed it. In other words, security employees, unlike police officers, act at their own peril.

A police officer has the right to arrest without a warrant where he reasonably believes that a felony has been committed and that the person arrested is guilty, even if, in fact, no felony has occurred. A private citizen, on the other hand, is privileged to make an arrest only when he has reasonable grounds for believing in the guilt of the person arrested and a felony has in fact been committed.[3]

Some states, however, do allow for citizen arrest in public order misdemeanors. Making a citizen's arrest, which must be recognized as the only kind of arrest that can be made by a security officer, is a privilege, not a right, and as such is carefully limited by law. Such limitation is enforced by the ever-present potential for either criminal prosecution or tort action against the unwise or uninformed action of a security professional.

4   Private Security Powers

4.1   Arrest

Arresting a person is a legal step that should not be taken lightly. A citizen's power to arrest another is granted by common law and in many jurisdictions by statutory law. In most cases, it is best to make an arrest only after an arrest warrant has been issued. Most citizen's arrests occur, however, when the immediacy of a situation requires arrest without a warrant. The exact extent of citizen's arrest power varies, depending on the type of crime, the jurisdiction (laws), whether the crime was committed in the presence of the arrester, or the status of the citizen (strictly a private citizen or a commissioned officer).

In most states, warrantless arrests by private citizens are allowed when a felony has been committed and reasonable grounds exist for believing that the person arrested committed it. *Reasonable grounds* means that the arrester acted as would any average citizen who, having observed the same facts, would draw the same conclusion. In some jurisdictions, a private citizen may arrest without reasonable grounds as long as a felony was committed.

Most states allow citizen's arrests for misdemeanors committed in the arrester's presence. A minority of states, however, adhere closely to the common-law practice of allowing misdemeanor arrests only for offenses that constitute a breach of the peace and that occur in the arrester's presence. A good source on state-specific legal issues related to security personnel is the National Association of Security and Investigative Regulators (www.iasir.org).

Although the power of citizen's arrest is very significant in the private sector because it allows security officers to protect their employer's property, there is little room for errors of judgment. The public police officer is protected from civil liability for false arrest if the officer has probable cause to believe a crime was committed, but the private officer (citizen) is liable if a crime was not committed, regardless of the reasonableness of the belief.

This distinction is illustrated by the case *Cervantez v. J.C. Penney Company*.[4] In this case, an off-duty police officer, moonlighting as a store detective for J.C. Penney Company, made a warrantless arrest of two individuals for misdemeanor theft. Later they were released due to lack of evidence. The plaintiffs sued the company and the officer for false arrest, imprisonment, malicious prosecution, assault and battery, intentional infliction of emotional distress, and negligence in the selection of its employee. The primary issue in the Cervantez case was whether the officer could rely on the probable-cause defense. The court's decision rested on whether the officer acted as a police officer in California or as a private citizen.

The store and the officer argued that the probable-cause defense was sound because the detective was an off-duty police officer and thus could arrest on the basis of probable cause. The plaintiffs argued that the store detective should be governed by the rules of arrest applied to private citizens and that the officer was therefore liable for his actions because no crime had been proven. The plaintiffs contended that the officer was employed as a private security officer, and thus his arrest powers were only those of a private citizen. The California Supreme Court ruled that the laws governing the type of arrest to be applied depend on the arrester's employer at the time of the arrest. Since the officer was acting as a store detective when he made the arrest, his arrest powers were no greater than those of a private citizen. Thus probable cause could not be used as a defense against false arrest.

Some states have avoided the problem of the Cervantez case by extending the probable-cause defense to private citizens. The most common extension involves shoplifting arrests. Many states have a mercantile privilege rule that allows the probable-cause defense for detentions but not for arrests. The law permits a private citizen or his employees to detain, in a reasonable manner and for a reasonable time, a person who is believed to have stolen merchandise so that the merchant can recover the merchandise or summon a police officer to make an arrest. Some states have extended this merchant clause to cover public employees in libraries, museums, or archival institutions.

The exact extent of the protection afforded to merchants and their employees or agents depends on the individual state's statutes. Some states offer protection against liability for false arrest, false imprisonment, and defamation; others offer protection against false imprisonment but not against false arrest. It is interesting to note that very few states allow a merchant to search a detainee. The private citizen's authority to search is unclear and will be discussed later in this chapter.

4.2 Detention

Detention is a concept that has grown largely in response to the difficulties faced by merchants in protecting their property from shoplifters and the problems and dangers they face when they make an arrest. Generally, detention differs from arrest in that it permits a merchant to detain a suspected shoplifter briefly without turning the suspect over to the police. An arrest requires that the arrestee be turned over to the authorities as soon as practicable and in any event without unreasonable delay.

All the shoplifting statutes refer to *detain*, not to *arrest*, a terminology probably derived from the thought that a distinction could be made between the two. The distinction is based on the fact that an arrest is for the purpose of delivering the suspect to the authorities and of exercising strict physical control over that person until the authorities arrive. A *detention*, or temporary delay, would not be termed an arrest as commonly defined. The distinction is difficult to defend but the statutes are clear. In Illinois, for example:

> *Any merchant who has reasonable grounds to believe that a person has committed retail theft may detain such person, on or off the premises of a retail mercantile establishment, in a reasonable manner and for a reasonable length of time for all or any of the following purposes:*
>
> *a. To request identification;*
> *b. To verify such identification;*
> *c. To make reasonable inquiry as to whether such person has in his possession unpurchased merchandise and, to make reasonable investigation of the ownership of such merchandise;*
> *d. To inform a peace officer of the detention of the person and surrender that person to the custody of a peace officer.*[5]

California was one of the first states to establish merchant immunity in a 1936 Supreme Court decision; in *Collyer v. S. H. Kress Co.*,[6] the court upheld the right of a department store official to detain a suspected shoplifter for 20 minutes.

Most statutes include the merchant, employee, agent, private police, and peace officer as authorized to detain suspects, but they do not include citizens at large, such as another shopper. Most of the statutes also describe the purposes of detention and the manner in which they may be conducted. These purposes are to search, to interrogate, to investigate suspicious behavior, to recover goods, and to await a police officer. The manner in which the detention is to be conducted is generally described as "reasonable" and for "a reasonable period of time."

The privilege of detention is, however, subject to some problems. There must be probable cause to believe that theft already has taken place or is about to take place before a merchant may detain anyone. Probable cause is an elusive concept and one that has undergone many different interpretations by the courts. It is frequently difficult to predict how the court will rule on a given set of circumstances that may at the time clearly indicate probable cause to detain. Second, reasonableness must exist both in time and manner of the detention or the privilege will be lost.

4.3   Interrogation

No law prohibits a private person from engaging in conversation with a willing participant. For public law enforcement, however, should the conversation become an *interrogation*, the information may not be admissible in a court of law. The standard is whether the statements were made voluntarily.

A statement made under duress is not regarded as trustworthy and is therefore inadmissible in court. This principle applies equally to police officers and private citizens.

A confession obtained from an employee by threatening loss of job or physical harm would be inadmissible and would also make the interrogator liable for civil and criminal prosecution.

The classic cases involving interrogation, generally applied to only public law enforcement officers, are *Escobedo v. State of Illinois*[7] and *Miranda v. Arizona*.[8] Today the Miranda case has become the leading case recognized by most American citizens in reference to "their rights." The facts of the case are these: On March 13, 1963, Ernesto Miranda was arrested at his home and taken to a Phoenix police station. There he was questioned by two police officers who, during Miranda's trial, admitted that they had not advised him that he could have a lawyer present during questioning. After two hours of interrogation, the officers emerged with a confession. According to the statement, Miranda had made the confession "with full knowledge of my legal right, understanding any statement I make may be used against me." His confession was admitted into evidence over defense objections during his trial. He was convicted of kidnapping and rape. On appeal, the Arizona Supreme Court upheld the conviction, indicating that Miranda did not specifically request counsel. The U.S. Supreme Court later reversed the decision based on the fact that Miranda had not been informed of his right to an attorney, nor was his right not to be compelled to incriminate himself effectively protected.

Although the principle behind the *Miranda v. Arizona* decision was the removal of compulsion from *custodial questioning* (questioning initiated by law enforcement officers after a person has been taken into custody or otherwise deprived of freedom), it generally applies only to public law enforcement officers. The police officer must show that statements made by the accused were given after the accused was informed of the facts that speaking was not necessary, that the statements might be used in court, that an attorney could be present, and that if the accused could not afford an attorney, one would be appointed for the accused prior to questioning. These "Miranda warnings" are not necessary unless the person is in custody or is deprived of freedom and is subject to interrogation. Based on this distinction, most courts agree that private persons are not generally required to use Miranda warnings because they are not public law enforcement officers.

In the case *In re Deborah C.*,[9] the California Supreme Court upheld the principle that private citizens are not required to use Miranda warnings and that statements made by the accused in citizen's arrests are admissible in a court of law. The court felt that the Miranda rationale did not apply to the retail store environment because store detectives lack the psychological edge that police officers have when the latter are questioning someone at a police station.

A few states require citizens to use a modified form of Miranda warnings before questioning, and some—a definite minority—prohibit questioning at all. Wisconsin law states, "[t]he detained person must be promptly informed of the purpose of the detention and be permitted to make phone calls, but shall not be interrogated or searched against his will before the arrival of a peace officer who may conduct a lawful interrogation of the accused person."[10]

In 1987 the case of *State of West Virginia v. William H. Muegge*[11] expanded the Miranda concept to private citizens in the state of West Virginia. Muegge was detained by a store security guard who observed Muegge place several items of merchandise in his pockets and proceed through the checkout aisle without paying for those items. The security guard approached Muegge, identified herself, and asked him to return to the store office to discuss the problem. The officer ordered Muegge to empty his pockets, which contained several unpaid-for items valued at a total of $10.65. The officer next read Muegge his "constitutional rights" and asked him to sign a waiver of rights. Muegge refused and asked for the assistance of a lawyer. The officer refused the request and indicated that she would call the state police. At some time either prior to the arrival or after the arrival of the state trooper, the defendant signed the waiver and completed a questionnaire that contained various incriminating statements. At the trial, the unpaid-for items were admitted without objection and the questionnaire was read aloud over the defendant's objection. Although the court felt that the specific Miranda warnings were not necessary, it ruled that whenever a person is in custodial control mandated by state statute (that is, merchant clauses), the safeguards protecting the constitutional right not to be compelled to be a witness against oneself in a criminal case apply.

4.4   Search and Seizure

A *search* can be defined as an examination of persons and/or their property for the purpose of discovering evidence of guilt in relation to some specific offense. The observation of items in plain view is not a search as long as the observer is legally entitled to be in the place where the observation is made. This includes public property and private property that is normally open to the public—for example, shopping malls, retail stores, hotel lobbies, and so on.

Common law says little about searches by private persons and is inconclusive. Searches by private persons, however, have been upheld by the courts where consent to search was given and where searches were made as part of a legal citizen's arrest. The best practice to follow is to contact police officials, who can then ask for a search warrant or search as part of an arrest. Because searches often need to be conducted on short notice without the aid of a police officer, however, it is important to understand several factors.

First, in a consent search, the searcher must be able to show that the consent was given voluntarily. Second, the search cannot extend beyond the area for which consent to search was given. It is advisable to secure a written agreement of the consent to search. Third, the person who possesses the item must give the consent. Possession, not ownership, is the criterion for determining whether a search was valid. Although many firms issue waivers to search lockers and other work areas, an officer must remember that the consent to search may be withdrawn at any time. If the consent is withdrawn, continuing a search might make the officer and the company liable for invasion of privacy. Some companies have solved this problem by retaining control over lockers in work areas. In this situation, workers are told that the lockers are not private and may be searched at any time.

A search made as a part of an arrest is supported by case law. In general, the principle of searching the arrestee and the immediate surroundings, defined as the area within which one could lunge and reach a weapon or destroy evidence, has been repeatedly held as constitutional. The verdict on searches incident to arrest by security officers is still mixed. In *People v. Zelinski*,[12] the California court disapproved of searches made incident to an arrest but did approve of searches for weapons for protective reasons. New York courts tend to support searches, indicating that private officers, like their public counterparts, have a right to searches incident to an arrest. In general, it appears that unless the security officer fears that a weapon may be hidden on the arrestee, the officer should wait until the police arrive to conduct a search unless the arrestee gives permission for such a search.

Even in the statutes governing retail shoplifting, the area of search is limited. Some states neither forbid nor condone searches; rather, they allow security personnel to investigate or make reasonable inquiries as to whether a person possesses unpurchased merchandise. In other states, searches are strictly forbidden, except looking for objects carried by the suspected shoplifter. Courts, however, generally favor protective searches where officers fear for their own safety.

4.5 The Exclusionary Rule

In an historic decision, the U.S. Supreme Court ruled that any and all evidence uncovered by public law enforcement agents in violation of the Fourth Amendment will be excluded from consideration in any court proceedings. That means that all evidence, no matter how trustworthy or indicative of guilt, will be inadmissible if it is illegally obtained. This landmark case (*Mapp v. Ohio*)[13] was the most important case that contributed to the development of the *exclusionary rule*, which states that illegally seized evidence (and its fruits) are inadmissible in any state or federal proceedings. *Weeks v. United States*[14] set the stage for the later, all-inclusive decision in *Mapp* by holding that evidence acquired by officials of the federal government in violation of the Fourth Amendment must be excluded in a federal prosecution. The Mapp case is clear in its application of the exclusionary rule to state and federal prosecutions. The question is, does the exclusionary rule apply to private parties? The determining case in this area is *Burdeau v. McDowell*.[15]

Unlike illegal searches conducted by public law enforcement officers, evidence secured by a private security officer conducting an illegal search is still admissible in either criminal or civil proceedings. In *Burdeau v. McDowell*, the U.S. Supreme Court said, "[i]t is manifest that there was no invasion of the security afforded by the Fourth Amendment against unreasonable searches and seizures, as whatever wrong was done was the act of individuals in taking property of another." If such evidence is admissible, why should private sector employees concern themselves with the legality of searches? Even though the evidence is admissible, security officers who conduct illegal searches may be subject to liability for other actions, including battery and invasion of privacy.

There is considerable controversy over the Burdeau case because some people fear that constitutional guarantees are threatened by the acceptance of evidence illegally obtained by private security personnel. It is clear that any involvement by government officials constitutes "state action" or an action "under color of law" and is limited by the constitutional restrictions that apply to public police actions. In *State v. Scrotsky*,[16] the New Jersey court excluded evidence obtained when a police detective accompanied a theft victim to the defendant's apartment to identify and recover stolen goods. The court held that "[t]he search and seizure by one served the purpose of both and must be deemed to have been participated in by both." The exclusionary rule is applied in this case, as in many others, to discourage government officials from conducting improper searches and from using private individuals to conduct them.[17]

In cases where private parties act independently of government involvement, the courts have not been so clear. In a significant case, *People v. Randazzo*,[18] the California court admitted evidence obtained by a merchant in a shoplifting case. The court did not deal with any questions of Fourth Amendment violation since there was no state action involved. The court held that redress for the victim of an unreasonable search conducted by a private individual not under color of law is a tort action, and thus the exclusionary rule does not apply. In *Thacker v. Commonwealth*,[19] the Kentucky court held that a private party acts for the state when that party makes an arrest in accordance with the state's arrest statute and thus would be subject to the exclusionary rule. On the other hand, following the *Burdeau* precedent, a federal district court found no state action in a case where the plaintiff alleged she was wrongfully detained, slapped, beaten, harassed, and searched by the manager and an employee of the store.[20] The plaintiff sued, alleging among other things that the employee, a security officer, was acting "under color of law" because he was licensed under the Pennsylvania Private Detective Act. The court rejected this argument and found that the Pennsylvania law "invests the licensee with no authority of state law."

In summary, although public police are clearly limited by constitutional restrictions, generally private security personnel are not so limited. Provided that they act as private parties and are in no way involved with public officials, they are limited by criminal and civil sanctions but are not bound at this time by most constitutional restrictions.

4.6 Use of Force

On occasion, security personnel must use force to protect someone or to accomplish a legitimate purpose. In general, force may be used to protect oneself or others, to defend property, and to prevent the commission of a criminal act. The extent to which force may be used is restricted; no more force may be used than is reasonable under the circumstances. This means that deadly force or force likely to create great bodily harm will not be allowable unless the force being used by the assailant is also deadly force or force likely to create great bodily harm. If the force exceeds what is deemed reasonable, officers and their employers are liable for the use of excessive force, which can range from assault and battery to homicide. This is the same degree of power extended to the ordinary citizen.

4.7 Self-Defense

In general, people may use reasonable force to protect themselves. The amount of force may be equal to, but not greater than, the force being used against them. In most states, a person can protect himself or herself, except when that person was the initial aggressor. Most states allow self-defense to be used by a person against whom force is being used.

4.8 Defense of Others

Security officers may protect others just as they protect themselves. However, two different approaches to defense of others are evident. In the first approach, the officer must try to identify with the attacked person. In this position, the officer is entitled to use whatever force would be appropriate if he or she were the person being attacked. If the officer happens to protect the wrong person—that is, the aggressor—the officer is liable regardless of his or her good intentions. In the second approach, the defender may use force when it is reasonable to believe that such force is necessary. In this case, the defender is protected from liability as long as he or she acted in a reasonable manner.

4.9   Defense of Property

In defense of property, force may be applied, but it must be short of deadly force, which is generally allowable only in cases involving felonious attacks on property during which loss of life is likely. As noted by Schnabolk, "one may use deadly force to protect a home against an arsonist but the use of deadly force against a mere trespasser would not be permitted."[21] Security officers acting in the place of their employers are empowered to use the same force that their employers are entitled to use.

4.10   Force Used During Arrest or Detention

Like the police, the private citizen security officer has the right to use reasonable force in detaining or arresting someone. Many states still follow the common-law principles that allow deadly force in the case of fleeing felons, but many others have restricted the use of deadly force. This restriction allows the use of deadly force only in cases where the felony is both violent and the felon is immediately fleeing. Figure 7.1 on the Use of Force Model has been widely used for training of police officers and has application for security personnel faced with various levels of suspect compliance.

4.11   Prevention of Crimes

To determine the amount of force a security officer may use to prevent crimes, the courts have considered the circumstances, the seriousness of the crime prevented, and the possibility of preventing the crime by other means. Under common law, a person can use force to prevent a crime. The courts have ruled, however, that the use of force is limited to situations involving felonies or a breach of the peace and that nonviolent misdemeanors do not warrant the use of force. Deadly force is justifiable in preventing a crime only if it is necessary to protect a person from harm. The ruling case is *Tennessee v. Garner*.

4.12   Use of Firearms

Most states regulate the carrying of firearms by private citizens. Almost all states prohibit the carrying of concealed weapons, whereas only half of them prohibit carrying an exposed handgun. Although all states excuse police officers from these restrictions, some states also exempt private security officers. Even in states that prohibit carrying concealed or exposed handguns, there are provisions for procuring a license to carry weapons in this manner.

5   Civil Law: The Controller for Private Security

5.1   Tort Law: Source of Power and Limits

A *tort* is a civil action based on the principle that one individual can expect certain behavior from another individual. When the actions of one party do not meet reasonable expectations, a tort action may result. In security applications, a guard may take some action to interfere with the free movement of some person. There is a basis for a suit no matter whether the guard knows those actions are wrong, is unaware that the actions are wrong, or is unaware that the actions are wrong but acts in a negligent manner.

Thus tort law may be invoked for either an intentional or a negligent act. In some cases, liability may be imposed even though an individual is not directly at fault. One

LEVEL V		
SUBJECT	**OFFICER**	**TECHNIQUES**
DEADLY FORCE ASSAILANT Is a person whose actions will probably cause death or great bodily harm.	DEADLY FORCE CONTROL TACTICS 1. Firearms 2. Other measures which could result in death or great bodily harm	1. Verbal Command (if time permits) 3. Weapon Retention/Take Back (Service Weapon) 2. Knife Defense 4. Firearms

LEVEL IV		
AGGRESSIVE ASSAILANT Is a person who performs physical actions, without weapons, that are aggressive and he/she demonstrates behavior that is likely to cause physical injury.	DEFENSIVE CONTROL TACTICS 1. Punches, kicks, & other strike/ blocking techniques/ to stop aggression 2. Intermediate tools 3. Other Non-Lethal tools (including firearms using ammunition defined in 720 ILCS 5/7-8(b) 1997	1. Verbal Command 6. Baton Chops and Jabs 2. Baton Retention 7. Intermediate Weapons 3. Weapon Retention/O.C. Spray (per department policy, other 4. Blocks/Strikes weapons authorized to carry (Baton and Empty Hands) stun-gun, taser, mace, etc.) 5. Escape Techniques

LEVEL III		
ACTIVE RESISTER Is a person who exhibits resistive movement to avoid physical control.	COMPLIANCE CONTROL TACTICS 1. Stunning techniques (with or without control instruments) 2. Take-downs 3. Control instruments techniques/leverage 4. Chemical agents 5. Canine deployment	1. Verbal Command 6. Baton Positions (on guard, 2. Pressure Points/Distractors strike ready, cross arm, and 3. Same Techniques as Level II, vertical) but with Torque 7. O.C. Spray 4. Driver Removal Techniques 8. Knifehand Transition (inside and outside hand) 9. Clamp Technique 5. Handshake Control

LEVEL II		
PASSIVE RESISTER Is a person who exhibits no resistive movement in response to verbal or other direction by the officer.	CONTACT CONTROL TACTICS 1. Joint manipulations/used to guide or direct the subject 2. Pressure sensitive area techniques	1. Verbal Command 4. Rear Wristlock 2. High Gooseneck 5. Armlock 3. Handshake Control 6. Control Applications

LEVEL I		
COOPERATIVE PERSON Is a person who is cooperative or can be developed into a cooperative individual.	COOPERATIVE CONTROL TACTICS 1. Officer presence 2. Verbal direction 3. Restraint devices	1. Verbal Command 5. Cuffed Search 2. Basic Alert Stance 6. Uncuffed Search 3. Basic Escort Position 7. Standing Cuff - Two on One 4. Standing Cuff - One on One

*Developed by Joe L. Smith, Police Training Specialist, Police Training Institute in 1999   Use of Force Scale, University of Illinois ©1999   10032

FIGURE 7.1 The use of force model. (Used with permission from the Police Training Institute, University of Illinois, Champaign.)

branch of this doctrine is *strict liability* and does not generally affect the security officer. Strict liability applies to a provider of defective or hazardous products or services that unduly threaten a consumer's personal safety. *Vicarious liability*, however, is of concern to enterprises that contract or employ security services. Vicarious liability is an indirect legal responsibility; for example, the liability of an employer for the actions of an employee.

5.2 Negligence

The Restatement of Torts[22] states that "[it] is negligence to use an instrumentality, whether a human being or a thing, which the actor knows, or should know, to be incompetent, inappropriate or defective and that its use involves an unreasonable risk of harm to others." This statement has particular importance to security employers and supervisors in hiring, supervising, and training employees.

In all cases of negligence, the plaintiff (the person who brings an action; the party who complains or sues) must prove the case by a preponderance of the evidence (more than 50 percent or "more likely than not") in all of the following areas:

1. An act or failure to act (an omission) by the defendant
2. A legal duty owed to the plaintiff by the defendant, the person defending or denying, and/or the party against whom relief or recovery is sought
3. A breach of duty by the defendant
4. A foreseeable injury to the plaintiff
5. Actual harm or injury to the plaintiff

A relatively new concept in the area of negligence is *comparative fault*. This concept accepts the fact that the plaintiff may have contributed to his or her own injury, such as being in a restricted area or creating a disturbance or some hazard. In the past, the theory of contributory negligence prevented the plaintiff from collecting for injuries and so forth if he or she contributed somehow to his or her own injury. In comparative negligence, the relative negligence of the parties involved is compared, and the plaintiff who may have contributed to the injury may get some award for part of the injury for which he or she is not responsible.

There are three types of comparative negligence statute: (1) pure approach, (2) the 50/50 rule, and (3) the 51 percent rule. In the pure approach, the plaintiff may collect something for injuries even if he or she was primarily responsible for the injuries. In theory, the jury could award the plaintiff 1 percent of the damages if he or she is found to have contributed 99 percent to the injury. Under the 50/50 rule, the plaintiff can collect for damages if he or she was responsible for no more than 50 percent of the negligence. In the 51 percent situation, the plaintiff's acts must not have contributed more than 49 percent of the situation in order to collect damages. Regardless of the rule followed, the degree to which the plaintiff is responsible for the end result is considered before judgments are pronounced. One example of the 50/50 rule is the following Illinois statute:

> *In all actions on account of bodily injury or death or physical damage to property, based on negligence … the plaintiff shall be barred from recovering damages if the trier of fact find that the contributory fault on the part of the plaintiff is more than 50% of the proximate cause of the injury or damage for*

which recovery is sought. The plaintiff shall not be barred from recovering damages if the trier of fact finds that the contributory fault on the part of the plaintiff is not more than 50% of the proximate cause of the injury or damage for which recovery is sought, but any damages allowed shall be diminished in the proportion to the amount of fault attributable to the plaintiff.[23]

The number of cases involving negligence in terms of firms providing adequate security has been increasing. Recent cases have resulted in awards of more than $1 million to plaintiffs in individual cases. More will be said about this issue later in the chapter.

5.3   Intentional Torts

An *intentional tort* occurs when the person who committed the act was able to foresee that the action would result in certain damages. The actor intended the consequences of the actions or at least intended to commit the action that resulted in damages to the plaintiff. In general, the law punishes such acts by compensatory judgments that exceed those awarded in common negligence cases. The most common intentional torts are described in this section.

5.3.1   Assault
Assault is intentionally causing fear of imminent harmful or offensive touching but without touching or physical contact. In most cases, courts have ruled that words alone are not sufficient to place a person in fear of harm.

5.3.2   Battery
Battery is intentionally harmful or otherwise offensive touching of another person. The touching does not have to be direct physical contact but may instead be through an instrument such as a cane or rock.

In addition, the courts have found battery to exist if "something" closely connected to the body but not actually a part of the body is struck.[24] In *Fisher v. Carrousel Motor Hotel, Inc.,* the plaintiff, Fisher, was attending a conference that included a buffet luncheon. While Fisher was in line, one of the defendant's employees snatched the plate from his hand and shouted that no Negro could be served in the club. The Texas court of appeals held that a battery can occur even though the subject is not struck. It ruled that, so long as there is contact with clothing or an object identified with the body, a battery can occur. From a security point of view, the contact must be nonconsensual and not privileged. Privileged contact is generally granted to merchants who need to recover merchandise; privilege is generally a defense against charges of battery if the merchant's actions were reasonable. If the touching were unreasonable, however, the plaintiff would have a case for battery. The same argument holds for searches: If a search is performed after consent has been given, no battery has occurred. If consent is not given, however, the search is illegal, and a battery has probably occurred.

5.3.3   False Imprisonment or False Arrest
False imprisonment or *false arrest* is intentionally confining or restricting the movement or freedom of another. The confinement may be the result of physical restraint or intimidation. False imprisonment implies that the confinement is for personal advantage rather

than to bring the plaintiff to court. This is one of the torts most frequently filed against security personnel.

5.3.4 Defamation

Defamation involves injuring the reputation of another by publicly making untrue statements. *Slander* is oral defamation; *libel* is defamation through the written word. The classic case of a security officer yelling "Stop, thief!" in a crowded store has all the necessary elements for slander if the accused is not a thief. Although it is generally true that truth is an absolute defense in defamation issues, the courts may also look at the defendant's motivation. True statements published with malicious intent can be prosecuted in some jurisdictions. In this age of high technology, the courts have now included in the libel category statements made on television or other broadcasts. It is apparent that the courts view these types of statements as being more permanent and as reaching broad audiences.

5.3.5 Malicious Prosecution

Malicious prosecution is groundlessly instituting criminal proceedings against another person. Malice is an essential element. To prove malice, the plaintiff must show that the primary motive in bringing about criminal proceedings was not to bring the defendant to justice. Classic cases include proceedings brought about to extort money or to force performance on contracts. Although there is no liability for reporting facts to the police or other components of the criminal justice system, if the prosecution resulted from biased statements of fact, incomplete reports, or the defendant's persuasion (political, sexual, religious, and so on), liability for malicious prosecution might be proved.

5.3.6 Invasion of Privacy

Intruding on another person's physical solitude, disclosing private information about another person, or publicly placing someone in a false light can be considered *invasion of privacy*. Four distinct actions fall into this category: (1) misappropriation of the plaintiff's name or picture for commercial advantage, (2) placing the plaintiff in a false light, (3) public disclosure of private facts, and (4) intrusion into the seclusion of another. For security purposes, invasion of privacy generally occurs during a search or during observation of an individual. If signs outside clothing store fitting rooms advise customers that they may be observed, some legal observers believe that shoppers should not expect privacy and thus cannot legitimately complain of invasion of privacy. Concern over liability for invasion of privacy is increasing; this liability may be the result of reference checks, background investigations, or the use of truth detection devices.

5.3.7 Trespass and Conversion

Trespass is the unauthorized physical invasion of property or remaining on property after permission has been rescinded. *Conversion* means taking personal property in such a way that the plaintiff's use or right of possession of chattel is restricted. In simpler terms, conversion is depriving someone of the use of his or her personal property.

5.3.8 Intentional Infliction of Mental Distress

This is intentionally causing extreme mental or emotional distress to another person. The distress may be either mental or physical and may result from highly aggravating words or conduct.

5.4   Security and Liability

In the past few years, the number of suits filed against security officers and companies
has increased dramatically. Predictions for the next 10 years indicate no further increase
but that the number of suits will continue at the present levels. One possible reason
for the leveling off of suits is that security managers have a better understanding of the
problems associated with liability situations today. The earlier increase may be partly
attributed to the growth of the security industry and to the public's demand for accountability and professionalism in the security area. Most cases filed against private security officers and operations belong in the tort category, as was mentioned earlier in this
chapter. The individual who commits a tort is called a *tortfeasor*, whereas the injured
party is called the *plaintiff*. The plaintiff may be a person, a corporation, or an association. Torts are classified as intentional, negligent, or strict liability. An *intentional tort*
is a wrong perpetrated by someone who intends to cause harm to another. In contrast, a
negligent tort is a wrong perpetrated by someone who fails to exercise sufficient care in
doing what is otherwise permissible. *Strict liability* imposes responsibility on a defendant for inherently dangerous products and acts, regardless of intent.

In most cases of negligence, the jury considers awarding damages to compensate
the plaintiff. The awards generally take into account the physical, mental, and emotional
suffering of the plaintiff, and future medical payments may be allowed for.

Punitive damages are also possible but are more likely to be awarded in cases of
intentional liability. Punitive damages are designed to punish the tortfeasor and to deter
future inappropriate behavior. Punitive damages are also possible in negligence cases in
which the actions of the tortfeasor were in total disregard for the safety of others.

5.5   Duty to Protect from Third-Party Crime

The area of civil liability is of great importance to the security industry because the
courts have been more willing to hold the industry legally responsible for protection
in this area than in others. This trend is particularly noticeable in the hotel and motel
industry, where owners are liable for failure to adequately protect guests from foreseeable criminal activity. In some circumstances, a hotel or motel owner might be held
accountable for failure to provide adequate protection from criminal actions. In *Klein
v. 1500 Massachusetts Avenue Apartment Corporation*,[25] a tenant who was criminally
assaulted sued the corporation. The decision centered on the issue that the landlord had
prior notice of criminal activity (including burglary and assault) against his tenants and
property. In addition, the landlord was aware of conditions that made it likely that criminal activities would continue. The court ruled that the landlord had failed in an obligation to provide adequate security and was thus liable.

A similar case was made against Howard Johnson's by the actress Connie Francis,
who was raped in a Howard Johnson's hotel room in 1974.[26] Francis alleged that the
hotel had failed to provide adequate locks on the doors. The jury awarded Francis more
than $1 million in damages.

Recent decisions (*Philip Aaron Banks, et al. v. Hyatt Corporation and Refco Poydras
Hotel Joint Venture* and *Allen B. Morrison, et al. v. MGM Grand Hotel, et al.*) have followed earlier landmark cases.[27] In the Banks case, a federal court held the hotel liable for
foreseeable events that led to the murder of Banks by a third party. Banks was shot only
four feet from the hotel door. The suit alleged that the hotel failed to provide adequate

security and to warn Banks of the danger of criminal activity near the hotel entrance. The jury awarded the plaintiffs $975,000, even though evidence was introduced that showed that the hotel had made reasonable efforts to provide additional protection in the area. The court stated that "the owner or operator of a business owes a duty to invitees to exercise reasonable care to protect them from injury," noting that "the duty of a business to protect invitees can extend to adjacent property, particularly entrances to the business premises, if the business is aware of a dangerous condition on the adjacent property and fails to warn its invitees or to take some other reasonable preventive action."

In the Morrison case, a robber followed Morrison from the hotel desk into the elevator after Morrison had cashed in his gambling chips and had withdrawn his jewelry and cash from the hotel's safe. The robber took Morrison's property at gunpoint and then knocked him unconscious. Morrison brought suit against the hotel for failing to provide adequate security, noting that a similar robbery had recently occurred. The federal appellate court supported Morrison's contention, saying, "a landowner must exercise ordinary care and prudence to render the premises reasonably safe for the visit of a person invited on his premises for business purposes." In *McCarthy v. Pheasant Run, Inc.*,[28] however, another federal court recognized that invitees who fail to take basic security precautions may not have cause for action against a hotel. The difference in the rulings in *McCarthy* and *Morrison* points out the need for security managers to be aware of decisions within their own states and federal jurisdictions.

The foreseeability issue has been applied to other areas of business in recent years. In *Sharpe v. Peter Pan Bus Lines*,[29] a Massachusetts court awarded $550,000 for a wrongful death attributed to negligent security in a bus terminal. The same basic concept of foreseeability was applied in *Nelson v. Church's Fried Chicken*.[30] In fact, the concept of foreseeability has been expanded beyond the narrow opinion that foreseeability is implied in failure to provide security for specific criminal behavior. This concept implies that, since certain attacks have occurred in or near a company, the company should reasonably be expected to foresee potential security problems and provide adequate security. In a recent Iowa Supreme Court decision, the court abolished the need for prior violent acts to establish foreseeability. In *Galloway v. Bankers Trust Company and Trustee Midlands Mall*,[31] the court ruled foreseeability could be established by "all facts and circumstances," not just prior violent acts. Therefore, prior thefts may be sufficient to establish foreseeability because these offenses could lead to violence. In another case, *Polly Suzanne Paterson v. Kent C. Deeb, Transamerica Insurance Co., W. Fenton Langston, and Hartford Accident & Indemnity Co.*,[32] a Florida court held that the plaintiff may recover damages for a sexual assault without proof of prior similar incidents on the premises.

5.6   Nondelegable Duty

Another legal trend is to prevent corporations from divesting themselves of liability by assigning protection services to an independent contractor. Under the principle of agency law, such an assignment transfers the liability for the service from the corporation to the independent contractor. The courts, however, have held that some obligations cannot be entirely transferred. This principle is called *nondelegable duty*. Based on this principle, contractual provisions that shift liability to the subcontractors have not been recognized by the courts. These contractual provisions are commonly called *hold harmless clauses*.

Take, for example, *Dupree v. Piggly Wiggly Shop Rite Foods, Inc.* The court decided that:

> *Public policy requires [that] one may not employ or contract with a special agency or detective firm to ferret out the irregularities of his customers or employees and then escape liability for the malicious prosecution or false arrest on the ground that the agency and/or its employees are independent contractors.*[33]

5.7   Imputed Negligence

Imputed negligence simply means that "by reason of some relation existing between *A* and *B*, the negligence of *A* is to be charged against *B*, although *B* has played no part in it, has done nothing whatever to aid or encourage it, or indeed has done all that he possibly can to prevent it. This is commonly called 'imputed contributory negligence.'"[34]

5.8   Vicarious Liability

One form of imputed negligence is *vicarious liability*. The concept of vicarious liability arises from agency law in which one party has the power to control the actions of another party involved in the contract or relationship. The principal is thus responsible for the actions of a servant or agent. In legal terms, this responsibility is called *respondeat superior*. In short, employers are liable for the actions of their employees while they are employed on the firm's business. Employers are liable for the actions of their agents, even if the employers do nothing to cause the actions directly. The master is held liable for any intentional tort committed by the servant when the servant's purpose, however misguided, is wholly or partially to further the master's business.

Employers may even be liable for some of the actions of their employees when the employees are neither at work nor engaged in company business. For example, consider the position of an employer who issues a firearm to an employee. The employee, at home and therefore off duty, plays with the firearm, which discharges and injures a neighbor. The neighbor may sue the employer for negligently entrusting a dangerous instrument to an employee or for the negligence in selecting a careless employee.

The principle of *respondeat superior* ("let the master respond") is well established in common law. It is not in itself the subject of any substantial dispute, and at those times when it becomes an issue in a dispute, the area of contention is factual rather than the doctrine itself. As was noted earlier, in the doctrine of *respondeat superior*, "[a] servant is a person employed by a master to perform service in his affairs, whose physical conduct in the performance of the service is controlled or is subject to the right of control by the master. The Minnesota court in *Graalum v. Radisson Ramp* has stated that the right of control and not necessarily the exercise of that right is the test of the relationship of master and servant. Basically, the issue revolves around the distinction between a person who is subject to orders as to how he does his work and one who agrees only to do the work in his own way."[35] There is no question that an employer (master) is liable for injuries caused by employees (servants) who are acting within the scope of their employment. This is not to say that the employees are relieved of all liability. They are in fact the principal in any action, but since the employee rarely has the financial resources to satisfy a third-party suit, an injured person will look beyond the employee to the employer for compensation for damages.

Clearly the relationship between master and servant under *respondeat superior* needs definition. Under the terms of the *Graalum v. Radisson Ramp* ruling, in-house security officers are servants, whereas contract security personnel may not be. In the latter case, as discussed previously, contract personnel are employees of the supplying agency, and in most cases, the hiring company will not be held liable for their acts. The relationship is a complex one, however.

If security officers are acting within the scope of their employment and commit a wrongful act, the employer is liable for the actions. The matter then turns on the scope of the officer's employment and the employer/employee relationship. One court described the scope of employment as depending on:

1. The act as being of the kind the employee is employed to perform
2. The act occurring substantially within the authorized time and space limits of the employment
3. The employee being motivated, at least in part, by a purpose to serve the master[36]

This is further refined in *Hayes v. Sears, Roebuck Co.*, in which the court found that if the employee is in pursuit of some purpose of his own, the defendant is not bound by his conduct, but if, while acting within the general scope of his employment, he simply disregards his master's orders or exceeds his powers, the master will be responsible for his conduct.[37]

Liability then is a function of the control exercised or permitted in the relationship between the security officer and the hiring company. If the hiring company maintains a totally hands-off posture with respect to personnel supplied by the agency, it may well avoid liability for wrongful acts performed by such personnel. On the other hand, there is some precedent for considering the hiring company as sharing some liability simply by virtue of its underlying rights of control over its own premises, no matter how it wishes to exercise that control. Many hiring companies are, however, motivated to contractually reject any control of security personnel on their premises in order to avoid liability. This, as was pointed out in *The Private Police*, works to discourage hiring companies from regulating the activity of security employees and the company that exercises controls (e.g., carefully examines the credentials of the guard, carefully determines the procedures the guard will follow, and pays close attention to all his activities) and may still be substantially increasing its risk of liability to any third persons who are, in fact, injured by an act of the guard.[38]

It is further suggested in this excellent study that there may be an expansion of certain nondelegable duty rules into consideration of the responsibilities for the actions of security personnel. As was discussed previously, the concept of the nondelegable duty provides that certain duties and responsibilities are imposed on an individual and for which that individual remains responsible even though an independent contractor is hired to implement them. Such duties currently encompass keeping the workplace safe and the premises reasonably safe for business visitors. It is also possible that the courts may find negligence in cases where the hiring companies, in an effort to avoid liability, have neglected to exercise any control over the selection and training of personnel, and they may further find that such negligence on the part of the hiring company has led to injury of third-party victims.

Vicarious liability requires a direct employer/employee relationship; it does not apply to cases in which an independent contractor is working for a firm. This is because the employer has no way of controlling the way an independent contractor performs the work. There are many exceptions to this rule, however. For example, the employer may be liable for the negligent selection of the contractor, or the employer may have exercised some day-to-day control over the employee.

5.9   Criminal Liability

Criminal liability is most frequently used against private security personnel in cases of assault, battery, manslaughter, and murder. Other common charges include burglary, trespass, criminal defamation, false arrest, unlawful use of weapons, disorderly conduct, extortion, eavesdropping, theft, perjury, and kidnapping. Security officers charged with criminal liability have several options in defending their actions. First, they might try to show that they were entitled to use force in self-defense or that they made a reasonable mistake, which would negate criminal intent. Other defenses include entrapment, intoxication, insanity, consent (the parties involved concurred with the actions), and compulsion (the officer was forced or compelled to commit the act). As has been already noted in previous discussions, a corporation or an association as well as an individual officer could be charged with criminal liability.

The reporting of crime is an area in which security officers are liable for criminal prosecution. In general, private citizens are no longer obliged to report crime or to prevent it. But some jurisdictions still recognize the concept of misprision of felony—that is, concealing knowledge of a felony. Such legislation makes it a crime to not report a felony. To be guilty of misprision of felony, the prosecution must prove beyond a reasonable doubt that (1) the principal committed and completed the alleged felony, (2) the defendant had full knowledge of that fact, (3) the defendant failed to notify the authorities, and (4) the defendant took affirmative steps to conceal the crime of the principal.

Security officers may also be liable for failure to perform jobs they have been contracted or employed to perform. If guards fail to act in a situation in which they have the ability and obligation to act, the courts suggest that they could be criminally liable for failure to perform their duties, assuming a criminal act is committed. At a minimum the guard is subject to tort liability.

Another issue in security work involves undercover operations. Many times security operatives are accused of soliciting an illegal act. Where security officers clearly intended for crimes to be committed, they may be charged with solicitation of an illegal act or conspiracy in an illegal act. This is in contrast to the public sector, where most police officers are protected by statute from crimes they commit in the performance of their duty. Thus only the private citizen may be charged with such an offense, and the only issue that can be contested is the defendant's intent.

Entrapment, which is solicitation by police officers, is another charge that may be leveled against security officers. While entrapment does not generally apply to private citizens (the case of *State v. Farns*[39] is frequently cited to prove that entrapment does not apply to private citizens), several states have passed legislation that extends entrapment statutes to cover private persons as well as police officers. Until the issue is resolved in the courts in the next few years, security officers involved in undercover operations should be careful to avoid actions that might lead to entrapment charges.

6 Recent Trends in Liability

As is evident from the listing of cases used to discuss security issues, case law continues to evolve. Although the basics attested to in the preceding discussions remain relatively constant, it is security managers' duty to follow current case-law thinking.

Recent cases in the area of vicarious liability include *Durand v. Moore* (Texas Court of Appeals, 1997), *Kirkman v. Astoria General Hospital* (New York Court of Appeals, 1994), and *Iglesia Cristiana LaCasa Del Senor Inc. v. L. M.* (Florida Court of Appeals, 2001). Cases out of California in 2000–01 focused on the issue of whether the acts were committed in furtherance of the employer's business or on the employee's subjective motivations (*University Mechanical v. Pinkerton's* [Superior Court of San Diego, 2001] and *Maria D. v. Westec Residential Security Inc.* [California Court of Appeals, 2000]).

A recent study of premises liability cases over the past 10 years was conducted by Liability Consultants, Inc., and reported in the October 2002 issue of *Security Management*. Figure 7.2 shows the average settlements for the cases examined between 1992 and 2001 by type of crime. The highest number of premises liability cases was filed in New York, followed by Texas and Georgia. Most cases were filed against condominiums, retail stores, and bars, with the largest number dealing with parking lot facilities. Still, it appears that business owners have learned from past cases, because the chances of prevailing in a liability suit of this type are just barely in favor of the defendant. Cases of interest include *Doe v. Kmart Corp.* (Circuit Court of Charleston County, South Carolina, 1997) and *Smith v. Sparks Regional Medication Center* (Arkansas Court of Appeals, 1998). In *Shadday v. Omni Hotels Management Corporation* (U.S. Court of Appeals Seventh Circuit, No. 06-2022, 2007), the court held that the Omni Hotel was not liable for the rape of a hotel guest by another guest. The court stated that the hotel could "hardly be required to have security guards watching every inch of the lobby every second of the day and night."

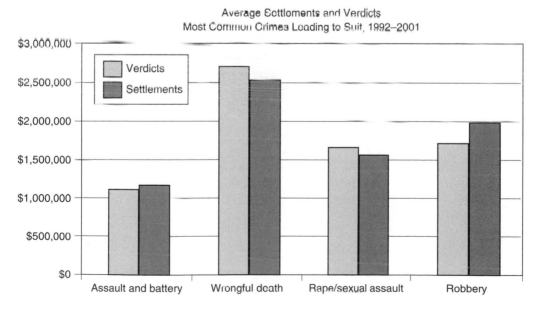

FIGURE 7.2 Settlement and verdict data. (Developed by Liability Consultants, Inc.)

7   Recent Trends in Privacy

With the growing use of software programs that monitor use and content of employees using company computers, there are those who have cited invasion of privacy as a legal concern. Most courts are following early precedents supporting employers and their right to monitor use. Decisions clearly conclude that the employer owns the software and hardware and thus has the right to monitor its use. In particular, the courts have ruled that some company information such as medical records, legal files, and financial statements must be protected from unauthorized viewing and possible manipulation. To ensure the security of these records, monitoring their use is essential. The courts have also determined that computer use logs are in fact legal records and may be admitted into court proceedings to substantiate company actions. The courts are clearly saying to employees that if you have something private to do, do it on your own time and with your own computer.[40]

8   New Laws

Many new laws impacting security and loss prevention are passed each year (some of which have been mentioned in earlier chapters), but two laws relating to privacy issues are worthy of note. The first, the Health Insurance Portability and Accountability Act (HIPAA), was passed in 1996. The Act is designed to ensure the security and privacy of medical records. The act provides for not only civil but also criminal penalties for breach of its provisions. The second law is the U.S. Financial Services Modernization Act of 1999. The Act establishes a duty for all financial services to protect the privacy of their customers.

These early efforts were the beginning of concern for ensuring personal privacy of records maintained by legitimate business but often compromised by criminals. More is said about this issue under the topic of identity theft in Chapter 18.

9   The Courts

The process of adjudication varies between civil and criminal courts. The differences occur in that the civil courts have no accused; rather, there are plaintiffs and defendants who believe that there is a cause for action rather than a violation of the law. The courts operate on many of the same rules, but the verdict in a civil case is by the preponderance of the evidence rather than by proof beyond a reasonable doubt.

9.1   The Procedure

In the event of an arrest, the accused must, by law, be taken without unnecessary delay before the nearest judge or magistrate. The court may proceed with the trial in the case of a misdemeanor charge unless the accused demands a jury trial or requests a continuance and such is ordered by the court.

If the charge is a felony, the judge or magistrate conducts a preliminary hearing, an informal process designed to determine whether reasonable grounds exist for believing that the accused committed the offense as charged. If such grounds do not appear, the accused will be discharged. If the judge finds that there are reasonable grounds for believing that the accused may have committed the offense as charged, the judge will "bind the accused over" for the action of the grand jury. The accused will be held in jail in the interim unless bond is paid, if the offense is bailable.

A grand jury is required by many states to consider the evidence in any felonious matter. Grand juries, usually consisting of 23 citizens, of whom 16 constitute a quorum, do not conduct a trial. They hear only the state's evidence. The accused may not be accompanied by an attorney into the hearing room and may not, in most cases, offer evidence in his or her own behalf. Misdemeanors are not handled by grand jury action but are usually prosecuted on an *information*, a document filed by the prosecuting attorney on receipt of a sworn complaint of the victim or a witness or other person who is personally informed about the circumstances of the alleged incident.

For a felony charge, the jury proceedings must result in a vote of at least 12 members for the accused to be indicted, and an indictment must be obtained in those jurisdictions that require it, even if it is determined that there are reasonable grounds for prosecution at the preliminary hearing. This procedure was instituted as a constitutional guarantee in federal cases as a safeguard against arbitrary prosecutorial action. Those states that have the same requirement are also motivated to provide protection at the state and municipal level.

If an indictment (also known as a *true bill*) is voted, the next step is the appearance of the accused before a judge who is empowered to try felony cases. At this time, the accused is confronted with the charges and is asked to plead. If the plea is guilty, the accused may be sentenced without further court action; if the plea is not guilty, the trial is set for some future date.[41]

10   Development of Case Law

Much of U.S. law, or more accurately its interpretation and hence its application, comes from the continuing judgments of the courts in cases all over the country. Most of the hundreds of cases heard daily are routine and, however significant they are to the participants, represent no particularly startling legal principle nor any significant upheaval in the day-to-day conduct of either the courts or the average person. Patterns in jurisprudence emerge, however, and landmark cases that had routine beginnings do appear.

It is essential for a lawyer to keep up with this flood of information, because legal practice is constantly reshaped by events in courtrooms around the country. Even the casual student with only a sporadic interest in the dynamics of the legal world should have some way of researching the latest events in areas of immediate concern.

10.1   Legal Research

Many sources of information are available to the researcher: legal encyclopedias, dictionaries, legal periodicals, and code books setting forth the statutes. The encyclopedias focus on legal principles and theories along with cases in which such principles predominate. There are also digests that index cases. This section following presents information on these sources, but the Internet and access to various legal research sites has made the area of legal research much easier for most casual learners.

10.2   Reporters

Perhaps the most useful sources are the bound volumes of reported cases, called *reporters*, that list the decisions of the appellate court. These decisions establish the precedents that are the cornerstone of the judicial system. Despite the large amount of available information, legal research is only as effective as the resources in the library or those obtainable through interlibrary loan. Legal research generally involves locating (1) the applicable statute, (2) the applicable case law, and (3) related articles in professional journals. Once the issue has been narrowed, the search for statutory law begins. Annotated criminal codes contain not only the statute but also brief notes and citations on court decisions that will be valuable in interpreting legal decisions. Federal statutes related to criminal law are found in the United States Code Annotated (USCA), Title 18, Crimes and Criminal Procedures.[42]

With the advent of the computer age, much of this legal research is simplified through the use of various computer sources. For example, Westlaw is a common computer-based subscription service available for a fee. Other information is available through the World Wide Web.

10.3   Case Reports

In legal writing, cases are frequently cited to show how a court applied a legal principle. Each such citation is followed by certain figures and abbreviations that are simply a convenient way to indicate the location of a description of a case's elements in a reporter. Cases are arranged with volumes for cases in each state. In addition to state reporters, a private publisher (West Publishing of St. Paul, Minnesota) has established what is termed the "national reporter system," in which blocks of states by geographical area are combined in various volumes. For example, appellate decisions from courts in Illinois, Massachusetts, Indiana, Ohio, and New York are contained in the Northeastern Reporter (N.E.) United States Reports. These are the official case reports of the U.S. Supreme Court and contain full transcripts of the majority opinions as well as other concurring or dissenting opinions in the Court's cases. The specifics of cases are summarized, and lists of the principals involved are given.

For a certain 1966 wiretapping case in Illinois, the citation is "*People v. Kurth*, 34 IL. 2d 387, 216 NE 2d 154 [1966]." Translated, this means that the decision of the appellate court in the case of *People v.* (versus, or against) *Kurth* can be found in the Illinois Reporter, second series, volume 34, on page 387; this same decision can be found in volume 216 of the Northeastern Reporter, second series, on page 154.

The reported decision indicates the contending parties, a synopsis of the case up to the time it appeared before the reviewing court, the decision of the court, the relevant points of law considered and decided by the court (in the opinion of the legal experts employed by the publisher), the majority opinion, and the minority opinion if there is one included. Other information includes dates, names of justices and contending attorneys, and even citations of the case if it has passed through prior appeals before the current one. For this wealth of information, the reporters are invaluable aids to any research of points of law and of the cases in which they are found.

10.4   Digests and Summaries

Another useful set of sources in researching legal issues are the digests and summaries. One of the most helpful is *Shepard's Acts and Cases by Popular Names*,[43] a digest that gives the references and citations necessary to find the legislation or court decisions.

Another source is *Corpus Juris Secundum*,[44] an encyclopedic compilation of criminal and civil law based on reported cases. The *Criminal Law Digest*[45] is a one-volume digest of leading court decisions. Each annual volume is cumulative from 1965, when the digest was first published. The *Digest* indexes the *Criminal Law Bulletin (CLB)*,[46] which gives specific information on cases. Still another source is the *Criminal Law Reporter*,[47] which has an alphabetical index of cases by subject matter and a straight alphabetical listing.

Once a case has been found, it is easy to find other related cases using *Shepard's Citations*.[48] This publication allows researchers to gather all the case citations that relate to issues in the known case. The legal road is filled with bumps and potholes. There is no easy way to deal with it. Alert security managers will keep abreast of the climate in their jurisdictions and of the latest developments. Rewards will come to the knowledgeable professional who has an acquaintance with the law and its changes. For the unwary or uncaring, the road can be troublesome indeed.

Liability costs, though remaining relatively high, will continue the downward trend that began in 1986. As was noted earlier, the downward trend may be attributable to better prepared security officers and managers, particularly to security managers, who are learning the value of risk management and making good use of proper training.

10.5   Computer-Based Legal Sources

The previously cited hardcopy sources have provided many legal scholars with invaluable assistance. Today's casual student will find that much of the information contained in these sources has been made accessible through various computer-based sites. The two most well-known and popular sites are Lexis-Nexis (www.lexis-nexis.com) and West Group (www.westpub.com). Another good site is Legal Resources (www.para-legals.org/LegalResources). In today's world of electronic communication, information on state laws may also be found through a computer search.

Summary

Although the area of law may appear complicated to many, it is one of the most important tools used by security personnel. A failure to understand offender rights, legal obligations of security personnel, and other legal matters can result in serious litigation involving employers as well as the employee.

The preceding materials present an overview of legal issues, but by no means should they be considered an adequate substitute for courses on criminal law, criminal procedure, contracts, and other related legal topics.

☐ ☐ ☐

Critical Thinking

Why do the courts continue to make distinctions between public law enforcement powers and private sector enforcement issues?

☐ ☐ ☐

Review Questions

1. Why is a practical knowledge of the law important to the security officer and the security manager?
2. What impact does tort law have on the private security industry?
3. What makes an arrest different from a detention?
4. What are the major legal differences between public police and private security officers?
5. Why is the legal term *respondeat superior* important to the contract security industry?
6. What is the difference between criminal law and civil law?
7. The private security industry may enforce criminal law, but it is restricted by civil law. How is this possible?

References

1. Michigan Revised Statutes, Section 338.1051-338.1083.
2. Pursley, Robert D., *Introduction to Criminal Justice*, 5th ed. (New York: Macmillan, 1991). p. 35
3. U.S. v. Hillsman, 522 F. 2d 454, 461 (7th Cir. 1975).
4. Cervantez v. J. C. Penney Company, 156 Cal. Rptr. 198 (1978).
5. 720 Illinois Compiled Statutes 5/16A-5.
6. Collyer v. S. H. Kress Co., 5 Cal. 2d 175, 54 p. 2d 20 (1936).
7. Escobedo v. Illinois, 378 U.S. 478, 84 S.Ct 1758, 12L.Ed.977 (1964).
8. Miranda v. Arizona, 384 U.S., 436, 86 S.Ct 1602, 16L.Ed.2d.691 (1963).
9. In re Deborah C., 1977 Rptr. 852 (1981).
10. Wisconsin Statutes Annotated, Section 943.50.
11. West Virginia v. William H. Muegge, 360 SE 2d. 216 (W.Va 1987).
12. People v. Zelinski, 594 P 2d 1000 (1979).
13. Mapp v. Ohio, 367 U.S. 643 (1961).
14. Weeks v. United States, 232 U.S. 383 (1914).
15. Burdeau v. McDowell, 256 U.S. 465 (1921).
16. State v. Scrotsky, 39 NJ 410, 416 189 A.2d 23 (1963).
17. People v. Jones, 393 NE 2d. 443 (1979).
18. People v. Randazzo, 220 Cal. 2d 268, 34 Cal. Rptr. 65 (1963).
19. Thacker v. Commonwealth, 310 Ky. 701, 221 SW 2d 682 (1949).
20. Weyandt v. Mason Stores, Inc., 279 F. Supp. 283, 287 (W.D. Pa. 1968).
21. Schnabolk, Charles., *Physical Security: Practices and Technology* (Boston: Butterworth-Heinemann, 1983). p. 74
22. Restatement of Torts, Second Section 307.
23. Illinois Revised Statutes, Ch. 110, sections 2–116.
24. Fisher v. Carrousel Motor Hotel, Inc., 424 SW 2d 627 (TX 1976).
25. Klein v. 1500 Massachusetts Avenue Apartment Corporation, 439 F 2d 477 (D.C. Cir. 1970).
26. Garzilli v. Howard Johnson's Motor Lodge, Inc., 419 F Supp. 1210, (D.CT. E.D.N.Y. 1976).
27. Philip Aaron Banks, et al. v. Hyatt Corporation and Refco Poydras Hotel Joint Venture, 722 F 2d 214 (1984); Allen B. Morrison, et al. v. MGM Grand Hotel, et al., 570 F. Supp. 1449 (1983).

28. McCarthy v. Pheasant Run, Inc., F 2d 1554 (1987).

29. Sharpe v. Peter Pan Bus Lines, No. 49694, Suffolk County, MA.

30. Nelson v. Church's Fried Chicken, 31 ATLA L. Rep 84 (1987).

31. Galloway v. Bankers Trust Company and Trustee Midlands Mall, No. 63/86-1879 Iowa Supreme Court (1988).

32. Polly Suzanne Paterson v. Kent C. Deeb, Transamerica Insurance Co., W. Fenton Langston, and Hartford Accident & Indemnity Co., 472 S. 2d 1210.

33. Dupree v. Piggly Wiggly Shop Rite Foods Inc., 542 SW 2d 882 (Texas 1976).

34. Prosser, W.L., *Handbook of the Law of Torts, Hornbook Series*, 4th ed. (St. Paul, MN: West, 1970). p. 458

35. Graalum v. Radisson Ramp, 245 Minn. 54, 71 NW 2d 904, 908 (1955).

36. Fornier v. Churchill Downs-Latonia, 292 Ky. 215, 166 SW 2d 38 (1942).

37. Hayes v. Sears, Roebuck Co., 209 P. 2d 468, 478 (1949).

38. Kakalik, James, and Wildhurn, Sorrel, *The Private Police* (New York: Crane, Russak & Co., 1977).

39. *State v. Farns*, 542 P.2d 725 (Kan. 1975).

40. Levine, D. E., "Content Monitoring and Filtering," *Security Technology & Design* (March 2003): 74.

41. Neubauer, D., *America's Courts and the Criminal Justice System* (Pacific Grove, CA: Brooks/ Cole, 1988).

42. *U.S. Code Annotated,* Title 18 Crimes and Procedures (St. Paul, MN: West), 50 vols., updated annually.

43. *Shepard's Acts and Cases by Popular Names* (Colorado Springs, CO: Shepard's/McGraw-Hill), updated annually.

44. Corpus Juris Secundum (New York: American Law Book Co.), 101 vols., updated annually.

45. Douglas, James A., and Benton, Donald S., *Criminal Law Digest* (Boston: Warren, Gorham & Lamont), updated annually.

46. Criminal Law Bulletin (Boston: Warren, Gorham & Lamont).

47. Criminal Law Reporter (Washington, D.C.: U.S. Bureau of National Affairs).

48. Shepard's Citations (Colorado Springs, CO: Shepard's/McGraw-Hill), updated annually.

8

Risk Analysis, Security Surveys, and Insurance

OBJECTIVES

The study of this chapter will enable you to:

1. Understand the use of risk management tools to determine the probability of an event occurring and the potential cost to the company should that event occur.
2. Identify traditional alternatives for optimizing risk management strategies.
3. Identify the role of insurance as a risk management strategy.
4 Know the basic types of insurance.

1 Introduction

Once security goals and responsibilities have been defined, as discussed in Chapter 3, and an organization has been created to carry them out, as discussed in Chapter 4, the ongoing task of security management is to identify potential areas of loss and to develop and install appropriate security countermeasures. This process is called *risk analysis*. Implicit in this approach is the concept of security as a comprehensive, integrated function of the organization. One part of this comprehensive, integrated job is the security survey, which is used to identify potential problem areas. More will be said about the survey later in this chapter.

A small business, particularly one with minimal loss potential or relative ease of defense, might adequately be served (as many are) by a good lock on the door and an alarm system or by a contract guard patrol.

This comprehensive view of the loss prevention function might be contrasted with more limited security responses such as:

- *One-dimensional security*, which relies on a single deterrent, such as guards or simple insurance coverage.
- *Piecemeal security*, in which ingredients are added to the loss prevention function piece by piece as the need arises, without a comprehensive plan.
- *Reactive security*, which responds only to specific loss events.

- *Packaged security,* which installs standard security systems (equipment, personnel, or both), without relation to specific threats, either because "everybody's doing it" or on the theory that packaged systems will take care of any problems that might arise. This is akin to prescribing a remedy without diagnosing the illness—like a broad-spectrum antibiotic that will kill any bacteria a patient has.

An integrated or systems approach to security is not always the desired solution. A small business, particularly one with minimal loss potential or relative ease of defense, might adequately be served (as many are) by a good lock on the door and an alarm system or by a contract guard patrol. Include some basic insurance and you might have a reasonable security package. But as the areas of loss increase and become more complex and as the ability to protect a growing company against those losses with one-dimensional responses decreases, it becomes increasingly necessary to adopt a more comprehensive security program. If security is not to be one-dimensional, piecemeal, reactive, or prepackaged, it must be based on analysis of the total risk potential. In other words, to set up defenses against losses from crime, accidents, or natural disasters, there must first be a means of identification and evaluation of the risks.

2   Risk Management

The first step in risk analysis involves recognizing the threats. It costs a company great sums of money to erect buildings to protect assets, information, and personnel. But compared to putting money into research and development, which is investing in the company's future, putting money into preventing a loss is only spending money to prevent something undesirable from happening. Although both investments involve risk, spending money on a product is dynamic and speculative and thus is a more interesting risk to take. Risks to real and intellectual property are generally overlooked or considered a necessary evil. Even when the risk is recognized, managers prefer to operate under the calculated risk theory. What is often overlooked in this process is the word *risk*. However, over the past several decades, businesses have been forced to come to terms with the potential consequences of taking security risks. The two alternative solutions, which should be complementary, are (1) investment in loss prevention techniques and (2) insurance.

Today the progressive manager recognizes that property risks are formidable and that they must be managed. Risk management may thus be defined as making the most efficient before-the-loss arrangement for an after-the-loss continuation of business. As a consequence, good insurance programs and security or loss prevention programs are in demand. The concept of *risk management* presents a sensible approach to this complicated problem: It allows risks to be handled in a logical manner, using long-held management principles. Insurance in and of itself is no longer able to meet the security challenges major corporations face. To meet these challenges, insurance companies have found loss prevention techniques and programs invaluable. A good risk management program involves four basic steps:

1. Identify risks or specific vulnerabilities.
2. Analyze and study risks, including the likelihood and degree of danger of an event.
3. Optimize risk management alternatives:
   a. Risk avoidance

  b. Risk reduction
  c. Risk spreading
  d. Risk transfer
  e. Self-assumption of risk
  f. Any combination of the above
 4. Study security programs (ongoing).

The approach must be total; there can be no shortcuts.

2.1 Asset Assessment

However, before considering threats, it is important to have a clear understanding of what assets are being protected. Assets may be as simple as a person or as complicated as billions of dollars' worth of materials, including people, buildings, machines, paperwork, and information stored in computer systems. More will be said about assets when we discuss the issue of criticality later in this chapter.

2.2 Threat Assessment

The first step in risk analysis is identifying the threats and vulnerabilities. Many threats to business are important to security, but some are more obvious than others. The key is to consider the specific vulnerabilities in a given situation. Each individual firm has problems and threats that are unique. For example, a retailing company may be less concerned about fire hazards than is a manufacturing firm that operates a foundry. A retailer will be concerned with shoplifting, whereas a horseshoe manufacturer might not be concerned about this problem if the horseshoes are not sold directly to the public. Employee theft, on the other hand, could be a big problem. Today it appears that drug use and abuse and workplace violence, along with computer integrity issues, could be security problems found to some extent in all organizations. More will be presented on these and other topics in later chapters.

Specific threats are not always obvious. Although it seems to be common sense to check doors, locks, and gates to control physical access, accessibility through walls made of inferior materials or through a poorly constructed door or doorframe is a less obvious consideration. Awareness of all the possibilities is the mark of a good security manager. The best manager can think like a thief and thus is able to consider policies to reduce the vulnerability of company property. Therefore, a manager must develop the ability to analyze vulnerabilities. A thorough analysis is comprehensive and accurate and leads to effective countermeasures. Once it has been completed, a vulnerability analysis—also called a *security survey* or *audit*—should be repeated on a regular basis.

2.3 The Security Survey

In the process of risk analysis that proceeds from threat assessment (identifying risk) to threat evaluation (determining the criticality and dollar cost of that risk) to the selection of security countermeasures designed to contain or prevent that risk, one of management's most valuable tools is the security survey (see Appendix D for sample surveys).

A security survey is essentially an exhaustive physical examination of a premises and a thorough inspection of all operational systems and procedures. Such an examination or survey has as its overall objective a facility analysis to determine the existing state of its security, to locate weaknesses in its defenses, to determine the degree of protection required, and ultimately to lead to recommendations for establishing a total security program.

Motivation to set the survey in motion should come from top management to ensure that adequate funds for the undertaking are available and to guarantee the cooperation of all personnel in the facility. Since a thorough survey will require an examination of procedures and routines in regular operation and an inspection of the physical plant and its environs, management's interest in the project is of the highest priority.

Whoever undertakes the survey should have training in the field and should also have achieved a high level of ability.

The survey may be conducted by staff security personnel or by qualified security specialists employed for this purpose. Some experts suggest that outside security people could approach the job with more objectivity and would have less of a tendency to take certain areas or practices for granted, thus providing a more complete appraisal of existing conditions. Others suggest that outsiders do not have a clear picture of the organization's internal workings. These opposite opinions may point to an operation that incorporates both external oversight utilizing internal security staff.

Whoever undertakes the survey should have training in the field and should also have achieved a high level of ability. It is also important that at least some members of the survey team be totally familiar with the facility and its operation. Without such familiarity, it would be difficult to formulate the survey plan, and the survey itself must be planned in advance to make the best use of personnel and to study the operation in every phase.

Part of the plan may come from previous studies and recommendations. These should be studied for any useful information they might offer. Another part of the survey plan will include a checklist made up by the survey team in preparation for the actual inspection. This list will serve as a guide and reminder of areas that must be examined, and once it has been drawn up, it should be followed systematically. In the event that some area or procedure was omitted in the preparation of the original checklist, it should be included in the inspection and its disposition noted in the evaluation and recommendation.

Since no two facilities are alike—not even those in the same business—no checklist exists that could universally apply for survey purposes. The following discussion is intended only to indicate those areas where a risk could exist. This discussion should be considered merely a guide to the kinds of questions or specific problems that might be handled.

2.4   The Facility

When analyzing security risks, the security manager should look at a number of aspects of the company, giving consideration as potential security problems to the following:

- *The perimeter*. Check fencing, gates, culverts, drains, lighting (including standby lights and power), overhangs, and concealing areas. Can vehicles drive up to the fence?
- *The parking lot*. Are employees' automobiles adequately protected from theft or vandalism? How? Is the lot sufficiently isolated from the plant or office to prevent unsupervised back-and-forth traffic? Are there gates or turnstiles for the inspection

of traffic, if that is necessary? Are these inspection points properly lighted? Can packages be thrown over or pushed through the fence into or out of the parking lot?

- *All adjacent building windows and rooftops.* Are spaces near these adjacencies accessible to them? Are they properly secured? How?

- *All doors and windows less than 18 feet above ground level.* How are these openings secured?

- *The roof.* What means are employed to prevent access to the roof?

- *The issuance of main entrance keys to all tenants in a building.* How often are entrance locks changed? What is the building procedure when keys are lost or not returned? How many tenants are in the building? What businesses are they in?

- *Any shared occupancy, as in office buildings.* Does the building have a properly supervised sign-in log for off-hours? Do elevators switch to manual, and can floors be locked against access outside of business hours? When are they so switched? By whom can they then be operated? Who collects the trash, and how and when is it removed from the building? Are lobbies and hallways adequately lighted? What guard protection does the building have? How can guards be reached? Are washrooms open to the public? Are equipment rooms locked? Is a master key system in use? How are keys controlled and secured? Is there a receptionist or guard in the lobby? Can the building be accessed by stair or elevator from basement parking facilities?

- *All areas containing valuables.* Do safes, vaults, or computer rooms containing valuables have adequate alarms? What alarms are in place to protect against burglary, fire, robbery, or surreptitious entry? Are computers protected from hackers and unauthorized employee use?

- *The off-hours when the facility is not in operation and all nighttime hours.* How many guards are on duty at various times of day? Are guards alert and efficient? How are guards equipped? How many patrols are there, and how often do they make their rounds? What is their tour? What is the guard communication system?

- *Controlling and supervising entry into the facility.* What method is used to identify employees? How are applicants screened before they are employed? How are visitors (including salespeople, vendors, and customers) controlled? How are privately owned vehicles controlled? Who delivers the morning mail, and when? How are empty mail sacks handled? Do you authorize salespeople or solicitors for charity in the facility? How are they controlled? Are their credentials checked? Who does the cleaning? Do they have keys? Who is responsible for these keys? Are the cleaners bonded? Who does maintenance or service work? Are their toolboxes inspected when they leave? Are their credentials checked? By whom? Are alarm and other technical and telephone company people allowed unlimited access? Is the call for their service verified? By whom? How is furniture or equipment moved in or out? What security is provided when this takes place at night or on weekends? Are messengers permitted to deliver directly to the addressee? How are they controlled? Which areas have the heaviest traffic? Are visitors claiming official status, such as building or fire inspectors, permitted free access? Are their credentials checked? By whom?

- *Keys and key control (traditional or electronic).* Are keys properly secured when they are not in use? Are locks replaced or recorded when a key is lost? Are locks and locking devices adequate for their purpose? Are all keys accounted for and logged? What system is used for the control of master and submaster keys? Is there adequate security to prevent unauthorized access and use of computer keying systems?

- *Fire.* Are there sufficient fireboxes throughout the facility? Are they properly located? Is the type and number of fire extinguishers adequate? Are they frequently inspected? How far is the nearest public fire department? Have they ever been invited to inspect the facility? Does the building have automatic sprinklers and automatic fire alarms? Are there adequate fire barriers in the building? Is there an employee fire brigade? Are fire doors adequate? Are "no smoking" signs enforced? Are flammable substances properly stored? Is there a program of fire prevention education? Are fire drills conducted on a regular basis?

- *Computer access.* What is the potential for loss of equipment? Which services will be denied if the computer is inoperable? What information is stored in the computer that could cause the organization loss of profits if it were compromised?

- *Video surveillance.* Is there a video surveillance system in place? Are cameras properly located and protected? Who monitors the system or is it monitored? What type of system has been designed for review and destruction of old video footage or digital records? What controls assure that images cannot be manipulated?

- *Computer systems.* Is the computer equipment properly protected from fire, water damage, and physical attacks? Is there a backup system? Are computer files properly backed up? Does the computer system have a backup power system or protection for power surges? What types of access controls exist? How is the system protected from unauthorized access? Are firewalls in place? How is the system protected from hackers? Is there a system to protect the computer from viruses?

For all its seeming length, this list contains only a sample of the kinds of questions that must be asked when conducting a survey of any facility. The list is only a general overview of some of the aspects to be covered.

2.5   General Departmental Evaluations

Each department in the organization should be evaluated separately in terms of its potential for loss. These departmental evaluations will eventually be consolidated into the master survey for final recommendations and action. Basic questions might be as follows:

- Is the departmental function such that it is vulnerable to embezzlement?
- Does the department have cash funds or negotiable instruments on hand?
- Does the department house confidential records?
- What equipment, tools, supplies, or merchandise can be stolen from the department?
- Does the department have heavy external and/or internal traffic?
- Does the department contain target items such as drugs, jewelry, or furs?
- What is the special fire hazard in the department or from adjacent areas?

These are questions that can serve to guide the survey in focusing on particular areas of risk in each department examined. Where particular risks predominate, special attention must be paid to providing some counteraction to remove them.

It is well to remember, especially when it appears that questions concerning the probity of company officers are posed, that the job of the security survey is not to make judgments on whether a criminal act is likely to occur but rather on whether it *could*.

2.5.1 The Personnel Department

Particular security problems are associated with personnel departments. Such concerns include:

- Can the department area be locked off from the rest of the floor and/or building after hours?
- How are door and file keys secured?
- Is the computer system accessible by individuals outside the personnel department? Can computer files be accessed from remote locations?
- Are files kept locked during the day when they are not in use?
- What system is followed with regard to the payroll department when employees are hired or terminated?
- What are the relationships between personnel and payroll staff?
- What are the employment procedures? How are applicants screened?
- How closely do personnel work with security on personnel employment procedures?
- Are new employees given a security briefing? By whom?
- Does the company have an incident-reporting system? Are employees aware of the program? Does the company have a follow-up security awareness training program?

Security of personnel files is of extreme importance. Normally these files contain information on every employee, past and present, from the president down. This information is highly confidential and must be handled that way. There can be no exceptions to this firm policy.

2.5.2 The Accounting Department

The accounting department has total supervision over a firm's money and will generally be the area most vulnerable to major loss due to crime. Certainly protective systems are in operation in this area from a company's founding, but these systems must be reevaluated regularly in light of ongoing experience to find ways of improving both their efficiency and security:

- Cashier
- Accounts receivable
- Accounts payable
- Payroll
- Company bank accounts

2.5.3 The Data Processing Department

Computer-related security problems are becoming more important as most companies increase their use of electronic data processing. In fact, it is rare for even the smallest companies to have no major computer operations in today's competitive environment. The importance of this area is stressed in Chapter 18, "Information Security Issues." The security manager should consider the following questions:

- Are adequate auditing procedures in effect on all programs?
- How are printouts of confidential information handled?
- What is the off-site storage procedure? How are such files updated?
- What is the system governing program access?
- How is computer use logged? How is the accuracy of this record verified?
- Who has keys to the computer spaces? How often is the list of authorized key holders evaluated?
- What controls are exercised over access? How often is the list of people authorized to enter updated?
- What fire prevention and fire protection procedures are in effect? What fire prevention and protection training is given employees? What is the number, location, and condition of fire extinguishers and the basic extinguishing system?
- Is there off-site backup hardware? How is it secured?
- Are there audits of downloads to laptop computers?
- How is remote access tackled for local area networks (LANs), wireless LANs (WLANs), or wide area networks (WANs)?
- What is done to determine access from outside sources through the Internet, if appropriate?

2.5.4   The Purchasing Department

Purchasing is an area subject to many temptations. Vendors often freely offer graft in the form of cash, expensive gifts, lavish entertainment, and luxurious vacations—all in the name of seeking the goodwill of the purchasing agent. Generally speaking, this is not a security matter unless the agent succumbs to the extent of paying for goods never delivered or paying invoices twice. If all the attention from vendors causes a purchasing agent to buy unwisely, that is a management concern in which security plays no role.

There are, however, some areas in the purchasing function in which security might be involved:

- What are the procedures preventing double payment of invoices? Fraudulent invoices? Invoices for goods never received? How often is this area audited?
- Are competitive bids invited for all purchases? Must the lowest bid be awarded the contract?
- What forms are used for ordering? For authorizing payment? How are they routed?
- Since purchasing is frequently responsible for the sale of scrap, waste paper, and other recoverable items, who verifies the amount actually trucked away? Who negotiates the sale of waste or scrap material? Are several prospective buyers invited to bid? How is old equipment or furniture sold? What records are kept of such sales? Is the system audited? What controls are placed on the authority of the seller?

2.5.5   *The Shipping and Receiving Departments*

Freight and merchandise handling areas are particularly troublesome because there is a great potential for theft in these areas. Close attention must be paid to current operations, and efforts must continually be directed to their improvement:

- What inspections are made of employees entering or leaving such areas?
- How is traffic in and to such areas controlled? Are these areas separated from the rest of the facility by a fence or barrier?
- Where is merchandise stored after receipt or before shipment? What is the security of such areas? What is the nature of supervision in these areas?
- What is the system for accountability of shipments and receipts?
- Is the area guarded?
- What losses are being experienced in these areas? What is the profile of such loss (type, average amount, time of day)?
- Is merchandise left unattended in these areas?
- Are truck drivers provided with restroom facilities separate from those of dock personnel? Are they isolated from them at all times to prevent collusion?
- How many people are authorized in security storage areas, and who are they?

2.6   Miscellaneous

Other general security concerns include:

- What records are kept of postage meter usage? What controls are established over meter usage?
- How is the use of supplies and materials controlled?
- How are forms controlled?

2.7   Report of the Survey

After the survey has documented the full scope of its examination, a report should be prepared indicating those areas that are weak in security and recommending measures that might reasonably bring the facility's security up to acceptable standards. On the basis of the status in the survey and considering the recommendations made, a security plan can now be drawn up.

In some cases, compromises have to be made. The siting of the facility or the area involved, for example, may make an ideal security program with full coverage of all contingencies too costly to be practical. In such cases, the plan must be restudied to find the best approach for achieving acceptable security standards within these limitations.

It must be understood that security directors will rarely get all of what they want. As in every department, they must work within the framework of the possible. Where they are denied extra personnel, they must find hardware that will help replace people. Where a request for more coverage by CCTV is turned down, they must develop inspection procedures or barriers that can serve a similar purpose. If at any time they feel that security costs have been cut to a point where the stated objective cannot be achieved, they are obliged to communicate that opinion to management, who will then determine whether to diminish the original objective or to authorize more money. It is important, however, that security directors exhaust every alternative method of coverage before going to management with an opinion that requires this kind of decision.

3   Operational Audits and Programmed Supervision

The Operational Audit (OA) should be distinguished from its simpler sister, the security survey. A security survey begins by developing a checklist of items that the security team feels are important. For example, are there adequate locks, alarms, and guard patrols? Do security breaches (that is, doors and windows) have adequate protection, and are they built of substantial materials? Although some security surveys involve a check of procedures, many do not. For example, it would be wise to ensure that check-in procedures at the warehouse are being followed.

The OA builds on the security survey. For many operations, a security survey may be conducted once a year, or even less frequently. The OA, however, is conducted regularly and frequently. An *operational audit (OA)* considers all aspects of the security operation on a continuing basis. The operational audit is a methodical examination, or audit, of operations. The purpose of the examination is threefold: (1) to find deviations from established security standards and practices, (2) to find loopholes in security controls, and (3) to consider means of improving the efficiency or control of the operation without reducing security.

Once the OA begins, it continues until someone in a position of authority decides that it is no longer necessary. The audit, through the process of Programmed Supervision (PS), requires that supervisors regularly report whether procedures are being followed and if those procedures are adequate.

Because the audit is an ongoing process achieved through program supervision, it is relatively inexpensive. An OA is based on the concept of programmed supervision, without which the audit would become nothing more than a simple security survey. *Programmed supervision (PS)* is a means of making sure that a supervisor or other employees go through a prescribed series of inspections that will ascertain that functions or procedures for which they are responsible are being properly executed. Supervisors are thus conducting OAs by evaluating their areas of responsibility on an ongoing basis.

A truly successful OA requires the supervisor to make the necessary inspection and to record specific recheckable findings, not just to record a simple checkmark as "yes" or "no." Some procedures might need to be amended as the work changes to meet new demands. The OA also requires supervisors to regularly report physical conditions (such as whether the doors are locked regularly as specified). A supervisor in a loading dock area should be required to check all steps in the shipping and receiving area. Where are truck drivers authorized to be during the loading or unloading of a truck? What procedures are followed to determine that the load count is accurate? How are broken parcels handled? The supervisor must answer each of these questions carefully and fully. As noted, the supervisor cannot simply respond with a "yes" or "no." The aggregate of several area OAs results in a divisional OA, and divisional OAs considered in aggregate are an entire company's OA.

The security survey is better than nothing, but the OA goes beyond an occasional survey. The security survey relies heavily on either the proprietary security force or on a contractor. The OA uses the company's management resources.

Using the information gained from vulnerability analysis, security surveys, and OAs, the security manager can develop a comprehensive security plan.

3.1 Probability

Once vulnerabilities have been identified through the use of the security survey or OA, it is essential to determine the probability of loss. For example, suppose that one vulnerability involves the theft of trade secrets. Within the area of trade secrets, subcategories of vulnerability are identified, including the loss of information from research and development through employee turnover or negligence. Should security dollars be spent to reduce the potential for such a loss? It is not possible to say until the probability has been assessed. Will a loss certainly occur if nothing is changed, or is the occurrence improbable? When security managers are confronted with a series of problems, they must determine which problems need immediate attention. *Probability* is a mathematical statement concerning the possibility of an event occurring. Is it possible to reduce security risks to a mathematical equation that can be used to determine probability? Unfortunately such mathematical precision must wait until various subjective security measures can be turned into numerical values. This has not yet occurred.

The best that can be done today is to make subjective decisions about probability. Such decisions should be based on data such as the physical aspects of the vulnerability being studied—for example, spatial relationships, location, and composition of the structure. Procedural considerations must also be studied. What policies exist? The history associated with the industry is of great importance, particularly the vulnerability being studied. Has the product been a target before? What is the current state of the art of thieving? Later in this book various physical security devices will be discussed. Each has its advantages, but the reality is that criminals, depending on their own education and level of determination, may find methods of overcoming each security device. How aware are potential thieves of the technology to defeat existing security devices?

3.2 Criticality

Probability cannot stand alone when the security manager analyzes which security problem to address first. For example, a certainty that someone will steal money from the company cafeteria might not warrant attention as immediate as the possibility that someone might tamper with the software used to maintain company inventory, purchasing, and order information, even when the probability of such tampering is only moderate. To help separate the vulnerabilities into still finer categories, security managers use the principle of *criticality*. The term has been defined as the impact of a loss as measured in dollars. As noted earlier in this chapter, the security manager must know what assets are being protected, including their relative value to the overall health of the organization. The concept has also been expanded to include how important the area, practice, or whatever is to the existence of the organization. The dollar loss is not simply the cost of the item lost but also includes:

- Replacement cost
- Temporary replacement
- Downtime
- Discounted cash

- Insurance rate changes
- Loss of marketplace advantage

Criticality is an extremely important concept for security managers to understand. In general, company executives who usually think in terms of cost/benefit analysis will not be interested in spending money for security if the cost is greater than the potential loss of money. Unfortunately, many security directors fail to explain that criticality is far more than just the direct cost of the items lost. Replacement costs include the new purchase price, the costs of delivery, installation costs, any additional materials needed during the installation, and other indirect costs.

A second major cost may be temporary replacement. Consider an attack on an electronic data processing (EDP) unit. If the main computer is damaged by sabotage or fire, the company will most likely need to process its data by leasing EDP equipment or through a time-sharing arrangement with a computer firm or another company. The cost of these temporary measures should be taken into consideration.

A third possible cost is downtime, the cost associated with not being able to continue business while the computer is inoperable. One possible cost in this category, depending on various company policies and union contracts, may be the wages for employees who are idled.

A fourth cost factor, discounted cash, is money lost when invested funds must be withdrawn from time certificates or other investments to pay for any of the afore-mentioned costs. For example, consider the loss of income on a $100,000 certificate of deposit, held at 12.9 percent interest, if the certificate is cashed early to pay delivery and installation costs.

A fifth cost involves the possible increase in insurance premiums associated with loss problems. Insurance rates will increase as losses go up.

Yet a sixth cost is the potential loss of marketplace advantage created by the loss of product markets due to sabotage, work slowdowns, and so forth. If the product is not available when consumers want to buy it, they will turn to alternatives. In some cases, they will stay with the competitor's product.

All six factors need to be added into the criticality cost. Many security managers are surprised to find that the criticality cost can be double the apparent cost of an item. Likewise, company managers often fail to consider these indirect costs.

3.3   The Probability/Criticality/Vulnerability Matrix

Criticality, much like probability, is a subjective measure, but it can be placed on a continuum. Consider the continuum for criticality and probability shown in Table 8.1. Using the rankings generated for probability and criticality and devising a matrix system for the various vulnerabilities, it is possible to quantify security risks somewhat and to determine which vulnerabilities merit immediate attention. Although some areas of importance may be obvious, some security executives will be surprised to find that other areas are more critical than they first surmised.

For example, consider the cash theft vulnerability matrix shown in Table 8.2. Cash theft has been chosen since it is simple to calculate criticality costs. By considering the gross sales of the firm and its current assets, we can determine the impact of the loss of cash from each of the areas listed. In addition, by considering the history of loss and the

Table 8.1 The Probability/Criticality Matrix

Probability	Criticality
1. Virtually certain	A. Fatal
2. Highly probable	B. Very serious
3. Moderately probable	C. Moderately serious
4. Probable	D. Serious
5. Improbable	E. Relatively unimportant
6. Probability unknown	F. Criticality unknown

Source: Richard J. Healy and Timothy J. Walsh, Industrial Security Management (New York: American Management Association, 1971), p. 17.

number and quality of security devices present, it is possible to estimate the probability of a cash theft.

Using the system presented in Table 8.1, alphabetical and numerical values can be assigned to each vulnerability area. For example, the manager's office might be categorized as A4, which indicates that the loss of $200,000 in a company with total current assets of $300,000 could be "fatal" and that the probability of the loss occurring is "probable" based on the amount of money tempting the thief and the level of security present (see Table 8.2). Each area may be classified in the same fashion. Then it is usually possible to rank the importance of addressing each area using criticality as the most important variable—for example, A1, A5, B3, B4, C1, D4, E2 (see Table 8.3). The only exception to this order of ranking occurs in the cases of F (criticality unknown) and 6 (probability unknown). If the security director cannot assign a probability or criticality to a certain item, the criticality should be assumed to be fatal and the probability virtually certain. To consider them otherwise is suicidal!

If a choice has to be made, criticality should take precedence over probability. The security director, however, should implement measures to reduce the threat to the improbable level whenever the measures are cost-effective.

3.4 Alternatives for Optimizing Risk Management

Once the security probability and criticality analysis has been completed and the security problems have been identified and ranked in importance, the security manager, in cooperation with company executives, must decide how to proceed. As noted earlier, there are several risk management alternatives: risk avoidance, risk reduction, risk spreading, risk transfer, and self-assumption of risk.

Risk avoidance is removing the problem by eliminating the risk. This can be accomplished by transferring responsibility to another area. For example, the manufacturing of a small micro chip by company *M* may be a security problem. To avoid the risk, company *M* decides to subcontract the manufacturing process to another firm that is better suited to handling this type of product security. Thus the risk for company *M* is avoided.

Risk reduction involves decreasing the potential ill effects of safety and security problems when it is impossible to avoid them. For example, as a result of a security

Table 8.2 Cash Theft Vulnerability Matrix

Building Location	Amount of On-Hand Dollars		Accountability Records		Area Has Physical Bounds		Area Locked		Positive Control on Admittance		Alarm Protection Devices		Surveillance Devices		Cash in Storage Container Kept		Bait Money Kept		History of Cash Loss	
	NBH	OT	NBH	OT	NBH	OT	NBH	OT	NBH	OT	NBH	OT	NBH	OT	NBH	OT	NBH	OT	NBH	OT
Manager's office	200,000	40,000	Y	Y	Y	Y	N	Y	N	Y	Y	Y	N	Y	Y	Y	Y	Y	N	N
Manager's secretary	300	300	Y	Y	N	N	Y	Y	Y	N	N	N	N	N	Y	Y	N	N	Y	Y
Cafeteria	2,000	0	N	Y	Y	Y	N	N	N	N	N	N	N	N	N	–	N	–	Y	Y
Loading dock	1,500	500	Y	Y	Y	Y	N	N	N	N	N	N	Y	Y	Y	Y	N	N	N	N
Visitor reception	100	100	N	N	N	N	N	N	N	N	N	N	N	N	N	N	Y	Y	N	Y

Data for a company with gross sales per year of $310,000 and total current assets of $300,000. NBH=Normal business hours; OT=Other times; Y=Yes; N=No.

Table 8.3 Probability/Criticality Assessment and Ranking

	Criticality		Probability	
	NBH	**OT**	**NBH**	**OT**
Manager's office	A	B	2	4
Manager's secretary	D	D	2	2
Cafeteria	C	–	1	–
Loading dock	C	D	1	2
Visitor reception	D	D	2	1
Suggested Rank Order				
Manager's office NBH			A2	
Manager's office OT			B4	
Cafeteria NBH			C1	
Loading dock NBH			C1	
Visitor reception OT			D1	
Visitor reception NBH			D2	
Loading dock OT			D2	
Manager's secretary NBH			D2	
Manager's secretary OT			D2	

survey and vulnerability analysis, the security manager has determined that company N has a high risk of money loss in the central budget office because there are no positive admittance controls and no alarms. Creating a policy for positive admittance and installing proximity alarm devices can reduce the risk. The risk is never totally eliminated, since the old adage "where there's a will, there's a way" applies to employees and outsiders who want to steal money.

Risk spreading is decentralizing a procedure or operation so that a security or safety problem at one location will not cause a complete loss. Suppose that company M is producing a microchip at a high risk of loss. It can spread its production risk by subcontracting some of the components to other companies or by producing the components at other sites owned by company M.

Risk transfer generally means removing the risk to the company by paying for the protection of an insurance policy. (Insurance options are discussed later in this chapter.)

Self-assumption of risk involves planning for an eventual loss without benefit of insurance. In all procedures to minimize risks, insurance should be considered a valuable addition to safety and security procedures.

Insurance should be considered a valuable addition to safety and security procedures.

3.4.1 The Cost-Effectiveness of Security

It is unlikely that any evaluation will ever absolutely determine the cost-effectiveness of any security operation. A low rate of crime—whether compared to past experience, to like concerns, or to neighboring businesses—is an indication that the security department is performing effectively. But how much is being protected that would otherwise be damaged, stolen, or destroyed? This can be any figure, from the total exposure of the entire organization to some more refined estimate based on the incidence of criminal attack locally or nationally, the average losses suffered by the industry in general, or the reduction in losses by the organization over a given period.

An estimate based on such figures might well serve as a practical guide to the usefulness of the security function. On the other hand, if a security operation costing $400,000 annually were estimated, by some formula using a mix of the data mentioned previously, to have saved a potential in theft and vandalism of $300,000, would it be deemed advisable to reduce the department's operating budget by $100,000 or more? Obviously not! This would be roughly analogous to reducing or canceling insurance because damage or loss and subsequent insurance recovery for a specific period or incident were less than the cost of the premium. Security can be considered insurance against unacceptable risks.

Studies on the role of security and related investments as part of corporate costs of risk conducted by the Risk and Insurance Management Society (RIMS) show that the share of the total cost for risk control in these areas has risen. The rise in percentage indicates management's growing awareness of the role security can and must play in the total package of risk control as well as strategies by the insurance industry to recover from losses incurred in the 1990s and events following 9/11, including the collapse of Enron, problems at WorldCom, and catastrophic storms like Katrina. The changes following 2001 have resulted in a now relatively healthy property and casualty insurance industry. This in turn has resulted in declines in rates in all segments of the industry in 2006 and continuing into 2007.[1]

Cost-effectiveness studies must be made, as part of a periodic review of protection systems, even though such studies cannot be used as a general rule in devising a magic formula for computing the cost per $1,000 actually saved in cash or goods that would otherwise have been lost. Such a review would consider, for example, the savings that could result from the substitution of functionally equivalent electronic or other gear for manpower (the most expensive deterrent) and the feasibility of taking such a step.

3.4.2 Periodic Review

Even after the security plan is formulated, it is essential that the survey process be continued. To be effective, a security plan must be dynamic. It must change regularly in various details to accommodate changing circumstances in a given facility. Only regular inspections can provide a basis for the ongoing evaluation of a company's security status. Exposure and vulnerability change constantly. What appears to be a minor alteration in operational routines may have a profound effect on the security of the entire facility.

3.4.3 Security Files

The survey and its resultant report are also valuable in the building of security files. From this evaluation emerges a detailed current profile of the firm's regular activities. With such a file, the security department can operate with increased effectiveness, but it should, by inspections and additional surveys, be kept current.

Such a database could be augmented by texts, periodicals, official papers, and articles in the general press related to security matters. Special attention should be paid to subjects of local significance. Although national crime statistics are significant and help to build familiarity with a complex subject, local conditions have more immediate import to the security of the company.

As these files are broadened, they will become increasingly useful to the security operation. Patterns may emerge, seasons may become significant, and/or economic conditions may predict events which should be security concerns. For example:

- Certain days or seasons may emerge as those on which problems occur.
- Targets for crime may become evident as more data is amassed. This can enable the security director to reassign priorities.
- A profile of the types and incidence of crimes—possibly even of the criminal—may emerge.
- Patterns of crime and their *modus operandi* on payday or holiday weekends may become evident.
- Criminal assaults on company property may take a definable or predictable shape or description, again enabling the security director to better shape countermeasures.

The careful collection and use of data concerning crime in a given facility can be an invaluable tool for the conscientious security officer. It can add an important dimension to the regular reexamination of the status of crime in the company.

Given the present atmosphere of litigation for failure to provide adequate security, the files showing an efficient security operation can be invaluable. On the other hand, poorly kept files can be as great a liability as well-kept files on a poorly designed security plan or poorly operated security organization.

4   Insurance

As noted earlier, one means of handling risks is *risk transfer*. Insurance is an option that is regularly pursued in the area of transfer. Yet far too many managers still cling to the mistaken notion that the most effective means of guarding against unforeseen business losses is insurance, and all too many still use insurance as a substitute for a comprehensive security program. The fallacy in this attitude is twofold.

> Insurance can never be a substitute for a security program.

In the first place, almost all casualty insurance companies have suffered losses in underwriting crime insurance. Most insurance companies have taken drastic steps to counter this trend. They have canceled or refused to renew policies of insured parties who have suffered losses from criminal activity, limited allowable coverage to a point well below replacement or even cash value of goods or property, limited the extent of coverage, set up limitations that exclude businesses in high-crime areas or in high-risk enterprises from any coverage at all, and increased premium rates.

In the second place, it is virtually impossible to insure against all the losses that could be incurred. Hidden damages in loss of company morale, customer confidence, and in interruption of vigorous participation in a highly competitive market are all serious, if not fatal, blows to any business and can never be recompensed.

Clearly, insurance can never be a substitute for a security program. In many cases, the very fact that assets are insured to some degree tends to reduce the proprietor's interest in instituting reasonable security procedures beyond those minimums specified in a policy. As an aspect of the overall picture, insurance also tends to reduce any interest the insured may have in capturing or prosecuting perpetrators of crimes, thus in effect encouraging the proliferation of like crimes.

4.1 The Value of Insurance in a Total Loss-Prevention Program

Insurance is certainly important. It is clearly necessary for any business that wants to be protected against loss—to spread the risk—but it must be thought of as a supportive, rather than the principal, defense against losses from crime. It is equally important to realize that insurance carriers provide coverage on the basis that the *estimated value (EV)* of loss is always less than the total of the premiums paid.

> Insurance must be thought of as supportive of security operations rather than as the principal defense.

4.2 Types of Insurance

There are many types of insurance. For the purposes of this discussion, however, the focus will be on only those types of insurance that play a prominent role in security or loss prevention.

4.2.1 Fidelity Bonds

Commonly referred to as *honesty insurance*, this coverage provides remuneration for losses due to employee dishonesty. There are those who believe that bonds are not insurance because:

1. Bonding always involves three parties, whereas insurance involves two parties.
2. The bond principal is in full control, whereas the insured really has no control over the event causing the loss.
3. Losses are not expected in surety bonding. Premiums are service fees for the use of the surety's name; in insurance, losses are expected and reflected in the premiums.
4. In bonding, the principal is liable to the surety for losses paid; in insurance, the insured does not agree to reimburse the insurer.

These arguments are worth noting, but they have no effect on the discussion presented here, because most authorities agree that fidelity bonding resembles insurance.

Though "blanket bonds" are in general use because they cover categories of employees and thus allow automatic coverage of new employees, name or position bonds are also popular because of the lower premium costs. The name bond covers only certain specifically named individuals; the position bond covers only those persons who hold a specific position within the company.

This type of coverage is frequently badly underestimated. In effect, the bonding company is guaranteeing the insured that bonded employees will perform in good faith—that is, that they will not commit any dishonest acts against their employer. If any so bonded employees violate this trust, the guarantor—the bonding company—will stand the loss up to the amount insured.

The investigation by the bonding company is valuable in that it provides a further check on the background of employees in sensitive positions, in addition to underwriting possible losses resulting from a violation of trust. Any employee with a past criminal history is excluded.

The losses from underbonding of employees are dramatic!

Most companies require that employees handling cash or high-value merchandise be bonded, but too many of these companies go along on a program calling for $5000, $10,000, or $25,000 bonds, failing to consider that, if bonding is deemed necessary, it must provide for protection against potential damage that such an employee can cause. For example, in situations where there is no system providing a regular, foolproof audit of cash and valuable merchandise, an employee might steal enormous sums over a period of time, even if the daily amount is relatively small.

The Surety Association of America publishes a list of losses from various kinds of businesses caused by bonded employees and the extent of fidelity coverage. The losses from underbonding of employees are dramatic. The association report clearly indicates the problem faced by business today. It also indicates that many businesses are not handling the problem with a coordinated systems approach. It might appear to be hindsight to point out that adequate bonding would have cost these companies the merest fraction of their ultimate losses. Yet we can assume that in most of these cases a more realistic evaluation of the exposure, risk, and insurance costs would have prevented these substantial losses.

With losses attributable to internal theft estimated in the billions of dollars, it is easy to see why fidelity bonds are thought of as high-priority coverage, especially since they provide particular protection in areas where exposure is generally the greatest. As important as this form of coverage is, it is essential that it be handled properly to provide the full protection of which it is capable.

It is important in cases involving bonded employees discovered in the act of theft that no arrangement concerning restitution be made with them without consulting the bonding company. Case files are filled with situations in which an employee agreed to pay back the value of stolen merchandise over a period of time. Typically a few payments are made and then the employee disappears. At that point, there is little or no likelihood that the bonding company will make good the loss. There may be good reasons to give an otherwise trusted employee a chance to make good on the larceny, but if restitution is the sole or at least the prime consideration, the entire matter should be left to the insurer, who is obliged to make good the loss to its extent or to the amount of the bond. Determination of the disposition of the perpetrator's case will be in the insurer's hands.

Generally speaking, few insurance carriers will allow use of inventory records in the initial stages of the claim to describe the amount of loss. Inventory shortages can result from clerical errors, poor record keeping, or shoplifting as well as from employee dishonesty. There is sufficient case law, however, to establish such records as a valid part of the claim in spite of the exclusionary clause. Insurance companies will ultimately deal with the issue and arrive at a mutually satisfactory settlement.

Insurance companies are not anxious to go to court in states where precedent has established the use of inventory records as valid in establishing the extent of claims, and they are reluctant to go to court and possibly establish such precedent in those states where it does not already exist.

4.2.2 Surety Bonds
Surety bonds, also called *performance bonds*, provide protection for failure to live up to contractual obligations.

4.2.3 *Storekeepers' Burglary and Robbery Policies and Mercantile Open-Stock Burglary Policies*

Insurance in these categories is streamlined for the particular establishment; thus premiums vary with the chosen coverage.

4.2.4 *Federal Crime Insurance*

A substantial number of businesses in this country have had some kind of problem with property insurance in any 12-month period. These problems include canceled policies, refusal to issue or renew insurance, prohibitive rates, and limiting coverage to well below the cash value of insured property.

In inner-city locations or in certain types of businesses, policies, when they are issued, substantially limit the insurer's liability—frequently to the point where the policy is virtually useless as support protection. The Federal Crime Insurance Program requires the participation of individual states and provides for federally funded crime insurance at reasonable rates, based on the size and accepted risk of the insured property.

To qualify for protection under this program, however, a business must establish certain minimum protective devices and procedures. The business must, in short, recognize that it can get the supportive protection that insurance offers, provided it makes at least minimal efforts to protect itself.

The program prescribes locks, safes, alarm systems, and other protective devices and establishes the kind of protection that various types of businesses must provide for themselves to qualify for this insurance. For example, gun stores, wholesale liquor and fur stores, jewelry firms, and drugstores must all have a central station alarm system; service stations must have a local alarm system; and so on. Small loan and finance companies, theaters, and bars—businesses rated as high risk—are also eligible for insurance under the program.

Not only does it provide for insurance coverage of premises otherwise difficult or impossible to insure adequately or reasonably, but it also focuses attention on the very real need for the insured to take positive steps to provide protection of the premises to prevent loss and to use insurance to defray those losses that do occur only when security measures fail. In short, it takes insurance from the front line of crime prevention—where it clearly cannot perform—and puts it into the reserve or backup position where it can.

4.2.5 *3-D Policies*

Comprehensive *dishonesty, destruction, and disappearance (3-D)* coverage is extremely flexible. Policies will vary in coverage and premiums based on the firm's needs. Possible areas covered may include burglary, robbery, employee theft, and counterfeit currency. These policies are designed to provide the widest possible coverage in cases of criminal attack of various kinds. The standard form is set up to offer five different kinds of coverage. The insured has the option of selecting any or all of the insuring agreements offered and of specifying the amount of coverage on each one selected. In addition to the coverage options in the standard form, 12 endorsements are also available to the manager who has a need for any or all of them.

The coverage available on the standard form consists of the following:

1. Employee dishonesty bond
2. Money and securities coverage on the premises

3. Money and securities coverage off the premises
4. Money order and counterfeit paper currency coverage
5. Depositors' forgery coverage

Additional endorsements available:

1. Incoming check forgery
2. Burglary coverage on merchandise
3. Paymaster robbery coverage on and off premises
4. Paymaster robbery coverage on premises only
5. Broad-form payroll on and off premises
6. Broad-form payroll on premises only
7. Burglary and theft coverage on merchandise
8. Forgery of warehouse receipts
9. Securities of lessees of safe deposit box coverage
10. Burglary coverage on office equipment
11. Theft coverage on office equipment
12. Credit card forgery

Obviously, the premium on this coverage will vary according to the number of options selected and the amount of coverage desired for each.

4.2.6 *Insurance Against Loss of Use and Extra Expense Coverage*

Most standard policies do not provide loss of use (the business or some suboperation ceases production, resulting in losses) or extra expense coverage (the business cannot afford to be down and therefore must pay for rental space and the like to continue operations). Since both these matters can represent a very substantial loss to most companies, consideration must be given to expanding the coverage provisions to include one or the other. Both of these losses can be covered either by endorsement or by additional policies that will provide that coverage on a broad basis.

Even a small fire in an office can render it inoperable for a substantial period of time due to smoke and water damage or damaged equipment. Even though all the damage is covered and will be taken care of, the interim period during which revenues may be lost and new facilities are occupied may be as expensive as the fire itself. In this scenario, loss of use or business interruption coverage would be suitable.

Here, too, there are options. A business interruption policy can be drawn up on a comprehensive basis, which means that it will cover a broad base of situations that might create a stoppage. Such a policy must, of course, be examined for types of incidents specifically excluded from coverage. On the other hand, such a contract might be drawn up in which the incidents covered are specified and perhaps limited to just a few potential hazards.

Basic insurance coverage for a specific loss often fails to provide coverage for business interruption costs.

The amount of coverage and the nature of recovery in business interruption contracts can be complicated. If recovery is on an actual loss basis, the insured must present a careful audit of actual demonstrable losses to the insurer in order to collect. If the policy is drawn as a valued loss contract, an accountant must certify the daily amount that would be lost if an interruption were to occur. This amount is entered as part of the contract. The premium and recovery are based on this amount, computed on the specified number of days to be covered for each interruption.

Recent court decisions point out the need to clearly state coverage. After the 2001 terrorist attacks, companies connected to the World Trade Center filed claims on their business interruption insurance polices. Courts found that only those with close and direct causal connections between the firm's loss of business and the attacks would be accepted. For example, a hotel claimed to have lost business as a result of grounded flights. This claim was rejected. On the other hand, a cleaning business that cleaned for firms in the Trade Center made a claim that was accepted.[2]

Extra expense coverage would be called for in a situation where the operation must immediately be transferred to another location and equipment rented until the damaged facility is back in operation. A good example is a newspaper, where the operation must continue in order to retain readership. If the business ceased operation even temporarily, subscribers would look elsewhere for their news.

4.2.7   Kidnap and Ransom Insurance

With the increase in international terrorism and the accompanying increase in kidnapping that went along with it, the demand for insurance covering executives against such incidents also increased. These policies generally cover all costs associated with the recovery of a kidnapped executive or relative, including costs of information and loss of ransom money. Some policies also cover the cost of lawsuits filed against the firm for inadequate protection and insufficient efforts to win release.

Such coverage requires that companies institute certain basic security measures:

1. Executives must maintain secrecy about the existence of coverage.
2. Every effort must be made to contact the police, the FBI, and the insurance company before payment is made.
3. Serial numbers on ransom money must be recorded.
4. A plan of action for dealing with kidnapping must be in place.

4.2.8   Fire Insurance

Though fire insurance is a must for homeowners, these once popular policies for business purposes have been, to a great extent, supplanted by broad coverage policies.

4.2.9   Business Property Insurance

These *special multiperil policies (SMPs)* generally offer coverage against a multitude of losses, including crime, property, liability, and machinery. In simple terms, this type of policy may be likened to homeowner's property insurance.

4.2.10   Liability Insurance

With the growth in the number of lawsuits filed against businesses each year for various negligent acts, the popularity of these insurance policies has grown. Coverage may include employer/employee, customer/employer, contracts, and professional services.

4.2.11   Workers' Compensation Insurance

This basic insurance provides for medical costs, lost wages, and rehabilitation of workers injured on the job. Death benefits are also available. In most states, this coverage is required by law.

4.2.12   Portfolio Commercial Crime Coverage

This form of coverage is replacing some of the individual policies listed previously. The policy is composed of standard modules and allows for up to 14 endorsements:

1. Employee dishonesty
2. Forgery or alteration
3. Theft, disappearance, and destruction
4. Robbery and safe burglary
5. Premises burglary
6. Computer fraud
7. Extortion
8. Premises theft and robbery outside the premises
9. Lessees of safe deposit boxes
10. Securities deposited with others
11. Liability for guests' property—safe deposit box
12. Liability for guests' property—premises
13. Safe depository liability
14. Safe depository direct loss

Portfolio commercial crime policies are effectively replacing many of the individual types of crime insurance.

4.3   Terrorism Risk Insurance Act of 2002

On November 26, 2002, President George W. Bush signed into law the Terrorism Risk Insurance Act of 2002. The Act established a temporary federal program to share with the private sector the burden of commercial property and casualty losses resulting from acts of terrorism. The Act was to sunset (cease to exist) on December 31, 2005, but was extended for two years and was once again set to sunset on December 31, 2007. However, Congress introduced the Terrorism Risk Insurance Revision and Extension Act (TRIREA) of 2007, which again extended the legislation. Specific information regarding this act may be found at *www.treasury.gov/trip*.[3]

The aftermath of 9/11 brought to light new concerns over the costs associated with mass destruction and who would pay for rebuilding.

In the business environment, a vast majority of small businesses are choosing not to purchase additional coverage. The Council of Insurance Agents and Brokers reports that less than 10 percent of the small business clients represented by their surveyed insurance brokers were interested in the expanded coverage. Two reasons for declining the coverage are expense and belief that the business would not be a terrorist target.[4]

The cost varies tremendously by company, ranging from a low of 2 percent of the value of the property being insured to a high of 150 percent. The average cost is 12 percent of the property value.[5]

4.4   How Much Insurance?

Since the options are essentially a choice between recovery of the cash value of the property or recovery of its replacement cost, there can be little hesitation in making a decision. Few experts disagree that insuring to the amount of replacement is clearly the wiser course to follow. When property is insured for its cash value only, there will almost inevitably be a loss to the insured unless property values decline enough to make up for the extra costs involved in replacement. The latter might include demolition of the remaining structure in the event of fire, clearing the site for rebuilding, or the declining value of the dollar. History shows us that property values, or more specifically building costs, rarely decline in this manner. Protection should therefore be arranged on the basis of resuming business as it was before the damage took place. This can normally be done only by insuring for the property's replacement cost.

Cost must be weighed against the risk and its consequences.

Replacement cost coverage is more expensive than cash value coverage because the insurer must set the premium sufficiently high to not only cover the estimated likelihood of a fire, for example, but to also try to anticipate the rate of increase in the cost of labor and materials in the reconstruction of the building in whole or in part.

Even insuring at replacement cost will not, as a rule, cover the full cost involved in a major disaster. Business interruption, extra expenses, site clearance, intervening passage of new and more exacting building codes—all add to the already inflated costs of replacing the existing structure so that business may resume as before as rapidly as possible.

There are many endorsements available to extend coverage to fully compensate for all expenses involved in replacement. They should all be considered in the light of individual needs. Obviously the greater the coverage, the higher the cost of coverage, but this cost must be weighed against the risk and its consequences.

CASE STUDY

The Arc Corporation's main plant is located in a mid-South city of about 50,000. It manufactures electrical and electronic appliances for sale under its own name and under other national store chain trademarks. It also makes components for use in the finished products of other manufacturers. It has a few branch plants in other parts of the country where it makes such items as plastic parts and shipping cartons for its own use from local raw materials.

Billing, accounting, and corporate offices are located in a larger city that offers financial facilities not available in the much smaller main plant city.

This corporation has no separate department to handle security matters. Each plant has a few uniformed guards to provide a minimum of security at night and on weekends and holidays, when the plants are not operating. The main plant has guards at gates used for receiving raw materials and shipping finished products, for vending machines and utility service trucks, and for related uses. It does not place guards at employee gates.

The guards are employees of the corporation. Most are former production employees who were injured on the job or are too infirm to operate machines. The captain of the guard at the main plant is a retired police captain who has had no training other than police training and on-the-job training for security. None of the individual guards has ever had training in the use of the firearms they carry. Guards are started at an hourly rate only slightly higher than the legal minimum wage.

There are no written guard manuals or guard post orders.

1. Does Arc have adequate security against employee dishonesty?

2. What initial action should the company take to establish adequate security?

3. What are the general objectives of a security survey?

4. What are the steps in security surveys?

5. Should a security department be allowed to police itself? State the reasons for your answer.

Summary

The area of risk analysis, as with law, can be complicated. Security managers who assume major responsibility for risk management should consider enrolling in courses directed toward risk management and insurance. To overlook the role of this important area of security is to move forward without a carefully developed plan. Dollars may be spent on security measures that have little impact on the actual protection of company assets while other assets remain vulnerable to destruction, theft, or other vulnerabilities.

Insurance has become part of the overall loss prevention plan supporting proper security planning. Security planning in turn has an impact on the cost associated with insurance. The more comprehensive the security plan, the lower the costs.

□ □ □ ▬▬▬▬▬▬▬▬▬▬▬▬▬▬▬▬▬▬▬▬▬▬▬

Critical Thinking

Why would a security loss prevention manager choose to hire an outside firm to review security operations and make recommendations for changes as well as insurance options rather than conduct the study internally?

▬▬▬▬▬▬▬▬▬▬▬▬▬▬▬▬▬▬▬▬▬▬▬ □ □ □

Review Questions

1. What is the difference between vulnerability to loss and loss probability?
2. What is meant by criticality of loss?

3. If a security countermeasure costs as much as or more than the loss being protected against for a given period, does it follow that the security measure should be discontinued because it is not cost-effective?

4. Why should accounting procedures be a part of a security survey? Why are security files significant in protection planning?

5. List four typical limited loss prevention responses.

6. What are the steps involved in a good risk management program?

7. What is an operational audit?

8. Do you agree with the statement that "Insurance must be thought of as a supportive rather than the principal defense against losses due to crime"? Why or why not?

9. Why is it important for the insured to clearly understand the terms describing criminal activity (for example, burglary or robbery)?

10. In terms of property insurance, define direct loss, loss of use, and extra expense losses.

11. What are the differences between specific and comprehensive property insurance policies? If you were a business executive, which would you prefer if you had to give priority to cost-effectiveness?

12. What were the problems that led to the establishment of the Federal Crime Insurance Program? What are some of the crime prevention measures prescribed by the program?

References

1. Treanor, Christopher, "Déjà Vu All Over Again: A Mid-Year P/C Outlook," *Risk Management,* July 2007.

2. Gosnell, Sean, "Disasters and the Law," *Canadian Insurance* (01/07) vol. 112, no. 1, p. 21.

3. "Interim Guidance Concerning Certain Conditions for Federal Payment, Non-U.S. Insurers, and Scope of Insurance coverage in the Terrorism Risk Insurance Act of 2002," Department of the Treasury, www.treasury.gov.press/releases/reports/interimguidance.htm, downloaded 3/24/2003 (checked for updates, 07/04/2007).

4. "Most Small Businesses Not Buying Terror Insurance," National Federation of Independent Businesses, www.nfib.com/cgi-bin/NFIB.fll/public?Advocacy/newsReleaseDisplay, downloaded 3/29/2003.

5. "Terrorism Insurance Meets Deadline Today," National Federation of Independent Business E-News, www.NFIB.com, downloaded 2/25/2003.

9

The Outer Defenses: Building and Perimeter Protection

OBJECTIVES

The study of this chapter will enable you to:

1. Recognize the basic tools of perimeter security.
2. Discuss the various types of lighting fixtures and systems.
3. Know the specifics involved in designing various types of barrier protection.

1 Introduction

The cause of security can be furthered simply by making it more difficult (or to be more accurate, less easy) for criminals to get into the premises being protected. These premises should then be further protected from criminal attack by denying ready access to interior spaces in the event that a determined intruder surmounts exterior barriers. This must be the first concern in security planning.

This basic concept is being applied to operations such as water treatment plants and electric substations, where in the past security was given barely a thought. Basic security protection is being implemented by these operations as a result of federal guidelines established following the events of 9/11. For additional information on these guidelines, see Chapter 1.

True, every security program must be an integrated whole, and each element must grow out of the specific needs dictated by the circumstances affecting the facility to be protected. But the first and basic defense is still the physical protection of the facility. Planning this defense is neither difficult nor complicated, but it requires meticulous attention to detail.

Whereas the development of computer protection programs and anti-embezzlement systems or even the establishment of shipping and receiving safeguards requires particularized sophistication and expertise, the implementation of an effective program of physical security is the product of common sense and a lot of legwork expended in the inspection of the area.

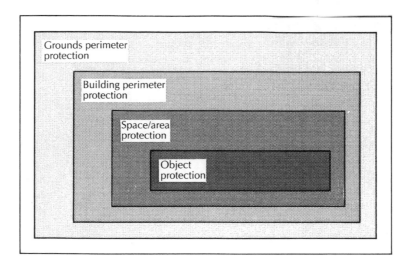

FIGURE 9.1 The four lines of protection. (From Don T. Cherry, Total Facility Control [Boston: Butterworth-Heinemann, 1986], p. 100.)

Physical security concerns itself with those means by which a given facility protects itself against theft, vandalism, sabotage, unauthorized entry, fires, accidents, and natural disasters. In this context, a *facility* is a plant, building, office, institution, or any commercial or industrial structure or complex with all the attendant structures and functions that are part of an integrated operation. An international manufacturing operation, for example, might have many facilities within its total organization.

In this new century, it is clear that old theories and devices may still be functional but they might not be effective enough in a good security program. This is often true with the use of burglar alarms and padlocks. Good systems combine access controls with advanced security technologies such as intrusion detection, video monitoring, smart cards, and biometrics. Integrate these systems within the company computer systems and you have an excellent beginning in a total asset protection program.

Physical security planning includes protection of: (1) the grounds around the building, (2) the building's perimeter, (3) the building's interior, and (4) its contents. Figure 9.1 illustrates these four lines of protection.

2   Barriers, Fences, and Walls

A facility's perimeter will usually be determined by the function and location of the facility itself. An urban office building or retail enterprise will frequently occupy all the real estate where it is located. In such a case, the perimeter may well be the walls of the building itself. Most industrial operations, however, require yard space and warehousing, even in urban areas. In that case, the perimeter is the boundary of the property owned by the company. But in either case, the defense begins at the perimeter—the first line that must be crossed by an intruder.

2.1   Barriers

Natural and structural barriers are the elements by which boundaries are defined and penetration is deterred. Natural barriers comprise the topographical features that assist

Table 9.1 Common Chain-Link Fence Characteristics

Characteristic	Option
Gauge	#9 (3.8 mm), #11 (3.0 mm)
Mesh	2 in. (50 mm), 1.6 in. (40 mm), 2.4 in. (60 mm)
Coating	Vinyl, galvanized
Tension wires	Wire, rail, cable (attached at top or bottom)
Support posts	Metal posts (see Federal Specifications RR-F-191H/GEN and RR-F-191/33)
Height	6 ft. (1.8 meters), 7 ft. (2.1 meters), 8 ft. (2.4 meters)
Fabric tie-downs	Buried, encased in concrete, staked
Pole reinforcement	Buried, encased in concrete
Gate opening	Swing, slide, lift, turnstile

Source: Gary R. Cook, "The Facts on the Fence," *Security Management* (June 1990): 86.

in impeding or denying access to an area. They could be rivers, cliffs, canyons, dense growth, or any other terrain or feature that is difficult to overcome. Structural barriers are permanent or temporary devices such as fences, walls, grilles, doors, roadblocks, screens, or any other construction that will serve as a deterrent to unauthorized entry.

It is important to remember that structural barriers rarely if ever prevent penetration. Fences can be climbed, walls can be scaled, and locked doors and grilled windows can eventually be bypassed through a resolute assault.

The same is generally true of natural barriers. They almost never constitute a positive prevention of intrusion. Ultimately all such barriers must be supported by additional security, and structural barriers of some kind should further strengthen most natural barriers. It is a mistake to suppose that a high, steep cliff, for example, is by itself protection against unauthorized entry.

2.2 Fences

The most common type of structural barrier, familiar to most, is the fence. The most common type of fencing normally used for the protection of a facility is chain link, although barbed wire is useful in certain permanent applications, and concertina barbed wire is occasionally used in temporary or emergency situations. In situations where aesthetics are the driving force, invisible fencing might be used. In this situation the barrier is not physical, but rather it is composed of some type of sensing system.

2.2.1 Chain Link

Chain-link fencing should meet the specifications developed by the U.S. Department of Defense in order to be fully effective. (See Table 9.1 for common characteristics of chain-link fences.) It should be constructed of a 9-gauge or heavier wire with twisted and barbed selvage top and bottom. The fence itself should be at least 6 feet tall and should begin no more than 2 inches from the ground. The bottom of the fence can be stabilized against an intruder crawling under or lifting it by tying it to rigid metal poles or concrete sills. The sills are usually precast with AWF #9 wires for ties. If the soil is sandy or subject to erosion, the bottom edge of the fence should be installed below ground level.

FIGURE 9.2 D.T.R. taut-wire intrusion detection systems, the solution for airport security and high-risk facilities. (Courtesy of Safeguards Technology, Inc.)

The fence should be stretched and fastened to rigid metal posts set in concrete with additional bracing as necessary at corners and gate openings. Mesh openings should be no more than 2 inches square. In addition, the fence should be augmented by a top guard or overhang of three strands of stretched barbed wire angled at 45 degrees away from the protected property (see Figure 9.2). This overhang should extend out and up far enough to increase the height of the fence by at least 1 foot to an overall height of 7 feet or more.

To protect the fence from washouts or channeling under it, culverts or troughs should be provided at natural drainage points. If any of these drainage openings are larger than 96 square inches, they too should be provided with physical barriers that will protect the perimeter without impeding the drainage.

If buildings, trees, hillocks, or other vertical features are within 10 feet of the fence, it should be heightened or protected with a Y-shaped top guard.

Amico (Alabama Metal Industries Corporation) has developed an extension of chain-link technology. The new fence, similar in appearance to traditional chain-link fencing, is actually a solid sheet of steel with holes cut in it. The construction makes this fence a less attractive target for many thieves. The major limitation to this product is cost; it is currently twice as expensive as traditional chain-link fencing.

Another product uses the standard chain-link fence and incorporates monitoring technology, putting the monitoring cables into the fence fabric. The fence is not noticeably different from standard chain-link fencing except for its built-in telemetry.[1]

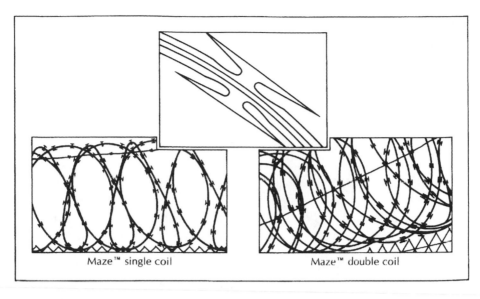

Maze™ single coil   Maze™ double coil

FIGURE 9.3 Concertina wire. (Courtesy of American Security Fence Corporation.)

2.2.2 Barbed Wire

When a fence consists of barbed wire, a 13.5-gauge twisted double strand with 4-point barbs 4 inches apart is generally used. These fences, like chain-link fences, should also be at least 6 feet high and in addition should carry a top guard. Posts should be metal and spaced no more than 6 feet apart. Vertical distance between strands should be no more than 6 inches, preferably less.

2.2.3 Concertina Wire

Concertina wire is a coil of steel wire clipped together at intervals to form a cylinder (see Figure 9.3). When it's opened, it forms a barrier 50 feet long and 24, 30, 36, 40, or 60 inches high. Developed by the military for rapid laying, it can be used in multiple coils. It can be used either with one roll atop another or in a pyramid with two rolls along the bottom and one on the top. Ends should be fastened together, and the base wires should be staked to the ground. Concertina wire is probably the most difficult fence to penetrate, but it is unsightly and is rarely used except in a temporary application. However, in recent years concertina wire has replaced traditional barbed wire as fence "top guards."

With the exception of concertina wire, most fencing is largely a psychological deterrent and a boundary marker rather than a barrier, because in most cases such fences can be rather easily penetrated unless added security measures are taken to enhance the security of the fence. Fences may deter the undetermined, but they will only delay the determined.

2.3 Walls

In some instances, masonry, stone, brick, or block walls can be used to form all or part of the perimeter barrier. Such walls may be constructed for aesthetic reasons to replace the less decorative barriers within that part of the facility.

In areas where masonry walls are used, they should be at least 7 feet high with a top guard of three or four strands of barbed wire, as in the case of chain-link fences.

Since concealment of the inside activity is offset by also cutting off the view of any activity outside the wall, extra efforts must be made to prevent scaling the wall. Ideally, the perimeter line should also be staggered in a way that permits observation of the area in front of the wall from a position or positions inside the perimeter. (Think Great Wall of China.)

2.4   Gates and Other Barrier Breaches

Every opening in the perimeter barrier is a potential security hazard. The more gates there are, the more security personnel or surveillance devices must be deployed to monitor the traffic through them. Obviously, these openings must be kept to a minimum.

During shift changes, more gates might be open and in use than at other times of the day when the smallest practical number of such gates are in operation. Certainly there must be enough gates in use at any time to facilitate the efficient movement of necessary traffic. The number can be determined only by a careful analysis of needs at various times of day, but every effort must be made to reduce the number of operating gates to the minimum consistent with safety and efficiency.

If some gates are not necessary to the operation of the facility or if changing traffic patterns can eliminate them, the openings should be sealed off and retired from use. Barriers can also include walk-in entrances where vehicle access must be restricted (see Figure 9.4).

2.4.1   Padlocking

Gates used only at peak periods or emergency gates should be padlocked and secured. If it is possible, the lock used should be distinctive and immediately identifiable. It is common for thieves to cut off the plant padlock and substitute their own padlock so they can work at collecting their loot without an alarm being given by a passing patrol that

FIGURE 9.4 Raised stainless steel bollards protect access to the U.S. Department of State headquarters. (Courtesy of Delta Scientific, Inc.)

has spotted an otherwise missing lock. A lock of distinctive color or design could compromise this ploy.

It is important that all locked gates be checked frequently. This is especially important where, as is usually the case, these gates are out of the current traffic pattern and are remote from the general activity of the facility.

2.4.2   Personnel and Vehicle Gates

Personnel gates are usually from 4 to 7 feet wide to permit single-line entry or exit. It is important that they not be so wide that control of personnel is lost. Vehicular gates, on the other hand, must be wide enough to handle the type of traffic typical of the facility. They may handle two-way traffic, or if the need for control is particularly pressing, they may be limited to one-way traffic at any given time.

A drop or railroad crossing type of barrier is normally used to cut off traffic in either direction when the need arises. The gate itself might be single or double swing, rolling or overhead. It could be a manual or an electrical operation. Railroad gates should be secured in the same manner as other gates on the perimeter except during those times when cars are being driven through it. At these times, the operation should be under inspection by a security guard.

Another effective vehicle control device is the spiked security track that allows for one-way traffic but is designed to puncture tires of vehicles traveling into the facility unless retracted by security personnel.

2.5   Miscellaneous Openings

Virtually every facility has a number of miscellaneous openings that penetrate the perimeter. All too frequently these are overlooked in security planning, but they must be taken into account because they are often the most effective ways of gaining entrance to the facility without being observed.

These openings or barrier breaches consist of sewers, culverts, drainpipes, utility tunnels, exhaust conduits, air intake pipes, manhole covers, coal chutes, and sidewalk elevators. All must be accounted for in the security plan.

Bars, grillwork, barbed wire, or doors with adequate locking must protect any one of these openings that has a cross-section area of 96 square inches or more. Sidewalk elevators and manhole covers must be secured from below to prevent their unauthorized use. Storm sewers must be fitted with deterrents that can be removed for inspection of the sewer after a rain.

2.6   Barrier Protection

For the barrier to be most effective in preventing intrusion, it must be patrolled and inspected regularly. Any fence or wall can be scaled, and unless these barriers are kept under observation, they will neutralize the security effectiveness of the structure.

2.6.1   Clear Zone

A clear zone should be maintained on both sides of the barrier to make any approach to the barrier from the outside or any movement from the barrier to areas inside the perimeter immediately visible. Anything outside the barrier, such as refuse piles, weed patches, heavy undergrowth, or anything else that might conceal someone's approach, should be eliminated. Inside the perimeter, everything should be cleared away from the barrier to create as wide a clear zone as possible.

Unfortunately, it is frequently impossible to achieve an uninterrupted clear zone. Most perimeter barriers are indeed on the perimeter of the property line, which means that there is no opportunity to control the area outside the barrier. The size of the facility and the amount of space needed for its operation will determine how space can be given up to the creation of a clear zone inside the barrier. It is important, however, to create some kind of clear zone, however small it might be.

In situations where the clear zone is necessarily so small as to endanger the barrier's effectiveness, thought should be given to increasing the barrier height in critical areas or to installing an intrusion detection device to give due and timely warning of an intrusion to an alert guard force.

2.6.2   Inspection

Once the perimeter defense and the clear zones have been established to the maximum that is possible and practical, it is essential that a regular inspection routine be set up. Gates should be examined carefully to determine whether locks or hinges have been tampered with; fence lines should be observed for any signs of forced entry or tunneling; walls should be checked for marks that might indicate they have been scaled or that such an attempt has been made; top guards must be examined for their effectiveness; miscellaneous service penetrations must be examined for any signs of attack; brush and weeds must be cleared away; erosion areas must be filled in; and any potential scaling devices such as ladders, ropes, oil drums, or stacks of pallets must be cleared out of the area. Any condition that could even in the smallest degree compromise the perimeter's integrity must be both reported and corrected. Such an inspection should be undertaken no less than weekly and possibly more often if conditions so indicate.

2.6.3   Hydraulic Defenses

Hydraulic defenses (barricades) are used to protect gates. These devices are designed to deploy in 1 to 3 seconds and can stop a 15,000-pound vehicle moving at 50 mph. In most cases the devices are installed in the roadway, where they are unobtrusive except for the outline of the top of the barrier, which is level with the surface into which it is installed.

2.6.4   Fence Protection Devices

Over the past decades, various devices have been designed to protect the integrity of fences. The earliest systems used electrification. Since those early days, the introduction of sensors to alert security staff of the presence of intruders has supplemented the use of fencing and in some cases replaced it. The most commonly used external intruder detection sensors are described here.

2.6.4.1   Fluid pressure   In this system, a fluid-pressure sensor (a small diameter tube sealed at one end and filled with fluid) is placed in the barrier. If a load is applied to the barrier, the tubes compress, placing force on the monitored fluid. This is useful for detecting people crossing open ground and is commonly used in military installations and tank farms.

2.6.4.2   Electromagnetic cable   This sensing device (see Figure 9.5) operates on the principle of electromagnetic capacitance. In simple terms, the cable creates an electromagnetic

FIGURE 9.5 A sensing device. (Courtesy of Southwest Microwave, Inc.)

field that is constant in output. If the field is interrupted by cutting or pressure on the cable, it can be sensed and reported. The cable is normally mounted on inner chain-link or mesh fences.

2.6.4.3   Fiber Optic Cable   A beam of pulsed light is transmitted through the cable, and this is sensed at the other end. If the cable is cut or interfered with, the pulsing stops and there are changes in amplitude. The application of the cable is similar to the electromagnetic cable. Some manufacturers of high-security fences, however, have incorporated the fiber optic cable into the hollow strand of their normal fence material, making it impossible to detect.

Fiber optic cable is finding many uses as a sensor. The sensing cable may be attached to a fence, buried alongside a pipeline, or used in conjunction with power or communications lines. The use of fiber optic cable allows monitoring of miles of fence, pipe, or transmission lines with no electronics or power in the field.

2.6.4.4   Capacitive Field Effect   A capacitive field effect sensor (see Figure 9.6) operates on the same principles as electromagnetic systems but uses electrical rather than magnetic fields. These systems are extremely sensitive and can be affected by snow and ice. Weeds and paper debris contacting the sensor wire will also trigger false alarms.

2.6.4.5   Active Infrared System (AIRS)   More will be said later about this system, but the basic premise behind it is a beam of infrared light sent to a sensor. If the beam is interrupted, the alarm sounds.

2.6.4.6   External Microwave   Used internally or externally, this system relies on sending microwaves and on the Doppler effect. When the sensor receives an unfamiliar return of waves, an alarm condition is noted. Most external systems, however, rely on the transmission of a microwave beam to a receiver. If the beam is interrupted or changed, an alarm sounds. More will be said about microwave sensors used internally in Chapter 11.

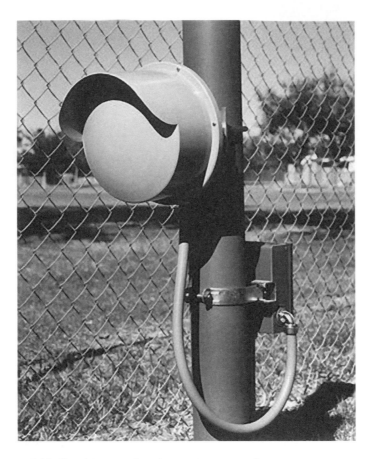

FIGURE 9.6 Capacitive field effect. (Courtesy of Southwest Microwave, Inc.)

2.6.4.7 Taut Wire This sensor, which is placed on the wires of a fence, relies on a pendulum that is in the off position until tension on the taut wire forces the pendulum to swing into the on position, tripping the alarm.[2]

3 Inside the Perimeter

Unroofed or outside areas within the perimeter must be considered a second line of defense because these areas can usually be observed from the outside so that targets can be selected before an assault is made.

In an area where materials and equipment are stored in a helter-skelter manner, it is difficult for guards to determine whether anything has been disturbed in any way. On the other hand, guards can readily observe neat, uniform, and symmetrical storage and detect any disarray at a glance.

Discarded machinery, scrap lumber, and junk of all kinds haphazardly thrown about an area create safety hazards as well as providing cover for any intruder. Such conditions must never be permitted to develop. Efficient housekeeping is a basic security practice.

3.1 Parking

Parking privately owned vehicles within the perimeter barrier should never be allowed. There should be no exceptions to this rule. Facilities that cannot or will not establish parking lots outside the perimeter barrier are almost invariably plagued by a high incidence of pilferage due to the ease with which employees can conceal goods in their cars at any point during the day. In addition, given today's heightened security concerns over terrorism, allowing cars that might be traveling bombs into the perimeter can be fatal.

In cases where the perimeter barrier encompasses the employee and visitor parking areas, additional fencing should be constructed to create new barriers that exclude the parking areas. Appropriate guarded pedestrian gates must, of course, be installed to accommodate the movement of employees to and from their cars.

The parking lot itself should be fenced and patrolled to protect against car thieves and vandals. Few things are more damaging to morale than the insecurity that an unprotected parking area in a crime-ridden neighborhood can create. According to Liability Consultants, Inc., the greatest number of negligent security lawsuits filed between 1992 and 2002 were the result of poor parking lot security.[3]

Company cars and trucks—especially loaded or partially loaded vehicles—should be parked within the perimeter for added security. This inside parking area should be well lighted and regularly patrolled or kept under constant surveillance.

Loaded or partially loaded trucks and trailers should be sealed or padlocked and should be parked close enough together and close enough to a building wall (or even back to back) that neither their side doors nor rear doors can be opened without actually moving the vehicles.

3.2   Surveillance

The entire outside area within the security barrier must be kept under surveillance at all times, particularly at night. Because goods stored in this area are particularly vulnerable to theft or pilferage, this is the area most likely to attract a thief's first attention. With planning and study in cooperation with production personnel, it will undoubtedly be possible to lay out this yard area so that there are long, uninterrupted sight lines that permit inspection of the entire area with a minimum of movement. (Surveillance is discussed in detail in Chapter 10.)

4   Lighting

Depending on the nature of the facility, protective lighting will be designed either to emphasize the illumination of the perimeter barrier and the outside approaches to it or to concentrate on the area and the buildings within the perimeter. In either case, it must produce sufficient light to create a psychological deterrent to intrusion in addition to making detection virtually certain in the event an entry is made. The *Code of Federal Regulations*[4] lists a specific requirement of 0.2 foot-candles (fc) for lighting protected areas within a perimeter. The National Parking Association recommends illumination of 6 fc at 30 inches above the parking floor in covered parking facilities. Open parking areas can get by with 2 fc, according to the Illinois Engineers Society North America (IESNA).[5] A foot-candle is a unit for measuring the intensity of illumination equal to 1 lumen per square foot—that is, the amount of light a single candle provides over 1 square foot (see Figure 9.7).

While light must provide a specified level of illumination, creating glare to deter intruders, it must also avoid casting annoying or dangerous light into neighboring areas. This is particularly important where the facility abuts streets, highways, or navigable waterways.

FIGURE 9.7 Foot-candle. (From Richard Gigliotti and Ronald Jason, *Security Design for Maximum Protection* [Boston: Butterworth-Heinemann, 1984].)

The system must be reliable and designed with overlapping illumination to avoid creating unprotected areas in the event of individual light failures. It must be easy to maintain and service, and it must be secured against attack. Poles should be within the barrier, power lines should be buried, and the switch box or boxes should be secure.

There should be a backup power supply in the event of power failure. Supplementary lighting, including searchlights and portable lights, should also be a part of the system. These lights are provided for special or emergency situations, and although they should not be used with any regularity, they must be available to the security force.

The system could be operated automatically by a photoelectric cell that responds to the amount of light to which it is subjected. Such an arrangement allows for lights to be turned on at dusk and extinguished at daylight. This can be set up to activate individual lamps or to turn on the entire system at once.

Other controls are timed, which simply means that lights are switched on and off by a clock. Such a system must be adjusted regularly to coincide with the changing hours of sunset and sunrise. The lights may also be operated manually.

4.1   Types of Lighting

Lamps used in protective lighting are either incandescent, fluorescent, metal halide, mercury vapor, quartz, or high- or low-pressure sodium. Each type has special characteristics suitable for specific assignments. Each lamp type offers differing effects on natural colors. The effect of the light on the color appearance of objects is measured by the *color-rendering index (CRI)*. Light with a low CRI makes colors appear less normal. The higher the CRI, the more the object appears normal. Sodium light has a low CRI, whereas metal halide has a high CRI.[6]

4.1.1   Incandescent

Incandescent bulbs are common light bulbs of the type found in homes. They have the advantage of providing instant illumination when the switch is thrown and are thus the most commonly used in protective lighting systems. Some incandescents are manufactured with interior coatings that reflect the light and with a built-in lens to focus or diffuse the light. Regular high-wattage incandescents can be enclosed in a fixture that will give much the same result.

4.1.2   Fluorescent

Fluorescents are generally of a mercury vapor type and are highly efficient, giving off approximately 62 lumens per watt. Most fluorescent lamps are temperature sensitive and thus have limited value for outdoor use in colder climates. In addition, the common flickering effect created by these lamps can have a disorienting effect on both security personnel and intruders. In addition, fluorescent lamps often interfere with radio reception.

4.1.3   Mercury Vapor Lamps

These common security lamps give out a strong light with a bluish cast. They are more efficient than incandescents because of a considerably longer lamp life. In general, these lamps can tolerate power dips of up to 50 percent. Lighting time, however, is considerable.

4.1.4   Metal Halide

These lamps are also very tolerant of power dips. As with mercury vapor lamps, the start-up time is long. A power outage of only 1/20th of a second is enough to knock this lamp offline.

4.1.5   Sodium Vapor Lights

Sodium lamps give out a soft yellow light and are even more efficient than mercury vapor lamps. They are widely used in areas where fog is a frequent problem, because yellow penetrates the mist more readily than does white light. They are frequently found on highways and bridges.[7]

4.1.6   Quartz Lamps

These lamps emit a very bright white light and snap on almost as rapidly as incandescent bulbs. They are frequently used at very high wattage—1,500 to 2,000 watts is not uncommon in protective systems—and they are excellent for use along the perimeter barrier and in troublesome areas (see Table 9.2).

4.1.7   Light-Emitting Diodes (Led)

LEDs are very small and are used predominantly on message signs. LEDs provide a sharper image than their incandescent predecessors. They do not have to be replaced as often but are more expensive. LED technology has advanced greatly in the past few years and now is being used in larger installations.

4.1.8   Electroluminescent

These lights are similar to their fluorescent cousins. However, they do not contain mercury and are more compact.[8]

4.2   Types of Equipment

No one type of lighting is applicable to every need in a protective lighting system, although manufacturers are continually working to develop just such a fixture.

Amid the great profusion of equipment on the market, four basic types are in general use in security applications: floodlights, searchlights, fresnel lenses, and streetlights (see Figure 9.8). (The first three of these might in the strictest sense be considered a single type because they are all basically reflection units in which a parabolic mirror directs the light in various ways. We will, however, deal with them separately.)

Table 9.2 Types of Luminaire Lamps Found in a Maximum-Security Environment

Lamp type	Mean Lumens per Watt	Start	Restrike	Nominal life of Lamp (hrs.)	Percent Lumen Maintenance at Rated Life	Color Discrimination
Incandescent	4 (21) 22*	Instant	Instant	750–1,000	85–90	Excellent
Fluorescent	35 (62) 100	Rapid	Rapid/ Instant[†]	7,500–10,000	70–90	Excellent
Metal halide	68 (80) 100	3–5 min.	10–20 min.	10,000–15,000	65–75	Excellent
Mercury vapor	20 (48) 63	3–7 min.	3–6 min.	16,000–24,000	50–75	Good
Sodium	92 (127) 140	4–7 min.	Instant[‡]	16,000–24,000	75–85	Fair
Xenon ARC	—	Rapid/ Instant	Instant	1,500	—	Excellent

Source: Richard Gigliotti and Ronald Jason, *Security Design for Maximum Protection* (Boston: Butterworth-Heinemann, 1984), p. 138.
*4 (21) 22:4=minimum mean; (21)=nominal rating for most protective lighting applications; 22=maximum mean.
[†]Low-temperature ballast must be considered.
[‡]Instant for most lamps if less than 1 minute of power interruption but a reduced lumen output.
—Used for searchlights only.

Streetlights are pendant lighting units that are built as either symmetrical or asymmetrical. The symmetrical units distribute light evenly. These units are used where a large area is to be lighted without the need for highlighting particular spots. They are normally centrally located in the area to be illuminated.

Asymmetrical units direct the light by reflection in the direction where light is required. They are used in situations where the lamp must be placed some distance from the target area. Because these are not highly focused units, they do not create a glare problem.

Streetlights are rated by wattage or even more frequently by lumens and in protective lighting applications may vary from 4,000 to 10,000 lumens, depending on their use.

4.2.1   Floodlights

Floodlights are fabricated to form a beam so that light can be concentrated and directed to specific areas. They can create considerable glare.

Although many floodlights specify beam width in degrees, they are generally referred to as wide, medium, or narrow, and the lamp is described in wattage. Lamps run from 300 to 1,000 watts in most protective applications. But there is a wide latitude in this, and the choice of one will depend on a study of its mission.

4.2.2   Fresnel Lenses

Fresnel lenses are wide-beam units, primarily used to extend the illumination in long, horizontal strips to protect the approaches to the perimeter barrier. Unlike floodlights and searchlights, which project a focused round beam, fresnel lenses project a narrow, horizontal beam that is approximately 180° in the horizontal plane and from 18° to 30° in the vertical plane.

These units are especially good for creating a glare for the intruder while the facility remains in comparative darkness. They are normally equipped with a 300- to 500-watt lamp.

Luminaire		Photometric designation	Typical distribution characteristics
Streetlight		Medium wide asymmetric	70° to 75°
Fresnel lens		Asymmetric, glare protection	
Searchlight	Pilot house control / Trunion	Extremely narrow beam	Less than 10°
Floodlight		Medium to wide beam	29° to less than 46°

FIGURE 9.8 Typical equipment for protective lighting.

4.2.3 Searchlights

Searchlights are highly focused incandescent lamps that are used to pinpoint potential trouble spots. They can be directed to any location inside or outside the property, and although they can be automated, they are normally controlled manually.

They are rated according to wattage, which may range from 250 to 3,000 watts, and to the diameter of the reflector, which can range from 6 inches to 2 feet (the average is around 18 inches). The beam width is from 3° to 10°, although this may vary in adjustable or focusing models.

4.2.4 Maintenance

As with every other element of a security system, electrical circuits and fixtures must be inspected regularly to replace worn parts, verify connections, repair worn insulation, check for corrosion in weatherproof fixtures, and clean reflecting surfaces and lenses. Lamps should be logged as to their operational hours and replaced at between 80 and 90 percent of their rated life.

4.2.5 Perimeter Lighting

Every effort should be made to locate lighting units far enough inside the fence and high enough to illuminate areas both inside and outside the boundary. The farther outside the boundary the lighted areas extend, the more readily guards will be able to detect the approach of an intruder.

Light should be directed down and away from the protected area. The location of light units should be such that they avoid throwing a glare into the eyes of the guard, do not create shadow areas, and create instead a glare problem for anyone approaching the boundary.

Fixtures used in barrier and approach lighting should be located inside the barrier. As a rule of thumb, they should be around 30 feet within the perimeter, spaced 150 feet apart, and about 30 feet high. These figures are, of course, approximations and will not apply to every installation. Local conditions will always dictate placement.

Floodlights or fresnel lenses are indicated in illuminating isolated or semi-isolated fence boundaries where some glare is called for. In either case, it is important to light from 20 feet inside the fence to as far into the approach as is practical. In the case of the isolated fence, this could be as much as 250 feet. Semi-isolated and nonisolated fence lines cannot be lighted as far into the approach because such lighting is restricted by streets, highways, and other occupancies. Because glare cannot be employed in illuminating a nonisolated fence line, streetlights are recommended.

Where a facility building is near the perimeter or is itself part of the perimeter, lights can be mounted directly on it. Doorways of such buildings should be individually lighted to eliminate shadows cast by other illumination.

In areas where the property line is on a body of water, lighting should be designed to eliminate shaded areas on or near the water or along the shoreline. This is especially true for piers and docks, where both land and water approaches must be either lighted or capable of being lighted on demand. Before finalizing any plans for protective lighting in the vicinity of navigable waters, however, you must consult the U.S. Coast Guard.

4.3   Gates and Thoroughfares

It is important that the lighting at all gates and along all interior thoroughfares be sufficient for the operation of the facility.

Because both pedestrian and vehicular gates are normally staffed by guards inspecting credentials as well as checking for contraband or stolen property, it is critical that the areas be lighted to at least 2 foot-candles. Pedestrian gates should be lighted to about 25 feet on either side of the gate, if possible, and the range for vehicular gates should be twice that distance. Street lighting is recommended in these applications, but floodlights can also be used if glare is strictly controlled.

Thoroughfares used for pedestrians, vehicles, or forklifts should be lighted to 0.10 fc for security purposes. Much more light may be required for operational efficiency, but this level should be maintained as a minimum, no matter what the conditions of traffic.

4.4   Other Areas

Open or unroofed areas within the perimeter, but not directly connected to it, require an overall intensity of illumination of about 0.05 fc (up to 0.10 fc in areas of higher sensitivity). These areas, when they are nonoperational, are usually used for material storage or for parking. According to many experts, particularly vulnerable installations in the area should not be lighted at all, but the approaches to them should be well lighted for at least 20 feet to aid in the observation of any movement.

Searchlights may be indicated in some facilities, especially in remote mountainous areas or in waterfront locations where small boats could readily approach the facility.

4.5   General

A well-thought-out plan of lighting along the security barrier and the approaches to it; an adequate overall level of light in storage, parking, and other nonoperational areas within the perimeter; and reasonable lighting along all thoroughfares are essential to any basic security program. The lighting required in operational areas will usually be much higher than the minimums required for security and will, therefore, serve a security purpose as well.

New lighting systems have proven effective in deterring crime. In San Diego, California, the installation of new security lighting in Spring Valley Park paid for the $17,250 investment in just six months by reducing burglaries at the community center that added up to a savings of more than $25,000. Other communities reported similar results with sodium systems: In Swampscott, Massachusetts, the Clark School (K-6) replaced its old incandescent security system with a low-pressure sodium system in hopes of reducing vandalism. The cost of the old system ran only $625 per year. The new system cost $1,725 to install. It paid for itself in just a little over a year, however, by saving the school $1,400 annually in vandalism-related costs.[9]

Can better lighting be sold to security management on the basis of cost-effectiveness? The preceding examples are indications of just how effective better lighting can be. In addition, high-pressure sodium lighting uses about 50 percent less energy to produce the same light as older incandescent streetlights. Sodium systems have a lumens-per-watt efficiency five or six times that of incandescent lighting and produce 106 percent more light than the most common mercury streetlights but use about 14 percent less electricity. Table 9.3 compares wattage ranges, lumens, and rated life for six basic lamp families.

Table 9.3 Six Basic Lamp Families

Type of Lamp	Wattage Range	Initial Lumens[†] per Watt Including Ballast Losses	Average Rated Life (Hours)
Sodium	35–1,000	15–130	7,500 24,000*
Metal halide	70–2,000	69–115	5,000–20,000
Mercury vapor			
Standard	40–1,000	24–60	12,000–24,000*
Self-ballasted	160–1,250	14–25	12,000–20,000
Fluorescent	4–215	14–95	6,000–20,000*
Incandescent	15–1,500	8–24	750–3,500

Source: John P. Bachner, "The Myths and Realities Behind Security Lighting," *Security Management* (August 1990): 109.

*Data are based on the more commonly used lamps and are provided for comparison purposes only. Actual results to be derived depend on factors unique to the specific products and installation involved. Consult manufacturers for guidance.

[†]Lumens (of light output) per watt (of power input) is a common measure of lamp efficiency. Initial lumens-per-watt data are based on the light output of lamps when new. The light output of most lamps declines with use. The actual efficiency to be derived from a lamp depends on factors unique to an installation. The actual efficiency of a lighting system depends on far more than the efficiency of lamps or lamps/ballasts alone. More than efficiency should be considered when evaluating a lighting system.

5 Planning Security

No business exists without a security problem of some kind, and no building housing a business is without security risk. Yet few such buildings are ever designed with any thought given to the steps that must eventually be taken to protect them from criminal assault.

A building must be many things in order to satisfy its occupant. It must be functional and efficient, achieve certain aesthetic standards, be properly located and accessible to the markets served by the occupant, and provide security from interference, interruption, and attack. Most of these elements are provided by the architect, but all too frequently the important element of security is overlooked.

> Good security requires thought and planning to achieve a carefully integrated system. Most security problems arise simply because no one has thought about them.

This is especially true where a company building is concerned. Because few architects have any training or knowledge in security matters, they design buildings that assist burglars or vandals by doing nothing to deter them. Because the architects' clients seldom consider security in the planning stages, buildings are erected that provide needless opportunities for crime.

Summary

Physical security devices are the most commonly thought of security measures. The discussion in this chapter covered security measures that are as old as medieval security concepts as well as new technologies that have improved these basic concepts. Clear zones, moats, and fences still exist but are now augmented with state-of-the-art sensors and computerized monitoring stations. The next two chapters focus on specific basic security measures that protect the interior as well as the exterior of facilities.

These basic tools are the fundamentals about which all security professionals should have at least conversational knowledge.

CASE STUDY

You are the security director for IBID International, a large manufacturer. You have assigned one of your staff to conduct a security survey of the company's exterior grounds. You have received the report and now must approve or disapprove each recommendation. Your approved recommendations will be presented to senior management for final approval and funding.

Critical Considerations

1. Senior management requires all expenditures over $10,000 to go to the capital expenditure committee (a six-month process).
2. Senior management is concerned about your large headcount.
3. Your personal bias is for security operations to be "low profile."
4. Your plant is in a low threat environment.
5. If approved, expensive items can be costed out over six years, according to company policy.

Physical Survey Report

1. There are no perimeter lights around company property. The city provides street-lights, causing deep shadows along the perimeter.
   Recommendation: Initiate a major perimeter lighting program involving place-ment of mercury vapor lights in such a manner as to effectively illuminate the property perimeter. *Cost:* $45,000
   APPROVE   DISAPPROVE

2. The property currently lacks any perimeter fence.
   Recommendation: Install 7-foot-high steel chain-link fencing topped with triple-strand barbed wire. This will prevent access to all but authorized personnel, visit-ors, etc. *Cost:* $800,000
   APPROVE   DISAPPROVE

3. At present employees and visitors park in three separate unguarded, unlighted, and open parking lots.
   Recommendations: To ensure protection of visitors and personnel and their vehicles, the following recommendations are made:
   - Establish regular security patrols of parking lots. *Cost:* $0 (change in patrol patterns)
   APPROVE   DISAPPROVE
   - Light parking lots to a level where vehicles can be clearly observed 24 hours a day. *Cost:* $15,000
   APPROVE   DISAPPROVE
   - Use closed-circuit cameras to monitor parking areas. *Cost:* $7,000
   APPROVE   DISAPPROVE
   - Place an emergency phone in each parking lot. *Cost:* $400
   APPROVE   DISAPPROVE
   - Establish a vehicle sticker program to aid in identifying authorized vehicles. *Cost:* $1,200
   APPROVE   DISAPPROVE
   - Combine all parking areas into one large lot for better overall protection. *Cost:* $125,000
   APPROVE   DISAPPROVE
   - Fence in the two existing parking areas for employees using electronic gates operated by an electronic pass system. *Cost:* $62,000
   APPROVE   DISAPPROVE
   - Purchase a scooter-type vehicle for parking lot patrols. *Cost:* $3,650
   APPROVE   DISAPPROVE

4. There is no access control at any of the four points of vehicle entry and exit.
   Recommendations: Establish all weather entry control points staffed 24 hours a day to control access on and off the plant property.
   - Five all-weather guard huts @ $10,000 each. *Cost:* $50,000
   APPROVE   DISAPPROVE
   - Sixteen new positions to staff all entry points. *Cost:* $200,000
   APPROVE   DISAPPROVE
   Narrative: You need to succinctly, clearly, and logically explain the rationale for each decision. The narrative should strive to briefly present each problem and the reasons the suggestions are being approved or disapproved.

Review Questions

1. What four lines of protection should be included in physical security planning?
2. How can the various openings in a perimeter be effectively protected and secured?
3. Why should parking not be allowed inside the controlled perimeter?
4. Discuss the different security applications for the various types of lighting equipment.
5. What considerations must be taken into account when installing a security lighting system?

References

1. "Security and the Chain Link Fence," *Security* (December 1996): 91.
2. Cumming, Neil, *Security: The Comprehensive Guide to Equipment Selection and Installation* (London: Architectural Press, 1987), pp. 70–109.
3. Anderson, Teresa, "Laying Down the Law: A Review of Trends in Liability Lawsuits," *Security Management* (October 2002): 43–51.
4. *Code of Federal Regulations Title 10* (Washington, D.C.: Government Printing Office, 1981).
5. Kangas, Scott, "Lighting the Way to Better Business," *Security Management* (September 1996): 83.
6. Ibid., p. 85.
7. Ibid., p. 84.
8. Ibid., pp. 85–86.
9. Bachner, John P., "The Myths and Realities Behind Security Lighting," *Security Management* (August 1990): 109–110.

10

Interior and Exterior Security Concerns

OBJECTIVES

The study of this chapter will enable you to:

1. Recognize the role of doors and windows as security risks.
2. Identify various types of locks and associated hardware.
3. Gain a basic understanding of surveillance equipment and its proper use in security operations.
4. Understand the significance of having security involved in building design and remodeling.

1 Introduction

Besides the clear-cut concerns for the perimeter and exterior security, other security vulnerabilities for the facility might be either part of the perimeter, part of the interior, or both. This chapter deals with security concerns that could be either interior or exterior problems, depending on the type of facility. For example, a freestanding retail outlet store has problems of perimeter security that include windows, doors, and roof. The same store located within the confines of a mall might not be as concerned with the windows and doors or with perimeter defense that must be overcome before the attacker can concentrate on the store, because the mall is a buffer.

2 Buildings On or As the Perimeter

When the building forms part of the perimeter barrier or when, as in some urban situations, the building walls are the entire perimeter of the facility, it should be viewed in the same light as the rest of the barrier or it should be evaluated in the same way as the outer structural barrier. It must be evaluated in terms of its strength, and all openings must be properly secured.

In cases of a fence joining the building as a continuation of the perimeter, there should be no more than 2 inches between the fence and the building. Depending on the placement of windows, ledges, or setbacks, it might be wise to double the fence height gradually to the point where it joins the building. In such a case, the higher section of the fence should extend 6 to 8 feet out from the building.

2.1 Windows and Doors

Windows and other openings larger than 96 square inches should be protected by grilles, metal bars, or heavy screening when they are less than 18 feet from the ground or when they are less than 14 feet from structures outside the barrier (that is, trees and other buildings). Doors that penetrate the perimeter walls must be of heavy construction and fitted with strong locks.

Since both the law and good sense require that there be adequate emergency exits in the event of fire or other danger, provision must be made for such eventualities. Doors created for emergency purposes only should have exterior hardware removed so that they cannot be opened from the outside. A remotely operated electromagnetic holding device can secure them, or they can be fitted with alarms so that their use from inside will be substantially reduced or eliminated.

2.1.1 Windows

It is axiomatic that windows should be protected. Since the ease with which most windows can be entered makes them ready targets for intruders, they must be viewed as potential weak spots in any building's defenses. Most forced break-ins are through window glass—whether such glass is installed in doors or windows.

In most industrial facilities, windows should be protected with grillework, heavy screening, or chain-link fencing. In some cases, however, caution dictates that windows may be needed as emergency exits beyond strict requirements of fire laws. Or, where they might be needed to lead in fire hoses, consideration should be given to hinging and padlocking protective coverings for easy removal.

2.1.1.1 **Burglary-Resistant Glass**   In applications such as prominent administration and office buildings, where architectural considerations preclude the use of such relatively clumsy installations as mesh or industrial screen, the windows can be immeasurably strengthened by the use of either UL-listed (which means that the material or item so designated has met the standards of Underwriters Laboratories, or UL) burglary-resistant glass or one of the brands of UL-listed polycarbonate glazing material. Both of these products are considerably more expensive than plate glass and are generally used only in areas where attack can be expected or where a reduction in insurance premium would justify the added expense (see Figure 10.1).

Standard plate glass can be given some measure of resistance if it is covered with a 4- to 6-millimeter cover of Mylar. This is a low-cost operation, but the Mylar needs to be replaced every five years. As little as a 2-millimeter cover of Mylar can keep glass from fragmenting. Thus the Mylar cover is good protection from flying shards associated with bombings. Since the first bombing of the World Trade Center and the bombing of the Murrah Federal Building in Oklahoma City, various studies have supported the need to mandate some type of coating for windows in buildings that might be targeted in terrorists attacks.

As opposed to tempered glass, which is designed to protect people from the danger of flying shards in the event of breakage, UL-listed burglary-resistant glass (frequently referred to as *safety glass*) resists heat, flame, cold, picks, rocks, and most other

FIGURE 10.1 Shatter-resistant film. (Courtesy of the www.ShatterGARD.com Glass Protection Experts.)

paraphernalia from the intruder's arsenal. It is a useful security glazing material because it is durable, weathers well, and is noncombustible. On the other hand, it is heavy, difficult to install, and expensive.

The plastic glazing sold under various trade names is optically clear, thin, and easy to install. Acrylic glazing material that appears as Plexiglas generally does not meet UL standards for burglar-resistant material; it is much stronger than ordinary glass, however, and has many useful applications in window security applications. It is also lighter in weight and cheaper than either safety glass or plastic glazing and, at 1¼-inches thick, is UL approved as a bullet-resistant barrier.

All these materials have the appearance of ordinary glass. Obviously, any window so hardened against entry must be securely locked from the inside to protect against intrusion from the outside. This implies a strong window frame and supporting construction.

2.1.1.2 "Smash and Grab" Attacks   Burglary-resistant glass is used to a considerable degree in banks and retail stores where there has been a very real need to prevent "smash and grab" raids on window displays and showcases.

It should be noted that UL-listed burglary-resistant glass is a laminate of two sheets of flat glass (usually ³⁄₁₆-inch thick) held together by a ¹⁄₁₆-inch layer of polyvinyl butyl, a soft, transparent material. In this thickness, laminated glass is virtually indistinguishable from ordinary glass; hence burglars may try with a hammer or iron bar to break what they suppose to be a plate-glass window. It is only after they have made a few unsuccessful tries that they realize the material is not penetrable.

Even though such attackers may flee empty-handed, the owners in such situations are left with windows with webs of cracks over the surface of the outer layer of glass, making replacement of the entire pane necessary in applications where appearance is important. Insurers in many cases require that laminated glass be clearly identified to discourage what would be a futile but damaging assault by the "smash and grab" attacker.

2.1.1.3 **Screening** It can also be important to screen windows. First, this might protect their use as a means by which employees can temporarily dispose of goods for later recovery. The smaller the goods being manufactured or available on the premises, the smaller the mesh in the screen must be to protect against this kind of pilferage.

Second, as was noted earlier, any windows less than 18 feet from the ground or less than 14 feet from trees, poles, or adjoining buildings should receive some protective treatment unless they are well within the perimeter barrier and open directly onto an area outside the building that is particularly well secured.

2.2 Doors

Every door, whether exterior or interior, must be carefully examined to determine the degree of security required. Such an examination will also determine the type of construction as well as the locking system to be used on each door.

The required security measures at any specific door will be determined by the operations in progress within the facility or by the value of the assets stored or available in the various areas. The need for adequate security cannot be overemphasized, but this security must be provided as part of an overall plan for the safe and efficient conduct of the business.

When this balance is lost, the business may suffer. Either the security function will be downgraded in favor of a more immediate convenience or the smooth flow of business will be impeded to conform to obtrusive security standards. Either of these conditions is intolerable in any business, and it is a management responsibility to determine the balance required in establishing systems that will recognize and accommodate production and security needs.

2.2.1 Door Construction and Hardware

Doors are frequently much weaker than the surface into which they are positioned. Panels may be thin, easily broken wood or glass. Locks may be old and ineffective. The door frame may be so constructed that a lever or a plastic card can be inserted between the door and the jamb to disengage the bolt in the lock. Even with a properly hung door, if the jamb is of soft material (unreinforced aluminum or light pine), it can be peeled or ripped away from the bolt. This technique is referred to as *spreading*. The locking bolt must throw at least an inch into the jamb for security applications. Heavy wood or metal doors with reinforced jambs can go a long way in reducing the potential for spreading.

In some cases, doors are entered by *pulling*, a technique whereby the lock cylinder is ripped from the door and the locking mechanism is operated through the opening left in its face. The installation of a special, hardened steel key cylinder guard can overcome this kind of assault. Or cylinders should be flush or inset to prevent their being wrenched out or "popped." Figure 10.2 illustrates common techniques of attacking doors and door frames.

Door hinges can also contribute to a door's weakness. Intruders can remove surface-mounted hinges with mounting screws or hinge pins exposed on the exterior side of

A. Jamb spreading by prying with two large screwdrivers.

D. Sawing the bolt with a hacksaw.

B. Use of an automobile bumper jack to spread the door frame. Standard bumper jacks are rated to 2000 pounds. The force of the jack can be applied between the two jambs of a door to spread them and to overcome by deflection the length of the latch throw.

E. Jamb peeling to expose the bolt.

C. Cylinder pulling with a slam hammer.

F. Forcing the dead bolt with a drift punch and hammer.

FIGURE 10.2 Common attack methods on doors and door frames. (Reprinted with permission of National Crime Prevention Institute, School of Justice Administration, University of Louisville, from Edgar et al., *The Use of Locks* [Boston: Butterworth-Heinemann, 1987], pp. 72–76.)

the door and gain entrance on the hinge side. To complicate the matter, the door can be replaced on its hinges after the intruder has finished and in most cases the intrusion will never be detected. Without any visible sign of forced entry, very few insurance policies would pay off on the stolen merchandise.

To prevent this unhappy chain of events, hinges should be installed with the screws concealed and with the hinge pins either welded or flanged to prevent removal.

2.3   Locks and Keys

2.3.1   Attacks Against Locks

Although direct forcible assault is the method generally used to gain entry, more highly skilled burglars may concentrate on the locks. This could be their only practical means of ingress if the door and the jamb are well designed in security terms and essentially impervious to forcible attack.

Picking the lock or making a key by impression are the methods intruders generally use. Both require a degree of expertise. In the former method, metal picks are used to align the levers, pins, discs, or tumblers as an authorized key would, thus enabling the lock to operate. Making a key by taking impressions is a technique requiring even greater skill because it is a delicate, painstaking operation requiring repeated trials.

Because both of these techniques are apt to take time, they are customarily used to attack doors located where the intruder may work undisturbed and unobserved for adequate periods of time. The picked lock rarely shows any signs of illegal entry, and often insurance is not collectible.

2.3.2   Locks as Delaying Devices

The best defense against lock picking and making keys by impression is the installation of special pick-resistant, impression-resistant lock cylinders or the use of magnetic cards (as commonly used in the hotel industry and discussed later in this chapter) in place of traditional keys. These lock cylinders are more expensive than standard cylinders but in many applications they could well be worth the added cost. Generally speaking, in fact, locks are the cheapest security investment that you can make. Cost cutting in their purchase is usually a poor economy since a lock of poor quality is virtually useless and effectively no lock at all.

The elementary but often overlooked fact concerning locking devices is that in the first place they are simply mechanisms that extend the door or window into the wall that holds them. If, therefore, the wall or the door itself is weak or easily destroyed, the lock cannot be effective.

In the second place, it must be recognized that any lock will eventually yield to an attack. They must be thought of only as delaying devices. But this delay is of primary importance. The longer an intruder is stalled in an exposed position while he or she works at gaining entry, the greater are the chances of discovery. Since many types of locks in general use today provide no appreciable delay to even the unskilled prowler, they have no place in security applications.

Even the highest-quality locking devices are only one part of door and entrance security. Locks, cylinders, door and frame construction, and key control are inseparable elements; all must be equally effective. If any one element is weak, the system breaks down.

All locks are essentially composed of three parts: the operating mechanism, the keying device, and the latch or bolt. Any number of combinations may be involved in any lock, and to understand a lock, one must understand the variety of items that exist in each of the essential parts.

2.3.3 Latches and Bolts

The simplest latch is the spring lock. Its value as a security device is negligible. Spring locks are designed primarily as latching devices to hold a door closed for privacy. Since the latch is spring-loaded and has a tapered side so it will slide smoothly over the strike plate, it can easily be opened with a plastic or celluloid strip or a credit card.

The next type of latch is the dead latch. This latching device combines the advantages of the spring lock with a means of protecting the latch from carding. The dead latch is a simple device that holds the spring latch in position when the door is closed. When the door is unlocked, the device is in an open position to allow the latch to operate as a simple spring latch. But when the door is locked, the strike plate depresses the device so that the spring latch becomes "dead": It will no longer move unless the operating device manipulates it. The basic problem with the dead latch as a security device is that the overall length of the latch is still not long enough to keep the door from being forced open by prying between the door frame and the door.

To overcome the problem of springing doors, a dead bolt lock is needed (see Figure 10.3). The dead bolt gets its name from the fact that it does not have a tapered side and is "dead" in the door, whether it is open or closed. The only way to manipulate a dead bolt is with an operating mechanism (key, electric switch, or the like). Dead bolts are generally long enough to overcome the problem of springing the door. Some intruders have attacked dead bolts with hacksaws, however, and cut their way through the brass alloy. To overcome this problem, the better dead bolts have a case-hardened pin in the center to frustrate the use of a hacksaw.

2.3.4 Keying Devices and Systems

Keying devices (which include lock and key) and the mechanisms they operate are many and varied in usage and style. A brief review of the types of keying and locking devices in general use and of their characteristics follows:

1. *Warded locks* are generally found in pre-World War II construction in which the keyway is open and can be seen through. These are also recognized by the single plate that includes the doorknob and the keyway. The security value of these locks is nil. These locks are found only in older construction and are becoming rare.

2. *Disc tumbler locks*, initially designed for use in the automobile industry, have been replaced in that industry with pin locks, combination, and proximity devices (discussed later in this chapter). Because the disc tumbler lock is easy and cheap to manufacture, however, its use has expanded to other areas such as desks, files, and padlocks. The life of these locks is limited due to their soft metal construction. Although these locks provide more security than warded locks, they cannot be considered very effective. The delay afforded is approximately 3 minutes.

3. *Pin tumbler locks* are in wide use in industry as well as in residences (see Figure 10.4). They can be recognized by the keyway, which is irregular in shape, and the key, which is grooved on both sides. Such locks can be master keyed in a number of ways, a feature that recommends them to a wide variety of industrial applications, although the delay factor is 10 minutes or less.

4. *Lever locks* are difficult to define in terms of security since they vary greatly in effectiveness. The best lever locks are used in safe deposit boxes and are for all practical purposes pickproof. The least of these locks are used in desks, lockers,

FIGURE 10.3 Common dead bolt locks. The bolt should extend at least 1 inch beyond the door edge. However, other locks that use an interlocking principle (for example, jimmy-resistant rim locks) also offer good security. If glass is within 40 inches of the lock, a double cylinder dead bolt (with keys needed to open both sides) should be installed. This makes it impossible for a criminal to break the glass and reach inside to unlock the door. Be certain to have the key readily available so that fast exits are possible in the event of an emergency.

and cabinets and are generally less secure than are pin tumbler locks. The best of this variety are rarely used in common applications, such as doors, because they are bulky and expensive.

2.3.5   Removable Cores

In facilities that require a number of keys to be issued, the loss or theft of keys is an ever-present possibility. In such situations, it might be well to consider removable cores on all locks. These devices are made to be removed if necessary with a core key, allowing a new core to be inserted. Since the core is the lock, this has the effect of rekeying without

FIGURE 10.4 Pin tumbler lock. (A) A cutaway of a pin tumbler lock showing the springs and tumblers. When the correct key is inserted into the lock, it will align all the tumblers in a straight line to allow the plug to turn and operate the locking mechanism. (B) Locked position. Notice how the spring is forcing the tumbler to project partway into the inner core (plug) of the lock, making it impossible for the plug to rotate. (C) Unlocked position. The tumbler is now outside the plug, thereby allowing it to be rotated. (Courtesy of Medeco Security Locks, Inc.)

the necessity of changing the entire device, as would be the case with fixed-cylinder mechanisms.

2.3.6   Keying Systems

Keys are generally divided into change, submaster, master, and occasionally grand master keys:

1. *The change key:* One key to a single lock within a master-keyed system.
2. *The submaster key:* Will open all the locks within a particular area or grouping in a given facility. In an office, a submaster might open all doors in the accounting

department; in an industrial facility, it might open all locks in the loading dock area. Typically, such groupings concern themselves with a common function, or they may simply be located in the same area even if they are not otherwise related.

3. *The master key:* Where two or more submaster systems exist, a master key system is established. Such a key would open any of the systems.

4. *The grand master key:* One that will open everything in a system involving two or more master-key groups. This system is relatively rare but might be used by a multipremises operation in which each location was master keyed, while the grand master would function on any premise.

Obviously, master and submaster keys must be treated with the greatest care. If a master key is lost, the entire system is threatened. Rekeying is the only really secure thing that can be considered, but the cost of such an effort can be enormous.

Any master-key system is vulnerable. Beyond the danger of loss of the master itself and the subsequent staggering cost of rekeying—or, even more unfortunate, of the use of such a key by enterprising criminals to loot the facility—there is the problem that it necessarily serves a lesser lock. Locks in such a system are neither pick-resistant nor resistant to making a key by impression.

On the other hand, relative security coupled with convenience may make such a system preferable in some applications but not in others. Only the most careful evaluation of the particular circumstances of a given facility will determine the most efficient and effective keying system.

2.3.7   Rekeying

In any sizable facility, rekeying can be very expensive, but there are methods of lessening the disruption and staggering cost that can be involved in rekeying. Outer or perimeter locks can be changed first, and the old locks can be moved to interior spaces requiring a lower level of security. After an evaluation, a determination of priorities can be made and rekeying can be accomplished over a period of time, rather than requiring one huge capital outlay all at once. Of prime importance is securing keys so that such problems do not arise.

2.3.8   Key Control

Every effort should be exerted to develop ways whereby keys remain in the hands of security or management personnel. In those cases where this is not possible or practical, there must be a system of inventory and accountability. In any event, keys should be issued only to demonstrably responsible persons who have compelling need for them. Though possession of keys is frequently a status symbol in many companies, management must never issue them on that basis.

Keys should never be issued on a long-term basis to outside janitorial personnel. The high employee turnover rate in this field suggests that this could be a dangerous practice. Employees of this outside service should be admitted by guards or other building employees and issued interior keys that they must return before leaving the building.

By the same token, it is bad practice to issue entrance keys to tenants of an office building. If this is done, control of this vital security point is lost. A guard or building employee should control entry and exit before and after regular building hours. If keys must be issued to tenants, however, the lock cylinder in the entrance should be changed every few months and new keys issued to authorized tenants.

The security department must maintain a careful, strictly supervised record of all keys issued. This record should indicate the name and department of the person to whom the key was issued as well as the date of issue.

A key depository for securing keys during nonworking hours should be centrally located, locked, and kept under supervision of security personnel. Keys issued on a daily basis or those issued for a specific, one-time purpose should be accounted for daily. Keys should be counted and signed for by the security supervisor at the beginning of each working day.

When a key is lost, the circumstances should be investigated and set forth in writing. In some instances, if the lost key provides access to sensitive areas, locks should be changed. All keys issued should be physically inspected periodically to ensure that they have not been lost, though unreported as such.

Master keys should be kept to a minimum. If possible, submasters should be used, and they should be issued only to a limited list of personnel especially selected by management. Careful records should be kept of such issuance. The list should be reviewed periodically to determine whether all those authorized should continue to hold such keys.

Before a decision can be reached with respect to the master and submaster key systems and how such keys should be issued, there must be a careful survey of existing and proposed security plans, along with a study of current and planned locking devices. Where security plans have been developed with the operational needs of the facility in mind, the composition of the various keying systems can be readily developed.

2.3.9   Locking Schedules

Door-locking schedules and responsibilities must be established and supervised vigorously. The system must be set up in such a way that a procedure for altering the routine to fit immediate needs is possible, but in all respects the schedule, whether the master or the temporary plan, must be adhered to in every detail. A breakdown in such a system, especially in large offices, institutions, or industrial facilities, could represent just the opportunity an alert criminal is waiting for.

2.3.10   Other Operating Mechanisms for Access Control

Besides the traditional key and lock, other mechanisms have been developed for access control purposes. The following are commonly used in security applications:

1. *Combination locks* are difficult to defeat since they cannot be picked and few experts can so manipulate the device as to discover the combination. Most of these locks have three dials that must be aligned in the proper order before the lock will open. Some such locks may have four dials for greater security. Many also have the capability of changing the combination quickly.

2. *Code-operated locks* are combination locks in which no keys are used. They are opened by pressing a series of numbered buttons in the proper sequence (see Figure 10.5). Some of them are equipped to sound an alarm if the wrong sequence is pressed. The combination of these locks can be changed readily. These are high-security locking devices. Because this type of lock can be compromised by "tailgating" (more than one person entering on an authorized opening), it should never be used as a substitute for a guard or receptionist.

FIGURE 10.5 Code-operated lock. (Courtesy of KABA, www.kaba-ilco.com.)

FIGURE 10.6 Card reader. (Courtesy of FlexIso-MifareCard/Indala.)

3. *Card-operated locks* (see Figure 10.6) are electrical or, more usually, electromagnetic. Coded cards are about the size of a credit card. These frequently are fitted with a recording device that registers time of use and identity of the user. The cards serving as keys also serve as company identification cards. As with code-operated locks, tailgating can occur with this type of lock as well. In addition, the readers identify

BACK **FRONT**

FIGURE 10.7 Proximity tags. (Photo courtesy of HID Corporation.)

the card, not the individual. The hotel industry has been making the switch from traditional key systems to the electronic locking systems over the past 15 years. The advantages of these systems are many, including the following:

- Security staff no longer need to spend hours rotating key cores and keeping detailed logs.
- Card keys can be programmed to function in a variety of ways.
- Lost cards can be deactivated in a matter of seconds.
- The systems often allow hotels to keep track of the time and number of entries at a given site.[1]

There are several types of card-operated systems on the market:

- *Magnetic coded cards* are of two basic designs. The first contains a flexible magnetic sheet sealed between two sheets of plastic. The second contains a magnetic strip along one edge of the card. The code is created by magnetizing spots on the sheet or strip. The code can be erased if it is exposed to a strong magnetic field. It is possible to duplicate the magnetic pattern and create false cards.
- *Wiegan Effect cards* rely on short-length magnetic wires embedded within the card. Cards contain up to 26 wire bits, which make millions of code combinations possible. The card is immune to demagnetization and difficult to copy.
- *Optical coded cards* contain bar codes similar to those found on products in most grocery stores. Early cards used the visible bar codes and were easy to duplicate. Today's product contains bar codes visible only under ultraviolet or infrared light.
- *Proximity cards* (see Figure 10.7) do not need to be inserted into a reader or scanned. These cards send a code to a receiver via magnetic, optical, or ultrasonic pulses.
- *Radio frequency identification (RFID)* is a form of proximity technology relying on radio frequency identification. The system has a signaling device (badge or tag) and readers. Coupled in an integrated system, data can be recorded and

managed by computer systems that track all types of information such as time admitted and number of entrances versus exits. Industry analysts predict that a large percentage of the access control market will be RFID-based in the future.

4. *Biometric systems* are designed to recognize biological features of the individual before access is granted. These systems are in fact identity verification systems that use personnel characteristics to verify identity. Though these systems bring the James Bond gadgetry to reality, they are also currently handicapped by problems relating to the fact that physical characteristics of people do change with physical injuries, stress, and fatigue. There are several types of this state-of-the-art technology:

- *Fingerprint recognition systems* (see Figure 10.8) optically scan a chosen fingerprint area and compare the scanned area with data in the file of the person to be admitted.

- *Signature recognition systems* rely on the fact that no two people write with the same motion or pressure. Although forgers can duplicate the appearance of the

FIGURE 10.8 Fingerprint recognition system. (Courtesy of KABA.)

signature, the amount of pressure and motions used in creating the signature will differ.

- *Hand geometry recognition systems* (see Figure 10.9) use the geometry of the hand. The system basically measures finger lengths and compares them with information in the authorized files.
- *Speaker verification systems* use the uniqueness of voice patterns to determine identification and control admittance. The system uses soundproof booths and

FIGURE 10.9 Hand geometry recognition. (Courtesy of Handkey II, Ingersoll-Rand, www.handreader.com.)

FIGURE 10.10 Eye retina identification system. (Courtesy of KABA.)

requires that the person to be identified repeat a simple phrase, usually four words in length.

- *Eye retina recognition systems* (see Figure 10.10) analyze the blood vessel pattern in the retina of the eye. These patterns vary widely, even between identical twins. The chance of false identification using this system is one in a million.

5. *Padlocks* are detachable, portable locks that have a shackle adapted to open for engagement through a hasp or chain. Padlocks should be hardened and strong enough to resist prying. The shackle should be close enough to the body to prevent the insertion of a tool to force it. No lock that will be used for security purposes should have fewer than five pins in the cylinder. Padlocks can be supplied with a function that prevents the withdrawal of a key until the lock is closed.

It is important to establish a procedure requiring that all padlocks be locked at all times, even when they are not securing an area. This will prevent the possibility of the lock being replaced by another to which a thief has the key.

The hardware used in conjunction with the padlock is as important as the lock itself. It should be of hardened steel, without accessible screws or rivets, and

FIGURE 10.11 Modern high-security lock with e-key access. (Photo courtesy of LA GARD, INC, A MASCO Company.)

bolted through the door to the inside, preferably through a backing plate. Shackles should be forged of hardened steel, ⅜ inch in both the heel and toe. The bolt ends should be burred.

6. *High-security locks.* Virtually every lock manufacturer makes some kind of special high-security lock that is operated by nonduplicable keys. A reliable locksmith or various manufacturers should be consulted in cases of such need.

7. The latest addition to new security access control hardware is the *iButton*. This device is an extension of the "smart card" technology being used by the banking industry. The iButton contains a hermetically sealed computer chip in a stainless steel container. The iButton can secure information and can provide information for security staff.[2]

It appears that as the technology allows, old systems are being supplanted by technology. One example of the ability to use old systems with new technology is the "electronic key" (see Figure 10.11). This key looks and is used like a regular metal key but contains the electronic characteristics of a smart card. The key does not have any cuts: It is an electronic key that can be fitted to existing door hardware.[3]

A 1996 study predicted that the then-popular existing magnetic strip cards would be phased out shortly after 2000. The same study predicted that in 2000 there would be 550 million smart cards.[4] The initial uses were in replacing store cards. However, this high-tech card now is accepted by credit card companies, banks, and others. Over half of all transactions in retailing and banking are now handled by smart card technology.

Other uses include access control for physical security, computer information access control, health care cards, access to mobile telephone networks, and multipurpose ID cards in colleges, universities, and workplaces.

2.3.11   Locking Devices

In the previous list we have considered the types of locks that are generally available. It must be remembered, however, that locks must work in conjunction with other hardware that affects the actual closure. These devices may be fitted with locks of varying degrees of security and may themselves provide security to various levels. In a security locking system, both of these factors must be taken into consideration before you determine which system will be most effective for specific needs.

1. *Electromagnetic locking devices* hold doors closed by magnetism. These electrical units consist of an electromagnet and a metal holding plate. When the power is on and the door secured, they will resist pressure of up to 1,000 pounds. A high frequency of mechanical failures with this type of lock can create problems. Inconvenienced employees will often block the door open or jam the door-bolting mechanism so that the lock no longer operates. Quality equipment, preventive maintenance, frequent inspections, and quick response to problems will minimize these issues.

2. *Double-cylinder locking devices* are installed in doors that must be secured from both sides, requiring a key to open them from either side. Their most common application is in doors with glass panels that might otherwise be broken to allow an intruder to reach in and open the door from the other side. Such devices cannot be used in interior fire stairwell doors, since in those cases firefighters break the glass to unlock the door from the inside.

3. *Emergency exit locking devices* are panic-bar installations allowing exit without use of a key. This device locks the door against entrance from the outside. Because such devices frequently provide an alarm feature that sounds when exit is made, they are fitted with a lock that allows exit without setting off the alarm when a key is used.

4. *Recording devices* provide a printout of door use by time of day and by the key used.

5. *Vertical throw devices* lock into the jamb vertically instead of the usual horizontal bolt. Some versions lock into both jamb and lintel. A variation of this device is the police lock, which consists of a bar angled to a well in the floor. The end of the bar contacting the door is curved so that when it is unlocked it will slide up the surface of the door, allowing the door to open. When it is locked, it is secured to the door at one end and set in the floor at the other. A door locked in this manner is virtually impossible to force.

6. *Electric locking devices* are installed in the same manner as other locks. They are activated remotely by an electric current that releases the strike and thus permits entrance. Many of these devices provide minimal security, since the engaging mechanisms frequently offer no security feature not offered by standard hardware. The electric feature provides a convenient method of opening the door; it does not in itself offer locking security. Because such doors are usually intended for remote operation, they should be fitted with a closing device.

7. *Sequence locking devices* are designed to ensure that all doors covered by the system are locked. The doors must be closed and locked in a predetermined order. No door can be locked until its designated predecessor has been locked. Exit is made through the final door in the sequence, and entry can be made only through that same door.

2.4   Roofs and Common Walls

An important though often overlooked part of the perimeter is the roof of the building. In urban shopping centers or even in small, freestanding commercial situations where the building walls are the perimeter, entry through the roof is common. Entry can be made through skylights or by chopping through the roof—an activity rarely detected by passersby or even by patrols.

Buildings sharing a common wall have also frequently been entered by breaking through the wall from a poorly secured neighboring occupancy. All of these means of entry circumvent normal perimeter alarm systems and can therefore be particularly damaging.

3   Surveillance Devices

Surveillance of a facility both internally and externally has traditionally been conducted by patrolling security personnel who watch for any signs of criminal activity. If they spot any trouble, they are in a position to take such action as necessary. Patrols cannot be everywhere, however, and with the present emphasis on cost-effectiveness, other methods have been introduced to supplement patrols. A wide variety of surveillance devices, including motion-picture cameras, sequence cameras, and CCTV monitors with video and digital cameras, are being used.

Effective surveillance systems are expected to produce two possible end results. First, a good system should produce an identifiable image of people engaging in criminal behavior or violating company policy. Second, the system should also serve as a deterrent. Although there is no way to determine how many attempts are discouraged because of the presence of these systems, one definite advantage is that surveillance systems generally mean lower insurance rates.

The major factor limiting the use of surveillance devices is the cost of installation and maintenance. In addition, some companies worry about the possible negative impact of these systems on employee morale, although this is becoming increasing rare as cameras become commonplace not only in the workplace but in public areas as well.

CCTV systems are the state-of-the-art surveillance devices and in most cases have replaced still and motion-picture systems. The CCTV systems coupled with recording (VCR) equipment or computers (digital systems) are exceptionally flexible (see Figure 10.12). The tapes or digital records can be erased and reused, a definite cost savings in comparison with other systems. In today's market, digital equipment has rapidly replaced VHS, which is viewed as too limiting because of intense maintenance, remote accessibility problems, and difficulty in integrating with other systems.[5] Problems associated with VHS are reduced or eliminated with digital technology.

Current technology developments have produced CCTV that is used for laparoscopic surgery. Improved lens design has also produced cameras that can identify objects within ¾ square foot from more than 100 miles in space. With the improved technology, the CCTV has become one of the most sought-after systems in the security market.

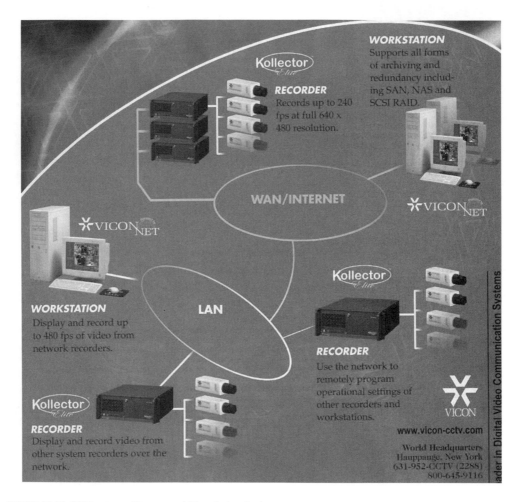

FIGURE 10.12 CCTV systems. (Courtesy of Vicon Industries.)

Technological advances allow CCTV technology to be used where it would not have been effective 10 years ago—in areas such as loading docks and automatic teller machines. The reduced size of the camera also allows for a greater number of applications (see Figure 10.13). Cameras may easily be placed in covert locations such as wall receptacles, clocks, and mannequins. The reduced price and improved reliability of color cameras have enabled banks, retail stores, museums, and others to add color evidence to their security capabilities.

The "starlight" cameras allow for good video reproduction at 0.0001 lux (the amount of light produced by stars on a clear night) compared to the previous 0.1 lux level. CCTV technology adds the ability to use thermal cameras with current systems. These cameras detect and transmit heat images. They will work in the light or in pitch-black environments.

Finally, the ability to network a widespread surveillance system and monitor multiple sites remotely from a central location is a reality (see Figure 10.14). Remote video management systems (RVMS) are now being used to monitor multiple VCRs and video-signaling devices at thousands of locations.[6] Modern integrated surveillance systems through the use of digital cameras connected worldwide via Wide Area Networks (WANs), Local Area

FIGURE 10.13 A first-generation smart camera. (Courtesy of Pelco, www.pelco.com.)

FIGURE 10.14 Control console. (Courtesy of Winsted Corp.)

Networks (LANs), and the Internet have truly expanded and revolutionized monitoring capabilities.

These improvements in CCTV technology have resulted in a move to replace or augment existing security systems with CCTV. However, as the demand for digital cameras continues to increase, analog CCTV equipment will eventually be phased out of use. This trend is predictable as security operations continue to integrate video, alarm systems, and access control into a seamless operation. Networking is becoming the technology via which we can build complete security systems that allow central stations to monitor operations around the world.

Once a decision has been made to purchase a system, careful planning must precede the purchase. Poor planning generally means wasted funds and a system that does not do the required job. Several questions should be asked before any purchase, among them the following:

- Is the camera to be visible and used as a deterrent to crime or hidden and used in civil or criminal prosecutions? Most businesses would rather prevent a crime than go to the effort and expense of prosecution; these businesses therefore prefer visible camera locations. In addition, hidden camera sites cost more because there is not only the investment in the camera but also expenses incurred in hiding the camera.

- What effect, if any, will the sun have on the operation of the system? Sunlight is variable in intensity, and good light conditions may deteriorate as the day progresses into dusk. In addition, sunlight can cause glare. A CCTV system may allow you to change the settings of the recording cameras to help adjust for changes in light intensity.

- Where is the best location for a camera? In banks, for instance, placement might be where customers do not immediately notice the camera. In many cases, this is accomplished by placing the camera over the exits. This permits narrow-angle coverage of an area where the subject must approach the camera directly at a time when he may be comparatively off-guard (for example, you might catch a bank robber removing his disguise). In these cases, the teller does not have to signal the camera until the robber is on the way out of the bank. When the camera is placed to photograph the teller and cashier area, attempting to trigger the camera manually may endanger the employee.

- Should the placement of the camera be high? High placement is not as efficient as it is often thought to be. Persons photographed from high locations might not be recognizable. A good spot is just high enough to see over obstacles and to protect the camera from curious observers.

- What type of lighting is in use? Sodium systems produce poor color accuracy. Ideally the camera system and lighting plan should be coordinated to allow for the most accurate recording of details.

A site survey is essential to effective planning. This survey is generally presented in the form of a diagram with the areas to be protected drawn to scale. The diagram should include blind spots, areas of high loss potential, exits, windows, cash registers, electrical outlets, and other items significant to the site. Lighting requirements can be determined using an illumination meter. Record the information on the diagram, and measure illumination at both the brightest and the darkest times of the day. Levels of light should generally not be below 20 to 40 or above 250 foot-candles (fc). If the level falls below 20 fc, you will need additional lighting or other camera equipment; if it rises above 250 fc, you will need special filters. Study the traffic flow to discover the greatest usage.

The future might increase the role of surveillance into the area of decision making. Manufacturers are developing cameras that not only watch and record but also interpret what they see. There are hints that cameras may soon be able to detect unattended baggage at airports, guess a person's weight, or analyze the way you walk.[7] The European Union is funding research in this area to include cameras and robots. According to Richard Bowden, University of Surrey professor, "If you have a robot with a camera that looks down a road and it knows it is normal behaviour for people to just walk along, then it will know that if somebody shimmies up a drainpipe, it is something the system has not seen before."[8]

Camera systems are increasingly becoming parts of company and community programs of protection. A Philadelphia neighborhood recently installed a $120,000 high-tech camera system that can detect suspicious activity, photograph faces and license plates from three blocks away, and eventually send real-time video straight to a police squad car.[9] In Baltimore, where 350 cameras were installed in 2005, violent crime in the areas with cameras has fallen 15 percent.[10]

4   Old Construction

Older buildings— particularly, though certainly not exclusively, office buildings—present a host of different and difficult security problems. Exterior fire escapes, old and frequently badly worn locks, common walls, roof access from neighboring buildings, unused and forgotten connecting doors—all increase the exposure to burglary.

It is vital that all such openings are surveyed and plans made for securing them. Windows not designated as emergency exits must be barred or screened. Where windows lead to a fire escape or are accessible to adjacent fire escapes, their essential security must be accomplished within local fire code regulations. Fire safety must be a primary consideration. In cases where prudence or the law (or both) dictate that locks would be a hazard to safety, windows should be alarmed and the interior areas to which these windows provide access must be further secured. Here, security can be likened to any army retreating to secondary or tertiary lines of defense to establish a strong and defensible position.

It is also well to consider the danger of attack from neighboring occupancies in shared space where entry might be made from low-risk, badly secured premises into a higher-risk area that might otherwise be well protected against a more direct attack.

5   New Construction

Modern urban buildings, though security conscious in varying degrees, present their own problems. Most interior construction is standardized. Fire and building codes are such that corridor doors can resist most attacks if the hardware is adequate. Corridor ceilings are fixed, and entrances to individual offices usually offer a fairly high degree of security.

On the other hand, modern construction creates offices that are essentially open-top boxes. They have solid exterior walls (though interior walls are frequently plasterboard) and a concrete floor. But nothing of any security value protects the top. The ceiling is simply a layer of acoustical tiles lying loose on runners suspended between partition walls. In the space above these tiles—between them and the concrete slab above—are vital air-conditioning ducts and wiring for power and telephones.

In effect, any given floor of a building has a crawl space that runs from exterior wall to exterior wall. This may not be literally so in every case, but the net result stands. It means that virtually every room and every office is accessible through this space. Once this crawl space is reached from any occupancy, the remaining offices on that floor are accessible.

Extending dividing walls up to the next floor will not solve the problem, because this drywall construction is easily broken through and, in any case, it must be breached to allow passage of all utilities. Alarms of various kinds, which are discussed later in this book, are recommended to overcome this problem.

6   Security at the Building Design Stage

Once a building has been constructed without proper security considerations, the damage has been done. Security weaknesses begin to manifest themselves, but at this point it is far too expensive to make basic structural changes to correct them. Guard services and protective devices that might not otherwise have been necessary must be instituted. In any event, there will be some expense for protection that could have been incorporated into the building's design before construction began. This kind of oversight can be very expensive indeed.

Unfortunately, we have not yet arrived at the point where the need for security from criminal acts is as automatic a consideration as the need for efficiency or profits. Architects' interest in design for protection of buildings and grounds is usually minimal. They traditionally leave such demands to their clients, who usually are unaware of the availability of protective hardware and who are rarely competent to deal with the problems of protective design.

This situation may be changing following the growing apprehension over possible terrorist attacks. Recent events, such as the destruction of the World Trade Center as well as attacks on buildings in many other countries, may prompt designers to consider incorporating security plans in their designs. As noted in Chapter 1, the construction industry, in response to issues raised in the review of the failure of the World Trade Center towers, has announced plans to revise its MasterFormat system to include more security concerns. MasterFormat is the work of the Construction Specifications Institute.

In addition, the crime rate and the growing awareness of the problem have directed more attention toward the important role that building design can play in security. There have been some efforts on the part of the federal government to accentuate the architect's role in security.

Under the umbrella of environmental security, concepts of crime prevention through environmental design (CPTED) have received added attention in recent years. Early work in this field concentrated on residential security, particularly in public housing, with Oscar Newman's major study of "defensible space" being a pioneering work.[11]

This approach to crime prevention through environmental design has important implications for private security. It seeks to bring together many disciplines—among them urban planning, architectural design, public law enforcement, and private security—to create an improved quality of urban life through crime prevention. In particular it encourages awareness of crime prevention techniques through physical design.

7 Security Principles in Design

Certain principles should always be considered in planning any building. Without them, it can be dangerously vulnerable. Some areas of consideration are listed here:

1. The number of perimeter and building openings should be kept to a minimum consistent with safety codes.
2. Perimeter protection should be planned as part of the overall design.
3. Exterior windows, if they are less than 14 feet above ground level, should be constructed of glass brick, laminated glass, or plastic materials, or they should be shielded with heavy screening or steel grilles.
4. Points of possible access or escape that breach the exterior of the building or the perimeter should be protected. Points to be considered are skylights, air-conditioning vents, sewer ducts, manholes, or any opening larger than 96 square inches.
5. High-quality locks tied to smart card technology should be employed on all exterior and restricted area doors for protection and quick-change capability in the event of cardkey loss.
6. Protective lighting should be installed.
7. Shipping and receiving bays should be widely separated from each other.
8. Exterior doors intended for emergency use only should be fitted with alarms.
9. Exterior service doors should lead directly into the service area so that nonemployee traffic is restricted in its movement.
10. Dock areas should be designed so that drivers can report to shipping or receiving clerks without moving through storage areas.
11. Employment offices should be located so that applicants either enter directly from outside or move through as little of the building as possible.
12. Employee entrances should be located directly off the gate to the parking lot.
13. Employee locker rooms should be located by employee entrance and exit doors.
14. Doors in remote areas should be fitted with alarms.

Summary

The basics of interior and exterior security theory remain constant, but the tools used to establish the systems have improved in recent years. Systems that integrate all aspects of security are becoming commonplace. Smart cameras work with monitors, switchers, recorders, access control devices, and computers to allow operators to efficiently monitor and control a multitude of locations from one central station operation. Biometric technology implementation is growing at a rapid pace and should continue to be an area of advancement in the security industry. Geoff Kohl, editor at SecurityInfoWatch.com, noted in 2007 that the security industry is still heavily focused on gates, fences, analog cameras, guards, and old reed-style contacts for intrusion detection. Although mag strip cards and security fencing may still define much of commercial security, it's rapidly moving beyond that. The industry as a whole is paying a lot more attention to technology.[12]

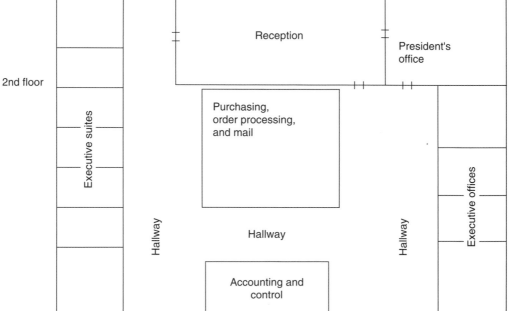

FIGURE 10.15 Floor plan of the IBID International Corporation.

CASE STUDY

You are the security director for IBID International, a large manufacturer. You have decided to conduct a security survey of the company's administrative building. You have received the security survey report form (see Appendix D) and a blueprint of the building (see Figure 10.15). Your approved recommendations will be presented to senior management for final approval and funding. Fill out the survey form. As you do so, look over the blueprint and note directly on your blueprint what and where you would make security improvements in the building and its interior.

Narrative: You should succinctly, clearly, and logically draw together your findings on the physical security survey. This narrative should briefly provide an overview of each problem and its recommended solution or correction.

Review Questions

1. What factors need to be considered when you are purchasing and installing locking devices for security purposes?
2. Describe the basic principles of an effective key control plan.
3. What are the two end results of an effective surveillance system?

References

1. Beaudry, Mark, "Locking In Hotel Security," *Security Management* (November 1996): 37.
2. "Access and Beyond: Read/Write Tokens Open New Possibilities," *Security* (December 1996): 23.
3. "Electronic Keys: Hardware Feel, High-Tech Benefits," *Security* (August 1996): 19.
4. "Market for Smart Cards to Increase 8-Fold by 2000," *Security* (January 1996): 15–16.
5. "Security Surveillance and Monitoring Systems to 2000," (April 1996), www.freedoniagroup.com.
6. Messenbrink, John, "The Digital rEVOLUTION," *Security*, downloaded 1/14/03, www.securitymagazine.com/security/cda/articleinformation/coverstory/bnpcoverstoryitem/0,5409,82693,00.html.
7. www.boston.com/business/technology/articles/2007/02/26/surveillance_cameras_latest_job_interpret_the_threats_they_see/.
8. *Security Management Daily,* February 28, 2007, excerpted from *Engineer* (02/26/07).
9. *Security Management Daily,* February 28, 2007, excerpted from *Philadelphia Inquirer* (02/26/07).
10. *Security Management Daily,* February 28, 2007, excerpted from *Columbus Dispatch* (02/25/07).
11. Newman, Oscar, *Defensible Space: Crime Prevention Through Urban Design* (New York: Macmillan, 1973).
12. Kohl, Geoff, "The Week That Was: A Recap, Feb. 3–9, 2007," listserve e-mail to rjfish@macomb.com (2/09/2007).

11

The Inner Defenses: Intrusion and Access Control

1   Introduction

Once the facility's perimeter is secured, the next step in physical security planning is to minimize or control access to the facility or building interior. The extent of this control will depend on the nature and function of the facility. The controls must not interfere with the facility's operation. It is theoretically possible to completely seal off access to a given operation, but it would be difficult to imagine how useful the operation would be in such an atmosphere.

Certainly no commercial establishment can be open for business while it is closed to the public. A steady stream of outsiders, from customers to service personnel, is essential to its economic health. In such cases, the security problem is to control this traffic without interfering with the function of the business being protected. Isolated manufacturing facilities must also provide for the traffic created by the delivery of raw materials, the shipping of fabricated goods, the provision of services, and of course the labor force, which may be operating in several shifts.

All such traffic tends to compromise the facility's physical security. But security must be provided, and it must be provided appropriately for the operation of the facility being served.

Within any building, no matter whether it is located inside a perimeter barrier or is a part of the perimeter wall, it is necessary to consider the need to protect against the internal thief as well as the potential intruder. Whereas the boundary fence is primarily designed to keep out unwanted visitors (not altogether forgetting its function in the control of movement of authorized personnel), interior security must provide some protection against the free movement of employees and others bent on pilferage as well as establishing a second line of defense against the unannounced intruder.

Since every building is used differently and has its own unique traffic composition and flow, each building presents a different security problem. Each must be examined and analyzed in great detail before an effective security program can be developed.

We cannot overemphasize that such a program must be implemented without in any way interfering with the orderly and efficient operation of the facility to be protected. It must not be obtrusive, yet it must provide a predetermined level of protection against criminal attack from outside or inside.

The first points of examination must be the doors and windows of buildings within the perimeter. These must be considered in terms of effectiveness, no matter whether the building walls form a part of (or in themselves constitute) the perimeter barrier (as we discussed in Chapter 9), or they are a true second defense line where the building under examination is completely within the protection of a barrier.

2   Doors to Sensitive Areas

Doors to telephone equipment rooms, computer installations, research and development, and other sensitive areas should be equipped with automatic door-closing devices and fitted with strong dead bolts and heavy latches.

In cases where an area is under heavy security but has any degree of traffic, it might be well to consider installing an electric strike to secure the operation and control the traffic. This kind of unit is a locking device that a security person controls remotely, permitting entry of a recognized, authorized person only when pressing a button to release the lock. Because it requires someone on hand at all times for its operation, this system can be expensive. It must be examined with the cost-versus-security equation in mind. Continuing development in biotechnology is providing other options that will be discussed later in this chapter.

Supply room and tool room doors should be secured whenever those rooms are not actually in use. Even when they are in use, entrance into these areas must be restricted. The usual construction of such restraints consists of either a "Dutch" door, in which the bottom half is secured, or a counter that can be closed off by heavy screening, chain-link fencing material, or reinforced shutters.

Special care should be taken in storing small items of value. Such merchandise or material is highly subject to theft by virtue of its value for resale or personal use combined with the ease with which it can be stolen. Although such items may be stored in a facility of any construction capable of providing security, it has been the experience of many firms that uniformly stacked rows, piles, or pallets of such items within a cage-type construction that provides instant eyeball inventory is the best protection. Such precautions will vary from business to business, but they must be carefully systematized to control this potentially troublesome area of loss.

3   Office Area Doors

Doors between production and office areas or between heavily trafficked areas and office spaces must be examined for the likelihood of their use for criminal purposes. Their construction and locking hardware will be determined by such a survey. In most cases, these passages will be minimum-security areas during regular working hours because there is usually a need for movement between these areas. When there is little or no use of the office area, these doors should be secured.

4   Traffic Patterns

When you're laying out the security plan, you must analyze doors for their function. In some cases, they will serve a dual purpose—for example, fire doors, which are designed to close automatically in the event of a fire. These doors, which may remain open at the discretion of management, must be fitted to form an effective and automatic barrier to the spread of fire. They may be desirable when fire doors separate a production area from a warehouse or storage area. During those times when the production area is in operation but the warehouse is not, such fire doors can perform a security function by remaining closed.

In other cases, doors must be examined in an effort to establish a schedule for their use. Employee entrances that are the authorized points of passage for all employees may be staffed by security personnel, depending on whether the control point is established there or farther out on the perimeter. These doors could be secured once the employees have entered, thus denying entrance to unauthorized visitors as well as preventing any employees from wandering out to the fence, the parking lot, or any other location where they might cache contraband for later pickup or transport.

It is axiomatic, however, that any door used as an entrance will in a time of emergency be used as an exit by some employees. This is true in apartments and office buildings and even in industrial facilities where the employees are thoroughly familiar with the premises. No matter what or how many designated emergency exits or procedures there are, in a time of tension or near panic some individuals will seek out the door with which they are most familiar. The entrance then must always be considered an emergency exit, and it should be equipped with panic hardware. To protect against surreptitious use, it should also be fitted with at least a local alarm.

The same, of course, is true of the designated emergency exits. These doors should, in addition, be stripped of all exterior hardware since they are not intended for operational use at any time.

Personnel doors leading to and from the dock area must be carefully controlled and supervised at all times when the dock is in use. These and dock doors must be secured when the area is no longer operational.

Fire doors in office buildings should be fitted with alarms to prevent surreptitious use and access to the interior. Use of public stairwells should be prohibited or discouraged unless doors from them open into reception areas.

5   Traffic Control

Controlling traffic in and out and within a facility is essential to the facility's security program. Perimeter barriers, locked doors, and screened windows prevent or deter the entry of unauthorized visitors. But because some traffic is essential to every operation, no matter how highly classified, provision must be made for the control of this movement.

Specific solutions will depend on the nature of the business. Obviously retail establishments, which encourage high-volume traffic and regularly handle a great deal of merchandise both in and out, have a problem of a different dimension from that of the industrial operation working on a highly classified government project. Both, however, must work from the same general principles toward providing the greatest possible security within the efficient and effective operation of the job at hand.

Controlling traffic includes identifying employees and visitors and directing or limiting their movements and controlling all incoming and outgoing packages as well as trucks and private cars.

5.1   Visitors

All visitors to any facility should be required to identify themselves. When they are allowed to enter after they have established themselves as being on an authorized call, they should be limited to predetermined, unrestricted areas. The obvious exception is in firms where the public has free access to the facility—for example, retail stores.

If possible, sales, service, and trade personnel should receive clearance in advance on making an appointment with the person responsible for them being there. Although this is not always possible, most businesses deal with such visitors on an appointment basis, and a system of notifying the security personnel can be established in a majority of cases.

Businesses that salespeople or tradespeople regularly call on unannounced should set aside a waiting room that can be reached without passing through sensitive areas. In some cases, it may be advisable to issue passes that clearly designate these people as visitors. If they will be escorted to and from their destination, a pass system is probably unnecessary.

Ideally, all traffic patterns involving visitors should be short, physically confined to keep visitors from straying, and capable of being observed at all points along the route. In spread-out industrial facilities, traffic patterns should take the shortest, most direct route that will not pass through restricted, sensitive, or dangerous areas and that will pass from one reception area to another.

To achieve security objectives without alienating visitors and without in any way interfering with the business's operation, any effective control system must be simple and understandable (see Figure 11.1). It must incorporate certain specific elements to accomplish its aims. It must limit entry to people who are authorized to be there and be able to identify such people. It must have a procedure by which persons may be identified as being authorized to be in certain areas, and it must prevent theft, pilferage, or damage to the installation's assets. It must also prevent injury to the visitor.

5.2   Employee Identification

Small industrial facilities and most offices find that personal identification of employees by guards or receptionists is adequate protection against intruders entering under the guise of employees. In organizations of more than 50 employees per shift or in high-turnover businesses, this type of identification is inadequate. The opportunity for error is simply too great. In 2004, the White House noted that there were "wide variations in the quality and security of forms of identification used to gain access to secure federal and other facilities where there is a potential for terrorist attacks."[1]

FIGURE 11.1 Visitor/contractor ID. (Courtesy of Temp Badge.)

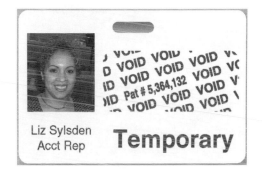

FIGURE 11.2 Employee identification card. (Courtesy of Temp Badge.)

With the continually changing technology, James Bond-type access controls are becoming common. Facial imaging, along with existing biometric identity and access control technology, will make it unlikely that access to secured areas will be gained by someone other than the person intended. The International Biometrics Group projects that facial recognition will represent more than $1.4 billion, or 19 percent, of the $7.4 billion non-AFIS (Automated Fingerprint Identification System) market by 2012. Fingerprint matching is predicted to represent 25 percent.[2]

Today the most practical and generally accepted system is the use of badges or identification cards (see Figure 11.2). Generally speaking, this system should designate when, where, how, and to whom passes should be displayed; what is to be done in case a visitor or employee loses the pass; procedures for retrieving badges from terminating employees; and a system for cancellation and reissue of all passes, either as a security review or when a significant and specific number of badges have been reported lost or stolen.

To be effective, badges must be tamper-resistant, which means that they should be printed or embossed on a distinctive stock that is worked with a series of difficult–to-reproduce designs. They should contain a clear and recent photograph of the bearer, preferably in color. The photograph should be at least 1 inch square and should be updated every two or three years or when there is any significant change in facial appearance, such as the badgeholder growing or removing a beard or mustache. The badge should, in addition, contain vital statistics such as date of birth, height, weight, color of hair and eyes, gender, and both thumbprints. It should be laminated and of sturdy construction. In cases where facility areas are set off or restricted to general employee traffic, the badge might be color-coded to indicate the areas to which the bearer has authorized access.

The latest entry into badge protection is holography. The introduction of holography into badge control systems reduces the chance of counterfeiting. Holograms incorporated with other technology advances from the past 15 years have produced an identification card system that is almost forgery-proof while incorporating computer accountability.

If a badge system is established, it will only be as effective as its enforcement. Facility guards are responsible for seeing that the system is adhered to, but they must have the cooperation of the majority of the employees and the full support of management. If the system is simply a pro forma exercise, it becomes a useless annoyance and would better be dispensed with.

Under the Department of Homeland Security Presidential Directive/HSPD-12, issued in August 2004, the federal government established a mandatory, government-wide standard for secure and reliable forms of identification issued by the federal government to employees and government contactors and their employees.[3]

5.3 Pass Systems

As we have just noted, all employees entering or leaving a facility or area should be identified and their authorization to be there should be checked. This can be achieved through one of many pass systems. Three possible systems are as follows:

- *The single-pass system,* in which a badge or pass coded for authorization to enter specific areas is issued to an employee, who keeps it until the authorization is changed or until he or she leaves the company.
- *The pass-exchange system,* in which an employee entering a controlled area exchanges one color-coded pass for another that carries a different color code specifying the limitations of the authorization. On leaving the area, the employee surrenders the controlled-area pass for the basic authorization identification pass. (In this system, the second pass never leaves the controlled area, thus reducing the possibility of switching, forging, or altering.)
- *The multiple-pass system,* the same as the exchange system, but it provides an extra measure of security by requiring that exchanges take place at the entrance to each restricted area within the controlled area.

5.4 Package Control

Every facility must establish a system for the control of packages entering or leaving the premises. However desirable it might seem, it is simply unrealistic to support as a workable procedure a blanket rule forbidding packages either in or out. Such a rule would be damaging to employee morale and in many cases would actually work against the efficient operation of the facility. Therefore, since transporting packages through the portals is a fact of life, the packages must be dealt with to prevent theft, misappropriation of company property, and concealment of dangerous materials (i.e., biological or chemical agents or bombs).

If it is deemed necessary, the types of items that may be brought in or taken out may be limited. If such is the case, the fact must be publicized and clearly understood by everyone.

Packages brought in should be checked for content. If possible where they are not to be used during work, they should be checked with the guard to be picked up at the end of the day. In most cases, spot-checking will suffice.

Whatever the policy concerning packages—whether they are to be checked or inspected—that policy must be widely publicized in advance. This is to avoid the appearance of discrimination against those whose packages are opened and examined or those that are denied entrance in conformity with company policy.

6   Files, Safes, and Vaults

The final line of defense at any facility is in the high-security storage areas where papers, records, plans, cashable instruments, precious metals, or other especially valuable assets are protected. These security containers will be of a size and quantity that the nature of the business dictates.

Every facility has its own particular needs, but certain general observations apply. The choice of the proper security container for specific applications is influenced largely by the value and the vulnerability of the items to be stored in it. Irreplaceable papers or original documents may not have any intrinsic or marketable value, so they might not be a likely target for a thief, but because they do have great value to the owners, they must be protected against fire. On the other hand, uncut precious stones or even recorded negotiable papers that can be replaced might not be in danger from fire, but they would surely be attractive to a thief. They must therefore be protected against theft.

In protecting property, it is essential to recognize that, generally speaking, protective containers are designed to secure against either burglary or fire. Each type of equipment has a specialized function and provides only minimal protection against the other risk. There are containers designed with a burglary-resistant chest within a fire-resistant container that are useful in many instances, but these too must be evaluated in terms of the mission.

Whatever the equipment, the staff must be educated and reminded of the different roles played by the two types of containers. It is all too common for company personnel to assume that a fire-resistant safe is also burglary-resistant and vice versa.

6.1   Files

Burglary-resistant files are secure against most surreptitious attacks. On the other hand, they can be pried open in less than half an hour if the burglar is permitted to work undisturbed and is not concerned with the noise created in the operation. Such files are suitable for nonnegotiable papers or even proprietary information, since these items are normally only targeted by surreptitious assault.

Filing cabinets with a fire rating of 1 hour and further fitted with a combination lock will probably be suitable for all uses except the storage of government-classified documents.[4]

6.2   Safes

Safes are expensive, but if they are selected wisely, they can be very important investments in security. Emphatically, safes are not simply safes. They are each designed to perform a particular job to provide a particular level of protection. The two types of safes of most interest to the security professional are the *record safe* (fire-resistant) and the *money safe* (burglary-resistant). To use fire-resistant safes for the storage of valuables subject to theft—an all too common practice—is to invite disaster. At the same time, it would be equally careless to use a burglary-resistant safe to store valuable papers or records because, if a fire were to occur, the contents of such a safe would be reduced to ashes.

Safes are rated to describe the degree of protection they afford. Naturally, the more protection the safe provides, the more expensive it will be. In selecting the best one for the requirements of the facility, you must consider a number of questions: How great is the threat of fire or burglary? What is the value of the safe's contents? How much protection time is required in the event of a fire or a burglary attempt? Only after these questions have been answered can a reasonable, permissible capital outlay for their protection be determined.

6.2.1   Record Safes

Fire-resistant containers are classified according to the maximum interior temperature permitted after exposure to heat for varying periods of time. A record safe with an Underwriters Laboratories (UL) rating of 350–4 (formerly designated "A") can withstand exterior temperatures building to 2,000°F for four hours without permitting the interior temperature to rise above 350°F.

The UL tests that result in the classifications are conducted to simulate a major fire with its gradual buildup of heat to 2,000°F, including circumstances where the safe might fall several stories through the fire-damaged building. In addition, an explosion test simulates a cold safe dropping into a fire that has already reached 2,000°F.

The actual procedure for the 350–4 rating involves the safe staying four hours in a furnace temperature that reaches 2,000°F. The furnace is turned off after four hours, but the safe remains inside until it is cool. The interior temperature must remain below 350°F during heating and cooling-off periods. This interior temperature is determined by sensors sealed inside the safe in six specified locations to provide a continuous record of the temperatures during the test. Papers are also placed in the safe to simulate records.

The explosion impact test is conducted with another safe of the same model that is placed for ½ hour in a furnace preheated to 2,000°F. If no explosion occurs, the furnace is set at 1,550°F and raised to 1,700°F over a ½-hour period. After this hour in the explosion test, the safe is removed and dropped 30 feet onto rubble. The safe is then returned to the furnace and reheated for one hour at 1,700°F. The furnace and safe then are allowed to cool, after which the papers inside must be legible and not charred.

Computer media storage classifications are for containers that do not allow the internal temperature to go above 150°F. This is critical because computer media begin to distort at 150°F and diskettes at 125°F.[5]

Insulated vault-door classifications are much the same as they are for safes except that the vault doors are not subjected to explosion or impact tests.

In some businesses, a fire-resistant safe with a burglary-resistant safe welded inside may serve as double protection for different kinds of assets (see Figure 11.3), but in no event must the purposes of these two kinds of safes be confused if there is one of each on the premises. Most record safes have combination locks, relocking devices, and hardened steel lock plates to provide a measure of burglar resistance. It must be reemphasized

FIGURE 11.3 Fire-resistant safe. (Courtesy of Diebold, Incorporated.)

that record safes are designed to protect documents and other similar flammables against destruction by fire. They provide only slight deterrence to the attack of even unskilled burglars. Similarly, the resistance provided by burglar-resistant safes is powerless to protect contents in a fire of any significance.

6.2.2 Money Safes

Burglary-resistant safes (see Figure 11.4) are nothing more than very heavy metal boxes without wheels; they offer varying degrees of protection against many forms of attack. A safe with a UL rating of TL-15, for instance, weighs at least 750 pounds, and its front face can resist attack by common hand and electric tools for at least 15 minutes. Other safes will resist not only attack with tools but also attack with torches and explosives.

Because burglary-resistant safes have a limited holding capacity, it is always advisable to study the volume of the items to be secured. If the volume is sufficiently large, it might be advisable to consider installing a burglary-resistant vault, which, although considerably more expensive, can have an enormous holding capacity.

6.2.3 Securing the Safe

Whatever safe is selected must be securely fastened to the structure of its surroundings. Police reports are filled with cases in which unattached safes, some as heavy as a ton, have been stolen in their entirety—safe and contents—to be worked on in uninterrupted concentration.

A convicted criminal told investigators how he and an accomplice had watched a supermarket to determine the cash flow and the manager's banking habits. They noted that the manager accumulated cash in a small, wheeled safe until Saturday morning,

FIGURE 11.4 Burglary-resistant safe. (Courtesy of Diebold, Incorporated.)

when he banked it. Presumably he felt secure in this practice since he lived in an apartment above the store and perhaps felt that he was very much on top of the situation in every way. One Friday night, the thief and his friend rolled the safe into their station wagon. They pried it open at their leisure to get the $15,000 inside.

Pleased with their success, the thieves were even more pleased when they found that the manager replaced the stolen safe with one exactly like it and continued with the same banking routine. Two weeks later, one man went back alone and picked up another $12,000 in exactly the same way as before.

It is becoming a common practice to install the safe in a concrete floor, where it offers great resistance to attack. In this kind of installation only the door and its combination are exposed. Because the door is the strongest part of a modern safe, the chances of successful robbery are considerably reduced.

6.3 Vaults

Vaults are essentially enlarged safes. As such, they are subject to the same kinds of attack and fall under the same basic principles of protection as safes.

Because it would be prohibitively expensive to build a vault out of shaped and welded steel and special alloys, the construction, except for the door, is usually of high-quality, reinforced concrete. There are many ways in which such a vault can be constructed, but however it is done, it will always be extremely heavy and at best a difficult architectural problem.

Typically vaults are situated at or below ground level so that they do not add to the stresses of the structure housing them. If a vault must be built on the upper stories of a building, independent members that do not provide support for other parts of the building must support it. It must also be strong enough to withstand the weight imposed on it if the building should collapse from under it as the result of fire or explosion.

The doors of such vaults are normally 6 inches thick, and they may be as much as 24 inches thick in the largest installations. Because these doors present a formidable obstacle to any criminal, an attack will usually be directed at the walls, ceiling, or floor, which must for that reason match the strength of the door. As a rule, these surfaces should be twice as thick as the door and never less than 12 inches thick.

If it is at all possible, a vault should be surrounded by narrow corridors that will permit inspection of the exterior but that will be sufficiently confined to discourage attackers' use of heavy drilling or cutting equipment. It is important that there be no power outlets anywhere in the vicinity of the vault; such outlets could provide criminals with energy to drive their tools.

6.4 Container Protection

Because no container can resist assault indefinitely, it must be supported by alarm systems and frequent inspections. Capacitance and vibration alarms are the types most generally used to protect safes and file cabinets. Ideally any container should be inspected at least once within the period of its rated resistance. CCTV surveillance can, of course, provide constant inspection and, if the expense is warranted, is highly recommended.

By the same token, safes have a greater degree of security if they are well lighted and located where they can be readily seen. Any safe located where it can be seen from a well-policed street is much less likely to be attacked than one that sits in a darkened back office on an upper floor.[6]

6.5 Continuing Evaluation

Security containers are the last line of defense, but in many situations, they should be the first choice in establishing a sound security system. The containers must be selected with care after an exhaustive evaluation of the needs of the facility under examination. They must also be reviewed regularly for their suitability to the job they are to perform.

Just as the safe manufacturers are continually improving the design, construction, and materials used in safes, so is the criminal world improving its technology and techniques of successful attack. Because of the considerable capital outlay involved in providing the firm with adequate security containers, many businesspeople are reluctant to entertain the notion that these containers may someday become outmoded. Not because they wear out or cease to function, but rather, because new tools and techniques have nullified their effectiveness. In 1990 a series of attacks on financial institutions in a major West Coast city in which the burglars used drainage tunnels to enter vaults from beneath the facilities pointed out that vaults are not impregnable.

In selecting security containers, it is important that the equipment conform to the needs of the risk, that it be regularly reevaluated, and that, if necessary, it be brought up to date, however unwelcome the additional dollar outlay.

7   Inspections

In spite of all defensive devices, the possibility of an intrusion always exists. The highest fence can be scaled and the stoutest lock can be compromised. A knowledgeable professional can contravene even highly sophisticated alarm systems. The most efficient system of physical protection can eventually be foiled.

It is necessary, therefore, to support each element of the system continually with another element; remember the concept of defense in depth. The ultimate backup surveillance must never be let down.

7.1   Guard Patrols

Visual inspections by irregular patrols through office spaces or an industrial complex, or constant CCTV surveillance of these same areas, are vital to the security program's success.

It is equally important to sweep the facility after closing time. "Hide-ins" are common in offices or retail establishments. These are thieves who conceal themselves in a closet or utility room and wait for the establishment to close and for everybody to go home. After hide-ins take what they are looking for, the only challenge is to break out. The chances of catching such thieves in premises protected only by perimeter alarms are remote indeed. They must be picked up on a sweep, when guards go through the entire facility from top to bottom or from east to west to see that everyone required to do so has left.

Specific duties of guards on patrol are discussed elsewhere, but in general, note that patrols should be made at least once each hour—more often if the area and the size of the guard force permit.

Guards must pay particular attention to any signs of tampering with locks, gates, fences, doors, or windows. The presence of piles of rubbish or materials should be noted for the possibility of concealment—particularly if they are near the perimeter barrier or in the vicinity of storage areas.

In patrolling office buildings, it is wise to stop occasionally for a long enough period of time to listen for any sounds that might indicate the presence of an intruder.

It is equally important that patrols in any facility be alert to any condition that might prove hazardous. These might be anything from an oil slick in a typically trafficked area to a heater left on and unattended. Conditions presenting an immediate danger must be corrected immediately; others must be reported for correction. All of them must be noted in the security log and on the appropriate form.

8   Alarms

To balance the cost factors in the consideration of any security system, it is necessary to evaluate the security needs and then determine how that security can—or more important, should—be provided. Because employing security personnel can be costly, methods must be sought to improve their efficient use and to extend the coverage they can reasonably provide.

Protection provided by physical barriers is usually the first area to be stretched to its optimum point before we start looking for other protective devices. Fences, locks, grilles, vaults, safes, and similar means of preventing entry or unauthorized use are employed to their fullest capacity. Since such methods can only delay intrusion rather than prevent it, security personnel are engaged to inspect the premises thoroughly and frequently enough to interrupt or prevent intrusion. To further protect against entry should both barrier and guard be circumvented, alarm systems are frequently employed.

Such systems permit more economical use of security personnel, and they may also substitute for costly construction of barriers. They do not act as substitutes for barriers as such. But they can support barriers of lesser impregnability and expense, and they can warn of movement in areas where barriers are impractical, undesirable, or impossible.

In determining whether a facility actually needs an alarm system, a review and evaluation of past experience of robbery, burglary, or other crimes involving unauthorized entry should be part of the survey preparatory to the formulation of the ultimate security plan. Such experience, viewed in relation to national figures and the experience of neighboring occupancies and businesses of like operation, may well serve as a guide for determining the need for alarms.

8.1   Kinds of Alarm Protection

There are three basic types of alarm systems providing protection for a security system:

- *Intrusion alarms* signal the entry of persons into a facility or an area while the system is in operation.
- *Fire alarms* operate in a number of ways to warn of fire dangers in various stages of development of a fire or to respond protectively by announcing the flow of water in a sprinkler system. Water flow indicates either that the sprinklers have been activated by the heat of a fire or that they are malfunctioning. (Fire alarms will be discussed in detail in the following chapter.)
- *Special-use alarms* warn of a process reaching a dangerous temperature (either too high or too low), of the presence of toxic fumes, or that a machine is running too fast. Although such alarms are not, strictly speaking, security devices, they may require the immediate reaction of security personnel for remedial action, and thus deserve mention at this point.

Alarms do not, in most cases, initiate any counteraction. They serve only to alert the world at large or, more usually, specific reactive forces to the fact that a condition exists for which the facility was fitted with alarms. However, many modern alarms are integrated with computer systems that can and do take predetermined actions in response to an alarm condition.

Alarm systems are of many types, but all have three common elements:

- *An alarm sensor:* A device that is designed to respond to a certain change in conditions, such as the opening of a door, movement within a room, or rapid rise in heat.
- 2. *A circuit or sending device:* A device that sends a signal about whatever is sensed to some other location. This may be done via an electrical circuit that transmits the alarm signal over a telephone, fiber optic lines, or through air waves.

- *3. An enunciator or sounding device:* A device that alerts someone that the sensor has detected a change in conditions. The device may be a light, a bell, a horn, a self-dialing phone, or a punch tape.

The questions that must be answered in setting up traditional simple alarm systems are:

1. Who can respond to an alarm fastest and most effectively?
2. What are the costs of such response as opposed to response of somewhat lesser efficiency?
3. What is the comparable predicted loss factor between these alternatives?

In modern integrated systems, the computer makes predetermined choices that include notification of appropriate personnel.

8.2   Alarm Sensors

The selection of the sensor or triggering device is dependent on many factors. The object, space, or perimeter to be protected is the first consideration. Beyond that, you must consider the incidence of outside noise, movement, or interference before deciding on the type of sensor that will do the best job. A brief examination of the kinds of devices available will serve as an introduction to a further study of this field.

8.2.1   Electromechanical Devices

Electromechanical devices are the simplest alarm devices used. They are nothing more than switches that are turned on by some change in their status. For example, an electromechanical device in a door or a window (their most common application) is held in the open, or noncontact, position when the door or window is closed (see Figure 11.5). Opening either of these entrances breaks the magnetic contact, engaging the device and thus activating the alarm.

Such devices operate on the principle of breaking the circuit. Since these devices are simply switches in a circuit, they are normally used to cover several windows and doors in a room or along a corridor. Opening any of these entrances opens the circuit and activates the alarm. They are easy to circumvent in most installations by jumping the circuit, or by tying back the plungers with string or rubber bands.

8.2.2   Pressure Devices

Pressure devices are also switches but are activated by applying pressure to them. This same principle is in regular use in buildings with automatic door openers. In security applications, they are usually in the form of mats. These are sometimes concealed under carpeting or, when they logically fit the existing decor, are placed in a strategic spot without concealment. Naturally, wires leading to them are hidden in some way.

8.2.3   Photoelectric Devices

Photoelectric devices use a beam of light, transmitted from as much as 500 feet away, to a receiver. As long as this beam is directed into the receiver, the circuit is inactive. As soon as this contact is broken, however briefly, the alarm is activated. These devices are also used as door openers.

FIGURE 11.5 (A) Recessed switches and magnets help make a neat and attractive installation. Because they are concealed, they are more tamper-resistant. (B) Larger switches are sometimes easier to install. Since they are recess mounted, they are hidden from view and their size is not noticeable. (C) Surface-mounted switches, although visible, are the least expensive and easiest to install. (Photo courtesy of Ademco.)

In security applications, the beam is modulated so that a flashlight or some other light source cannot circumvent the device, as can be done in nonsecurity applications. For greatest security, ultraviolet or infrared light is used—although an experienced intruder can spot even these unless an electronic flicker device is incorporated into the device. Obviously the device must be undetectable, because once the beam is located, it is an easy matter to step over or crawl under it.

In some applications, a single transmitter and receiver installation can be used—even when they are not in a line of sight—by a mirror system reflecting the transmitted beam around corners or to different levels. Such a system is difficult to maintain, however, since the slightest movement of any of the mirrors will disturb the alignment and the system will cease operating.

8.2.4 Motion-Detection Alarms

Motion-detection alarms operate by radio frequency or ultrasonic wave transmission (see Figure 11.6). The radio frequency (or microwave) motion detector transmits waves throughout the protected area from a transmitting to a receiving antenna. The receiving antenna is set or adjusted to a specific level of emission. Any disturbance of this level by absorption or alteration of the wave pattern will activate the alarm.

FIGURE 11.6 Motion-detector alarms. (From Robert Barnard, *Intrusion Detection Systems* [Boston: Butterworth-Heinemann, 1981], p. 125.)

The false-alarm rate with this device can be high because the radio waves will penetrate the walls and respond to motion outside the designated area unless the walls are shielded. Some such devices on the market permit an adjustment whereby the emissions can be tuned in such a way to cover only a single area without leaking into outside areas, but these require considerable skill to tune them properly.

The ultrasonic motion detector operates in much the same way, as does the radio frequency unit, except that it consists of a transceiver that both transmits and receives ultrasonic waves. One of these units can be used to cover an area, or they may be used in multiples where such use is indicated (see Figure 11.7). They can be adjusted to cover a single, limited area or broadened to provide broad area protection.

The alarm is activated when any motion disturbs the pattern of the sound waves. Some units come with special circuits that distinguish between inconsequential movement (such as flying moths or moving drapes) and an intruder.

Ultrasonic waves do not penetrate walls and are therefore unaffected by outside movement. They are not affected by audible noise in itself, but such noises can sometimes disturb the wave pattern of the protective ultrasonic transmission and create false alarms.

Passive infrared motion detectors do not transmit a signal for an intruder to disturb. Rather, moving infrared radiation is detected against the radiation environment of the room (see Figure 11.8). This detector is designed to sense the radiation from a human body. Sunlight, auto headlights, heaters, and air-conditioning units can trigger false alarms.

Dual-tech motion sensors combine the traits of passive infrared detectors with either microwave or ultrasonic technology.

8.2.5 Capacitance Alarm Systems

Also referred to as *proximity alarms*, capacitance alarm systems are used to protect metal containers of all kinds. This alarm's most common use is to protect a high-security storage area within a fenced enclosure. To set the system in operation, an ungrounded metal object (such as the safe, file, or fence mentioned previously) is wired to two oscillator circuits that are set in balance. An electromagnetic field is thus created around the object to be protected. Whenever this field is entered, the circuits are thrown out of balance and

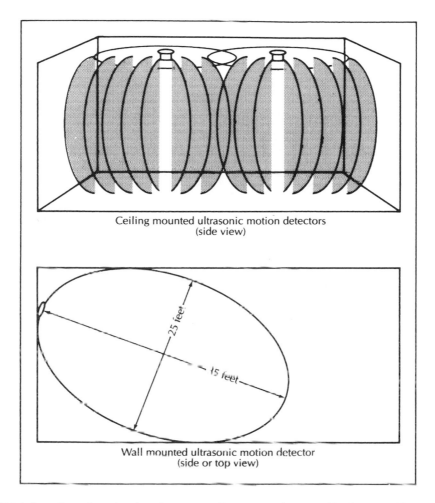

Ceiling mounted ultrasonic motion detectors
(side view)

Wall mounted ultrasonic motion detector
(side or top view)

FIGURE 11.7 Indoor ultrasonic motion-detection patterns. (From Don T. Cherry, *Total Facility Control* [Boston: Butterworth Heinemann, 1986], p. 134.)

the alarm is initiated. The electromagnetic field may project several feet from the object, but it can be adjusted to operate only a few inches from the object when traffic in the object's vicinity is such that false alarms would be triggered if the field extended too far.

8.2.6   Sonic Alarm Systems

Known variously as *noise detection, sound,* or *audio alarms,* sonic alarm systems operate on the principle that an intruder will make enough noise in a protected area to be picked up by microphones that will in turn activate an alarm. This type of system has a wide variety of uses, limited only by the problems of ambient noise levels in a given area. The system consists simply of a microphone set in the protected area that is connected to an alarm signal and receiver. When a noise activates the alarm, a monitoring guard turns on the receiver and listens in on the prowler.

Such a system must be carefully adjusted to avoid setting off the alarm at every noise. Usually adjustment is set to sound the alarm at sounds above the general level common to the protected area. The system is not useful in areas where background noise levels are so high that they will drown out the anticipated sounds of surreptitious entry. This

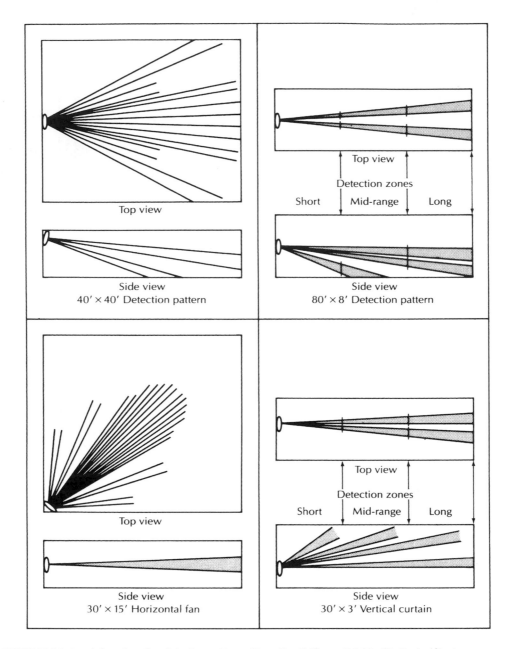

FIGURE 11.8 Indoor infrared motion-detection patterns. (From Don T. Cherry, *Total Facility Control* [Boston: Butterworth-Heinemann, 1986], p. 135.)

device may also come with a sound discriminator that evaluates sounds to eliminate false alarms.

8.2.7 *Vibration Detectors*
Vibration detectors provide a high level of protection against attack in specific areas or on specific objects. In this system, a specialized type of contact microphone is attached to objects such as works of art, safes, or files, or to surfaces such as walls or ceilings.

Any attack on, or movement of, these objects or surfaces causes some vibration. This vibration is picked up by microphones, which in turn activate alarms. These units may be adjusted for sensitivity, which is set according to application and environment. Here again, discriminator units are available to screen out harmless vibrations. These units are very useful in specific applications because their false alarm rates are very low.

Certain additional alarm devices are currently in use as perimeter protection, as discussed in Chapter 9.

Some of the alarm sensors discussed in the preceding paragraphs can be defined as providing point protection. Electromechanical devices, capacitance alarms, and pressure devices, for instance, will be activated only when a specific area (point of entry) has been crossed, a door or window has been opened, or an object has been moved. On the other hand, ultrasonic, microwave, and passive infrared alarm systems protect large spaces, even entire rooms, against intrusion. These "volumetric" alarms, however, can be triggered by any number of environmental factors normally present in the protected space. Each alarm system has different strengths and weaknesses, and to assure effective performance, the total environment should be analyzed before selecting the specific system. Table 11.1 briefly summarizes the factors that affect these systems.

8.2.8   Alarm Monitoring Systems

Currently available monitoring systems are:

- *The central station:* This is a facility set up to monitor alarms indicating fire, intrusion, and problems in industrial processes. Such facilities are set up for a number of clients; all are serviced simultaneously. On the sounding of an alarm, a team of security officers may be dispatched to the scene and the local police or fire department may be notified. Depending on the nature of the alarm, on-duty plant or office protection is notified as well. Such a service is as effective as its response time, its alertness to alarms, and the thoroughness of inspection of premises fitted with alarms.

- *Proprietary system:* This functions in the same way as a central station system except that it is owned and operated by the company rather than a contractor and is located on company property. Response to all alarms is generally by the facility's own security or fire personnel.

- *Local alarm system:* In this case, the sensor activates a circuit that in turn activates a horn, a siren, or even a flashing light located in the immediate vicinity of the area fitted with alarms. Only guards within hearing distance can respond to such alarms, so their use is restricted to situations in which guards are so located that their immediate response is assured. Such systems are most useful for fire alarm systems because they can alert personnel to evacuate the endangered area. In such cases, the system can also be connected to local fire departments to serve the dual purpose of alerting personnel and the company fire brigade to the danger as well as calling for assistance from public firefighting forces.

- *Auxiliary system:* In this system, installation circuits are connected to local police or fire departments or 911 centers by leased telephone lines. The dual responsibility for circuits and the high incidence of false alarms have made this system unpopular with public fire and police personnel. In a growing number of cities, such installations are no longer permitted as a matter of public policy.

Table 11.1 What Detector to Select: Space Protection Guide

Environmental and Other Variables	Ultrasonic	Passive Infrared	Microwave
Vibration	No problem with balanced processing, some problem with unbalanced	Very few problems	Can be a major problem
Effect of temperature change on range	A little	A lot	None
Effect of humidity change on range	Some	None	None
Reflection of area of coverage by large metal objects	Very little	None unless metal is highly polished	Can be a major problem
Reduction of range by drapes, carpets	Some	None	None
Sensitivity to movement of overhead doors	Needs careful placement	Very few problems	Can be a major problem
Sensitivity to small animals	Problem if animals close	Problem if animals close but can be aimed so beams are well above floor	Problem if animals are close
Water movement in plastic storm drain pipes	No problem	No problem	Can be problem if storm drainpipes very close
Water noise from faulty valves	Can be a problem, but very rare	No problem	No problem
Movement through thin walls or glass	No problem	No problem	Needs careful placement
Drafts, air movement	Needs careful placement	No problem	No problem
Sun, moving headlights through windows	No problem	Needs careful placement	No problem
Ultrasonic noise	Bells, hissing, some inaudible noises can cause problems	No problem	No problem
Heaters	Problem only in extreme cases	Needs careful placement	No problem
Moving machinery, fan blades	Needs careful placement	Very little problem	Needs careful placement
Radio interference, AC line transients	Can be problem in severe cases	Can be problem in severe cases	Can be problem in severe cases
Piping of detection field to unexpected areas by AC ducting	No problem	Very few problems	Can be problem when radar is close and sensor pointed at it

(Continued)

Table 11.1 Continued

Environmental and Other Variables	Ultrasonic	Passive Infrared	Microwave
Radar interference	Very few problems	Very few problems	Can be problem when radar is close and sensor pointed at it
Cost per square foot, large open areas	In between	Most expensive	Least expensive
Cost per square foot, divided areas, multiple rooms	Least expensive	Most expensive	In between
Range adjustment required?	Yes	No	Yes
Current consumption (size of battery required for extended standby power)	In between	Smallest	Largest
Interference between two or more sensors	Must be crystal controlled and/or synchronized	No problem	Must be different frequencies

Source: Aritech Corp.
This list is intended as a guide only and does not represent absolutes but suggests areas for consideration.

- *Local alarm-by-chance system:* This is a local alarm system in which a bell or siren is sounded with no predictable response. These systems are used in residences or small retail establishments that cannot afford a response system. The hope is that a neighbor or a passing patrol car will react to the alarm and call for police assistance, but such a call is purely a matter of chance.
- *Dial alarm system:* This system is set to dial a predetermined telephone number or numbers when the alarm is activated. The number(s) selected might be the police, the subscriber's home number, or both. When the phone is answered, a recording states that an intrusion is in progress at the location so fitted with alarms. This system is relatively inexpensive to install and operate, but because it is dependent on general phone circuits, it could fail if the line(s) being called were busy or if the phone connections were cut.

8.3   Cost Considerations

The costs involved in setting up even a fairly simple alarm system can be substantial, and the great part of this outlay is not recoverable should the system prove inadequate or unwarranted. Its installation should be predicated on exposure, concomitant need, and on the manner of its integration into the existing or planned security program.

This last point is important to consider because the effectiveness of any alarm procedure lies in the response it commands. As elementary as it sounds, it is worth repeating that most alarms take no action; they only notify that action should be taken. There must therefore be some entity near at hand that can take that action. Too often, otherwise effective alarm systems are set up without adequate supportive or responding personnel.

FIGURE 11.9 In-depth physical security. (From Don T. Cherry, *Total Facility Control* [Boston: Butterworth-Heinemann, 1986], p. 148.)

This is at best wasteful and at worst dangerous. The best systems are integrated with computers so that the computer can initiate action while waiting for human response.

In many instances, alarm installations are made to reduce the size of the guard force. This is sometimes possible. At least if the current guard force cannot be reduced in number, those additional guards needed to cover areas now fitted with alarms will no longer be required.

Good business practice demands that the expense of alarm installations be undertaken only after a carefully considered cost and effectiveness analysis of all the elements. If the existing security personnel can cover the security requirements of the facility, no alarm system is needed. If they can cover the ground but not in a way that will satisfy security standards, more guards are needed or the existing force must be augmented by an alarm system to extend their coverage and their protective ability. The costs and effectiveness must be studied together with an eye toward the efficient achievement of stated objectives.

Summary

Almost all sources of the security equipment industry predict growth, indicating that use of technology and equipment to supplement security staffs is growing. Today a great deal of new technology and equipment are available to the security manager. Some of it is useful, some not, but none of it is better than the use to which it is put or the system into which it is integrated. No equipment can stand on its own. It can be used only if it is employed properly, fully, and effectively, and to be effective, all the components of the security system must work together. Figure 11.9 shows the security devices and types of barrier protection commonly used for each line of defense.

□ □ □ ▬▬▬▬▬▬▬▬▬▬▬▬▬▬▬▬▬▬▬▬▬▬▬▬▬▬▬▬▬▬▬▬

Critical Thinking

Knowing about the various security techniques that are available to protect assets, is it possible to develop a virtually attack-proof security system? Is this even desirable? What are the potential problems, if any?

▬▬▬▬▬▬▬▬▬▬▬▬▬▬▬▬▬▬▬▬▬▬▬▬▬▬▬▬▬ □ □ □

A reasonable level of security cannot necessarily be assured with a single line of defense. Depending on the level of security desired, you might require several layers of protection in an integrated system.

Review Questions

1. What are the elements necessary for an effective visitor access control system?
2. Explain the characteristics of each of the common types of alarm systems.
3. Give an example of a situation in which a motion-detection alarm might be deployed effectively. Under what circumstances would an ultrasonic system be chosen over a radio frequency system?
4. Describe how passive infrared detectors operate. What environmental variables must be considered to assure proper operation?

References

1. Homeland Security Presidential Directive/HSPD-12, Office of the Press Secretary, White House, August 27, 2004, www.whitehouse.gov/news/releases/2004/08.
2. "Face in Hand; Biometrics Company Bioscrypt to Merge with A4Vision Facial Recognition Company,"*Security Magazine*, e-mail list serve January 23, 2007.
3. Homeland Security Presidential Directive/HSPD-12.
4. Diebold Direct Security Catalog (Canton, OH: Diebold, 1990), p. 10.
5. Ibid.
6. Jeffery, C.R., Hunter, R.D., and Griswold, J., "Crime Prevention and Computer Analysis of Convenience Store Robberies in Tallahassee, Florida," *Florida Police Journal* (1987): 65–69.

12

Contingency Planning, Fire Protection, Emergency Response, and Safety

1 Introduction

No facility protection program is complete without clear, well-defined policies and programs confronting the possible threat of fire or any other natural or human-made disaster. Planning for such contingencies is the responsibility of top management, but unfortunately in most situations the task of carrying out the emergency response falls specifically on security. In the best of all possible worlds, the responsibility for disaster planning is assigned to a fire department and a safety department, allowing security to focus on security-related matters. Regardless of the functional placement of responsibility, security, fire, and safety personnel must work together when they are confronted with disasters.

According to an IOMA Safety & Security Reports briefing, 39 percent of U.S. companies lack a basic crisis plan and 56 percent have not conducted crisis drills or simulation in the last year (2006). If Senator Joseph Lieberman has his say, disaster preparedness will by legislation become a business responsibility. Under an amendment to a 9/11 bill passed by the House, the Department of Homeland Security and the American National Standards Institute would formulate a set of "best practices" for disaster preparedness that businesses will have a choice of adopting. The proposal includes a certification process to verify compliance.[1]

According to Dennis F. Sigwart, current and future security professionals should be aware of the absolute necessity of disaster planning and preparedness as a viable component of the many facets (fire, earthquake, explosions, flood, and so forth) they will have to confront as a practitioner. Those assigned disaster preparedness tasks must continually play the "what happens if?" game.[2]

Fire, safety, and emergency (contingency) planning is designed to anticipate what might happen to endanger people or physical property and to take the necessary preventive measures, as well as to make provision—through appropriate hardware and/or personnel response—for prompt and effective action when an emergency does occur.

Though the emphasis in this chapter (as in most actual practice) is on physical safeguards, it is important to emphasize the human aspect of fire, safety, and emergency protection. Disastrous losses often occur not from the failure or absence of physical safeguards but from human error—the failure to close a fire door, to maintain existing protection systems in good working condition, to inspect or report hazards, and, at the management level, to ensure through continuous employee education and training that the organization remains prepared at any time for any emergency. The Occupational Safety and Health Administration (OSHA), National Fire Protection Association (NFPA), and Life Safety Codes dictate certain safety requirements for all businesses. In addition, the NFPA, Factory Mutual, and Underwriters Laboratories (UL) have established standards for fire and safety that have been adopted by many state and local governments. These standards have been important in helping various insurance companies establish their rating systems.

2   Contingency Planning

The Association of Contingency Planners (ACP), an association dedicated to the evolution of business continuity, describes contingency planning in the following way: "Business continuity planning integrates knowledge from related disciplines such as information technology, emergency response, and crisis communications to create a strategy that ensures a business will remain resilient in the face of adversity."[3]

The purpose of contingency planning is simple. Essentially, contingency planners work to prepare their business, organization, or institution to be better able to mitigate any disruption to normal business activities. As an example, if a natural occurrence (hurricane, fire, or earthquake) disrupts normal business activities, having plans in place for responding to and recovering from the disaster will allow for a faster recovery, thus reducing the amount of time the business is disrupted.

For our purposes, we will discuss contingency planning in the construct of four major components: emergency response, crisis management, business recovery, and business resumption. The fundamental elements of each component and the need for an effective, integrated contingency planning process will be addressed. Furthermore, categories and types of crises, along with basic preparation and awareness needs, will be discussed. The reader will note that emergency response, crisis management, business recovery, and business resumption processes have much in common (for example, communications requirements); however, each is handled as a standalone process.

2.1   Security and the Contingency Planning Process

The traditional role of security in the contingency planning process has been to develop emergency evacuation plans for the business and to respond to emergency or crisis situations. Acting as the eyes and ears for an organization, business, or facility and maintaining a 24-hour-day, seven-day-a-week presence, the security organization is best positioned to respond to and manage a crisis. As crises escalate, they are best managed by a multidisciplinary team.

Because of the ever-ready posture of many security organizations and the increased emphasis on emergency preparedness and contingency planning following the tragic events of September 11, 2001, in New York City and Washington, D.C., many security departments have expanded their contingency planning capabilities to include our four major components of emergency response, crisis management, business recovery, and business resumption.

Depending on the scope of the effort, a contingency planning program can take into consideration many activities, events, conditions, and processes. Depending on the business's size and complexity, the process of contingency planning can be quite extensive. Planning for a contingency generally means assessing and understanding all aspects of the business, particularly the business-critical processes and supporting information systems. To do this effectively requires the participation of many people from different disciplines. This includes management, employees, suppliers, and sometimes even customers. It may also include representatives from external organizations such as an insurance underwriter or the local fire departments.

Having so many people involved and from the many different functional disciplines calls for establishing common parameters. For the plan to be effective, everyone involved must have a common understanding of the contingency planning program's elements and objectives, and all must have a common understanding of the process. The first consideration in establishing common parameters is to develop a set of common definitions of terms. When discussing any aspect of contingency planning it is essential that all parties have a common understanding of what is being discussed. Just what does someone mean when they refer to crisis management, business recovery, or any other element of the contingency planning process?

The following contingency planning terms are defined in such a way as to be useful for any organization in establishing a common baseline, points of reference, and common jargon for the contingency planning process. Definition of terms must be part of the organization's formal or institutionalized contingency planning process to ensure continuity of planning and success in achieving common preparedness objectives:

- *Business continuity:* Minimizing business interruption or disruption caused by different contingencies. Keeping the business going. Business continuity plans encompass actions related to the way an organization prepares for, manages, recovers, and ultimately resumes business after a disruption.
- *Business recovery:* Refers to the short-term (less than 60 days) restoration activities that return the business to a minimum acceptable level of operation or production following a work disruption. Commonly used interchangeably with the term *disaster recovery*.
- *Business resumption:* The long-term (more than 60 days) process of restoration activities after an emergency or disaster that return the organization to its

pre-event condition. (Keep in mind that restoration to the exact pre-event condition might not be necessary or even desirable. However, making this determination might not be possible without proper planning or going through the actual resumption process.)

- *Contingency:* An event that is possible but uncertain in terms of occurrence or that is likely to happen as an adjunct to other events. Contingencies interrupt normal business activities. In some cases the disruption is minor; in others the disruption can be catastrophic.

- *Contingency planning:* The process of planning for response, recovery, and resumption activities for the infrastructure, critical processes, and other elements of an organization based on encountering different contingencies.

- *Crisis management:* The process of managing events of a crisis to a condition of stability. This task is best accomplished by an integrated process team (IPT) made up of members from different disciplines throughout the organization. When formed, the team becomes the organization's crisis management team (CMT) and serves as the site, business, or organization deliberative body for emergency response and crisis management planning and implementation.

- *Critical processes:* Activities performed by functions, departments, or elements within a business or organization that, if significantly disrupted due to an incident, emergency, or disaster, would have an adverse impact on organizational operations, revenue generation ability, production and/or distribution schedules, contractual commitments, or legal obligations.

- *Emergency response:* The act of reporting and responding to any emergency or major disruption of the business organization's operations.

2.2   Contingency Planning Program

The purpose for contingency planning is to better enable a business or organization to mitigate disruption to the enterprise. Should disruptions occur, and they do all too often, the enterprise must be able to resume normal business activities as quickly as possible. The inability to restore normal operations will have an adverse economic impact on the enterprise. The extent of the impact will correspond to the extent of the disruption or damage. It the damage is severe and the mitigation of such damage has not been properly planned for, the effect could be catastrophic. Essentially, the business could fail.

Essentially, contingencies fall into three categories:

- Those that impact the business infrastructure (fire, severe weather, earthquakes: see the definition of hazards further in this section), causing physical damage.

- Those that impact people, such as accidents, seasonal illnesses (influenza), epidemics, or pandemics, causing harm to employees and rendering them unavailable to work.

- Those that impact the reputation of the business (such as a product defect leading to a recall), causing resources to be diverted from normal operations to recovery and/or restoration. Each contingency has the potential to disrupt normal business operations to some degree. A minor building fire may disrupt operations in a limited way for only a couple of days, whereas a major fire could destroy an entire factory, completely stopping operations for an extended period.

Contingency planning is a continuous process requiring periodic updates and revisions as appropriate to, and consistent with, changing business conditions. It is not something that can be done once and put away only to be retrieved when needed. It also involves implementing and maintaining awareness and training elements. Personnel with contingency planning responsibilities require periodic familiarization with plans and processes as well as training on new techniques and methods. The process of contingency planning should be designed to achieve the following:

- Secure and protect people. In the event of a crisis, people (employees, visitors, customers, and suppliers) must be protected.
- Secure the continuity of the core elements of the business (the infrastructure and critical processes) and minimize disruptions to the business.
- Secure and protect all information systems that include or affect supplier connections and customer relationships.

The remaining sections of this chapter present and explain elements of the contingency planning process and program (see Figure 12.1).

2.3 Contingency Plans

Contingency plans formally establish the processes and procedures to protect employees, core business elements, critical processes, information systems, and the environment in the event of an emergency, business disruption, or disaster. These plans should be developed and designed to consider specific categories and types of emergencies and disasters and address the mitigation, preparedness, and response actions to be taken by employees, management, and the organizations charged with specific response and recovery tasks. These plans should contain basic guidance, direction, responsibilities, and administrative information and must include the following elements:

- *Assumptions:* Basic assumptions must be developed to establish contingency planning ground rules. As a baseline for planning, it is best to use several possible "worst-case" scenarios relative to time of event, type of event, available resources, building/facility occupancy, evacuation of personnel, personnel stranded on site, and environmental factors such as weather conditions and temperature. Furthermore, consideration should be given to establishing response parameters for emergency events. Define (for your enterprise) what constitutes a minor emergency, a major emergency, and a disaster.
- *Risk assessment and vulnerability analysis:* Identify known and apparent vulnerabilities and risks associated with the type of business and the enterprise's geographic location. Make an assessment of risk and vulnerabilities prior to developing or upgrading contingency plans. All planning will be accomplished in accordance with a thorough understanding of actual and potential risks and vulnerabilities. For example, in a petroleum refining facility, contingency plans for petroleum spillage, contamination, and fires must be considered. Furthermore, if the facility is located in an earthquake zone, planning must address associated hazards. The risk assessment and vulnerability analysis must also include an assessment of enterprise-critical relationships. That means involving suppliers and

Contingency planning and business continuity program

Site emergency response plan (hazmat plan & fire prevention plan)	Site crisis management plan	Site business recovery & resumption plans	Vital records program	Information systems, telecommunications, and facilities	Executive protection
Escalated response	Transition to bus. cont. team	Written process contingency plans			
Communications	Initial assessment	Recovery strategies approved by management			
Accountability	Incident containment	Critical process identification			
Evacuation					
Emergency response	Responsibilities notifications activation	Management guidance & analysis			
Employee education					
Focus: People	Focus: Decision processes	Focus: Maintaining revenue stream			

Business impact analysis (Identify process owners, information system dependencies, financial impact, maximum allowable downtimes)
Risk assessment & vulnerabilities analysis
Corporate and business unit requirments

OSHA requirements

FIGURE 12.1 Elements of a business continuity planning program. This chart depicts the building blocks of contingency planning and a business continuity program and their relationship to each other.

customers in the contingency planning process. If a critical supplier or many key suppliers are not also prepared for various potential contingencies, their inability to recover will adversely impact your enterprise.

- *Types of hazards:* Planning for each and every type of hazard is not practical nor is it desirable. Grouping them into similar or like categories will allow you to plan to address categories of hazards. Since many hazards have similar consequences and result in like damages, it is best to plan for them in categories. The following is a list of common hazards: medical emergencies; fires; bomb threats; high winds; power interruptions; floods; hurricanes; snow and ice storms or blizzards; hazardous materials issues; aircraft crashes; civil disorders; earthquakes; terrorist threats or activities; workplace violence; explosions; and tornados.

- *Critical process identification:* Critical processes must be ranked in accordance of criticality and importance to the enterprise's productivity and survivability. The process of recovery must be focused on critical processes that, when resumed, will restore operations to a minimal acceptable level. In essence, these processes are identified to be the first processes restored in the event of a major interruption to business operations. Failure to restore them presents the greatest possibility of damage or loss to the enterprise and could lead to the loss of a competitive edge, market share, or even the enterprise's viability.

- *Business impact analysis:* A business impact analysis must be accomplished to accurately determine the financial and operational impact that could result from an interruption of enterprise operations. Moreover, all critical interdependencies, those processes or activities on which critical processes depend, must be assessed to determine the extent to which they must be part of the contingency planning process.

- *Emergency response:* All participants in the emergency response process, particularly emergency responders, must understand their roles. Expectations and responsibilities of emergency response personnel must be well defined and documented. Guidance for all employees on how to react in the event of an emergency and what their individual and collective responsibilities are must be documented and shared. Organizational responsibilities must also be established to include the development of department-level emergency plans, generally for midsize and large organizations. Events such as building evacuation and role-call assembly need to be well defined so that, in the event of an actual emergency, there is no confusion or uncertainty as to what must be accomplished.

- *Incident management and crisis management:* As an incident escalates, a crisis management team (CMT) should assume responsibility for managing the crisis. How this process works and who has what responsibilities must be clearly stated in the contingency plans. In the event of an actual emergency, some unauthorized people will attempt to manage the incident or participate in crisis management; however, they should not have any role in this process unless they were previously identified and trained as part of the CMT. Without established and well-defined incident management protocols and procedures, chaos is likely to erupt. Essentially, incident management and crisis management personnel must be trained and must understand their responsibilities. Where practical, backup supporting personnel should be identified and trained in the event that primary personnel are not available or are disabled.

- *Incident/event analysis:* After an event occurs and the situation is stable, conduct an analysis of what occurred and the reason it occurred to determine the immediate extent of damage and the potential for subsequent additional damage.

- *Business resumption planning:* The process of planning to facilitate recovery of designated critical processes and the resumption of business in the event of an interruption should be performed in two parts. The first part focuses on business recovery in the short term; the second part focuses on business restoration in the long term. This process will also include establishment of priorities for restoring critical processes, infrastructure, and information systems.

- *Post-event evaluation:* An assessment of preceding events to determine what went well, what did not go so well, and what improvements to existing plans need to be made must also be part of the process. Learning from real events is an unfortunate opportunity. There is no better way to learn how to handle an emergency than to actually handle one.

3   Emergency Response

When an emergency occurs, and unfortunately emergencies occur at even the most prepared businesses, being able to respond effectively is critical. The type and nature of emergency that can occur vary widely. From a medical emergency, where an employee becomes injured or sick, to a natural or manmade disaster causing extensive damage to buildings and equipment, being prepared to respond will usually lessen the damage or impact of the event.

Preparedness takes many forms. Being prepared to respond to a medical emergency is different from being prepared to respond to a natural disaster. The medical emergency might only require applying first aid to a victim, or it could require the assistance and services of medical professionals. A natural disaster could require support from emergency medical services along with law enforcement, fire departments, and search-and-rescue operations as well as hazardous materials crews.

When planning for emergencies, group types of emergencies into like categories so that planning is accomplished for only categories of emergencies as opposed to each and every possible emergency. This strategy recognizes the similarities of various types of emergency and is efficient in terms of creating fewer but flexible actual plans.

The purpose of preparing an emergency response plan is to document the planning accomplished in preparation for an emergency. This documentation provides the ground rules for emergency response activities. It also provides a reference for all who need to know how the process works. The plan will identify general and specific responsibilities for emergency response personnel and for all employees, both management and nonmanagement. Having a plan in place will assist emergency response personnel in their effort to return the business to normal operations.

- *Reporting emergencies:* Employees must know how, and to whom, emergencies should be reported. If handling an emergency is beyond an organization's internal capability, additional external assistance can be sought. For example, a seriously ill employee may require immediate medical attention. If paramedic capabilities exist within the company, the in-house paramedics should be the first responders. If the situation calls for more sophisticated expertise and capabilities, call external emergency medical services.

- *Communications and warning systems during an emergency:*

  1. *Fire alarm systems:* These systems are generally the most widely used. Linked to a variety of sensor detectors and manual pull stations, fire alarms do just that—sound an alarm. These systems are sufficiently unique in sound and volume as to clearly indicate the need for building and facility evacuation. Employees must be conditioned to respond immediately.

  2. *Public address systems:* These systems can be used to augment the fire alarm system. Announcements can be made alerting employees to the danger of fire. Announcements alerting employees to other types of dangers can also be made. Public address systems are particularly useful during emergencies in which a building or facility evacuation is just the opposite of what is needed. For example, in the event of a chemical discharge or other environmental hazard, it might be necessary to keep people inside the facility and shut down all air movement systems, thus preventing employees from exposure to hazardous airborne substances. Since employees are conditioned to evacuate a building or facility when a fire alarm is sounded, they can be conditioned to wait and listen for specific instructions provided over a public address system.

  3. *Floor wardens:* The use of employees to augment the emergency notification system has a great deal of value. Specially selected and trained employees can be given responsibility to act to spread the word to evacuate a building or facility during an emergency. Assigning each one a specific area of responsibility (or floor, hence the term *floor warden*) ensures complete coverage of the building or facility. Communications between floor wardens and emergency response personnel or a security emergency operations center can be easily established. Floor wardens can be alerted by pager, cell phone, or other means (including a variety of wireless devices) in the event of an emergency and can be instructed to react to the specific situation. Floor wardens can and should be empowered and trained to react on their own in the event that they recognize danger. Give authority to floor wardens to evacuate a building or facility based on their judgment and assessment of an emergency situation. In the event of a complete communications failure, it might be necessary to empower floor wardens to dispatch people to a safe environment.

  4. *Security officers:* Since security officers are generally located throughout the facility, they are usually the first responders. Here officers can assess the situation and make a determination whether additional assistance is necessary. In some cases, they might not be able to make an assessment and may require support from others. For example, in the event of a hazardous chemical spill, it will be necessary to have an expert in environmental and safety issues on the scene to make the assessment. It may even be necessary for a hazardous materials (hazmat) crew to respond to handle the event. Cleanup of a chemical spill should be done only by skilled and certified personnel. Clearly defining who has what response capabilities and responsibilities will impact the effectiveness of any response.

- *Department-specific emergency plans:* It is best to have one emergency response plan for each company facility. These plans should be incorporated into a master plan and provide a common framework for all sub-elements of the plan. A key sub-element of an emergency plan is the individual departments' emergency plans. Those plans must specifically identify the following information:

  1. Common and unique responsibilities in the event of an emergency to include:

     A roster of department employees

     Emergency contact/notification roster (not all emergencies occur during working hours so it might be necessary to reach people at home)

  2. Identify floor wardens

  3. Evacuation routes, procedures, and assembly areas

  4. Role-call instructions

  5. Procedures for evacuation of people who require assistance

  6. People identified as members of a search-and-rescue team

  7. Additional manager- or employee-specific responsibilities

- *Incident management:* Personnel trained in handling emergencies should manage the incident at the scene. If the incident escalates to a crisis, a company CMT should be convened to manage the crisis. The senior emergency response person at the scene should manage the incident with the assistance of specialists as appropriate.

- *Evacuation and assembly:* A critical objective during any emergency is employee safety. In the event it is necessary to evacuate a building or facility, it is essential to have an established and orderly process. Once a warning system sounds the notice to evacuate, employees must be aware of pre-established procedures for quick evacuation, including primary and alternate evacuation routes and where they should assemble. Maps or diagrams with this information should be included in the plan and posted throughout the work area. A floor warden or an employee with the assignment to facilitate evacuation should make a sweep of the area prior to their own evacuation to ensure that all personnel have exited the building or facility. Once everyone is in the predetermined assembly area, a roll call must be taken. Primary, secondary, and tertiary responsibilities should be assigned to ensure that someone is available to take role call and report the results to security. If someone did not evacuate the facility, a search-and-rescue team or other emergency personnel may be required to reenter the facility and provide assistance.

- *Emergency evacuation drills:* The efficient and complete evacuation of personnel from a building or facility in the event of an emergency is such an important event that periodic drills should be conducted to reinforce the process and its importance. At least annually, each building or facility should undergo an evacuation drill where employees respond to a warning and completely evacuate the building or facility. A role call should be conducted and results reported to security and senior management.

- *Search and rescue:* In the event of serious damage such as a fire or collapse of building, it might be necessary to search for persons not accounted for. Search and rescue are the responsibility of responding emergency personnel who have proper protective equipment. Persons not trained in search-and-rescue techniques or who do not have proper equipment should not enter hazardous areas and conduct searches.

- *Return to work:* The process for returning to work after a crisis should also be included in the emergency plan. After any incident that requires employees to leave their work area and evacuate a building or facility, a process for having them return to work is necessary. For example, in the event of a false fire alarm where employees have evacuated a building, a means of communicating to them an all-clear, safe-to-return-to-work signal is needed. This can be accomplished in many ways. Public address announcements can be made, or plant protection personnel can go to assembly areas directing employees to return to work. As appropriate, other methods may also be employed. In the event there is actual damage and employees cannot return to work, a process should be established to identify who makes the decision to send employees home as well as how that information is communicated to them and how they are kept apprised of event updates. For example, if a building was severely damaged due to fire and cannot be occupied for several days, posting daily direction and guidance for employees on the company Website or on an emergency toll-free phone line will allow employees to call each day for specific instructions. For this to be effective, employees must know this process, know the phone number to call or Website to access. Like all other processes, this one must be updated regularly.

- *After action:* When any incident occurs that necessitates evacuation or results in injuries or major damage or presents the possibility of major business interruption, an after-action report must be prepared. The primary focus is twofold:

  1. Document the events, circumstances, and chronology.
  2. Prepare a "lessons learned" review. Include key personnel involved in responding to and managing the emergency so as to assess what occurred and how could it have been better handled.

4 Crisis Management

Emergencies, contingencies, business interruptions, and other unplanned events happen. Sometimes the event itself is a crisis, such as a fire burning a building or facility. In other cases, an incident not responded to or managed properly at the scene may turn into a crisis. For example, failing to respond promptly to that small fire could allow it to turn into a large fire.

Crisis management is the process of managing events in a crisis to a condition of stability. Crisis management is *not* incident management. Emergency response personnel at the scene of an incident manage the incident. If the incident escalates, becoming a crisis, it is then necessary to have a different group take charge. Ideally, a crisis management team, or CMT, consisting of experienced personnel from multiple disciplines, would come together to manage the incidents that develop beyond the capability and decision authority of emergency response personnel. Essentially, the CMT manages the crisis to closure.

After emergency response planning, crisis management planning is the next step in the continuum of the contingency planning process. A crisis management plan should address the following activities and concerns:

- *Crisis management teams:* Managing a crisis can't be left to emergency personnel only. When an incident escalates into a crisis, the situation becomes more complex, affecting different aspects of the business if not the entire business, and thus requires different skills to manage. Employees with a broad understanding of the enterprise and its mission, goals, and objectives are much better suited to manage a crisis than those with a more narrow perspective of the business. Ideally, a CMT is like an integrated process team: Skilled professionals representing different disciplines come together on a short-term basis to work on a specific issue or task. In the case of CMTs, the task is to serve as a deliberative body to plan and prepare for a crisis and, when a crisis occurs, manage that crisis so as to mitigate damage or its impact. CMTs should include members with expertise in the following areas: security, human resources, site management, safety and environmental and safety services, business management, and communications.

- *Disaster operations:* In the event of a crisis or disaster, it is to be expected that some personnel might not be able to immediately leave the site. For example, following an earthquake the surrounding area might not be safe for travel. Employees may have no choice but to seek shelter at the workplace for hours or days. Furthermore, emergency personnel could be needed on site for an extended period to assist in recovery operations. It's essential to be prepared to deal with scenarios such as this one. Preparation will include ensuring that sufficient supplies to meet the needs of a reasonable number of stranded or support personnel are on hand and that sufficient food, water, medical supplies, and emergency sanitation and shelter facilities are available. All these items can be acquired and placed in long-term storage providing that they are regularly checked for serviceability and spoilage and maintained within the expected shelf life. During a crisis, there is typically a great deal of uncertainty. Consequently, it will be necessary to communicate to employees, keeping them as up to date as possible about the situation and events and providing guidance concerning their safety and work expectations. In such situations, employees are naturally anxious. Prompt and clear communications can help reduce their anxiety and keep them informed. Communication may need to extend beyond the duration of a crisis into an undefined subsequent period. Using the previously discussed emergency contact and notification number or company Website can be very effective. Messages can be updated regularly as needed so that the information is current. Also, information broadcast on local news radio stations can reach a large population of employees. At the point when an incident escalates into a crisis, the CMTs become involved managing the crisis to closure. At some point, a deescalation of events will occur and eventually the crisis will terminate. If the impact of or damage from the crisis is significant, the CMT will commence restoration activities. These activities may be led by the CMT or passed on to a business continuity team, as discussed further in the next section.

- *Media relations:* During a crisis, it is possible that the local, national, or even international media will become interested in events. For example, large industrial fires always draw the attention of local media. Natural disasters also draw much media attention. Even isolated events such as incidents of workplace violence can draw significant media attention. It is therefore important to have a media relations plan. The company media representative should be part of the CMT. Since there is always a degree of unpredictability during a crisis, it is best that all CMT members understand how to deal with the media and be prepared to do so, should they be thrust into such a situation.

- *Damage assessment:* During a crisis, emergency personnel will make ongoing damage assessments, reporting the status to the CMT. These assessments are useful in determining actions to be taken next. However, these assessments are situational and, due to the circumstances and nature of a crisis, do not have the luxury of thoroughness. The true extent of damage is not determined until after the crisis has terminated and a complete building, facility, or site assessment can be made. Immediately following a crisis, a damage assessment for infrastructure safety and functionality must be made. Without this, a return-to-work decision cannot be made. The damage assessment is also the starting point for all restoration and resumption activities.

- *Business continuity teams:* Earlier we discussed the transition of responsibility from a CMT to a business continuity team. This is an important step in the effort to resume business. The CMT's focus is on managing through the crisis; the focus of the business continuity team (BCT) is recovery and resumption. The role of a BCT is discussed further in the next section.

- *After action/post event assessments:* After every crisis, an assessment of what occurred should be conducted. The chronology and circumstances of the event will be recorded. The CMT will review what went well and what did not. Performance to plan will be reviewed and a lessons-learned document will be created for all team members and supporting personnel to review and hopefully learn from.

5   Business Continuity

Earlier in this chapter, we defined business continuity as the effort to minimize business interruption or disruption caused by different contingencies. When contingencies occur, business recovery and resumption need to happen as rapidly as possible. In essence, business must continue. Business disruptions can be costly and even catastrophic. Customers, shareholders, and stakeholders demand that the business remain viable. Preparation to deal with contingencies is a critical component of keeping the business going and maintaining the viability of the enterprise.

Business continuity is a two-stage process. *Business recovery* is the first stage; *business resumption* is the second. The recovery effort is the process of getting the business up and running again but only in a minimally acceptable condition. It is not recovery to a pre-event condition; it is recovery to create product, make deliveries to customers, and accomplish the basic activities to keep the business going.

The business resumption stage is the effort to recover from a contingency and resume business in a pre-event condition. This is not to say that all critical and other processes will be exactly the same as they were pre-event. Resumption planning may call for new or modified processes. The intent is to resume business operations to a level similar to the pre-event operations level but not necessarily exactly the same.

A business continuity team, or BCT, should be established to oversee the development of business resumption plans. Representatives from each of the major business functions should be part of this team. Manufacturing, business management, finance, engineering, information technology, human resources, legal, and other major areas and disciplines within the business need to participate. Business resumption teams lead the effort and planning process to ensure that the business is prepared to recover from contingencies and resume full business operations. In some cases it may be necessary to have a major supplier or customer participate as a member of this team.

Business recovery and resumption planning have common elements. The difference is the stage of recovery and the time necessary to get there. The following are common elements of the processes for business recovery and resumption:

- *Business impact analysis of critical processes and information systems:* The most fundamental aspect of recovery and resumption planning is conducting a business impact analysis of critical processes. Critical processes must first be identified. Knowing what they are and having the BCT agree to their criticality will allow for proper planning and prioritization. Failure to properly identify critical processes can lead to wasted time, effort, and money. Even worse, noncritical processes may be given priority over critical processes, leading to further delays in recovery and causing unnecessary expenditure of resources. It's not uncommon for organizations to identify their processes as critical when, on further examination, they are determined not to be critical. Process owners have a tendency to believe *all* their processes are critical. This is precisely why it is necessary to have the BCT make this assessment. In developing recovery and resumption plans, the following areas must be considered and addressed:

  1. *Define critical processes:* Each major business area, function, and discipline should provide to the BCT a listing of all critical processes. The BCT should then review these processes for criticality and prioritize them, creating an official critical process list. Planning for recovery of the critical processes is the primary concern. Noncritical processes should be recovered and resumed after the critical processes. Resource and time limitations do not allow for resumption of all processes at the same time. Processes critical to the business must have top priority. Any processes determined not to be critical should be planned for during the later stages of the resumption effort.

  2. *Critical process interdependencies:* As part of the critical process assessment, particular emphasis must be placed on information systems and process interdependencies. For example, a process owner might not determine an information system, in and of itself, to be critical. However, if it supports a critical process and that critical process can't be completely restored without the information system, that information system itself becomes critical. Examining processes as part of a system is essential to assessing criticality. Interdependencies need to be identified to properly assess their criticality to the business. Other interdependencies may exist in the form of relationships with organizations outside the enterprise. These too must be considered. Various methodologies can be used to estimate potential impact of a contingency or disaster on a critical process. When considering the criticality of a process, you must address the financial effect, operational effect, and any less tangible or quantifiable concerns, such as customer satisfaction.

  3. *Resources:* Critical process recovery requires an assessment of resources. Planning for process restoration means considering what resources might no longer be available and will need to be acquired or obtained to get the critical process up and functional again. What type of facilities will be needed, and where? Will additional hardware, software, or equipment be required? Will

people capable of managing and working the processes be available? Will there be effective means of communications? If not, what must be done to provide a minimum capability of communications until full communications can be restored? These are some of the resource issues and questions the team must grapple with.

4. *Mitigation strategies:* For processes identified as critical, pre-event actions can be taken to help mitigate the impact, both operationally and financially, of interruptions to the business. In developing contingency plans for critical processes, strategies will become apparent that may be implemented prior to an event to lessen the impact of an event if and when it occurs. A cost/benefit analysis may be required to assess the feasibility of implementing a pre-event action and, if the analysis shows it to be an effective action, it should be taken. For example, an old building not built to current building codes could be vulnerable to damage from an earthquake. If that building supports a critical process, it might be more cost-effective to retrofit the building with the necessary structural supports and bring it into compliance with current standards than to risk severe damage in the event of an earthquake, which could render a critical process inoperative.

- *Vital records:* The ability to recover vital records is critical to the recovery and restoration process. Having a vital records protection and management program will enable the recovery of essential information during a contingency.

- *Customers and suppliers:* The importance of considering input, participation, and impact to customers and suppliers cannot be overstated. Any business continuity planning must take into consideration customer and supplier relationships.

- *Communications:* Communicating during the recovery and resumption process can be just as important as communications during other phases of a contingency. Employees who have been affected by the events of a crisis or disaster need to be kept abreast of developments affecting them and their employment. Customers and suppliers need to understand the progress made toward resumption of business, because it could have a serious impact on their operations. Even the external worlds of stakeholders and shareholders have an interest in these events.

- *Lessons learned:* There is an old adage that lightning doesn't strike twice in the same place. If only that were certain, true, and applicable to the critical processes of a business; however, it is not. Therefore, much can be learned from each phase of managing and recovering from a contingency. Documenting the process of recovery and restoration will help identify the things learned, both good and bad, and will go a long way toward dealing with other crises when they occur.

6 Business Recovery

The previous section addressed areas and issues common to resumption and recovery aspects of the total contingency planning process. This section discusses areas specific to recovery and the short-term process of resuming normal business operations.

Recovery plans focus on getting the business up and running. In essence, this involves the actions that need to be taken within the first 30 to 60 days to restore critical processes and resume operations. These should be the most critical processes focused on infrastructure, product delivery, and keeping damage or loss to an absolute minimum. As difficult as it might be, people need to be part of this equation. For example, should a natural disaster occur and cause severe damage to a building or facility, there is a good chance that some key employees might have experienced something similar in the past. Some could be preoccupied with their own issues of recovery and restoration and might not be able to support the company. Generally, you can expect this number to be limited to a few, but it could be a critical few. Part of the critical process planning should take this into consideration and identify alternatives.

Vital records recovery is very much part of the recovery process. Being able to access off-site records storage, both hard copy and electronic, is critical to expediently moving this process forward. Many companies use outsource providers to handle, store, and retrieve their vital records. This process allows for separate storage, away from company facilities, and reduces the possibility of damage to or destruction of these records. Many capable and reliable companies throughout the world perform vital records handling, storage, and recovery for organizations.

7 Business Resumption

Issues and areas of focus and concern that are common with recovery and resumption were addressed earlier. This section discusses areas specific to resumption and the long-term process of resuming normal business. Long-term priorities are addressed in business resumption plans with the intention of restoring operations to a pre-event condition. Restoration to a pre-event condition does not necessarily mean that all is the same or equal to the conditions prior to contingency occurrence, crisis, or disaster. During the process of recovery and restoration, it may be learned or discovered that the implementation of a critical process or other processes can be accomplished differently in the sense that improvements can make the process more efficient and more cost-effective. Consequently, changes can and should be made. Furthermore, it may be learned that some processes can be eliminated altogether. Recovery and resumption in many ways are similar to a reengineering process. Process owners are usually the best source of ideas, and as they participate in resumption they may develop new approaches and methods to implementing and executing their process.

If the process is a simple one, changes can be implemented quickly, with little or no additional review from management or the BCT. If the process is a complex one that affects or is dependent on other processes, a cost/benefit analysis is warranted to accurately assess the impact of any proposed changes.

In this chapter the authors have attempted to provide a framework for understanding the complexities of contingency planning and the development of contingency plans. A particular point we attempt to make lies with the importance of planning for *categories* of contingencies. It is a daunting task to attempt to plan for each and every possible contingency. However, contingencies can be grouped into categories and planned for accordingly. This allows for consistency in preparedness and best utilization of resources. Types of contingencies develop and change over time as societies and organizations change and progress. Prior to the 20th century, nuclear contamination was not a concern, but today countries with nuclear power-generation capabilities have in place extensive contingency plans that are regularly tested. More common hazards such as severe weather and other natural events have caused enough damage to drive organizations to better preparedness. State and local governments, along with private enterprises in states like California and Mississippi, spend large sums of money preparing to mitigate the effects of earthquakes and hurricanes.

8 Pandemics

Furthermore, not so common hazards drive governments and private organizations to take mitigating measures. Pandemic preparedness currently is getting much attention as the H5N1 Avian Flu virus continues to spread in both birds and people (at this writing), mostly in Asia.[4] Pandemics are not new; they have been with us since man's earliest times. They don't occur frequently, but when they do the effects can be devastating. The last devastating pandemic occurred in 1918. The Spanish flu affected more than 30 percent of the world's population,[5] killing between 50 and 100 million people and disrupting the normal lives of societies around the globe.[5]

Planning for a pandemic requires an emphasis on people. The focus is planning to keep employees, and their families, healthy and in the workplace, where they can be productive. Pandemics affect people, not infrastructure. However, without people, operating an infrastructure is at best difficult and could be nearly impossible. Consider running the air transportation infrastructure without people. With a 30 percent reduction in the number of air traffic controllers, pilots, and maintenance personnel, would this system work effectively, or would it even work at all? How would your business be affected if air transportation operations were limited or shut down for 30 days?

The Centers for Disease Control and Prevention (CDC) has created a Pandemic Severity Index to assist local and state governments in assessing the severity of a viral outbreak. The level will help officials determine the extent of school closure, quarantines, and work-from-home assignments.

- Category 1 involves fewer than 90,000 deaths and would not require school closures.
- Category 2 and 3 would recommend school closures and limiting personal contact for up to one month.
- Category 4 or 5 would potentially involve over 1.8 million deaths, school closures of up to three months, and limits on public events.[6]

9 Fire Prevention and Protection

Although all industry-specific vulnerabilities should be considered in contingency planning, the threat of fire is universal. Because fire is also one of the most damaging and demoralizing hazards, fire prevention and control must be a major part of any comprehensive loss prevention program. The following materials are designed to provide an overview of this important area. For a complete discussion on fire, seek out professional literature for each topic (arson, fire suppression, or fire prevention).

For someone who has administrative oversight of fire issues, it is important to note that any defense against fire must be viewed in two parts. First, *fire prevention,* which is usually the major preoccupation of most businesses, embodies controlling heat sources and eliminating or isolating the more obviously dangerous fuels. However, this commendable effort to prevent fire must not be undertaken at the expense of an equal effort for the second part of defense, *fire protection.*

Fire protection includes not only the equipment to control or extinguish fire but also the devices that will reduce the effect of fire in relationship to the building, its contents, and particularly its occupants. Fire doors, firewalls, smokeproof towers, fireproof safes, nonflammable rugs and furnishings, fire detector and signaling systems—all are fire protection components that are essential to any fire safety program.

9.1 Security Personnel

One of the key elements in fire prevention and protection is security personnel. Though a smoke detector senses smoke and a heat detector senses heat, the human brain senses much more. The trained security officer can think, problem solve, and sense what detectors cannot. We can often sense when someone is having a bad day. Likewise, we can also sense when the building just "doesn't feel right." There are no detectors to tell you that the exits are blocked or the exit doors are not opening properly.

9.2 Vulnerability to Fire

There are no fireproof buildings, though frequently the term is misapplied. However, there are fire-*resistant* buildings, meaning one that will not collapse quickly under fire conditions and that does not readily add fuel to the fire. But combustible materials such as furnishings, paneling, stored flammable materials, and so on inside a fire-resistant building can make ovens out of buildings, generating heat of sufficient intensity to destroy everything inside. Eventually such heat can even soften the building's structural steel to such an extent that part or all of the building collapses. By this time, however, the collapse could endanger only outside elements because many things inside, with the possible exception of certain fire-resistant containers and other metal or fire-resistant items and their contents, will already have been destroyed.

Heat was a major factor in the collapse of the World Trade Center. The heat generated by the burning jet fuel resulted in expansion and thus weakening of the steel superstructure. Coupled with the intense pressure of the burn, the building began to collapse. The weight of the collapsing structure created additional weight on the lower floors, eventually resulting in the collapse of the entire structure.

The particular danger of this situation is that although wood frame construction is recognized for the fire hazard it represents, many otherwise knowledgeable people are oblivious to the potential dangers from fire in steel and concrete construction. We have a normal tendency to think that because something does not burn, it is safer. The misconception is that steel is better in a fire situation than wood. This is not always the case.

We cannot be blind to the fact that steel has it shortfalls. Though wood will ignite at between 400 and to 600 degrees, steel will start losing strength at 600 degrees and loses 40 percent of its strength at 1,110 degrees, well within the temperatures that develop in common fires. Though wood will burn, the sheer mass of wood needed to match the strength of steel in any given construction project could mean that a wooden structure will withstand a fire longer.[7]

9.3 Fireload

The degree of fire exposure in any fire-resistant building is dependent on its fireload: the amount of combustible material that occupies its interior spaces. Fireload is often misunderstood when we look at different occupancies. We tend to look at some businesses as more hazardous due to their operation rather than taking into count their fireload. There could be more concern for a processing plant that fabricates steel products because of the intense heat present in the fabrication process than for a doctor's office or hospital. A factory atmosphere catches our interest due to electrical equipment, machinery, and stock. But what is the true fireload? A doctor's office could warehouse many years of patient records, files, and X-rays that could create a greater fireload than a factory. A hospital, with its clean and safe environment, needs supplies and replacement equipment. There could be storerooms of additional beds, furniture, and records. An in-house laundry department with workers' and patients' bedding and gowns will add fireload. We need to look past a facility's fundamental operation to see *what* will burn.

In the case of multiple occupancies where general businesses, retail, and residential units are under one roof, as in a large office building, no one office manager can control the building's fireload. In such an environment, new furniture, decorative pieces, drapes, carpeting, unprotected insulated cables, or even volatile fluids for cleaning or lubricating are moved through the building every day. The building fireload may continue to increase without much thought from most of its occupants.

9.4   The Nature of Fire

The classic triangle frequently referred to in describing the nature of fire consists of heat, fuel, and oxygen. This triangle has been augmented by the fire tetrahedron theory, which adds a fourth element: chemical reaction, pyrolysis, or vaporization. *Pyrolysis* is the decomposition of solids to the point where they give off enough flammable vapors and gases to form an ignitable mixture. In liquid fuels the process is called *vaporization*. Flammable gases require no pyrolysis because they are already in a form capable of combining with oxygen. If all four components exist, normally there will be a fire; remove or reduce any one component and the fire will be reduced or extinguished (see Figure 12.2).[8]

Fuel and oxygen are always present. It would be difficult to imagine any facility that had no exposed combustible items, and air most certainly will be present. Only sufficient heat and the chemical breakdown associated with it are missing, and these factors can be readily supplied by a careless cigarette or faulty wiring, two of the most common causative factors. In fact, an almost infinite number of heat sources can complete the deadly tetrahedron and start a fire raging in virtually any facility.

Every fire prevention program begins with the education of staff and visitors because it is nearly impossible to change existing fireload problems overnight. Yet every fire prevention program must also work to control the amount and nature of the fireload or fuel and institute programs to prevent the occurrence of any heat buildup, whether from careless smoking or from sparks from a welding torch. This is actually a two-pronged approach: First, control ignition sources; second, set fireloads at appropriate working levels.

9.5   Byproducts of Fire

Contrary to popular opinion, flame or visible fire is rarely the killer in deaths from fire. Death is usually caused by smoke or heat or from toxic gas, explosion, or panic. Several such byproducts accompany every fire; all must be considered when defenses are being planned.

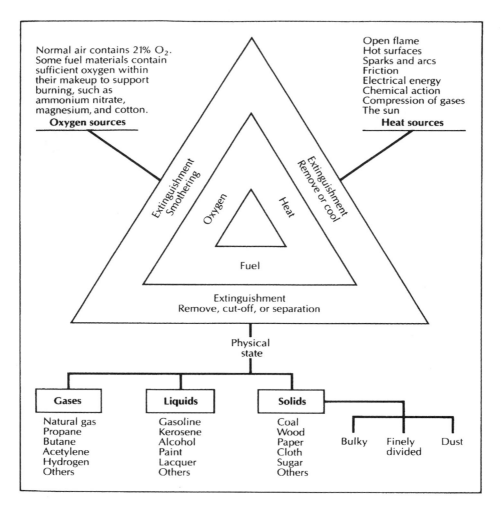

FIGURE 12.2 The fire triangle.

Smoke will blind and asphyxiate in an astonishingly short time. Tests have been conducted in which smoke in a corridor reduced the visibility to zero in two minutes from the time of ignition. A stairway 2 feet from a subject in the test was totally obscured.

Fire gases, composed mostly of carbon dioxide and carbon monoxide, make up a large part of smoke. Still, most persons have a relatively lax attitude about smoke in comparison to fire. We need to understand that smoke is actually unburned fuel and gases that are still flammable. Though most people would not walk into a kitchen when gas is coming out of the four burners of the stove, the same people often fail to think of smoke in the same terms. Firefighters are taking a much harder look at how those burning gases add to and extend a fire.

Heat plays an important part in the destructive capabilities of fire and its spread. A small fire that does not consume large amounts of fuel can produce large amounts of destructive heat. A fire that may just consume a sofa or chair can produce heat damage many times greater than the cost of the fire-involved item. Heat is also the main means by which fire travels. Flames do not cause a fire to move across an area, room, or building.

It is the heat associated with the flames that leads to fire spread. Furthermore, heat can travel great distances and heights without flames to start new points of ignition.

Ignition temperature is the temperature at which a solid fuel will ignite without direct flame contact. Most materials we use in our everyday lives have an ignition temperature somewhere between 400 and 600 degrees, well below the temperatures developed in a fire. If we take one of these fuels and put it in an oven that has no flame, when the fuel reaches its ignition temperature, it will ignite. No flame is required to start combustion. The point is that it does not matter where the fire is; the important question is, where is the heat going? For example, in a high-rise building, a fire that starts in a basement where someone has left the stairwell doors open allows heat from the fire to travel to the upper floors of the building. Once the heat reaches that 400–600 degree range on those upper floors, fire will develop. It does not matter that the original fire is located 300 feet below the 30th floor—fires will start!

Fire evolves through three stages: incipient, free burning, and smoldering. The *incipient stage* is the moment the fire begins, when fuel, air, and an ignition source all come together at the right rate for the correct period of time. Picture the instant a match falls into a trash can. There is little heat and little smoke, and you can stand right in front of the trash can with no real concern. In the *free-burning stage* the fire is doing just what it wants; it has plenty of fuel and air. However, as flames continue to develop with heat increasing, your ability to be close to the fire will be almost nil. In the *smoldering stage* air has been reduced or fuel is dwindling to the point where there is no visible flame, just an entire area filled with tremendous heat.

The plan of how to "fight" a given fire for extinguishment is determined by the stage that the fire is in. Another determining factor will be whether the fire is confined or unconfined.

Most fires in a commercial setting will be of a confined nature. An unconfined fire would be similar to a camp fire. The fire is doing just what it wants; the heat is going up, the smoke is going up, it is doing what it naturally does. We could walk right up to that fire and warm our hands or put the fire out by simply pouring a bucket of water on it. But take that same fire and put it in a room, confine it, and the heat and smoke still go up until they hit the ceiling, then they start moving laterally. The smoke and heat will no longer allow you to directly access the fire. This is why the fire stage and whether the fire is confined or unconfined are so important in determining how a fire should be fought and the amount of extinguishment time that will be involved.

9.6 Classes of Fire

All fires are classified into one of five groups. It is important that these groups and their designations are widely known because the use of various kinds of extinguishers depends on the type of fire to be fought (see Figure 12.3):

- *Class A*. Fires of ordinary combustible materials, such as wastepaper, rags, drapes, and furniture. These fires are most effectively extinguished by water or water fog. It is important to cool the entire mass of burning material to below the ignition point to prevent rekindling.
- *Class B*. Liquid fuel fires such as gasoline, grease, oil, or volatile fluids, with the exception of some cooking oils. In this type of fire an oxygen displacement effect such as carbon dioxide (CO_2) or other fire extinguishing agent is used. A stream of

Kind of fire	Approved type of extinguisher							
Decide the class of fire you are fighting …	**Foam** Solution of aluminium sulphate and bicarbonate of soda	**Carbon Dioxide** Carbon Dioxide gas under pressure	**Pump tank** Plain water	**Gas cartridge** Water expelled by carbon dioxide gas	**Multi-purpose dry chemical**	**Ordinary dry chemical**	**Dry powder**	**Wet chemical**
A **Class A fires** Ordinary combustibles • Wood • Paper • Cloth etc.	●		●	●	●			
B **Class B fires** Flammable liquids, grease • Gasoline • Paints • Oils etc.	●	●			●	●		
C **Class C fires** Electrical equipment • Motors • Switches etc.		●			●	●		
D **Class D fires** Combustible metals • Magnesium • Sodium • Potassium etc.							●	
K **Class K fires** • Cooking oils • Fats								●

How to operate

Foam: Don't spray into the burning liquid. Allow foam to fall lightly on fire.

Carbon Dioxide: Direct discharge as close to fire as possible, first at edge of flames and gradually forward and upward.

Pump tank: Place foot on footrest and direct stream at base of flames.

Dry chemical: Direct at the base of the flames. In the case of class A fires, follow up by directing the dry chemicals at the material that is burning.

Wet chemical: Direct at the base of the flames.

FIGURE 12.3 Use of fire extinguishers.

water on such fires would simply serve to spread the substances, with disastrous results. Water fog, however, is excellent because, if applied by properly trained personnel, it cools without spreading the fuel.

- *Class C*. Fires involving live electrical equipment such as transformers, generators, or electric motors. The extinguishing agent is nonconductive to reduce the firefighter's danger of electrocution. Electrical power should be disconnected before beginning extinguishing efforts, because you are basically extinguishing the Class A or B fuel around the energized equipment.

- *Class D*. Fires involving certain combustible metals such as magnesium, sodium, and potassium. Dry powder is usually the most, and in some cases the only, effective extinguishing agent. Because these fires can only occur where such combustible metals are in use or production, they are fortunately rare.

- *Class K*. In recent years studies have found that some cooking oils produce too much heat to be controlled and extinguished by the traditional Class B extinguishing agents. Class K fires and extinguishers deal with cooking oil fires.

9.7   Extinguishers

The security department must evaluate the fire risk for each facility or department and determine the types of fires most likely to occur. Although the potential for all types of fires exists and should be planned for, certain production areas are more likely than others to have a specific type of fire. This condition should be considered when assigning extinguishers to the department or facility. Every operation is potentially subject to Class A and C fires, and most are also threatened by Class B fires to some degree.

Having made such a determination, security must then select the types of fire extinguishers most likely to be useful. The choice of extinguisher is not difficult, but it can be made only after determining the nature of the risks. Extinguisher manufacturers can supply all pertinent data on the equipment they supply, but the types in general use should be known. It is important to know, for example, that over the years the soda/acid and carbon tetrachloride extinguishers have been prohibited. They are no longer manufactured. An extinguisher that must be inverted to be activated is no longer legal.

There are a number of considerations in choosing fire extinguishers to be used in a given facility. First, what type of fire do you anticipate? Second, how compatible is the fire extinguisher with the environment and personnel who are going to use it? Is the fire-extinguishing agent inside the fire extinguisher going to do more harm than the fire? Are personnel of a size and stature to handle such an extinguisher?

Fire extinguishers must be matched with the type of fire they will be effective on. Again, all extinguishers have their good and bad points to consider:

- *Dry chemical*. These are designed for Class B and C fires.
- *Multipurpose dry chemical*. These extinguishers are designed for use on Class A, B, and C fires.
- *Dry powder*. This is used on Class D fires. It smothers and coats.
- *Foam extinguishers*. These are effective for Class A and B fires where blanketing is desirable.
- CO_2. Used on Class B or C fires, CO_2 has no lasting cooling effect due to the fact that the gas dissipates so quickly, making flashbacks of fires a concern.

- *Wet agents.* New clean water-based wet agents have been developed for different classes of fires. They are cleaner than the powders and more desirable in some occupancies. It is necessary to match the proper extinguisher with the type of protection desired.

Halogenated agents, though no longer in production, do have substitutes taking their place. Research the proper substitution agent to meet protection needs.

After extinguishers have been installed, a regular program of inspection and maintenance must be established. A good policy is for security personnel to visually check all devices once a month and to have the extinguisher service company inspect them twice a year. In this process, the serviceperson should retag and if necessary recharge the extinguishers and replace defective equipment (see Figure 12.4). It is a good idea to check with your extinguisher servicepeople to find out when routine service requires the fire extinguishers to be discharged or emptied. This is a good time to do employee and fire brigade training because the company will be paying for refill service. It is a good cost-saving measure.

9.8   Fire Alarm Signaling Systems

Early notification is the key to fast, loss reduction, and lifesaving extinguishment of fire. If a fire is discovered in the very first stages before it develops, it can be extinguished with a minimal amount of exposure to personnel and use of extinguishing agents. For example, should a fire develop in a waste can and quickly activate a sensor, a person could easily and safely approach it with a handheld extinguisher and extinguish it. This is the general concept of detection and signaling systems and fire extinguishers on the premises that could be used by trained personnel. The simple rule is small fire, small extinguishment; large fire, large extinguishment. Should that waste can fire go undetected and develop, lateral extension would not allow personnel to safely approach it and on-premises extinguishing units would not be adequate for extinguishment. Delays in fire detection and alarm notification have been one of the major causes of large loss of life and property fires.

Fire Extinguisher Checklist

No.	Location	Description and size	Fully charged	Operable	Sealed	Comments
1	Sheet metal shop	CO_2 15	yes	yes	yes	Hanging bracket should be replaced

Date ___3-2-04___   Signed ___J. Pendleton___

FIGURE 12.4 Fire extinguisher safety checklist.

Most fires are discovered by our senses. We see them, smell them, and sometimes hear them. Normally we are left with nothing more than the chance for human discovery. A fully functional high-tech alarm system (see Figure 12.5) gives early detection 24 hours a day, 365 days a year. If someone is on the premises or not, notification can occur.

A total fire alarm system, like intrusion alarms, can be viewed as consisting of the signaling system and the alarm and sensor system. The alarm system discovers the fire and activates a circuit, and then the signaling device notifies those concerned of the danger.

When determining the type of alarm system to utilize, check with code requirements, seek recommendations from insurance carriers, and evaluate unique features of the premises and operation. You will discover that some systems have better sensitivity, reliability, maintainability, and stability than others. Though on the surface all detectors appear to do what you want, realize that some do a better job in certain situations. For example, it might not be advantageous to have a highly sensitive sensor in a highly contaminated area, because this could cause numerous false alarms. Also in areas such as computer rooms you'll want a sensor that will activate before heat or smoke develop.

FIGURE 12.5 Elements of a fire alarm system. (Courtesy of EST, www.est.net/std.)

9.8.1 Sensors

Sensors (detectors) can be categorized by what they sense. By looking at what fire produces, we can class sensors as flame detectors, smoke detectors, and heat detectors. Again, you should evaluate the premises to determine the type of detector that meets code and the specific needs of the area to be protected.

Today the terms *sensor, detector,* and *initiating device* are synonymous. This is a device that "initiates" a signal to activate an alarm system. This device should be viewed as nothing more than a switch, similar in principle to a light switch. When we turn on a light switch, the light comes on. Similarly, when initiating devices are activated, they can cause alarms to sound, signals to be sent, and even safety features of the premises to be activated. These devices can be automatic: smoke detectors, heat detectors, or flame detectors. They can also be manual, such as a pull station. Alarm systems will be incorporated with other safety systems such as a sprinkler system. Flow switches are initiating devices that are placed in the piping of sprinkler systems to send a signal indicating that water is flowing and the system has activated. Sprinkler systems can be incorporated into the alarm system as any initiating device.

Flame detectors are used in locations where signals must be sent before heat and smoke develop. They are often found in computer and high-tech areas. Flame detectors are "line of sight" detectors, meaning that they must be located in varying spots in the area to be protected because they must "see" the flame. They respond to either ultraviolet or infrared light. Some detectors today are produced with both ultraviolet and infrared sensors in them to reduce false alarms.

Smoke detectors are broken into two groups: photoelectric and ionization. Photoelectric smoke detectors are either beam or refraction type. Beam smoke detectors operate on the principle of a light and a receiver. Once enough smoke or fire byproduct breaks the beam of light, the device activates. The refraction type of detector has a blocker between the light and the receiver and operates with the principle that once there is enough smoke in the detector, the light signal refracts (reflects) around the blocker to the receiver. Ionization-type detectors monitor the air around them constantly. Once enough fire byproducts enter the detector, the contaminants will complete a circuit that sends the alarm signal.

Heat detectors can be grouped as fixed temperature or rate of rise. Fixed temperature detectors activate at a predetermined temperature. Rate-of-rise detectors activate at changes in heat in the area in which they are located. Heat detectors are slower to react than other detectors, but they have less chance for false alarms and are durable in many applications.

Fixed temperature detectors can be the following types: fusible link, frangible bulb, continuous line, and bimetallic. Rate-of-rise detectors are categorized as either pneumatic, rate compensation, or thermoelectric.

9.8.2 Signal Devices

The signal sent by initiating devices will send a signal to the system control unit that processes the alarm. This is often referred to as the *main control panel*. These main panels are electrically powered and have a secondary backup source of battery power or a generator.

The system control unit sends signals via circuitry to various components of the system. It could retransmit the signal to a signaling system and activate on-premises safety features. For example, a system could be designed so that when a heat detector is activated, horns will go off in the building to notify the occupants, a signal will be sent via telephone wires to an alarm monitoring location, fire doors in the building will shut to compartmentalize the fire, and heating and cooling units will shut down to stop the spread of smoke and toxic gases. Signaling systems are broken into five categories: local, auxiliary, remote station, proprietary, and central station.

Local systems do not retransmit the alarm anywhere. This is always a concern because there is a fear that people will assume that a response to the alarm is coming. Workers, residents, and employees must be made aware of the operation of this system. Most codes today require systems to be retransmitted, but many are still in place since their initial installation.

Auxiliary systems are utilized in communities that have a municipal alarm system. Building alarms are connected to a system owned and operated by the municipality. The signal may be transmitted to a fire station or a central receiving location.

Remote station systems are ones that lease phone-line service to transmit the alarm signal to a location. This is nothing more than a phone line, the same as you have in your home.

Proprietary systems are those that are owned and operated by the building or complex owner. A series of buildings or warehouses on the same location would have their alarm systems send a signal to an owner-controlled location such as a security office. This office would monitor the entire area. Once a signal is received, company personnel would retransmit the alarm via phone.

A central station system is one that is independently owned and operated by an alarm company. It may be located in the immediate town or city or across the country. Signals are transmitted via phone lines to a continually manned location that then contacts the proper responding agency. This is one of the more popular systems due to the fact that many cities have decided not to take on the responsibility of receiving alarms and instead have privatized systems.

Whenever alarm and signaling systems are on the premises, representatives of the property should view an acceptance test after the system is installed. Service tests should be conducted at required or recommended intervals and documentation should verify the testing.

9.8.3 Automatic Sprinkler Systems

Similar to alarm systems, sprinkler systems provide buildings with around-the-clock protection. Ninety-six percent of fires in buildings equipped with sprinkler systems are either extinguished or held in check until responding agencies arrive. The 4 percent of failure is due to human error, design, maintenance, or the result of an explosion that has rendered the system inoperative.

Concerns regarding sprinkler systems are the high cost of installation, especially retrofitting them to existing buildings, and water damage. As the popularity of plastic pipe increases and the fire codes allow more of their use, the cost of sprinkler system installation is coming down. If you calculate the cost of smoke and heat damage in a fire and the amount of water damage done by fire personnel with fire hoses, you'd realized that the fears of sprinkler system water damage are unfounded. Good sprinkler system design will eliminate those fears. Many codes require sprinkler systems in certain occupancies, and over a period of time the savings in insurance coverage can justify their use. Interfacing the sprinkler system with a detection system can control water damage.

Sprinkler systems are classified into five groups: wet, dry, pre-action, deluge, and cyclic. Wet systems have water in them all the time, right up to the sprinkler head mounted in the ceiling or wall. The sprinkler heads are made to open individually at a given temperature, determined by code or requirements of the occupancy. Once they open, they do not close again. To discontinue water flow, the source of water must be shut off.

A dry system has no water in it. The water is held back by a valve that is kept in the closed position by air pressure or an electric valve. This system is used mainly to protect unheated areas. It is more cost-effective to heat the valve room than an entire warehouse used for cold storage.

Pre-action systems incorporate a detection system, which can eliminate concerns over water damage and false activation of the system. A valve holds back water in the system. The valve is activated by initiating devices (detectors) in the area. Once the detector senses the fire, the valve is opened and the system is charged. The sprinkler head must also open for water to be discharged. In this case, two steps are required to discharge water. Multidetector circuits could be added to require multiple steps for system activation.

A deluge system is similar to a pre-action system except all the sprinkler heads are in the open position. It is obvious that water damage in this case is not a concern. Due to the nature of the situation or occupancy, extinguishment far outweighs other issues. Once the detector senses a fire, the valve opens and all sprinkler heads discharge.

A cyclic sprinkler head is more of a head type than a system. The opening and closing of a cyclic sprinkler head is controlled by a thermostat that is part of the sprinkler head. When the thermostat reaches a predetermined temperature, it opens; once it falls below that temperature, it closes. Cyclic sprinkler heads are one of the rare sprinkler heads that do not need to be replaced after a fire unless they're damaged. One drawback to the cyclic sprinkler head is that though many thought it helped reduce water damage, it was troublesome in that it often just discharged enough water to keep the fire in the smoldering state, generating smoke.

9.9   Education in Fire Prevention and Safety

Educating employees about fire prevention, fire protection, and evacuation procedures should be a continuous program. Ignorance and carelessness are the causes of most fires and of much loss of life. An ongoing fire safety program will inform all employees and help keep them aware of the ever present and very real danger of fire.

Such a program would ideally include fire and evacuation drills. Since such exercises require shutting down operations for a period of time and can lead to the loss of expensive production time, management is frequently cool toward them. Indoctrination sessions for new employees and regular review sessions for all personnel, however, are essential. Such sessions should be brief and involve only small groups.

In many businesses visitors and guests should also be made aware of fire and evacuation plans. Pamphlets describing plans as well as placards that indicate the location of fire exits in relation to the placards should be available. In the case of hotels and other facilities that have resident clientele, the law demands such actions. In the recent nightclub deaths in Chicago and West Warwick, Rhode Island, patrons were unable to escape the facilities due to panic and lack of orientation to their surroundings. Perhaps better marking of emergency exits with properly working emergency exit hardware would have reduced the number of fatalities.

9.9.1 *Employees as Firefighters*

Because the danger of fire, with its concomitant risk to life and property, affects every employee, many experts feel that the responsibility in case of fire is a shared one. The exception to this rule is when the firm has a well-trained fire unit. Few experts would disagree that everyone must be educated in the principles of fire prevention and protection, including indoctrination in evacuation procedures and on reporting a fire. But beyond this, there is little agreement on what employees should be asked to do in the event of fire.

Some business offices set up a system of floor wardens whose job it is to pass the word for evacuation and who then sweep their area of responsibility to see that it is clear of personnel, that papers are deposited in fireproof containers, and that high-value, portable assets are removed from the premises.

Others take the view that their employees were not hired to act as emergency supervisors. Many firms of this latter persuasion ask that certain minimal functions be performed by the employees who are on hand but do not assign roles to specific people. Examples might be a policy of having employees return tapes to a fireproof container in the computer area or secure fire-resistant safes in the accounting or cashier's office before they evacuate. This responsibility would fall on the personnel in these areas at the time of an alarm and would or should take little time to accomplish. When the signal for evacuation is given, no time should be lost in vacating the building.

Many professionals feel that office employees should never be asked to do more than see to their own safety by making an orderly retreat along predetermined escape routes. Only in the most extreme emergency—and then only if they are otherwise trapped—should employees engage in fighting a fire of any magnitude. They can be expected to make an effort to put out a wastebasket fire or a small blaze in a broom closet, but even in these cases the alarm must be given as first priority. Any fire that threatens to involve a major part of an office or other parts of the building should be left to professionals (company fire units, security personnel, or the fire department). Obviously all such situations are matters of on-the-spot judgment. Policies covering every situation are difficult, if not impossible, to predetermine.

The situation is quite different in industrial fire operations. In such facilities, the formation of a fire brigade composed of a few selected and trained employees is a fairly common practice. There is general agreement that the nature of their employment in industrial areas makes these employees more competent to handle firefighting assignments, which are in many cases not that far removed from their regular work.

The exact size of each fire protection organization will vary according to the size and function of each facility. Very large facilities or those whose fire risks are high due to the nature of the operations may have a full-time fire department. In smaller or less hazardous facilities, regular employees are organized into fire brigades that are broken down, usually by departments or areas, into fire companies. These companies are assigned to given areas for purposes of fire protection, fire prevention, and firefighting. They are also available, as part of the fire brigades, to work in any other area of the plant if a fire occurs that requires more personnel than the assigned company can provide.

The size of the brigade will depend on the size of the plant, the nature of the risk involved, and the willingness to take on that risk. It will also be affected by the general availability, size, competence, and response capability of the public firefighting facilities in the neighboring areas. Whatever the size, however, the brigade must consist of people sufficiently well trained and familiar with the plant operation and layout to fight fires effectively in any part of the facility if such a need arises. They may be an incipient fire brigade or an interior fire brigade. Incipient fire brigades are trained to handle fires in their earliest stages. The use of fire extinguishers by employees may be all the involvement this group will have. Interior fire brigades are trained and equipped to the level of many fire departments. OSHA as well as other standards should be evaluated to determine the level of training required for an interior fire brigade.

The plant engineer and the maintenance crew should certainly be included in the brigade. Their knowledge in servicing valves, pumps, and other machinery is invaluable in emergency situations.

9.9.2 Evacuation

9.9.2.1 Evacuating Industrial Facilities

Evacuation plans for an industrial facility are relatively simple to design because most buildings within the perimeter are one-, two, or, in rare cases, three-story buildings. Fire exits can be readily identified for such a plan of action. Because they are occupied by personnel of a single company or under that company's jurisdiction, a single plan involving all personnel can be drawn up. And because in most cases aesthetic considerations are not a prime concern in the design of the industrial building, fire escapes can be constructed in any way for the greatest safety.

Although many of these buildings have elevators, most of which serve the dual purpose of hauling freight and personnel, these elevators are not necessarily the prime means of moving to and from the upper level as they are in high-rise office buildings.

Generally, these buildings can be cleared in minutes. This is not to say that an evacuation plan is not needed. It is, and it must be widely distributed and clearly understood. Most industrial buildings are more open, the exits are more visible—more a part of employees' unconscious orientation and, therefore, more a part of the natural traffic flow—than these elements are in many other types of construction. Again, accountability of all personnel is necessary once evacuation is completed.

9.9.2.2 Evacuating High-Rise Buildings

Evacuation from high-rise urban buildings is quite a different story. In this situation, employees come to work and leave regularly by elevator. Yet if there is a fire, they are told they must not use the only means of entrance and exit they really know—the elevator.

In most cases, employees have never been on the fire stairs. They may have only a vague idea where those stairs are located, but in a time of emergency—a time of anxiety bordering on panic, when instinctual behavior is the most natural—they are asked to vacate the premises in a way that to them is very unnatural indeed.

Even in wide-open industrial facilities where orientation is quick and easy, there will always be some people who will pass a clearly marked exit to get to the employee door they are used to using. This is much more likely to happen in buildings with windowless corridors and fire exits—however clearly lighted and marked—that are well off employees' normal traffic pattern. A good emergency lighting system can do much to reduce this potentially life-threatening problem.

To overcome this problem, which must be overcome until such time as elevators are made safe to use in fires, it is advisable to walk all employees as a drill from their desks to the nearest fire exit and to the nearest secondary exit they would use in case their first escape route was cut off by fire or smoke. In addition, the use of "You Are Here" placards can assist those who become disoriented in a building in finding the nearest safe exit.

This orientation could be done over a period of time with small groups at each drill. It is important that the drill actually start at an employee's desk or office so that the route as well as the location of the exit are made clear.

People need to be educated that in some occupancies elevators are programmed not to operate once the fire alarm system activates. Though they're dramatic on the news, roof evacuations are difficult, slow, and subject to many factors that make it the least desirable evacuation. People should be taught to move *down,* and if down is not possible, laterally to another exit and then down. Roof evacuation should be the last consideration.

9.9.2.3 **Planning and Training**   Evacuation plans must be based on a well-considered system and on thorough and continuing education. They should also be based on indoctrinating employees in the principles of fire safety, stressing that they are to make their own way to the proper exit and leave as quickly and as calmly as possible.

Adults do not respond well to being lined up like children at a fire drill and marched down the fire stairs. Though people might be inclined to follow a leader under many circumstances, when it comes to a concept as simple as vacating the premises, a leader has no purpose or place. Employees will rebel or even panic if they feel restrained or regimented in their movements toward the exit.

In setting up plans for evacuation, it might be a good idea to review and evaluate the circumstances of a given facility and then ask a few questions:

1. Are routes to exits well lighted, fairly direct, and free of obstacles?
2. Are elevators posted to warn against their use in case of fire? Do these signs point out the direction of fire exits?
3. Are disabled persons provided for?
4. Do corridors have emergency lighting in the event of power failure?
5. Who makes the decision to evacuate? How will personnel be notified?
6. Who will operate the communication system? What provisions have been made in case the primary communication system breaks down? Who is assigned to provide and receive information on the state of the emergency and the progress of the evacuation? By what means?
7. How will everyone be accounted for? Do we know that everyone is out of the building? How do we verify that?

10   Safety and Loss Control

Safety consciousness in business and industry did not begin with the establishment of OSHA in 1970, but it is largely a product of the 20th century. Prior to the Industrial Revolution early in the 19th century, workers were independent craftspeople. If they suffered economic loss due to accident or illness rising out of prolonged exposure to a particular work environment, the problem was the craftsperson's, not the employer's. This attitude generally prevailed during the rapid expansion of the factory system in America throughout the 19th century. Only toward the latter part of the 19th century did it begin to become obvious that factories were far superior in terms of production capability to the small handicraft shops, yet they were often inferior in terms of human values, health, and safety.

The atmosphere of reform that gained impetus after the turn of the century resulted in, among other new laws, the first effective Workmen's Compensation Act in Wisconsin in 1911. Compulsory laws on workmen's compensation followed in many states after the U.S. Supreme Court upheld their constitutionality in 1916. Even the most hardheaded employers found that their costs dictated compliance with the spirit of the law.

As a result of this growing concern for industrial safety, there followed a long downward curve in work-connected accidents and injuries that lasted through the period between the two world wars and continued into the 1950s. By 1958 this trend had leveled off, and by 1968, for the first time in more than 50 years, the curve began to rise again.

Fourteen thousand occupational fatalities and more than 2 million disabling, work-connected injuries each year seemed to be considerably more than the number that might one day be arrived at as the irreducible minimum. The result throughout the 1960s was increasing federal concern with establishing standards of occupational safety and health. Prior to that decade, only a few federal laws, such as the Walsh-Healey Public Contracts Act, had been passed, with most legislation in this area being left to the states. During the 1960s a number of laws were passed—the McNamara-O'Hara Service Contracts Act, the Federal Construction Safety Act, and the Federal Coal Mine Health and Safety Act, among others—all dealing with safety and health standards in specific fields and under specific circumstances. Public Law 91-596, known as OSHA, which was signed into law on December 29, 1970, was the first legislation that attempted to apply standards to virtually every employer and employee in the country.

10.1   OSHA Standards

Generally speaking, OSHA requires that an employer provide a safe and healthful place for employees to work. This is spelled out in great detail in the Act to avoid leaving the thrust of the legislation in any doubt. Though much of the language in the Act is technical in nature and largely couched in legalese, the thrust of the legislation is absolutely clear and unambiguous in what is known as the "General Duty" clause, which states that each employer "shall furnish to each of his employees a place of employment free from recognized hazards that are causing or likely to cause death or serious physical harm to his employees" and that, further, the employer "shall comply with all occupational safety and health standards promulgated under this Act."[9] Much of the rest of the Act deals with procedures and standards of safety and is, in places, difficult to follow.

It speaks of free and accessible means of egress, of aisles and working areas free of debris, of floors free from hazards. It gives specific requirements for machines and equipment, materials, and power sources. It specifies fire protection by fixed or portable systems, clean lunchrooms, environmental health controls, and adequate sanitation facilities. Whereas in past years employers might contend in all sincerity that their facilities met community standards for safety and cleanliness, with the enactment of OSHA these standards have been formalized to describe minimum levels of acceptability. Although employers might also contend that some specific demands of the Act are unclear, there is no mistaking the purpose of the Act: "The Congress declares to be its purpose and policy to assure so far as possible every working man and woman in the nation safe and healthful working conditions and to preserve our human resources."

Perhaps the strongest resistance to OSHA in its first years was the complaint that some of the basic standards went too far or were unnecessary. In May 1978 the U.S. Supreme Court ruled that the agency could not conduct surprise workplace inspections without a proper warrant.[10] And with growing criticism from that time period, the OSHA administration has continually sought the elimination of "Mickey Mouse" standards that have no direct bearing on improving safety in the workplace.

In 1988 OSHA issued the Hazard Communication Standard, which states that all employees have the right to know what hazards exist in their place of employment and what to do to protect themselves from the hazards. Simple labels and warnings on containers are not enough. Employers must have a program to communicate more detail on all hazards, including a Material Safety Data Sheet (MSDS) that must be available for each chemical at the work site. Each MSDS contains seven sections:

1. Product identification and emergency notification instructions
2. Hazardous ingredients list and exposure limits
3. Physical and chemical characteristics
4. Physical hazards (that is, fire, explosion) and how to handle them
5. Reactivity—what the product might react with and whether it is stable
6. Health hazards—how the product can enter the body, signs and symptoms of problems, and emergency first-aid steps
7. Safe handling procedures

10.2 Setting Up the Safety Program

H. W. Heinrich, an outstanding pioneer in safety studies, held that unsafe acts caused 85 percent of all accidents and that unsafe conditions caused the remaining 15 percent.[11] Therefore, if these acts could be modified, the accidents would be sharply reduced. Today safety supervisors agree that unsafe acts are the principal villain and that the system's approach to safety is the only real way to control losses. It is necessary, however, for management to get the system together and implement a strong, active program so that it is effective. Safety problems are caused, they do not just happen, and each problem can be identified and controlled.[12]

In developing a safety program, you need to address the "three Es." They are engineering, education, and enforcement. First, you must build and develop a good program. Second, everyone needs to be educated abut the program and the part he or she plays in it. Third, the program must be enforced to see that it is followed.

Accidents, by our definition, refer to property damage as well and in aggregate can amount to substantial cost for the company that fails to keep them under control. In fact, an effective loss control program can be an organization's best moneymaker when it can be shown that the actual cost of accidents may be anywhere from 6 to 50 times as much as the money recovered from insurance. Uninsured costs in building damage, production damage, wages to the injured for lost time, clerical costs, cost of training new workers and supervisors, and extra time all mount up. By controlling such incidents through careful study of hazards and the introduction of safety programs to deal with the hazards, the profit picture will be immeasurably improved. In a company operating at a 4 percent profit margin, the sales department would have to generate sales of $1,250,000 just to compensate for an annual loss of $50,000 in incidents.

10.3 Finding the Causes of Accidents

The causes of accidents should be determined before they occur. Because accidents don't "just happen" but are *caused,* the conditions that cause them can be known and controlled. It is therefore of the greatest importance that management deal vigorously with issues that can cause an accident. Unsafe acts and unsafe conditions will ultimately cause accidents if they are allowed to continue.

Unsafe acts will be discovered and corrected only when immediate supervisors are alert to the problems. They must set up systems for closely observing all workers while they are performing their jobs, especially those in hazardous jobs. To do this, they must have a job safety analysis at their disposal. This analysis divides each job into component parts, and each part is studied for the hazards it can present.

Unsafe conditions are uncovered through constant inspection. Such conditions do not disappear entirely because they have been taken care of once. Unsafe conditions are continuously created by the operation of the facility. Normal wear and tear, careless housekeeping, initial bad design, or simply the deterioration that results from inadequate maintenance or caused by cost cutting all create unsafe conditions that have high potential loss factors. Early discovery of unsafe conditions is essential to good loss control, and the procedure is simply inspection, inspection, inspection.

10.4 Identification and Control of Hazards

OSHA standards (or equivalent state standards) provide the baseline for a company's safety program. A bewildering catalog of standards has already developed, and new ones are constantly being added. Checklists (available from OSHA, the National Safety Council, insurance carriers, and other sources) can provide the starting point for detailed inspections to identify hazards. The confusion that might accompany a consideration of all the standards begins to sort itself out when inspections zero in on only those standards that apply to specific operations and conditions.

A safety program should include periodic inspections scheduled at regular intervals. Figure 12.6 is an example of a monthly checklist for inspection. In addition, looking for safety hazards and violations should be part of the day-to-day activity of both safety professionals and security personnel. Some hazards that might be present in any business facility are shown in Table 12.1.

10.5 A hazardous Materials Program

In addition to the seven steps in safety planning, particular types of businesses dealing with hazardous substances should have a hazardous materials program. As a minimum, it is necessary to:

1. Identify the hazardous materials you have and where they are.
2. Know how to respond to an accident involving hazardous materials.
3. Know how to deal with spills.
4. Set up appropriate safeguards.
5. Train employees to deal with hazardous materials.

As discussed earlier, MSDSs are designed specifically to help identify the nature of potential hazards. These data sheets are obtainable from vendors of hazardous materials or equipment.

Monthly Safety Check

Dept. _____ Date _____

Supervisor _____

Indicate discrepancy by ☒

General area	
Floor condition	
Special purpose flooring	
Aisle, clearance/markings	
Floor openings, require safeguards	
Railings, stairs temp./perm.	
Dock board (bridge plates)	
Piping (water-steam-air)	
Wall damage	
Ventilation	
Other	
Illumination—wiring	
Unnecessary/improper use	
Lights on during shutdown	
Frayed/defective wiring	
Overloading circuits	
Machinery not grounded	
Hazardous location	
Other	
Housekeeping	
Floors	
Machines	
Break area/latrines	
Waste disposal	
Vending machines/food protection	
Rodent, insect, vermin control	
Vehicles	
Unauthorized use	
Operating defective vehicle	
Reckless/speeding operation	
Failure to obey traffic rules	
Other	
Tools	
Power tool wiring	
Condition of hand tools	
Safe storage	
Other	

First aid	
First aid kits	
Stretchers, fire blankets, oxygen	
Fire protection	
Fire hoses hung properly	
Extinguisher charged/proper location	
Access to fire equipment	
Exit lights/doors/signs	
Other	
Security	
Doors/windows, etc. secured when required	
Alarm operation	
Department shut down security	
Equipment secured	
Unauthorized personnel	
Other	
Machinery	
Unattended machines operating	
Emergency stops not operational	
Platforms/ladders/catwalks	
Instructions to operate/stop posted	
Maintenance being performed on machines in operation	
Guards in place	
Pinch points	
Material storage	
Hazardous & flammable material not stored properly	
Improper stacking/loading/securing	
Improper lighting, warning signs, ventilation	
Other	

FIGURE 12.6 Monthly safety checklist.

10.6   Management Leadership

Management's attitude toward safety filters down through the entire company. Top management's concern will be reflected in that of the supervisors; in turn, the supervisor's attention to safety will affect the individual employee's attitude. Management is responsible not only for a basic policy providing a work environment free of hazards, which should be embodied in an executive policy statement, but also for active leadership. This can be expressed by holding subordinates responsible for accident prevention

Table 12.1 Common Safety Hazards

1. Floors, aisles, stairs, and walkways

   - Oil spills or other slippery substances that might result in an injury-producing fall.

   - Litter-obscuring hazards such as electrical floor plugs, projecting material, or material that might contribute to fueling a fire.

   - Electrical wire, cable, pipes, or other objects crossing aisles that are not clearly marked or properly covered.

   - Stairways that are too steep or have no nonskid floor covering, inadequate or nonexistent railings, poor lighting, or are in a poor state of repair.

   - Overhead walkways that have inadequate railings, are not covered with nonskid material, or are in a poor state of repair.

   - Walks and aisles that are exposed to the elements and have not been cleared of snow or ice, are slippery when wet, or are in a poor state of repair. Aisles may be blocked with stock or items that reduce employees' ability to exit safely or get emergency equipment where needed.

2. Doors and emergency exits

   - Doors that are ill fitting, stick, and might cause a slowdown during emergency evacuation.

   - Panic-type hardware that is inoperative or in a poor state of repair.

   - Doors that have been designated for emergency exit but that are locked and not equipped with panic-type hardware.

   - Doors that have been designated for emergency exit but that are blocked by equipment or debris.

   - Missing or burned-out emergency exit lights.

   - Nonexistent or poorly marked routes leading to emergency exit doors.

3. Flammable and other dangerous materials

   - Flammable gases and liquids that are uncontrolled in areas in which they might constitute a serious threat.

   - Radioactive material not properly stored or handled.

   - Paint or painting areas that are not properly secured or that are in areas that are poorly ventilated.

   - Gasoline pumping areas located dangerously close to operations that are spark-producing or in which open flame is being used.

4. Protective equipment or clothing

   - Workmen in areas where toxic fumes are present who are not equipped with or not using respiratory protective apparatus.

   - Workmen involved in welding, drilling, sawing, and other eye-endangering occupations who have not been provided with or are not wearing protective eye covering.

   - Workmen in areas requiring the wearing of protective clothing due to exposure to radiation or toxic chemicals but who are not using such protection.

   - Workmen engaged in the movement of heavy equipment or materials who are not wearing protective footwear.

   - Workmen who require prescription eyeglasses who are not provided with or are not wearing safety lenses.

5. Vehicle operation and parking

   - Forklifts that are not equipped with audible and visual warning devices when backing.

   - Trucks that are not provided with a guide when backing into a dock or that are not properly chocked while parking.

(Continued)

Table 12.1 Continued

- Speed violations by cars, trucks, lifts, and other vehicles being operated within the protected area.
- Vehicles that are operated with broken, insufficient, or nonexistent lights during the hours of darkness.
- Vehicles that constitute a hazard due to poor maintenance procedures on brakes and other safety-related equipment.
- Vehicles that are parked in fire lanes or that block fire lanes and emergency exits or fire protection equipment and system access.

6. Machinery maintenance and operation
    - Frayed electrical wiring that might result in a short circuit or malfunction of the equipment.
    - Workers who operate, process, or work near or on belts, conveyors, and other moving equipment who are wearing loose-fitting clothing that might be caught and drag them into the equipment.
    - Presses and other dangerous machinery that are not equipped with the required hand guards or with automatic shutoff devices or dead-man controls.

7. Welding and other flame- or spark-producing equipment
    - Welding torches and spark-producing equipment being used near flammable liquid or gas storage areas or being used in the vicinity where such products are dispensed or are part of the productive process.
    - The use of flame- or spark-producing equipment near wood shavings or oily machinery or where they might damage electrical wiring.
    - Followup inspection should be done periodically at intervals to make sure there are no smoldering heat sources.

8. Miscellaneous hazards
    - Medical and first aid supplies not properly stored, marked, or maintained.
    - Color coding of hazardous areas or materials not being accomplished or not uniform.
    - Broken or unsafe equipment and machinery not being properly tagged with a warning of its condition.
    - Electrical boxes and wiring not properly inspected or maintained, permitting them to become a hazard.
    - Emergency evacuation routes and staging areas not properly marked or identified.

Source: Eugene Finneran, *Security Supervision: A Handbook for Supervisors and Managers* (Boston: Butterworth-Heinemann, 1981).

and in such visible ways as plant tours, letters to employees, safety meetings, posters, prompt accident investigations, and personal example. (When visiting a hard hat area, for example, the president of the company should also put on a hard hat.)

General safety rules must be established and published in the employee handbook or manual. Safety rules should be continually reviewed and updated.

10.7   Assignment of Responsibility

Responsibility for the safety program should be clear and personal. In the small company, this responsibility might rest with the owner. It will generally be an added responsibility of the supervisors in companies with fewer than 100 employees.

In larger companies, safety should be a responsibility assigned to a ranking member of management who can delegate the authority to oversee the program to a safety director (who may be called the safety professional, safety engineer, or safety supervisor, depending on his or her qualifications and the nature of the operation). In many companies, safety is a responsibility of the security director, who will often have a safety specialist as a subordinate. (In virtually all circumstances, there is a close relationship between safety and security.)

10.8   Training

All employees must be initially and periodically trained in both general safety principles and safe work practices in their specific jobs. Safety rules such as requirements to wear protective clothing (gloves, headgear, respirators, shoes, eye protection, and such) should be clearly explained and promptly enforced. The importance the company attaches to safety should particularly be emphasized in new employee training, but it is also important to pay attention to regular employees, including the "old timers" who did not grow up with safety awareness as part of their conditioning. Certificates for completing classes should be given to employees at the workplace to show the program's importance to management.

In addition, there are specific training requirements in the OSHA standards (such as those involving the operation of certain types of equipment). Employers and employees should be aware of those standards that apply in their specific workplace.

10.9   Emergency Care

Under OSHA, all businesses are required, in the absence of an infirmary or hospital in the immediate vicinity, to have available a person or persons trained in first aid, along with first aid supplies. Where employees are exposed to corrosive materials, procedures for drenching or flushing the eyes and body should be provided in the work area.

Procedures should be established for handling injury accidents without confusion or delay. The extent of these preparations will, of course, depend on the nature of the business and the types of hazards.

10.10   Employee Awareness and Participation

Developing safety and health awareness is one of the primary goals of OSHA. Active steps by management, such as those suggested in this chapter, are essential to involve all employees in the need to create a safe work environment.

Safety awareness has an added benefit for both the employer and employees in that it tends to carry over into a concern for off-the-job safety. Accidents away from the work environment account for more than half of all injuries, and the ratio of deaths is higher in off-the-job accidents by a ratio of 3:1. Carrying safety practices from the job to activities away from the job is an aspect of safety training that is receiving increasing emphasis from today's safety professionals (see Table 12.2).

Summary

With the advent of OSHA, the attention focused on safety in the workplace created many new attitudes about the place of loss control within organizations. Many companies that had at best paid lip service to concepts of safety that are commonplace today

Table 12.2 Typical Human Problems as a Result of Disaster and Potential Agencies for Assistance

Requirement	Provider(s)
Shelter	Civil Defense and Red Cross
Food	Red Cross and civic groups
Water	Civil government
Emergency care	Hospitals and clinics
Medical evaluations	Hospitals and health agencies
Personal protection	Police and National Guard
Illumination	Public utilities
Communications	Citizen band radio and National Guard
Transportation	National Guard, local trucking and bus companies
Property protection	Police, auxiliary police, and National Guard

Source: Dennis Sigwart, "Disaster Planning Considerations for the Security/Safety Professional: A Historical Interface," in John Chuvala III and Robert Fischer, eds., *Suggested Preparation for Careers in Security/Loss Prevention*, 2nd ed. (Dubuque, IA: Kendall/Hunt 1999).

came to see that safety, like security, is good business and that a well-managed loss control program would produce gratifying savings in a potentially costly area of company operations. But it must be noted that a well-managed safety program goes well beyond simply complying with OSHA standards.

In addition to recognizing OSHA standards, many companies have also placed more emphasis on fire prevention and protection. Some companies have even established their own fire departments, which are often better equipped than some municipal departments. Although there is some recognition of the importance of contingency planning, far too few firms that have anything beyond a contingency plan that sits on a shelf in the CEO's office. Even in companies with crisis management teams, the members often do not meet to discuss how the team would function in an actual situation.

The most progressive firms offer the team members, fire brigades, and employees an opportunity to preplan (contingency planning) through mock exercises that replicate industrial disasters, explosions, fires, or tornado alerts. The end result is a better prepared team of employees. Unfortunately, many firms have not gone this far.

Contingency planning might not have been a traditional security process, but in today's global business environment the security organization is assuming a much greater role and responsibility for its implementation. Even prior to the events of 9/11 many organizations were becoming more conscious of the need to have contingency plans. A complete contingency planning program has three major elements:

- Emergency response
- Crisis management
- Business continuity: Business recovery and business resumption

Emergency response activities involve responding to an incident, crisis, or disaster and managing that incident at the scene. Should an incident escalate to the crisis or disaster stage, a CMT should take over managing the crisis to its conclusion. If the crisis or disaster does cause damage to a company building, facility, or operation, the CMT should hand over to a BCT the responsibility of recovery and resumption. After a disaster, it is critical that the business recovers and resumes normal (pre-event) operations as soon as possible. Customers, shareholders, and stakeholders expect nothing less. Executive management has the obligation to ensure that contingency planning is properly considered and addressed within their company. The consequences of not planning for contingencies can be catastrophic and bring up numerous liability issues.

□ □ □ ▆▆▆▆▆▆▆▆▆▆▆▆▆▆▆▆▆▆▆▆▆▆▆▆▆▆▆▆▆

Critical Thinking

What is the relationship between safety issues, fire prevention and firefighting, other emergencies, and the process of contingency planning? Can a business be successful without having contingency plans?

▆▆▆▆▆▆▆▆▆▆▆▆▆▆▆▆▆▆▆▆▆▆▆▆▆▆▆ □ □ □

Review Questions

1. What are the classes of fire, the fuels needed to ignite each, and the extinguishing agents that can be used in each class?
2. In what ways is an ionization detector different from a smoke, infrared, or thermal detector?
3. What are the key elements of any contingency plan?
4. What should be the role of security in developing a contingency plan?
5. When management is developing a plan for emergency evacuations, what things need to be considered?
6. What is OSHA, and what effect has it had on company safety operations?

References

1. Block, Robert, "Pushing Disaster Preparedness the Lieberman Way," *Wall Street Journal* Online, 02/09/07.
2. Sigwart, Dennis F., "Disaster Planning Considerations for the Security/Safety Professional: A Historical Interface," in John Chuala III and Robert Fischer, eds., *Suggested Preparation for Careers in Security/Loss Prevention,* 2nd ed. (Dubuque, IA: Kendall/Hunt, 1999).
3. www.acp-international.com/; for contact information, mailto:chairman@acp-international.com.
4. http://pandemicflu.gov/plan/pandplan.html.
5. http://en.wikipedia.org/wiki/Spanish_flu.
6. Pugh, Tony, "Rating System Develop to Gauge Pandemics," *Houston Chronicle,* (February 2, 2007), A10.
7. *Firefighter's Handbook,* 2nd ed. (Clifton Park, New York: Thomson Delmar Learning, 2004), Chapter 13.

8. Bryan, John L., *Fire Suppression and Detection Systems* (New York: Macmillan, 1982), pp. 11–12.

9. General Industry: Safety and Health Regulations, Part 1910 (U.S. Department of Labor, OSHA, 1974).

10. *Marshall v. Barlow's,* 98 Sct. Rptr. 1816 (1978).

11. Heinrich, H. W., *Industrial Accident Prevention* (New York: McGraw-Hill, 1959).

12. Ibid.

13

Internal Theft Controls and Personnel Issues

OBJECTIVES

The study of this chapter will enable you to:

1. Understand the complexity of relative honesty.
2. Develop strategies to manage employee honesty.
3. Understand the relationship between security and human resources personnel.
4. Know the basics of background checks.
5. Understand the operation of various lie detection devices and integrity tests.
6. Know the rights of employees confronted with wrongdoing in the workplace.
7. Identify problem areas where employee theft is most likely.

1 Introduction

It is sad but true that virtually every company will suffer losses from internal theft—and these losses can be enormous. Early in this new century, even large corporate giants such as Enron, WorldCom, and Martha Stewart were affected by internal corruption that reached the highest levels of the organization. *Security* reports that in the retail business alone, 1 in every 27 employees is apprehended for theft from their employer. Internal theft in the retail business outstrips the loss from shoplifting by approximately 7.9 times.[1] Loss Prevention Consultants reported the significance of the employee-theft problem. Their study, based on confessions of 345 employee thieves, documents a combined shrinkage of more than $1 million over a four-year period. The study notes that employee theft is not seasonal and that accessibility rather than need triggers the desire to steal. The report notes, however, that 51 percent of the thieves over 41 years of age reported that they stole to satisfy financial needs. Younger employees tend to steal gadgets, whereas older thieves take money.[2]

The significance of employee theft is pointed out in a 2007 University of Florida and National Retail Federation report. Dr. Richard Hollinger, the report's lead author, reported that $19.5 billion was lost to retailers thanks to thieving employees.[3]

2   What Is Honesty?

Before considering the issue of dishonest employees, it is helpful to understand the concept of honesty, which is difficult to define. Webster says that honesty is "fairness and straightforwardness of conduct, speech, etc.; integrity; truthfulness; freedom; freedom from fraud." In simple terms, honesty is respect for others and their property. The concept, however, is relative. According to Charles Carson, "Security must be based on a controlled degree of relative honesty" because no one fulfills the ideal of total honesty. Carson explores relative honesty by asking the following questions:

1. If an error is made in your favor in computing the price of something you buy, do you report it?
2. If a cashier gives you too much change, do you return it?
3. If you found a purse containing money and the owner's identification, would you return the money to the owner if the amount was $1? $10? $100? $1,000?[4]

Honesty is a controllable variable, and how much control is necessary depends on the degree of honesty of each individual. The individual's honesty can be evaluated by assessing the degree of two types of honesty: moral and conditioned. *Moral honesty* is a feeling of responsibility and respect that develops during an individual's formative years; this type of honesty is subconscious. *Conditioned honesty* results from fearing the consequences of being caught; it is a product of reasoning. If an honest act is made without a conscious decision, it is because of moral honesty, but if the act is based on the conscious consideration of consequences, the act results from conditioned honesty.

It is vital to understand these principles because the role of security is to hire employees who have good moral honesty and to condition employees to greater honesty. The major concern is that the job should not tempt an employee into dishonesty.

Unfortunately there is no sure way by which you can recognize potentially dishonest employees. Proper screening procedures can eliminate applicants with unsavory pasts or those who seem unstable and therefore possibly untrustworthy. There are even tests that purport to measure an applicant's "honesty index." But tests and employee screening can only indicate potential difficulties. They can screen out the most obvious risks, but they can never truly vouch for the performance of any prospective employee under circumstances of new employment or under changes that may come about in life apart from the job.

The need to carefully screen employees has continued to increase. In today's market, there are many individuals who have been called the "I deserve it!" generation. According to a study by the Josephson Institute for the Advanced Study of Ethics, "cheating, stealing and lying by high school students have continued their alarming, decade-long upward spiral." The Institute, which conducts nonpartisan ethics programs for the Internal Revenue Service, the Pentagon, and several major media organizations and educators, states that their findings show "evidence that a willingness to cheat has become the norm and that parents, teachers, coaches and even religious education have not been able to stem the tide." To support the research, the Institute notes that in 2002, 37 percent of high school youth reported that they would be willing to lie to get a good job, compared to 28 percent in 2000 and 25 percent in 1992. Seventy-four percent of high school students reported they cheated on tests during 2002, compared to 61 percent in 1992.[5] The good news is that the 2006 results reported a decline of those who reported cheating on a test to 60 percent. The 2006 study found that young people believe that ethics and character are important but are cynical about whether a person can be ethical and succeed.[6]

3 The Dishonest Employee

Because there is no fail-safe technique for recognizing the potentially dishonest employee on sight, it is important to try to gain some insight into the reasons that employees steal. If some rule of thumb can be developed that will help identify the patterns of the potential thief, it would provide some warning for an alert manager.

There is no simple answer to the question of why heretofore honest people suddenly start to steal from their employers. The mental and emotional processes that lead to this behavior are complex, and motivation can come from any number of sources.

Some employees steal because of resentment over real or imagined injustice that they blame on management indifference or malevolence. Some feel that they must maintain status and steal to augment their incomes because of financial problems. Some steal simply to tide themselves over in a genuine emergency. They rationalize the theft by assuring themselves that they will return the money after the current problem is solved. Some simply want to indulge themselves, and many, strangely enough, steal to help others. Some employees steal because no one cares, because no one is looking, or because absent or inadequate theft controls eliminate the fear of being caught. Still others steal simply for excitement.

3.1 The Theft Triangle

A simplified answer to the question of why employees steal is depicted in the theft triangle. According to this concept, theft occurs when three elements are present: (1) motive, (2) desire, and (3) opportunity.

In simple terms, *motive* is a reason to steal. Motives might be the resentment of an employee who feels underpaid or the vengefulness of an employee who has been passed over for promotion. *Desire* builds on motive by imagining the satisfaction or gratification that would come from a potential action: "Taking a stereo system would make me feel good because I always wanted a good stereo system." *Opportunity* is the absence of barriers that prevent someone from taking an item. Desire and motive are beyond the scope of the loss prevention manager; opportunity, however, is the responsibility of security.

A high percentage of employee thefts begin with opportunities that are regularly presented to them. If security systems are lax or supervision is indifferent, the temptation to steal items that are improperly secured or unaccounted for might be too much to resist for any but the most resolute employee.

Many experts agree that the fear of discovery is the most important deterrent to internal theft. When the potential for discovery is eliminated, theft is bound to follow. Threats of dismissal or prosecution of any employee found stealing are never as effective as the belief that any theft will be discovered by management.

3.2 Danger Signs

The root causes of theft are many and varied, but certain signs can indicate that a hazard exists. The conspicuous consumer presents perhaps the most easily identified risk. Employees who habitually or suddenly acquire expensive cars and/or clothes and who generally seem to live beyond their means should be watched. Such persons are visibly extravagant and appear indifferent to the value of money. Even though such employees might not be stealing to support expensive tastes, they are likely to run into financial difficulties through reckless spending. Employees may then be tempted to look beyond their paychecks for ways to support an extravagant lifestyle.

Employees who show a pattern of financial irresponsibility are also a potential risk. Many people are incapable of handling their money. They might do their jobs with great skill and efficiency, but they are in constant difficulty in their private lives. These people are not necessarily compulsive spenders, nor do they necessarily have expensive tastes. (They probably live quite modestly since they have never been able to manage their affairs effectively enough to live otherwise.) They are simply people unable to come to grips with their own economic realities. Garnishments or inquiries by creditors could identify such employees. If there seems a reason to make a credit check, it might reveal the employee's tangled state of affairs.

Employees caught in a genuine financial squeeze are also possible security problems. If they have been hit with financial demands due to illness in the family or if they have heavy tax liens, they could find the pressures too great to bear. If such a situation comes to the attention of management, counseling is in order. Many companies maintain funds that are designated to make low-interest loans to employees in such cases. Alternatively, some arrangement might be worked out through a credit union. In any event, employees in such extremes need help fast. They should get that help both as a humane response to their needs and as a means of protecting company assets.

In addition to these general categories, you should note specific danger signals:

- Gambling on or off premises
- Excessive drinking or signs of other drug use
- Obvious extravagance
- Persistent borrowing
- Requests for advances
- Bouncing personal checks or problems with creditors

3.3   What Employees Steal

The employee thief will take anything that might be useful or that has resale value. The thief can get at the company funds in many ways, directly or indirectly, through collusion with vendors, collusion with outside thieves or hijackers, fake invoices, receipting for goods never received, falsifying inventories, payroll padding, false certification of overtime, padded expense accounts, computer records manipulation, overcharging, undercharging, or simply by gaining access to a cash box.

This is only a sample of the kinds of attacks that can be made on company assets using the systems set up for the business's operation. It is in these areas that the greatest losses can occur. Thefts are frequently based on a systematic looting of the goods and services in which the company deals and the attendant operational cash flow.

Significant losses do occur, however, in other, sometimes unexpected, areas. Furnishings frequently disappear. In some firms with indifferent traffic control procedures, this kind of theft can be a very real problem. Desks, chairs, computers and other office equipment, paintings, rugs—all can be carried away by the enterprising employee thief.

Office supplies can be another problem if they are not properly supervised. Beyond the anticipated attrition in pencils, paper clips, notepads, and rubber bands, these materials are sometimes stolen in case lots. Many firms that buy their supplies at discount are in fact receiving stolen property. The market in stolen office supplies is a brisk one and is becoming more so as the prices for this merchandise soar.

The office equipment market is another active one, and the inside thief is quick to respond to its needs. Computers always bring a good price, as do calculators and equipment used to support computers.

Personal property is also vulnerable. Office thieves do not make fine distinctions between company property and that of their fellow workers. The company has a very real stake in this kind of theft because personal tragedy and decline in morale follow in its wake. Although security personnel cannot assume responsibility for losses of this nature since they are not in a position to know about the property involved or to control its handling (and they should so inform all employees), they should make every effort to apprise all employees of the threat. They should further note from time to time the degree of carelessness the staff displays in handling personal property and send out reminders of the potential dangers of loss.

3.4 Methods of Theft

A 2007 report by Gaston and Associates pointed out that the American Management Association believes that 20 percent of business failures were the result of employee dishonesty. The same report stated that the Association of Certified Fraud Examiners estimates that 6 percent of total revenue losses for most companies are due to employee fraud of some type.[7] Therefore, there is a very real need to examine the shapes the dishonesty frequently takes. There is no way to describe every kind of theft, but some examples can give an idea of the dimensions of the problem:

1. Payroll and personnel employees collaborating to falsify records by using nonexistent employees or by retaining terminated employees on the payroll
2. Padding overtime reports and kicking back part of the extra unearned pay to the authorizing supervisor
3. Pocketing unclaimed wages
4. Splitting increased payroll that has been raised on signed, blank checks for use in the authorized signer's absence
5. Maintenance personnel and contract servicepeople in collusion to steal and sell office equipment
6. Receiving clerks and truck drivers in collusion on falsification of merchandise count (extra unaccounted merchandise is fenced)
7. Purchasing agents in collusion with vendors to falsify purchase and payment documents (the purchasing agent issues authorization for payment on goods never shipped after forging receipts of shipment)
8. Purchasing agent in collusion with vendor to pay inflated price
9. Mailroom and supply personnel packing and mailing merchandise to themselves for resale

10. Accounts payable personnel paying fictitious bills to an account set up for their own use

11. Taking incoming cash without crediting the customer's account

12. Paying creditors twice and pocketing the second check

13. Appropriating checks made out to cash

14. Raising the amount on checks after voucher approval or raising the amount on vouchers after their approval

15. Pocketing small amounts from incoming payments and applying later payments on other accounts to cover shortages

16. Removal of equipment or merchandise with the trash

17. Invoicing goods below regular price and getting a kickback from the purchaser

18. Manipulating accounting software packages to credit personal accounts with electronic account overages

19. Issuing (and cashing) checks on returned merchandise not actually returned

20. Forging checks, destroying them when they are returned with the statement from the bank, and changing cash account records accordingly

21. Appropriating credit card, electronic bank account, and other electronic data

3.5 The Contagion of Theft

Theft of any kind is a contagious disorder. Petty, relatively innocent pilferage by a few spreads through a facility. As more people participate, others will follow until even the most rigid break down and join in. Pilferage becomes acceptable—even respectable. It gains general social acceptance that is reinforced by almost total peer participation. Few people make independent ethical judgments under such circumstances. In this microcosm, the act of petty pilferage is no longer viewed as unacceptable conduct. It has become not a permissible sin but instead a right.

In the last century the docks of New York City were an example of this progression. Forgetting for the moment the depredations of organized crime and the climate of dishonesty that characterized that operation for so many years, even longshoremen not involved in organized theft had worked out a system all their own. For example, for every so many cases of whisky unloaded, one case went to the men. Little or no attempt was made to conceal this pilferage. It was a tradition, a right. When efforts were made to curtail the practice, labor difficulties arose. It soon became evident that a certain amount of pilferage would have to be accepted as an unwritten part of the union contract under the existing circumstances.

This is not a unique situation. The progression from limited pilferage through its acceptance as normal conduct to the status of an unwritten right has been repeated time and again. The problem is, it does not stop there. Ultimately pilferage becomes serious theft, and then the real trouble starts. Even before pilferage expands into larger operations, it presents a difficult problem to any business. Even where the amount of goods taken by any one individual is small, the aggregate can represent a significant expense. With the costs of materials, manufacture, administration, and distribution rising as they are, there is simply no room for added, avoidable expenses in today's competitive markets. The business that can operate the most efficiently and offer quality goods at the lowest prices because of the efficiency of its operation will have a huge advantage in the market-place. When so many companies are fighting for their economic lives, there is simply no room for waste—and pilferage is just that.

3.6   The Moral Obligation to Control Theft

When we consider that internal theft accounts for at least twice the loss from external theft (that is, from burglars and armed robbers combined), we must be impressed with the scope of the problem facing today's businesspeople. Businesses have a financial obli-gation to stockholders to earn a profit on their investments. Fortunately there are steps that can be taken to control internal theft. Setting up a program of education and control that is vigorously administered and supervised can cut losses to relatively insignificant amounts.

It is also important to observe that management has a moral obligation to its employees to protect their integrity. Management should take every possible step to avoid presenting open opportunities for pilferage and theft that would tempt even the most honest people to take advantage of the opportunity for gain by theft.

This is not to suggest that each company should assume a paternal role toward its employees and undertake their responsibilities for them. It is to suggest strongly that the company should keep its house sufficiently in order to avoid enticing employees to acts that could result in great personal tragedy as well as in damage to the company.

4   Program for Internal Security

As with all security problems, the first requirement before setting up protective systems for internal security is to survey every area in the company to determine the extent and nature of the risks. If such a survey is conducted energetically and exhaustively, and if its recommendations for action are acted on intelligently, significant losses from internal theft will be a matter of history. (Security surveys and their companion, the operational audit, were discussed in detail in Chapter 8.)

4.1   The Need for Management Support

Once concerns have been identified, it is especially important that the strong support of top management be secured. To implement needed security controls, certain operational procedures may have to be changed. This will require cooperation at every level, and cooperation is sometimes hard to get in situations where department managers feel their authority has been diminished within their sphere of responsibility.

The problem is compounded when changes determined to be necessary cut across departmental lines and even serve to some degree to alter intradepartmental relationships. Affecting systems under such circumstances requires the greatest tact, salesmanship, and executive ability. Failing that, it might be necessary to fall back on the ultimate author-ity vested in the security operation by top management. Any hesitation or equivocation on the part of either management or security at this point could damage the program before it has been initiated.

This does not, of course, mean that management must give security carte blanche. Reasonable and legitimate disagreements will inevitably arise. It does mean that proposed security programs based on broadly stated policy must be given the highest possible priority. In cases where conflict of procedures exists, some compromise may be necessary, but the integrity of the security program as a whole must be preserved intact.

4.2 Communicating the Program

The next step is to communicate necessary details of the program to all employees. Many aspects of the system may be proprietary or on a need-to-know basis, but because part of it will involve procedures engaged in by most of or all company personnel, they will need to know those details in order to comply. This can be handled by an ongoing education program or by a series of meetings explaining the need for security and the damaging effects of internal theft to jobs, benefits, profit sharing, and the company's future. Such meetings can additionally serve to notify all employees that management is taking action against criminal acts of all kinds at every level and that dishonesty will not be tolerated.

Such a forceful statement of position in this matter can be very beneficial. Most employees are honest people who disapprove of those who are criminally inclined. They are apprehensive and uncomfortable in a criminal environment, especially if it is widespread. The longer the company condones such conduct, the more they lose respect for it, and a vicious cycle begins. As they lose respect, they lose a sense of purpose. Their work suffers, morale declines, and at best effectiveness is seriously diminished. At worst they reluctantly join the thieves. A clear, uncompromising policy of theft prevention is usually welcomed with visible relief.

4.3 Continuing Supervision

Once a system is installed, it must be constantly supervised if it is to become and remain effective. Left to their own devices, employees will soon find shortcuts, and security controls will be abandoned in the process. Old employees must be regularly reminded of what is expected of them, and new employees must be adequately indoctrinated in the system they will be expected to follow.

There must be a continuing program of education if expected results are to be achieved. With a high turnover within the white-collar workforce, it can be expected that the office force, which handles key paperwork, will be replaced at a fairly consistent rate. This means that the company will have a regular influx of new people who must be trained in the procedures to be followed and in the reasons for these procedures.

4.4 Program Changes

In some situations, reasonable controls will create duplication of effort, cross-checking, and additional paperwork. Because each time such additional effort is required there is an added expense, procedural innovations requiring it must be avoided wherever possible, but most control systems aim for increased efficiency. Often this is the key to their effectiveness.

Many operational procedures, for a variety of reasons, fall into ponderous routines involving too many people and excessive paper shuffling. This can increase the possibility of fraud, forgery, or falsification of documents. When the same operational result can be achieved by streamlining the system and incorporating adequate security control, it should be done immediately.

Virtually every system can be improved and should be evaluated constantly with an eye for such improvement, but these changes should never be undertaken arbitrarily.

Procedures must be changed only after the changes have been considered in the light of their operational and security impact, and such considerations should further be undertaken in the light of their effect on the total system.

No changes should be permitted by unilateral employee action. Management should make random spot checks to determine whether the system is being followed exactly. Internal auditors and/or security personnel should make regular checks on the control systems.

4.5   Violations

Violations should be dealt with immediately. Management indifference to security procedures is a signal that they are not important, and where work-saving methods can be found to circumvent such procedures, they will be. As soon as any procedural untidiness appears and is allowed to continue, the deterioration of the system begins.

It is well to note that, although efforts to circumvent the system are frequently the result of the ignorance or laziness of the offender, a significant number of such instances are the result of employees probing for ways to subvert the controls to divert company assets to their own use.

4.6   Personnel Policies for Internal Security

There is no greater need for cooperation between two departments than that between human resources and security and loss prevention. The job for loss prevention is much simpler when the right person is hired. Though human resources reviews all applications and maintains all records on employees, the security department should be responsible for conducting thorough background checks on specific employee positions. It would be desirable to background all employees, but the amount of employee turnover or volume of new hires often makes such a comprehensive program an impossibility.

4.7   Human Resources and the Screening Process

Internal security's objective is preventing theft by employees. If all employees were of such sterling character that they could not bring themselves to steal, security person nel would have little to do. If, on the other hand, thieves predominated in the mix of employees, the system would be sorely tried, if indeed it could be effective at all. Basic to internal security effectiveness is the cooperation of that majority of honest personnel performing as assigned and in so doing refusing to initiate or collaborate in conspiracies to steal. Without this dominant group, the system is in trouble from the start.

The first line of internal security defense is the human resources department, where bad risks can be screened out by use of reasonable security procedures. Screening is the process of finding the person best qualified for the job in terms of both skills and personal integrity. This process may or may not involve a background check (which will be discussed later), but it must include at least a basic check of an applicant's references and job history.

In some industries, especially those with high technical requirements, screening can be a problem because qualified personnel may be difficult to find. Resistance can come from the human resources department when an otherwise qualified applicant is disqualified on the marginal grounds of a potential security problem. Security management must undertake the job of convincing objectors that a person who may later embezzle from the company is a poor risk from many points of view, no matter how highly qualified that person is in the specific skills required.

Rejecting bad risks must be done on the basis of standards carefully established in cooperation with the human resources director. Once established, these standards must be met in every particular circumstance, just as proficiency standards must be met. Obviously such standards require review from time to time to avoid dealing with applicants unjustly and placing the company in the position of demanding more than is either realistically possible or available. Even here, however, a bottom line must be drawn. At a certain point, compromises and concessions can no longer be made without inviting damage to the company.

Such a careful, selective program will add some expense to the employment procedure, but it can pay for itself in terms of reduced losses, better employees, and lower turnover. And the savings in terms of potential crimes that were averted, though incalculable, can be thought of as enormous.

4.8   Employment History and Reference Checking

The key to reducing internal theft is ensuring the quality of employees employed by the facility. The problem, however, will not be eliminated during the hiring process, no matter how carefully and expertly selection is made. Systems of theft prevention and programs of employee motivation are ongoing efforts that must recognize that elements of availability, susceptibility, and opportunity are dynamic factors in a constant state of flux. The initial approach to the problem, however, starts at the beginning, in the very process of selecting personnel to work in the facility. During this process, a knowledgeable screener who is aware of what to look for in the employment application or résumé can develop an enormous amount of vital information about a prospective employee. Some answers are not as obvious as they once were, and the ability to perceive and evaluate what appears on the application or résumé is more important than ever since application forms are more restrictive in what they can ask.

Privacy legislation coupled with fair employment laws drastically limits what can be asked on the employment application forms. The following federal legislation relates directly to hiring and dealing with employees:

- Title VII of the Civil Rights Act of 1964
- Pregnancy Discrimination Act of 1978
- Executive Order 11246 (affirmative action)
- Age Discrimination in Employment Act
- National Labor Relations Act
- Rehabilitation Act of 1973
- Vietnam Era Veterans' Readjustment Assistance Act of 1974
- Fair Labor Standards Act of 1938 (The Wage and Hour Law; being revised as of this writing)
- Federal Wage Garnishment Law
- Occupational Safety and Health Act of 1970
- Immigration Reform and Control Act of 1986

- Employee Polygraph Protection Act of 1988
- Consolidated Omnibus Reconciliation Act of 1985 (COBRA)
- Worker Adjustment and Retraining Notification Act (Plant Closing Law)
- EEOC Sexual Harassment Guidelines
- Americans with Disabilities Act (for a more complete list, see Table 13.1)

In some aspects, these regulations had a streamlining effect, eliminating irrelevant questions and confining questions exclusively to those matters relating to the job applied for. The subtler kinds of discrimination on the basis of age, sex, and national origin have been largely eliminated from the employment process. In making these changes to protect the applicant, state and federal laws have created new dilemmas for employers and their security staffs.

Various federal and state laws prohibit criminal justice agencies (police departments, courts, and correctional institutions) from providing information on certain criminal cases to noncriminal justice agencies (for example, private security firms or human resources departments). The Fair Credit Reporting Act requires that a job applicant must give written consent to any credit bureau inquiry.

All states have some type of privacy legislation meeting the guidelines set forth in the Federal Privacy Act of 1976. The most controversial portion of the Act states "that information shall only be used for law enforcement and criminal justice and other lawful purposes." The crux of the issue is the way that "other lawful purposes" is defined. Does this meaning include human resources departments and private security operations? The verdict is mixed. Human resources, security, and loss prevention operations must be aware of the interpretation of the privacy legislation in each state in which they operate. Recent legislation, as discussed in Chapter 1 regarding the Department of Homeland Security, has allowed government agencies and private security firms greater access to criminal histories, financial records, and medical records.

Understandably there is some confusion regarding the rules governing employment screening. In spite of such confusion, the preemployment inquiry remains one of the most useful security tools employers can use to shortstop employee dishonesty and profit drains. Security management should consult with legal counsel to determine which laws relate to their locality and establish firm and precise policies regarding employment applications and hiring practices.

Generally speaking, look for, and be wary of, applicants who:

1. Show signs of instability in personal relations
2. Lack job stability: a job hopper does not make a good job candidate
3. Show a declining salary history or are taking a cut in pay from the previous job
4. Show unexplained gaps in employment history
5. Are clearly overqualified
6. Are unable to recall or are hazy about names of supervisors in the recent past or who forget their addresses in the recent past

If the job applied for is one involving the handling of funds, it is advisable to get the applicant's consent to make a financial inquiry through a credit bureau. Be wary if such an inquiry turns up a history of irresponsibility in financial affairs, such as living beyond one's means.

Table 13.1 Who Is Protected, Who Is Affected? Federally Covered Employers and Protected Classes

Legislation	Race/Color	National	Origin/Ancestry	Sex	Religion	Age	Disabled	Union	Covered Employers	Federal Agency
Title VII Civil Rights Act	X	X	X	X					Employers with 15+EEs; unions, employment agencies	EEOC
Equal Pay Act (EPA) as amended			X						Minimum wage law coverage ("administrative employees" not exempted)	EEOC
[a]Age Discrimination in Employment Act (ADEA)						X	40+		20+EEs (unions with 25+members), employment agencies	EEOC
*Age Discrimination Act of 1975 (ADA)						X			Receives federal money	EEOC
*Executive Order 11246.11141	X	X		X	X	X			All federal contractors and subcontractors	OFCCP
*Title VI Civil Rights Act	X	X		X	X				Federally-assisted program or activity—public schools and colleges also covered by Title IX	Funding Agency and EEOC
*Rehabilitation Act of 1973							X		Receives federal money: federal contractor, $2,500+	OFCCP
National Labor Relations Act (NLRA)	X	X		X	X	X		X	ER in interstate commerce	NLRB

Act					Coverage	Enforcement
Civil Rights Act of 1866	X	X			All employers	Courts
Civil Rights Act of 1871	X	X			Private employers usually not covered	EEOC
Revenue Sharing Act of 1972	X	X	X	X	State and local governments that receive federal revenue sharing funds	OFCCP
Education Amendments of 1972 Title IX		X			Educational institutions receiving federal financial assistance	Dept. of Education
Vietnam Era Vets Readjustment Act—1974				X	Government contractors—$10,000+	OFCCP
Pregnancy Discrimination Act of 1978		X			All employers 15+EEs	EEOC-OFCCP
Fair Labor Standards Act					Includes minimum wage law and equal pay act with DOL complex method of coverage	
*Rehabilitation Act of 1973			X		Receives federal money: federal contractor, $2,500+	OFCCP
Americans with Disabilities Act of 1990			X		Covers employers with 15 or more employees	EEOC

(*Continued*)

Table 13.1 Continued

Legislation	Race/Color	National Origin/Ancestry	Sex	Religion	Age	Disabled	Union	Covered Employers	Federal Agency
Federal Privacy Act of 1976								Federal agencies only	
Freedom of Information Act								Federal agencies only	
Family Educational Rights and Privacy Act								Schools, colleges, and universities, federally assisted	
Immigration Reform Act of 1986								All employers	INS

EE = Employee; ER = Employer; EEOC = Equal Employment Opportunity Commission; OFCCP = Office Federal Contract Compliance Programs; NLRB = National Labor Relations Board; DOL = Department of Labor; INS = Immigration and Naturalization Service.

*Applies to federal agencies, contractors, or assisted programs only.

aMandatory retirement eliminated except in special circumstances.

Table 13.2 Examples of Acceptable and Unacceptable Inquiries for Preemployment Screening

Subject	Unacceptable Inquiries	Acceptable Inquiries
Address or duration of residence	Do you own or rent your home?	What is your place of residence? How long have you resided in this state or city?
Age	How old are you? What is your birth date? What are your children's ages? Dates of attendance or completion of elementary or high school.	Are you 18 years of age or older? If not, state your age. If hired, can you show proof of age? If under 18, can you submit a work permit after employment?
Arrest and convictions records	Have you ever been arrested?	Have you been convicted of a crime? If so, give details.
Birthplace, citizenship	Of what country are you a citizen? Are you naturalized or a native-born citizen? What date did you acquire citizenship? Please produce your naturalization or first paper. Are your parents or spouse naturalized or native-born United States citizens? What date did your parents or spouse acquire United States citizenship?	Are you authorized to work in the United States? Can you, after employment, submit verification of your legal Right to work in the United States? Statement that such proof may be required after employment.
Disability	What is your corrected vision? Have you ever been unable to cope with job-related stress? Do you have a disability that would interfere with your ability to perform the job? When will your broken leg heal? Can you stand? Can you walk? How many days were you sick last year? Have you ever been treated for mental illness? Do you have asthma? Do you have any physical disabilities or handicaps? Questions regarding receipt of workers' compensation	Do you have 20/20 corrected vision? How well can you handle stress? How did you break your leg? Can you stand for 5 hours? Can you walk 20 miles in one day? Can you meet the attendance requirements of this job?
Discharge from military service	Did you serve in the armed forces of another country? Did you receive a discharge that was less than honorable?	Have you ever been a member of the United States armed services or in a state militia? If so, what branch? If so, explain your Experience in relation to the Position for which you are applying.
Education		Describe your academic, vocational, or professional education as it relates to this position. What private or public schools did you attend?

(Continued)

Table 13.2 Continued

Subject	Unacceptable Inquiries	Acceptable Inquiries
English language skills	What is your native language? How did you acquire your foreign language skill?	What foreign language do you read, write, and/or speak fluently?
Experience		Inquiries include those regarding work experience.
Marital status, number of children, child care, sex	Are you married? single? divorced? Separated? What is your spouse's name? Where is your spouse employed? What is your spouse's salary? What are your child care plans? Who can we contact in case of emergency? (This question can be asked after a person has been hired.) Do you wish to be addressed as Miss? Mrs.? Ms.? Questions regarding pregnancy, child-bearing, or birth control.	Information such as this, which is required for tax, insurance, or Social Security purposes, may be obtained after hiring. Lawful inquiries include those regarding one's ability to travel if the job required it. However, all applicants must be asked the same question.
Notice in case of emergency	Name and address of person to be notified in case of accident or emergency. (Information obtained after the applicant has been hired.)	Name and address of person to be notified in case of accident or emergency. Name and address of a relative or spouse to be notified in case of accident or emergency.
Name	Please state your maiden name. If you have worked under another name, state that name and dates.	Have you ever worked for this company under a different name? Is additional information relative to change of name, use of an assumed name or nickname necessary to enable a check on your work record? If yes, explain.
Organization, activities	List all clubs, societies, and lodges to which you belong.	Please state your membership in any organization(s) that you feel is/are relevant to your ability to perform this job.
Physical description, photograph	Questions as to applicant's height and weight. Require applicant to affix a photograph to application. Request applicant at his or her option to submit a photograph. Require a photograph after interview but before employment. Inquiries include those that are not related to job requirements.	Any questions that have an impact on one's ability to perform the job requirements. Statement that photograph may be required after employment.

(Continued)

Table 13.2 Continued

Subject	Unacceptable Inquiries	Acceptable Inquiries
Race, color, religion, or national origin	Questions as to applicant's race or color. Questions regarding applicant's complexion or color of skin, eyes, hair. Questions regarding applicant's religion. Questions regarding religious days observed. Does your religion prevent you from working weekends or holidays? Questions as to nationality, lineage, ancestry, national origin, descent, or parentage of applicant, applicant's parents, or spouse.	Statement by employer of regular days, hours, or shifts to be worked.
References	Questions of applicant's former employers or acquaintances that elicit information specifying the applicant's race, color, religious creed, national origin, ancestry, physical handicap, medical conditions, marital status, age, or sex.	Who referred you for a position here? Names of persons willing to provide professional and/or character references for applicant.

Application forms should ask for a chronological listing of all previous employers which will provide a list of firms to be contacted for information on the applicant as well as show continuity of career. Any gaps could indicate a jail term that was "overlooked" in filling out the application. When checking with previous employers, verify dates on which employment started and terminated.

References the applicant submits must be contacted, but they are apt to be biased. After all, since the person being investigated submitted their names, they are not likely to be negative or hostile. It is important to contact someone, preferably an immediate supervisor, at each previous job. Such contact should be made by phone or in person.

The usual and easiest system of contact is by letter, but this leaves much to be desired. The relative impersonality of a letter, especially one in which a form or evaluation is to be filled out, can lead to generic and essentially uncommunicative answers. Because many companies as a matter of policy, stated or implied, are reluctant to give someone a bad reference except in the most extreme circumstances, a written reply to a letter will sometimes be misleading.

Over the past several years the letter has often been replaced with an e-mail. What have been noted as pitfalls of the letter apply to e-mail as well. However the ease of use and virtually no-cost benefits often put this form of reference check at the top of many budget-conscious managers' preferred means of contact.

On the other hand, phone or personal contacts can become considerably more discursive and provide shadings in the tone of voice that can be important. Even when no additional information is forthcoming, this method may indicate when a more exhaustive investigation is required.

4.9 Backgrounding

It may be desirable to get a more complete history of a prospective employee, especially in cases where sensitive financial or supervisory positions are under consideration. In-depth investigations will involve extra expense but could well prove worthwhile. *Backgrounding*, which involves a discreet investigation into the past and present activities of the applicant, can be most informative.

An estimated 90 percent of all persons known to have stolen from their employers were not prosecuted. Thus a thorough investigation of potential employees is certainly justified, especially people being considered for jobs with responsibility for significant amounts of cash or goods or those seeking management positions in shipping, receiving, purchasing, or accounting.

Also of note, personnel and security experts agree that 20 percent of any given workforce is responsible for 80 percent of personnel problems of every variety. If backgrounding can turn up this kind of recorded or known employee behavior, it is well worth the expense.

Backgrounding is also utilized to investigate employees being considered for promotion to positions of considerable sensitivity and responsibility. Such persons might have been the very model of rectitude at the time of employment but could since have had financial reverses threatening their lifestyles. If a background investigation uncovers such information, a company is in a position to offer assistance to that employee if it so desires, relieving both strain and need, which can lead to embezzlement. Such action can boost company morale as well as reduce the potential for theft committed out of desperation.

With today's access to the Internet, security staff can subscribe to any number of Internet investigative resources. The cost associated with these services ranges from as low as $25 to several hundred dollars per inquiry. The cost is often a reflection of the depth of the inquiry. Common resources include:

- www.instantpeoplecheck.com
- www.yourownprivateeye.com
- www.uscriminalcheck.com
- www.accuratecredit.com
- www.web.public.records-now.com

4.10 Integrity and Lie Detection Tests

Another option in lieu of a full background investigation is the use of various integrity and lie detection tests. According to some experts, in states where their use is legal, these tests can be useful tools in determining the past and current records of candidates for employment or promotion to sensitive positions.

Using integrity and lie detection tests is controversial, as is the discussion among practitioners about the relative merits of different types of tests. Many security professionals look on integrity tests as invaluable tools but generally agree that their use should be restricted to the hands of competent, trained professionals to get productive results.

The three main categories of integrity and lie detection tests are (1) the polygraph, (2) the Psychological Stress Evaluator (PSE), and (3) the Personal Security Inventory (PSI). The first two are machines that operate on the same basic physiological principle. The third is a psychological pencil-and-paper test. Controversial recent entries into the area of truth and stress detection are infrared heat scanner and magnetic resonance imaging (MRI) brain scans.

The polygraph, PSE, MRI scan, and infrared face scan operate on the premise that lying creates conflict, which in turn causes anxiety leading to stress reactions. Stress reactions typically include increased respiration, increased pulse rate, higher blood pressure, digestive disorders, perspiration, temperature change, muscle tension, and pupil dilation. The polygraph and the PSE measure some of these changes. Most polygraphs measure galvanic skin response, blood pressure, and respiration. The PSE measures changes in voice quality from tension in the vocal cords. The readouts of both devices may be recorded on paper tape and the responses to various questions analyzed in terms of the charted reactions, which are compared with reactions to simple test questions establishing an individual's normal response to lying. Digital readouts are now more common, and although the PSE has not been as well publicized as the polygraph, portable PSEs are now available. Manufacturers claim that the digital device is the world's first portable lie detector.[8]

Do these machines really work? The controversy over this question continues to draw attention in professional publications. The Employee Polygraph Protection Act of 1988 strictly limits the use of the polygraph to certain industries and for specific purposes. It prohibits preemployment polygraphs by all private employers except those whose primary business is providing security personnel for the protection of currency, negotiable securities, precious commodities or instruments, or proprietary information. Companies that manufacture, distribute, or dispense controlled substances may use the polygraph for any employee having direct access to the manufacture, storage, distribution, or sale of these controlled substances.

To determine whether the polygraph or PSE is worth using in a security operation, various questions need to be considered, such as: What is a lie? According to the *American Heritage Dictionary of the English Language*, a lie is a statement or statements that one knows to be false, especially if made with the intent to deceive. Because a lie is really a subjective evaluation, what these machines record is what a person *believes* to be a lie. In addition, because the machines measure only stress, the subject must believe that the machine works so that enough stress is produced to record.

Because these machines simply measure the physiological symptoms of stress, other stressors may also be recorded. For example, a question concerning drug history may evoke a dramatic response from a subject who has lost a close relative to drug abuse. The subject's physical condition at the time of the test can also influence the tracings. Fatigue, alcohol, and other drugs are the biggest culprits in this category, but even simple things like needing to use the bathroom or suppressing a cough can affect the tracings.

Can someone beat the machine? The answer is both simple and complex. A subject can affect the tracing of the machine by saying prayers or counting holes in acoustic tiles, but a good examiner can and will note these changes. Although the machine registers only physiological changes and thus cannot be beaten, the accuracy of the machine is determined solely by the quality of the examiner.

Problematic to the issue of accuracy, then, is the training of examiners. Training can range from as little as six weeks to as long as six months. Still, a 2003 National Academy of Sciences report concluded that research on the polygraph's efficacy was inadequate.[9]

What is the role of these devices if such doubts can be cast on their accuracy and on the skill of examiners? Jerome Skolnick, noted criminologist, suggests that their result should be used "to open up leads to further investigation of information rather than being itself prima facie evidence."[10]

Much case law regarding the use of the polygraph has been added since the 1988 Polygraph Act. Still, the polygraph's advocates are striving for national recognition for the professional use of the instrument through improving standards for operators. For example, in Illinois, a licensed school must certify polygraph operators before they can operate a machine. Even so, Illinois does not allow polygraph evidence to be presented in its courts.

As for the PSE, the question remains whether polygraph case law will apply to this type of testing as well. Since both machines operate on the same principles, it is likely that much of the established case law relating to the polygraph might be applicable to the PSE. It is interesting to note, however, that during the past 10 years, little has changed in reference to the use of the PSE, but the polygraph continues to struggle to survive under legal fire.

As previously mentioned, the PSI is a psychological pencil-and-paper exam. Many variations of this test exist throughout the United States (for example, the California Personality Inventory [CPI], the Minnesota Multiphasic Personality Inventory [MMPI], Inwald Personality Inventory [IPI], Wonderlic), but they all have common traits. These tests are designed to evaluate prospective employees for honesty and integrity, alcohol and other drug abuse, and violence or emotional instability. Most of these tests can be administered on company property and are relatively inexpensive. The test questions are designed to make consistency (veracity) checks by comparing responses and to provide clues for the psychologist evaluating the personality of the potential employee tested. For example, a typical question might be as follows:

You are riding on a bus. A sign indicates "No Smoking." A person sits down next to you and lights a cigarette. What would you do?

1. Inform him that he is not allowed to smoke.
2. Point out the "No Smoking" sign.
3. Move to another seat.
4. Get off the bus.
5. Say or do nothing.

Adherents of this system claim a high degree of accuracy for such tests when they are conducted by properly trained personnel. Table 13.3 provides a list of pointers that can be used in evaluating pencil-and-paper tests.

It is important for security managers to research the limitations on the use of each of these instruments in their state. Some states forbid their use as a requirement for employment but permit such testing to be used on a voluntary basis. Other states forbid their use under any circumstances.

In general, organized labor has lobbied diligently for legislation banning the use of so-called integrity testing and lie detectors for all industrial or commercial applications, their efforts proving successful with the passage of the 1988 Polygraph Act. The American Polygraph Association, which opposes the use of the PSE on grounds that it has not yet proved itself, has endorsed legislation setting stricter standards for polygraph operators but naturally fights labor's stand on the issue.

Despite the 1988 Polygraph Act limitations on preemployment usage, many firms continue to use the polygraph in various types of investigations. Firms so using these

Table 13.3 Scrutinizing Vendor Pencil-and-Paper Tests: Twelve Pointers in Evaluating a Test's Relevance for Meeting Your Hiring Goals

1. Beware of tests for which little or no validation research exists.
2. Beware of tests that claim they "only replace the polygraph."
3. Beware of studies that are not based on the predication model of validation.
4. Beware of studies that do not tell you how many people were incorrectly predicted to have job problems.
5. Beware of tests that claim to predict dangerous or violent behavior or tendencies.
6. Beware of studies that report "significant" correlations as evidence of their validity.
7. Beware of studies that use small numbers of people to predict important job-performance outcomes.
8. Beware of studies that have not been cross-validated.
9. Beware of claims that tests are valid for use with occupational groups for which validation studies have not yet been conducted.
10. Beware of studies based on questionnaires or tests filled out anonymously.
11. Beware of studies that have not used real job candidates as subjects in their validation efforts.
12. Beware of tests whose validation studies have been designed, conducted, and published only by the test developer or publishing company without replication by other, totally independent, psychologists or agencies.

Source: From materials developed by Dr. Robin Inwald, Hilson Research Inc., February 1988.

machines have generally found them to be useful. The federal government still performs tens of thousands of polygraph tests each year.[11]

According to the 1988 Polygraph Act, the polygraph may be used on existing employees under the following circumstances:

1. In connection with an ongoing investigation involving economic loss or injury to the employer's business (that is, theft, embezzlement, or misappropriation)
2. If the employee has access to the property that is the subject of an investigation
3. If the employer has reasonable suspicion that the employee was involved in the accident or activity under investigation
4. If *before* the test the employer provides to the employee the specifics of the inquiry, that is, what incident is being investigated and the reason the employee is being tested

Even if the employer meets these criteria, employees cannot be disciplined or discharged solely on the basis polygraph results or for refusing to take the polygraph test.

Because such examinations cost from $50 to $150, depending on the length of the test, not every firm will find it practical to use them. Firms finding the expense acceptable usually limit the polygraph's application to particularly sensitive investigations and then only after deciding whether the risk is such that the expense is warranted. Even so, these companies first explore whether they can be satisfied by an evaluation based on other, less expensive methods.

Of recent interest is the use of MRI technology to scan brain activity. Functional MRI technology expands the traditional static picture MRI to allow for a series of scans that show changes in the flow of oxygenated blood preceding neural events. The theory is that lying requires more cognitive effort than telling the truth. The test is too expensive for general commercial use at this time due to an estimated cost of $10,000 for an examination. For more information see www.noliemri.com.

Whatever decision the security manager makes regarding the use of integrity tests, he or she would be well advised to consult a reputable firm to learn what such examinations involve.

Recent concerns following the September 11, 2001, attacks on the World Trade Center have researchers looking for ways to detect deception at airports. The problems associated with traditional polygraphs and the PSE have been discussed. Scientists' recent work has applied the same theory of lying and stress to new technology. In this instance a heat-sensitive camera spots possible deceit by looking for telltale increases in body temperature around the eyes. Such a device could be of value to airport security personnel. Although the research team was led by experts from the Mayo Clinic and Honeywell Laboratories, polygraph authorities question the utility of the device until further testing is completed.[12] As of 2007 it appears that the same stress pitfalls are present in this new technology. TSA personnel might be targeting nervous but harmless travelers as well as those who might be terrorists.[13]

4.11   The Americans with Disabilities Act

The Americans with Disabilities Act (ADA) is a federal statute requiring employers to focus on the *abilities* of applicants rather than on their disabilities. For this reason, inquiries about medical conditions or medical tests before a job offer is made are prohibited. Offers can, however, be made contingent on successful completion of medical examinations. Employers must make certain that medical, psychological, and physical agility examinations come at the end of the hiring process rather than at the beginning. Currently the ADA does not protect the following categories: drug abusers; homosexuals and bisexuals; persons who engage in aberrant sexual behavior; compulsive gambling, theft, or pyromania; persons whose disorders have been caused by drug abuse; or persons whose disabilities are only temporary. It should be noted that tests for illegal drugs are not subject to the ADA's restrictions on medical examinations.[14]

Job announcements, descriptions, and applications should be carefully reviewed to ensure that they conform to the ADA requirements concerning the description of each position's essential functions. All staff involved in recruiting, hiring, and personnel processing and decision making generally should be trained to ensure that they understand and conform to all ADA requirements. In the end, employers should hold persons with disabilities to the same performance standards as other employees.[15]

4.12   Drug Screening

Few areas of preemployment screening provoke the strong reactions that drug screening does. Two major issues usually raised about this type of testing concern invasion-of-privacy arguments and the problem of the risk of false positives. (The issues related to drug screening will be dealt with in more detail in Chapter 15.)

4.13   Other screening options

In addition to the screening tools already discussed, other sources of information can provide details of the applicant's background that might prove valuable in making a hiring decision.

Credit reports not only reflect an applicant's financial situation and stability, they also provide other useful information such as past addresses and previous employers. The legal restrictions of the Federal Fair Reporting Act must be complied with if a person is denied employment as the result of information discovered through this source.

Motor vehicle records are easily obtained and can aid in identifying high-risk employees by noting the number and types of driving violations.

Civil litigation records provide detailed, documented records of an applicant's personal history, background, and financial relationships. These records also document previous injury complaints. They may also provide clues to other employment problems not filed as criminal charges, such as theft, fraud, or serious misconduct.

There are many other possible sources of information, but time and space considerations do not allow for total coverage in an introductory text like this one. As noted earlier, numerous Websites are willing to provide information for a price.

4.14   Hiring Ex-Convicts and Parolees

It should be strongly noted here that rigid exclusionary standards should never be applied to hiring ex-convicts or parolees who openly acknowledge their past records. Such a policy would be at best unjust and at worst irresponsible. These people have served their sentences. Their records are available in situations in which employment is being sought. To turn them away solely on the basis of their past mistakes would be to force them back into a criminal pattern of life in order to survive.

Although people with criminal backgrounds might well be unacceptable to certain companies, a rigid policy refusing all such people employment would deny companies many potentially good employees who deserve a chance to show that they have rehabilitated themselves. Experience has shown that these employees, knowingly hired in the right positions and properly supervised, are not only acceptable but are frequently highly responsible and trustworthy. They should be given an opportunity to reestablish themselves in society.

4.15   Employee Assistance Programs

One innovation in coping with employee problems relating to, among other things, honesty, alcohol and other drug problems, and depression has been the advent of the employee assistance program, or EAP. According to Tom Pope, "At a time when substance abuse, mental health problems, and other stresses beset the American work force, an effective employee assistance program can be a wise investment."[16] Today more than 90 percent of the *Fortune* 500 companies have introduced EAPs.[17] Programs vary with the type and size of company. Some companies provide full-service, in-house operations, whereas some smaller firms restrict the type of service and contract with professional EAP firms.

The fact is that EAPs are proving valuable for some firms. McDonnell-Douglas reports a 34 percent reduction in absences in comparison to its corporate counterparts without EAPs. In the area of attrition of drug users, McDonnell-Douglas displays a job dropout rate from 40 percent in their control group to 7.5 percent in the EAP participants. Other firms also report success: Chicago Bell, General Motors, HARTline, and so forth. Many of these employers believe that improving family life will also reflect positively in the workplace.[18] For a discussion on EAPs, see Chapter 15, "Violence and Drug Use in the Workplace."

4.16 Continuity of the Screening Program

When a company makes a systematic and conscientious effort to screen out dishonest, troublesome, incompetent, and unstable employees, it has taken a first and significant step toward reducing internal theft. It is important that the program continue on a permanent basis.

Care must be taken to avoid relaxing standards or becoming less diligent in checking applicants' backgrounds and employment histories. There is a tendency to lose sight of all the dimensions of the problem if the security program makes substantial inroads into the loss factor. Past problems are too soon forgotten, and carelessness follows closely behind. Active supervision is always necessary to maintain the integrity of this essential aspect of every security program.

CASE STUDY

A security survey conducted for the Assets Corporation recommended a complete revamping of the activity and aims of the Human Services Department. At present the department deals only with plant personnel hiring. The office manager finds and hires all office personnel, sidestepping Human Services. The Human Services manager merely records these employees after they are hired.

The Assets Corporation uses one application form for all employees, regardless of job classification. The legal-size application form was copied 10 years ago from one used by the Human Services manager in a prior job. It contains one line to record the applicant's race and another to record religion. It also asks for three nonrelative references and a listing of all prior employment, with only the years of such employment required. No skill-related tests are given. The Human Services Department bases the employment decision on a review of the application and an interview with Human Services staff.

In a pending court case, the Assets Corporation has been charged with discharging a secretary on the basis of race. This employee stated on her application form that she had a high school diploma and could type 60 words a minute. After employment, her typed letters showed many uncorrected errors, including typing errors, misspelled words, and poor knowledge of business terms. This poor performance continued despite the availability of a comprehensive word processing program. She responded to all criticism by claiming racial discrimination on the part of her supervisor. She was verbally discharged, and no written record was kept of her poor performance.

- How could Assets protect itself from allegations such as those made by the discharged stenographer?
- What changes in Human Services Department practice should the survey have recommended regarding content of the application form? Decision making process to hire employees? Clerical applicant tests?

Though employee screening and background checks can reduce later problems with employee performance and dishonesty, time and money often restrict the amount of effort in these important areas. Even tools such as polygraph and paper-and-pencil tests that are used in place of personal record checks are not universally accepted.

One thing, however, is clear: Employees who have options and feel treated like part of a team will not usually become security problems.

5 Procedural Controls

5.1 Auditing Assets

Periodic personal audits by outside auditors are essential to any well-run security program. Such examinations discover theft only after the fact, but they will presumably discover any regular scheme of embezzlement in time to prevent serious damage. If these audits, which are normally conducted once a year, were augmented by one or more surprise audits, even the most reckless criminal would hesitate to try to set up even a short-term scheme of theft.

These audits normally cover an examination of inventory schedules, prices, footings, and extensions. They should also verify current company assets by sampling physical inventory, accounts receivable, accounts payable (including payroll), deposits, plant assets, and outstanding liabilities through an ongoing financial audit. In all these cases, a spot check beyond the books themselves can help establish the existence of legitimate assets and liabilities, not empty entries created by a clever embezzler.

5.2 Separation of Responsibility

The principle of separation of responsibility and authority in matters concerning the company's finances is of prime importance in management. This situation must always be sought out in the survey of every department. It is not always easy to locate. Sometimes even the employee who has such power is unaware of the dual role. But the security specialist must be knowledgeable about its existence and suggest an immediate change or correction in such operational procedures whenever conflict appears.

An employee who is in the position to both order and receive merchandise or a cashier who authorizes and disburses expenditures are examples of this double-ended function in operation. All situations of this nature are potentially damaging and should be eliminated. Such procedures are manifestly unfair to company and employee alike. They are unfair to the company because of the loss that they might incur; they are unfair to the employee because of the temptation and ready opportunity they present. Good business practice demands that organizations studiously avoid such invitations to embezzlement.

It is equally important that cash handling be separated from the record-keeping function. Cashiers who become their own auditors and bookkeepers have a free rein with that part of company funds. The chances are that cashiers will not steal, but they could and might. They might also make mathematical mistakes unless someone else double-checks the arithmetic.

In some smaller companies, this division of function is not always practical. In such concerns, it is common for the bookkeeper to act also as cashier. If this is the case, a system of countersignatures, approvals, and management audits should be set up to help divide the responsibility of handling company funds from that of accounting for them.

5.3   Promotion and Rotation

Most embezzlement is the product of a scheme operating over an extended period of time. Many embezzlers prefer to divert small sums on a systematic basis, feeling that the individual thefts will not be noticed and that therefore the total loss is unlikely to come to management's attention.

These schemes are sometimes frustrated either by some accident that uncovers the system or by the greed of the embezzlers, who are so carried away with success that they up the ante. But while the theft is working, it is usually difficult to detect. Frequently the thief is in a position to alter or manipulate records in such a way that the theft escapes the attention of both internal and external auditors.

This can sometimes be countered by upward or lateral movement of employees. Promotion from within, wherever possible, is always good business practice, and lateral transfers can be effective in countering possible boredom or the danger of reducing a function to rote and thus diminishing an employee's effectiveness. Such movement also frustrates embezzlers. When they lose control of the books governing some aspect of the operation, they lose the opportunity to cover their thefts. Discovery inevitably follows careful audits of books they can no longer manipulate. If regular employee transfers were a matter of company policy, no rational embezzler would set up a long-term plan of embezzlement unless a scheme was found that was audit-proof—and such a thing is highly unlikely.

To be effective as a security measure, such transfers need not involve all personnel, since every change in operating personnel brings with it changes in operation. In some cases, even subtle changes may be enough to alter the situation sufficiently to reduce an embezzler's totality of control over the books. If such is the case, the swindle is over. The embezzler may avoid discovery of the previous looting, but he or she cannot continue without danger of being unmasked.

In the same sense, embezzlers dislike taking vacations. They are aware of the danger if someone else should handle their accounts, if only for the two or three weeks of vacation, so they make every effort to pass up holidays. Any manager who has a reluctant vacationer should recognize that this is a potential problem. Vacations are designed to refresh employees' outlook. No matter how tired they may be when they return to work, vacationers are refreshed emotionally and intellectually. Their effectiveness in their jobs has probably improved, and they are, generally speaking, better employees for having taken time off. The company benefits from vacations as much as the employees do. No one should be permitted to pass up authorized vacations, especially someone whose position involves control over company assets.

5.4   Computer records/electronic mail and funds transfer/fax

The computer has become the most powerful tool for record-keeping, research and development, funds transfer, electronic mail, and management within most companies today.

It is essential that computers and their support equipment and records be adequately protected from the internal thief.

Besides the computer, the transfer of information using Wi-Fi, wireless phones, and other electronic devices is an everyday occurrence. This is such an important area of security that additional coverage is provided in Chapter 18, "Computers, Information, and Information Systems Security."

5.5 Physical Security

It is important to remember that personnel charged with responsibility for goods, materials, and merchandise must be provided the means of properly discharging that responsibility. Warehouses and other storage spaces must be equipped with adequate physical protection to secure the goods stored within. Authorizations to enter such storage areas must be strictly limited, and the responsible employees must have means to further restrict access in situations where they feel that the security of goods is endangered (see Chapter 11 for a discussion of pass systems).

Receiving clerks must have adequate facilities for storage or supervision of goods until they can be passed on for storage or other use. Shipping clerks must also be able to secure goods in dock areas until they are received and loaded by truckers. Without the proper means of securing merchandise during every phase of its handling, assigned personnel cannot be held responsible for merchandise intended for their control, and the entire system will break down. Unreasonable demands, such as requiring shipping clerks to handle the movement of merchandise in such a way that they are required to leave unprotected goods on the dock while filling out the rest of an order, lead to the very reasonable refusal of personnel to assume responsibility for such merchandise. And when responsibility cannot be fixed, theft can result.

5.5.1 The Mailroom

The mailroom can be a rich field for a company thief. Not only can it be used to mail out company property to an ally or to a prearranged address, but it also deals in stamps—and stamps are as good as money. Therefore any office with a heavy mailing operation must conduct regular audits of the mailroom.

Some firms have taken the view that the mailroom represents such a small exposure that close supervision is unnecessary. Yet the head of the mailroom in a fair-sized Eastern firm got away with more than $100,000 in less than three years through manipulation of the postal meter. Only a firm that can afford to lose $100,000 in less than three years should think of its mailroom as inconsequential in its security plan. In addition, recent events related to bioterrorism make mailroom security an even greater responsibility.

5.5.2 Trash Removal

Trash removal presents many security problems. Employees have hidden office equipment or merchandise in trash cans and then picked up the loot far from the premises in cooperation with the driver of the trash-collecting vehicle. Some firms have had a problem when they put trash on the loading dock to facilitate pickup. Trash collectors made their calls during the day and often picked up unattended merchandise along with the trash. On-premises trash compaction is one way to end the use of trash containers as a safe and convenient vehicle for removing loot from the premises.

Every firm has areas that are vulnerable to attack. What and where they are can only be determined by thorough surveys and regular reevaluation of the entire operation. There are no shortcuts. The important thing is to locate the areas of risk and set up procedures to reduce or eliminate them.

5.5.3 Kidnap, Ransom, and Extortion

Kidnapping is a serious threat in many parts of the world. South America, Latin America and the Caribbean, central Africa, parts of Eastern Europe, the Middle East, and South Asia all experience significant incidents of kidnapping, ransom, and extortion. South America is the continent with the most incidents of kidnapping, ransom, and extortion. Sadly, in several South American countries, kidnapping has become a "cottage industry." According to ASI Group,[19] Brazil, Ecuador, Venezuela, Colombia, and Peru together experienced more than 230 incidents of kidnapping and extortion in the fourth quarter (October, November, and December) of 2006. Include Latin America and the Caribbean and these numbers increase during the same period by another 140 incidents.

Most of these kidnappings were for money, but more than 50 were for political purposes. Kidnappings for money range from the "express kidnapping" (which is relatively unsophisticated and lasts for only a few hours or days and includes a trip or trips to an ATM) where the kidnappers continue to withdraw monies from the victim's account until the account is emptied, to very sophisticated kidnappings that are well-planned and target specific wealthy executives, politicians, high-profile persons, and in some cases, travelers. Kidnapping is a favored practice for terrorist groups as a means of financing their organizations. Perhaps the best-known terrorist group in the Western Hemisphere is the Revolutionary Armed Forces of Colombia; in Spanish they are known as the Fuerzas Armadas Revolucionarias de Colombia, or FARC. Along with drug trafficking, the FARC finances itself through kidnapping, ransom, and extortion.[20]

Kidnappings in the Middle East, particularly in Iraq, are done primarily for political purposes and often with disastrous results. Unlike kidnapping for ransom, political kidnappings often end with the death of the victim. Consider the kidnapping of Paul Johnson, Jr., an employee of Lockheed Martin Corporation working in Saudi Arabia. In June 2004, shortly after being kidnapped by Al Qaeda, an international alliance of militant Sunni jihadists,[21] Johnson's body was found decapitated in Northern Riyadh. No ransom was sought; the terrorist captors chose to make a murderous political statement with the execution of an American.

As the threat of kidnapping, ransom, and extortion continues to grow throughout the world, companies and security executives are faced with few choices: discontinue conducting business in high-risk areas, which is unlikely; provide increased physical security and executive protection support, which is costly and reduces but does not eliminate the risk; or obtain insurance to help mitigate the cost and effects of kidnapping, ransom, and extortion. Increased security augmented with insurance helps a company better manage the risks associated with such events.

There are several underwriters for kidnapping, ransom, and extortion insurance polices. These policies generally cover all costs associated with the recovery of a kidnapped executive, employee, or relative, including costs of information, fees for professional negotiators, and loss of ransom money. Some policies also cover the cost of lawsuits filed against the firm for inadequate protection and insufficient efforts to win release. Such coverage requires that companies institute certain basic security measures:

- Executives must maintain secrecy about the existence of coverage.
- Every effort must be made to contact the police, the Federal Bureau of Investigation, and the insurance company before payment is made.
- A plan of action for dealing with kidnapping must be in place.

Along with these policies come the crisis management and negotiation services of international business risk consultancy companies. Most insurance providers have working agreements with at least one risk consultancy company specializing in negotiating kidnapping, ransom, and extortion incidents. Part of the insurance coverage includes use of their services. If a kidnapping, ransom, or extortion situation does occur, the importance of utilizing the services of companies that have expertise in this area cannot be overstated. They are staffed with skilled, experienced professionals, many of whom have spent much of their career working on such cases. Of course the best way to deal with kidnapping, ransom, or extortion is to prevent the occurrence in the first place. This is easier said than done, but preventative steps can be taken to help mitigate the risks.

6   When Controls Fail

On occasion, a company is so beset by internal theft that it seems to have gotten totally out of hand. In such cases, it is often difficult to localize the problem sufficiently to set up specific countermeasures in affected areas. The company seems simply to "come up short." Management is at a loss to identify the weak link in its security, much less to identify how theft is accomplished after security has been compromised. Here then is an examination of some steps that such an out-of-control organization can take.

6.1   Undercover Investigation

Many firms similarly at a loss in every sense of the word have found it advisable to engage the services of a security firm that can provide undercover agents to infiltrate the organization and observe the operation from within.

Such agents may be asked to get into the organization on their own initiative. The fewer people who know of the agents' presence, the greater the protection and the more likely they are to succeed in investigations. It is also true that when large-scale thefts take place over a period of time, almost anyone in the company could be involved. Even one or more top executives could be involved in serious operations of this kind. Therefore secrecy is of great importance. Because several agents may be used in a single investigation and because they may be required to find employment in the company at various levels, they must have, or very convincingly seem to have, proper qualifications for the level of employment they are seeking. Over- or under-qualification in pursuit of a specific area of employment can be a problem, so they must plan their entry carefully. Several agents may have to apply for the same job before one is accepted.

Having gotten into the firm's employ, agents must work alone. They must conduct the investigation and make reports with the greatest discretion in order to avoid discovery. But they are in the best possible position to get to the center of the problem, and such agents have been successful in a number of cases of internal theft.

These investigators are not inexpensive, but they earn their fee many times over by breaking up a clever ring of thieves. It is important to remember, however, that such agents are trained professionals. Most of them have had years of experience in undercover work of this type. Under no circumstances should a manager think of saving money by using employees or well-meaning amateurs for this work. Such a practice could be dangerous to the inexperienced investigator and would almost certainly warn the thieves, who would simply temporarily withdraw from their illegal operation until things cooled down, after which they could return to the business of theft.

6.2   Prosecution

Every firm has been faced with the problem of establishing policy regarding the disposal of a case involving proven or admitted employee theft. They are faced with three alternatives: to prosecute, to discharge, or to retain the thief as an employee. The policy that is established is always difficult to reach because there is no ready answer. There are many proponents of each alternative as the solution to problems of internal theft.

However difficult it might be, every firm must establish a policy governing matters of this kind. The decision about that policy must be reached with a view to the greatest benefits to the employees, the company, and society as a whole. An enlightened management would also consider the position of the as-yet-to-be-discovered thief in establishing such policy.

6.3   Discharging the Thief

Most firms have found that discharge of the offender is the simplest solution. Experts estimate that most employees discovered stealing are simply dismissed. Most are carried in the company records as having been discharged for "inefficiency" or "failure to perform duties adequately."

This policy is defended on many grounds, but the most common are as follows. While there is some validity in all of these views, each one bears some scrutiny:

1. *Discharge is a severe punishment, and the offender will learn from the punishment.* Experience does not bear out this contention. A security organization found that 80 percent of the known employee thieves they questioned with polygraph substantiation admitted to thefts from previous employers. Now it might well be argued that because they had not been caught and discharged as a result of these prior thefts, the proposition that discharge can be therapeutic still holds or at least has not been refuted. That may be true, and it should be considered.

2. *Prosecution is expensive.* Prosecution is unquestionably expensive. Personnel called as witnesses may spend days appearing in court. Additional funds may be expended investigating and establishing a case against the accused. Legal fees may be involved. But can a company afford to appear so indifferent to significant theft that it refuses to take strong action when it occurs?

3. *Prosecution would create an unfavorable public relations atmosphere for the company.* Many experienced managers have found that they have not suffered any decline in esteem. On the contrary, in cases where they have taken strong, positive action, they have been applauded by employees and public alike. This is not always the case, but apparently a positive reaction is usually the result of vigorous prosecution in the wake of substantial theft.

4. *Reinstating the offender in the company—no matter what conditions are placed on the reinstatement—will appear to be condoning theft.* Reinstatement is sometimes justified by the circumstances. There is always, of course, a real danger of adverse reaction by the employees, but if reinstatement is to a position not vulnerable to theft, the message may get across. This is a most delicate matter that can be determined only on a case-by-case basis.

5. *If the offender is prosecuted and found not guilty, the company will be open to civil action for false arrest, slander, libel, defamation of character, and other damages.* As far as civil action is concerned, that possibility must be discussed with counsel. In any event, it is to be hoped that no responsible businessperson would decide to prosecute unless the case was a very strong one.

6.4   Borderline Cases

Even beyond the difficulty of arriving at a satisfactory policy governing the disposition of cases involving employee theft, there are the cases that are particularly hard to adjudicate. Most of these involve the pilferer, the long time employee, or the obviously upright employee in financial difficulty who steals out of desperation. In each case, the offender freely admits guilt and pleads being overcome by temptation. What should be done in such cases? Many companies continue to employ such employees, provided they make restitution. The employees are often grateful, and they continue to be effective in their jobs.

In the last analysis, individual managers must determine policy in these matters. Only they can determine the mix of toughness and compassion that will guide the application of policy throughout.

It is hoped that every manager will decide to avoid the decision by making employee theft so difficult and so unthinkable that it will never occur. That goal may never be reached, but it is a goal to strive for.

CASE STUDY

Consider the following actual case study, and then decide how you would answer the questions posed at the end.

J. Jones, a salesman traveling his territory in his own car, receives a travel allowance of 34.5 cents a mile from his company to pay all car expenses. The vehicle is also used as a second family car when he is at home. He considers the 34.5-cents-a-mile figure too low.

Jones reclaims this and other travel expenses in a monthly expense account. In this account he is required only to list total miles driven each day, with a total of miles for the month. He always claims total miles each month, business and personal, by making a small daily false increase in mileage driven on company business. Around Christmas his personal expenses are higher and his company car travel is less. His practice then is to arbitrarily add extra miles to his expense account for November and December.

The company pays expense accounts each month without auditing them. External auditors select a few salespersons each year for expense account audit. The salesperson knows this because any errors located in this random audit are reported to them and the errors (plus or minus), are corrected.

Jones arbitrarily increased one month's expense account total by $200. He knew he could keep this if his expense accounts were not chosen for the audit that year. If caught in an audit, he knew it would simply be attributed to an error in addition on his part.

Jones's total increase of reported expenses over actual expenses this year was about 5 percent. He has no unusual expenses of a nonrecurring nature.

1. Who ultimately pays the padded 5 percent in Jones's expense accounts?
2. Which of Carson's principles (see page 288) is the company ignoring in its established expense reimbursement policy?
3. In future years, will Jones's expense account padding (under present reimbursement policies) probably stay the same, increase, or decrease?
4. What minimum action should the company take to prevent expense account padding?

Review Questions

1. What are some of the common danger signals of employee dishonesty?
2. Discuss procedural controls for decreasing the incidence of employee theft in specific departments.
3. What should management's role be in effecting internal security?
4. Should employees be prosecuted for stealing? Why?
5. Discuss the differences between personnel screening and backgrounding.
6. What areas of federal legislation must be considered when conducting reference checks and employment histories?
7. Discuss the role of lie detection in backgrounding of employees.
8. What impact has the Americans with Disabilities Act had on employee selection?

References

1. Zalud, Bill, "2002 Industry Forecast Study Security Yin-Yang: Terror Push, Recession Drag," *Security* (January 2002).
2. "Weak Awareness Secures Sky-High Theft Figures,"*Security* (August 1990): 13.
3. Grannis, Kathy, "Retail Losses Hit $41.6 Billion Last Year, According to National Retail Security Survey," National Retail Federation, www.nrf.com.
4. Carson, Charles P., *Managing Employee Honesty* (Boston: Butterworth-Heinemann, 1977).
5. The Ethics of American Youth, 2002 Report Card, Josephson Institute of Ethics, www.josephsoninstitute.org/Survey 2002.
6. Josephson Institute of Ethics, "2006 Josephson Institute Report Card on Ethics of American Youth: Part One, Integrity."
7. www.insurecast.com/html/crime_insurance.asp, downloaded 7/9/2007.
8. www.pimall.com, downloaded 7/9/2007.
9. www.newyorker.com/2007/007/02.

10. *The Use of Polygraphs and Similar Devices by Federal Agencies: Hearing Before a Subcommittee on Government Operations, House of Representatives* (Washington, D.C.: Government Printing Office, 1974), p. 29.

11. www.newyorker.com/reporting 2007/07/02.

12. Shachtman, Noah, "Liar, Liar, Eyes on Fire?" *Wired* (January 2002), downloaded 3/6/03, www.wired.com/news/technology/0,1282,49458,00.html.

13. www.newyorker.com.

14. U.S. Equal Employment Opportunity Commission, *Facts About the Americans with Disabilities Act*; U.S. Equal Employment Opportunity Commission, *The ADA: Your Responsibilities as an Employer*; U.S. Equal Employment Opportunity Commission, *The ADA: Questions and Answers*.

15. Fyfe, James J.; Greene, Jack R.; Walsh, William F.; Wilson, O.W.; and McLaren, Roy Clinton, *Police Administration*, 5th ed. (New York: McGraw-Hill Companies, 1997); *Pre-employment Screening Considerations and the ADA* (1997),
    http://janweb.icdi.wvu.edu/kinder/pages/pre_employment_screening.html; U.S. Equal Employment Opportunity Commission, *Facts About the Americans with Disabilities Act*; Gilbert Casella (1995, October 10), *ADA Enforcement Guidance: Preemployment Disability-Related Questions and Medical Examinations* (EEOC Notice Number 915.002), www.eeoc.gov/docs/preemp.txt.

16. Pope, Tom, "An Eye on EAPs," *Security Management* (October 1990): 81.

17. Contact, "Is An Employee Assistance Program (EAP) a Good Idea for My Client Companies?" downloaded 1/14/03, www.contactbhs.com/brokers/brokers/brokers10.html.

18. Pope.

19. www.asiglobalresponse.com/.

20. http://en.wikipedia.org/wiki/Revolutionary_Armed_Forces_of_Colombia.

21. http://en.wikipedia.org/wiki/Al_Qaeda.

Specific Threats and Solutions

In this final section of the book, attention is directed at specific security threats. Many of these threats are common to all types of organizations, whereas some, such as retail, are limited to a subcategory. Although there are many threats, we have given their own chapters to the areas of terrorism, retail theft, transportation and cargo security, workplace violence and drugs, and information security. In addition, we briefly cover traditional problems such as burglary, robbery, labor disputes, espionage, and piracy in a single chapter. Finally, the section ends with a chapter on the future of security.

The impact of homeland security on the industry was primarily covered in Chapter 1. However, where the impact of the Department of Homeland Security has touched these topics, the following chapters provide additional comment.

□□□
□□□ **14**
□□□

Transportation and Cargo Security

OBJECTIVES

The study of this chapter will enable you to:

1. Understand the growing importance of security in the transportation industry.
2. Discuss the changes that have occurred in the airline industry since September 11, 2001.
3. Identify some of the technology that is being used to improve security in the transportation industry.
4. Discuss the role of the federal government in establishing security standards in the area of transportation security.

---

1 Introduction

The first thought of most Americans regarding transportation security has to do with airlines and the hijackings that resulted in the destruction of the World Trade Center in 2001. Still, transportation security has been a growing security problem since 1970, when the U.S. Senate Select Committee on Small Business estimated that almost $1.5 billion in direct loss was attributable to cargo theft.[1] By 1975 the U.S. figure had reached $2.3 billion; by 1990 it had climbed to $13.3 billion, according to Federal Bureau of Investigation (FBI) figures. These figures do not reflect pilferage and unreported crimes, which represent a minimum of 5 to 10 times the amount of the reported crimes. Worldwide, cargo losses have been estimated at $30 billion.[2] In 2006 the FBI reported that an estimated $15 billion to $30 billion was lost to cargo theft in the United States. In March 2006, the category "cargo theft" was added to the FBI's Uniform Crime Reporting (UCR) System through a provision of the USA PATRIOT Improvement and Reauthorization Act.[3]

The indirect costs of claims processing, capital tied up in claims and litigation, and market losses from both nondelivery and underground competition from stolen goods can cost between two to five times the direct losses.[4] This equates to an estimated $2 to $5 for every $1 of direct loss—a $30 billion to $150 billion annual loss to the U.S. national economy. Worldwide this can amount to another $60 billion to $150 billion.

The problem continues to increase in severity. According to the FBI, cargo theft has become a significant concern, as noted by the government's focus on including it as its own category in the UCR. The shipment of goods is vital to the economy and ultimately to the country's survival. Since the 1970 figures were established, the international transportation systems using containers that can be transported by truck, ship, and rail has developed to the extent that land bridges, particularly in the United States, have been thoroughly established. These land routes carry millions of dollars in goods from other countries over our rail system on stack trains through the United States. The liability for the contents of these containers, moving via land bridge, is shared among a multitude of ocean carriers, rail companies, and truckers. The security concerns for the safe handling of this movement of goods are many and include many different groups: rail police, state and local police, and customs officials as well as other federal authorities.

Still, cargo security is only one part of the concern in the 21st century. The Department of Homeland Security (DHS) has made the transportation business one of many priorities in efforts to protect citizens from the threat of terrorism. As noted in Chapter 1, transit agencies have taken serious steps to improve security for passengers. The problems are enormous in a system that relies on public accessibility and rapid movement.

2   The Role of Private Security

Because it appears that cargo theft is more a problem of "inside jobs" than "highway robbery," it seems that by far the greatest burden falls on the security apparatuses of the private concerns involved.[5] It is true that public law enforcement agencies must make a greater effort to break up organized fencing and hijacking operations, and they must find a way to cut through their jurisdictional confusion and establish more effective means of exchanging information. But the bulk of the problem lies in the systems now employed to secure goods in transit.

On the other hand, public transportation problems require carefully planned cooperative ventures between public law enforcement and private security. The very nature of public transportation requires that private security protect the infrastructure of transit companies while public law enforcement provides protection of the public's highways. Heightened security of the early 21st century due to increased threats of terrorism resulted in public law enforcement personnel providing security for railroad bridges and at public transit terminals.

There is no universally applicable solution to this problem. Every warehouse, terminal, and means of shipment has its own particular peculiarities. Each has weaknesses somewhere, but certain principles of cargo security, when they are thoughtfully applied and vigorously administered, can substantially reduce the enormous losses so prevalent in today's beleaguered transport industry.

A good loss prevention manager must recognize that the key to good cargo security is a well-organized cargo-handling system. As Louis Tyska and Lawrence Fennelly note, cargo loss exists whenever the "three C's of cargo theft" are present.[6] The three C's are confusion, conspiracy, and the common denominator (the dishonest employee). Confusion is a primary ingredient and represents the loss prevention specialist's opportunity to reduce theft. Confusion arises when an adequate policy does not exist or, if it does exist, when it is not followed. Tyska and Fennelly identify the following activities as great contributors to the confusion variable:

1. Personnel entering and exiting the specific facility. These people include everyone from repair people to regular employees.
2. Movement of various types of equipment—for example, trucks, rail cars, and lift trucks.
3. The proliferation of various forms of paper—freight bills, bills of lading, manifests, and so on.

Conspiracy builds on confusion when two or more people take advantage of their positions and the confusion to steal. Many major cargo security losses would not occur, however, without the common denominator: the dishonest employee. When the security manager is dealing with more than cargo pilferage, monitoring the employee is essential. The manager must be aware of the preceding variables. By eliminating any one variable, opportunities for theft are reduced.

3 Accountability Procedures

The paramount principle is *accountability*. Every shipment, whatever its nature, must be identified, accounted for, and accounted to some responsible person at every step in its movement. This is difficult in that the goods are in motion and there are frequent changes in accountability, but this is the essence of the problem. Techniques must be developed to refine the process of accountability for all merchandise in transit. Technology has now advanced to the point where much merchandise can be tracked using geographic positioning systems (GPS).

3.1 The Invoice System

This accountability must start from the moment the shipper receives an order. As an example of a typical controlled situation, we might refer to a firm that supplies its salespeople with sales slips or invoices that are numbered in order. In some cases paper invoices are still used, but in today's world of technology, the computer form has replaced much of the old paper world. Whether invoiced using paper or the computer, this step in establishing a record is very important if any control is to be maintained over product order and delivery. Without proper records, either numbering of hard copies or computer entries, sales slips could be destroyed and the cash, if any, pocketed; or they could be lost so that the customer might never be billed. When these invoice forms are tracked, every invoice can and should be accounted for. Even forms that have been spoiled by erasures or physical damage should be voided and returned to the billing department.

Merchandise should only be authorized for shipment to a customer on the basis of the regular invoice. This form is filled out by the salesperson receiving the order and is sent to the warehouse or shipping department. The shipping clerk signs one copy, signifying that the order has been filled, and sends it to accounts receivable for billing purposes. The customer signs a copy of the invoice, indicating receipt of the merchandise, and this copy is returned to accounts receivable. It is further advisable to have the driver sign the shipping clerk's copy as a receipt for the load. In some systems, a copy of the invoice is also sent directly to an inventory file for use in inventory and audit procedures. Returned merchandise is handled in the same way but in reverse.

In this simplified system, there is a continuing accountability for the merchandise. If anything is missing or unaccounted for at any point, the means exist whereby the responsibility for the loss can be located. Such a system can be effective only if all numbered invoices are strictly accounted for and merchandise is assembled and shipped only on the basis of such invoicing. The temptation to circumvent the paperwork for rush orders or emergencies frequently arises, but if a company succumbs, losses in embezzlement, theft, and/or lost billing can be substantial.

Similarly, transport companies and freight terminal operators must insist on full and uninterrupted accounting for the goods in their care at every phase of the operation—from shipper to customer.

The introduction of the computer, bar coding, scanners, radio frequency identification (RFID), and electronic signature technology has made a reality of the process of accounting for merchandise from the point of purchase by the wholesaler to delivery at the retail outlet. Bar coding provides not only the information discussed in the previous paragraphs but also additional information that allows security to trace losses to the specific persons with responsibility for the merchandise at the time of the loss.

3.2   Separation of Functions

Such a system can still be compromised by collusion between or among people who constitute the links in the chain leading from order to delivery unless we make efforts to establish a routine of regular, unscheduled inspection of the operations down the line and, depending on the nature of the operation, regular inventories and audits. It is advisable, for example, for the shipper to separate the functions of selecting the merchandise from stock from those of packing and loading. This will not in itself eliminate the possibility of collusion, but it will provide an extra check on the accuracy of the shipment. And as a general rule, the more people (up to a point) charged with the responsibility and held accountable for merchandise, the more difficult and complex a collusive effort becomes.

To clearly fix accountability, it is advisable to require that each person who is at any time responsible for the selecting, handling, loading, or checking of goods sign or initial the shipping ticket that is passed along with the consignment. In this way, errors, which are unfortunately inevitable, can be assigned to the person responsible. Obviously any disproportionate number of errors traced to any one person or to any one aspect of the shipping operation should be investigated and dealt with promptly.

Similarly, at the receiving end, the ticket should be delivered to a receiving clerk. Appropriate personnel who verify the count of merchandise received without having seen the ticket in advance should then unload the truck. In this way, each shipment can be verified without the carelessness that so frequently accompanies a perfunctory count that comes with the expectation of receiving a certain amount as specified by the ticket. It will also tend to eliminate theft in the case of an accidental, or even intentional, overage. Since the checkers do not know what the shipment is supposed to contain, they cannot rig the count.

3.3   Driver Loading

Many companies with otherwise adequate accountability procedures permit drivers to load their own trucks when the driver is taking a shipment. This practice can defeat any system of theft prevention because drivers are accountable only to themselves when such a method of loading is in effect. This practice should never be condoned. It is worth the investment of time to have others check the cartons tendered to the driver. The potential losses in theft of merchandise by overloading or future claims of short deliveries would almost certainly exceed the costs involved in the time or personnel required to institute sensible supervisory procedures.

3.4   Theft and Pilferage

3.4.1   *Targets of Theft*

An analysis of claims data from the transportation industry shows that a few very specific commodities attract the attention of pilferers and thieves. These items, often referred to as "hot products," are items that are in demand and easily disposed of, such as computers, entertainment equipment, name-brand clothing and footwear, perfume, jewelry, cigarettes, and prescription drugs.[7]

But overall the kinds of things stolen vary considerably, depending on the location and the nature of the merchandise. Thieves might prefer to steal part of a shipment of clothing, but if none is available, they might just as vigorously pursue a truckload of dog food as long as there is a means of disposing of it. Anything can be stolen if the thief is given an opportunity. Anything that has a market—and nothing would be shipped unless a market existed—can be considered attractive to a thief.

It is important for transportation industry managers to recognize that all merchandise is susceptible to theft but at the same time to know the high-loss items at their locations so that they can exert extra efforts to secure such goods. It is also useful to know that motor carriers are the victims of more than 75 percent of the theft-related losses, rail and maritime carriers account for almost 25 percent, and air cargo losses make up the difference.[8]

3.4.2   *Pilferage*

According to the U.S. Department of Justice, as much as 80 percent of cargo theft losses are the result of a series of minor thefts.[9] The exact amount, however, cannot be established because of extensive nonreporting of these crimes. Thefts of this nature are generally held to be impulsive acts, committed by persons operating alone who pick up an item or two of merchandise that is readily available when there is small risk of detection. Typically the pilferer takes such items for personal use rather than for resale, because most of those who are termed "pilferers" are unsystematic, uncommitted criminals and are unfamiliar with the highly organized fencing operations that could readily dispose of such loot.

Such pilferage is always difficult to detect. Because it is a crime of opportunity, it is rarely committed under controlled circumstances that can either pinpoint the culprit or gather evidence that would later lead to discovery. Generally the items taken are small and readily concealed on the person or easy to transport and conceal in a car.

Pilferage is usually aimed at items in a freight or cargo terminal awaiting transshipment. In such instances, merchandise may be left unprotected on pallets, handcarts, or dollies awaiting the arrival of the next transport. In this mode, the goods are highly susceptible to pilferage as well as to a more organized plan of theft.

Broken or damaged cases offer an open invitation to pilferage if supervisory or security personnel fail to take immediate action. Accidental dropping of cases to break them open is a common device used to get at the merchandise they contain. If each such case is carefully logged—listing the name of the person responsible for the damage as well as the names of those who instantly gather at the scene—a pattern may emerge that will enable management to take appropriate action.

Whatever form pilferage takes, it can be extremely costly. Although each individual instance of such theft may be relatively unimportant, the cumulative effect can be enormous. Eighty percent of an estimated total direct loss of $30 billion worldwide adds up to a staggering bill for petty theft.

3.4.3   Deterring Pilferage

Here again, accountability controls can provide an important deterrent to pilferage loss. If one person is responsible for merchandise at every stage of movement or storage, the feasibility of this kind of theft can be substantially reduced.

In cases where it does occur, a rapid and accurate account of the nature and extent of such loss can be an invaluable tool in indicating the corrective action to be taken. Properly supervised accountability controls can locate the point along the handling process where losses occurred, and even in cases where they will not identify the culprit, these controls will underscore any weaknesses in the system and indicate trouble areas that need more or different security application.

Movement of personnel in cargo areas must be strictly controlled. All parcels must be subject to inspection at a gate or control point at the entrance to the facility. Private automobiles must be parked outside the area immediately encompassing the facility and beyond the checkpoint. All automobiles should be subject to inspection on departure if a parking area inside the boundaries of the facility is provided.

Every effort should be made to keep employee morale high in the face of such security efforts. Though some managers have expressed an uneasiness about inspections and strict accountability procedures, fearing that they might damage company morale, it should be pointed out that educational programs aimed at acquainting employees with the problems of theft and stressing everyone's role in successful security have resulted in boosting morale and in enlisting the aid of all employees in the security effort.

Here, as in other areas of security, employees should be encouraged to report losses immediately. They must never be encouraged to act as informers or asked to report on their coworkers. If they simply report the circumstances of loss, it is the job of security to carry forward further investigation or to take such action as seems indicated.

3.4.4   Large-Quantity Theft

Though the point-to-point trafficking of merchandise utilizing storage containers has reduced the amount of petty theft, the number of load thefts has increased. According to a report prepared by Todd Roehrig and Treven Nelson, at least two cargo containers disappear from the Port of Los Angeles every day.[10] The FBI reports that freight trailer losses range between $12,000 and $3 million, depending on the type of load.[11] Thefts in such amounts are no longer in the category of pilferage but rather theft engaged in by one or more persons who are in it for profit via resale through traffickers in stolen goods.

Thieves may or may not be employees, but because in either case they need information about the nature of the merchandise on hand or expected, they will usually find accomplices inside who are in a position to have that information. They are interested in knowing what kinds of cargo are available in order to make a decision about what merchandise to hit, depending on its value and on the demands of the fencing organization with which they deal.

Dealers in stolen goods are subject to the vagaries of the marketplace in the same way legitimate businesspeople are. Whereas a certain kind of merchandise may find a ready market today, it may move slowly tomorrow. Such dealers are anxious to move their goods rapidly, not so much because of fear of detection (even if they are found, mass-produced goods of any nature are difficult if not impossible to identify as stolen once they find their way into other hands) but because they generally want to avoid the overhead and the attention created by a large warehousing operation.

3.4.5 Removal of Goods

Once the thieves have the information, they need to arrange to take over the merchandise and remove it from the premises. To do this, they will usually try to work with some employee of the warehouse or freight terminal.

In cases where accountability procedures are weak or inadequately supervised, thieves have few problems. In tighter operations, they may try to bribe a guard, or they might forge the papers of an employee of a customer firm. They might even create confusion, such as a fire in a waste bin or a broken water pipe, to divert attention for those few moments needed to accomplish the actual theft. Generally the stolen goods are taken from the facility in an authorized vehicle driven either by the thieves, who have false identification papers and forged shipping documents, or by an authorized driver who is more often than not working with the thieves.

3.4.6 Disposal of Stolen Goods

Disposal of the goods usually presents no problem, because it is customary for thieves to steal from an order placed for any one of certain kinds of merchandise. The loot is normally pre-sold. In a July 2006 press release on cargo theft, FBI Unit Chief Eric Ives describes a cargo theft enterprise that is well organized at regional and even national levels. The organization includes the thieves, brokers (fences), drivers ("lumpers"), and a specialist at foiling antitheft locks.[12]

Principally for this reason, cooperation between private security and public law enforcement is extremely vital to the war against cargo theft. No thief will continue to steal unless there is a ready market for the stolen goods. In the hearings of the Select Committee on Small Business, one of the most inescapable conclusions was that the fences were the kingpins behind the majority of the thefts taking place. They dictated the nature of the merchandise to be taken, the price to be paid, and the amount wanted. They directed the thefts without ever becoming involved—in many cases never even seeing the merchandise they bought, warehoused, and sold. Without the fences, many of whom are otherwise legitimate businesspeople, the markets would shrink, the distribution networks would disappear, and losses would be dramatically reduced.

Another possibility discovered by a major retailer has been the theft of merchandise by employees who either sell merchandise at local flea markets or advertise it in local newspapers. One individual reportedly stole electronic items and developed a business through advertising in local papers for some time before getting caught.

Unfortunately, only sporadic efforts have been made to break up the big fencing operations, and the business of thievery thrives. Any assistance that private security can give to public law enforcement by way of instant and full reports on thefts can help combat these shady operations, and all private industry will benefit immeasurably in the long run.

3.5   Terminal Operations

Terminal operations are probably more vulnerable to theft than are other elements of the shipping system. Truck drivers mingle freely with personnel of the facility, and associations can readily develop that lead to collusion. Receiving clerks can receipt goods that never arrive; shipping clerks can falsify invoices; and checkers can overload trucks, leaving a substantial percentage of the load unaccounted for and therefore disposable at the driver's discretion.

Here again, these thefts can be controlled with a tight accountability system, but too often such facilities fail to install such a procedure or to follow up on it after it is in effect. This is poor economy, even under the most difficult situations when seasonal pressures are at their highest.

Railway employees on switching duty at a freight terminal can also divert huge amounts of goods. They can easily divert a car to a siding accessible to thieves who will unload it at an opportune time. This same device can be employed to loot trucks that have been loaded for departure the next morning. Unless these trucks are securely locked and parked where they are under surveillance by security personnel, they can be looted with ease. Drivers can park their trucks unlocked near a perimeter fence for later unloading unless the positioning and securing of the vehicle is properly supervised.

In all cases, a professional thief is someone with a mission. Such people cannot be deterred by the threat of possible detection. They recognize the possibility, accept the risk, and make it their business to circumvent detection. Only alert and active countermeasures will serve to reduce losses from their efforts.

3.6   Surveillance

There must be strict guard surveillance at facility entrances and exits as well as patrol activity at perimeters and through yards, docks, and buildings. Key control must be tight and painstakingly supervised. Cargo should be stored in controlled security areas that are enclosed, alarmed, and burglar-resistant. High-value cargo should be stored in high-security areas within the cargo area. Special locks, alarms, and procedures governing access should be employed to provide the highest possible security for these sensitive goods. The use of CCTV and other surveillance technology is covered in Chapter 10.

Shipments of unusual value should be confidential, and only those employees who are directly concerned with loading or unloading or transporting such shipments should be aware of their schedules. Email and fax information about such movements should be restricted, and trailer numbers should be covered while the vehicle is in the terminal. Employees involved with such shipments in any way should be specially selected and further indoctrinated in the need for discretion and confidentiality.

3.7   A Total Program

Adequate physical security installations supported by guard and alarm surveillance will go a long way toward protecting the facility from the thief or terrorist, but these measures must be backed by proper personnel and cargo movement systems, strict accountability procedures, and continuing management supervision as well as presence to ensure that all systems are carried out to the letter. Regular inspections of all facets of the operation, followed by prompt remedial action if necessary, are essential to the success of the security effort.

4 Planning for Security

It is important to the security of any transportation company, shipper, or freight terminal operation to draw up an effective plan of action to provide for overall protection of assets, whether general cargo or people. The plan must be an integrated whole wherein all the various aspects are mutually supportive.

In the same sense, in large terminal facilities occupied by a number of different companies, all individual security plans must be integrated to provide for overall security as well as for the protection of individual enterprises. Without full cooperation and coordination among participating companies, much effort will be expended uselessly and the security of the entire operation could be threatened.

Such a plan should establish area security classifications. Designated parts of the building or the total yard area of the facility should be broken down into controlled areas, limited areas, and exclusion areas. These designations are helpful in defining the use of specific areas and the mounting security classifications of each.

4.1 Controlled, Limited, and Exclusion Areas

Controlled areas are those restricted as to entrance or movement by all but authorized personnel and vehicles. Only part of a facility will be designated a controlled area, because general offices, freight receiving, personnel, restrooms, cafeterias, and locker rooms may be used by all personnel, some of whom would be excluded if these facilities were located within an area where traffic was limited. Within the controlled area itself, all movement should be controlled and under surveillance at all times. A fence or other barrier should additionally mark it, and access to it should be limited through as few gates as possible.

Limited areas are those within the controlled area where an even greater degree of security is required. Sorting, handling broken lots, storage, and reconstituting cases are vulnerable functions that might be handled in these areas.

Exclusion areas are used only for handling and storing high-value cargo. They normally consist of a crib, vault, cage, or room within the limited area. The number of people authorized to enter this area should be strictly limited, and the area should be under surveillance at all times. Since such areas should be locked whenever they are not actually in use, careful key control is of extreme importance.

4.2 Pass Systems

All employees entering or leaving the controlled area should be identified, and their authorization to be there should be checked. Each employee should be identified by a badge or pass, using one of the several systems discussed in Chapter 11.

4.3 Vehicle Control

Controlling the movement of all vehicles entering or leaving a controlled area is essential to the security plan, as is checking the contents. See Figure 14.1. All facility

FIGURE 14.1 A truck cargo inspection. (Photo courtesy Zistos Corporation, Hauppauge, NY, www.zistos.com.)

vehicles should be logged in and out on those relatively rare occasions when it is necessary for them to leave the controlled area. They should be inspected for load and authorization.

All vehicles entering the controlled area should be logged and checked for proper documents. The fastest and most efficient means of recording necessary data is optical readers that record information digitally in the company's computer system or a camera system such as a Regiscope, which will record all the required information digitally on a single photograph or record. This information should include the driver's license, truck registration, trailer or container number, company name, waybill number, delivery notice, a document used to authorize pickup or delivery, time of check, and the driver's picture if it is not on the driver's license.

The seal on inbound loaded trailers should be checked, and the driver should be issued a pass that is time-stamped on entering and leaving the area and that designates the place for pickup or delivery.

All vehicles leaving the area should surrender their passes at the gate where their seals will be checked against the shipping documents. Unsealed vehicles will be inspected, as will the cabs of all carriers leaving the facility. Partial load vehicles should be returned to the dock from time to time on a random basis for unloading and checking cargo under security supervision. They should also be sealed while they are in the staging area.

Loading and unloading must be carefully and constantly supervised since it is generally agreed that the greater part of cargo loss occurs during this operation and during the daylight hours.

4.4   Other Security Planning

The security plan must also specify the persons who have access to security areas, and it must specify the various components necessary for physical security, such as barriers, lighting, alarm systems, fire protection systems, locks, and communications. It must detail full instructions for the guard force. These instructions must contain both general orders applicable to all guards and special orders pertaining to specific posts, patrols, and areas.

There must be provision for emergency situations. Specific plans for fire, flood, storm, or power failure should be part of the overall plan of action. You should also specify people to call in an emergency.

After the security plan has been formulated and implemented, it must be reexamined periodically for flaws and for ways to improve it and keep it current with existing needs. Circulation of the plan should be limited and controlled. It must be remembered that such a plan, however well conceived, is doomed from the outset unless it is constantly and carefully supervised.

4.5   Security Surveys

Security managers of freight terminals or companies engaged in shipping are continually occupied with surveys of the facility under their security supervision. Security surveys were discussed in detail in Chapter 8.

An initial survey must be made to formulate the security plan governing the premises. It should be thorough enough to detect the smallest weaknesses in the operation and to provide the information needed to prepare adequate defenses. Further surveys will be necessary to evaluate the effectiveness of the established program, and follow-up surveys should determine whether all regulations and procedures are being followed. Additional surveys may be necessary to reevaluate the security picture following changes in operational procedures in the facility or to make special studies of particular features of the security plan.

4.6   Inspections

In addition to these surveys, essentially designed to evaluate the security operation as a whole or to reevaluate it in the light of changing conditions, the security manager should make regular inspections of the facility to check on the performance of security personnel and to check the operating condition of the facility. Such inspections should include potential trouble areas and should not overlook a check of fire equipment and alarm systems.

4.7   Education

If the security plan is to succeed, it must have the full cooperation and support of all employees in the facility. Only a continuing program of education in the meaning and importance of effective security can achieve this goal in every phase of the business.

All personnel should be indoctrinated at the time of their employment, and a continuing program should be instituted to update the staff on current and anticipated problems. More advanced courses on procedures might be instituted for management personnel. Part of this program should be devoted to educating employees about the importance of security to each individual and job.

Security reminders are also important to keep the subject of security constantly alive in everyone's minds. Prominently hung posters, placards, and notices are all effective devices for getting the message across. Leaflets or pamphlets covering more details can be distributed to employees in their pay envelopes.

5   Cargo in Transit

5.1   The Threat of Hijacking/Sabotage

Although the crime itself is dramatic and receives much publicity, armed hijacking of entire tractor-trailers with full loads of merchandise represents only 1 percent of the losses suffered by the shipping industry as a whole. This is not to say that it is a minor matter. On the contrary, such a crime is of extreme importance to the carrier taking the loss, because the enormity of the theft represents a huge financial blow in one stroke, whatever its significance in the overall percentages.

However, little can be done by a driver who is forced over by a car carrying armed and threatening hijackers. When it comes to that point, the driver has little choice but to comply. The load is lost, but hopefully the driver is unhurt. There is little that private security can do in such cases, and it is indeed fortunate that the incidence of such crimes is as low as it is. The matter is in the hands of public law enforcement agencies and must be handled by them.

If there is cause to believe that hijacking of a load is an imminent possibility, trucks should be scheduled for nonstop hauls and rerouted around high-risk areas. Schedules should be adjusted so that carriers do not pass through high-risk areas at night. In extreme cases, trucks might be assigned to travel in pairs or in larger convoys. Company cars can follow very high-value loads that are deemed especially vulnerable. Two look-alike trucks might make it more difficult to pinpoint the specific desired shipment. Such procedures constitute selective protection at best since they can be used only infrequently and are impractical for general application. The second driver, however, would be assigned the task of identifying the persons, the vehicle used, and so on and of reporting the hijacking if it occurs.

5.2   Global Positioning Systems

With the development of accurate, commercially available GPS tracking systems, it is now possible for trucking firms and individuals to track vehicles in a cost-effective, real-time, mapping and reporting environment. Such systems make it possible to know when a truck is not following planned routes or spending too much time stopped.

5.3   Personnel Qualifications

The cardinal rule in the management of a transportation concern is that employees assigned to line hauling duties must be of the highest integrity. Drivers and helpers must be carefully screened before they are hired, and personnel and security managers must carefully evaluate them before they are given this critical responsibility. An irresponsible driver can cost the company all or part of a load, and whether the loss is unintentional or the result of the driver's carelessness, the cost to the company will be the same.

Many cases have been reported where drivers set themselves up as victims of a hijack. This is difficult if not impossible to prevent unless the honesty of the driver is unquestionable—an attitude that can be determined only by a careful screening process and regular analysis of the person's behavior and performance. Any changes in a driver's demeanor or lifestyle should be noted, since deterioration of morale or a basic change in attitude toward the job might lead to future problems.

5.4 Procedures on the Road

All employees should receive specific instructions about procedures to be followed in every predictable situation on the road. The vehicle should be parked in well-lighted areas where it can be observed. It should be locked at all times, even if the driver sleeps in the cab. Trailers should be padlocked as well as sealed. A high-security seal, requiring a sizable tool to remove it, should always be used on valuable shipments that are parked overnight.

Drivers must be instructed never to discuss the nature of their cargos with anyone. Thieves frequently hang out at truck stops, hoping to pick up information about the nature of loads passing through. All too often, the most innocent conversations among truckers can lead to the identification of a trailer containing high-value merchandise that, when it is spotted, becomes a target.

The driver should never deviate from the preplanned route. In the case of a forced detour or a rig breakdown or if in any way the schedule cannot be met, the driver must notify the nearest terminal immediately.

Trucks should be painted on the top as well as on the sides to facilitate identification by helicopter in the event of theft.

5.5 Seals

Among the many seals available today, the one in most common use is the metal railroad boxcar type. This is a thin band of metal that is placed and secured on the trailer in such a manner that the door or doors cannot be opened without breaking the seal, thus revealing that the doors have been opened and a theft has, or may have, taken place. They are easy to break and must be broken when the destination has been reached and the merchandise is unloaded. They in no way secure the doors but are placed there simply as a device to indicate whether the doors have been opened at any point between terminal stops. Each seal is numbered and should identify the organization that placed the seal (see Figure 14.2).

All doors on a trailer must be sealed. Trucks or trailers with multiple doors may habitually load by only one, in which case doors not in regular use may carry the same seal for months at a time with only the rear being regularly sealed and unsealed.

POLY LOK II (PLASTIC STRAP SEAL)   TAPERED LOK (CABLE SEAL)   TRANS LOK (BOLT SEAL)

FIGURE 14.2 Security seals in common use. (Courtesy of E. J. Brooks Company.)

Seal numbers must be recorded in a permanent log as well as in the shipping papers. The dock superintendent or security personnel should be responsible for recording seal numbers and affixing seals on all trucks. The seals should be positioned in such a way that locking handles securing the door cannot be operated without actually breaking the seal. Some truck or railway car locking devices are so large that several seals may have to be used in a chain to properly seal the carrier. In this case all seal numbers must be recorded.

5.5.1 Resealing

Trailers loaded to make several deliveries along the route must be resealed after each stop. To accomplish this, enough seals must be issued to be placed on the truck after each delivery is made. In this case, the truck is sealed at the point of origin and the seal number logged and entered in shipping documents. The additional, as yet unsealed seals are also logged, and the numbers to be used at designated points of delivery are entered in the shipping documents.

When the first checkpoint is reached, the receiving clerk verifies the truck's seal number. After the merchandise is unloaded, the consignee, not the driver, as directed by the shipping documents, affixes the next seal. This procedure is followed at all stops, including the last one. There, a seal is affixed to the now empty vehicle, which may return to the point of origin, where the seal will again be checked against the shipping documents.

Empty trailers should also be sealed immediately after being unloaded. This practice will discourage the use of empties to remove unauthorized material from dock areas, and it does not preclude the necessity of physical inspection of all vehicles leaving the controlled areas.

5.5.2 Seal Security

All seals must be held under the tightest possible security at all times. Previously unissued seals should be logged and secured on receipt. They should then be issued in numerical order, and the assignment of each should be duly noted in the log. The seal supply should be audited daily; a careful check to account for each seal, issued or not, should be made at the same time. Without such regular inventories, the entire system can be seriously compromised. As a further part of such audit, all seals that are damaged and cannot be used, as well as seals taken from incoming vehicles, should be logged and secured until they can be destroyed.

5.5.3 Modern Technology and Seals

As with most areas of security, technology has entered the picture. Whereas metal and plastic seals can be tampered with, the new electronic seals require advanced technological information before criminals can compromise their integrity. In addition, the new system avoids the problems associated with the distribution of stocks of seals to depots and ensuring their safe storage. The electronic seals work much like electronic locks and can be monitored by the push of a button.[13]

6   Special Issues in Airline Security

In the aftermath of September 11, 2001, the airline industry fell under close scrutiny by the U.S. government. What had gone wrong with passenger screening? How did hijackers

FIGURE 14.3 Airport security has become increasingly important in the years since 9/11. (Courtesy of BEI Security, Inc.)

board the planes? These questions prompted other questions relating to airline security in general (see Figure 14.3).

The problems associated with security for airlines and overlapping responsibilities among airlines, customs, police, and airport security have confounded airports. Still, most airlines have a well-developed security program to combat cargo thefts.

6.1   Increased Security Measures

Even before 9/11, airport security had been increased throughout the world. The United States, though increasing security, often lagged behind security operations in other countries. However, the U.S. Federal Aviation Administration has for many years provided training for airport police officers. In recent years the Airport Law Enforcement Agency Network (ALEAN) has taken a lead in organizing programs and communication among airport police departments. The FBI has also increased its interest in aviation security issues. However, even with the increased emphasis on security issues, the perceived quality of security screening, of passengers in particular, has been found inadequate. As a result the U.S. government passed the Airport Security Federalization Act of 2001.

6.2   Specific Solutions for a Specific Problem

On November 6, 2001, the U.S. House of Representatives passed Senate Bill 1447, "An Act to Improve Aviation Security." The Act, known as the Airport Security Federalization Act of 2001, soon set into motion the federalization of airport security. The Act placed the responsibility for civil aviation security functions with an Under Secretary of Transportation. The Secretary's specific functions include the following:

- Receive, assess, and distribute intelligence information related to transportation security.
- Assess threats to transportation.
- Develop policies, strategies, and plans for dealing with threats to transportation security.
- Make other plans related to transportation security, including coordination of countermeasures with appropriate departments, agencies, and instrumentalities of the U.S. government.

- Serve as the primary liaison for transportation security to the intelligence and law enforcement communities.
- Supervise all airport security and screening services using Federal uniformed personnel.[14]

There are other functions listed in the Act, but it is clear that airport security is now firmly under the control of the U.S. government. This approach follows that developed in other countries, which have also been combating air crimes for several decades.

In March 2003 the FBI announced that selected airports would receive antimissile technology to protect against shoulder-launched missiles fired at planes taking off or landing. The program was prompted by the attack on an Israeli plane over Kenya in November 2002.[15]

In November/December 2006, the Transportation Security Administration (TSA) began a program of additional screening of employees at Chicago's O'Hare International and Midway airports. Workers, including delivery truck drivers, city workers, and food vendor employees, had been required to show identification or swipe security badges through electronic readers to gain access to security areas; they are now required to face extra measures to include inspection of vehicles and pat-downs. The TSA is imposing this increased security at more than 100 airports.

The TSA is also developing additional personnel to serve as "bomb-appraisal officers." These individuals are part of the TSA bomb-appraisal officer program, which is based on a quick psychological screening of passengers through the use of observation techniques.[16]

In 2007 the U.S. government began asking foreign countries to allow pilots to carry guns in the cockpit when they fly overseas. Though a similar program, now more than four years old, allows thousands of U.S. pilots to carry guns on domestic flights, some countries are wary of allowing armed pilots on international flights. Congress cut $11.5 million from the last two budget requests for armed pilots because the program was not spending all its allocation.[17] Thousands of pilots have opted for the training, but many are not interested in being armed.

Even with the emphasis on airline security measures, problems continue to be found. Though passenger suitcases loaded onto flights are regularly screened for explosives, other cargo that fill the bays is not generally screened. The disparity has been noted in Congress, where some representatives are calling for all air cargo to be inspected at the same level as baggage. The estimated cost of the program would be $6 million. The TSA argues that current standards are sufficient to prevent a bomb from getting on board. Security officials argue that a security zone surrounding the cargo packages during their journey from source to destination is sufficient.[18]

7   Other Transportation Industry Responses to Terrorism

7.1   Bus Transportation

The American Bus Association (ABA) established its Anti-Terrorism Action Plan in 2002. The association sought to increase awareness of potential hijackers and improve security plans for transit companies, including protection of the bus industry infrastructure. As noted in Chapter 1, cooperative ventures among the federal government, local law enforcement, and local bus companies have placed cameras throughout the bus system, including on board buses and in terminals. At the 2005 ABA board meeting, board members were informed that the DHS had provided $50 million in security grants to the bus industry.[19] In 2007 the TSA provided support for intercity bus operations through the Intercity Bus Security Grant Program as part of the DHS Infrastructure Protection Program. The Intercity Bus Security Grant Program is designed to assist fixed route intercity and charter bus services.[20]

7.2 Maritime Operations

The U.S. Coast Guard has provided major leadership in this arena, calling for the inspection of high-risk cargos at the point of shipment. Agreement among more than 100 governments has led to the International Ship and Port Facility Security Code.

The Coast Guard has also stepped up its inspections efforts. Sea marshals are assigned to "high interest" vessels arriving and departing from U.S. ports. Additional DHS measures are discussed in Chapter 1.

7.3 Amtrak and Local Commuter Trains

The public rail system is struggling with controls. Terminals have been secured to some extent by limiting access to underground areas. Increased presence of security personnel is apparent. Tickets are now checked before passengers are allowed into final waiting areas, and in some operations positive identification is being requested.

The DHS has on occasion requested local, state, or National Guard units to assist in monitoring key bridges and terminal facilities.

In response to questions regarding the application of airline security measures to rail passengers, the DHS has spent $7 million to test screening equipment that would reliably stop terrorist attacks similar to those on the Madrid and London rail systems. The 2006 tests showed that the technologies tested each had significant problems. Many devices triggered excessive false alarms; some took too long to screen passengers. Robert Jamison, deputy director of the TSA, said there are no plans to put the tested technologies to work. However, the assessment of the testing program concluded that the effort to screen rail passengers needed significant investment. With over 12 million passengers traveling on U.S. subways and rail lines each day, the need is great.[21]

In Los Angeles the Metropolitan Transportation Authority, which manages the city's subway system, is considering adding security. To date the system has been known for a lack of traditional subway components such as turnstiles, gates, attendants, and police officers and has relied on surveillance cameras. However, a late 2006 incident where mercury was spilled on a platform and remained undetected for eight hours has convinced MTA officials that additional security may be needed.[22]

7.4 Oil and Gas

Transportation of oil and gas, as well as other liquids and gases, is completed through millions of miles of pipelines. The Department of Transportation's Office of Pipeline Safety (OPS) began inspecting the system in 2002. The OPS is also requiring pipeline operators to develop plans to reduce risks and respond to disasters in areas where pipeline failures would have the greatest impact on populations or ecological systems.

In 2006 a liquid natural gas facility in Massachusetts had its security breached by intruders who slipped through the fence and took pictures of themselves standing on the storage tank stairwell. The incident was recorded by CCTV, but the company waited five days to file a report with Massachusetts authorities. Massachusetts Representative Edward Markey noted, "This incident raises serious questions about the adequacy of the perimeter security and surveillance monitoring in place at this facility." At the time, Markey was a senior member of the House Homeland Security Committee and the House Energy and Commerce Committee.[23]

Summary

One of the fastest-growing crimes appears to be theft of merchandise in transit. Even with gains in reducing petty pilferage, new containerized transportation has brought on new problems, including the theft of entire containers of merchandise. Control of merchandise during transit is often difficult but, through proper employee screening and security applications, the problem can be controlled. However, given the financial incentives for thieves, it is unlikely that the problem will ever be eliminated.

Airport security has undergone federalization in the United States, due primarily to the increased threat of terrorist attacks, similar to operations in other countries, but it would be unwise to consider applying all these security concepts to all transportation and cargo security problems. Still, given the events of the past few years, where passenger trains and buses have been attacked in European countries, additional scrutiny is certainly called for.

□ □ □ ▬▬▬▬▬▬▬▬▬▬▬▬▬▬▬▬▬▬▬▬▬▬▬▬▬▬

Critical Thinking

What are the real issues that need to be considered in implementing additional security measures on public transportation in the United States?

▬▬▬▬▬▬▬▬▬▬▬▬▬▬▬▬▬▬▬▬▬▬▬▬ □ □ □

Review Questions

1. Why is it said that the greater burden in preventing cargo thefts falls on private security rather than on public law enforcement?
2. Describe the operation of an invoice system that would establish accountability for all merchandise in shipments.
3. What are some policies and procedures that would be effective in deterring pilferage?
4. Define controlled areas, limited areas, and exclusion areas.
5. Offer procedures for the control of the movement of and contents in all vehicles entering or leaving a controlled area.
6. Describe the measures governments and companies have taken in response to terrorism.

References

1. *Crime Against Small Business: A Report of the Small Business Administration Transmitted to the Select Committee on Small Business, United States Senate* (Washington, D.C.: Government Printing Office, 1969).

2. Salkin, S., "Safe and Secure?," *Warehousing Management* (December 1999).

3. "Cargo Theft's High Cost," FBI press release 07/21/06, downloaded 7/11/2007.

4. U.S. General Accounting Office, *Report by the Comptroller General of the United States: Promotion of Cargo Security Receives Limited Support* (Washington, D.C.: U.S. General Accounting Office, 1980).

5. "It's a Crime," *Viewpoint*, Vol. 24, No. 2 (1999), downloaded 12/12/02, www.aais.org/communications/viewpoint/vp24_2.htm.

6. Tyska, Louis, and Fennelly, Lawrence, *Controlling Cargo Theft* (Boston: Butterworth-Heinemann, 1983), pp. xxvii–xxix.

7. Atkinson, W., "How to Protect Your Goods from Theft," *Logistics Management and Distribution Report* (March 2001).

8. "It's a Crime."

9. U.S. Department of Justice, "1332 Charging Theft from Interstate Shipment-Dollar Thresholds, Local Efforts," *Criminal Resource Manual* 1332 (October 1997), downloaded 12/12/02, www.usdoj.gov/usaoo/eousa/foia_reading-room/usam/title9/crim01332.htm.

10. Roehrig, Todd, and Nelson, Trevan, "Cargo Theft," downloaded 12/12/02, www.ucalgary.ca/MG/inrm/industry/theft.htm.

11. "Cargo Theft's High Cost," FBI.

12. Ibid.

13. "Smart Tags, Seals Computerized Advantages," *Security* (March 1997): 65.

14. Mayhew, Claire, "The Detection and Prevention of Cargo Theft," *Trends and Issues in Crime and Criminal Justice* (Australian Institute of Criminology, September 2001).

15. "FBI: Airports to Take Anti-missile Measures," CNN.com (March 31, 2003), downloaded 4/4/03, http://cnn.travel.printthis.clickability.com/pt/cpt?actions=cpt&expire=-1&urlIC=5857474&t.

16. Security Management Daily, February 28, 2007, excerpted from *Chicago Tribune*, (02/27/07).

17. Frank, Thomas, "U.S. Asks to Arm Pilots Abroad," *USA Today*, www.usatoday.com/travel/news/2007-02-07-us-pilots-guns_x.htm.

18. Lipton, Eric, "Security Debate Centers on Tougher Standards for Inspections of Air Cargo," *The New York Times*, February 8, 2007.

19. Chairman Young, Pundit Tony Blankley, "DHS Official & Fuel Expert Address ABA Board Members at Fall 2005 meeting," www.buses.org/Press_Room_the_report_newsletter/2126.cfm.

20. "Intercity Bus Security Grant Program," www.tsa.gov/join/grants/ibsgp.shtm.

21. Frank, Thomas, "Security Devices Falter in Rail Tests," *USA Today*, usatoady.com/news/nation/2006-02-13-rail-security_x.htm.

22. Guccione, Jean, and Blankstein, Andrew, "Call for More Security Inside Los Angeles's Subway System," *Christian Science Monitor*, 02/12/07.

23. Crocker, Michael, "Platforms, Pipelines, and Pirates," *Security Management*, June 2007 pp. 77–86.

Violence and Drug Use in the Workplace

1   Introduction

Workplace violence has become a growing concern for security managers over the past two decades. There have always been some problems associated with violence in the workplace, but recent decades have focused additional attention on this serious problem. Whether the violence is the result of a personnel problem such as disciplinary action, salary dispute, or termination or if it's of a domestic nature, such as a "love triangle," employees do bring their problems to work. Far too often the pressures result in some form of violence against fellow employees, employers, or the work facility.

In addition to traditional concepts of workplace violence, the late 1990s saw serious problems with violence in our schools. Columbine High School and Little Rock will be remembered for many years, as will recent shootings at an Amish school in 2006 and Virginia Tech University in 2007—the worst mass shooting in school history. No one had thought about the possibility of violence becoming murderous on our school properties. The murders at these and other schools brought the public's focus on schools. Schools and government bodies responded with safe school studies and grants. Many schools have dramatically improved their access systems, locking doors, assigning identification systems, and in some cases installing metal detectors.

Though the response to school violence was swift, the reality is that schools remain the safest environment for children. According to the findings of *The Final Report and Findings of the Safe School Initiative* (May 2002), the Department of Education reported that there are almost 60 million children in American schools. The Safe School Initiative study was able to identify only 37 incidents of targeted school-based attacks committed by 41 individuals over a 25-year period. The increased security can do nothing but improve safety, but care must be taken not to create an environment that children and parents view as harsh.

This chapter also discusses drug use in the workplace. Unfortunately, drug abuse and violence in the workplace are often found together. For smaller companies, workplace substance abuse costs Americans over $100 billion annually and causes companies to incur a 300 percent increase in medical benefits.[1] Substance abuse is also an ongoing problem in the school setting. In 2004 the U.S. public school systems reported 32,641 incidents of distribution of illegal drugs and 131,267 incidents of possession or use of alcohol or illegal drugs. The forces that cause frustration that leads to violence also contribute to substance abuse. In turn, substance abuse often leads to a lack of control and violent behaviour.

Webster defines *violence* as an "[unwanted] exertion of physical force so as to injure or abuse" or a "vehement feeling or expression." Encompassed within this broad definition are subtle forms of harassment, threats, intimidation, and sabotage, as well as overt acts of violence and temper tantrums. According to Joseph Kinney, workplace violence includes four broad categories:

- Threat
- Harassment
- Attack
- Sabotage

1.1   Threat

Threat involves an expression of an intention to inflict injury. A threat can be an intimidating stare, posture, or verbal exchange. An intimidating stare or posture is less obvious and, therefore, can be more subtle; a verbal exchange is more direct and obvious. The key is to determine whether the threat was made in jest or with malice aforethought. In all cases, threats should not be tolerated in the workplace.

1.2   Harassment

Harassment in general involves a behavior designed to trouble or worry someone. For example, sexual harassment often causes people to fear the loss of their jobs if they resist or report it. Harassing behavior can be something like putting grease on a coworker's chair or phone, feces in or on their desk, or graffiti on bathroom walls or making phone calls with immediate hang-ups.

1.3   Attack

Attacks involve the use of unwanted force against someone in order to cause harm. To attack is to make contact in an unwanted manner such as spitting, choking, punching, slapping, and grabbing. The key word is *unwanted*. Like threats, attacks, even in harmless fun, should not be tolerated in the workplace.

1.4   Sabotage

Sabotage involves the destruction of an employer's property, tools, equipment, and products to hinder the manufacturing process, which can ultimately affect a company's profits. For example, take the case of a factory worker who attacked a conveyor and shut down production for a half day. Although this action occurred due to drug ingestion, the initial factor leading to this incident was employee game playing. Another example is the General Motors employee nicknamed "Edward Scissorhands" by other factory workers, who would often cut power to the plant to halt production. The worker was motivated by frustration and anger over the GM workforce reductions that caused this employee and others to work longer hours and weekends to meet production schedules.

> Employees do bring their problems to work!

2   Violence and the Workplace

2.1   The Phenomenon of Workplace Violence

Workplace violence is not new and in fact reached a high point during the late 1890s and early 1900s with the growing union movements, but the focus of the violence has changed greatly over the years. Today's workplace is too often the focus of random acts of violence that on the surface appear to have no logical cause. A study of the phenomenon and underlying factors should make it possible for the security manager to prevent violence or intervene in a potential problem area before violence occurs.

Each day a newspaper, magazine, radio, or television reports another act or occurrence of workplace violence in America. According to the 2001 National Crime Victimization Survey, the number of workplace violence incidents has been slowly declining since 1993. It is perhaps coincidental that the decline parallels major companies' efforts to combat the increase in workplace violence that occurred in the 1980s and early '90s.[2] In each case the victims are new and the lives shattered are real. Who are the victims? Victims range from those directly involved to those indirectly involved, such as first responders, family, friends, and colleagues. According to the U.S. Department of Justice, between 1993 and 1999 over 1.7 million Americans were victims of violent crime while working.[3] Total cost to the victimized workers is 1,751,100 lost workdays, or 3.5 days per crime. This missed work cost the workers over $55 million in lost wages, not including days covered by sick and annual leave.

Of the victims, men are more likely than women to experience violence. Women are just as likely to be victims of theft. Over 30 percent of the victims were faced with armed offenders, of whom almost one-third were armed with a handgun. Sixteen percent of the victims suffered physical injuries, with 10 percent requiring medical care.

Sixty percent of workplace violence occurs in private companies. Though government employees make up only 18 percent of the total U.S. workforce, 50 percent of the victims of violence worked for federal, state, or local government units. Table 15.1 (page 350) shows the reported locations of violent crime between 1993 and 1999.

There are three primary reasons for the upsurge in workplace violence during the 1980s and '90s. First, there is society's general acceptance of using violent means to deal with emotions and negative feelings. In other words, those who use violence as a form of personal communication believe their behavior is an acceptable way to deal with emotions and problems. Children of the 1980s and '90s, who will one day become the employees of America, are generally seen as an aggressive and potentially violent bunch. It is not uncommon to witness classroom and schoolyard mediation sessions designed to prevent shooting, stabbing, and gangland violence on campus. A study of teachers in 1949 revealed their primary concerns to be student tardiness, smoking, and ditching class on occasion. The same study conducted in 1995 reveals a much different and more alarming picture. The primary concerns of today's teachers include the availability of weapons and their use on campus, violence in general, drugs and alcohol use and abuse among students, and finally, the breakdown of the family structure.

> In 1998, taxicab drivers risked dying on the job at a rate 36 times that of the national average.

A second factor is the general availability of guns and the mass media's glamorous and accepted portrayal of their use to remedy a wrong done or to seek revenge. According to Joseph Kinney, "The availability of guns, the experience that people have in using such weapons, and the perception that such use is legitimate have created circumstances encouraging weapons use."[4] Eighty percent of all workplace homicides were committed with firearms.[5] Between 1996 and 2000, 3,829 people were homicide victims while at work. The three most risky places to work based on chance of death through homicide are retail operations, service industries, and government. The most dangerous occupation was that of a taxicab driver. In 1998 a taxicab driver risked dying on the job at a rate of 36 times that of the national average.[6]

Finally, economic factors also contribute to workplace violence. According to Michael Mantell, "the rising tide of workplace violence incidents points to two carefully linked factors: people and money."[7] Today, perhaps more than ever, workers feel vulnerable, especially in corporate America. Even a "secure" government job is becoming a less secure place to work as the privatization and reengineering movements take hold. Teams of employees often find themselves processing each other out of a job as unnecessary steps are eliminated. Workers are more apt to turn to violence to deal with emotions and negative feelings toward coworkers and the employing organization.

It is unfair, however, to suggest that all employees will act out violently against coworkers or the organization. To the contrary, some aggressors just commit suicide. According to the Bureau of Labor Statistics, 213 employees committed suicide on the job between 1992–1997.[8] Even when grievance or employee appeal processes are used to redress the sources of problems, acts of violence continue to rise. For example, a former postal employee in the Royal Oaks, Michigan, post office killed four postal workers and himself although an arbitration process, albeit lengthy, had been invoked to help him get his job back.

No matter the type of workplace violence, it is destructive. It not only attacks the very fabric of the organization, it also serves to polarize and frighten the workforce, which can negatively affect productivity and employee satisfaction.

According to Dr. Charles Labig, there are six common sources of violence on the job:

- Strangers, who are typically involved in the commission of a crime or who have a grudge against the business or an employee

- Current or past customers
- Current or former coworkers who commit murder
- Current or former coworkers who threaten and assault
- Spouses or lovers involved in domestic disputes
- Those infatuated with or who stalk employees[9]

2.2   The Work Environment and Violence

One key finding in a Northwestern National Life Insurance survey on workplace violence was a strong correlation between job stress and workplace violence. Many factors must be considered in this formula—for example, employee/employer relations, leadership styles, communication patterns, and job security. These factors need to be explored and understood in the context of potential workplace violence. Demeanor and tone can contribute to an employee's feelings and job satisfaction. The traditional McGregor Theory X leader often contributes to work-related problems such as stress attacks, headaches, insomnia, ulcers, nightmares, and anxiety bouts.

In the 1990s, William Lunding stated: "To survive and thrive . . . [leaders] need to shift their thinking from 'kick butt' to compassion, from suspicion to trust, from a 'no-brainer' to a learning environment."[10] Generally speaking, employees like to work in an environment where and for leaders who view their employees as an integral and important part of the organization in furthering its mission. Working for a management structure that trusts and respects its employees' opinions will naturally make the work environment less stressful. Still, workers cannot be left to their own imaginations and direction. Mantell's analogy says it well:

> *Employees in [an organization] are much like blades of grass that together make up a vast green lawn. Given the proper amount of attention, "care and feeding" if you will, nurturing, and exposure to warmth, this "lawn" will flourish. Left to grow unchecked, without careful supervision, control and planning for the future, many parts of the lawn will wither and die or grow completely out of control.[11]*

As a society, we have become increasingly attached to our work. Often, the nature of our work defines who we are, what we are, and what social status we enjoy in the community. In most social conversations, soon after "How are you?" comes "What do you do for a living?" More than ever, people are judged not so much by who they are but by what they do for a living. People who are unemployed often avoid social functions to avoid answering the inevitable questions. Simply stated, for many employees, success at work means success at life.

An organization provides many human needs, from pay to provide for food and shelter to benefits to provide for protection of not only the employee but his or her family as well. In essence, the organization provides security, stability, and structure, which, in turn, provide friendships and sometimes love in the workplace, self-respect and a sense of competency, and ultimately belonging. After a while, and particularly if one is a long-term employee, one begins to count on the organization to provide a standard of living. Consider what happens when an employer takes a person's job away for cause or due to downsizing. This type of rejection, particularly for an emotionally unstable person who identified his or her self-worth and self-esteem with the job, can become potentially explosive.

"We watch in amazement as people make requests of their employer they probably wouldn't make of their own mother, including … education, recreation, [specialized] medical care, psychological care, and plenty of tangible and intangible 'warm fuzzies' that help people pull themselves out of bed and head out to work."[12] We need to recognize that the loss of stature—real or perceived—income, or opportunity, such as with a job change, job loss, or demotion, can be devastating to a person's sense of well-being. A job loss can severely attack an individual's self-esteem and sense of identity, causing the person to lash out either overtly or covertly at the organization or individual who caused the pain.

> *"The workplace murderer is likely to be a Caucasian male, using an exotic weapon, such as an Uzi, an AK-47, or Samurai sword, legally acquired."*
> —Tom Harpley, National Trauma Services

2.3   Profiling Violent Behavior

The well-established profile for violent behavior in the workplace, and perhaps the prevailing view, according to Tom Harpley of National Trauma Services, is as follows: "The workplace murderer is likely to be a Caucasian male [between 25 and 40 years of age], using an exotic weapon, such as an Uzi, an AK-47 or Samurai sword, legally acquired."[13] Although this may be the prevailing view, there is little supporting evidence that it is an accurate profile or that certain kinds of persons can be identified with violent behavior. Typecasting is unrealistic in the work world. Violence is not the result of a particular type of person but rather a mixture of experiences and emotions reinforced over time, sparked by some event that causes violence. Still, there are certain common behavioral characteristics or predictors that can be used to recognize a person's potential for violent behavior:

- *Disgruntled over perceived injustices at work.* This type of employee will be angry, upset, and annoyed about such things as pay, benefits, working conditions, discipline, and the way management operates. It is not uncommon for such an employee to feel paranoid, persecuted, or conspired against. This type of employee is readily recognizable as one who takes up causes almost to the extreme either on his or her own behalf or for a coworker who is reluctant to come forward.

- *A loner who is socially isolated.* This type of employee does not appear to have any outside interests; he or she identifies their self-worth and self-esteem with the job and avoids socializing during lunchtime, breaks, and other social functions. When someone attempts to seek them out to invite them, they seem more than just shy.

- *Poor self-esteem.* This type of employee lacks the self-esteem necessary to move ahead and will often become easily frustrated and has difficulty accepting constructive criticism. It is not uncommon for this type of employee to be extremely pessimistic, carrying around with him or her a personal collection of stories of hurt, rejection, and powerlessness.

- *Angry.* This type of employee is easily angered and often blows his or her cool for even the smallest of reasons. It is not uncommon for this type of employee to escalate into a full-blown rage from a seemingly normal conversation. It would not be uncommon for this type of employee to have a criminal history.

- *Threatening.* This type of employee takes pleasure in directly threatening, harassing (including sexually), or intimidating coworkers that he or she does not like and the organization as a whole. Statements such as "you will be sorry for what you said" or "revenge is sweet" are not uncommon among the many statements this type of employee will make.

- *Interested in media coverage of violence.* This type of employee has an excessive interest in the mass media's coverage of violence and can often be heard quoting articles about workplace violence episodes. It is not uncommon for this type of employee to suggest that if the same act occurred where he or she worked, management would finally take notice. An employee of this nature might even attempt to copycat other acts of workplace violence.

- *Has asked for help before.* This type of employee has indirectly or directly asked for help from the organization's employee assistance program, a coworker, or a supervisor.

- *Collects weapons.* This type of employee collects weapons, particularly guns, and may often brag about his or her collection. It would not be uncommon for this employee to have subscriptions to such magazines as *Soldier of Fortune* or *Survivalist.* This employee might also have a fascination with the military.

- *Unstable family life.* This type of employee has either grown up in a dysfunctional family, had a chaotic childhood, or has no support system on which to fall back. This type of employee may disrespect animals and may have abused them as a child.

- *Chronic labor/management disputes.* This type of employee has a long history of ongoing labor/management disputes or has numerous unresolved physical or emotional injury claims. It is not uncommon for this employee to take management's instructions as suspect. This employee will routinely violate organizational policies and procedures.

- *Stress.* This type of employee shows constant signs of stress or is a chronic complainer who always seems to feel overburdened by the pace, the workload, or the physical or psychological demands of the job. It is not uncommon for this employee's true personality to come out under stress; this may be the exact person one sees each day: aggressive, uncompromising, and belligerent.

- *Migratory job history.* This type of employee has bounced from job to job in a relatively short time. In fact, a history of migratory jobs should be caught at the preemployment interview and rigorously questioned.

- *Drug and alcohol abuse.* This type of employee will show signs of alcohol and other drug abuse, which is traditionally characterized by bloodshot, drooping, or watery eyes; impairment in speech or motor skills; and an unusually disheveled appearance.

- *Vindictive.* This type of employee will be vindictive in his or her actions or words. This type of employee will not leave well enough alone and will often attack the character of a person or organization even though the problem has been resolved. This employee is a typical organizational sniper who takes pleasure in watching others dodge the bullets. It is not uncommon for this employee to feel little or no remorse after hurting someone.

Table 15.1 Reported Locations of Violent Crime, 1987–1992

Place Where Victimization Occurred	Rate Per 1,000
Type of work setting	
Private company	9.9
Government employee (federal, state, or local)	33
Self-employed	7.4
Other (i.e. Working without pay)	11
Location where victimization occurred	Percentage of victimizations occurring at work where victim identified location
Restaurant, bar, or nightclub	13
Office, factory, or warehouse	14
Other commercial establishment	23
On school property	9
Parking lot/garage	11
On public property (such as streets and parks)	22
Other	8

Source: Violence and Theft in the Workplace, U.S. Department of Justice.

> Violence is not the result of a particular type of person but rather a mixture of experiences and emotions reinforced over time.

These characteristics are not all-inclusive and will require updating as new clues are developed. Unfortunately, the behavioral patterns of a typical perpetrator of workplace violence are frequently apparent, though often noted only in retrospect. These behavioral characteristics alone or in combination with one another do not necessarily guarantee that an individual will become violent. In other words, they should not be considered a guarantee of violent behavior. However, they can, and often do, act as an early warning system, so that preventive intervention techniques can be used before it is too late. All supervisors, human resource professionals, and staffing specialists should be trained to identify and properly handle these behavioral characteristics when they manifest themselves either independently or jointly in an employee.

2.4 Basic Levels of Violence

Once a person decides to act out, violence can take many forms. Experts generally agree that it manifests itself in three levels of intensity:

- *Level 1.* Subject actively or passively refuses to cooperate with superiors; spreads rumors and gossip to harm others; frequently argues with coworkers; is belligerent toward customers and clients; constantly swears; and, finally, makes unwanted sexual comments.
- *Level 2.* Subject argues increasingly with customers, coworkers, and supervisors; refuses to comply with the organization's policies and procedures; sabotages equipment and steals the organization's property for revenge; verbalizes the wish

to hurt coworkers and supervisors; sends sexual or violent messages to coworkers and supervisors; and, finally, regards self as victimized by management—"me against them."

- *Level 3*. Subject frequently displays intense anger; recurrent suicidal threats; recurrent physical fights; destroys or sabotages company property; uses weapons to harm others; and, finally, commits murder, rape, or arson.

> *"Violence does not occur in a vacuum. It is the result of an escalating process, rather than of one sudden event."*[14]
>
> —Charles Labig

2.5   Preventing Workplace Violence

An ounce of prevention is worth a pound of cure. The need for prevention is so apparent that the Centers for Disease Control (CDC) issued an alert in 1993 requesting organizations to prevent workplace violence, particularly workplace homicide. The purpose of the alert was to (1) identify high-risk occupations and workplaces, (2) inform organizations and employees about the risk, and (3) encourage organizations to gather statistics and to take active intervention measures.

> *"The single biggest deterrent to violence in the workplace is careful hiring [and screening]."*
>
> —Joseph Kinney

Both the CDC, through its division the National Institute for Occupational Safety and Health (NIOSH), and OSHA are deeply involved in research and training initiatives in the area of violence in the workplace. Both groups have produced major works reporting statistics as well as suggesting methods to reduce the potential for work-related violence. (See www.osha.gov/SLTC/workplaceviolence/index.html or www.cdc.gov/niosh/homepage.html for additional resources.)

Investing in the prevention of violence in the workplace is as vital to a business as investing in research and development. According to Joseph Kinney, the key step in preventing workplace violence is to look for a history of violence in a person's background.[15] Mantell supports Kinney's suggestion: "The single biggest deterrent to violence in the workplace is careful hiring [and screening]."[16] The process of backgrounding and screening employees was thoroughly addressed in Chapter 13.

Even with proper hiring processes, employees can still become disillusioned and violence may still occur. An organization that fails to prepare for the likelihood of violence can be faced with regulatory sanctions, costly litigation, and the loss of faith among once trusting employees. Under no circumstances should an organization believe that it is immune from workplace violence. An organization that is proactive on the issue of workplace violence should consider the development of a violence intervention and contingency team (VIACT). Such recognized employers as the United States Postal Service, General Dynamics, International Business Machines Corporation, Honeywell, Minnesota Mining and Manufacturing, Kraft General Foods, General Motors, and the Elgar Corporation have formed VIACTs to address violent acts because of past violent incidents. At the least, the teams will communicate to all employees that the organization is genuinely concerned about their welfare and is doing everything possible to prevent and defuse potentially violent situations.

2.6   The Violence Intervention and Contingency Team

Since all organizations are different, forming a VIACT to prevent and respond to violent situations will require some degree of tailoring to fit the organizational structure. Ideally, members of the team should include, but not be limited to, the following: management, human resources, health and safety, facilities, medical, legal, public relations, and security. The team's primary goal is to ensure that all available resources are used at the earliest opportunity to prevent and respond to potentially violent situations. The team must meet regularly and should become subject-matter experts.

> The team's primary goal is to ensure that all available resources are used at the earliest opportunity to prevent and respond to potentially violent situations.

2.6.1   Pre-Violence Mission

The team should lead the way in developing policies and procedures that make it absolutely clear to all employees that the organization will not tolerate threats, acts of sabotage, intimidation, harassment, stalking, or violent acts in the workplace. A key component is to communicate to employees that they will be held accountable for their actions and that the organization will cooperate fully with local law enforcement in dealing with any person involved in workplace violence.

The team should also work to develop a cooperative liaison and open communication with local law enforcement, fire support, and emergency medical service agents. The team should examine the capabilities and responsiveness of these agencies and detect shortfalls, and if any exist, arrange for an alternative or coordinated response.

Finally, the team should identify intervention processes to prevent workplace violence, formulate education and awareness programs, and ensure that employees have access to world-class resources that can help prevent or defuse violence in the workplace.

2.6.2   Post-Violence Mission

Once an incident has occurred, the team should convene to review incidents involving the potential for violence or to recommend corrective actions or intervention strategies. If a violent situation arises or the potential for violence is imminent, the team should convene to review the possibility and seriousness of a violent episode; examine administrative, disciplinary and medical options; and examine legal alternatives such as seeking arrest, committing to a medical or mental facility, issuing no trespass warnings, or getting an injunction against harassment. In all situations involving workplace violence, the team should recommend a timely and decisive response to any violent behavior or act or sabotage.

The VIACT should know when to meet. Prematurely convening a team may frustrate team members and discredit the entire mission. The team should convene when the nature of the threat, harassment, attack, or act of sabotage is unique and falls outside the scope of the organization's normal progressive disciplinary policy. In sum, the VIACT should be the organization's single point of contact with local law enforcement, regulatory bodies, and the media. They should be the information-gathering center for the organization, in turn separating and disseminating factual information.

2.6.3   Strategies for Dealing with Potential Violence

An important part of the VIACT mission is to protect employees from harm and limit liability and regulatory sanctions against an organization. Toward that end, the team should recommend a swift protection strategy after a violent incident occurs. An organization must consider serious all acts of violence and sabotage until proven otherwise and appropriate action must be taken to protect employees and property from further harm or damage. In other words, an organization should take whatever action is reasonable and necessary to contain the violent act and minimize the risk of harm to employees and, secondarily, to property. The violent perpetrator should be managed or removed from the organization's premises as quickly as possible.

Particular attention should be given to employee(s) who is (are) directly threatened. Appropriate measures will vary according to the circumstances of each threat and may include, but are not limited to, the following:

- Involving local law enforcement
- Protecting the threatened individual's work environment (e.g., increasing security)
- Staggering or changing the individual's work shift
- Allowing the individual to park inside the facility or plant
- Transferring the individual to another work area, building, or site
- Having the individual escorted to and from their vehicle or home
- Relocating the individual to another facility out of the region, temporarily or permanently
- Advising the individual to alter their daily routine and remove its predictability

The team should consider the following options concerning a violent perpetrator:

- Changing the shift or transferring to another location
- Suspension with pay pending further investigation
- Immediate referral to a medical department or the organization's employee assistance program (EAP)
- Retirement
- Voluntary mutual separation
- Progressive discipline
- Involuntary termination of employment (for cause)

2.7   Perpetrators' Rights

Alleged perpetrators have rights. The case law in this area suggests that an employer can be found liable for defamation of character if it mistakenly reports the perpetrator as violent when the evidence suggests otherwise. To avoid a claim of defamation of character, an organization should begin its investigation by discussing the allegations with the individuals who have personal knowledge of the violent incident; it should not rely on hearsay information. Moreover, if an employer discharges an employee without validating the fact that the employee is violent, the employer can be found liable for wrongful discharge. After a threat or actual act of violence occurs, employers should suspend the alleged perpetrator pending further investigation.

2.8   Intervention Strategy

Mantell offers what he calls the *workplace violence spectrum* (see Figure 15.1), a proactive strategy for recognizing, dealing with, and defusing a potentially violent act before it is too late. The key to using the spectrum is for an organization to look at all employees to determine as accurately as possible where on the spectrum each employee falls:

- *The normal employee.* The normal employee is a person who gets along with others and resolves conflict in a constructive manner and, therefore, does not pose a threat of workplace violence.

- *The covert employee.* The covert or closet employee engages in silent, hidden, or behind-the-scene activities designed to be disruptive to the workplace. This employee might sabotage equipment, leave notes, vandalize property, or leave disturbing voicemail messages or threatening faxes.

- *The fence-sitter employee.* The fence-sitter is on the border between covert tactics and actual violence. This employee's actions will be more direct and confrontational. In some cases, he or she might not take steps to hide his or her identity.

- *The overt employee.* The overt employee will act out directly and openly against the organization or person perceived to have caused him or her harm. This employee can be highly volatile and ready to strike at any moment.

- *The dangerous employee.* The dangerous employee is the potentially homicidal employee, bent on causing destruction and threatening the lives of not only him- or herself but of others as well. In short, this employee is a ticking bomb waiting to explode.

Proactive intervention begins with the covert employee. The strategy is to identify the covert employee before he or she reaches the fence-sitter stage of the continuum and to direct the employee back to the normal range of behavior. An organization should apply as many resources as necessary to identify the covert employee. Anonymous hotlines, investigative techniques such as covert surveillance cameras, and education and awareness programs for employees are all methods to identify the covert employee. Once the covert employee is positively identified, the organization can prescribe many forms of intervention to push the employee back to a normal employee state. Forms of intervention include psychological counseling, EAPs, grievance hearings, time away from work to relieve stress and pressure (e.g., vacation, personal or medical leave), intervention sessions, or progressive discipline designed to coach.

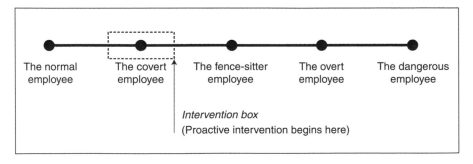

FIGURE 15.1 Workplace violence spectrum. (From Michael Mantell, *Ticking Bombs: Defusing Violence in the Workplace* [Burr Ridge, IL: Irwin Publishing, 1994]. Intervention box and strategy developed by the researcher.)

2.8.1 Intervention Education

Intervention education is defined as reaching out to an employee before it is too late to do so no matter where they fall on the continuum. More specifically, intervention education means immediately recognizing and correcting unsatisfactory behavior and performance patterns before they get out of hand. Once they're out of control, the result can be termination of employment or worse—violence. Intervention education is the key to eliminating the sparks of future workplace violence. Violent behavior clues are usually evident, as noted earlier. "Prevention begins with careful observations and continual communication, the most accessible, viable and logical alternative to letting a problem fester."[17]

Intervention begins with establishing open communications with all employees and providing an anonymous reporting channel for complaints about aberrant behavior. If employees believe they can speak openly and honestly with the organization, it can serve as a pressure release valve, blowing off steam when the pressure and stress get to be too much to handle. In other words, allowing employees to vent their feelings is an effective way to reduce job pressure and stress that can lead to violence.

To reduce stress in the organization, employees should believe they have five inalienable rights:

1. Freedom of speech
2. Credit for work performed
3. Strong support
4. Reliable guidance
5. Solid leadership

Humor that is not harassing or combative should also be encouraged in the workplace. Research shows that the positive effects of laughter can be enormous. Employees should also be encouraged to relax.

2.8.2 The Intervention

Any form of intervention must be tempered by the realization that violence could occur. You should quickly learn to expect the unexpected when it comes to an intervention session. Don't be fooled into thinking that violence always involves physical contact. Verbal threats, abusive language, and acts of intimidation can sometimes be more threatening than physical contact.

Always consider personal safety before an intervention session. If you believe that the intervention session could be confrontational, contact the organization's security department so the necessary security countermeasures can be put in place, or consult the guidance manual for addressing violent acts in the workplace.

During the intervention session, always face the employee and sit as close to the exit as possible; never allow the employee to sit between you and the door in case an escape is necessary. Remove all potentially dangerous items from the intervention area. If appropriate, have a second person in the hearing room during the intervention session. Not only can this provide a calming effect, but it can also act as a force presence. Women provide a calming effect when it comes to male-to-male hearings. Finally, have available tissues and business cards with the organization's EAP phone number.

Intervention must be tempered by the realization that violence could occur.

Handling an intervention session can be difficult given the fact that people in general do not like or handle confrontation well. It is important to recognize that the intervention session can be laden with emotion on both sides. The session should be made as much a positive experience for the employee as possible. It is also helpful to offer a beverage as an icebreaker.

There is no one best way to conduct an intervention session. However, how you begin the session will often determine its outcome. As a result, begin with something like the following statement: "Listen, the organization and I do not want to fire you. However, you are here because of your unsatisfactory behavior. Do you understand how you arrived at this stage?" It is appropriate to wait for a response at this point, then say something like. "The organization's goal is to help you become the best employee you can be. However, the organization needs your help to accomplish this goal. Do you understand what we are saying?"

Intervention can be a positive experience if you quickly remove the immediate threat of being fired from the employee's mind. Once the threat has been removed, move to get the employee to accept responsibility for improving his or her unsatisfactory behavior. If the employee responds, "I understand what you mean and I am sorry," you have arrived at the acceptance stage. Now move quickly to solidify ideas for improvement. Employees who believe their suggestions are included in the improvement solution are more apt to take ownership of their behavior and voluntarily seek to improve it. It is also important to recognize when an expert is needed. Some employees bring deep-seated emotional problems to the intervention session. If this is the case, refer the employee to the organization's EAP.

If the intervention session involves progressive discipline that requires some form of documentation, such as a written reminder, the session should be rehearsed prior to the employee's arrival, to ensure a smooth delivery of the letter's contents. Always remain genuine and authentic during the session. Do not speed through the written reminder. Take the time necessary to explore each paragraph with the employee. Wait for questions, and answer them as you can. The session should not be dictatorial, in which the organization imposes sentence on the employee. The session should be designed to get the employee to accept and voluntarily correct their behavior. Be firm but polite and respectful. Do not be surprised if the employee gets emotional.

As a rule, do not give the written reminder to the employee when he or she walks into the intervention session. In the employee's mind, this could be an ominous start to an otherwise productive session. Instead, talk each paragraph out, as an actor would a script. In this way, the employee will be focusing not on the letter but the session's intent.

If the employee is represented under a collective bargaining agreement and requests union representation, wait until representation arrives before proceeding. At the conclusion of the intervention session, give the employee a copy of the written reminder as a capstone of the conversation. For written material, it is wise to have the employee cosign the letter. If a union representative is present, have the representative sign the letter as well.

Research suggests that an effective system of disciplinary due process will reduce workplace violence. Many instances of workplace violence have been the result of some perceived injustice at work. Due process gives the employee a chance to work out his or her differences. Using the intervention strategy and recommendations, the organization can effectively intervene in a positive and productive manner. Finally, leaders within an organization must learn to understand human behavior. It is not what you say that makes employees respond, but rather *how* you say it.

Finally, do not expect all employees to behave alike. Learn to recognize their strengths and weaknesses and respond accordingly. To be a successful leader, you must adopt a separate and sometimes distinct approach for each employee.

3   Drugs in the Workplace

Many U.S. citizens view drugs as a recent crisis, but the use of drugs in the workplace has been a problem for many years. In fact, historically, private enterprise has pioneered most of the programs in drug detection, rehabilitation, and prevention. The federal government has adopted a policy that makes some drugs illegal and drug usage unacceptable. Support for the federal policy has been forthcoming from all segments of society, including federal government, state government, and business.

American business leaders share a consensus that illegal drugs have become pervasive. The exact costs associated with the drug problem in the workplace are not known, but the estimates are staggering. It is estimated that alcohol and other drug (AOD) use costs American business $140 billion every year ($80 billion for alcohol-related costs and $60 billion for illicit drug-related costs) in lost productivity, accidents, employee turnover, and related problems.[18] According to the U.S. Bureau of Labor Statistics, employers are spending between 5 percent and 15 percent of company health-care budgets on substance abuse problems.[19] In 1990 General Motors estimated that it lost $1 billion to substance abuse and that the costs associated with drug abuse raised the price of a GM car by $400.[20]

About 74.8 percent of current illegal drug users are employed, three-fourths of them full time, and 17.1 percent of unemployed persons used an illicit drug. Furthermore, 8.2 percent of full-time workers and 10.3 percent of part-time workers use illegal drugs. In addition, 8.4 percent of full-time workers and 10.4 percent of unemployed persons have engaged in heavy drinking in the past month.[21] Among 18-to-25-year-old full-time employees, 16.6 percent have used an illicit drug in the past year, including significant illegal use of marijuana and psychotherapeutic drugs. According to Gregory M. Louis-Nunt, president of a firm specializing in employee assessment and evaluation, 44 percent of employees who are entering the job market have used an illegal drug within the past 12 months.[22]

According to OSHA, psychotherapeutic drugs are also on a distinctive rise in the workplace due to anxiety, stress, and neurotic disorders comprising nonfatal injuries. The combination of these three disorders results in the largest median time away from work, more than any other nonfatal injuries combined. The professions with the most nonfatal injuries are construction, agriculture, forestry, fishing, private industry, and mining.

Drug use and abuse is broadly distributed across occupations and industries; however, prevalence varies. Table 15.2 shows the prevalence of current illicit drug use and current levels of heavy drinking among 14 industries.[23] Data from 2005 show that illegal drug use was greatest among workers in the occupations of construction; food preparation, waiters, waitresses, and bartenders; transportation and material moving; and other services. Heavy alcohol use was also relatively high among these occupations as well as among handlers, helpers, and laborers and precision production and repair.[24]

Table 15.2 Percentage of Full-Time Workers, Ages 18–49, Reporting Illicit Drug and Heavy Alcohol Use, by Occupation

Occupation Category	1997 Illicit Drug Use	Heavy Alcohol Use
Executive, administrative, and managerial	8.9	7.1
Professional specialty	5.1	4.4
Technicians	7.0	5.1
Sales	9.1	4.1
Administrative support	3.2	5.1
Protective services	3.0	7.8
Food Preparation, waiters, waitresses, bartenders	18.7	15.0
Other service	12.5	11.4
Precision production and repair	4.4	11.6
Construction	14.1	12.4
Extraction and precision production	4.4	5.5
Machine operators and inspectors	8.9	9.0
Transportation and material moving	10.0	10.8
Handlers, helpers, and laborers	6.5	13.5

Source: Office of Applied Studies, SAMHSA, *National Household Survey on Drug Abuse* (1997).

A 2006 report published in the *Journal of Applied Psychology* estimated that 17.7 million employees (14.1 percent of the U.S. workforce) used illicit drugs in 2005, with 14.1 million using enough to get "high." Marijuana was the most commonly used illicit drug, taken prior to and during work hours.[25]

3.1 The Impact of Drug Use

Substance abusers, as compared to nonabusers, are more likely to have a negative impact on the company or business in a variety of ways, including increased theft, decreased productivity and quality control, increased incidence of accidents and injuries, increased absenteeism, high turnover rate, and increased costs due to personal problems.

3.1.1 Theft
Many security administrators say that drug abuse and theft go hand in hand. Drug users often steal from employers and fellow employees to support their habits. Criminal activities, including vandalism, often result in increased legal costs for the firm. Lawsuits, legal fees, and court costs are added expenses when drug use leads to theft, vandalism, and other criminal behavior.

3.1.2 Productivity, Quality Control, Accidents, and Injuries
Several years ago during a break period, one line employee for a major corporation was slipped drugs in his drink for laughs. The joke got out of control when the employee threw a bucket into a conveyor. Fifty percent of the operation was shut down. The company lost several hours of work while still paying employees who were idled by the incident. In general, substance abusers, compared to nonabusers, are involved in many more job mistakes and are more likely to have lower output and work shrinkage.[26]

Substance abusers also experience three to four times more on-the-job accidents and are responsible for 40 percent of all industrial fatalities.[27] A study reported in the *Journal of Drug Education* found that employees who tested positive for cocaine or marijuana had a significantly higher rate of on-the-job accidents and injuries.[28]

Horror stories abound. In 1983 the National Transportation Safety Board identified marijuana as the cause of the fatal crash of an aircraft, and in 1989 the Exxon *Valdez* captain was using alcohol while on the job. In 1991 a New York subway operator crashed his train near a station in Manhattan; five people were killed and 215 others were injured. The operator admitted that he had been drinking prior to the crash. His blood alcohol content was found to be 0.21—more than twice the legal limit.[29] In July 2002 two America West pilots were fired after being stopped at the gate by security personnel, who smelled alcohol on their breath and prevented the two pilots from boarding the 124-passenger airliner. Both pilots possessed blood alcohol levels over the legal limit of 0.08.[30]

3.1.3 Absenteeism and Turnover Rate

Overall, substance abusers are late to work three to four times more often, absent five to seven times more often, and are three to four times more likely to be absent for longer than eight consecutive days. Also, they use three times more sick leave.[31] Alcohol is the major drug problem in this regard. According to the Substance Abuse Prevention Network, alcoholism causes 500 million lost workdays each year.[32] A study found that employees who were marijuana or cocaine users also had a higher rate of absenteeism (78 percent and 145 percent more absenteeism, respectively) compared with other employees.[33] At GM the average substance abuser works only 140 out of 240 working days before entering treatment.[34]

Substance abusers also have higher turnover rates. According to a recent nationwide study of workers ages 18 to 49, those who reported having three or more jobs in the previous year were about two times more likely to be current or past-year illicit drug users and/or heavy drinkers than those who had two or fewer jobs. Variation occurred depending on the industry and occupation.[35]

3.1.4 Personal Problems

Approximately half the employees who have personal problems are substance abusers of one type or another. Substance abusers use three times more medical benefits, file five times more workers' compensation claims, and increase premiums for the entire company for medical and psychological insurance. Also, substance abusers are seven times more likely to experience wage garnishments and are more often involved in grievance procedures, taking up both union and organization time and resources.[36]

3.2 Drug Testing

One solution to the drug problem is drug testing and proper advertising. The words "Must have a clean drug history" will discourage those who have drug problems from applying. The federal government recognized the importance of preemployment drug screening with the passage of the Drug Free Workplace Act of 1988.

A 1991 Gallup poll found that 71 percent of the respondents agreed that companies have the right to test job applicants before hiring them.[37] The majority (68 percent) of the largest employers in the United States have adopted drug screening for all new employees.

Table 15.3 Percentage of Full-Time Workers, Ages 18–49, Reporting Workplace Drug Testing Programs, by Occupation

Occupation	At Hiring	Random	Upon Suspicion	Post-Accident
Managerial	33.5	24.1	30.3	27.2
Professional specialty	26.9	14.3	17.9	15.2
Technicians	38.0	19.5	30.3	26.4
Sales	28.9	18.7	23.9	19.8
Administrative support	42.6	24.6	31.3	26.0
Protective services	74.0	60.4	68.9	56.0
Waiters, waitresses	19.1	16.7	19.0	18.1
Other service	37.3	19.6	24.0	20.9
Precision production	56.1	34.9	41.6	38.0
Construction	25.8	25.7	22.4	27.2
Machine operators	58.0	30.8	38.2	48.7
Transportation	62.7	52.9	47.6	54.7
Laborers	49.2	32.0	38.7	45.3

Source: Office of Applied Studies, SAMHSA, *National Household Survey on Drug Abuse* (1994-B, 1997).

As company policies change to testing all new employees, the proportion of those testing positive tends to drop.[38]

According to a 1996 survey of 961 businesses conducted by the American Management Association, 81 percent of those surveyed said they had a workplace drug testing program, compared to only 52 percent in 1990. Many more businesses are performing drug tests even though they are not required to do so. For example, only about 23 percent of manufacturing businesses are required to test, but up to 89 percent do test. Table 15.3 shows the percentages of the occupations that perform drug testing. Of the companies that performed drug testing, 90 percent used urine analysis, 7 percent used blood analysis, and 3 percent used hair analysis.[39]

Through drug testing it is possible to identify the use of a variety of drugs, both illicit and licit. Substances that are commonly tested for are alcohol, amphetamines, barbiturates, benzodiazepines, marijuana, cocaine, methadone, methaqualone, opiates, phencyclidine (PCP), and testosterone-like anabolic steroids. Presence of other substances can also be tested.

Once introduced into the body, drugs are biotransformed and eventually eliminated from the body through excretion. The presence of drugs or their metabolites can be detected in urine, blood, and body tissues through various types of testing technology. Table 15.4 provides a listing of common drugs and the number of days that they are typically detectable.[40]

The National Institute on Drug Abuse (NIDA) has established standards for drug-testing laboratories that should ensure quality testing. Several types of drug screening are available. Two of the most frequently discussed are urinalysis and blood testing. Both tests are intrusive and require that someone monitor the removal of material to be tested. To counter the problems of intrusiveness, some firms prefer to use pencil-and-paper tests. Various types of pencil-and-paper tests claim to provide an indication of previous or present drug use. Additional information on these tests can be found in Chapter 13.

Table 15.4 Detection Period Range Chart (Urine Only)

Drug	Period Range
Alcohol	1/2–1 day
Amphetamines ("crank," "speed")	2–4 days
Barbiturates	
Amobarbital, pentobarbital	2–4 days
Phenobarbital	Up to 30 days
Benzodiazepines, e.g., Xanax®, Royhypnol®	Up to 30 days
Cocaine ("coke," "crack")	12–72 hours
Marijuana	
Casual use, to 4 joints per week	5–7 days
Daily use	10–15 days
Chronic, heavy use	1–2 months
Opioids	
Dilaudid®	2–4 days
Darvon®	6–48 hours
Heroin (morphine is measured)	2–4 days
Methadone	2–3 days
Phencyclidine (PCP)	
Casual use	2–7 days
Chronic, heavy use	Several months
Quaalude®	2–4 days

Source: Darryl S. Inaba, William E. Cohen, and Michael E. Holstein, *Uppers, Downers, All Arounders,* 3rd ed. (Ashland, OR: CNS Publications, 1997).

Three basic drug-testing formats are common. The first and most popular is enzyme immunoassay (EIA). The most widely used of the EIA tests is the EMIT developed by Syva Corporation. The EIA uses urine samples and can be used to screen for up to 10 drugs. A second format is the radioimmunoassay (RIA). Although similar to EIA, it uses radioactivity rather than a color change as an indicator for a positive test. These first two formats cost between $5 and $30 per sample. The third is a combination of gas chromatography and mass spectrometry (GC-MS). This test is 99.9 percent accurate and is the only test accepted by most courts as prima facie evidence of drug use. Although it is an extremely accurate test, the GC-MS is not widely used for screening purposes. The cost of $100 per sample is prohibitive. However, it is often used as a confirmatory test when positive results occur using a cheaper and less accurate method.

Other types of screening tests are:

- Thin layer chromatography
- Agglutination
- Fluorescence polarization immunoassay

On-site drug testing is likely to make it easier for companies to test for drugs. Disposable tests for alcohol and other drug use are now available at reasonable costs. Roche Diagnostic Systems is marketing its OnTrakTesTcup that purports to test for morphine, cocaine, tetrahydrocannabinol (THC), and amphetamines from a urine sample cup. The results are developed within 3 to 5 minutes and are indicated by a plus or minus sign on the urine container.[41]

Unfortunately, the high-profile publicity surrounding the introduction of drug testing has allowed violators to develop a counter-educational movement in an attempt to beat the screening systems. Smuggling "clean" urine into the bathroom is widely practiced. With careful monitoring, this should be almost impossible; however, some employees have devised very clever schemes that may escape notice, such as carrying a plastic bag of "clean" urine under the arm. In addition, cocaine users know that it stays in the system for a maximum of 72 hours; thus it is possible to abstain just prior to urine testing so that the test results are negative for cocaine use.

Another test is radioimmunoassay of hair (RIAH). This test requires that the individual provide several strands of hair, which are then tested for drugs. The procedure initially involves testing using the radioimmunoassay technique. If the results are positive, a confirmatory test is performed using the extremely accurate GC-MS technique.

Major advantages of this test are:

- The collection, transportation, preservation, and storage of hair samples are simple and relatively nonintrusive processes as compared to other types of drug testing.
- It is less prone to tampering.
- Human hair maintains a 90-day record of drugs ingested into the body, and thus drug use can be detected as far back as three months.
- A laboratory can determine the date when a drug was last used within seven days.
- Hair can also be matched to the owner with the exactness of fingerprints.
- Contrary to popular belief, the use of special shampoos cannot "beat the test," because the analysis is performed on the cortex of the hair.

Although RIAH test results have been challenged in court, it has predominantly been judged a valid and reliable test.[42] Prevalence of RIAH testing in the workplace has been increasing in the past few years, in part because of the mentioned advantages as well as the fact that it has become less expensive. The average cost is approximately $45. Companies such as GM, Blockbuster Video, and Anheuser-Busch routinely use RIAH for drug testing.

Drug testing is an excellent way to reduce problems in the work environment. It not only weeds out drug abusers at the time of hiring, but it allows employers to detect drug abuse among current employees. The rights of individual privacy are often of less significance than the importance of public health and safety. With appropriate policies and procedures, the accuracy of drug testing is greatly enhanced. This includes having a chain of custody for handling the specimen, a policy for a second confirmatory test for all positive results from the initial screen, and use of a medical officer to review the results.

The U.S. military reports that it administered 420,687 urine tests to active duty personnel in 2001.[43] These mandatory tests have been credited with the reduction of drug use, improved job performance, and a reduction in accidents.

3.3 Spotting Drug Use

Besides the problems of reduced efficiency, increased absenteeism, and accident proneness, supervisors should look for other signs of drug use. Watching for drug use or intoxication on the job is not easy, because there are many different types of drugs and drug-dependent people. Reactions differ with the type of drug and often with the personality and problems of the individual user.

The most commonly abused drug is still alcohol. However, the use of marijuana in the workplace has also been common for many years. In recent years the use of cocaine has increased to rival marijuana in many locations. According to the Substance Abuse Information Network, of those who call the cocaine helpline, 75 percent report using drugs on the job and 64 percent admit that drugs adversely affect their job performance.[44] Other drugs commonly abused in the workplace are amphetamines, barbiturates, benzodiazepines, methaqualone, opiates, and phencyclidine (PCP).[45] The following descriptions represent only a sample of signs of which supervisors should be aware.

3.3.1 Crack Cocaine
A simple aluminum drink can is crushed in the middle, and holes are punched in the can with a nail. Crack is placed over the holes and lighted. The user smokes the drug by inhaling the smoke through the open tab end of the can. When the user is finished, the can is discarded.

3.3.2 Cocaine
Small vials are often placed in the employee's wallet, along with supporting paraphernalia such as a straw, a pocket mirror, and a razor blade. In addition, small safes made to look like soft drink cans or fire extinguishers are becoming popular hiding places.

3.3.3 Other Methods
Drug users have long used tinfoil, old prescription bottles, and zip-top bags. Table 15.5 provides a list of indications of possible chemical abuse.[46]

3.4 The Components of a Comprehensive Substance Abuse Program

In 1988 the federal government passed the Comprehensive Drug-Free Workplace Act. All companies administering federal grants and contracts are obligated to follow the Act's guidelines, listing countermeasures to reduce the costs associated with employee drug use and abuse. The Act sets forth the following requirements:

1. Development of a clear drug-free workplace policy. This policy must clearly state the reason it is needed (for example, safety, product quality), the company's expectations regarding employee behavior, the rights and responsibilities of employees, and the type of action that will be taken if drug use or possession is suspected or discovered.

2. Establishment of continuing drug education and awareness programs. Firms are expected to provide educational programs aimed at ensuring that employees understand the drug policies and their consequences. In addition, supervisors must be trained to identify and deal with employees suspected of drug use or possession.

3. Implementation of an employee assistance program (EAP) or other appropriate mechanism. Through the employee assistance program, the employer is able to help employees who have a substance abuse problem rather than resort to immediate termination. This is accomplished by referral for evaluation and treatment/ rehabilitation. There are many ways to set up an EAP, including establishing a program at or near the worksite or buying EAP services from an outside provider.

4. Reporting to the federal government any convictions related to drug crimes committed in the workplace.

Table 15.5 Indications of Possible Chemical Abuse

Common signs

- Changes in attendance patterns at work
- Change from typical capabilities, such as work habits, efficiency, self-discipline, mood, or attitude expression
- Poor physical appearance, including lack of attention to dress and personal hygiene
- Unusual effort to cover arms in order to hide needle marks
- Association with known drug users
- Increased borrowing of money from friends or family members; stealing from employer, home, or school
- Heightened secrecy about actions and possessions.

Specific indications

Narcotics

- Appearance of scars ("tracks") on the arms or back of hands, caused by injecting drugs
- Constricted pupils
- Frequent scratching of various parts of the body
- Loss of normal appetite
- Immediately after a "fix," user may be lethargic or drowsy, that is, "on the nod," an alternating cycle of dozing and awakening
- Restlessness; sniffles; red, watery eyes; and yawning, which disappear soon after drug is administered
- Users often have syringes or medicine droppers, bent spoons or metal bottle caps, small glassine bags or tinfoil packets

Depressants

- Behavior like that of alcohol intoxication, with or without the odor of alcohol on the breath
- Sluggishness, difficulty in thinking and concentrating
- Slurred speech
- Faulty judgment, moody
- Impaired motor skills
- Falls asleep while at work

Common signs

- Anxiety, weakness, tremors, sweating, insomnia relieved by another dose

Stimulants

- Excessively active, irritable, nervous ("wired"), or impulsive
- Abnormally long periods without eating or sleeping, with the likelihood of being or becoming emaciated
- Repetitive, unpurposeful behavior
- Dilated pupils
- Chronically runny nose, respiratory problems related to snorting cocaine
- Users may have straws, small spoons, mirrors, and razor blades

Psychedelics (hallucinogens)

- Behavior and mood vary widely; the user may sit or recline quietly in a trancelike state or may appear fearful or even terrified
- Difficulty in communicating
- Profound changes in perception, mood, and thinking
- May experience nausea, chills, flushing, irregular breathing, sweating, and trembling of hands after consuming the drug

Phencyclidine (PCP) and related drugs

- User is likely to be uncommunicative and exhibit a blank, staring appearance, with eyes repeatedly flicking from side to side

(Continued)

Table 15.5 Continued

- High-stepping, exaggerated gait
- Increased insensitivity to pain
- Amnesia
- Profound changes in perception, mood, and thinking, which can include self-destructive behavior and can mimic an acute schizophrenic disorder

Marijuana
- Shreds of plant material in pockets, along with bobby pins or other small clips used to hold end of cigarette (joint), cigarette papers, pipes
- Intoxicated behavior
- Lethargy, inability to concentrate
- Impaired motor skills
- Distorted sense of time and distance that would make driving hazardous

Source: Charles R. Carroll, *Drugs in Modern Society* (Dubuque, IA: Brown & Benchmark Publishers, 1997).

Drug testing and treatment are not required by the Act. However, many companies provide exceptional treatment plans through their EAPs. In addition, many firms have initiated some type of drug testing in pre-employment or post-employment to reduce problems associated with employee use of drugs.

3.4.1 Pre-Employment Drug Testing

When companies conduct preemployment screening, they should adopt the following guidelines:

1. Notify the applicant of the company's policy of drug screening.
2. Make sure the test results are valid by using a reputable laboratory.
3. Ensure confidentiality.

3.4.2 Post-Employment Drug Testing

As with all policies, the key is that the policy is well written and communicated to the employees in a clear manner. Expectations regarding the use of drugs and the penalties associated with that use must be clearly stated. The policy should specify under what conditions an employee will be expected to submit to drug testing (for example, after an on-the-job accident).

All policies and procedures for drug testing should (1) be consistently administered; (2) explain prescription drug use, including the types of drugs that need to be declared to company supervisors; (3) require substantive proof of drug use; and (4) be consistent with statutory or regulatory requirements, collective bargaining agreements, and disability discrimination provisions.

In addition to drug testing, some companies have also adopted the use of undercover operatives to discover possible drug trafficking and use in the workplace. Some firms use camera systems, ranging from simple hidden cameras to more elaborate hidden or open observations.

Further information on development of policies and procedures for a comprehensive substance abuse program can be obtained from the Center for Substance Abuse Prevention Workplace Helpline (1-800-WORKPLACE).

Summary

As the statistics indicate, workplace violence has been decreasing over the past decade, but there were 674 workplace homicides, or 11 percent of all workplace deaths, in 2000. And as noted earlier, 25 percent of all homicides between 1975 and 2005 were work related. These figures are much too high. Organizations' efforts through VIACT programs and other plans have had the desired positive impact. However, we must continue to look for better ways of reducing this major workplace problem.

Drugs in the workplace continue to be a concern, many times contributing to the violence issue as well as to absenteeism and substandard production. Testing of applicants and incumbent employees is becoming more widespread. The loss of time on the job as well as job-related injuries caused by drug impairment have brought these issues to the forefront. Security must continue to monitor the workplace for illegal drug use and make sure that employees with problems are either placed into EAPs or, when illegal activity is discovered, discharged and criminally prosecuted.

□ □ □ ▬▬▬▬▬▬▬▬▬▬▬▬▬▬▬▬▬▬▬▬▬▬

Critical Thinking

Although drug use is illegal, some people believe it is a personal decision and should not be penalized. Shouldn't the individual worker have the option of using drugs whenever or wherever they choose? If they are impaired at work or become violent, the employer should terminate their employment, not send them to assistance programs!

Consider the above statement and comment.

▬▬▬▬▬▬▬▬▬▬▬▬▬▬▬▬▬▬▬▬▬▬ □ □ □

Review Questions

1. What is a VIACT?
2. Can the potential for violence be identified?
3. What are the steps that should be taken before an intervention is initiated?
4. What is an EAP?
5. Name the various typologies of possible problem employees.
6. Name at least three things that an employer should look for that could indicate possible drug use on the job.
7. Is there any difference in the incidence of drug abuse among various types of jobs? If so, which occupations have the greatest problems?
8. What are the major problems associated with drug abuse and the workplace?

References

1. www.sba.gov.
2. "Violence in the Workplace," *National Crime Victimization Survey*, December 2001.
3. Ibid.

4. Kinney, Joseph, *Violence at Work* (Englewood Cliffs, NJ: Prentice-Hall, 1995). p. 1.

5. "Violence in the Workplace."

6. "Workplace Violence," Occupational Safety and Health Administration, U.S. Department of Labor, downloaded January 28, 2003, www.osha.gov/oshinfo/priorities/violence.html.

7. Mantell, Michael, *Ticking Bombs: Defusing Violence in the Workplace* (Burr Ridge, IL: Irwin Publishing, 1994), p. 53.

8. "Fatalities to Young Workers and All Workers by Event and Exposure," U.S. Bureau of Labor Statistics, downloaded January 28, 2003, www.stats.bls.gov.

9. Labig, Charles, *Preventing Violence in the Workplace* (New York: AMACOM, 1995).

10. Yates, R. E., "The Healing Manager," *San Diego Union* (1993), p. Cl.

11. Mantell, *Ticking Bombs*, p. 136.

12. Ibid., p. 33.

13. Baron, Anthony, *Violence in the Workplace: A Prevention and Management Guide for Business* (Ventura, CA: Pathfinder Publishing of California, 1993), p. 88.

14. Labig, *Preventing Violence*, p. 16.

15. Kinney, *Violence at Work*, p. 125.

16. Mantell, *Ticking Bombs*, p. 1.

17. Baron, *Violence in the Workplace*, p. 139.

18. U.S. Department of Health and Human Services, "Creating a Drug-Free Workplace" (Rockville, MD: Center for Substance Abuse Prevention, 1995), p. 3; Darryl S. Inaba, William E. Cohen, and Michael E. Holstein, *Uppers, Downers, All Arounders,* 3rd ed. (Ashland, OR: CNS Publications, 1997), p. 349.

19. Bush, Loren L., "Preventing the Artful Dodge," *Security Management* (June 1996): 83.

20. Schlaadt, Richard G. and Shannon, Peter T., *Drugs: Use, Misuse and Abuse* (Englewood Cliffs, NJ: Prentice Hall, 1998), p. 56.

21. Office of Applied Studies, SAMHSA, *National Household Survey on Drug Abuse* (1997), www.samhsa.gov.

22. Louis-Nont, Gregory M., "Alternatives to Drug Testing," *Security Management* (May 1990): 48–50.

23. SAMHSA.

24. Ibid.

25. Frone, Michael R., "Prevalence and Distribution of Illicit Drug Use in the Workforce and in the Workplace: Findings and Implications from a U.S. National Survey," *Journal of Applied Psychology* (2006): 834–869.

26. Inaba, Cohen, and Holstein, p. 349.

27. Ibid., p. 349; "Substance Abuse in the Workplace,"*HR Focus* (February 1997): 1, 4ff.

28. Carroll, Charles R., *Drugs in Modern Society* (Dubuque, IA: WCB Brown & Benchmark Publishers, 1997), p. 434.

29. National Clearinghouse for Alcohol and Drug Information, "Why Have a Drug-Free Workplace? It's Important to Our Organization," Employee Fact Sheet #1 (1995).

30. Polk County, Florida, "Airline Tells Pilots in Alcohol Arrests They Will Be Fired" (2002), www.polkonline.com/stories/070402/sta_pilots.shtml.

31. Inaba, Cohen, and Holstein, p. 349.

32. Substance Abuse Data Base, *Drugs in the Workplace* (1997), www.dol.gov.

33. Carroll, p. 434.

34. Schlaadt and Shannon, p. 56.

35. Hoffman, John P., Brittingham, Angela, and Larison, Cindy, *Drug Use Among U.S. Workers: Prevalence and Trends by Occupation and Industry Categories* (Rockville, MD: Substance

Abuse and Mental Health Services Administration, U.S. Department of Health and Human Services, Public Health Service, May 1996), p. 9.

36. Carroll, p. 434; Inaba, Cohen, and Holstein, p. 349.

37. *Drug/Alcohol Facts: Why Drug-Testing Programs?* (1990), www.usaor.net/users/mdt/drug-facts.htm.

38. *American Management Association Research: Workplace Drug Testing and Drug Abuse Policies* (1996), www.amanet.org/ama/survey/drugtest.htm.

39. SAMHSA.

40. Inaba, Cohen, and Holstein, p. 354.

41. "On-site Testing New Screening Trend,"*Security* (October 1996): 83.

42. McBay, A., *Legal Challenges to Testing Hair for Drugs: A Review* (1996), http://big.stpt.usf.edu/~journal/mcbay2.html.

43. Department of Defense Urinalysis Report (2002), usmilitary.about.com/library/milinfo/milarticles/bldrugtests-2.htm.

44. Substance Abuse Data Base, *Drugs in the Workplace* (1997), www.dol.gov/dol/asp/public/programs/drugs/said.htm.

45. Liska, Ken, *Drugs and the Human Body*, 5th ed (Upper Saddle River, NJ: Prentice Hall, 1997), p. 422.

46. Carroll, p. 428.

47. Homicide Trends in the U.S., USDJ, *Bureau of Justice Statistics*, www.ojp.usdop.gov/bjs/homicide/city.htm, downloaded 7/12/2007

16

□□□ □□□ □□□

Retail Security

OBJECTIVES

The study of this chapter will enable you to:

1. Understand the relationship between shoplifting and internal theft in the retail environment.
2. Be able to identify various methods of shoplifting.
3. Understand the problems associated with checks and credit and debit cards.
4. Have a working knowledge of how to reduce retail shrinkage associated with shoplifting and internal theft.

1 Introduction

At the retail end of the distribution chain, merchants are beset on all sides by assaults on their profit-and-loss positions. The very nature of retailing demands that quantities of merchandise be attractively displayed in easily accessible areas. The public can roam at will and handle much of the merchandise. Every effort is made to create a desire to possess the displayed merchandise and to make the possession as effortless as possible.

Of course, the merchant expects payment for the goods. Others—customers and employees alike—sometimes overlook that aspect of the transaction, and the merchant takes a loss. Generally each such loss is relatively small, but the aggregate damage to the business from such erosion of inventory can be enormous. It is estimated that retailers lost approximately $32.3 billion in 2001 to such activities as bad checks, shoplifting, internal theft, general inventory problems, and over the past five years, shop-return frauds.[1] In 2006, the National Retail Federation reported an estimated $41.6 billion loss to retailers.[2]

Add to these problems the issues of targeting by terrorists and retailers have their hands full. Chapter 1 covered the topics of retail targets and homeland security, but it is worth noting that retailers have been targeted for terror but not by traditional terrorists. The 2002 sniper attacks in the Washington, D.C., area required retailers to take additional precautions to protect their customers. In 2007, Sulejman Talovic shot five people outside the Pottery Barn Kids and Cabin Fever stores in Salt Lake City's Trolley Square shopping mall.[3] According to an article in *Loss Prevention Magazine*, some chains dispatch loss prevention personnel to rooftops in affected areas to monitor parking lot activity and allow for rapid response to potential problems.[4] Though this action might seem extreme, many malls and general retailers have indicated increased interest in the International Council of Shopping Centers (ICSC) security guidelines that suggest increased foot patrols and the checking of delivery shipments, delivery personnel, and retail employees.

As in the past, the employee contributes more to losses than does the shoplifter. The International Mass Retail Association reports that 40 percent of retail loss is from employees, whereas 33 percent is from shoplifting.[5] Drugs have become associated with both shoplifters and employees thanks to the extent that 46 percent of shoplifters and 55 percent of employees, when apprehended, showed evidence of drug use.[6]

Most businesses are subject to problems of inventory shortages, but few feel the problem as acutely as do retailers. They necessarily deal in merchandise that must be received, stored, and moved from warehouse or storage rooms to display areas on the selling floor. All these operations pose a risk of loss from breakage or other damage, pilferage, or quantity theft. Even inadequate or careless record keeping can effectively "lose" merchandise that fails to show up on proper inventory records. According to one regional retail security manager, the inventory problem, coupled with computer records, has become his major concern. Merchandise on display is fair game for shoplifters during the day, and when the day is over, the whole cycle begins again.

The three principal sources of loss to the retailer are external losses from theft, internal losses from employee dishonesty, and losses that come from carelessness or mismanagement. In the aggregate, these losses are referred to as *shrinkage*. As noted, loss prevention executives reported that they believe 40 percent of shrinkage is due to employee theft. Thirty-three percent is attributable to shoplifting, whereas approximately 20 percent is due to administrative error. The remainder may be related to vendor theft.[7]

A fourth source of loss has recently become apparent. *Return fraud* is estimated to cost retailers about $1 billion a year. Return fraud is cynically called "borrowing" merchandise. These shop returns are a growing problem for retailers. The cause of this new threat to retail profits is the industry's own generous return policies. While the problem was first noticeable approximately 15 years ago, it is only recently that the costs involved began to draw real attention.[8]

Every area of loss must be counteracted in some way or retailers may find that although gross business is booming, they are barely able to break even. The arithmetic is as simple as it is familiar, but it bears repeating. Convenience store C sustains a $5,000 shrinkage loss. If that shortage is viewed as lost net profit and the store is operating on a 3 percent profit margin, sales must increase by $166,666.66 just to recoup the $5,000 loss.[9] The National Retail Security Survey for 2006 reported that American retail businesses lost $32.8 billion that year to shoplifting and employee theft.[10] Retailers attempt to make up for a portion of the shrinkage by passing the cost along to the customer, but the end result may be reduced sales and thus reduced profits. The National Retail Security Survey reports that inventory losses in the retailing sector remain constant at around 1.6 percent of retail sales.[11]

Generally, shortage control procedures apply to retailers of every kind—from all-night restaurants to department stores. Legal considerations, surveillance techniques, cash register control, and the many other factors involved in a security program for a retailing facility are much the same (see Figure 16.1). The details vary, and every establishment must ultimately make its own determination of what is best for its own application, but

FIGURE 16.1 Security "gateway" at a retail outlet. (Courtesy of Checkpoint Systems, Inc.)

the basics are much the same throughout the trade. However, it is worth noting that the 2000 Retail Theft Trends Report lists the following categories of items as most often shoplifted: compact discs, athletic shoes, apparel, earrings, and beauty products.[12] Consumer goods with "street hot" logos and brand names are almost always attractive targets.

As noted in Chapter 1, a new problem for retailers is the potential targeting of retail establishments – in particular malls – by terrorist organizations. However, as of this writing the perception of problems have not been real. Many retailers have taken some measures to assure the public that facilities are safe; we can only hope that such measures, while increasing the level of security, are really not needed.

2 Shoplifting

Retailing today demands that merchandise be prominently displayed and exposed so that customers can see it, touch it, pick it up, and examine it. Because displaying merchandise is such a successful sales technique, there is little likelihood that merchandise will ever go back behind the counter in the great majority of stores that now display it so invitingly. Some stores, however, are finding ways to make it more difficult to steal openly displayed items. These techniques and procedures are discussed later in this chapter, in the section entitled "Preventive Measures." Displaying merchandise in this way is hardly a theft-proof practice, but theft must be controlled if profit margins are to be maintained. Shortages from shoplifting are not likely to be eliminated, but they must and can be reduced through a thoughtful and energetic security program.

2.1 Extent of Shoplifting

It is difficult to accurately assess the full dimension of the shoplifting problem. Few shoplifters are apprehended, and of those who are, even fewer are referred to the police.

In fact, the most optimistic studies of retail effectiveness in spotting shoplifters indicate that stores that do a good security job apprehend no more than 1 out of every 35 shoplifters. (Another report estimates that the figure is only 1 in 200.) Using 2005 statistics from Hayes International, it appears that roughly 1 of over 250 shoplifters was apprehended. This figure is based on an average of $126.87 per shoplifting incident, apprehensions of 607,457, and an estimated loss from shoplifting at $11.1 billion.[13] Stores with vigilant personnel report a relatively high level of shoplifting, whereas analogous concerns (in terms of store type, location, and size) with indifferent antishoplifting programs report few such incidents.

Information provided by one major retailer from its Midwestern region provides an excellent profile of shoplifting activity. The number of shoplifting apprehensions is consistent between April and September. Beginning in October this number climbs until it reaches a peak level in December. In contrast, January provides the lowest number of apprehensions, which increases gradually until April. Shoplifting apprehensions by day of the week are consistent, with the exception of Saturdays, when apprehensions are approximately 50 percent higher than they are during the week. Sundays are the slow days. Most shoplifting apprehensions are made between 1:00 P.M. and 7:00 P.M., with the period between 4:00 P.M. and 7:00 P.M. contributing the greatest amount of activity.

Of the items recovered, cosmetics leads all departments, followed by jewelry, women's wear, electronics, sporting goods, men's wear, and shoes. This pattern of experience has been frequently reported. It appears that where the vulnerability remains constant, the potential for shoplifting remains constant, ultimately varying only with the effectiveness of the security measures. The unhappy lesson is simple: If you look for a shoplifter, you will find one.

2.2   Methods of Shoplifting

Shoplifting is conducted in every imaginable way; the ingenuity of the shoplifter is legendary. By and large, the great majority of thefts are simple and direct, involving nothing more sophisticated than putting the stolen merchandise into a handbag or a pocket. But there are certain methods beyond the simple taking of items that are in general use and should be anticipated, including:

1. The "bloomer" technique—using large, baggy clothes such as bloomers or pantyhose that can be filled like shopping bags.
2. The clothing technique—slitting pockets in coats or jackets, or hiding merchandise inside a coat or up a sleeve.
3. The fitting room technique—wearing stolen clothes under the thief's own clothing.
4. Hiding items in purses or umbrellas.
5. Palming—placing small items in the palm of the hand.
6. The bag technique—using shopping bags, sometimes even using the store's own bags.
7. The packaging technique—hiding items within other prepackaged items; for instance, placing jewelry (cotton and all) into toothpaste boxes. In other situations, merchandise such as an infant car seat is removed from its box and replaced with several CD players. The package is retaped and taken through the checkout.

8. Wearing the item in plain view and walking out with large items.

9. Grabbing an item and running.

10. Booster boxes and cages—boxes designed with special spring lids in which merchandise can be concealed, or cages that are worn by women to make them appear pregnant.

11. Hiding items in books, newspapers, or magazines.

12. Crotch—a technique used by females whereby an item is held in place by the thighs under a skirt or dress.

13. Ticket switching or destruction.

According to ongoing research by Commercial Service Systems, Inc., the techniques used vary with individual preference and type of establishment. For example, purses are most commonly used for concealment of merchandise in supermarkets, followed by the use of pockets and by carrying items under clothes. It is estimated that the purse is used 26 to 33 percent of the time, pockets 17 to 30 percent, and clothing 12 to 24 percent. We must keep in mind, however, the self-fulfilling prophecy: What one looks for most, one finds most often!

2.3 Who Shoplifts

Shoplifters come in all sizes and ages and are of either sex. Generally they are broken down by type into amateur, professional, drug user, and thrill seeker. Of these, amateurs are by far the largest in number.

Amateurs come from every economic group and represent every level of education. Their thefts are generally impulsive, although a significant number of them find some kind of economic (or more often emotional) satisfaction in their action, and they become virtually indistinguishable from professionals. The rest of them have no particular pattern of theft and may only steal once or, at most, a handful of times. Individually they do not represent a severe threat to the retailer, but the cumulative effect of such thefts, however motivated, can be very damaging.

The frequent repeaters ultimately become more methodical in their thefts and soon become a real problem. Among this group are those compulsive thieves known as kleptomaniacs—people who are unable to overcome their desire to steal. Such driven souls are very rare and do not make up a significant number or dollar loss to the retailing community.

Professional shoplifters are a very real danger. Their methods are well planned and practical; often they work with partners. *This Is My Job* is the appropriate title of a videotape prepared by a professional shoplifter. The professional approaches shoplifting just as a dancer studies dance or a ballplayer plays ball. They appear to be ordinary shoppers in every way, carefully fitting into the environment of the stores they single out. They select merchandise with high resale value and a ready market. They are well connected with fences and lawyers. They are in every sense suppliers in the subsystem of illegal merchandising. They are the first people in the chain of underworld retailing, and their activities are damaging to the legal storekeeper in a number of ways. Not only do they create severe losses for the legitimate retailer, but they also set up a system whereby they are effectively in competition with their victims' own goods.

Drug users, trapped by their addiction, must find a regular source of funds to supply their needs. They turn to many sources for their insatiable demands, but shoplifting is often the easiest. Thefts of $500 a day or more may be required to supply an individual's habit. Typically, merchandise is stolen for fencing at between 10 and 20 percent of its retail value. In other cases it may be stolen and returned for a refund. Either way, the store suffers substantial losses.

Thrill seekers are more often than not teenagers who shoplift as a gesture of defiance or under peer pressure to do something daring. Shoplifting lists are still used to initiate new members into certain gangs or groups.

Over the years, various reports have found that approximately 50 percent of the people apprehended for shoplifting are adults, 60 percent are under 30 years of age, and 80 percent are under 40. Females account for at least 50 percent of shoplifting incidents. Nevertheless, the statistics are contradictory: Females dominate the overall statistics, but males account for the majority of juvenile shoplifters. The main difference seems to be that females outnumber males in the adult shoplifting segment. Once again, the self-fulfilling prophecy may have some effect on these statistics: Security professionals have stereotyped the housewife as a major shoplifting threat. In addition, females are in the stores more often than males and therefore may be overrepresented in the apprehension statistics. All socioeconomic classes are represented in shoplifting; unlike most criminal activity, the lower socioeconomic classes do not predominate. Rather, shoplifting is a crime of the working and middle classes, who are not generally motivated by need. Instead shoplifting is often a crime of greed. This contention is supported by the fact that many items recovered from shoplifters are luxuries.

2.4   Detecting the Shoplifter

Professional shoplifters will not be deterred by the normal means that would discourage the great bulk of amateurs from stealing. Only a well-trained security staff can apprehend them. Such detectives must learn to blend in with the normal routine of the average customer in a given store at a given time of day. They must learn the different patterns of a secretary on a lunch hour, a bored matron who shops to kill time, and the energetic early morning customer with a specific mission in mind. They must observe the difference in pace of customers in the 10 A.M. crowd and the hurry-to-get home 5:30 P.M. shoppers. After learning the techniques of anonymity, the detective must learn what to look for—how to spot a potential shoplifter.

A large Midwestern store developed a list of some of the signs to look for; it includes the following:

1. *Packages.* A person carrying a great many packages; empty or open paper bags; clumsy, crumpled, homemade, untidy, obviously used before, poorly tied packages; unusual packages; knitting bags; hat boxes; zipper bags; newspapers; magazines; schoolbooks; folded tissue paper; briefcases; and brown bags with no store name on them.
2. *Clothing.* Coat or cape worn over the shoulder or arm; coat with slit pockets; ill-fitting, loose, bulging, unreasonable, and unseasonable clothing.
3. *Actions.* Unusual actions of any kind: extreme nervousness; strained look; aimless walking up and down the aisles; leaving the store but returning in a few minutes;

walking around holding merchandise; handling many articles in a short time; dropping articles on the floor; making rapid purchases; securing empty bags or boxes; entering elevators at the last moment or changing one's mind and letting the elevator go; excessive inspection of packages; examining merchandise in nooks and corners; concealing merchandise behind purse or package; placing packages, coat, or purse over merchandise; using stairways; loitering in vestibules.

4. *Eyes*. Glancing without moving the head, looking out from beneath a hat brim, studying customers instead of merchandise, looking in mirrors, glancing up from merchandise quickly from time to time, glancing from left to right in cross aisles.

5. *Hands*. Closing hands completely over merchandise, palming, removing ticket and concealing or destroying it, folding merchandise, holding identical pieces for comparison, working merchandise up sleeve and lowering arm into pocket, placing merchandise in pocket, stuffing hands in pocket, concealing ticket while trying on merchandise, trying on jewelry and leaving it on, crumpling merchandise.

6. *At counters*. Taking merchandise from counters but returning repeatedly, taking merchandise to another counter or giving it to a minor, standing behind a crowd and taking merchandise from counters by reaching through the crowd, placing merchandise near an exit counter, starting to examine merchandise then leaving the counter and returning to it, holding merchandise below counter level, taking merchandise and turning back to counter, handling a lot of merchandise at different counters, standing a long time at counter.

7. *In fitting rooms*. Entering with merchandise but no salesperson, using room before it has been cleared, removing hangers before entering, entering with packages, taking in two or more identical items, taking in items of various sizes or of obviously wrong sizes, gathering merchandise hastily without examining it and going into fitting room.

8. *In departments*. Sending clerks away for more merchandise, standing too close to dress racks or cases, placing shopping bag on floor between racks, refusing a salesperson's help.

9. *Miscellaneous*. Requesting questionable refunds; acting in concert —separating and meeting, setting up lookouts, interchanging packages, following companion into fitting room independently.[14]

Obviously, many of these are the actions of a perfectly well-intentioned person, but they may indicate a shoplifter, especially if several such indications appear in the actions of one person. In such cases surveillance is essential.

2.5 Preventive Measures

2.5.1 Surveillance

The key to successful shoplifting prevention is surveillance. Impulse theft, which represents 95 percent of shoplifting incidents, is motivated by availability, desire, and opportunity. Availability is a basic fact of life in modern retailing. Desire is not just a private matter of individual character, but also a factor of the merchant aggressively selling his wares. Neither of these factors can be controlled to a significant degree, nor should they be in retailing. But opportunity can be controlled.

Shoplifters characteristically snatch loot when they think they are alone and not being observed. An attentive sales staff occasionally asking if they can help, or rearranging merchandise in the vicinity of a customer acting in any unusual manner, can discourage most amateurs. Supervisors moving about the floor can also be effective in making known to potential shoplifters that they may be observed at any time. Obviously such store personnel are primarily concerned with serving customers. But they can be effective deterrents to shoplifting as well if they are aware of the problem and alert to any signs that might indicate a problem. In short, any method that increases the would-be shoplifter's fear of being caught will significantly decrease the temptation to steal. The public address system call "security to department five," whether real or false, brings terror to the shoplifter since there is no way of knowing where department five is located or if the would-be shoplifter has been spotted. One professional shoplifter indicated that when he hears this call he always ditches the merchandise and leaves the store immediately. The last thing a potential shoplifter wants to hear from store staff is, "I am sure I'll see you if you need me."

2.5.2 Closed-Circuit Television

As was noted in an earlier chapter, CCTV can either catch someone in an illegal act or prevent the act. (See Figure 16.2.) It may have a place in retail security, but is it for deterrence or apprehension? Most merchants prefer to prevent theft rather than deal with the trouble and cost of prosecution.

FIGURE 16.2 CCTV surveillance integrated system. (Photo compliments of Verint, Loronix Video Solutions.)

Systems designed to prevent shoplifting must be obvious to shoppers. In most cases, the cameras are placed in observable locations with signs noting their presence. Some systems use flashing lights on the cameras throughout the store, to show shoppers that the system is operating.

To be effective, the system must make shoppers believe that they are being watched all the time. In addition, however, the shoplifter must know that apprehension is likely and will result in prosecution.

The use of CCTV for apprehension of shoplifters may be a greater burden than most retail managers want to assume. Not only is it troublesome and costly to be constantly in court for prosecution, but CCTV cameras and systems that are designed for apprehension are more expensive than those designed for deterrence. The cost of the apprehension type is greater because the quality of the images must be good enough for recognition of individuals. These images should also be recorded to show shoplifters that they were caught in the act. Whereas the deterrence systems can get by using dummy cameras, a system for apprehension needs full coverage. In addition, apprehension systems require additional personnel to monitor the system, whereas deterrent systems do not require constant monitoring. For all these reasons, most CCTV systems in retail stores are primarily deterrents, but they also serve as an aid to apprehension.

2.5.3 Electronic Article Surveillance

The current state-of-the-art technology in retail security is electronic article surveillance (EAS). The first systems were sold in 1971, and their growth in popularity has been steady ever since. These systems have at least three components: tags, sensors, and alarm.

Tags are of various types, but two systems (Senormatic and Checkpoint Systems) and their tags currently dominate the industry. The first is a VHF/microwave system. In this system, the tag contains a semiconductor that, when radiated by the transmitter frequency, reradiates or reflects a signal at the receiver. The second system uses a magnetic field rather than radio waves. Here the tag contains a magnetized strip that is sensed by a magnetometer. Most tags are designed to be reused, but newer systems have tags that can be desensitized and thrown away. The most familiar system uses a large plastic tag that is attached to clothing with a metal pin. The device can be removed only with a special tool and can be reused. These tags not only aid apprehension but also serve as prevention devices. The systems serve as a deterrent by decreasing the opportunity to steal.

Although the tagging system has been valuable in reducing shoplifting losses, it is not possible to tag every item in a store. Perhaps the deterrent value of the system is greater than the apprehension value, however. Recent developments allow the placement of EAS targets next to bar codes where they can be deactivated as the bar code is read. Other EAS manufacturers have found ways to include the EAS target in the package in an inactive state. The retailer who purchases the item will then have the option of activating the target for use with the EAS system. This will save retailers time and money in placing targets on merchandise.

In its *Electronic Article Surveillance Industry Report*, the Home Center Institute reports that EAS is 75 percent effective against the average shopper but that it deters only 15 percent of "social misfits" and 10 percent of professional shoplifters.[15] Most large retailers now use some type of EAS like the system shown in Figure 16.3.

FIGURE 16.3 Electronic article surveillance (EAS) detector. (Courtesy of Checkpoint Systems, Inc.)

2.5.4 Radio Frequency Identification

The latest addition to the retail arsenal is *radio frequency identification (RFID)*. Wal-Mart is currently piloting RFID tags at its stores and plans to introduce the asset-tracking technology into the United Kingdom in the near future. RFID is a multifunctional system that not only allows for article surveillance but also tracking to merchandise, inventory control, and pricing. Predictions are that this new technology (also used for access control, toll highway pass systems, and pass systems for use in retail environments such as McDonald's) will be used more and more as its benefits are discovered by other areas of industry.

RFID relies on radio frequency waves passing between a reader and a card or tag. Although currently more expensive than EAS for bar code technology, RFID has become a mainstay for identification applications and data collection.[16]

2.5.5 Mirrors

Convex mirrors, which are in wide use throughout the United States, may be useful in avoiding collisions of people or shopping carts rounding corners, but they have a limited use in the detecting shoplifters and may even hurt the program by creating an atmosphere of unwarranted confidence. Such mirrors distort the reflected scene in such a way that it is virtually impossible to see the details of action—and in shoplifting it is the detail of merchandise concealment that is of prime importance. Without a clear, precise image of what was taken and how it was concealed or where, it would be foolhardy, and possibly costly in legal fees, to confront a customer as a shoplifter.

On the other hand, flat mirrors of a decorative design might be built into the decor of the store at strategic spots that might otherwise be difficult to observe or keep under surveillance. Such mirrors, presenting a clear, undistorted image, can be very useful in the security effort.

2.5.6 Signs

There is considerable controversy over the use of signs warning of the results of shoplifting as a deterrent. Many merchants take the view that such signs are an insult to the great majority of honest shoppers who may become incensed and take their business elsewhere. Other merchants subscribe to the theory that such signs have no effect on honest people since they clearly are not those to whom the message is addressed but that they will remind those with larceny in mind of the gravity of their offense and thus deter them. There does not seem to be a clear-cut resolution of these viewpoints except to say that there is no evidence anywhere that the posting of such warnings has ever had any effect on the incidence of shoplifting.

2.5.7 Displays of Merchandise

Merchandise displays must be appealing to attract customers, but they can also be secure to prevent theft. Symmetry in certain kinds of items displayed can be important in enabling the clerk or floor personnel to tell at a glance if any of the items are missing. Thin, almost invisible wires that in no way detract from the display can secure small items to the display rack. Dummy items look exactly like the actual merchandise and should be used when possible. Fountain pens can be displayed in a closed case, with two or three different models on counter chains outside for handling and testing. A relatively recent addition to the display strategy is called the "bull pen." A specific type of high-vulnerability merchandise such as electronic equipment is situated within the store in such a manner that customers can enter in only one or two locations, which are staffed at all times. A sales representative will also be present in the bull pen to assist with customer questions. There are thousands of items and countless ways to display them to catch the customer's attention. Each such display must accommodate some means to provide security for the goods it presents.

High-value merchandise is now being displayed in units that require store personnel to unlock the display for customer retrieval of merchandise. In other instances cards identify the merchandise (sometimes too big to load into a cart and sometimes of high value) for the customer to present to the cashier upon checkout.

2.5.8 Checkout Clerks

These clerks should check all merchandise for signs of switched or altered price tags. Customers should never be permitted to carry out unwrapped or unbagged merchandise. All purchases should be wrapped or bagged, and if the additional precaution of stapling is taken, the receipt should be stapled to the package.

Checkers in supermarkets must check shopping carts for merchandise on the bottom shelf. They should further check all merchandise purchased for possible concealment of other goods. This includes paper bags holding purchases of produce. Pilfered items may be concealed beneath the apples or potatoes these bags contain.

2.5.9 Refunds

Refunds should be issued on the return of merchandise with the original sales slip. Since these slips are frequently misplaced, full particulars, including the name and address of the customer, should be entered on the appropriate refund form if the customer insists on a cash refund. The original of the form, signed by the clerk making out the form, the customer, and the authorizing supervisor, should be presented to the customer for cashing at a refund window or other location handling such matters. The register operator should never permit cashing of refunds at cash registers on the floor because this practice could invite embezzlement. Unfortunately, this last practice is not applied in all operations, because customer relations are more important than the irritation caused by red tape. The clerk who handled the transaction should turn in a copy of the refund authorization at the end of the day's business. All such refund forms should be numbered and accounted for, including damaged ones.

All customers must cash their own refunds, to avoid the possibility of forged slips supposedly being cashed by store personnel as a service to a nonexistent customer.

The refund system should be further checked by periodic audits of all refund forms used and unused and by contact with the customer so refunded. The company should regularly send out letters to a certain percentage of customers who have received refunds, asking whether the service was adequate and if their request for refund was promptly and courteously complied with. If such letters are returned as undeliverable or if the customer denies having received a refund, an investigation of refund procedures is indicated.

Much of the cash refund system has been displaced with refunds on credit. Here the refund is made back to the original card as a credit to that cardholder's account.

2.5.10   Arrest

Many issues are involved in arresting a shoplifter. Chief among them, after considerations of justice and fair play, is the ever-present possibility of liability for false arrest or imprisonment, slander, or unreasonable detainment. Because the laws pertaining to shoplifting vary from state to state and because they are still subject to changes to conform to an equitable balance between the merchant's needs and the general public's protection, it is essential that the retailer seek legal advice to guide company policy in such matters.

Every store management team should develop a specific set of instructions that should be taught to employees in such a way that adherence to them will be automatic in every covered instance. Any variation from approved procedure in dealing with shoplifting incidents can subject the store to severe financial reverses and damaging public relations consequences. All personnel must conform to the established policy. Since under the doctrine of *respondeat superior* the owner is liable for all employees' actions while they are on the job, we'll use the term *merchant* in this discussion, even though employees usually perform most of the actions herein described.

Under common law, merchants operate in a most dangerous legal minefield. Although tort law allows property owners the privilege of defending their property against theft and even allows them to repossess their goods if they have been wrongfully removed from the premises, this privilege is not absolute and is limited in scope. The privilege is entirely dependent on the fact of wrongful taking. If the suspicion of theft turns out to be groundless, the privilege vanishes and the merchant is vulnerable to a tort action that can result in substantial damages, both compensatory and punitive. The basis for such actions may be one or more of five torts that were discussed in Chapter 7.

The complexities of the legal climate governing the war against shoplifting require a sensitive understanding and a thorough briefing by an attorney experienced in the field. Store policies on procedures of arrest and detainment must be predicated on legal advice and must then be followed to the letter. As a general rule, it should be noted that, in cases of detainment where neither a confession of guilt nor a form releasing the store from any liability has been signed, it will be necessary to prosecute to avoid the suit for false arrest that would be likely to ensue.

2.5.11 Prosecution

The argument over when and whom to prosecute shows no sign of abating; certainly there appears to be little agreement among security professionals. The skew is probably more toward a tough attitude than otherwise, but every shade of opinion has its adherents.

Every study undertaken on the subject has shown that the rate of recidivism is enormous. The Bureau of Justice Statistics' latest study reports that 67.5 percent of prisoners released in 1994 were rearrested within three years. Isolating property offenders, the rate increased to 73.8 percent. Such a figure suggests that neither arrest nor the fear of arrest is a very effective deterrent.

3 Checks and Credit/Debit Cards

The boom in private checking accounts that has been a part of the American economic scene for the past 45 years has led us to the point where business analysts and economists continue to predict a cashless economy within the foreseeable future. At that time, they suggest, even checks will become passé, and all transactions will be based on debits and credits handled through instant recording of the exchange of goods or services by centralized computers. Such computers would register a credit to an employee's account, credit where appropriate to various government agencies, and debit the account of the employer in the amount specified on payroll information. This process is already available through electronic filing of IRS tax returns and through various credit card companies, in cooperation with some major retail chains.

All obligations of the employee—from mortgage payments to the expenses of a vacation trip—would be handled in the same manner by a simple series of ledger entries in an interlocking central computer system. The automatic debit systems for checking accounts on mortgages, car loans, and insurance payments are with us now. Personal bank checks in use today are a crude and primitive version of this predicted, streamlined system.

With personal checking accounts the rule rather than the exception, it would appear that the physical handling of cash has been delegated solely to the banks. That day has not, of course, arrived, but it seems close. Even today almost 90 percent of all business transactions are handled by check or debit and credit accounts.

In today's world, people use credit and debit cards in supermarkets, for online purchases and airport baggage carts, and at movie theaters, museums, and fast-food restaurants, to name only a few business uses. As noted in Chapter 9, the use of the smart card is increasing, too. As the card with detailed customer and account information becomes commonly available, it is predicted that the old-fashioned check and cash will become relics of the past.

In 2003, for the first time, credit and debit card payments in stores were greater than use of cash and checks, according to a study by Dove Consulting. The breakdown showed that credit cards were used 21 percent of the time and debit cards 31 percent, with checks adding only 15 percent to the total use. According to a 2004 study by the Raddon Financial Group, 54 percent of customers have used a debit card monthly.[17]

The most common debit card also serves as a credit card. Whether debit or credit, the merchant must make sure that the cardholder and purchaser are the same. The signature on the card and credit card slip must match. If the transaction is a debit, the user must enter a personal identification number (PIN). These transactions are checked against the available balance in the individual's checking account and authorized when there are sufficient funds. Merchant liability is eliminated because the funds are automatically transferred from the buyer to the merchant's account.[18]

The consumer use of debit and credit cards has not gone unnoticed by the criminal element. Hackers are shopping for personal data at major retailers. Chain stores like T. J. Maxx and Marshalls have reported that hackers had broken in and potentially had access to a wide range of financial information from their customers. Attacks against retailers are increasing as financial institutions have made it more difficult for hackers to compromise their computer security systems. Current retail payment systems are not designed with security in mind; hackers do find weak links.[19]

The extent of the problem is indicated by a report from the Privacy Rights Clearinghouse, which stated that more than 100 million personal financial records were compromised through 440 reported data breaches between 2004 and 2006. While the retail industry is playing catch-up, criminals are figuring out who has the weak links. Many retail firms comply with the Payment Card Industry Data Security Standard that calls for encrypting customer information and installing computer firewalls, but not all participate. According to Visa, only one-third of the major retailers comply with the standard. The recent problems with T. J. Maxx point out the potential problem: More than 40 million credit and debit card numbers were exposed. In another example, Family Dollar (a Matthews company) does not accept credit cards but does use debit cards and checks, which are handled by a third party. Banks could make it easier for the retailers by including fingerprint scan technology to authenticate card users, but they are often unwilling to invest in the technology.[20]

3.1   The Nature of a Check

Although the check may become obsolete at some point in the future, it is still a means of transacting business. No good security manager would presume to neglect this important business tool.

A check is nothing more than an authorization to the holder of funds or the bank to debit the account of the authorizer and to credit the named person or the bearer in the amount specified. Provided that sufficient funds are available in the debited account, the exchange is made either in cash or by crediting the account of the payee. This system is really only a version of the most rudimentary kind of bookkeeping accomplished by the exchange of tons of paper in a never-ending chain of authorizations.

Checks can and have been written on almost anything and in every conceivable form. Their legality as a negotiable instrument is in no way dependent on the usual check form in common use today. As a practical matter, many banks refuse checks other than those written on the forms they provide, simply because their procedure for processing the enormous volume they are called on to record does not allow for personal eccentricities. The day when Robert Benchley, a popular humorist of the 1930s and 1940s, could write checks in the form of risqué poems on wrapping paper is gone, not because such a check duly signed and clear in intent is not a legal instrument for transferring funds but because few people would cash it.

Checks are in such wide use today because they are safe and convenient. Because cash can almost never be identified if it is lost or stolen, once gone it is gone forever. Checks, on the other hand, have no negotiable value except as they are drawn and signed by the payer.

Forgery is, of course, a problem, but that is of considerably less risk than the loss of cash, which requires no criminal expertise of any level for its disposal.

Checks are invaluable as receipts of payments made and for recording an individual's accounts for tax and other purposes.

Only the designated payee can theoretically use checks. Therefore if a drawn check is lost or mutilated, payment can be stopped by notification to the bank and a new check can be drawn. Checks lost or stolen in the mail can be handled in the same way, whereas mailed cash is always at considerable risk of nondelivery because of theft, loss, or destruction.

Checks are a ready source of cash at any time. Many people are cautious about carrying substantial amounts of cash for fear of loss or theft. In the event a situation requiring funds arises, a check can provide the necessary money.

From the retailer's point of view, checks are a boon because customers will buy what appeals to them at the moment and handle the transaction with the stroke of a pen. People who buy only with cash tend to be considerably more restrained in their buying habits. They are limited by the amount of cash they are carrying, and the psychological restraints imposed by the actual doling out of cash are considerably more persuasive than are those involved in check transactions. People are cautious when handling cash, which has a reality that is automatically translated into food and doctor bills, car payments, and the like. On the other hand, check cashers are usually bigger buyers who allow their impulses to have greater sway in retail situations.

3.2 Checks and the Retailer

Bad checks of various kinds add to a merchant's cost of doing business. Forgeries or fraudulent checks are a direct loss of both merchandise and cash. Checks that are ultimately collectable but that are returned by the bank for any number of reasons present a huge administrative headache in making the collection. Even though a majority of such checks are soon made good—often after a single letter or phone call—the cost of such follow-up and double handling, as well as the additional cost of collection agencies if such are required, may bring the cost of each returned check to between $25 and $30. The charge for any returned check is usually added on to the eventual collection, but most retailers feel that they do not collect the full amount. Such returns actually cost them in direct and indirect losses.

3.3 Check and Credit/Debit Card Approval

3.3.1 Checks

The two most important and relatively simple steps that merchants can and must take in approving checks are a thorough examination of the check itself and a positive identification of the check casher (see Figures 16.4 and 16.5). Neither of these steps will screen out the accomplished forger or the skilled bank check artist, nor will they eliminate the problem of honest but careless people issuing checks that are returned because of insufficient funds. But they will reduce, or possibly eliminate, a great deal of the most persistent losses.

Retailers are not obliged to cash checks. They do so in their own interests, as a service. If a casher's check looks dubious, the check should be refused. Since retailers will cash most checks presented, however, they must know what to look for. They must

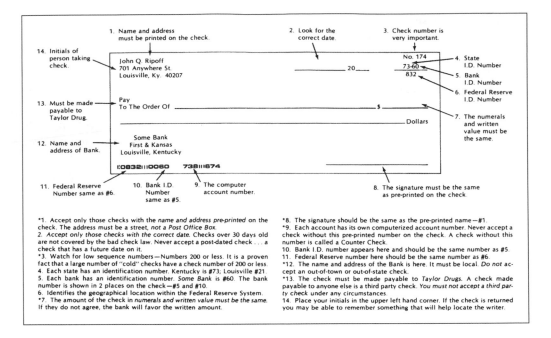

1. Name and address must be printed on the check.
2. Look for the correct date.
3. Check number is very important.
14. Initials of person taking check.

John Q. Ripoff
701 Anywhere St.
Louisville, Ky. 40207

No. 174
73-60
832

4. State I.D. Number
5. Bank I.D. Number
6. Federal Reserve I.D. Number

Pay
To The Order Of _____ $_____

13. Must be made payable to Taylor Drug.

7. The numerals and written value must be the same.

_____ Dollars

12. Name and address of Bank.

Some Bank
First & Kansas
Louisville, Kentucky

⑈08321⑈0060   738⑈⑈674

11. Federal Reserve Number same as #6.
10. Bank I.D. Number same as #5.
9. The computer account number.
8. The signature must be the same as pre-printed on the check.

*1. Accept only those checks with the *name and address pre-printed* on the check. The address must be a street, *not a Post Office Box*.
2. *Accept only those checks with the correct date.* Checks over 30 days old are not covered by the bad check law. Never accept a post-dated check . . . a check that has a future date on it.
*3. Watch for low sequence numbers—Numbers 200 or less. It is a proven fact that a large number of "cold" checks have a check number of 200 or less.
4. Each state has an identification number. Kentucky is #73; Louisville #21.
5. Each bank has an identification number. *Some Bank* is #60. The bank number is shown in 2 places on the check—#5 and #10.
6. Identifies the geographical location within the Federal Reserve System.
*7. The amount of the check in *numerals and written value must be the same*. If they do not agree, the bank will favor the written amount.

*8. The signature should be the same as the pre-printed name—#1.
*9. Each account has its own computerized account number. Never accept a check without this pre-printed number on the check. A check without this number is called a Counter Check.
10. Bank I.D. number appears here and should be the same number as #5.
11. Federal Reserve number here should be the same number as #6.
*12. The name and address of the Bank is here. It must be local. *Do not accept an out-of-town or out-of-state check.*
*13. The check must be made payable to *Taylor Drugs*. A check made payable to anyone else is a third party check. *You must not accept a third party check* under any circumstances.
14. Place your initials in the upper left hand corner. If the check is returned you may be able to remember something that will help locate the writer.

FIGURE 16.4 Check procedure: accepting a check. (Courtesy of Taylor Drug Stores.)

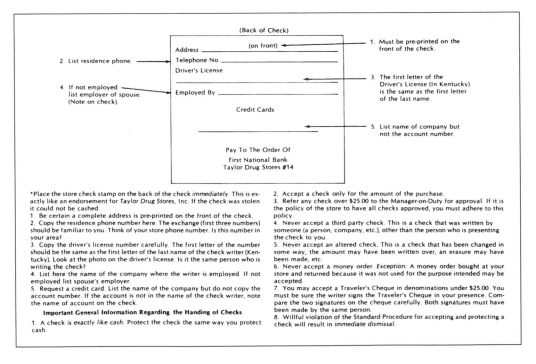

(Back of Check)

1. Must be pre-printed on the front of the check.

Address _____ (on front)
Telephone No. _____
Driver's License

2. List residence phone.

3. The first letter of the Driver's License (In Kentucky) is the same as the first letter of the last name.

Employed By _____

4. If not employed list employer of spouse. (Note on check).

Credit Cards

5. List name of company but not the account number.

Pay To The Order Of
First National Bank
Taylor Drug Stores #14

*Place the store check stamp on the back of the check *immediately*. This is exactly like an endorsement for *Taylor Drug Stores, Inc.* If the check was stolen it could not be cashed.
1. Be certain a complete address is pre-printed on the front of the check.
2. Copy the residence phone number here. The exchange (first three numbers) should be familiar to you. Think of your store phone number. Is this number in your area?
3. Copy the driver's license number carefully. The first letter of the number should be the same as the first letter of the last name of the check writer (Kentucky). Look at the photo on the driver's license. Is it the same person who is writing the check?
4. List here the name of the company where the writer is employed. If not employed list spouse's employer.
5. Request a credit card. List the name of the company but do not copy the account number. If the account is *not* in the name of the check writer, note the name of account on the check.

Important General Information Regarding the Handing of Checks

1. A check is *exactly like cash*. Protect the check the same way you protect cash.

2. Accept a check only for the amount of the purchase.
3. Refer any check over $25.00 to the Manager-on-Duty for approval. If it is the policy of the store to have all checks approved, you must adhere to this policy.
4. Never accept a third party check. This is a check that was written by someone (a person, company, etc.), other than the person who is presenting the check to you.
5. Never accept an altered check. This is a check that has been changed in some way, the amount may have been written over, an erasure may have been made, etc.
6. Never accept a money order. *Exception:* A money order bought at your store and returned because it was not used for the purpose intended may be accepted.
7. You may accept a Traveler's Cheque in denominations under $25.00. You must be sure the writer signs the Traveler's Cheque in your presence. Compare the two signatures on the cheque carefully. Both signatures must have been made by the same person.
8. Willful violation of the Standard Procedure for accepting and protecting a check will result in *immediate dismissal*.

FIGURE 16.5 Check-cashing procedure: protecting a check. (Courtesy of Taylor Drug Stores.)

examine the check to verify the date, the amount drawn both numerically and in script, the customer's name and address, the bank's name, the customer's signature, and the endorsement if it is a third-party check of any kind, including payroll or government checks.

They must also reassure themselves that the customer is properly identified. Generally any official document that describes the holder and bears a signature can be accepted as adequate identification. One that also includes a suitably laminated (or otherwise affixed) photograph is even better. An artful forger can fabricate such documents, but because forging of this kind requires some equipment and skill, it is not a widespread or general practice.

Driver's licenses, passports, national (major) credit cards, birth certificates, and motor vehicle registrations are all acceptable forms of identification. Club or organization membership cards, Social Security cards, hunting licenses, and employee passes are not valid as dependable pieces of identification because they are easily obtained or duplicated.

The best identification is by an authorization system established by the store itself. Credit cards or check-cashing cards issued by the store provide a running record of the customer's account and serve as nearly positive identification for check-cashing purposes. The cost of establishing such a system can be well worth it in stores suffering from substantial losses due to fraudulent or other uncollectible checks.

The information used to identify a customer should, in all cases, be entered on the back of the check for future reference. If, for example, a vehicle registration is accepted, its number should be entered on the check along with other relevant information.

3.3.2 Credit and Debit Cards

Again, though merchants are not obligated to honor credit and debit cards, there are few businesses that do not handle most major cards in today's business environment. In most cases the cards represent fewer risks than checks. Still, merchants need to adopt simple methods to assure that card users are who they claim to be.

As with check-cashing policies, stores need to properly identify card users by asking for identification and comparing card signatures to signatures on other forms of identification such as the driver's license. However, recent increased use of "swipe" devices has reduced the opportunity for register operators to ask for identification.

As the business environment turns more "cashless" and checkless, credit and debit cards will dominate retail transactions. The good news is that with electronic data transfer, retailers can be assured that customer accounts are either adequate to cover the sales cost or guaranteed by the credit card company.

3.3.3 Biometric Authentication Payment

Pay by Touch, a biometric authentication payment company, demonstrated a biometric payment system at the National Retail Federation's 96th Annual Convention & Expo 2007. The customer only needs to press an index finger on a small scanner and punch in his or her phone number. The computer does the test, looking for the previously established consumer "wallet" and then debiting the customer's bank account. In 2007 over 3.5 million people were using Pay by Touch accounts, which are available in 3,000 retail locations in 44 states.[21]

3.3.4 ID Equipment and Systems

Equipment to record any check casher exists to help the retailer. Camera devices that photograph the customer simultaneously with the check can be used to record the transactions. Instruments to record thumbprints on the check without the use of ink also serve in this capacity. With the introduction of the automatic fingerprint identification systems (AFIS) in many states, the ability to identify individuals from only a thumbprint has improved greatly.

These devices are as effective as the system established for their use. If they are used carefully in accordance with a designated procedure, they can provide a useful record for the merchant. By their very presence, these systems tend to discourage check passing by thieves, although they will by no means eliminate it.

Electronic check verification systems, using computer interlink capabilities, also give some merchants the ability to check individual checks against lists of problem check writers; in some cases, this technology even allows for verification of the solvency of the account on which the check is drawn.

By integrating AFIS and camera systems along with bank interlink capabilities, technology is moving toward a system that should reduce merchants' economic losses from check-cashing, credit card, and various other frauds utilizing fake identification.

3.3.5 Store Policy

Every store must set and maintain its own policy for handling checks. Certainly the policy should be reviewed and adjusted as necessary, but it must be strictly adhered to as long as it is in force. Employee indoctrination and continuing education are essential to the success of any check control program.

As a guide, though certainly not as a rigid rule, merchants should consider certain limitations. The retailer should not accept the following:

1. Third-party checks. Payment can be stopped on such checks and the merchant's recourse is only to the customer, not to the payer.
2. Checks drawn on out-of-town banks. Such checks are difficult to verify, and the time involved in clearance is such that, if it is fraudulent, the customer has long disappeared before the check is returned.
3. Checks over a certain amount above purchase.
4. Checks for cashing, other than government or payroll checks.
5. Checks for cashing without adequate predetermined documents of identification.
6. Checks for cashing drawn on other than personal checks imprinted with the name and address of the customer.

If such rules are followed, the loss from bad checks should be small, provided all checks are themselves carefully examined by the cashiers.

It is generally agreed that a merchant should never suffer losses greater than 0.05 percent of the face value of checks cashed, although some do in fact have losses as high as 1 percent. Such a drain on the resources of any company is clearly intolerable. To correct these losses, you must establish reasonable controls and a program of employee education.

4   Internal Theft

4.1   Methods of Theft

The list of ingenious techniques dishonest employees use in stealing is endless. Whatever systems are installed to control inventory shrinkage from internal theft, some clever employee will find a way around them. Theft is limited only by the imagination of the perpetrator. And the problem is very real. According to the 14th annual retail theft survey conducted by Jack L. Hayes International, on a per-company basis, 1 in every 27 employees was apprehended for theft from their employer.[22]

To better understand the scope and nature of the problem, it is important for managers to familiarize themselves with some of the ways in which employees steal. Familiarity alone will not stamp out this problem, but it will aid in focusing on the areas of greatest danger and help to establish some countermeasures. Warehousing operations have become a major liability as mega-regional warehouses have become more prominent in large retail operations. Many stores are assigning an increased security priority to these facilities. (For more information on warehouse and cargo security, see Chapter 14.)

The following sections describe some of the most common methods of employee theft.

4.1.1   Cash Registers

One method of employee theft involves some kind of juggling with the cash register contents. Since cashiers and managers both have access to customer cash to be deposited in registers that record the transaction, there are literally thousands of opportunities to manipulate the accounting before individual sales or even the receipts of the day are posted. Cash never recorded as received is clearly much harder to locate or identify as missing than is cash or merchandise that has been entered and later stolen.

Methods of theft with the register usually involve the regular theft of small sums by under-ringing the amount received. This involves ringing $9 for a $10 purchase, for example, and pocketing the difference at the end of the day before leaving work. An even cruder method is to ring up "no sale" or "void" instead of the amount paid from time to time and to pocket the cash received at the sale. The assignment of one till for each cashier rather than having several cashiers operating out of the same drawer has reduced the opportunities to steal because the cashier is responsible for balancing the drawer at the end of the day. The use of CCTV to randomly monitor cashier stations can help reduce under ringing and no-sale problems. The widespread use of price-scanning technology has also reduced the cashier's ability to skim cash.

From time to time, employees have an opportunity to remove the tape from their registers shortly before the day's end. They put in a fresh tape and ring up all sales accurately. When they check out, they pocket all the proceeds on the new tape, destroy it, and hand in the prematurely removed old tape as their record of the day's receipts. They have effectively gone into business for themselves on company time and at company expense. Several cases of such "private enterprises" have involved managers buying their own registers and, either alone or in collusion with another employee, setting up an additional checkout lane during a few hours of heavy traffic.

4.1.2   The Giveaway

According to several regional discount store security managers, the giveaway is the largest employee theft problem because it is extremely difficult to detect. Checkers in supermarkets have been discovered giving away large amounts of merchandise to fellow employees when they check out by ringing up only a small fraction of the value of the merchandise. In other cases, they have similarly accommodated friends or family members.

In many reported cases, various store clerks set themselves up as traders, exchanging stockings for another clerk's shoes or blouses for costume jewelry, for example.

In a somewhat similar approach, employees have been found who, after selling an item for its regular price, enter it as having been sold to an employee at the regular discount price. The seller then pockets the difference.

4.1.3   Price Changing

Every kind of merchant must be alert to price changing by employees and customers alike. Employees can alter price tags and buy the merchandise on their own or in collusion with an outside confederate. The growing use of the uniform product code (UPC) as a part of the prepackaged merchandise has reduced the opportunity for customer ticket switching on some merchandise. The ability of employees to change the price in the computer so that it is scanned at a lower price, however, is still possible. One retail security manager indicated that employees have been caught changing the UPC price entry toward the end of the day, indicating that the item is going on sale, so that a confederate might purchase that item at a lower price. The next morning the employee changes the UPC back to the original price, indicating that the sale was a mistake.

4.1.4   Vendor Kickbacks

Employee collusion with vendors in receipting more merchandise than is delivered is common in every business and particularly cannot be overlooked in retail establishments.

4.1.5   Refunds

In cases where refund controls are inadequate, it is a simple matter for employees to write up refund tickets and submit them for cash, either in person or through a confederate. As noted in the introduction to this chapter, the use of store goods that are eventually returned for refund has become a major problem for retailers.

4.1.6   Merchandise Theft

Another common method of theft is employees transporting items of merchandise to their cars in the course of the day. This is often done in several trips or perhaps by accumulating items in one package to be removed just after the store opens or before it closes. If package control procedures are in operation, such employees may purchase an inexpensive item or two and carry out the package with the legitimate sales slip for authorization.

4.1.7   Stocking

Stocking crews have an excellent opportunity to steal enormous amounts of merchandise during the off-hours when they are typically working. The "box and buy" technique is one that provides stock crews with great opportunities. A large item of relatively low cost is removed from the box and placed on the shelf as a display. High-priced items are then placed in the box, which is resealed. The next morning the employee or confederate enters the store and purchases the box supposedly containing the lower-priced item.

4.1.8   Embezzlement

Embezzlement in retail establishments takes on many forms, and merchants must take precautions to prevent it. The first and most important countermeasure that every store should establish is a firm employment policy that includes careful screening of every job applicant. These procedures, discussed in another chapter, may seem burdensome and even more costly than the more cursory checking used by too many stores, but in the long run, they will pay for themselves many times over.

The other basic countermeasure is enlightened supervision. Supervision to confirm that all established procedures are being followed, as well as regular audits of their effectiveness, is vital to the success of any retail security program. No system of controls can be effective if it is not adhered to, and unless it is supervised, it may soon fall into disuse.

4.2 Controls

4.2.1 *Shopping Services*

Retailers have long used shopping service investigations that audit salespeople's efficiency, effectiveness, and honesty and are one of the most accurate methods of determining the conduct of their operations. Such an audit is not inexpensive but has established itself as sufficiently effective in reducing theft and improving personnel performance to pay for itself many times over.

The tests conducted by shopping services or their shoppers usually note the employee's appearance, manner, helpfulness, and "salespersonship" as well as checking for any signs of dishonesty.

Dishonesty testing consists of creating situations in which the employee could easily steal or fail to ring up cash. The employee is then observed or audited by a "shopper" representing the merchant to check on performance under these circumstances. The situations created are in no way construed as entrapment or enticement but represent recreations of normal situations that could be anticipated in the regular course of business. Since shoppers making these tests are unknown to the employees, employee reactions to the tests can be taken as indications of their performance in similar situations with any customer. A full report is submitted after each such test for the manager's reference and review.

Most stores contract for such services on a yearly basis at a set fee with the understanding that inspections will be made with a certain prescribed frequency. In this way, store management has some confidence that an ongoing audit made by objective outside investigators will help uncover inadequate or dishonest performance by sales employees and cashiers.

4.2.2 *Security Audit or Survey*

The store manager and security representative should, at a minimum, conduct an annual audit of operations. The security survey is discussed in Chapter 8.

4.2.3 *Shipping/Receiving Controls*

As in other types of business, the receiving and shipping areas of any retail operation are particularly sensitive. Since the lifeblood of the business flows across these areas many times in the course of a year, it is essential that there be full accountability for all movement of merchandise, that a perpetual inventory be an integral part of the system, and that the areas be restricted to people who are specifically authorized to be there.

All loaded or unloaded merchandise should be subject to periodic spot checks, including, from time to time, a complete unloading and recounting of merchandise already loaded. Cargo seals should be secured and inventoried regularly. All broken shipments should be investigated and secured. All loading and unloading procedures should be supervised.

Maintain a restroom and lounge area for drivers, separate from the facilities used by stockroom, warehouse, or dock personnel, and insist on maintaining this separation. Do not permit drivers to enter storage or merchandise-handling areas.

Your procedures' effectiveness should be audited from time to time by introducing errors into various operations. For example, the number of cases to be shipped might be purposely invoiced incorrectly to see if the checker catches the error, or truck seals might be logged and noted on invoices incorrectly to verify the alertness of the personnel involved.

4.2.4   Trash Removal

Trash removal has always been a problem because it provides an efficient means of removing merchandise from the premises without detection. It is important to have a supervisor on hand when trash is loaded for removal, and it is especially important that trash collection for removal be conducted in a separate area from loading or receiving dock areas. In some instances, it would be wise to inspect the dumpsters after hours. The use of clear plastic trash bags has reduced the potential for removal of some articles, because they are clearly visible through the plastic.

4.2.5   Package Control

It is important that some kind of control procedure be established to inspect packages removed from the premises by employees. Retail outlets have a particularly difficult time with this problem because employees have regular access to large amounts of merchandise, much of it small enough to be easily portable. Receipts must accompany every purchase removed from the premises, and all packages should be subject to full inspection by security personnel.

4.2.6   Employee Morale

The state of employee morale is the key factor in any merchant security program. If employees are totally familiar with all store rules and policies, if they feel that they are appreciated as human beings as well as store employees, if they feel they are an important functioning part of the organization, they will respond with increased efficiency and the problem of dishonesty will diminish. It is essential that management bear in mind that along with its desire to receive reports from up the ladder, it must reciprocate by communicating back down the same ladder. Communication must be a two-way path.

Employees should be motivated to perform, not compelled to do so. Tom Peters refers to "ownership" of the job. The employees should feel that the job is truly important and that they contribute to the firm's profitability. This can be accomplished only by clear statements of policy, supervision insisting on compliance to those policies, and intelligent leadership.[23] In this atmosphere, morale should grow, and the company should prosper.

4.2.7   Civil Recovery

One means of reducing merchants' shrinkage figures is through use of the court system to recover losses. Civil recovery is not a new idea. In fact, the concept goes back to common law. What are new are the statutes that make it easier for merchants to collect for damages resulting from theft. The first such act was passed in 1973 by the state of Nevada. The statutes have passed the test of time and the courts. In 1986, in the case of *Payless Drug Store v. Brown*, the court found that the statute did not violate civil rights or due process.[24]

Summary

Retail security, facing the same problems in the 21st century that it always has, is also faced with the growing problems associated with e-trade. However, for the traditional retail establishments, the problems remain the same. The tools for discovering, preventing, and apprehending internal thieves and shoplifters continue to improve each year. Still, improved technology has not drastically reduced retail shrinkage; thieves continue to find methods to defeat even the best electronic devices.

Finally, the belief that shopping malls could be potential targets for terrorists must be taken seriously. As a result of these concerns, most large retailers have increased surveillance and patrol presence, particularly in large malls.

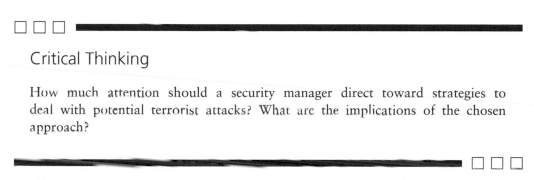

Critical Thinking

How much attention should a security manager direct toward strategies to deal with potential terrorist attacks? What are the implications of the chosen approach?

Review Questions

1. Describe some of the common shoplifting techniques.
2. What are common preventive measures that can be used in a retail store to help reduce the incidence of shoplifting? How effective is each of these measures?
3. What are the legal implications that accompany the arrest of a shoplifter?
4. What are the implications of the growing use of credit and debit cards?
5. Identify check-cashing policies a retail store might set up to reduce its losses from bad checks.
6. Discuss this statement: "The state of employee morale is the key factor in any store's security program."

References

1. Kolettis, Helen, "Guarding the Shelves,"*Security* (February 14, 2002), downloaded 1/15/03, www.securitymagazine.com.
2. www.nrf.com, downloaded 7/2/07.
3. "Utah mall shooter survived Srebrenica massacre," blogs.usatoday.com/ondeadline/2007/02/utah_mall_shoot.html.
4. Rogers, King, "Emerging Trends in Loss Prevention," *Security Technology & Design* (March 2003): 30.
5. "Employee Monitoring," IMRA Research Report, International Mass Retail Association, downloaded 1/15/03, www.imra.org/public/pages/index.cfm?pageid=2519.
6. "Substance Abuse Linked to Increased Problems on the Job,"*Security* (April 1991): 10–11.

7. "Employee Monitoring."

8. Neuborne, Ellen, "Burned Retailers Are Fed Up: Clamping Down," *USA Today* (June 3, 1996): B16.

9. Parker, Edward M., "An Inconvenient Problem," *Security Management* (July 1990): 26.

10. www.nrf.com, 7/2/07.

11. Ibid.

12. "Better Watch Out,"retailindustry.about.com/od/statistics_loss_prevention/1/aa112399.htm.

13. Shoplifting, www.hayesinternational.com/ts_shplftng.html.

14. Curtis, Bob, *Security Control: External Theft* (New York: Chain Store Publishing Corporation, 1971), pp. 75–77.

15. "Retail Security,"*Security* (March 1996): 11.

16. Mesenbrink, John, "Shopping for RFID,"*Security* (October 29, 2002), downloaded 1/15/03, www.securitymagazine.com.

17. Dahl, Judy, "We Love Our Debit Cards," http://hffo.cuna.org/1243333.

18. "Debit Cards," Credit Card Processing Services, downloaded 1/15/03, www.mcvisa.com/debi.html.

19. Swartz, Jon, "Tech Experts Plot to Catch Identity Thieves," *USA Today* (February 9, 2007).

20. Shain, Andrew, "Breaches of Cards on Pace for Record: Recent Break-In Shows Vulnerability of Security," *The Charlotte Observer* (January 21, 2007).

21. Allison, Melissa, and Soto Ouchi, Monica, "In Touch with the Future: Payment by Fingerprint Ready for Checkout Near You,"*The Seattle Times* (January 19, 2007): D1.

22. Zalud, Bill, "Outsiders, Insiders and Theft,"*Security* (August 22, 2002), downloaded 1/15/03, www.securitymagazine.com.

23. Peters, Tom, *Thriving on Chaos: Handbook for a Management Revolution* (New York: Harper & Row Publishers, 1987).

24. *Payless Drug Store v. Brown*, Oregon Supreme Court, 1986.

17

Terrorism and Other Tools of Destruction

This chapter is primarily the work of Dr. Vladimir Sergevnin, editor of the Illinois Law Enforcement Executive Forum journal and research manager of the Illinois Law Enforcement Training and Standards Board Executive Institutes, as well as previous work on terrorist tactics by Dr. Robert Fischer, with coauthors Colonel Fred Berger, U.S. Army, ret., and the late Dr. Bruce Heininger. Portions of this chapter were published as "Terrorism: Nothing New—A Predictive Model for Handling Terrorists Incidents," Illinois Law Enforcement Executive Forum Special Edition 2(1): 2002.

OBJECTIVES

The study of this chapter will enable you to:

1. Understand the problems associated with defining terrorism.
2. Briefly discuss the evaluation of terrorist tactics.
3. Identify major terrorist organizations.
4. Know the various motivations for adopting terrorist tactics.
5. Identify some of the tools being used to combat terrorism.

1 Introduction

With the events of September 11, 2001, the U.S. and world community became explosively aware of the power of terrorism as a tool of war. Although terrorism is not a new tool of war, the sheer magnitude of the attack on the World Trade Center has assured terrorist groups of recognition beyond that horrendous event. This attack, the most significant on the continental United States since 1812, made a deep impact on the U.S. government, the people's collective psychology, and the national security industry. Today, there is virtually no organization, agency, or business in the United States that does not have, in one way or another, a security plan for terrorist attack. Nationally there are thousands of agencies and institutions, training entities, universities and colleges, and Websites providing information, research, education, and recommendations related to terrorist incidents and appropriate security. It can be explained only because the threat of terrorist acts against the United States has significantly elevated since the end of the 1980s, along with an increased level of public awareness. All this has created a tremendous increase in counterterrorism investments on individual, local, and governmental levels. According to recent data, in 2007 the U.S. total military expenditure was 48 percent of the world military spending at $1.36 trillion, with NATO at 23 percent, China at 9 percent, Russia at 4 percent, and Iran at 0.5 percent.[1]

The Western world has heavily invested in a so-called "war on terror" with mostly vague and predominately controversial results. Ideologically, the last century generally saw decentralized terrorist groups converge into anti-Western and anti-Christian movements which do not require constant operational communications but produce an unlimited stream of individual terrorist recruits and cells by means of self-indoctrination and radicalization via advanced channels of communications. Geopolitically, the United States transformed from a firm ally of the Muslim world fighting against the Soviet Union during the war in Afghanistan to a definite enemy for many Muslim countries. Iraq has since became a new epicenter for *jihad* against the Western powers. Two consecutive invasions by Christian superpowers, with different political systems, ensured Muslim's public opinion that these aggressions are religiously motivated. Tactically, the terrorist movement shifted from targeting governmental officials and military to killing civilians at an unprecedented scale, using the effective, precise, and flexible potential of the suicide mission. Al-Qaeda and it leaders not only survived the most widespread and best-equipped hunt; they became ideological and tactical leaders and icons for thousands and thousands of followers.

Terrorism will be a major world concern for the visible future, although the hype factor may be more significant than the actual probability of becoming a victim. In 1986 only 12 U.S. citizens were killed and 100 wounded in worldwide international terrorism. In 1987 the number killed dropped to 7, with only 40 wounded. By 1989, 16 U.S. citizens were killed and only 19 wounded.[2] In 1995, 70 attacks were directed toward U.S. businesses abroad[3] and 10 U.S. citizens were killed. The following numbers of U.S. citizen deaths caused by international terrorism from 1995 to 2000 provides some explanation as to why terrorism was not a priority for the U.S. government prior 9/11: 1996, 25; 1997, 6; 1998, 12; 1999, 5; and 2000, 19.[4] Between January 2005 and May 2006 there were only 9 American civilians wounded as a result of terrorist attacks, and in 2006, 28 American citizens were killed while overseas.

In 2006 in the European Union countries there were fewer than 500 terrorist incidents, whereas Islamist-authored attacks accounted for less than 1 percent of the recorded incidents over the same period.[5]

Still, the loss of even one life and the fear associated with becoming a victim cannot be overestimated. With the events of the mid-1990s, including the bombing of the Federal Building in Oklahoma City, the 1993 bombing of the World Trade Center in New York, the capture of the Unibomber, and the bombing at the Olympics in Atlanta, terrorism reached the forefront of the American public's interest. Experts agreed that terrorism in the United States was just beginning. Their predictions proved too accurate, as evidenced by perhaps the most spectacular terrorist attack to date, the 2001 destruction of the twin towers and World Trade Center complex using hijacked commercial airplanes.

The impact of all this on the corporate United States is very significant. Terrorists have targeted 20 of the top 25 U.S. firms, and terrorism has had an impact on almost all international firms. The largest firms have taken security precautions. An analysis of U.S. business victimization by terrorist attack demonstrated that almost every type of U.S. business overseas has been targeted.[6] Terrorism threats made against the Fortune 1000 companies increased from 17 in 1998 to 40 in 2003.[7]

One of the newer (but certainly not new) trends in terrorist attacks on companies has been assault on executives, primarily kidnapping for ransom. Risk insurance, and the provision of related risk and crisis management services, has become an established industry; it is estimated that as much as $100 million in premiums is paid globally each year.[8] (Chapter 8 provides additional information on terrorism insurance.)

This practice has been common in many foreign countries in sub-Saharan Africa, Eastern Europe, Central Asia, the Balkans, and the Middle East and is also increasing in the United States. The problem seems to be related to the increase in terrorism throughout the world. To be able to develop adequate protection for executives, security managers must understand the terrorist problem and the strategies of various terrorist leaders.

Although the number of terrorists is small, their actions have a great deal of impact. Throughout the world there are more than 42 major terrorist organizations, each varying in size from a few members to several hundred.[9] In all, there are more than 3,000 members. According to the Office of International Criminal Justice at the University of Illinois at Chicago, there were 300 extremist groups operating around the globe fewer than 10 years ago.[10] However, only four or five such groups have enough members and support to be transnational threats.

The real problem arises from terrorist sympathizers. Most of these groups have support from various governments and thus have access to automatic weapons, surface-to-air missiles, antitank weapons, and sophisticated bombs. In 1988 Pan Am Flight 103 was blown from the air over Scotland by a bomb. In 2002 SAM handheld missiles targeted a commercial jetliner flying over Africa. Luckily the aircraft took evasive action and survived.

Why does terrorism exist? Although political terrorism often appears irrational and unpredictable to victims and observers, it is very rational from the terrorist point of view. Basic to most terrorist theory is that violence will bring the uncommitted masses into the conflict on the side of right—of course, the terrorist point of view. Terrorist actions are violent because:

1. They show the strength of the group.
2. They are provocative, causing the general population to pay attention to the group's activities.

> Today terrorism is a very viable method of attracting not only local but also national or world attention through the mass media.

In the last few years, terrorist organizations have shifted their focus from governments to business and other soft targets. Since 1975, targeting of businesses has become more widespread, even in the United States. According to Global Terrorism Database, between 1998 and 2003 terrorists targeted 17 businesses in the United States.[11] Attacks on private businesses in New York and Chicago and on the West Coast are indicative of this trend. Terrorists use the rich nation/poor nation argument, whereby multinational and other large companies are portrayed as exploiters of the poor. Many of these large companies are rich enough to pay enormous ransoms, and in the past, they have paid the ransoms. Coupled with government target hardening (increased security measures such as state-of-the-art hardware), this makes companies more attractive targets. Because of these trends, businesses are more vulnerable to terrorism than at any time in the past.

Despite this vulnerability, the cost of the additional security measures must always be justified because businesses are profit-oriented. In many cases, CEOs view the cure as worse than the disease, and many are unwilling to give up their personal liberty and freedom for protection. These same CEOs generally are unwilling to concede that their firms could be targets of terrorists. In addition, many corporations are willing to pay ransoms rather than invest in protective measures, because they believe that a ransom will work out cheaper than constantly spending money on security.

The United States and many other countries, however, have adopted a posture of not making concessions to terrorists. Following the destruction of the World Trade Center, President George W. Bush declared a worldwide war on terrorism. The vast majority of the world's governments joined him.

2   Current Issues

The last decade has seen tremendous changes in international terrorism activities all over the world. The recent history of international terrorism attacks, from the World Trade Center to the hostage situation in Beslan, Russia (2004) and the Glasgow airport bombing attempt (2007), has activated mass media and expert attention, reminding citizens over the globe that international terrorism is not distant from each of us and is capable of affecting national and global security. International cooperation in countering terrorism is becoming very strong. When the United States launched Operation Enduring Freedom in October 2001, a total of 136 countries offered a range of military assistance.

There is definite abuse in the use of the term *terrorism* by mass media and various political groups and movements. Despite the tremendous amount of research and publications, international terrorism remains a phenomenon that is not clearly understood, adequately analyzed, or effectively controlled. The limited scope of international terrorism analysis can be explained by political, ideological, and behavior approaches, which easily can overshadow the real substance of the phenomenon.

Present-day international terrorism is quite different from old-fashioned terrorist acts, such as assassinations (Archduke Franz Ferdinand in 1914) or bombing (Russian Emperor Alexander II in 1881). Modern forms of international terrorism are more lethal and suicidal, more ideologically religious, and more technologically advanced. Incidents of international terrorism caused around 1,500 deaths worldwide in the period 1991 to 1996.[12] Generally speaking, the human life value vacuum of international terrorists has also struck humankind at the beginning of the 21st century.

According to the U.S. Department of State, three trends in terrorism were identified in 2006: (1) emergence of more decentralized operatives or groups involved in terrorism activities; (2) "sophistication" of terrorist activities through informational technologies and Internet finance; and (3) convergence of terrorist activity and international crime.[13]

The lack of coordinated efforts at the international level means that various countries' security agencies must assume some of the initiative in establishing partnerships on the basis of similar approaches and standards.

This chapter is an attempt to make a contribution to the United States' ongoing international terrorism preparedness effort. It is designed for academic and pedagogical purposes to provoke interest and controversy. This chapter will demonstrate to students how international terrorism is defined and will shape the conclusions they reach about terrorist characteristics and counterterrorism implications.

3   Historical Background

International terrorism has existed throughout the history of humans and society. Modern terrorism has evolved from several epicenters, which we explore here.

3.1   Europe

Europe is a motherland of modern terrorism. Members of a radical society or Jacobins' club of revolutionaries promoted the Reign of Terror in France, and other extreme measures were active mainly from 1789 to 1794. French revolutionaries used terror as a remedy for political transformation:

> *One of the original justifications for terror was that man would be totally reconstructed; one didn't have to worry about the kinds of means one was using because the reconstruction itself would be total and there would be no lingering after-effects ...*[14]

Terror Is the Order of the Day, or *Que la Terreur soit a L'ordre du jour* (Carlyle, 2002), was designed as a temporary domestic policy oriented on suppression of the enemies of the French Revolution, but its legacy provided international implications for more than two centuries. The original purpose of terror was to eliminate any opposition to the revolutionary Jacobins' regime and to consolidate power. The latest applications of governmental or state terrorism can be found in Soviet Russia (Civil War, 1918–1921), Communist China (Great Proletarian Cultural Revolution, 1966–1969), and Cambodia (Khmer Rouge Regime, 1975–1979).

These early experiments with state or governmental terrorism outlined several important objectives of this method of governing, as Table 17.1 shows.

From the French revolutionaries who employed the strategies of international terrorism against European countries to Russian terrorists that carried us into the 19th and 20th centuries, we can observe a steady trend to gain political and ideological objectives. Marxism reinforced this orientation.

Considerable numbers of leftist and right-wing terrorist organizations were formed in the late 1960s in Europe, including Germany's Red Army Faction (RAF), France's Action Directe, Italy's Red Brigades, and German neo-Nazism.

3.2   Marxism

Karl Marx, along with Friedrich Engels, developed the communist doctrine of the class struggle, which has been a major agency of historical change. They theorized that the capitalist system would inevitably, after the period of the dictatorship of proletariat, be superseded by a socialist state and classless communist society. A dictatorship of the proletariat is necessary to ensure the removal of the capitalist society. The dictatorship is above the law because it *is* the law and therefore can be unlimited. By introducing the First International Working Men's Association of communist organizations in 1864, Marx and Engels launched the idea of international or global socialist revolution, employing any necessary means of class struggle, including terrorist tactics, against dominant classes. The international character of the proletarian revolution was derived from the international development of the capitalist society.[15]

Table 17.1 Terrorism as a Method of Governance

	Oppression	Consolidation	Reconstruction	Threat Orientation
France	Monarchy, clergy, aristocracy, and common people	A dictatorship operating through the Committee of Public Safety, the Jacobins	Introducing new rule through the Revolutionary Tribunal	Anyone who disagreed with the Jacobins was a "threat to the Republic"
Russia	Monarchy, clergy, aristocracy, owners, landlords, farmers, intelligentsia, church	Power around the Communist Party and Lenin, dictatorship of proletariat	Introducing communist values and priorities	Anyone who disagreed with the Communists was an "enemy to the people"
China	Communist party officials, state leaders, "wrong-headed intellectuals," farmers, intelligentsia	Regained control over the Communist Party by Mao Zedong through Red Guards and Cultural Revolution	Destroying "outdated," "counterrevolutionary" values. Reeducating intellectuals by sending them for hard labor	Anyone who disagreed with Mao's group was sent to the countryside
Cambodia	Owners, entrepreneurs, intellectuals, city dwellers, military and state officials	Power around Pol Pot and Angkar (organization)	"Purify the Khmer race," create classless society	Anyone who doesn't want to be part of Red Khmer society will be exterminated

3.3 Russia

Russia has a long history of coexisting with political terrorism and lives under fear of terror. Russian anarchist Peter Kropotkin promoted the fundamental philosophical basis for utilization of terrorism as the tool for revolution, proclaiming the concept "propaganda of the deed." Sergei Nechaev might be called the extremist forerunner of modern Russian terrorism; Dostoevsky used him as a model for the revolutionary protagonist of *The Devils*. Nechaev was the father of political terror, which he developed as a revolutionary tool as early as 1869, when he published the *Revolutionary Catechism*, in which he defined a revolutionary as:

> A man who is already lost ... he has broken all links with society and the world of civilization, with its laws and conventions, with its social etiquette and its moral code. The revolutionary is an implacable enemy, and he carries on living only so that he can ensure the destruction of society.[16]

For Nechaev, when it came to revolution, the end always justified the means. He believed that a terrorist must be:

> ... hard towards himself, he must be hard towards others also. All the tender and effeminate emotions of kinship, friendship, love, gratitude, and even honor must be stifled in him by a cold and single-minded passion for the revolutionary cause. There exists for him only one delight, one consolation,

one reward and one gratification—the success of the revolution. Night and day he must have but one thought, one aim—merciless destruction. In cold-blooded and tireless pursuit of this aim, he must be prepared both to die himself and to destroy with his own hands everything that stands in the way of its achievement.[17]

This trend became even stronger 10 years later when the rebel group named itself the People's Will (*Narodnaya Volya*), the name under which the radicals were responsible for the assassination of Alexander II in 1881. The objective of the group was to cause a coup or overthrow the Russian government. They believed that the assassinations would be the trigger for revolution and would finally change the order of the regime.

The Bolsheviks and Lenin inherited terrorist approaches and converted them into state policy. The communist state developed two main types of terrorism. First, there was the internal policy of using terror for the benefit of establishing a so-called "dictatorship of proletariat." The goal was to suppress and physically eliminate opposing forces in the country and convince the population to be loyal to the new regime. In September 1918 the Russian communist government officially announced the policy of "Red Terror." Hundreds of thousands died; millions were scared.

Second, they supported the idea of international terrorism with the goal of causing destruction and chaos, resulting in a world communist revolution. There were many cases of state supported terrorist actions. Soviet secret police (NKVD, OGPU, KGB) even established a special department that was in charge of the elimination of popular political figures worldwide (e.g., the assassination of Leon Trotsky in August 1940).

Stalin developed terrorism as one of the most powerful tools of state policy, but individual and group terrorism was almost unknown under Stalin, Khrushchev, and Brezhnev. Isolated acts of terrorism by individuals (e.g., the explosion in Moscow's subway in January 1977) got the state security agencies' (KGB and MVD) attention, and terrorists were arrested and executed almost immediately.

3.4 Ireland

Ireland has been one of the longstanding centers of modern terrorism. At the end of the 19th century the Irish Republican Brotherhood (originally formed by Irish immigrants in New York City) launched a campaign of assassinations and bombing against the British, whom they considered oppressors. The Easter Rising of 1916 helped to establish the Irish Republican Army, which was the main political and terrorist organization pushing for the formation of the Irish Free State.

Terrorism related to Northern Ireland has significantly diminished in recent years, with the Provisional IRA, Dissident Irish Republican terrorist groups, and the main Loyalist groups ceasing their terrorist campaigns and engaging in the peace process. On May 8, 2007, the Northern Ireland Executive was successfully restored with the creation of a new government under a power-sharing agreement between nationalist and Unionist political parties.

3.5 Palestine

A new chapter of international terrorism was opened in the 1960s with the establishment of the Palestine Liberation Organization (PLO), led by Yassir Arafat. This Palestinian group vowed to fight the war of attrition against the occupying Israeli forces. In 1982 the Soviet Union initiated and sponsored the International Conference of the World Center for Resistance to Imperialism, Zionism, Racism, Reaction, and Fascism, which was held in Tripoli. This meeting resulted in the formation of a committee consisting of the Soviet Union, Libya, Cuba, Iran, Syria, and North Korea. The goal of this committee was the establishment of international terrorist training programs to prepare fighters to battle against all type of oppressors, primarily the United States.[18]

In 2007, an important transformation of power happened in Palestine. Hamas, a radical Islamist political group, forcibly seized control of Gaza from rival Fatah, an essentially secular Palestinian group. Therefore, for the first time, the significant part of Palestinian territories—the Gaza Strip—is under the authority of a radical group that regularly uses terrorist tactics.[19]

3.6 Chechnya

In 1999 Islamic justice was established in Chechnya. Terrorism, including a series of bombings in Moscow (where several hundred people were killed), erupted. After that, several thousand Islamic militants, armed members of a Chechen Muslim fundamentalist group whose aim was to merge Dagestan with neighboring Chechnya in a single Islamic state, invaded Dagestan. Russia responded with police and military attacks by federal forces, and the militants retreated; the incident contributed to Russia's decision to invade Chechnya later in 1999. International extremist organizations, including Osama bin Laden and other criminal associations, back the Chechen terrorists.

The territory of Chechnya is used to host and train terrorists from Arab countries and some Western European countries. The numerous terrorist groups are free and go unpunished and make raids in the territory of Russia. In 1999 20 terrorist acts in the Russian Federation were registered by the MVD security agency. In 2001 representatives of terrorist organizations were registered by the Federation of Small Businesses (FSB) in 49 of 89 states in Russia, and in 2001, the terrorist groups twice attempted to gain access to Russian nuclear munitions dumps. Security agencies do not exclude the possibility that terrorist groups may directly attack nuclear installations.

For the last three years terrorist attacks have mutated from Chechnya to other republics in the region. During this period there have been several extremely sophisticated and well-coordinated attacks. Internationally funded Chechen-led groups returned to hostage taking as a terrorist tactic in the raid on Beslan's School in September 2004, in which 334 people were killed, including 186 children. Chechen terrorist groups shifted from mostly military operations to the following tactics: random attacks on military installations; random attacks on tourists and the deliberate killing of foreign-aid workers; incidents of kidnapping, hostage taking, and bombing of apartment buildings (from 1999 to 2005 more than 5,000 people were kidnapped by Chechen terrorists); and terrorist attacks on economic infrastructures, including energy distribution, transportation, and banking.

3.7 Terrorism in the 21st Century

Since the beginning of the communist rule in Russia, state sponsors of terrorism have provided political, financial, operational, and military support to terrorist groups around the world. Without such states, terrorist groups would not have the same level of stability and ideological support. The limited success of international efforts materialized in

2003 when Libya renounced terrorism and abandoned its WMD programs. North Korea shut down its nuclear program in 2007.

Diminishing the volume of state sponsorship for terrorist groups forces them to explore links with transnational and national organized crime entities. Several countries are taking steps in preventing this symbiosis. In June 2000, the Anti-Terrorist Center of the Commonwealth of Independent States (Armenia, Azerbaijan, Belarus, Georgia, Kazakhstan, Kyrgyzstan, Moldova, Russia, Tajikistan, Turkmenistan, Ukraine, and Uzbekistan) was established with the purpose of coordinating counterterrorism measures in the territory of the former Soviet Union. In November 2001, the main organized crime administration of the criminal police service at the MVD established a special section for fighting terrorism and extremism. National police offices in the seven federal districts have already set up terrorism sections. The officers intend to cooperate with foreign law enforcement bodies in carrying out antiterrorist activities.

In 2007, the U.S. State Department included the following countries as sponsors of terrorism: Sudan, Cuba, Iran, and Syria. Venezuela was certified by the Secretary of State as "not fully cooperating" with U.S. counterterrorism efforts.[20]

There is very little evidence that Cuba is currently active in international terrorism. The State Department described Iran as the most active state supporter of terrorism. Iran and Syria continue to support groups such as Hamas and Hizballah and, according to President George W. Bush, Iran supports al-Qaeda.

4 Implications of a Changing World

Law enforcement officials around the world have reported a significant increase in the range and scope of international terrorist activity since the early 2000s. This is in contrast with the 1990s, when the total number of terrorist incidents worldwide declined, but the percentage of terrorist acts resulting in fatalities has grown.[21]

Recently the number of incidents has grown from about 11,000 in 2005 to around 14,000 in 2006, and fatalities are up from about 14,500 to about 20,500.[22] According to the Department of State, in 2006 the number of terrorist incidents globally increased 25 percent in comparison with 2005.[23]

The level and severity of this activity and the accompanying growth in the power and influence of international terrorist organizations have raised concerns among governments all over the world—particularly Western democracies—about the threat terrorists pose to democracy and stability in many countries and to the global economy. In 2006, mainly in Iraq and Afghanistan, terrorist incidents claimed more than 20,000 lives, which is 5,800 more deaths than in 2005. International terrorist networks have been quick to take advantage of the opportunities resulting from the revolutionary changes in world politics, business, technology, and communications that have strengthened democracy and free markets and brought the world's nations closer together.

The end of the Cold War resulted in the shift of political and economic relations not only in Europe but also around the world. This change opened the way for substantially increased trade, movement of people, and capital flows between democracies and free-market countries and the formerly closed societies and markets that had been controlled by the Soviet Union. These developments have allowed international terrorists to expand their networks and increase their cooperation in illicit activities and financial transactions. Terrorists have taken advantage of transitioning and more open economies to establish financial ventures that are helpful in budgeting international terrorist activities: training camps, "sleeper cells," and purchase of weaponry and explosives.

International terrorists have extended their reach by building globe-circling infrastructures. Lebanese Hizballah, whose presence now reaches most of the continents, has led the way. But other terrorist organizations, with agendas as diverse as that of the Palestinian group Hamas or the Sri Lankan Liberation Tigers of Tamil Eelam, have their active presence far from the lands where their objectives are focused.[24] And of course, following the bombing of the World Trade Center in September 2001, al-Qaeda has taken its place as a major world terrorist "player."

Present-day terrorist networks are loosely structured, acting without an operational structure and with regular connections across the globe. They are bound by shared extremist ideology or experiences. Some of these networks are directly connected to al-Qaeda, but most are autonomous, and both work to carry out terrorist attacks and are influenced by radical beliefs shared over the Internet. The terrorists draw their motivation from sporadically delivered messages articulated by leadership icons such as Osama bin Laden.

Revolutionary advances in information and communications technologies have brought most of the world population closer together. Terrorist networks just as easily use modern telecommunications and information systems. Sophisticated communications equipment greatly facilitates international terrorist activities, including coordination of terrorist acts, and affords terrorists sufficient security from law enforcement counterterrorist operations.

Through the use of digital technologies, international terrorists have an unprecedented capability to obtain, process, and protect information from law enforcement investigations. They can use the interactive capabilities of advanced computers and telecommunications systems to plot terrorist strategies against U.S. representatives and institutions all over the globe, to find the most efficient routes and methods for financial transactions, and to create international virtual networks. Some terrorist networks are using advanced technologies for counterintelligence purposes and for tracking law enforcement operations.

The modern megatrend of globalization and the reduction of barriers to the movement of people, commodities, and financial transactions across borders have enabled international terrorist networks to expand their global reach. International terrorist groups are able to operate increasingly outside traditional models, take quick advantage of new opportunities, and move more readily into the most vulnerable areas of the Western world. The major international terrorist groups have become more global in their operations and have developed more threatening goals. Since the end of the Cold War, terrorist groups from Middle Eastern countries have increased their international presence and worldwide networks or have become involved in more lethal terrorist acts. Most of the world's major international terrorist groups are aiming toward the United States.

5   In Search of a Definition for International Terrorism

Numerous attempts to produce a general definition of terrorism have been more focused on terrorism as a concept (converging it with intentions and justifications) than a term and consequently include the damaging impact from ideologies and political partisanships.

The first recorded definition of the term *terrorism* was given in the 1795 supplement of the *Dictionaire of the Academe Français* as *system regieme de la terror*. The Jacobins used the term when speaking and writing about themselves.

At present there is no precise or widely accepted definition of international terrorism, or terrorism. The difficulty in defining derives from (1) highly politicized usage of terrorism and terrorism-related terminology for national or ideological purposes; (2) vagueness of boundaries for terrorist acts in comparison with crime, military actions, use of force, or threat; and (3) attempts to infuse a concept into a term rather than defining a phenomenon. Alex Schmid surveyed more than 100 definitions of terrorism and found two characteristics of the definition:

- An individual is being terrorized.
- The meaning of the terrorist act is derived from its target and victims.[25]

These characteristics show that we are experiencing only the initial stage in scientific analysis of the phenomenon. There are many approaches to analyzing and defining international terrorism, and we should mention the most influential.

5.1 Political Approaches

Political analysis of international terrorism views it as one of the instruments in a political process. The Marxist-Leninist ideology and many other revolutionary factions accept terrorism, including international terrorism, as a legitimate instrument in the class struggle. For Marxist-Leninists the political goal justifies the means. The political goal is above any law or moral code in the current society. These ideologies believe that it is not immoral for social revolutionaries to use terrorism, because it leads to fulfillment of the political goal.

Governmental institutions of the United States are implementing the political approach in analyzing and defining terrorism. Information pertaining to the political definition of terrorism is contained in Title 22 of the United States Code, Section 2656f(d). That statute contains the following definitions:

- The term *terrorism* means premeditated, *politically* motivated violence perpetrated against noncombatant targets by subnational groups or clandestine agents, usually intended to influence an audience.
- The term *international terrorism* means terrorism involving citizens or the territory of more than one country.
- The term *terrorist group* means any group practicing, or that has significant subgroups that practice, international terrorism.

The U.S. government has employed this definition of terrorism for statistical and analytical purposes since 1983. At the same time, not all terrorist acts have political motivation. This approach excludes those whose motivation is religious or personal and who are not trying to change any political institution in the foreign society.

5.2 Criminal Approaches

Most terrorists claim to be not criminals but freedom (religion, ideology, special interest) fighters. However, almost all terrorist acts are characterized by criminal violence, which violates criminal codes and is punishable by the criminal justice system of the state. In this case, terrorism is defined as "a *crime*, consisting of an intentional act of *political violence* to create an atmosphere of *fear*."[26] Some definitions of international terrorism include just violence, but a few years ago, for example, the Islamic Army in Yemen warned foreigners to leave the country if they valued their lives but did not actually carry out its threat.[27] Using a criminal justice approach, we will find no terrorism, because any of the acts will simply be crimes.

5.3   Militaristic Approaches

Several international lawyers see a possible solution to the dilemma in a definition of the laws of war. If the laws of war will be applied to terrorists, they will be treated as soldiers who commit atrocities in international armed conflicts.[28] If this approach is utilized, we have to treat our own citizens as people in the war zone to prevent possible terrorist acts. Furthermore, not all terrorist acts have an international character.

5.4   The Physiological Approach

The physiological approach suggests a tendency to imitate behavior that is successful in delivering a message to the public. This approach analyzes the power of inspiration drawn from the media. David G. Hubbard concludes that much of terrorist violence is rooted not in the psychology but in the physiology of the terrorist, partly the result of "stereotyped, agitated tissue response" to stress.[29] From this approach, international terrorism is targeted more at an audience or the public in general rather than the immediate victims. But this definition excludes those terrorist acts that targeted one person, or a very limited circle of the public, or the military. In this regard the violence against the U.S. battleship *Cole* would not be considered terrorism.

The psychological approach is not interested in the political or social contexts of international terrorists but in the terrorists' personalities, their recruitment, and their induction into terrorist organizations, beliefs, attitudes, motivations, and careers.

Some researchers view terrorism as a "syndrome." Recent results have thus far found little support for the syndrome view. The psychological nature of terrorism's users is consistent with the tool view, affording an analysis of terrorism in terms of *goal and means* psychology.[30]

The weak points of this approach are that the analysis isolates the phenomenon from the social and political context of international terrorism, and a slight presumption is made that international terrorists are born, not made.

5.5   Group Behavior

Another productive approach describes terrorism as rational strategy decided by group.[31] This approach is rather close to the political one because it requires collective decision making in the utilization of terrorist tactics to reach group goals. Group behavior is wider than the political approach because it can include, for example, criminal acts of international terrorism, in which the goals will not be political.

Very often the definitions of terrorism mention only "groups" or clandestine agents as an active core of this type of activity. But in this case we're excluding state-sponsored international terrorism.

To understand international terrorism, we must always assess what exactly constitutes terrorism and the definition in use. International terrorism, or terrorism, has to be analyzed as an instrument, not a concept.

5.6   The Multifactor Approach

International terrorism preferably can be viewed as a multidimensional phenomenon. It would be misleading to analyze it by a single-cause approach. International terrorism can be attributed to the same type of events as social revolution, revolt, uprisings, and any kind of political, social, ideological, or religious unrest. Terrorism in general, and international terrorism in particular, is an instrumental phenomenon and as a remedy could be utilized for multiple causes, forces, organizations, and individuals.

6   Terrorism as a Tactic, Instrument, or Method

Terrorism is a term describing a method or instrument of utilizing violence, intimidation, threat, and fear against an individual, a populace, or a government. Terrorists use a wide range of force, violence, and brutality with the purpose of manipulating human behavior and illegally reaching their goals.

These goals are diverse but can be grouped into the following categories:

- Political—change of regime, overthrow the government, *coup d'etat*, damage relations between countries, disgrace the political system
- Social—upset the social order
- Economic—damage the economic order; upset the budget, interrupt vital supplies such as oil, gas, and electricity
- Ethnic and religious—fundamentalist sects, racism, genocide, spread of new beliefs
- Ideological
- Personal

Categorizing and separating domestic from international terrorism depends on the target (domestic or international) or forces (individual, group, criminal, military, state sponsored). Any kind of individual, global, regional, or local player can use terrorism. We have to separate terror as application of fear for criminal or insane purposes from political terrorism, which has a definite objective: gaining political power. Application of fear is a universal method used in military operations, and the criminal justice systems (punishment).

Terrorism in general covers a wide range of criminal acts with a focus on use of violence and destruction or threat of violence and destruction to inculcate fear. The acts are undertaken by an individual, an organized group, or a state, driven by generally ethnic, religious, nationalist, separatist, political (including governing), ideological, mentally deviant, and socioeconomical motivations. It is a vast area of crime with a flavor of nontraditional motivation.

Numerous publications describe international terrorism as terrorist acts with international goals, targets, and consequences[32] or as acts committed by a group or individual that is foreign-based and/or directed by countries or groups outside the United States or whose activities transcend national boundaries. See Table 17.2 for a typology of international terrorism.

These definitions are not accurate because, for example, stealing of diplomatic mail should be included. International terrorism is a term describing the utilization of fear and intimidation, including violence, brutality, and invasion of privacy, across national boundaries with the purpose of political, social, economic, ideological, religious, ethnic, or cultural change.

Table 17.2 Typology of International Terrorism

Typology of International Terrorism	Origin	Targets	Tactics	Consequences
Social revolutionary	Connection to foreign country	Western society, culture and religion in general, targets abroad, overthrowing foreign governments, or home targets of foreign origin such as riots against foreigners, embassies, companies, burning refugee shelters, and the ransacking of embassies-although such acts were supported, or instigated, by the State.	Bombs and explosives	Panic
Nationalist-separatist	Acts transcend national boundaries			Social and political disorder
Ideological			Assassinations	
Religious fundamentalist			Armed assaults	Economic and financial loss
State sponsored			Kidnappings	
Organized crime			Barricade and hostage situations	Mass media pressure on the governments
Military				
Left/right extremism			Hijackings Insurgency Hostage taking Coup d'Etat, Guerilla warfare Clandestine networks Sabotage communications	Impulse for domestic terrorism

The concept of traditional "war" requires the mobilization of political, financial, and industrial resources for the development and production of modern weapons.

The concept of traditional "international terrorism" requires the mobilization of political, financial, and industrial resources for the development and production of modern homeland security and defense. It is much more expensive because instead of a front, we have an unlimited number of potential targets.

Terrorism requires more efforts in the political sphere, that may eliminate potential grounds for terrorism activity.

7 Characterizing Modern Terrorism

7.1 Ideological Shift

At the end of the 19th century and beginning of the 20th, the dominant form of international terrorism was an ideological one. The phenomenon of ideological terrorism was brought to the global stage via bombings and the extermination of "enemies of communism" beginning from around 1917. These acts were perpetrated by such states as the Soviet Union and of late by groups such as the Red Army Faction, Red Brigades, and the Japanese Red Army. The end of the Cold War resulted in the shift from antidemocratic or anticapitalist, Marxist-based, ideologically motivated international political terrorism to ethnic and religious terrorism.

One of the reasons that the ethno-religious type of international terrorism has become dominant is the globalization of the Western type of economy and culture in traditionally culturally and economically endemic countries, such as in the Middle East region and Asia. International terrorism has an anti-American, anti-Western trend because these countries view the spread of "global Western economy and culture," an increasing U.S. presence in the Middle East (Israel, Iraq, Afghanistan) and the Pacific Rim, Western development of the Caspian oil reserves (Uzbekistan, Kazakhstan, Azerbaijan), and flourishing Western technological development in the Middle East and Pacific Rim as a threat to their powers and traditional ways of governing. It's not surprising, then, that many of the international terrorist organizations are state sponsored.

Marxism was a dominant basis for terrorist ideology (1848 to the end of the 1980s). Communist ideology sought a global communist revolution through initiating riots, uprisings, and coups against imperialism and "weak bourgeois national governments." The period from 1848 to 1917 saw political parties and trade-union organizations sponsored by individuals and opposition groups. From 1917 to the end of the 1980s was a period characterized by state-sponsored ideological "warfare," the states being mainly the Soviet Union and Warsaw Pact states.

International terrorism networking was established through the First, Second, Third, and Fourth International and national communist or totalitarian organizations. The First International, as it was to be called, was formed in 1864 in London and was composed of various elements: French, Italian, and British. Marx composed the Inaugural Address of the International, which is now considered a historic document. The organization stood for efforts of workers against anarchists and middle-class reformers of the time.

The Second International was founded in 1889 in Belgium. The primary members were German and Russian social democrats. The group worked to advance labor legislation and to strengthen the democratic socialist movement. It failed in its primary concern, the prevention of war. With the outbreak of World War I, the International collapsed.

The Third or Communist International was created in 1919 under the leadership of Lenin. This group's goal was to bring about world revolution. The group was not supported by many mainstream socialists and was dissolved in 1943.

The role of ideology is still significant, and old-fashioned "revolutionary" organizations continue to exist, such as the Turkish Revolutionary People's Liberation Party-Front and the Peruvian Sendero Luminoso (Shining Path). But the dominant terrorist ideology has an ethno-religious character. The spread of ethno-religious ideology is a basis for international terrorism based on ethno-religious conflicts in the Caucasus, Balkans, Middle East, South Asia, and central Africa.

Table 17.3 A Comparison of Communism and Radical Islam

Communism	Radical Islam
Worldwide communist state	Worldwide Islamic state
Equality	Equality
Common property	Sharing property
Class struggle results in overthrowing capitalism	Faith struggle (jihad) results in overthrowing of Russian capitalist society
Anti-Semitism	Anti-Semitism
State terror against "enemies of the state"	Terror against "infidels"
Terror against "enemies of state"	International terror against imperialists, occupiers
International terror against imperialists	

A comparison of communist and radical Islamic ideology demonstrates some close similarities and explains its attractiveness in many countries formerly sympathetic to socialism, as Table 17.3 demonstrates.

Ethno-religious ideological activities are very often state-sponsored, which gives them more informational stability and coordination. Ethnic ideology deals with ethnic identity, solidarity, self-determination, and domination. Religious ideological activities usually are oriented toward establishing "the pure and the only true religion" and aimed at spreading certain beliefs and defeating modern Western ideology.

The 21st century is promising to be a century of an ideological war for radical religious indoctrination opposing Free World ideology, beliefs, and values. It will be fought by all means of propaganda in the format of modern channels of communication.

Modern terrorist organizations realized much earlier than Western governments the power of propaganda. Unlike communist propaganda, democratic governments are generally hesitant to make aggressive ideological responses because of the religious underlining of the radical Islamic propaganda. It should be realized that counter-ideological measures can be more effective than military ones and should focus on promoting democratic values; providing a Western view on events inside Islamic countries—supporting education and social activity, especially for women; controlling terrorist virtual communications; and depicting terrorists as criminals, not freedom fighters.

Terrorist organizations use Websites to conduct psychological warfare, generate publicity, and disseminate propaganda as well as for data mining, fundraising, recruitment and mobilization, networking, planning and coordination, and sharing information on their activities, organization, plans, and political, religious, and social goals to glorify their actions. In 2005 there were more than 4,300 Websites with terrorist affiliations and content; in 2006 the FBI counted as many as 6,000 extremist Websites. Since January 2006, the primary clearinghouse for jihadist information releases has been an Internet outpost called the Al-Fajr Center. The Al-Fajr Center has many divisions that are devoted to hacking, intelligence, propaganda, publications, multimedia, and cybersecurity. Other influential online groups are the Ansar e-Group, the Jihadi Brigades, and the Global Islamic Media Front, also known as GIMF.[33] Some recent reports conclude that Internet chat rooms are now major venues for recruitment and radicalization by terrorist groups like al-Qaeda, and video-hosting Websites like YouTube broaden the outreach.[34] According to the FBI, in 2006 Al-Sahab, al-Qaeda's official media component, released

48 propagandist videos with various focus topics, the most al-Qaeda ever released in one year.[35]

For the majority of terrorist organizations, the destruction of American and Western values and establishing a "true religious order" worldwide is the main goal of these ideological activities. Law enforcement and security forces can concentrate their efforts on isolating radicals in the community using a nonbiased approach within and outside the department, outreach to ethnic groups (communication with ethnic representatives), and recruitment from ethnic groups.

7.2 Organizational Shift

There are three basic organizational levels of international terrorism:

1. Individual international terrorism often has criminal motivation (e.g., revenge, intimidation, and any other personal motives). It is close to organized crime activities. It is difficult to detect this type of terrorist. Even mentally retarded individuals have carried out some individual international acts.

2. Group terrorism requires organization and some type of leadership, recruitment, training, and retention of members.

3. State terrorism is one of the political tools utilized by a government, which establishes a specific agency or uses a legitimate state institution for gaining domestic or international benefits for the regime.

The current shift in the organizational sphere is increasingly away from state-sponsored international terrorist activities and toward groups of terrorists. The process of decentralization of international terrorism was initiated by several factors. The modern world relies on very close economic and political interrelations between countries. It is a tremendous political and economic disadvantage for any state to associate itself with international terrorist activities. Libya and Iraq are strong examples of governments that made all possible efforts to disassociate themselves from terrorist incidents. In May 2002 Libya agreed to pay $2.7 billion compensation for the Lockerbie, Scotland, bombing and has tied the money to the lifting of U.S. and United Nations sanctions. Libya continues to deny involvement in the explosion that downed Pan Am Flight 103 in 1988 and killed 259 passengers and crew along with 11 Lockerbie residents.

The methods by which states sponsor international terrorism and support "isolated" groups are almost untraceable. In November 2002 the FBI was investigating whether a charitable contribution by Saudi Princess Haifa al-Faisal, wife of Bandar bin Sultan, the Saudi ambassador to the United States, may have indirectly benefited two of the September 11, 2001, terrorist hijackers. Because these groups cannot rely on open sponsorship from state agencies, they turn more to involvement with international and domestic organized crime syndicates and self-financing. International terrorist groups are more isolated and loosely organized than in the past, when under the influence of Soviet bloc sponsorship they were more or less interconnected and had a centralized structure.

7.3 Geographical Shift

International terrorism once threatened Americans only when they were outside the country. The primary source of this terrorism was known as the Soviet bloc. Today international terrorists attack Americans on their home soil. There is more than just one major source of international terrorist activity. International terrorism has gained a global character. Oceans or borders cannot stop it.

The Near East and South Asia are the regions responsible for 90 percent of the nearly 300 high-casualty attacks in 2006 that killed 10 or more people. Of the 14,000 reported attacks, 45 percent—about 6,600—occurred in Iraq, where approximately 13,000 fatalities—65 percent of the worldwide total—were reported for 2006. Violence against civilians in eastern and sub-Saharan Africa, especially in Sudan and Nigeria, rose 64 percent in 2006, increasing to 422 from the approximately 256 attacks reported for 2005. The number of reported incidents in 2006 fell in Europe and Eurasia by 15 percent from 2005, for South Asia by 10 percent, and for the Western Hemisphere by 5 percent. The nearly 750 attacks in Afghanistan during 2006 are 50 percent more than the nearly 500 attacks reported for 2005 as fighting intensified. The overall number of people injured in terrorists' incidents rose substantially—54 percent—in 2006, with most of the rise stemming from a doubling of the reported number of injuries in Iraq since 2005.[36]

7.4   Tactical Shift

In the past, international terrorism used more single assassinations and hostage situations. Airline hijackings have become unpopular among international terrorists because few countries will let hijacked planes land, and chances are very high that they will be deported back to the country from which the international terrorist incident originated. Only 19 states have extended their support to include asylum to aviation hijackers.[37]

> According to the U.S. State Department, the number of international terrorist attacks in 2001 declined to 346, down from 426 the previous year.

A total of 3,547 persons were killed in international terrorist attacks in 2001. In 2000, 409 people died in terrorist attacks.[38] International terrorism became more lethal. Most of the international groups are turning to indiscriminate killings of civilians. In the 1990s a terrorist incident was almost 20 percent more likely to result in death or injury than an incident two decades ago.[39] As we enter the 21st century, terrorism has become more destructive and focuses on mass causalities, tremendous loss of property, and financial and economic downfall. Terrorists also shifted their focus to "soft targets," such as schools and hospitals. In 2006, attacks on children were up more than 80 percent, with more than 1,800 children killed or injured.[40]

International terrorist missions became more suicidal. In the past, terrorist groups did not exclude the possibility of becoming victims of counterterrorist security measures. Terrorist groups today are recruiting young volunteers to carry out violent acts. It is much harder to deal with this kind of terrorist, because they do not recognize the natural concept of respect for human life. Some of the traditional law enforcement tactics in these cases will not work. International incident and casualty figures bear this out (see Table 17.4).

Table 17.4 International Incident and Casualty Figures

	1996	1997	1998	1999	2000	2001
Incidents	296	304	274	395	426	346
Casualties	3,225	914	6,694	939	1,205	4,655

Most international terrorist groups have shifted to the following tactics:

- Random attacks on military and diplomatic installations
- Random attacks on tourists and the deliberate killing of foreign-aid workers
- Incidents of kidnapping, hostage taking, and bombing of apartment buildings have become frequent in the republics of the former Soviet Union
- Terrorist attacks on economic infrastructures, including energy distribution, transportation, banking, and tourism, have become routine in, for example, Colombia
- Bomb threats

Another significant tactical focus shift is suicide bombing. A suicide attack is an operational method in which the very act of the attack is dependent upon the death of the perpetrator. The typical type of bombing attacks carried out in the 1970s and 1980s were time bombs. This modus operandi often failed due to early or late detonation without many people concentrated in the immediate vicinity of the explosion or as an outcome of early detection by law enforcement or civilians prior to detonation. Later, during the 1990s, terrorist organizations started to use remote controls to detonate their explosives. The remote control provided the bomber with the ability to detonate the bomb with optimal timing to cause the maximum number of casualties and damage.

The suicide attack, like the smart bomb, is the most sophisticated tactic used by terrorist organizations, because it provides the perpetrator with control of both the timing and the location of the attack and, therefore, produces the maximum number of casualties and damage. Globally in the 1980s there were 4.7 suicide attacks per year, whereas in 2001 there were 81; 2002, 91; 2003, 99; 2004, 163; and 2005, 460. Eighty percent of suicide attacks since 1968 occurred after 9/11, with jihadis representing 31 of the 35 responsible groups.

7.5 Technological Shift

From relatively primitive means of technology (guns, explosives, and conventional weaponry), international terrorism shifted to highly sophisticated technologies such as weapons of mass destruction and chemical and biological weapons. According to the U.S. State Department, for instance, Iran, seen as the most active state sponsor of terrorism, has been aggressively seeking a nuclear arms capability.[41] North Korea decided in December 2002 to restart nuclear installations at Yongbyon that were shut down under the U.S.-North Korea Agreed Framework of 1994. Three atomic reactors will be able to produce 207 kilograms of plutonium annually, which is enough for the manufacture of nearly 30 atomic bombs per year.[42]

Modern Islamic terrorists have expressed interest in developing the capability to exploit cyber vulnerabilities to disrupt banking communications and important infrastructures such as transportation, medical services, and others which will have an economic costs and to undermine public confidence. Some terrorist Websites provide instructions on how to create and spread viruses, develop malicious code, and promote hacking plans. One such online community calling itself "Electronic Jihad," in October 2006, claimed it had designed and used a hacking program to synchronize a distributed denial-of-service attack against an Israeli Website.[43] Businesses and corporations are addicted to easily compromised protocols and commercial Internet products to manage networks increasing the probability of and vulnerability to cyber attacks by terrorists.

7.6   Organized Crime Shift

One of the more significant shifts since the early 1970s has been the growing involvement of organized crime groups with terrorist organizations. For example:

- In Peru from the late 1980s until the early 1990s, the extremist Sendero Luminoso insurgents profited from protecting coca fields and extorting drug traffickers operating in the Andean region they controlled.

- In Western Europe, members of the terrorist Kurdistan Workers' Party (PKK) in Turkey have engaged in drug trafficking and other crimes to help finance local operations.

- In Colombia, since the late 1980s, Marxist insurgents have not been able to rely on financial support from Cuba and Russia. Some insurgent fronts of the Revolutionary Armed Forces of Colombia (FARC) and the National Liberation Army (ELN) generate substantial revenue by taxing and protecting coca cultivation, cocaine processing, and drug shipments in the areas they control. The U.S. government estimates that the FARC may earn as much as half its revenue from involvement in the Colombian drug trade.[44]

With the substantial decline in state-sponsored international terrorism support, many terrorist networks reach out to criminal networks to acquire arms and supplies that cannot be obtained through more traditional or legitimate channels. International organized criminal groups are well connected to outside "gray" arms merchants, transportation coordinators, money launderers, and other specialists who can provide the weapons and other logistics support once given by state sponsors. International organized crime groups cannot exist without corrupt contacts in law enforcement agencies, which are crucial in smuggling operations of weapons and other contraband for terrorist groups.

7.7   Characterizing International Terrorist Groups

This original form of terrorist activity began to spread in the second half of the 20th century with the increase in the number of terrorist organizations and the expansion of social support for terrorism. In the recent Abu Mus'ab al-Suri and Umar Abd al-Hakim's 1,600-page publication, *The Call to Global Islamic Resistance* (2005), which is among the most frequently mentioned jihadi strategy books, they make a strong statement that the future of jihad lies with individuals and small terrorist groups, with no chains connecting them to al-Qaeda leadership.[45]

This form of terrorist activity involves hiring participants for different terrorist organizations, personnel training on methods and ways of conducting terrorist acts, and preparation for the forthcoming terrorist acts—rehearsals for terrorist acts, separate stages of terrorist operations, and so on. The common practices in recruiting a jihadist are (1) identifying individuals with appropriate ideology; (2) indoctrination; (3) cultivating the desire for jihad; and (4) training and preparation for the terrorist act.

This form also involves establishing contacts with other terrorist groups and creating and maintaining connections with organized crime institutions, representatives of illegal firearms businesses, and drug dealers. A high level of secrecy and specialization of terrorist group participants according to different functions (e.g., hiring personnel, recognizers, warriors, production specialists of combat substances and cover documents, secret apartment maintenance staff) is common for organized terrorist activity. There are certain characteristics of international terrorist groups, which we'll explore now.

7.7.1 Seeking Political Gain

Hatred and the quest for political changes or status quo outside their own country dictate more international terrorist networks' decisions than any other single motive. It is this consuming desire for political power that typically drives and sustains international terrorism.

7.7.2 Motivation

In 1974 Dr. Frederick Hacker reported to the U.S. Congress House Committee on Internal Security Hearing on Terrorism that all terrorists fall into three basic motivational groups:

- Criminal—motivated mainly by personal gain
- Mentally deranged—personal motivation, often accompanied by delusions or hallucinations
- Political—motivation toward a real or imagined strategic goal

Islamic fundamentalists (i.e., Osama bin Laden) demonstrate political and often mentally deranged characteristics.[46] The current shift in motivation is from Marxist-based ideology to ethnic nationalism and religious extremism.

According to Jerrold M. Post (1984), religious international terrorists are more dangerous than the average political or social terrorists, who have a mission that is somewhat measurable in terms of public attention or government reaction; the religious terrorist can justify the most horrific acts "in the name of Allah," for example.[47] Terrorism that is religiously motivated is growing quickly, increasing the number of killings and reducing the restraints on mass indiscriminate murder. For religious terrorists, as for social revolutionary terrorists, violence is morally justified and legitimate. See Table 17.5 for information on terrorist motivations.

7.7.3 Seeking Publicity

Almost all international terrorist groups are seeking publicity to promote themselves and their agendas and to discredit those in opposition to them. International terrorist groups are highly motivated to publicize every act of terrorism, to show the state's inability to control terrorist activities. The propaganda of terrorism is connected with attempts to gain public approval of a terrorist activity as a form of political fight, with substantiation of its legal use and also with direct initiative calls to terrorist activities, which may lead to real commitment of criminal actions and involve separate individuals or groups committing severe violent crimes. These appeals are realized verbally or by distributing written or visually demonstrative materials.

7.7.4 Requiring Member Loyalty Through Ideological, Religious, Ethnic, and Other Considerations

Terrorists generally believe that they have to accomplish some global mission, such as communist revolution, liberating Palestine, continuing jihad, or the like.

Table 17.5 Terrorist Motivations

Motivation	Agents of Violence	Activities
Nationalism-separatism	Separatist and regional autonomy movements, ethnically-based contenders for power	Anti-government, intercommunal violence, attacks on peacekeepers
Religious	Extremist fundamentalists (Islamists, Hinduists, Tamils)	Mass casualty attacks on civilian targets, suicide attacks
Ideology (Belief in political cause)	Right and left wing extremists	Hate propaganda, anti-immigrant violence, bombing
Single issue	Animal rights, environmentalists, anti-abortion extremists	Sabotage, mail bombs
State sponsored	Oppressive regimes	Sabotage and use of chemical weapons
Mentally ill	Individual	Bombings (Unabomber), hijackers

Source: B. Hoffman, "Terrorism Trends and Prospects," in Lesser, I., Hoffman, B., Arquilla, J., Ronfeldt, D., Zanini, M., and Jenkins, B., *Countering the New Terrorism* (RAND Corporation, 1999).

7.7.5 Structure

Generally, international groups maintain a structure with defined leadership-subordinate roles, through which the group's objectives are achieved. Recently, because more groups are based on religious motives and may lack political or nationalistic agenda, they have less need for hierarchical structure. International terrorist groups have a tendency to rely on loose affiliations with like-minded groups in different countries.[48]

7.7.6 Tactical Diversity

Typically, international terrorist groups are utilizing more than one method of violent act—suicide bombings, bombings, assassinations, sabotage communications, armed assaults, kidnappings, barricade and hostage situations, and hijackings.

7.7.7 Assistance

With the creation of large terrorist institutions, terrorist assistance is becoming more important in the overall system of terrorism. Main variations of this assistance are extremist groups financing and providing the means for terrorism, providing facilities for training their members, and harboring and hiding them after they commit terrorist acts. This assistance can be used by states (so-called terrorism sponsors) as well as by representatives of business circles and ethnic and other social groups that express sympathy to terrorist organizations or support them because of their common political interests. There may also be direct involvement with extremist organizations in conducting tasks of legal political institutions to influence their enemies.

7.7.8 Organizational Maturity

In most cases, international terrorist groups have a high level of organizational stability and do not depend on the continuing participation of one or a few individuals for their existence. For example, Osama bin Laden's organization was designed during the 1980s as a worldwide recruitment and support network for the purpose of resisting the former

Soviet Union's occupation of Afghanistan. Bin Laden's Organization was backed with financial aid from the United States, Saudi Arabia, and other states.

It is important to appreciate that Osama bin Laden's organizational structure is complex by design. During the 1980s resistance fighters in Afghanistan developed a worldwide recruitment and support network. In the early 1990s this network, which equipped, trained, and funded thousands of Muslim fighters, came under the control of Osama bin Laden. Al-Qaeda ("The Base") is a network of groups spread throughout the world, with a presence in Algeria, Egypt, Morocco, Turkey, Jordan, Tajikistan, Uzbekistan, Syria, Xinjiang in China, Pakistan, Bangladesh, Malaysia, Myanmar, Indonesia, Mindanao in the Philippines, Lebanon, Iraq, Saudi Arabia, Kuwait, Bahrain, Yemen, Libya, Tunisia, Bosnia, Kosovo, Chechnya, Dagestan, Kashmir, Sudan, Somalia, Kenya, Tanzania, Azerbaijan, Eritrea, Uganda, Ethiopia, and in the West Bank and Gaza.

As hierarchy, al-Qaeda is organized with bin Laden, the emir-general, at the top, followed by other al-Qaeda leaders and leaders of the different groups. Horizontally, it is integrated with 24 constituent groups. The vertical integration is formal; the horizontal integration, informal. Immediately below bin Laden is the Shura Majlis, a consultative council. Four committees report to the Shura Majlis: (1) military, (2) religious-legal, (3) finance, and (4) media. Members of these committees conduct special assignments for bin Laden and his operational commanders. Operational effectiveness at all levels is reached by compartmentalization and secrecy. Though the organization has evolved considerably since the U.S. embassy bombings in Africa in 1999, the basic structure of the consultative council and the four committees remains intact.[49]

In addition, almost all the international terrorist organizations have developed a training function.

7.7.9   Violent Nature

Terrorist groups routinely utilize violence to advance and protect their interests. These groups are ruthless and suicidal in protecting their interests from rivals and law enforcement alike. Unprecedented violence—bombings, hostage taking, contract killings, kidnappings, and large-scale massacres—has increased with competition for political, ideological, and religious purposes.

7.7.10   Weaponry

For many years international terrorism analysts did not believe that terrorists were willing to use weapons of mass destruction (WMD). But present-day reality shows that religious extremists and sects with messianic or apocalyptic mindsets have a tendency to use WMD or any kind of equivalent approaches. Such religious groups as al-Qaeda and Aum Shinrikyo are inclined to use equivalents of WMD. The September 11, 2001, attacks by al-Qaeda and Aum Shinrikyo's sarin attack on the Tokyo subway system on March 20, 1995, demonstrated this new shift in the utilization of new terrorist technologies.

To complicate this already critical situation, with the collapse of the Soviet Union the possibility of nuclear terrorism has increased. As reported by the Center for Strategic and International Studies (CSIS), "The current trafficking situation shows disturbing upward trends, substantial quantities of materials are likely to remain at large, and the potential for an accident or use of smuggled nuclear materials probably is increasing." The seriousness of potential nuclear losses is evident from the number of thefts reported by Russian Interior Ministry officials. They reported 27 thefts of nuclear materials in 1993 and 27 incidents in 1994. Globally from 1993 to 2003, 540 attempts at illegal nuclear materials trading, including 182 incidents with materials that can be used in assembling nuclear weaponry, were registered.[50]

Dirty bombs pose an ongoing terrorist threat that the United States must be prepared to counter. The representative of the 9/11 Commission stated in 2004 that al-Qaeda is still interested in using a radiological weapon or "dirty bomb." This was confirmed in September 2006 by a statement by the then leader of al-Qaeda in Iraq, Abu Hamza al-Muhajir.[51]

This tendency to use unconventional weapons shows the international terrorism asymmetry—the use of unconventional weapons against expected conventional weapons. In many instances this shift requires the development of connections with arms dealers, or those who can manufacture arms. (The Chechen terrorists have connections with a machine-gun manufacturer in Kovrov, Russia, for example.) International terrorism groups are involved in such organized crime activity as weapons smuggling.

7.7.11   *Financing*

Financial support to international terrorist groups comes from many sources, including state sponsorship, organized crime, and drug and human trafficking. Most Marxist and leftist terrorist organizations are suffering now from a lack of funding due to the disintegration of the USSR and Warsaw Pact countries. As we mentioned, today international terrorists' funding and logistical networks cross borders, are less dependent on state sponsors, and are harder to disrupt with economic sanctions.

Funds can be moved to terrorists in many ways. For one, it can be done through financial institutions such as banks that have secret accounts. For example, half of 15,000 accounts of Clearstream Clearinghouse in Luxemburg are unpublished. This institution is suspected of moving Osama bin Laden's money. Among the international banks with the most secret accounts are Citibank (271), Barclays (200), Crédit Lyonnais (23), and Japanese company Nomura (12). Also, there are 2,000 investment companies, banks, and subsidiaries of banks—mainly British, German, American, Italian, French, and Swiss—with unpublished accounts.[52] Western Union and similar businesses are able to send money worldwide in 15 minutes, and no bank account, background check, or ID is required to send less than $1,000. According to the U.S. Treasury, al-Qaeda, Hamas, and other terrorist groups use Muslim charities for financial transactions. The Holyland Foundation charity of Richardson, Texas, has been used to support the families of Arab suicide bombers on the West Bank affiliated with Hamas.[53]

7.8   Terrorism Prevention

Since 9/11 the U.S. has made visible progress in terrorism prevention planning and education. However, the modern history of international terrorism shows that it is not realistic to eliminate it or to control it, but it is possible to reduce it. For this purpose, it is not enough to just improve antiterrorism legislation to solve the problems created by terrorism globally. This is because the laws on terrorism are aimed to suppress terrorist activity and to punish those who are responsible, but it is much more important to prevent such activity from occurring in the first place. Even a successfully conducted antiterrorist operation with the terrorists' capture and apprehension cannot compensate its damages and cannot be evaluated completely positively, because it shows missed opportunities to prevent such an act.

A lot of negative consequences occur during the preparation stage of a terrorist act. Usually other crimes are committed before a terrorist attack (e.g., burglary; illegal weapons possession; acquisition of explosives, toxins, and radioactive substances). A substantial number of groups and even layers of society are getting involved in various negative criminal consequences; social tension is increasing; international, interethnic, and religious controversies are growing; legal nihilism is spreading; and opponent aggression is increasing. The most effective prevention, and of course the most expensive and difficult, is early prevention. Today, the U.S. government focuses on several main activities that can promote terrorism prevention strategies and tactics:

1. Analyze, localize, and minimize those social, political, financial, and other factors that create fertile ground for international terrorism. It is necessary for these purposes to study thoroughly this phenomenon and its roots and reasons. Studying and explaining motives of the widespread cases of international terrorism and subsequent data gathering and assessment can play an important role in determining sets of problems that need to be solved in the near future—economic, social, and political.

2. One of the effective remedies in terrorism prevention activities by security agencies is implementing programs that reward individuals for information that leads to the prevention of terrorist acts or that leads to apprehension of people committing such acts.

3. Launch an information campaign designed to disclose the criminal and violent nature of terrorist groups and organizations. Build public awareness about the legal consequences of participation in any activities related to terrorism.

4. Develop public safety programs to protect vulnerable objects and locations.

5. Enhance community participation in "terrorist watch" programs.

6. Improve intelligence by increasing the cooperation between law enforcement agencies worldwide.

7. Enhance information sharing by centralizing and increasing the protection of the integrated information system of security forces globally.

8. Improve training for security forces by developing realistic antiterrorist action scenarios and organizing regular exercises for security forces and citizenry.

9. Foster coordination between security forces and communities on the basis of model local, state, and federal plans of responding to terrorist attacks.

10. Develop a general policy of covering terrorism through the mass media. Legal issues of mass media participation in antiterrorism activities have not been thoroughly illustrated. Law enforcement agencies should try not to broaden the scale of psychological war. If pro-terrorism statements appear, and unfortunately they do, they strengthen terrorists' courage. Agencies shouldn't mix terrorism with politics and ideology and should not depict it as an international plot against the United States as a whole. Wrongful and contradictory understandings of causes and roots of international terrorism developed as a result of insufficient antiterrorism actions in Russia.

Political leaders of the United States consider counterterrorism one of the most important state tasks. Some of the main trends in this activity are legislative improvement, strengthening cooperation between communities and law enforcement agencies, creation of special task forces, increasing federal agencies' personnel, dealing with terrorism problems, and providing better technical equipment.

> U.S. security agencies trying to put pressure on the forces supporting terrorism will use all available resources, including military ones, to their full extent, to punish terrorism, to assist and collaborate with other countries, and not allow weakness in dealing with terrorists.

International intelligence gathering is coordinated through Interpol today. Interpol's involvement in the fight against international terrorism materialized during the 54th General Assembly in Washington in 1985, when Resolution AGN/54/RES/1[54] was passed, calling for the creation of a specialized group within the then Police Division to "coordinate and enhance cooperation in combating international terrorism." Interpol's multinational police cooperation process has a three-step formula for dealing with terrorism, a formula all nations must follow: (1) pass laws specifying that the offense is a crime; (2) prosecute offenders, and cooperate in other countries' prosecutions; and (3) furnish Interpol with and exchange information concerning the crime and its perpetrators.[55]

The challenges for the intelligence community are enormous: Uncovering "sleepers" currently residing in both urban and rural settings is crucial to disrupting and preventing the next attack, as there seems little doubt that we must expect another attack. The truly global nature of the terror threat cannot and must not be confined to profiling of an ethnic group. The global nature of the organization means that greater efforts and communication must come from intelligence communities around the globe.

8   Specific Threats and Responses

8.1   Executive Protection

Countermeasures against terrorism for businesses are not as costly as executives may believe. Of course, no program can entirely guarantee protection against attack. But a business can take action to lessen its attractiveness as a target. In general, executive protection programs include target hardening, bodyguard operations, and training sessions to teach executives how to avoid being identified as targets and what to do if they become targets. The key to success in executive protection is preplanning for a possible attack. One successful approach has been the crisis management team (CMT).

A company's CMT is made up of a carefully selected group of experts in a variety of fields who meet several times a year to discuss how to prevent attacks and what to do if an executive is kidnapped or if the firm receives another type of threat (for example, a bomb threat). In general these teams are composed of a senior executive, a team leader, a security executive, a police liaison, a medical consultant, a lawyer, a financial adviser, a communications expert, and a terrorist liaison.

Each team member brings specific knowledge that will be crucial should a threat be received. The senior executive is responsible for making the final decisions. The security executive must coordinate security operations for the facilities involved to protect other employees or company property. The police liaison is responsible for seeing that the authorities are fully apprised of the situation and that the company cooperates with the civil authorities to its fullest ability. The medical consultant must have access to medical files on each executive so that a medical profile can be developed to help the kidnappers keep the victim in good health.

The lawyer interprets what actions the company can take without violating company policy or various laws. This is particularly vital when multinational corporations are involved in negotiations with foreign countries. In the past, several firms that cooperated with terrorists in an attempt to recover kidnapped executives found that the governments involved prohibited such negotiations and subsequently confiscated the firms' assets. The financial adviser is necessary to determine how and whether funds can be pulled together to meet demands. Ideally most firms do not have $1 million in cash simply lying around. Rather, firms invest their capital in equipment, stocks, and bonds. The communications expert handles any direct communications desired by the terrorists. In many cases the authorities may handle this operation.

The terrorist liaison may be the most difficult member to recruit; this person must understand terrorist organizations and their intentions. The terrorist liaison must analyze the terrorists' demands and predict their responses to the company's actions. In general, a psychologist, psychiatrist, or sociologist fills this role.

Regardless of what actions a firm takes to prevent or respond to terrorist attacks, it is most important that some action be taken. The problem must be recognized, and some type of planning must follow. According to Joseph Marog, manager of the Counterterrorism Training Program for the Defense Intelligence Agency's Joint Military Intelligence Training Center, there are six trends that security managers should consider when developing security programs:

1. Terrorism will remain a persistent international problem. "Not only will it not go away, but it is continually evolving."
2. There will be an emergence of transient groupings of terrorists such as those involved in the World Trade Center bombing.
3. Terrorists will increasingly use "soft targets" such as businesses.
4. Attacks will become more lethal.
5. More attacks will go unclaimed.
6. The lines will become less clear between domestic and foreign terrorism.[56]

8.2   Bombs and Bomb Threats

Any business, industry, or institution can become the victim of a bombing or a bomb threat. Most telephone bomb threats—approximately 98 percent—turn out to be hoaxes. The target of the threat, however, has no way of knowing whether a real bomb has been planted. Contingency planning is necessary for an organization to be able to protect its personnel and property from the hazards of an explosion. In the absence of a specific response plan, the bomb threat will often cause panic. This may be the precise result the caller seeks.

Controlling access to the facility; having adequate perimeter barriers and lighting; checking all parcels and packages; locking areas such as storerooms, equipment rooms, and utility closets; and taking note of any suspicious persons or of anyone not authorized to be in an area are all measures that can thwart a bomb planter as well as a thief or other kind of intruder.

Contingency plans should specify who will be responsible for handling the crisis and delegating authority in the event a bomb threat is received. The officer in charge of responding to a bomb threat must be someone who will be available 24 hours a day. A control center or command post provisioned for communication with all parts of the facility and with law enforcement agencies should also be designated. All personnel who will be involved in the bomb threat response must receive training in their assignments and duties. Plans should be in writing.

8.3 Telephone Operator's Response

The telephone operator's role is critical in handling the bomb threat call. The operator should receive training in the proper response so as to elicit from the caller as much information as possible. The two most important items of information to be learned are the expected time of the explosion and the location of the bomb. The operator should remain calm and attempt to keep the caller talking as long as possible in hopes of gaining information or clues that will aid investigators. The caller's accent, tone of voice, and any background noises should be noted. Many organizations provide telephone operators with a bomb threat report form for recording all information (see Figure 17.1).

CHECKLIST WHEN YOU RECEIVE A BOMB THREAT

Time and date reported: _____

How reported: _____

Exact words of caller: _____

_____

_____

Questions to ask: _____

1. When is bomb going to explode? _____

2. Where is bomb right now? _____

3. What kind of bomb is it? _____

4. What does it look like? _____

5. Why did you place the bomb? _____

6. Where are you calling from? _____

Description of caller's voice: _____

Male _____ Female _____ Young _____ Middle age _____ Old _____ Accent _____

Tone of voice _____ Background noise _____ Is voice familiar? _____

If so, who did it sound like? _____

_____

Other voice characteristics: _____

Time caller hung up: _____ Remarks: _____

_____

_____

Name, address, telephone of recipient: _____

_____

_____

FIGURE 17.1 Telephone bomb threat information form.

After receiving a bomb threat call, the operator must inform the designated authority within the organization (the chief of security, for example). Law enforcement authorities and others in the organization will be notified in turn according to the written contingency plans.

8.4   Search Teams

A decision must be made whether to conduct a search of the premises and how extensive the search should be. If possible, employee teams rather than police or fire department officers should conduct the search. Employees are familiar with their work area and can recognize any out-of-place object. An explosive device may be virtually any size or shape. Any foreign object, therefore, is suspect.

Basic techniques for a two-person search team include the following:

1. Move slowly and listen for the ticking of a clockwork device. (It is a good idea to pause and listen before beginning to search an area, to become familiar with the ordinary background noise that is always present.)

2. Divide the room to be searched into two halves. Search each half separately in three layers: floor to waist level, waist to eye level, and eye to ceiling level.

3. Starting back to back and working toward each other, search around the walls at each of the three height levels; then move toward the center of the room.

If a suspicious object is found, it must not be touched. Its location and description should be reported immediately to designated authorities. A clear zone with a radius of at least 300 feet should be established around the device (including the floors above and below). Removal and disarming of explosive devices should be left to professionals. Those assigned to search a particular area should report to the control center after completing the search.

8.5   Evacuation

Evacuating the facility for any reason, particularly in response to a bomb threat, is a drastic reaction to the potential danger. There clearly are situations when such an extreme course is indicated, but such a decision should never be undertaken lightly. It is essential that a thorough and exhaustive dialogue relative to this complex problem be undertaken at the earliest opportunity so that plans and policies may be formulated prior to any actual pressure caused by such an emergency. Many experts in the field argue that a total evacuation is rarely if ever indicated. The argument concerns the risk of exposing a great number of people to the blast when the location of the bomb is unknown. Whenever personnel are moved about in large groups, the possibility of exposure to injury is increased. Moreover, the movement of large numbers under the threat of bombing can create panic—a very dangerous situation.

A bomber who has shown familiarity with the facility by placing a bomb on the premises can be assumed to be familiar with normal and perhaps even abnormal or emergency traffic patterns of that facility. The bomber has probably placed the bomb in such a way as to create the greatest possible injury and havoc. In such a situation, total evacuation might serve only to expose the greatest number of employees to injury and death.

It has also been found that hoaxers or mischief-makers may be encouraged by a mass evacuation to repeat such calls and to subject the facility to a string of bomb threats.

The decision whether to evacuate will be made by management of the threatened facility, often in conjunction with law enforcement officials. It may be decided to evacuate the entire facility, only the areas in the vicinity of the suspected bomb, or (unless a device has actually been discovered) not to evacuate at all. Detailed plans are necessary to ensure safe and orderly evacuation. Personnel should leave through designated exits and assemble in a predetermined safe area. Elevators should not be used during evacuation. Doors and windows should be left open for increased venting of the explosive force.

When authorities have determined that the bomb threat emergency has ended, all personnel who have been notified of the threat should be informed that normal operations are to resume.

9   Other Specific Response Issues in the United States

For additional information on specific responses to terrorist threats in the United States, see Chapter 1 on homeland security. Chapter 1 provides information on responses by the federal, state, and local government; private sector companies; and joint responses.

9.1   Al-Qaeda

Al-Qaeda, the self-proclaimed terrorist group that destroyed the World Trade Center, continues to be a major concern for the Department of Homeland Security. In 2007, the U.S. intelligence community identified al-Qaeda as the most serious terrorist threat to the homeland, with plans of high-impact plots and attempts to acquire and employ chemical, biological, radiological, or nuclear material in attacks where they would not hesitate to use them.

DHS continued to encourage homeland businesses, security, and law enforcement agencies to be vigilant. Because al-Qaeda has been careful and meticulous in its planning of attacks in an effort to inflict the greatest number of casualties, DHS believes that there are indicators that an organization or facility has been targeted by the group. In its Information Bulletin 03-004, "Possible Indicators of Al-Qaeda Surveillance," the department lists the following indicators:

- Unusual or prolonged interest in security measures or personnel, entry points and access controls, or perimeter barriers such as fences or walls
- Unusual behavior such as staring at or quickly looking away from personnel or vehicles entering or leaving designated facilities or parking areas
- Observation of security reaction drills or procedures
- Increase in anonymous telephone or email threats to facilities in conjunction with suspected surveillance incidents, indicating possible surveillance of threat reaction procedures
- Foot surveillance involving two or three individuals working together
- Mobile surveillance using bicycles, scooters, motorcycles, cars, trucks, sport utility vehicles, boats, or small aircraft
- Prolonged static surveillance using operatives disguised as panhandlers, demonstrators, shoe shiners, food or other vendors, news agents, or street sweepers not previously seen in the area
- Discreet use of still cameras, video recorders, or note taking at nontourist-type locations

- Use of multiple sets of clothing or identification or the use of sketching materials
- Questioning of security or facility personnel

9.2 Nuclear and Radiological Threats

Though it is impossible to accurately predict the extent of threat from nuclear or radiological devices, the fear is real. An attack on a nuclear power facility (see Figure 17.2), though unlikely, could be catastrophic. Given the comments earlier in this chapter referring to the loss of radioactive materials from the now defunct Soviet Union, the fear is substantiated. To support this fear, on May 2, 2002, José Padilla was arrested at Chicago's O'Hare International Airport. Padilla, returning from Pakistan, was suspected of plotting to use a "dirty bomb" in the United States.[57] Still, the probability of any individual or company being the victim of such a fearsome device is minimal.

9.3 Bioterrorism

The threat of bioterrorism in the United States is real. The anthrax scares in Washington, D.C., on November 14, 2001, and in Florida, New Jersey, and New York in 2001 and 2002 brought the reality home. Bioterrorism is the use of biological agents to produce illness or death in people, animals, or plants. These agents can be distributed by air or as contaminants in food or water, and gas masks (see Figure 17.3) can be used by first responders, military, and civilians in the event of a wide scale strike.

The Centers for Disease Control and Prevention (CDC) has identified biologics that can be used as weapons, including anthrax, smallpox, botulism, Ebola, and several other lesser-known diseases. Only with rapid identification and containment can these biologics be controlled. Many excellent Internet sites provide detailed information for anyone interested in learning more about bioterrorism (see Appendix B).

9.4 Chemical Agents

Although not biologics, chemical agents can perform the same actions as viruses, toxins, and fungi/bacteria. Chemical agents include poisonous gas, liquids, and solids. One of

FIGURE 17.2 Nuclear power plant.

FIGURE 17.3 Gas masks for civilian use. (Courtesy of IBN Protection Property, www.domesticfront.com/potomic.)

the best-known chemical agents, used during World War I and most recently in Iraq on Kurdish resistance groups, is mustard gas. This gas attacks the skin, eyes, lungs, and even the gastrointestinal tract.

9.5 Cyber Terrorism

Almost everyone who uses the Internet can relay stories of virus problems, identity theft, and other issues, but most are not aware of the possibility that terrorists might use viruses or physical attacks to shut down the Internet. The media has publicized the use of the Internet by terrorists for communication and electronic transfer of funds. But will terrorists ever consider attacking the Internet? The answer is a resounding yes. According to a CIA report to the U.S. Senate Select Committee, al-Qaeda has expressed the intention of developing skills necessary for an effective cyber attack.

Despite the CIA report, only three federal agency computer systems were able to pass General Accounting Office security evaluations. Though some of the trouble may be associated with agency problems, flawed software products have left holes in otherwise well-planned systems.

The solution may come from the recently established Common Criteria (CC), an international program attempting to establish standards against which security products may be evaluated to provide assurance of the products' security features.[58]

10 The Future

During 2002, despite the capture or death of many al-Qaeda and other extremist leaders, there were 12 major terrorist attacks worldwide, killing at least 300 people. According to Control Risks Group, a private consulting firm that evaluates international business risks, the global community should expect "more of the same." Car and truck bombings will be the most common method of attack. The firm predicts that the major targets will be the United States and British and Israeli military and diplomatic facilities. Other sites include businesses frequented by foreign visitors such as shopping malls, restaurants, bars, and supermarkets. Infrastructure facilities such as energy companies and transportation (including oil refineries) may continue to be targeted. Still other targets identified by Control Risks' report are commercial shipping and aviation, schools, and churches, as well as individual Western leaders.

□ □ □

Critical Thinking

What is your definition of terrorism? Defend your position. Is it possible to find arguments to defend the use of terrorism as a tool in waging war? Consider the American Revolution and its use of tactics in combating the British.

□ □ □

Review Questions

1. Where did the first "terrorist" groups first appear? What was the reason for such activities?
2. Discuss trends in terrorism over the past two decades.
3. Outline a proper response to a bomb threat.

References

1. Richardson, L., "Terrorist Rivals: Beyond the State-Centric Model," *Harvard International Review*, XXIX(1) (Spring 2007): 66–68.
2. Cunningham, C. William, Strauchs, J. John, Van Meter, W. Clifford, *The Hallcrest Report II: Private Security Trends, 1970–2000* (Boston: Butterworth-Heinemann, 1990), p. 173.
3. "Reports Shed Light on Terrorist Threat," *Security Management* (November 1996): 12.
4. Berry, Nicholas, "Targets of Terrorists" (2007), www.cdi.org/terrorism/moretargets.html.
5. Richards, J., "Europe and the Nature of the Terrorist Threat in 2007" (July 16, 2007), http://intellibriefs.blogspot.com/2007/07/europe-and-nature-of-terrorist-threat.html
6. Alexander, D. *Business Confronts Terrorism: Risks and Responses* (WI: The University of Wisconsin Press Terrace Books, 2004): p. 23.
7. "Top Security Threats and Management: Issues Facing Corporate America, 2003 Survey of Fortune 1000 Companies," www.asisonline.org/newsroom/surveys/pinkerton.pdf, retrieved July 16, 2007.
8. Pharoah, Robyn, *An Unknown Quantity: Kidnapping for Ransom in South Africa* (Institute for Security Studies, 2005), www.iss.co.za/index.php?link_id=24&slink_id=1029&link_type=12&slink_type=12&tmpl_id=3.
9. "Country Reports on Terrorism: Released by the Office of the Coordinator for Counterterrorism" (April 30, 2007), www.state.gov/s/ct/rls/crt/2006/82738.htm.
10. "Terrorist Threat," *Security Management* (November 1996):12.
11. Global Terrorism Database, http://209.232.239.37/gtd2/browse.aspx?what=target.
12. Wilkinson, P., "Why Modern Terrorism? Differentiating Types and Distinguishing Ideological Motivations," in Charles W. Kegley, Jr., ed., *The New Global Terrorism: Characteristics, Causes, Controls* (Upper Saddle River, NJ: Prentice Hall, 2003), pp. 106–138.
13. Country Reports on Terrorism 2006, U.S. Department of State (April 2006), www.terrorisminfo.mipt.org/pdf/Country-Reports-Terrorism-2006.pdf.
14. Henderson, H., *Global Terrorism: The Complete Reference Guide* (New York: Checkmark Books, 2001).

15. Trotsky, L., "On the Ninetieth Anniversary of the *Communist Manifesto*," in Karl Marx and Frederic L. Bender, eds., *The Communist Manifesto* (New York: W.W. Norton & Company, 1988), pp. 139–145.

16. Courtois, S., Werth, N., Panne, J., Paczkowski, A., Bartosek, K., Margolin, J., *The Black Book of Communism: Crimes, Terror, Repression,* 4th printing, Harvard University Press Cambridge.

17. Nechaev, S., "Catechism of a Revolutionary," www.geocities.com/countermedia/5.html.

18. Holms, J., and Burke, T., *Terrorism* (New York: Pinnacle Books-Kensington Publishing Corporation, 2001).

19. Friedman, G., "The Geopolitics of the Palestinians," *Geopolitical Intelligence Report* (June 19, 2007). Online: www.stratfor.com.

20. "Country Report on Terrorism 2007," U.S. Department of State (April 30, 2007), www.state.gov/s/ct/rls/crt/2006/82736.htm.

21. Hoffman, B., "Terrorism Trends and Prospects," in I. Lesser, B. Hoffman, J. Arquilla, D. Ronfeldt, M. Zanini, and B. Jenkins, eds., *Countering the New Terrorism* (RAND Corporation, 1999).

22. Urbancic, Frank C., Acting Coordinator for Counterterrorism; Travers, Russ, Deputy Director of the National Counterterrorism Center, Washington, D.C., April 30, 2007. Online: http://www.state.gov/s/ct/rls/rm/07/83999.htm.

23. National Counter Terrorism Center Report" (May 29, 2007), http://wits.nctc.gov/crn2/cgi-bin/cognos.cgi.

24. Pillar, Paul R., "Terrorism Goes Global: Extremist Groups Extend Their Reach Worldwide," *The Brookings Review* (Fall 2001): 34–37.

25. Schmid, A., *Political Terrorism* (1983), cited by C. Simonsen and J. Spindlove, *Terrorism Today: The Past, the Players, the Future* (Upper Saddle River, NJ: Prentice Hall, 2000).

26. "Terrorism: Can You Trust Your Bathtub?" Terrorism Research Center (September 12, 1996), downloaded 1/13/03, www.terrorism.com.

27. Whitaker, B., "The Definition of Terrorism," *Guardian Unlimited* (May 7, 2001), www.guardian.co.uk/elsewhere/journalist/story/0%2C7792%2C487098%2C00.htm.

28. Jenkins, B., "International Terrorism: The Other World War," in Charles W. Kegley, Jr., ed., *The New Global Terrorism: Characteristics, Causes, Controls* (Upper Saddle River, NJ: Prentice Hall, 2003), pp. 15–26.

29. Hubbard, David G., *Winning Back the Sky: A Tactical Analysis of Terrorism* (San Francisco: Stonybrook, 1986).

30. Kruglanski, Arie W., and Fishman, Shira, "Terrorism Between 'Syndrome' and 'Tool,'" *Current Directions in Psychological Science,* 15(1) (February 2006): 1–48.

31. Crenshaw, M., "Questions to Be Answered, Research to Be Done, Knowledge to Be Applied," in Walter Reich, ed., *Origins of Terrorism: Psychologies, Ideologies, Theologies, States of Mind* (Cambridge, MA: Cambridge University Press, 1990), pp. 247–260.

32. Jenkins, B., and Kegley, Jr., C., "The Characteristics, Causes, and Controls of the New Global Terrorism: An Introduction," in Charles W. Kegley, Jr., ed., *The New Global Terrorism: Characteristics, Causes, Controls* (Upper Saddle River, NJ: Prentice Hall, 2003), pp. 1–14.

33. Katz, R., Director, SITE Institute Testimony before the House Armed Services Committee Terrorism, Unconventional Threats and Capabilities Subcommittee United States House of Representatives: "The Online Jihadist Threat" (February 14, 2007), http://armedservices.house.gov/pdfs/TUTC021407/Katz_Testimony021407.pdf.

34. Web on Terror (July 6, 2007), http://expertlancer.com/web-of-terror-part-1-extremists-take-to-the-net/.

35. Mueller, R., Statement Before the Senate Select Committee on Intelligence (January 11, 2007), www.fbi.gov/congress/congress07/mueller011107.htm.

36. "Report on Terrorist Incidents, 2006," National Counterterrorism Center (April 30, 2007), http://wits.nctc.gov/reports/crot2006nctcannexfinal.pdf

37. D'Arcy, P., *Law Enforcement Executive Forum*, Terrorists, Enemies of Mankind (March 2002).

38. Patterns of Global Terrorism, U.S. State Department Report, 2002.

39. *Countering the Changing Threat of International Terrorism,* report from the National Commission on Terrorism, Washington, D.C. (June 2000), downloaded 1/24/03, www.fas.org/irp/threat/commission.html.

40. Urbancic, Frank C., Acting Coordinator for Counterterrorism; Travers, Russ, Deputy Director of the National Counterterrorism Center. Washington, D.C., April 30, 2007, www.state.gov/s/ct/rls/rm/07/83999.htm.

41. Lee, R., and Perl, R., *Terrorism, the Future, and U.S. Foreign Policy*, Congressional Research Service, downloaded 1/24/03, www.fas.org/irp/crs/IB95112.pdf.

42. Niksch, L., *North Korea's Nuclear Weapons Program*, Congressional Research Service, downloaded 1/24/03, http://fas.org.

43. United States Institute for Peace Press, "Terror on the Internet: The New Arena, The New Challenges," 2006; Global Issues Report, "Electronic Jihad Group Coordinates Sophisticated Hacking Attacks," October 10, 2006.

44. *Countering the Changing Threat of International Terrorism, 2000.*

45. Brynjar, Lia, "Al-Suri's Doctrines for Decentralized Jihadi Training" (February 2007), www.jamestown.org/news_details.php?news_id=217.

46. Fischer, R., Berger, F., and Heininger, B., "Terrorism: Nothing New—A Predictive Model for Handling Terrorist Incidents," *Law Enforcement Executive Forum* (March 2002): 23+.

47. Hudson, R., and Majeska, M., *The Sociology and Psychology of Terrorism: Who Becomes a Terrorist and Why?*, Federal Research Division, Library of Congress, Washington, D.C. (1999), downloaded 1/27/03, www.neuromaster.com/LOsocpsyterrorism/spt_12.htm.

48. *Countering the Changing Threat of International Terrorism.*

49. Spindlove, Jeremy R., "Terrorism and Countering the Threat," *Law Enforcement Executive Forum* (March 2002).

50. Newsru (April 26, 2005), www.newsru.com/world/26apr2005/bomb.html.

51. "Dirty Bomb Vulnerabilities Taff Report," Permanent Subcommittee on Investigations, United States Senate, Washington, D.C., 2007. Released in conjunction with the Permanent Subcommittee on Investigations, July 12, 2007, hearing, p. 1.

52. Komisar, L., "Tracking Terrorist Money—Too Hot for U.S. to Handle," Pacific News Service (October 2001), downloaded 1/24/03, www.alternet.org/story.html?StoryID=11650.

53. Frank, A., "On the Terrorist Money Trail," downloaded 1/24/03, www.evesmag.com/terroristmoney.htm.

54. Resolution AGN/54/RES/1 (Washington D.C.: U.S. 54th General Assembly, 1985).

55. Spindlove.

56. "Terrorism: Assessing the Threat," *Security Management* (September 1996): 40–42.

57. Kushner, Harvey, ed., "Introduction," *American Behavioral Scientist* (February 2003).

58. Uner, Eric, "The Threat of Cyber Terrorism Is Real; It's Only a Matter of When," *Security Products*, (February 3, 2003): 26.

59. "The Shape of Things to Come," *Security Management* (March 2003): 20.

18

Computers, Information, and Information Systems Security

OBJECTIVES

The study of this chapter will enable you to:

1. Identify various computer products.
2. Discuss possible attacks on computer systems and software.
3. Discuss options for protecting computers and information from fraudulent use and theft.

1 Introduction

Computers and information systems have traditionally been treated as something that the security or loss prevention director needed to consider as a vulnerability, but the 21st century has brought about a revolution in security operations. The following discussion on computers and information systems[1] (IS) security focuses primarily on the services provided by the traditional roles of security in protecting computers. However, the trend is for security technologies to rely on the very computers that they are designed to protect. For example, information technology (IT) has brought CCTV, used primarily for surveillance, of age. Technologies such as biometrics[2] have made possible video monitoring in the areas of facial and physical characteristics recognition, fire and smoke detection, and advanced alarm monitoring. With this growing integration of technology and the security operation, the traditional dichotomy associated with security and information technology often creates problems.

In 1946, the U.S. Army developed the Electronic Numerical Integrator and Calculator (ENIAC), the first viable full-scale computer. At that time, computers were mysterious boxes utilized by scientists and thought to be the top-secret weapons of generals. Today, scientific pocket calculators have greater computing power than the ENIAC, and most kindergarten kids know how to use a computer[3] or some type of handheld personal digital assistant (PDA) computing device, particularly those designed for electronic games.

Computers have become an important part of peoples' lives, becoming an integral part of the way we work, teach, learn, and even play.

In government and business, computers are used to process, store, and transmit vast amounts of information. Information processing used to take days or weeks for workers to compile, whereas today, computers perform the same task in mere minutes, translating into greater efficiencies and greater productivity. Moreover, information systems are becoming primary methods of communication. Email, instant messaging, and Voice-over-Internet Protocol (VoIP) (essentially using computers and the Internet for voice communications, until recently the exclusive capability of telephones and telephone companies) are common and in many cases essential means of effective and efficient communications.

The criminal justice sector also relies on computers. Since 1924, the FBI has been responsible for keeping the nation's fingerprint and criminal history records. In 1967, the National Crime Information Center (NCIC) was established. Today, the FBI has a computer system they call the Investigative Data Warehouse (IDW), described as a one-stop shop that gives FBI agents from anywhere in the world instant access to a database containing more than 650 million records. The search capability of this system has been described as an "Über-Google."[4]

In the private sector, banks, insurance agencies, and credit-rating agencies also process enormous volumes of computer data. For example, in the early part of this decade, it was estimated that TRW Data Systems of California collected, stored, and sold access to information containing the credit histories of more than 90 million Americans. Banks, department stores, jewelry stores, and credit card companies pay this organization a subscription fee to access such information on current and potential customers. Today, Choicepoint, a leading information broker, aggregates personal data for sale to the government and the private sector. The firm maintains more than 17 billion records of individuals and businesses, which it sells to an estimated 100,000 clients, including 7,000 federal, state, and local law enforcement agencies (March 30, 2005, estimates).[5] Likewise, every major insurance company in America collects and stores information on past, current, and future policyholders.

Telemarketing and mail-order professionals similarly buy, sell, and repackage such information like so many tangible products. The countless pieces of junk mail stuffed in Americans' mailboxes each day attest to the proliferation of such information brokers. Information brokers sell personal data to companies that then target mail campaigns to people who might be interested in their products.

The Dow Jones News/Retrieval Service offers stock market quotations and reports on business and economic forecasts, plus profiles of companies and organizations. It provides its subscribers not only news and stock market indexes but also games and other forms of entertainment. Each of these information services is available to anyone with a computer, a modem, and a phone.

However, as with all great advances, there is a downside. Computer technology is changing so fast that equipment and software are often outdated before or as soon as they are installed, having a negative impact on a company's profit margin. This is especially true of microcomputers.[6]

Of greater importance for the security professional are the criminal activities associated with the misuse of computers and the technology supported by them. Early in the 21st century, one of the fastest-growing problems in this arena is identify theft. Problems that did not exist 25 years ago are commonplace today. For example, 25 years ago, few people had any fear of computer viruses. Today, several major firms are in the business of protecting from destructive viruses not only company computers but also the computers used at home.

2   CSO, CISO, and CIO Interactions

Information and information systems have become so critical to the efficient operation of business and government that organizations have put in place senior executives to direct strategic and tactical operations associated with creating, processing, transmitting, storing, and protecting information. Virtually all major corporations and government organizations have in place chief information officers (CIOs) and chief information security officers (CISOs). These executives either hold a seat in the C-suite (a term used to refer to corporate and organizational positions of the chief executive level for a particular function, the most common being the chief financial officer [CFO], the chief executive officer [CEO], and in the security profession, the chief security officer [CSO]) or directly report to someone with "chief" responsibilities.

The CIO and CISO work closely with the CSO and in most organizations have distinctively separate responsibilities. Where the CIO is responsible for the delivery of information services capabilities to the company, its workforce, and other stakeholders, the CISO is responsible for the security of those information systems and the information contained within. In more traditional companies, the CSO is responsible for determining the sensitivity of information and is responsible for the protection of information when it is not residing within an information system.

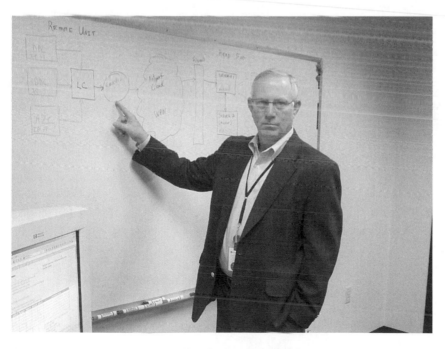

FIGURE 18.1 Wesley Eller, Manager of Security Systems for Deere & Company, reviews a network problem. (Courtesy of Deere & Company.)

More specifically, CSOs have been, and often still are, responsible for the protection of information when it is in other than electronic form. For example, much information exists in the form of paper documents. These documents, when containing pages of sensitive information, require protection. This protection usually is accomplished with more traditional security methods such as locked containers, files, and safes kept in secure or protected company areas where unauthorized persons are not allowed physical access. These traditional security methods help prevent compromise or theft of sensitive company or organization information. In some companies and organizations, the CISO duties are assigned to the CSO; however, it is more common to see them separated or to see a CISO reporting to a CSO.

Furthermore, CSOs are often charged with the responsibility of working with the creators of information and with intellectual property attorneys to determine and assign some level of sensitivity to information. Information has different degrees of value and sensitivity. Some information is routine business information with no particular sensitivity or value; other information contains trade secrets or strategic data that is of high value to the organization and perhaps even provides the organization with a unique competitive advantage. To properly protect sensitive information, it is essential to be able to identify that information which is truly sensitive and separate it from less valuable information by virtue of a physical separation or a process of uniquely identifying (marking) that sensitive information so it is clear to the possessor just how sensitive that information is. Moreover, the CSO is generally charged with developing procedures for protecting information determined to be sensitive when not contained within information systems and with ensuring that the workforce understands how to protect sensitive information.

Essentially, the CIO, CSIO, and CSO are collectively responsible for protecting the confidentiality, integrity, and availability of all company or organization information. Confidentiality of information is the process of ensuring that only authorized persons have access to protected information and that same information is used only for authorized purposes. Integrity of information is the process of ensuring that the information is not manipulated in an unauthorized way or corrupted, thus diminishing its value and utility to the organization. Availability of information is the process of making information available for authorized business use to authorized persons when they need access to perform work on behalf of the company or organization. Properly maintaining information in these three conditions—confidentiality, integrity, and availability—is particularly complex and difficult for information residing on electronic information systems.

Cooperation among the CIO, CISO, and CSO is critical if the organization is to successfully protect information and information systems. This importance is best expressed by CIOs' reported responses to the 2003 *CIO Magazine* survey. According to this report, security, which had once been on the bottom half of the CIO spending lists, had moved to the fourth highest priority. Only systems and process integration and finding ways to lower costs are ahead of security—and even those priorities are of concern to the CSO.[7]

3   Types of Computer Systems

Regardless of the type of computer system a given agency or company is using, it has four common elements: input, processing, storage, and output.

Input refers to entering data and programs into the computer. This can be accomplished by using a keyboard, mouse, scanner, voice recognition software, or telecommunications methods such as traditional phone lines or wireless transmissions. *Processing* transforms the input into machine instructions. These instructions then exist in executable form within the computer. Hardware components such as the central processing unit (CPU), memory, and basic input/output system (BIOS) affect the computer's ability to process the input. *Storage* is a generic term that refers to the areas of a computer and associated media that store information such as data and programs. Examples of storage include internal or main memory, tapes, diskettes, zip drives, hard disks, CD-ROMs, and memory sticks. *Output* is any on-screen result or printed report generated by the computer. Output devices are printers, monitors, and communication data.[8]

Microcomputers, minicomputers, mainframe computers, and supercomputers are the four general categories of computer systems available today. What separates these categories from one another is how much information each computer can store, the system's processing speed of the system, and its size.[9]

3.1 Microcomputers

These are the smallest and least expensive of the four computer categories. The term became common in the 1980s but now has mostly been replaced by the term *personal computer*. These machines are designed primarily for individuals or small businesses. Such systems can fit either on or beside a person's desk.[10] Within this category are two types of computers: personal computers (PCs) and workstations.[11]

3.1.1 Personal Computers

These machines can sit on a desk or stand on the floor or are portable and are either IBM- or Apple-compatible. Both systems can operate easy-to-use programs such as word processing, spreadsheets, and data management programs.[12]

Nonportable PCs require an AC outlet and weigh more than 20 pounds. These systems do not have special installation requirements (e.g., extra air conditioning or heavy-duty wiring). With desktop and floor-standing computers, the user can add circuit boards to the system to add functionality, such as boards for modems, scanners, video capture systems, and fax machines. The following are nonportable PCs:

- *Desktops* are machines that can fit on a single table or desk. A potential difficulty with this type of system is how much space the cabinet "footprint" occupies.[13]

- *Floor-standing computers* are those in which the system cabinet sits as a "tower" on the floor next to the desk.[14]

Portable computers do not require an AC outlet. Instead, these machines operate from a battery. Weight for portables ranges from 0.5 pound to 20 pounds. Portable systems are designed to be used in transit and have no special installation requirements. The following are portable PCs:

- *Laptop computers* or *notebook computers*, which get their name from their size, roughly that of a thick paper notebook; they weigh between 2 and 18 pounds. These systems have a flat display screen that can display mono or color images. These machines can easily be tucked into a briefcase, backpack, or simply under a person's arm.[15]

- *Mobile computing devices* weigh less than 1 pound. These computers are also called *handhelds* and are useful in specific situations. They include smart phones, electronic organizers, palmtop computers, PDAs, and other personal communicators.[16]

Although these computers are used at home or during travel, most also have the ability to be used as remote terminals to access company information. Through the Internet, it is not unusual for company employees to access company records and email from home. Given the ability of hackers to access home computers that are "always on" the Internet, security executives need to consider how to protect proprietary systems from well-meaning employees who need remote access to systems and data.

3.1.2   Workstations

Workstations look like desktop PCs but are more powerful. These systems cost between $10,000 and $150,000.[17]

3.2   Minicomputers

Minicomputers make up the middle class of computer size and power. They are popular with small to medium-sized businesses because they can be used as servers and do not require special installation. *Servers* are central computers that hold data and programs for many PCs or terminals, called *clients,* which are linked by a computer network. The entire network is called a *client/server network.*[18]

3.3   Mainframes

Mainframe systems occupy specially wired, air-conditioned rooms and are the oldest category of computer. Mainframe computers are capable of great processing speed and data storage, allowing multiple users to utilize the system simultaneously. Because of their costs (between $50,000 and $5 million), large organizations use these systems, operating them with a staff of professional programmers and technicians.[19]

3.4   Supercomputers

The largest and most powerful computers are called *supercomputers.* Such computers are high-capacity machines that also require special air-conditioned rooms and specially trained staff. They are the fastest calculating devices ever invented. To achieve this capability, cost (typically from $225,000 to more than $30 million) is set aside to achieve the maximum capabilities that technology has to offer. Because of the cost, these machines are used primarily by government, large companies, and universities.[20]

4   Networks

With increasing numbers of computers in the workplace, employees and employers want to be able to share computer resources. This sharing of resources typically includes proprietary or sensitive data, printers, and other types of applications. Because of this need, networks were developed. A network is two or more computers connected together.[21]

4.1　Local Area Networks

Local area networks (LANs) consist of two or more computers physically connected with some type of wire or cable (normally coaxial or fiber optic) that forms a data path over which information is transferred. Communication to a computer on the LAN is instantly broadcast to all the computers connected to the LAN.[22]

The most popular LAN communication protocols are Ethernet, Token Ring, and ARCnet. The Xerox Corporation developed Ethernet. When using the Ethernet protocol, computers must ensure that there is no traffic on the network before they are allowed to transmit information. IBM developed both the Token Ring and ARCnet protocols. LANs using these protocols pass a special data frame (or token) around the network in a predetermined order to enable data transmission. Under ARCnet, the order of token movement is based on a network address; in Token Ring networks, it relies on the physical placement of devices.[23]

Because of the way LANs are wired and the protocols they use, communication is limited to a short distance. This is not a major limitation; organizations and businesses have discovered that as much as 80 percent of their communications occur within a limited geographic area. This geographic area is frequently within the same department, office, building, or group of buildings.[24]

4.1.1　Wireless LANs

New technology has lead several major organizations to adopt wireless LANs (WLANs). One popular brand of wireless technology often used to provide Internet access in airports, cafés, and hotels is Wi-Fi. These networks operate on the open air, eliminating hardwire applications and their limitations. Though the systems offer added flexibility in connectivity, because users are not tied to telephone or other hard lines they present real problems for security officers assigned to protect assets. The federal government will not allow any government-funded agency to introduce wireless technology until security is improved.

4.1.2　Wide Area Networks

It was generally recognized in the 1970s and 1980s that computers in different locations need to talk with one other. This led to the development of wide area networks (WANs). WANs are more powerful networks that can function across wide geographic areas at greater speeds than LANs. Most WANs are connected via telephone lines, although a variety of other technologies, such as satellite links, are used as well. Because telephone lines were used in this system, WANs do not allow multiple computers to share the same communication line, as is possible with LANs.[25]

4.1.3　The Internet

For years, WANs used the X.25 protocol developed by the Consultative Committee for International Telephone and Telegraph, whereas LANs utilized different protocols. Because LANs communicate with Ethernet, Token Ring, and ARCnet, and WANs use X.25, these networks cannot communicate directly with each other.

The Department of Defense started a network in the 1970s called ARPAnet. This system allowed LANs and WANs to communicate with one another using a new communications rule called the Internet Protocol (IP) packet. Today, ARPAnet has evolved into the Internet, which still uses the protocol developed for ARPAnet.[26]

IP sends information across networks in packets, each containing between 1 and approximately 1,500 characters, which creates two problems. First, most information transfers are longer than 1,500 characters. Second, when data exceeds 1,500 characters, the IP breaks the information into packets. These individual packets are then transmitted, which can lead to further problems. Packets can get lost or damaged in transit or may arrive out of sequence.[27]

The Transmission Control Protocol (TCP) was developed to deal with the problems of IP. TCP divides the information into packets, sequentially numbers each packet, and inserts some error control information. Each sequentially numbered packet is then addressed to the recipient. IP then transports the information over the network. When the host computer receives the packets, TCP then checks for errors in transmitting. If errors occur, TCP asks for that particular packet to be resent. Once all the packets are received correctly, TCP will use the sequence numbers to reconstruct the original message.[28]

Many services are available on the Internet. Electronic mail (e-mail) allows individuals to send and receive messages from anyone on the Internet. Telnet allows people to log on to a remote computer and use the resources of that system if they have a valid account. Finger services allow people to ask for information about a particular user. Usenet is a system of discussion groups in which individual articles are distributed throughout the world. File Transfer Protocol (FTP) allows people to copy or move files from one computer to another. Gophers provide a series of menus from which a person can access virtually any type of textual information. The World Wide Web (the Web, or WWW) is a hypertext-based tool that allows people to retrieve and display data. Utilizing both graphics and hypertext (data linked to other data), the Web is one of the most popular tools on the Internet. This is only a sampling of the services provided by the Internet.[29]

As noted earlier, although the Web has made life easier, it has also brought with it many new problems. Anyone using the Web is well aware of the spam problem, cookies, and viruses. These are minor problems compared to the possibility that someone could steal your identity by stealing personal information that you share while online. In the first half of 2006, Symantec reported 2,249 documented new vulnerabilities, representing an increase of 18 percent over the previous period and the highest volume of vulnerabilities recorded for any reporting period.[30]

5   The Database Problem

There is little doubt that the data collected for business has become the backbone of most organizations. (*Note:* In this chapter, the authors frequently use the terms *information* and *data* interchangeably, depending on the context of the situation or description.) The need for data management resulted in the creation of data management personnel or IT departments. Because data is stored in computers, the management and security of these systems has created more problems for security than any other threat in recent years. Some 30 years ago, the security department simply controlled access to the computing center, restricting access to only those few who needed to work in the center. Today, control of access is much more complex. The task of safeguarding these assets has many parts. As previously mentioned, the three major aspects include (1) integrity: making sure that data is changed only in intended ways, (2) confidentiality: making sure that only authorized individuals view the information, and (3) availability: making sure the data is available when needed to authorized persons.

But even when proper measures are in place to assure these aspects of security, there are still two problems. First, even authorized users sometimes use data improperly (deliberately or accidentally). Second, unknown flaws in policy and its implementation can allow for unintended data access and data changes.

CIOs stress the importance of accountability in maintaining database integrity. This accountability should determine who did what to which data when and by what means. The CSO generally agrees with this approach. The answer rests in a simple concept: Because technical systems are involved in storing data, technical systems must be involved in *safeguarding* the data. Such a program should do the following:

- Send notification when someone changes data or permissions.
- Keep a record of all changes to data or permissions.
- Know what data was changed, when, and by whom.
- Know who has viewed certain data and when.
- Generate periodic reports on who accessed certain tables.
- Investigate suspicious behavior on certain tables.
- Know who modified a set of tables over a period of time.
- Automate procedures across multiple servers.[31]

5.1 The Need for Computer Security

What is computer security? People normally answer that it is protecting computers and information from some type of theft. Though true, this is only part of the answer. Earlier in this chapter we mentioned the need to protect information residing on computers or within information systems in the context of the confidentiality, integrity, and availability of such information. This too is a form of computer security; it requires protecting access to the computer, allowing only authorized persons. Furthermore, computer security must also deal with other hazards such as natural disasters (fires, floods, accidents, and so forth), essentially physically protecting them from harm. In fact, the *American Heritage Talking Dictionary* defines *security* as freedom from risks and dangers.[32]

Unfortunately, the type of crimes committed on a grand scale are often also perpetrated on a small scale. Computer crimes that startled people a few years ago for their uniqueness and scope are now being mirrored in many communities across the nation.[33] According to a *Newsweek* report, independent hackers account for 82 percent of all Web attacks. Seventy-five percent of the problems come from disgruntled employees; this includes independent hackers. Other attacks come from competitors, accounting for between 25 and 35 percent of the problems. Among this group are domestic and foreign corporations and some foreign governments. The number of hacks in 2002 reached 87,000 worldwide, with the United States being the biggest target, followed in number of attacks by Brazil, Britain, Germany, and Italy.

According to an American Society for Industrial Security (ASIS) International survey, sponsored by the ASIS Council on Safeguarding Proprietary Information, during the period of July 1, 2000, through June 30, 2001, U.S. companies lost up to $59 billion in proprietary information and intellectual property.[34] Furthermore, e-commerce online retailers also suffered losses of more than $2 billion from the cost of purchases made with stolen credit cards (identity theft). Other types of Web scams occurring during the following year (2002) involved:

- Internet auctions
- Shop-at-home and catalog sales
- Internet access services
- Foreign money offers
- Internet info and adult services
- Business opportunities
- Computers
- Web site design[35]

5.2   Classic Methods for Committing Computer Crimes

An initial entry into a business's computers often requires virtually no expertise. For employees, it is a routine matter, especially if security measures are not used. For non-employees, it may be as easy as dialing a published telephone number and then using an obvious password such as "system" or "test." Once connected to the computer, the criminal has a wide range of methods available to disrupt system activity or to observe, steal, or destroy information.

5.2.1   Data Manipulation or Theft

Changing data during or after input into a computer system is the simplest, safest, and most common method of committing computer crime. Any size of business is vulnerable. It can be performed by anyone associated with or having access to the processes for creating, recording, transporting, encoding, examining, checking, converting, or transforming the data that is eventually entered.[36] Data theft has become a major precursor for identity theft. Insiders often sell data files to an individual, who then uses the information to "steal" identities. (See the following section on identity theft.)

5.2.2   The Salami Technique

This descriptive term implies trimming off small amounts of money from many sources and diverting these slices into one's own or an accomplice's account. This form of crime is most common in banking environments with a large number of savings and/or checking accounts and automated financial processing. By creating a new program or altering an existing one, an employee can randomly deduct one to five cents from a few thousand different individual accounts. The accumulated sums can then be withdrawn by normal methods from his or her receiving account.[37]

5.2.3   The Trojan Horse

Appropriately named after the hollow horse given to the city of Troy, Trojan horse programs initially appear legitimate and will behave as though they were doing what the computer operator expects. However, the Trojan horse contains either a block of undesired computer code or another computer program that allows it to do to the system detrimental things of which the operator is not aware, such as infecting a machine with a virus, worm, bomb, or trapdoor. Remember, a Trojan horse program appears innocent and attracts users by inviting them to load it as some type of software. In reality, Trojan horse programs are not software but ruses designed to penetrate a computer system so that a program of the penetrator's choosing can become active.[38]

5.2.4 Viruses

According to the popular press and the world in general, a virus is any hidden computer code that copies itself to other programs. In the computer field, a *virus* is a set of unwanted instructions executed on a computer and resulting in a variety of effects. Currently there are over 10,000 known computer viruses.[39] The term *virus disruption* is used to categorize computer viruses.[40]

Viruses fall into one of four categories based on the type of damage that the virus inflicts: innocuous viruses, humorous virus, altering viruses, and catastrophic viruses. *Innocuous viruses* cause no noticeable disruption or destruction in the computer system. When humorous text or a graphic message is displayed without causing any damage or loss of data, then a *humorous virus* has infected the system. Categories three and four cause damage to the data stored in the computer system. *Altering viruses* change system data subtly (e.g., moving a decimal to a different place or adding or deleting a digit). When sudden widespread destruction of data both on the computer system and on the peripheral devices occurs, the machine is possibly infected with a *catastrophic virus*.[41]

5.2.5 Worms

Some people regard worms and viruses as the same type of program. Each has a replication mechanism, an activation mechanism, and an objective. Nevertheless, viruses and worms are very different kinds of programs. Viruses just infect programs, but worms take over computer memory and deny its use to legitimate programs.[42]

5.2.6 Hostile Applets

A new danger exists when you use the Web to obtain information. The danger is from so-called hostile applets that utilize a Java-enabled Web browser. Java is Sun Microsystems' scripting language. Just as viruses perform a variety of tasks without the user's knowledge, so do hostile applets. The effects can range from mild distraction to data loss.[43]

5.2.7 Bombs

Like the Trojan horse method, a bomb is a computer code a programmer inserts into legitimate software. There are two types of bombs: time bombs and logic bombs. A date or time triggers a *time bomb*, whereas some event, perhaps the copying of a file, triggers a *logic bomb*.

There are several advantages to using bombs. The built-in delay makes the program harder to trace. Perpetrators can plan the event for maximum effect, with the delay allowing the bomb to be copied into backup files. Also, some companies implant bombs in their software. If customers fall behind in payments or if customers attempt to copy the program, the bomb is set off and the program stops or the system is halted.[44]

5.2.8 Trapdoors and Back Doors

Doors allow programmers extensive access to test systems while they are being developed, allowing programmers access that would normally be denied. There are two types: trapdoors and back doors. *Trapdoors* are intentionally created and are normally inserted during software development. These doors are supposed to be removed once the software is completed. Unintentional access to software code is referred to as a *back door*.[45]

5.2.9 Time Stealing

This is one of the most common forms of computer crime because people do not consider the cost of accessing a computer without authorization. Any access uses the computer's resources (hardware, memory, software, peripherals), which costs money. Time stealing is comparable to driving another person's car (using his gas and putting wear and tear on the vehicle) without his or her knowledge.[46]

5.2.10 Electronic Eavesdropping

Tapping without authorization into communication lines over which digitized computer data and messages are being sent is electronic eavesdropping. Using technologically advanced listening devices, eavesdropping can be done on traditional telephone lines and even satellite transmission networks. If the data transmitted are not encoded, capturing and transforming the data is equivalent to using a clandestine tape recorder to record a standard telephone conversation.[47]

5.2.11 Software Piracy

Providing software for computers is big business. Software programs can cost from a few dollars to thousands of dollars. For this reason, some people are willing to copy software and resell it or give it away. This unauthorized copying of copyrighted computer programs is referred to as *software piracy*. It has been estimated that for each legitimate copy of a software package sold, between 4 and 30 additional copies are made illegally. Although most copied programs are not resold, they deny vendors and software developers profits that they should have accrued through legal sale of their intellectual property.[48]

5.2.12 Scavenging Memory

Information contained in buffers or random access memory is kept until the space is written over or the machine is turned off. This fact allows a person gaining access to these areas to search for sensitive data that may be left from previous operations.[49]

5.2.13 War Driving

This self-attached term refers to hackers who drive around locating wireless network points of entry to computers or networks. With today's technology, anyone with a laptop and powerful wireless card can enter a company's wireless network. As the range of the wireless systems increases, so do the threats from the war driver.[50]

5.2.14 Identity Theft

Using information stolen from computer databases, criminals are committing criminal acts that impact on the people whose identities are stolen. Though using false identification is an old method of criminal activity, the ability to access all types of information on the computer has given this old problem an entirely new life.

Between November 1999 and September 2001, the Federal Trade Commission (FTC) received 94,100 complaints from victims of identity theft. Complaints show the types of criminal activity as well as the consequences to the victims the identity thief caused. The following list suggests some of the more common losses:

- Cash theft using ATMs
- Electronic check fraud
- Denial of credit

- Financial service charges for overdrafts
- Lost time in dealing with the aftermath
- Criminal investigation, arrest

A study by the California Public Interest Research Group and the Privacy Rights Clearinghouse reported an average of 175 hours of lost time (over a month of activity) in attempting to correct errors caused by identity theft. Of the reports to the FTC on money losses, 200 individuals reported losses of between $5,000 and $10,000, with an additional 200 persons reporting losses of more than $10,000. The American Banking Association (ABA) reports that 29 percent ($197 million) of its check fraud losses were attributable to identity theft. Two major credit card associations reported to the U.S. General Accounting Office losses of $144.3 million in 2000, up 43 percent from 1996. A 2001 report by Celet Communications projected that losses to financial institutions from identity theft would exceed $8 billion by 2004.[51] In January 2006, a Reuters news report concluded that identity theft cost U.S. consumers 4 percent more in 2005 than the $54.4 billion it cost in 2004.[52]

5.3   Federal Computer Legislation

The Computer Fraud and Abuse Act of 1986 (CFAA) was the first truly comprehensive federal computer crime statute and was an extension of Federal Statute 18 U.S.C. 1030, enacted in 1984. The CFAA was amended in 1986, 1988, 1989, and 1990. This law covers only federal interest computers. A *federal interest computer* is one that is owned, leased, or operated by or for the federal government, contains federally protected information, or is used in interstate commerce.[53]

This act contemplates six offenses:

- The unauthorized access of a computer to obtain information relating to national security with an intent to injure the United States or give advantage to a foreign nation
- The unauthorized access of a computer to obtain protected financial or credit information
- The unauthorized access into a computer used by the federal government
- The unauthorized interstate or foreign access of a computer system with an intent to defraud
- The unauthorized interstate or foreign access of computer systems that results in at least $1,000 aggregate damage or modifies or impairs medical records
- Fraudulent trafficking in computer passwords affecting interstate commerce

Penalties range from $5,000 to $100,000 or twice the value obtained by the offense, whichever is higher, or imprisonment from 1 to 20 years, or both. These violations are investigated by the FBI's National Computer Crime Squad (NCCS), which was authorized by the CFAA.[54]

The CFAA covers all phases of computer crime, including hacking, misuse of passwords, and bulletin boards. Electronic trespassers now commit a felony when they enter a federally related computer with intent to defraud. The malicious damage felony violation applies to any hacker altering information in that computer. Preventing other legal users from accessing the computer is also defined as a felony.

The CFAA has a far-reaching new provision regarding electronic bulletin boards. It is now a misdemeanor for any bulletin board operator to provide "any password or similar information through which a computer may be accessed without authorization." This includes any sharing of information with other board users on ways to break into computers.[55]

Immediately following 9/11, the U.S. government passed the USA PATRIOT Act mentioned in Chapter 1. Part of its mandate deals with computer records and the Internet. Combating identity fraud is one of the act's primary goals, covered in Title III. Because false identities were found on a number of terrorists involved in the World Trade Center attack and because the terrorists used identity fraud in financing their efforts, the government has required financial institutions to increase efforts to prevent theft of information that allows for identity theft.[56]

6   Computer Systems Protection

Security professionals must protect from damage or loss information contained within their organizations' computer systems. The system might contain any of the following components: an electronic data processing (EDP) center, a LAN, a WLAN, a WAN, or a PC. Regardless of the type of system, the security professional's dilemma is balancing convenience in using the system against protecting the system from disasters, systems failures, or unauthorized access. Disaster-recovery planning, identification, and access control of software and data, encryption, and physical security are the four facets of computer protection.[57]

6.1   Disaster-Recovery Planning

Disasters such as fires, floods, and earthquakes are potential hazards to essential computer systems. Because these threats are unpredictable, businesses must develop contingency or disaster-recovery plans. Contingency planning requires more than an occasional emergency drill; such plans must cover all business functions, including, but not limited to, emergency response requirements, personnel resources, hardware backup, software and data file backup, and backup for related and special activities.[58]

6.1.1   Contingency Procedures

Every company should have procedures for dealing with emergencies, whether natural or manmade. Without such planning, the initial response might be a knee-jerk reaction that could lead to people being injured or killed and damaged or destroyed data, software, and hardware. To guard against counterproductive knee-jerk reactions, companies must implement contingency planning. Prior comprehensive planning is the first line of defense against all types of disaster.[59]

6.1.1.1   **Computer Center Location**   As a rule, computer centers should not be in a basement, below grade level, or on first-floor sites. This prevents the entry of surface water into the center. In addition to avoiding areas that are prone to flooding, don't place computer centers in sites along known geological fault lines. If this is not possible, make sure that the building is constructed using approved earthquake-proof practices.

Certain areas of any building present problems for security. First-floor sites are most vulnerable to forcible attack, surreptitious intrusion, civil commotion, or terrorist attack. The top floor also presents opportunities for illegal activities. People can enter the facility through skylights or by cutting through the roof.

Ideally, from a security standpoint, computer centers should be within a company-owned area at least 200 feet from the closest public access. If the building houses other types of businesses, the computer center should be on a floor completely occupied by the company, and the floor above and below the site should also be company occupied. If a new site is being selected, the preferred location is either rural or suburban.[60]

6.1.1.2 **Fire Protection** Buildings housing computer centers should be of noncombustible construction to reduce the chance of fire. These facilities must be continuously monitored for temperature, humidity, water leakage, smoke, and fire. Most building codes today require that sprinkler systems be installed.

Remember that water and electrical equipment do not mix. It is preferable to install a dry pipe sprinkler system rather than a wet pipe system. Dry pipe systems allow water into the pipes only after heat is sensed. This avoids potential wet pipe problems, such as leakage. In addition, fast-acting sensors can be installed to shut down electricity before water sprinklers are activated. Sprinkler heads should be individually activated to avoid widespread water damage.

Another type of fire-suppression system uses chemicals instead of water. Once this system is utilized it must be recharged. FM-200 is similar to Halon, which is no longer available, but with no atmospheric ozone-depleting potential. Carbon dioxide flooding systems are also available but should never be used. Carbon dioxide suffocates fire by removing the oxygen from the room. Though this effectively extinguishes most fires, it also suffocates people still in the affected area.

All chemical fire-suppression systems are relatively expensive and require long and complex governmental approval to install. Neither chemical fire suppression system protects people from smoke inhalation, nor can they deal effectively with electrical fires. They are, however, the only fire-suppression systems that do not require computer equipment to be turned off, assuring the quickest possible return to normal operations.

There should be at least one 10-pound fire extinguisher within 50 feet of every equipment cabinet. At least one 5-pound fire extinguisher should also be installed for people unable to handle the larger units. These extinguishers should be filled with either FM-200 or carbon dioxide. None of these agents requires special cleanup.

Install at least one water-filled pump-type fire extinguisher to use for extinguishing minor paper fires. Employees should be trained and constantly reminded not to use water extinguishers on electrical equipment because of the possibility of electric shock to personnel and damage to the equipment. They should also be discouraged from using foam, dry chemical, acid-water, or soda-water extinguishers. The first two are hard to remove and the others are caustic and will damage computer components.[61]

6.1.1.3 **Personnel Issues** Crisis management focuses on the swift and effective action of personnel. This means that anyone involved in the emergency response plan must be adequately trained and kept up-to-date on any changes in procedures. When ranking emergency response procedures, protection of life is the most important, followed by protection of property, and finally limitation of damage. One way to verify that employees are familiar with and have current knowledge of the contingency plan is to conduct periodic drills.[62]

6.1.2   Hardware Backup

Most people think contingency planning and hardware backup are the same thing. This is not the case. Hardware backup is only one element of contingency planning. In this phase, classifying possible disruptions is useful so that hardware backup strategies can be developed. There are three categories of disruptions: nondisasters, disasters, and catastrophes.

Nondisaster disruptions are normally system malfunctions or other failures. *Disasters* cause the entire facility to be inoperative for longer than one day. *Catastrophes* entail the destruction of the data processing facility. In this last category, a new facility must be built or an existing alternate structure must be identified to be used as the computer center.[63]

Once the extent of the disruption is ascertained, the company must make arrangements for alternate locations in which to conduct their computer operations. Alternative locations are categorized into hot, warm, and cold sites. *Hot sites* are fully configured and ready to operate within several hours. *Warm sites* are partially configured but are missing the central computer. Because the central computer is missing, these sites are less expensive than hot sites. However, it may take several days or weeks to locate and install the main computer and any other missing equipment necessary for operation. Once the equipment is installed, these sites can be operational within several hours. The least expensive sites are referred to as *cold sites*. These locations are ready to receive equipment but do not have any components installed in advance. Cold sites take at least several weeks to become operational.

The major factors in choosing the right "temperature" of the three types of site are the company's needs in terms of activation time and cost. All companies must also have a way of alerting personnel of a disruption and telling employees which site to report to for work. Computer personnel must also be trained to operate the hardware at the new site. Finally, the hardware must be compatible with the equipment that was damaged or destroyed.[64]

6.1.3   Software and Information Backup

Software includes operating systems (e.g., DOS, Windows, and Unix), programming languages (C, Pascal, Ada, COBOL, and so forth), utilities (virus checkers, security programs, and batch files), and application programs (word processors, databases, accounting programs, and so forth). Keep in mind, if the hardware at the alternate site is not compatible with the computers at the company, the software will not operate.

Information and software are both less tangible and more dynamic than hardware. To protect these elements, it is necessary to consider both the physical storage environment and the frequency of change in data. Backing up information and software can protect the company from loss. Regardless of the approach, backing up data involves copying files onto machine-readable media. The backup media can be tapes, diskettes (pretty much obsolete), hard drives, or CD-ROMs. At this point the diskette drive has been replaced by removable "finger style" hard drives.

Information and software should be stored at on- and off-site locations. Many large organizations employ a tiered strategy, using several levels of backups to achieve a balance of safety and convenience. Ideally, a business should have four sets of backup files, with one set of files staying on-site and three sets of files being stored off-site.

On-site files should be housed in a fire-resistant safe designed for computer media. These files are the most recently created backup files until replaced by newer generations. Next, there is an off-site local backup location. This location is normally within a half-mile radius of the computer site. Files at this site are stored in a fire-resistant vault and accessed daily for rotation. Backup files are retained there for one week.

Once files leave the off-site local storage facility, they are moved to an off-site remote location, which is a minimum of 5 miles from the computer center. This site also contains a fire-resistant vault designed for computer media and is accessed weekly. The remote location is used to retain remaining backup files in active use for more than one week. Finally, any permanent records that need to be retained for several years are removed to archival storage. Archival facilities should be more than 50 miles away from the original computer site. The vault should be fire- and earthquake-resistant. From a security standpoint, as the storage facility becomes more remote, accessibility decreases and security increases.[65]

6.1.4   Backup for Related and Special Activities

Besides protecting computer hardware and software, source documents must be protected. Source documents contain information transformed into machine-readable data from which printouts are generated. The printouts are referred to as either *human-readable output* or *hard copies*. This output is used to help in furthering the organization's business activities. Source documents should be copied or backed up in the event of loss or destruction so that the basic information can be reconstructed in an emergency. Backing up may take the form of duplicate copies, photocopies, microfilm, microfiche, or many other media.[66]

6.1.5   Identification and Access Control of Software and Data

People used to believe that only highly skilled technicians could gain illicit access to computers. This illusion has been shattered by many well-publicized news stories. Today, many people believe that any individual possessing basic computer skills can break into a computer system. Because of this perception and the fact that it has occasionally been proven correct, organizations must now go to tremendous lengths to protect their software and data.[67]

Computer systems can use three methods to determine if a person has a legitimate right to access the system. The three categories are:

- What a person has: cards, keys, and badges
- What a person knows: personal identification numbers (PINs), passwords, and digital signatures
- Who a person is: physical traits

Each of these authentication methods is designed to make impersonation difficult.[68]

6.1.5.1   **What a Person Has**   Some systems require that an employee insert cards, a key, or a badge into the machine before it will allow access to data. Credit cards, debit cards, cash machine cards, and ID badges are examples of cards. Cards can contain either a magnetic strip or a computer chip. Cards containing a computer chip are referred to as *smart cards*. With this system, the operator must insert the card before the machine will allow that person to access any information. With a key-lock system, a person must unlock the computer to use the system. This is one of the most popular types of security features found on PCs. Most PCs have a key-lock installed that allows the authorized user to lock out the keyboard. When the system is locked, keyboard input is not recognized.[69]

Cards, keys, or badges can be lost, stolen, or counterfeited.[70] In addition, the key-locks on PCs can be disabled if a person can remove the machine's case. This drastic method is seldom necessary, because most PC locks use the same type of key. If someone has a computer with a key-lock, it is possible that his or her key can open or close the lock on an unauthorized computer.[71]

6.1.5.2 **What a Person Knows** PINs, passwords, and digital signatures fall under the category of what a person knows. These security features work with any computer system. PINs work in conjunction with various types of card systems (e.g., ATM cards or phone cards). With this system the user inserts a card and then enters the PIN, a security number known only to the user. Passwords are special words, codes, or symbols required to access a computer system; they work in conjunction with access logs. Access logs keep track of who got in, how often they tried to enter, when they entered (date, time, and even location), and when they left, whereas passwords allow an operator into the system.

To discourage the misuse of passwords, companies should require passwords to contain at least eight characters that could be any combination of symbols, capital and lowercase letters, and numbers. Easily guessed or obvious passwords should be discouraged. Finally, the company may assign passwords to employees that are meaningless numbers, letters, or both. If the system requires a high degree of security, a password should be used only once.

The last "what a person knows" category, digital signatures, is relatively new. This system uses a public/private key system. One person creates the signature with a public key, and the receiver reads it with a second, private key. The "signature" is a string of characters and numbers that a user signs to an electronic document.[72]

The two biggest pitfalls of the "knows" systems are associated with passwords and PINs. Passwords can be guessed. People have a tendency to use real words or dates (their name, birth date, friends' or children's names, user initials, Social Security numbers, and so forth). Some system operators even fail to replace the default password. PINs and passwords are frequently written down by employees in convenient places that are easily discovered by others.[73]

6.1.5.3 **Who a Person Is** Biometric methods are utilized in this category. *Biometrics* encompasses the science of measuring individual body characteristics. Fingerprints, hand geometry, retinal patterns, voice recognition, keystroke dynamics, signature dynamics, and lip prints are common methods used to identify authorized users. In each of these methods, the computer compares the item being scanned with a copy of the item stored in the computer's memory. If the compared items match, the computer allows access. If not, the person is denied entry. Biometric techniques are not usually found on PCs, because they require expensive equipment to be connected to the computer. This equipment limits mobility, which restricts its use with portable computers.[74]

6.2   Encryption

The best way to protect any type of data is to encrypt it. This also happens to be one of the best ways to protect data on portable machines, like laptop computers. Encryption scrambles the information so that it is not usable unless the changes are reversed. Today there are at least five different methods for encrypting data. One, Data Encryption Standard (DES), is a 56-bit algorithm. This standard was first published in 1977 and is used to protect federal unclassified information (in this usage, *unclassified* means sensitive information not falling within "Classified" e.g. secret or top secret parameters). Commercial users have adopted it. DES is used in financial applications to protect electronic fund transfers and by the Internet to encrypt information.

In 1978, a 512-bit key was developed that uses the Rivest, Shamir, and Adleman (RSA) algorithm. Another encryption algorithm is Pretty Good Privacy (PGP). Using both the International Data Encryption algorithm (IDEA) and the RSA algorithm, PGP is available over the Internet and has become something of a de facto standard for encryption on the Internet.

A new algorithm called Skipjack has been developed by the National Security Agency (NSA) to replace DES. Placed in a computer chip, this algorithm is referred to as a *clipper chip*. One enhanced clipper chipset is called Capstone. These chips allow law enforcement and other agencies with access to the algorithm key to break encrypted information. The Communications Assistance for Law Enforcement Act (CALEA) preserves law enforcement's ability, pursuant to court order or other lawful authorization, to access communications and associated call-identifying information. CALEA mandates that law enforcement agencies have the legal right to break encryption algorithms.

One last system utilizes both encryption and digital signatures to protect email. This system is called Privacy Enhanced Mail (PEM) and uses both DES and RSA algorithms to encrypt e-mail messages.[75] In 1996, the U.S. government mandated that all exported data had to be set at 128-bit encryption. Both Netscape and Internet Explorer have updated browsers that use the 128-bit encryption basis.[76]

6.3   Physical security

Physical security places barriers in the path of attackers to deter them from attacking, delay them if they decide to attack, and deny them access to high-value targets should they succeed in penetrating the security system. There are two methods of security planning: traditional planning and strategic planning. *Traditional* methods start from the outside perimeter and work inward, whereas *strategic* methods are applied in just the opposite way.[77]

6.3.1   *Electronic Data Processing Centers*

EDP centers have the same physical security needs as any other business or industrial establishments. Most EDP centers use the traditional security approach, beginning with the protection of the grounds around the building, then proceeding to the building's perimeter, the building's interior, and the building's contents.[78]

With an EDP center, the outer shell provides perimeter protection and includes walls, fences, or partitions. Entrance protection restricts entry points to the EDP center. Doors and other entry points should be restricted to locations essential for safe evacuation in an emergency. A receptionist or security officer should be stationed at each entry point during all hours that the department is working.

Compartmentalizing a computer center into clearly defined rooms according to function (control, central processor, test and maintenance, storage, media library, forms, printing, waste) provides additional security. It enables access to each area to be controlled and restricted to authorized personnel. Electronic access control mechanisms such as badge-reading locks should be installed. Badges should only be issued to personnel who need to be in a given area; badges can also be time-stamped to restrict access to authorized times.

In all circumstances, the computer room should be limited to operations personnel. Protection of these critical areas should follow the principle of "authorized access only." Only people specifically necessary to its operation are allowed into the computer room. This should be the only room where programs, data, and computer equipment are all brought together. Extremely tight control of this room is imperative if the integrity and confidentiality of the data and programs are to be preserved. Install detection intrusion devices to monitor these critical areas when not occupied. These devices are usually wired directly to the department or company security office station to alert, identify, and monitor the location of an intruder.[79]

6.3.2   Personal Computers

Security used to be much easier when we only had EDP centers. These centers were and still are centralized, containing mainframes or supercomputers. Today, there are a multitude of personal computer systems. These systems range from minicomputers to pocket PCs. In addition, many of these stand-alone PCs are connected to form either LANs, WLANs, or WANs. Furthermore, the user community is mobile and needs access to ever-increasing online resources.[80] For this reason, traditional security methods are inappropriate and inadequate. To protect PCs, the strategic method, where protection starts from the computer and works toward the perimeter, is best.[81]

Access to a company's personal computers, like all other corporate computers, should be limited to authorized users only. If all the computers are in a central location, restrict entry to this area using methods similar to the security measures used in EDP centers.

With LAN and WLAN systems, begin security procedures by locking up everything that can be physically secured. With the strong trend toward concentrating control at hubs, the LAN and WLAN systems become increasingly vulnerable. With LANs, make sure that the wiring closets are secured with an appropriate lock system. Another entry point for obtaining data from a LAN system is through the wiring itself. In most companies, the wiring is hidden in the ceiling, walls, or under the carpet, giving a wiretapper a choice of points of entry. All original, necessary wiring needs to be documented and diagrammed. By routinely checking the diagrams against existing wiring, new or suspicious additions will alert security to a potential problem.[82] With WLANs, problems are even greater. More will be said about protecting these state-of-the art wireless systems later.

For any PCs placed on a person's desk, a lock-down system attaching the equipment to the desk must be installed. There are four types of lock-down systems: cages, plates, cables, and alarms. These various systems discourage theft of the equipment. Do not neglect to ensure that equipment covers are tamper-resistant. Some criminals are now removing computer chips taken from inside computers' cases and reselling them.[83]

In a similar vein, portable computers have become a popular item to steal. During the Gulf War, a laptop computer was stolen from a military staff officer's automobile in England. This machine's hard drive contained detailed plans for Great Britain's participation in the war. A common scam in many hotels, motels, and airports is for a person in front of an individual with the targeted portable computer to slow the line. If the target puts the notebook computer down, an accomplice standing behind the intended victim picks up the notebook and walks away. The first line of defense against that theft is "street smarts." This basically means keeping the computer in your constant physical possession.[84]

Besides protecting the computer itself, security must also be concerned with storage media (discs, USB flash drives, and so forth). People do transport storage media between work and home, even if company policy forbids the practice. Though not really used anymore, diskettes and computer tape cassettes are small enough to fit into a shirt pocket, and new media like thumb drives are even smaller. Even if the work environment is secure, the home environment is not. Media can also be lost between work and home. If the information contained is sensitive or irreplaceable data or programs, such a loss could be catastrophic. Employees can also alter the data, taking it back to the office to be used to update the central computer. This incorrect data would then affect the entire organization.[85]

7 Content Monitoring and Filtering

The following discussion is based on an article by D. E. Levine, "Content Monitoring and Filtering," that appeared in *Security Technology – Design* (March 2003): 70-74.

Less than a decade ago, companies paid little attention to monitoring network use, whether LAN, WAN, WLAN, or the Internet. Today, with the widespread use of the Internet, companies cannot ignore looking at who is using the service and what they are doing while on the network. Traditional security wisdom devoted time to monitoring specific types of activity. Unfortunately, experience has shown that traditional solutions are not always effective.

Vulnerabilities due to remote access through the networks fall into several major categories:

- *Hacking.* These technologically experienced computer users keep finding ways to enter and misuse corporate data and systems.
- *Voice systems.* Interconnectivity of computers and telephone systems have opened opportunities for computer techies to abuse telephone and voice systems.
- *Remote and traveling employees.* A company's "road warriors" need access to company data and computers, but maintaining security while allowing such remote access is a challenge.
- *Disgruntled employees.* Although not a new threat, the computer provides such employees with new opportunities to strike back at employers.

In a recent survey by the American Management Association, 75 percent of its members reported regularly monitoring employee phone calls, email, and Internet use.[86] The number-one rule in such activities is to inform the employees of the company's policies. The courts have ruled that employers have a right to monitor their own systems, but employees have the right to be informed regarding such monitoring activities.

7.1   Possible Security Solutions

Traditionally, security has relied on a well-written company policy to enforce access controls and handle computer abuse problems. In recent years, information monitoring has been added to the available tools. However, until recently, most monitoring was restricted to looking for destructive or prohibited content that entered the company computer network. Today, security and IT managers are just as concerned about what goes out. Software packages allow companies to block out entertainment, gaming, pornography, and other nonwork-related sites while still allowing Internet access for company-related work.

7.2   Network Security Policy

Although this might be old information for some, it is vital that companies have a clear statement of network use. The establishment of a Network Security Policy (NSP) is critical in developing other solutions. Employees need to know their rights as well as the company's expectations. Most NSPs define the problem, set the requirements, discuss solutions, and set out punishment for infractions.

Although many NSPs are written from scratch, some companies sell model policies that can be modified. In some cases, firms or consultants will gladly sell their services to assist an organization in the development of these policies.

7.3   Appropriate Use Policy

Closely allied to the NSP is the Appropriate Use Policy (AUP). This document aids the NSP by clearly delineating what the company believes is appropriate use of company computers, software, networks, and email.

7.4   Virus Scanning

Most computer users are at least familiar with the concept of scanning for viruses. Some form of antivirus software should protect every computer system or stand-alone computer. As noted earlier, there are thousands of virus threats every year, making it almost impossible for the end user to keep current. A number of companies provide virus-scanning software. Among these are McAfee, Symantec, Computer Associates, Panda, and Trend Micro. It is important to remember that although these programs are generally effective, no developer can claim to be 100 percent effective, because new viruses appear regularly.

7.5   Email Filtering Software

Because of problems (e.g., spam) noted earlier, email filtering software has become common in many company security programs. Both CSOs and CIOs are interested in this type of software, just as they are in the solutions discussed previously. Most commercial software allows the end user to set rules or protocols that mail must meet. When the email fails to meet these criteria, it is blocked. Some of the more popular vendors include:

- IM Message Inspector (www.elronsoftware.com)
- Email Filter (www.surfcontrol.com)
- Imira Screening (www.ulead.com)

- Mailwasher (www.mailwasher.net)
- Eblaster 3.0 (www.spectorsoft.com)
- Eudora (www.eudora.com)

7.6   Web Monitoring Software

Just as email software allows you to monitor and block email that fails to meet certain criteria, Web monitoring software allows the end user to monitor what Websites employees are using and for how long. Some software allows the user to filter or restrict access to certain sites. Many schools use this type of software to block pornographic and other adult content Websites from their systems.

Some of the more popular vendors in this area are:

- Websense (www.websense.com)
- IM Web Inspector (www.elronsoftware.com)
- Surfcontrol Web Filter (www.surfcontrol.com)

7.7   Spam Filtering

Some authorities estimate that between 50 and 70 percent of the email received each day is spam. This may be one of the biggest problems, or more accurately, annoyances, associated with Web use. This specialized email-filtering software blocks email based on keywords, sender's address, mail content, or other specified criteria. Vendors include the following:

- Spam Killer (www.mcafee.com)
- Spam Assassin (www.spamassassin.org)

7.8   Computer Forensic Investigations

Another tool in combating a variety of computer crimes is investigations. Some individuals, primarily consultants, specialize in forensic investigations associated with computer crimes. These individuals are often self-taught computer users from the public law enforcement sector, security, or IT.

These experts can trace email, viruses, and other computer transactions. When the I Love You virus was trailed, it led investigators to the Philippines and the originator. Investigators have traced mails from bomb threats as well as viruses. The investigator follows the trail using information stored in the receiving computer to post offices that handled the transmission. Investigators commonly use tools such as Whois or Better-Whois. These database search engines look for databases of registrars that record online users and their IP. Ultimately, the investigator finds the initiating machine. The next step is to determine who used the machine at the time the message was drafted.

Unfortunately, the tracing process is usually not this easy, because most computer users know methods to send false trails. Spoofing, or making the email appear that it is from someone else, is common. Remailing is also designed to cause investigators additional grief. Stealing email accounts is another means of protecting the criminal's identity. It would be nice if there was always an easily followed audit trail, but the reality is that smart programmers find ways to get around security protection. It takes time for the investigator to discover these new techniques.[87]

As noted earlier in this chapter, the use of WLANs is expanding. As these wireless systems, with their advantages, become more widespread, CIOs and CSOs are challenged to protect the information that is transmitted over the airwaves. Tools currently available to detect unauthorized access to the WLAN include vulnerability scanners (software) such as Ping and other well-known network discovery technologies. These software packages can detect points of access but will not identify the perpetrator. However, point-of-access information is vital to security efforts, since hackers need open ports to operate.

8   Dealing with Identity Theft

From a security position, the recent increase in identity theft presents unique problems. Identity theft is defined as using the identity information of another person to commit fraud or engage in other unlawful activities. Criminals are stealing identities by raiding databases containing information on legitimate company customers. The schemes may be old-style or high-tech. For example, a simple theft of personal information by a help desk worker resulted in thousands of individual identity thefts by his accomplices. The worker used his position at a credit-checking firm to access credit reports. The worker sold the credit reports to accomplices, who then sold the Social Security numbers and names of the individuals to identity thieves. In another scam, an identity theft ring placed a cohort as a temporary employee at a company's world headquarters. The employee, using access codes needed for work, accessed executive records. Using the pilfered Social Security numbers, names, and birth dates, the ring obtained credit cards. When apprehended the ring had charged more than $100,000 to the cards. In yet another case, an employee of a major insurance firm stole 60,000 personnel records, selling them over the Internet. A simple ad announced the sale of thousands of names and Social Security numbers. The going price for an individual identity can be less than $100. The bottom line is that personal information is only as safe as the company securing it.

What do identity thieves do with the information? Among other things, the following are their most frequent activities:

- Open new credit card accounts
- Take over existing credit card accounts
- Apply for loans
- Rent apartments
- Establish services with utility companies
- Write fraudulent checks
- Steal and transfer money from existing bank accounts
- File bankruptcy
- Obtain employment using the victim's name

Organizations can no longer ignore this problem. The number of victims has become too great and the federal government has taken an interest in protecting citizens' personal information.

The proper action regarding identity theft depends on the level of potential victimization. Companies need to find ways to protect the information that they gather, whether it's company information or private client information. Users (customers) need to know what to do if and when they become victims.

8.1 Safeguarding Corporate Information

John May, consultant and author specializing in identity theft, makes the following recommendations:

- Properly dispose of personal information. These documents should be shredded.
- Conduct proper background checks on all individuals with access to personal information.
- Limit the number of temporary agencies working within your organization.
- Develop guidelines on handling personal information.
- Train the staff on information security.
- Limit the use of Social Security numbers. Don't use Social Security numbers on identification cards, time cards, or paychecks.
- Limit access to personal information to those who have a legitimate reason for access.
- Secure personal employee information in locked files or with proper password access or through file encryption.
- Implement and enforce password security measures.
- Change passwords on a regular basis.

8.2 Protecting Your Identity

John May also has suggestions for protecting your own identity. While there are no totally fail-safe programs, the following will reduce personal risks.

- Invest in a personal shredder. Shred all personal information, credit card statements, cancelled checks, and preapproved credit card offers.
- Purchase a mailbox with a locking mechanism.
- Review your monthly bills promptly.
- Order a copy of your credit report at least once each year. (There are three major credit bureaus: TransUnion, Experian, and Equifax.)
- Keep a record of all your accounts—numbers, expiration dates, telephone numbers, and addresses.
- Opt out of preapproved credit card offers by calling 1-888-567-8688.
- Minimize the amount of information you carry in your wallet or purse. Don't carry a Social Security card.
- Cancel any seldom used cards. Limit the number of cards you use.
- Don't leave outgoing checks or paid bills in your residential mailbox. Take them to the post office.

Much of the preceding information is from Johnny R. May, "Feeling Vulnerable? Corporate and Personal Identity-Theft Protection Procedures," *Security Products* (March 2003): 30–31.

8.3   When You Are the Victim

The FTC recommends the following should you become a victim of identity theft:

- Contact the fraud departments of the three major credit bureaus to report the theft of your identity. Ask that a fraud alert be placed on your file and that no new credit be authorized without your personal consent.
- Contact the security department of those organizations where your accounts have been accessed. Close those accounts. Put passwords on any new accounts.
- File a report with the local police. Get a copy of the report for your own protection, showing the date and time the theft was reported.

The FTC has created a simple fraud affidavit that can be sent to all financial institutions to alert them of the potential of fraud from stolen identities.

8.4   Education and Training

Companies should educate employees about the problem of identity theft, how to prevent it, and what to do if victimized. Orientation opportunities should be conducted until all employees understand the significance of the problem to individuals and the company. Awareness can be increased through traditional techniques such as posters, brochures, or booklets. The use of email alerts is also encouraged.

9   Other Data Resource Vulnerabilities

Though the focus of this chapter has been on computers, other company assets can also present vulnerabilities to data theft. Sharp Electronics reports that many IT and security managers did not recognize the potential risks associated with copiers, faxes, and scanners. Survey results indicate that 77 percent of the respondents did not know that copier and printers contain hard drives. Sixty-five percent said that copiers and printers presented little or no risk to data security.

What most users, including security and IT personnel, do not realize is that document information in these devices remains in memory until memory needs eventually overwrite the data. Peter Cybuck, senior manager of Business Development at Sharp, suggests the following to provide proper security for these vulnerabilities:

- Limit access to copiers, printers, fax machines, and scanners to authorized users only.
- Install network-based software to monitor use and flag abuse.
- Protect your devices from hacking by using secured network interfaces.
- Automatically erase document data.
- Protect confidential information from accidental or intentional viewing and distribution.[88]

Summary

The world of computers and the information that is stored, processed, analyzed, and disseminated by them is constantly changing. The progress achieved in this dynamic field has improved the general state of the world, but there are always people who use the technology for personal gain or criminal activity. CIOs, CISOs, and CSOs must work together to protect the companies and the individuals that they serve. Identity theft must be curtailed and large-scale transfers of money for terrorist purposes must be controlled.

□ □ □ ▬▬▬▬▬▬▬▬▬▬▬▬▬▬▬▬▬▬▬▬▬▬▬▬▬▬▬

Critical Thinking

What problems are created when a company decides that laptop computers are a better option for employees than desktop versions? What are the advantages of such a program as well as potential pitfalls?

▬▬▬▬▬▬▬▬▬▬▬▬▬▬▬▬▬▬▬▬▬▬▬▬▬ □ □ □

Review Questions

1. Why is it safe to assume that computer crime will increase in the years ahead?
2. What are some of the vulnerabilities unique to computer systems?
3. What are LANs? What are WLANs?
4. What significance does the term *password* have in the area of computer security?
5. What is the World Wide Web?
6. How do LANs, WLANs, and the Web present security issues?
7. What are some of the management principles basic to computer security?

References

1. See http://en.wikipedia.org/wiki/Information_systems. An information system (IS) is the system of people, data records, and activities that process the data and information in a given organization, including manual processes or automated processes.
2. See http://en.wikipedia.org/wiki/Biometric. Biometrics (ancient Greek: *bios* ="life," *metron* = "measure") is the study of methods for uniquely recognizing humans based on one or more intrinsic physical or behavioral traits.
3. Covington, P.A., *Computers: The Plain English Guide*, 3rd ed. (Jackson, MI: QNS Publishing, 1991).
4. CBS Evening News, "FBI's New Data Warehouse A Powerhouse," August 30, 2006, www.cbsnews.com/stories/2006/08/30/terror/printable1949643.shtml.
5. From Wikipedia, the free encyclopedia; http://en.wikipedia.org/wiki/ChoicePoint.
6. Fischer, R.J. and Green, G., *Introduction to Security*, 6th ed. (Boston: Butterworth-Heinemann, 1998).
7. Cosgrow, Ware and Lorraine, "The Survey: What You Have to Say," *CIO Magazine* (April 1, 2003), downloaded 4/2/2003, www.cio.com/archive/040103/results_content.html?printversion= yes.
8. Carroll, J.M., *Computer Security*, 4th ed. (Boston: Butterworth-Heinemann, 1996); Cobb; Covington.

9. Sawyer, S.C. Williams, B.K. and Hutchinson, S.E., *Using Information Technology: A Practical Introduction to Computers and Communications* (Chicago: Irwin, 1995).

10. Clontz; Covington; Rothman, S., and Mosmann, C., *Computer Uses and Issues* (Chicago: Science Research Associates, 1985).

11. Sawyer, Williams, and Hutchinson.

12. Covington; Sawyer, Williams, and Hutchinson.

13. Sawyer, Williams, and Hutchinson.

14. Ibid.

15. Ibid.

16. Sawyer, Williams, and Hutchinson.

17. Ibid.

18. Covington; Rothman and Mosmann; Sawyer, Williams, and Hutchinson.

19. Covington.

20. Covington; Sawyer, Williams, and Hutchinson

21. Amoroso, E.; and Sharp, R., *PCWeek: Intranet and Internet Firewall Strategies* (Emeryville, CA: Ziff-Davis Press, 1996); Cobb; Covington; H. Hahn and R. Stout, *The Internet Complete Reference* (St. Louis: Osborne McGraw-Hill, 1994); D. E. Levine, "Local Area Network Security," in A. E. Hutt, S. Bosworth, and D. B. Hoyt, eds., *Computer Security Handbook*, 3rd ed. (New York: John Wiley and Sons, 1995), pp. 22.1–22.21.

22. Amoroso and Sharp; Cobb; Covington; Levine, "Local Area Network Security."

23. Amoroso and Sharp; Levine, "Local Area Network Security."

24. Amoroso and Sharp; Cobb; Covington; Levine, "Local Area Network Security."

25. Amoroso and Sharp; Covington; Hahn and Stout; Levine, "Local Area Network Security."

26. Amoroso and Sharp; Hahn and Stout; E. Krol, *The Whole Internet: Users' Guide and Catalog* (Sebastopol, CA: O'Reilly and Associates, 1992).

27. Amoroso and Sharp; Krol.

28. Hahn and Stout; Krol.

29. Hahn and Stout.

30. Symantec Report; dated Sept. 25, 2006, *Vulnerabilities in Desktop Applications and Use of Stealth Techniques are on the Rise*, Cupertino, Calif.

31. Mazer, Murray S., "Data Access Accountability: Who Did What to Your Data When?" A Lumigent Data Access Accountability Series, White Paper, Lumigent Technologies, Inc. (2002), downloaded 4/4/2003, www.lumigent.com.

32. *American Heritage Talking Dictionary*, SoftKey, 1996.

33. Boni, William C., and Kovacich, Gerald L., *I-Way Robbery* (Boston: Butterworth-Heinemann, 1999). p. 28.

34. See www.asisonline.org/newsroom/pressReleases/093002trends.xml, September 30, 2002 (New York).

35. "The Dark Side of the Internet,"*Newsweek* (March 17, 2003): special insert.

36. Clontz; Magel; Schweitzer.

37. Clontz; Magel.

38. Carroll; Clontz; Levine, D. E., "Viruses and Related Threats to Computer Security," in A. E. Hutt, S. Bosworth, and D. B. Hoyt, eds., *Computer Security Handbook*, 3rd ed. (New York: John Wiley and Sons, 1995), pp. 19.1–19.24; F. Simond, *Network Security: Data and Voice Communications* (New York: McGraw-Hill, 1996).

39. Computer virus information, see www.uhd.edu/computing/uss/virus.htm.

40. Carroll; Clontz; K. Dunham (1996), *Introduction to Viruses*, www.iste.org/~iste/antivirus/intro.htm; Levine, "Viruses and Related Threats"; Sawyer, Williams, and Hutchinson; Simond.

41. Clontz; Levine, "Viruses and Related Threats."
42. Clontz; Levine, "Viruses and Related Threats"; Simond.
43. Clontz; H. Hoffman, "Hostile Applets: The Dark Side of Java," *Computer Shopper* (October 1996): 80.
44. Carroll; Clontz; Levine, "Viruses and Related Threats"; Sawyer, Williams, and Hutchinson; Simond.
45. Clontz; Levine, "Viruses and Related Threats."
46. Clontz; Magel.
47. Ibid.
48. Clontz; Rothman and Mosmann.
49. Kabay, M.E., "Penetrating Computer Systems and Networks," in A.E. Hutt, S. Bosworth, and D.B. Hoyt, eds., *Computer Security Handbook*, 3rd ed (New York: John Wiley and Sons, 1995), pp. 18.1–18.55; Schweitzer.
50. Mattox, Marc, "Worried About Wireless?," *Security Products* (February 2003): 30+.
51. "Green Link: The Threat of Terrorism and the Role of Financial Institutions," *Security Products* (February 2003): 38–41.
52. Reuters news report, January 31, 2006, "Identity theft losses grow; Web a small factor," http://news.com/Identity+theft+losses+grow,+Web+a+small+factor/2100-1029_3-6033610.html
53. Carroll; Clontz; M. D. Rasch, *Legal Lessons in the Computer Age* (1996), www.securitymanagement.com/library/000122.html.
54. Carroll; Clontz; Federal Bureau of Investigation National Computer Crime Squad (1996), www.fbi.gov/compcrim.htm.
55. Clontz; Magel.
56. Mattox.
57. Sawyer, Williams, and Hutchinson.
58. Clontz; A. E. Hutt, "Contingency Planning and Disaster Recovery," in A. E. Hutt, S. Bosworth, and D. B. Hoyt, eds., *Computer Security Handbook*, 3rd ed. (New York: John Wiley and Sons, 1995), pp. 7.1–7.35; Sawyer, Williams, and Hutchinson.
59. Clontz; Hutt.
60. Carroll; Clontz.
61. Carroll; Clontz; F. N. Platt, "Computer Facility Protection," in A. E. Hutt, S. Bosworth, and D. B. Hoyt, eds., *Computer Security Handbook*, 3rd ed. (New York: John Wiley and Sons, 1995), pp. 12.1–12.24.
62. Carroll; Clontz; Hutt.
63. Clontz; Hutt.
64. Clontz; Hutt; Sawyer, Williams, and Hutchinson.
65. Clontz; Hutt.
66. Ibid.
67. Clontz; Sawyer, Williams, and Hutchinson; M. E. Walsh, "Software and Information Security," in A. E. Hutt, S. Bosworth, and D. B. Hoyt, eds., *Computer Security Handbook*, 3rd ed. (New York: John Wiley and Sons, 1995), pp. 14.1–14.20.
68. Clontz; Kabay; Sawyer, Williams, and Hutchinson.
69. Bologna, G.L., "Computer Crime and Computer Criminals," in A.E. Hutt, S. Bosworth, and D.B. Hoyt, eds., *Computer Security Handbook*, 3rd ed. (New York: John Wiley and Sons, 1995), pp. 6.1–6.31. Clontz; Kabay; Sawyer, Williams, and Hutchinson.
70. Kabay.
71. Clontz.

72. Carroll; Clontz; J. R. David, "Security for Personal Computers," in A. E. Hutt, S. Bosworth, and D. B. Hoyt, eds., *Computer Security Handbook*, 3rd ed. (New York: John Wiley and Sons, 1995), pp. 21.1–21.21; D. B. Hoyt, "Security of Computer Data, Records, and Forms," in A. E. Hutt, S. Bosworth, and D. B. Hoyt, eds., *Computer Security Handbook*, 3rd ed. (New York: John Wiley and Sons, 1995), pp. 15.1–15.24; Kabay; Sawyer, Williams, and Hutchinson.

73. Clontz; David; Hoyt; Kabay.

74. Clontz; Kabay; Sawyer, Williams, and Hutchinson.

75. Clontz; L. J. Freeh, "Impact of Encryption on Law Enforcement and Public Safety" (June 26, 1996), downloaded 7/25/96, www.fbi.gov/congress/encrypt/encrypt.htm; Levine, "Viruses and Related Threats"; J. Rothfeder, "Hacked! Are Your Company Files Safe?"*PC World* (November 1996): 170–182; Simond; V. Sussman, "Policing Cyberspace,"*U.S. News & World Report* (January 1995): 55–60.

76. Levine, D.E., "Assessing Your Encryption Options," *Security Technology & Design* (March 2003): 56–62.

77. Clontz, *National Crime Prevention Institute, Understanding Crime Prevention* (Boston: Butterworth-Heinemann, 1986).

78. Clontz; Fischer and Green; National Crime Institute.

79. Magel.

80. Clontz; Simonds.

81. Clontz; National Crime Institute.

82. Clontz; Simonds.

83. Carroll; Clontz; David.

84. Carroll; Clontz; Stone.

85. Clontz; Simonds.

86. Moses, Jeffrey, "Checking Employees' Phone, Email and Internet Usage,"*National Federation of Independent Business E-News* (April 3, 2003), downloaded 4/4/2003, www.NFIB.com.

87. Poole, Tim, and Hansen, James, "Tips for Tracking the E-Mail Trail," *Security Management* (January 2001): 42–47.

88. Cybuck, Peter, "Machine Talk," *Security Products* (March 2003): 34.

Selected Security Threats of the 21st Century

1 Introduction

The preceding chapters have highlighted some of the most important aspects of the security and loss prevention field. The discussions in the past few chapters centered on security in areas such as terrorism, retailing, and cargo and transportation security as well as on the devices and techniques used to reduce potential losses. This chapter examines several of the security threats common to many businesses. Although these threats are common to many businesses in the United States, with one possible exception they are not vulnerabilities that will be faced by every firm.

2 Economic or White-Collar Crime

Today, the concept of white-collar or economic crime is familiar to most of us. The deceptions of executives at Enron, WorldCom, and Martha Stewart made the news as we entered the 21st century. Along with the corporate misconduct at these corporations, accounting giant Arthur Andersen was humiliated in its alleged failure to apply proper accounting practices in its dealings with Enron. The junk-bond market and insurance scams are regularly reported in the news media. Ivan Boesky and other names are familiar for their involvement in various financial scams. We know that white-collar crime is against the law, yet there is no legal definition for it, and it does not appear as part of the criminal code (although some of the crimes committed by white-collar criminals, such as embezzlement, are codified). The FBI defines white-collar crime as "those illegal acts which are characterized by deceit, concealment, or violation of trust and which are not dependent upon the application or threat of physical force or violence. Individuals and organizations commit these acts to obtain money, property, or services; to avoid payment or loss of money or services; or to secure personal or business advantage."[1]

Government and the private sector keep declaring war on white-collar crime, yet they have failed to define what they are fighting. The problem is that white-collar crime is a social abstraction, not a legal concept. Morality and society's commitment to equal justice are more a part of the white-collar crime issue than is a true legal definition. Though some white-collar crimes are violations of criminal laws, others are violations of regulatory statutes and general standards of moral conduct. The most recent addition to the legal toolkit is the Sarbanes-Oxley Act of 2002, which addresses securities fraud. Corporate executives and auditors now face prison time if they knowingly submit false financial reports, alter or destroy records, or fail to maintain a proper audit trail.

Still, the way corporate "wrongdoers" are handled appears to be lax as evidenced by the lack of harsh penalties faced by executives at Enron, Arthur Andersen, and Martha Stewart. A good example is the Credit Suisse First Boston settlement. Accused of a pervasive scheme to siphon tens of millions of dollars from customers' trading profits in 2000, the company (according to the Securities and Exchange Commission (SEC)) had failed to observe "high standards of commercial honor." The SEC fined them $100 million. Still, no one was charged with a crime.[2]

Executives generally do not go to jail. According to a University of California Irvine and New York's St. John's University study, executives who stole more than $100,000 got an average of 36.4 months in prison, whereas burglars received an average of 55.6 months, car thieves 38 months, and first-time drug offenders 64.9 months. Ironically the total cost from all bank robberies in 1992 totaled $35 million, about 1 percent of the estimated cost of Charles Keating's fraud at Lincoln Savings and Loan a few years earlier.[3]

Though we are familiar with traditional white-collar crime activities, the newest entries, compliments of a shrinking global environment, are transnational white-collar scams. Today criminals, terrorists, warlords, and drug barons can reach freely around the globe. According to Michael Robert, editor of *Threat Level*, a newsletter devoted to corporate security issues, "Mafia-like organizations are springing up like daisies all through what used to be the Warsaw Pact."[4] Perhaps one of the best-known activities in this area is the Nigerian money scam.

2.1 Definitions

Edwin H. Sutherland made the first mention of white-collar crime as a concept in 1939 at an American Sociological Society conference. He defined white-collar crime as "an offense committed by a person of respectability and high social status in the course of his [or her] occupation." In 1970 Herbert Edelhertz presented a newer and perhaps more descriptive definition: an "illegal act or series of acts committed by nonphysical means and by traditional notions of deceit, deception, manipulation, concealment or guile to obtain money or properties, to avoid the payment or loss of money or property, or to obtain a business or personal advantage."[5] Edelhertz's definition has been widely accepted because it relies more on the perpetrator's actions than it does on economic social status. By including regulatory issues as well, his description also has no restriction to criminal offenses. Experience has shown that white-collar offenses are not limited to the rich and powerful and that the offenses need not arise out of the context of one's occupation.

Regardless of which of the definitions one chooses for white-collar crime, the concept today has the following common elements:

1. It is an illegal act committed in the context of a lawful occupation.
2. It generally involves deceit, deception, manipulation, and breach of trust.
3. It does not rely on physical force.
4. It has the acquisition of money, property, or power as the primary goal.

2.2   Impact

Although the crime itself may be nonviolent, the end result could be violent (an industrial plant knowingly allows carcinogenic waste to pollute water; a pharmaceutical corporation knowingly sells a weight loss drug that has potentially harmful effects on the heart). Thus the nonviolent statement is only appropriate to the means of delivery or action necessary, not to the end results. As Gilbert Geis says, "corporate criminals deal death not deliberately, but through inadvertence, omission and indifference."[6]

The exact extent of white-collar and economic crime is difficult to establish. A lack of standard classifications and definitions, coupled with limited reporting of workplace crime, contributes to the problem of accurate measurement. Over the past 25 years, five studies have identified the need for indexes to accurately measure economic crime and its true impact on society. But there is still no progress! "Security executives told the Hallcrest research staff that their companies' incident or crime loss reporting system was incomplete or nonexistent." One key security executive with one of the nation's largest corporations said, "We probably know of only 1 fraud out of every 10 that is occurring or has occurred."[7]

White-collar crime will continue to be a growing problem into the 21st century. A relatively recent $1.1 million loss was the result of collusion between the contracting company vice president and the security firm vice president. Even security is not immune from participating in white-collar crime.

3   Burglary and Robbery

Burglary and robbery have remained, in terms of the number of incidents, two of the most persistent crime problems in the United States. All types of establishments are subject to their attack, but certain businesses are more prone to these crimes than are others. Obviously banks and retail stores have more to fear from robbery than do manufacturing firms. Before discussing these two problems, we should define them; far too often people use the terms *burglary* and *robbery* interchangeably. *Burglary* is committing a crime through stealth by entering a building or other structure. In most cases, the crime committed is larceny (theft), but burglars also commit rape and arson among other felonies. *Robbery*, on the other hand, is a crime of force or threat of force. Though burglars do not like to confront people, robbers work by creating fear or by forcing people to give up their property. Although burglary may involve different kinds of crimes, robbery is strictly a crime comprising only two offenses: theft, and assault or battery.

Statistics presented in the Uniform Crime Report (UCR) indicate that the growth of these two crimes has decelerated; however, both are difficult crimes to deal with. Robbery has the potential of physical harm that all firms must consider. Burglary has the problem of insolvability because less than 2 percent of all burglary cases are solved, and the recovery rate for stolen property is less than 4 percent.

3.1 Burglary

According to the FBI's UCR, burglary accounted for over 20 percent of all property crimes in 2005, with an average loss of $1,725 per incident.[8] Even though the number of incidents has decreased over past two decades, burglary costs Americans billions of dollars annually. Because burglary is the most frequently occurring crime, it is essential that every business take particular care to protect itself against this form of crime.

3.2 The Attack

A burglary attack on a retail establishment is similar to such attacks on other types of facilities except that the burglar's job is simplified by the ease with which the premises can be inspected before the attack. The physical layout, store routines, police patrols, and internal inspections (if any) can be easily assessed by a burglar posing as a customer. For a more exhaustive survey, the burglar might even pose as a building or fire inspector and make a minute examination of alarm installations, safe location, interior lock construction, and every other detail of the defenses.

Assuming that the burglar finds a weak point, he or she enters through a door or window, through the roof, or possibly from a neighboring occupancy. Most successful burglaries (and more than 90 percent of detected attempts are successful) are made without forced entry. Curiously enough, the greatest numbers are made through the front door or main entrance.

A considerably smaller number of burglaries involve the stay-in (a "shopper" in a retail situation, for example) who gathers the loot, then breaks out and is gone before the guards or police can respond to an alarm.

3.3 Merchandise as Target

Most burglaries involve the theft of high-value merchandise, although any goods will do in the absence of big-ticket items. Police reports repeatedly show the most astonishing variety of goods that have been targeted by enterprising thieves. Anything from unassembled cardboard cartons to bags of flour is fair game. Obviously such merchandise would hardly be considered high-risk assets, but it cannot be overlooked, because possible burglars of loot come in all sexes, races, and sizes and what might seem to one as cumbersome and unprofitable could be remarkably appealing to another.

3.4 Cash as Target

Cash is naturally the most sensitive asset and the most eagerly sought, but because it is usually secured in some manner, it represents the greatest challenge to the burglar.

Stores keeping supplies of cash on hand are particularly susceptible, especially before payday. If such stores customarily cash payroll checks as a service to their employees, a burglar can assume that adequate cash must be on hand in anticipation of the next day's demands. Particular care must be taken in such cases if there is no way to handle cash needs other than to store it on the premises overnight. Every other avenue should be explored before the decision is made to keep substantial supplies of cash on hand overnight.

Because any cash will normally be held in a safe, it requires some degree of expertise to get at it. Boring, jimmying, blasting, and even carrying away the entire safe are the methods most commonly used. Few burglars are sufficiently skilled to enter a safe by manipulating the combination, so applied violence is the normal approach. Unfortunately, even in cases where an attack is unsuccessful, the damage to the container is likely to be severe enough to require its replacement. This is equally true in all areas where entry is made or attempted. The high cost of repairing damage to buildings and equipment can be almost as harmful as the loss in cash or merchandise.

3.5 Physical Defense Against Burglary

Burglary defense has been widely studied for years, and several strategies have been developed to combat this crime. The most common approach is referred to as *target hardening*. Simply speaking, this means that the basic security precautions outlined in the preceding chapters are applied to the facility, including attention to door construction, locks, alarms, and surveillance devices.

It is always wise to let potential burglars know that the facility is well protected. In most cases, a burglar will avoid facilities where the chance of getting caught is great, instead seeking out other locations that are not as well protected.

Another defense against burglary that has met with some success is *reducing the value of merchandise*. This approach usually includes marking company property with company identification tags or recording serial numbers that are easily traced. Because many fencing operations will turn away merchandise that is well marked and thus identifiable, burglars prefer merchandise that has no identifiable numbers.

In addition, some communities have developed "sting" operations—that is, fencing operations run by law enforcement officials. These operations require large outlays of cash but have proven effective in closing down major theft rings. Firms suffering substantial losses from theft should consider working with local officials in developing sting operations.

3.5.1 Alarms

Alarms of some kind can make the difference between an especially effective burglar-proofing program and one that provides only minimal protection. The type of alarm providing the best results is a matter of some disagreement, but there is little disagreement over the effectiveness of having some kind of system, however simple. Several alarm systems are covered in Chapter 11.

Many stores report satisfaction with local alarm systems. They feel that the sound of the signaling device scares off the burglar in time to prevent the looting of the premises. Many police and security experts feel such alarms are ineffective because the response to the signal is only by chance and because such a device serves to warn the intruder rather than aid in capture. Because most managers are less interested in apprehending thieves than they are in preventing theft and because local systems are inexpensive and can be installed anywhere, they continue to be widely used. Certainly they are preferable to no alarm system at all. With the relatively inexpensive dial alarm systems and national central-station paid services, many retailers and homeowners have replaced older, less reliable systems with new state-of-the art technology.

Whether the outer perimeter should be fitted with alarms and whether space coverage alarms should be used are matters peculiar to each facility. This issue must be carefully studied and determined by the manager. But it is always important to have the safe fitted with an alarm in some way.

3.5.2   Safes

The location of the safe within a premises will depend on the facility's layout and location. Many experts agree that the safe should be located in a prominent, well-lighted position, readily visible from the street, where it can be seen easily by patrols or by passing city police. In some premises—especially where no surveillance by passing patrols can be expected—it is generally recommended that the safe be located in a well-secured and alarm-rigged inner room that shares no walls with the exterior of the building. Floors and ceilings should also be reinforced. The safe should be further protected by a capacitance alarm. The classification of the safe and the complexity of its alarm protection will be dictated by the amount of cash the safe will be expected to hold. This should be computed on the maximum amount to be deposited in the safe and the frequency with which such maximums are stored therein.

3.5.3   Basic Burglary Protection

Obviously the amount of protection and the investment involved in it will depend on the results of a careful analysis of the risks involved in each facility. There is no single way—no magic solution—to the problem of burglary. Every system and each element of that system must be tailored to the individual premises.

Managers must evaluate the incidence of burglary in their neighborhoods as well as the efficiency and response time of the police. They must consider the nature of the construction of the building and the type of traffic in the area. Consideration must also be given to the ease with which merchandise can be carried off and by what probable routes. Managers must consider the reductions in insurance premiums provided by various security measures. The advice of city police in antiburglary measures and their experience in analogous situations should be sought out. In short, homeowners, retailers, and other businesses owe it to themselves to learn as much as they can about coping with the problem of burglary and dealing with it as forcefully, economically, and energetically as possible.

3.6   Robbery

Although the number of robbery incidents has declined in recent times, robbery remains a serious crime because of the potential harm to its victims. Deaths in convenience store holdups make this point all too clear! However, convenience stores have taken a proactive approach to robbery reduction. According to the Bureau of Justice Statistics, the overall rate of robbery has remained relatively low since 1973.[9] Attention to the following points is credited with most of the reduction:

- Employee training programs
- Proper cash control; extensive use of "drop" safes with signs noting that there is no more than $50 in the register during the day and $30 at night

- Visibility measures, including proactive work with police agencies offering police substations in conjunction with store operations; other programs allow police to write up reports at convenience stores
- Use of technology—for example, CCTV and silent panic alarms

Aside from private individuals, retailers and banks take the brunt of these attacks. Because less than a third of all robbers are arrested, retailers are obliged to take measures to protect themselves from this most dangerous crime.

3.6.1 The Nature of Robbery

The incidence of robbery varies only slightly according to geographical location, and the occurrence of such incidents is fairly constant throughout the week. The daily peak of robberies is at 10:30 P.M. Those stores remaining open all night, however, suffer the majority of robberies between midnight and 3:00 A.M. More than 90 percent of the money stolen is taken from cash registers, and 8 out of 10 robbers are armed with handguns. Eight out of 10 assailants are generally under 30, and of these, the vast majority are male. Although weapons (or the threat of harm) are used, violence is generally carried out in less than 5 out of 100 cases. Eighty percent of the fatal cases occur in situations in which store personnel did nothing to motivate the attack. And while lone robbers carry out 60 percent of all robberies, 75 percent of the death or injury occurrences take place in situations involving two or more robbers.

We thus find that the robber is most apt to be a young man working alone, carrying a pistol, and threatening employees with bodily harm unless they hand over the money from cash registers. He rarely carries out his threats—probably because the employees wisely comply with his demands—unless accompanied by a partner, in which case he is very likely to cause death or injury without provocation. The deaths of convenience store employees during holdups with multiple assailants clearly illustrate this trend.

3.6.2 Robbery Targets

Robbers are typically criminals making a direct assault on people responsible for cash or jewelry. Their targets may be messengers or store employees taking cash for deposit in the bank or bringing in cash for the day's business. Robbers frequently enter stores a few minutes before closing and hold up the managers for the day's receipts, or they may break into stores before opening and wait for the first employees, whom they force to open safes or cash rooms. In some cases, managers or members of their families have been kidnapped or threatened in order to coerce access to company cash.

Delivery trucks and warehouses can also be targets of robbers. These latter cases require several holdup people working together, and they are a very real threat and do occur. The majority of cases, however, are still carried out by the lone bandit attacking the cash register.

Businesses most frequently attacked are supermarkets, drugstores, jewelry stores, liquor stores, gas stations, and all-night restaurants or delicatessens.

3.6.3 Cash Handling

Probably the major cause of robbery is the accumulation of excessive amounts of cash. Such accumulations not only attract robbers who have noticed the amount of cash handled but they are also more damaging to business if a robbery does occur.

It is essential that only the cash needed to conduct the day's business be kept on hand, and most of that should be stored in safes. Cash should never be allowed to build up in registers, and regular hourly checks should be conducted to audit the amounts each register has on hand.

Every store should make a careful, realistic study of actual cash needs under all predictable conditions, and the manager should then see to it that only that amount plus a small reserve is on hand for the business of the day. Limits should also be set on the maximum amount permitted in each register, and cashiers should be instructed to keep cash only to that maximum. Overages should be turned in as often as necessary and as unobtrusively as possible.

In large-volume stores, a three-way safe is an invaluable safety precaution. Such safes provide a locked section for storage of two or three hours' worth of money that may be called on for check cashing or other cash outlays. The middle section has a time lock that is not under the control of any of the store personnel and has a slot for the deposit of armored-car deliveries or cash buildups. Cash register trays are stored in the bottom compartment.

Movement of cash buildups from registers to the safes should be accomplished one at a time, and every effort should be made to conceal the transfer. This is particularly important at closing time when registers are being emptied. The sight of large amounts of cash can prove irresistibly tempting to a potential robber.

3.6.4   Cash-Room Protection

If the store has a cash room, it must be protected from assault. Basic considerations as to location and alarming were outlined in the discussion on antiburglary measures earlier in this chapter, but an additional precaution to protect against robbery should also be noted: The room itself must be secure against unauthorized entry during business hours. If possible, you should draw up a list naming the people authorized to enter the cash room and under what conditions. It should be made clear that there are to be no deviations from these authorizations under any circumstances.

The door to the room must be secure in itself and securely locked. If fire regulations indicate the need for additional doors, they should be equipped with panic locks and have alarms fitted to them. The entrance should be under the control of a designated person who, through a peephole or other viewing device, can check people who want to enter. In larger facilities, an employee at a desk outside the room can control entrance, although this arrangement should be studied carefully before implementation because a robber could force such an employee to permit entrance unless the position is protected from the threat of attack.

3.6.5   Opening Routine

Because the potential for robbery is always present when opening or closing the store, it is important that a carefully prescribed routine be established to protect against that possibility.

At opening, the employee responsible for this routine should arrive accompanied by at least one other employee. The second employee should stand well away from the entrance while the manager prepares to enter. The manager should check the burglar alarm, turn it off, and enter the store. The interior, including washrooms, offices, back rooms, and other spaces that might offer concealment to robbers, should also be checked. After a specific, preestablished time, the manager should reappear in the main entrance and signal the second person with a predetermined code.

This code, which should be changed periodically, should be given both in voice and in some hand signal or gesture such as adjusting clothing or smoothing hair. One coded reply and gesture should indicate that all is clear; another should indicate trouble. It is important that this code be innocent and reasonable sounding to allay any suspicions on the part of robbers (if any are present).

If assistants get the danger sign, they should reply with something to the effect that they will return after getting a paper, checking the car, or buying a cup of coffee. The assistants should then proceed slowly and deliberately to a predetermined location and call the police. Experienced security experts all stress the value of carrying a card with the number of the police station.

3.6.6   Transporting Cash

Because a basic principle in robbery protection is minimizing cash on hand, from time to time money will necessarily have to be moved off the premises to a bank. Ideally this should be done by an armored-car service. If this cannot be done because of cost or unavailability of such service, efforts should be made to get a police escort for the store employee acting as messenger.

In any event, messengers so assigned must be instructed to change their routes; they should also be sent out at different times of day and if possible on different days of the week. They should regularly change the carriers in which the money is stored. It might be anything from a brown paper bag to a toolbox. They should stay on well-populated streets and move at a predetermined speed. The bank should be notified of their departure and given a close estimate of the time of arrival.

3.6.7   Closing Routine

Shortly before closing time, the manager should make a check of all spaces, similar to that conducted during opening. An assistant should watch unobtrusively for any unusual activity on the part of departing customers. When all registers have been emptied and the money locked up, the assistant should wait in the parking lot and watch as the manager completes the closing routine. When the manager has checked the alarm and locked up, the assistant will be free to go. If the manager signals trouble during any of this routine, the assistant should follow the same routine as at opening.

3.6.8   Other Routines

Because any entry into a store leads to a potential for robbery, it is important that the manager never try to handle it alone. In a number of instances, robbers have phoned managers and reported damage or a faulty alarm ringing in order to lure the managers into opening the store. The managers are then in a position to be coerced into opening the safe or at least into providing a bypass of the alarm system. If so notified, the manager should phone the police and/or the appropriate repair people and wait for them to arrive before getting out of his or her car. A manager should never try to handle the matter without some backup present.

3.6.9   Employee Training

A fully cooperative effort by all employees is essential to any robbery prevention program. Properly indoctrinated employees will know how to use a silent, "hands-off" alarm, if such an installation is deemed advisable. They will learn to question people loitering in unauthorized areas. They will be alert to suspicious movements by customers and will know what to do and how to do it if they are aware that a holdup is in progress in some other part of the store. They will remain cool and make mental notes of the robbers' appearance for later identification. They will cooperate with the robbers' demands to an acceptable minimum. They will not under any circumstances try to fight back or resist. If possible, they will hand over the lesser of two packs of money if that choice is open, but they will never do so if there is the slightest chance that the robbers will notice. They will remain alert to the possibility of robbery, and if they are involved in one, they will make careful observations for assistance in apprehending the criminals.

3.6.10   Robbery Prevention

By incorporating some of the ideas already discussed in this chapter, several companies have developed robbery prevention programs. These are comprehensive plans designed to make stores less attractive targets for robbers, to protect employees, and to assist officials in apprehension.

The primary goal of these programs is to make the store less attractive to potential robbers. One successful strategy has been to publicize the fact that the store has a robbery prevention program and does not keep large amounts of money in cash registers and that employees do not have the combination to the drop safe. Today it is not unusual to see large signs stating these facts placed in plain view in many stores. This program became essential to several major convenience store and gas station chains during the early 1970s when a rash of robberies left several employees dead. The importance of such programs again dramatically came to public attention with the rash of slayings associated with convenience stores in the 1990s.

Cash register location has also been carefully studied. In general, it is advisable to locate cashiers in areas where they are visible from the street but where the register drawer and cash transactions are not easily observed by passersby.

After a robbery has occurred, employees are often supplied with forms that ask for specific details about the robber's appearance and voice and show pictures of various weapon types as an aid to identification. Though it might not be possible to describe a robber in the police jargon (for example, 6 feet, 2 inches; 200 pounds; light complexion, dark brown hair), it is possible to use descriptive aids that will allow the police to develop such a description. Because many people are not practiced enough to guess someone's specific height, such information is often not reliable. Employees can be trained, however, to match a person's height to reference points in the store or to other people. For example, employees might notice how the robber's height compared to their own or might observe that the robber came up to a certain point on a doorway. Weight and build might be better described by comparing the robber with another person—perhaps the investigating police officer or the store manager. In addition, employees must realize that the best information concerning the robbery is the escape mode. Did the robber leave on foot, on a motorcycle, or in a car? Only one employee should try to follow the robber after allowing the robber time to get far enough away so that the employee is not in jeopardy.

As in the case of burglary, there is no absolute solution to the problem of robbery, but this does not mean that firms must accept robbery as a business given. It has been shown that we can reduce robbery attempts by careful management procedures and by certain physical security measures.

4   Labor Disputes

If a facility is faced with a deteriorating labor-management relationship during negotiation of a new union contract, it might be necessary to review those security measures designed to protect personnel and property during unusual periods.

With the passage of the National Labor Relations Act and the Norris LaGuardia Act in the early 1930s, followed by similar legislation in many industrial states, a change in strike profiles began that has continued to the present. Whereas violence occurs with significant frequency, it is not generally planned or used in a tactical way by modern management or organized labor. Still, in specific disputes and local situations, violence may be intentionally generated.

Spontaneous violence occurs in almost every strike situation except the most mild. Dealing promptly and effectively with these sudden crises is critical in preventing the entire mood and complexion of the strike from becoming violent.

4.1   Security's Role

Security directors should review every element of the company's strike plans with their departments to ensure that the staff is totally familiar with the job to be performed and that every member of the staff is adequately trained to perform as necessary. They should be certain that all security personnel are aware that their role is to protect personnel and property only and that they are not to participate in any way in the elements of the dispute, which is strictly between management and the participating union.

In clarifying policy and getting approval of specific plans of action from responsible management, foresight is indicated. The earlier the protection system is established, the better. Many elements will require time and considerable concentration from the executives who will later be occupied with handling the labor problem and therefore may not be available for consultation.

Here is a checklist of some possible measures as a guide to the development of a more thorough plan that will apply more specifically to a given facility:

1. Secure all doors and gates not being used during the strike and see that they remain secured.
2. Remove all combustibles from the area near the perimeter—both inside and outside.
3. Remove any trash and stones from the perimeter that could be used for missiles.
4. Change all locks and padlocks on peripheral doors of all buildings to which keys have been issued to striking employees.
5. Recover keys from employees who will go out on strike.
6. Nullify all existing identification cards for the duration and issue special cards to workers who are not striking.

7. Check all standpipe hoses, fire extinguishers, and other firefighting equipment after striking workers have walked out.

8. Test sprinkler systems and all alarms—both fire and intrusion—after striking workers have walked out.

9. Consider construction of barriers for physical protection of windows, landscaping, and lighting fixtures.

10. Move property most likely to be damaged well back from the perimeter.

11. Be certain all security personnel are familiar with the property line and stay within it at all times when they are on duty.

12. Guards are not to be armed, nor are guards to be used to photograph, tape, or report on the conduct of the strikers. The only reports will relate to injury to personnel or property.

13. Notify employees who will continue to work to keep the windows of their automobiles closed and their car doors locked when they are moving through the picket line.

14. Consider the establishment of a shuttle bus for nonstriking employees.

15. Establish, in advance, which vendors or service people will continue to service the facility, and make arrangements to provide substitute services for those unwilling to cross the picket line.

16. Keep lines of communication open.

17. Because functional organizational lines may be radically changed during the walkout, find out who is where and who is responsible for what.

4.2 Right to Picket

The federal and state courts, along with the Labor Management Relations Act, protect picketing on public property as an exercise of the right of free speech and free assembly. Although picketing is protected, there are established rules restricting both the purposes and the methods used by picketing unions. The employer, nonstriking employees, customers, suppliers, service personnel, management staff, and visitors have a right to enter and leave the business without obstruction. There is no right to picket on private property.

However, it is important to remember that union officials and pickets have the right to talk to anyone entering or leaving company facilities. On the other hand, the nonunion individuals, truckers, managers, and so on also have the right to not engage in conversation. There is also no law against passing out pamphlets or leaflets on public property.

The responsibilities of security officers generally do not involve pickets unless they extend onto company property. Pickets are usually the responsibility of public law enforcement.

4.3 Pre-Strike Planning

The best place to begin handling a strike is long before one is anticipated. The company should have comprehensive written strike and work-stoppage procedures. These policies should be reviewed annually. Education of all management personnel, especially security, is a must.

4.4   Law Enforcement Liaison

Because a portion of the responsibility in dealing with strikes falls on the shoulders of local law enforcement agencies, it is essential that security and police personnel understand each other's mutually supportive roles. At least one company person, usually security management or someone from human services, is assigned as a liaison to ensure a common understanding of company roles and law enforcement expectations. Such relationships should be cultivated over time and not wait until a strike situation. Similar relationships should be developed with local fire, telephone, city services, and so on.

5   Espionage

Espionage usually brings about thoughts of spies sneaking into a company's private vaults and copying or stealing formulas or products. Government spies, typified by James Bond, working in glamorous settings, retrieve government secrets. The reality is somewhat different, but in a world of increasing corporate competition and computer-based data storage, the problem of espionage is increasing. The spy's tools may have transitioned to the computer and other sophisticated technology, but many of the people are Cold War participants, now working for private firms.

Still, the issue of what constitutes espionage is gray. Competitive intelligence (also a form of espionage) involves legal means of data collection. This ranges from analyzing publicity documents to schmoozing representatives or researching securities filings and news reports. It does not involve illegal means. The following quotation from a 2001 *Business Week* publication illustrates the point well: "Companies that engage in corporate spying see a payoff in increased revenue, costs avoided, and better decision-making."[10]

Research and development investment in the United States was about $174 billion in 1996. In 1994 the FBI reported that its economic counterintelligence unit had information that nearly 50 percent of research and development firms had a trade-secret theft, and 57 percent reported repeat or multiple thefts. An employee most often accomplished the thefts. FBI Director Louis Freeh noted that the cost to U.S. business for all types of espionage was more than $100 billion annually.[11] Corporations have gathered information on products, pricing, research, and corporate strategies for years from media reports, public financial statements, and other open-source research materials. In today's market, more and more companies seem to be turning to the dark area of industrial espionage. According to James Chandler, executive director of the National Intellectual Property Law Institute, "We have seen industry after industry collapse after losses of intellectual property." An American Society for Industrial Security (ASIS) report found that 700 cases of theft of intellectual property at 310 companies were discovered during 1993.

Although espionage is not a new threat, the fall of the Soviet Union in the 1990s prompted increased activity. The 2005 case of Hewlett-Packard executives spying on employees and each other as well as members of the press may be the current pinnacle of unethical practices. In this case the espionage was used against the company's own people in an attempt to find out who was leaking company information to reporters. In a recent American Management Association and ePolicy Institute survey of 526 companies, 76 percent reported that they monitor Website connections used by workers; 26 percent have fired workers for "misusing" the Internet; and 6 percent have fired workers for misusing office phones.[12]

Probably the most embarrassing case in recent years occurred in 1994, when the FBI arrested Aldrich Ames on espionage charges. Ames had been working for the CIA for more than 31 years and spying for the Soviet government since 1986. Ames passed secret CIA information on Russian agents working for the U.S. government to the KGB, resulting in the deaths of some compromised agents. Ames was paid millions of dollars by his KGB contacts during the years that he provided them with intelligence information. The case shows that any organization can be victimized.

One of the biggest cases of industrial espionage was filed in December 1996 against a purchasing chief for General Motors after he defected to Volkswagen. The former GM employee is accused of taking thousands of pages of confidential documents, slides, computer disks, and price lists. Specifically, the former GM employee is accused along with two other GM associates of taking plans for a superefficient car factory. VW then opened a plant similar to the GM plan.[13] VW has also been the target of espionage. In September 1996 the company discovered a night-vision video camera and satellite uplink transmitter hidden in its Wolfsburg, Germany, testing facility.[14]

The full extent of the problem is not known, because many corporations do not disclose problems. Companies fear that disclosure of problems will hurt their image with stockholders and customers. A recent survey of Fortune 1000 companies, conducted by ASIS, estimates that the theft of intellectual property may amount to more than $300 billion each year.[15]

Those cases that are known tell a story of great financial gain for the agency or company acquiring information, while the victim suffers bankruptcy in some cases. Ellery Systems, Inc., of Boulder, Colorado, a software developer, went out of business when an employee allegedly transferred 122 computer files with source codes from Ellery Systems computers to his own startup company. In 1994 Genetics, Inc., was the victim of a theft of a patented drug formula. FBI agents posing as Russian agents discovered the theft. The two thieves contacted the agents in an attempt to sell the formula.[16]

To counter these espionage trends, the U.S. House Judiciary Committee approved the Economic Espionage Act of 1996; the legislation was sponsored by the U.S. Justice Department.[17] The Department of Justice has prosecuted several major cases since the introduction of the Act. Insiders played a major role in the espionage cases, providing information for pay to interested third parties. In one case an insider sold information to rival company Four Pillars Enterprises of Taiwan. The insider received a six-month sentence while Four Pillars Enterprises was fined $5 million. This was the first case tried under the new law but not the last.

Following the implementation of the 1996 Act, the U.S. government has successfully prosecuted offenders, with the most recent case occurring in 2007, when a naturalized American citizen of Chinese heritage was convicted of conspiring to export classified defense technology to China. Chi Mak was employed by Power Paragon, a California defense contractor, part of L-3 Communications.[18] The actual data he shared with foreign nationals was export controlled. The U.S. Arms Export Control Act places restrictions on the sale of certain technologies with military applications. Such technology sales or transfers must have prior approval by the U.S. Department of State.[19]

In a 2004 presentation before the International Security Managers Association in Scottsdale, Arizona, Deputy Director Bruce Gebhardt highlighted the importance of dealing with economic espionage. Over $250 billion per year is lost in the theft of trade secrets and technologies. Counterfeiting of U.S. products by overseas competition costs at least the same. The number of countries now spying against U.S. companies has increased, with many countries using students and business executives to gather information. However, approximately 75 percent of the cases involve company insiders.[20]

6 Piracy

Though certainly not a new problem, the copying of copyrighted materials by unauthorized means is one that has grown with the increase in the amount of material produced for public consumption. A police raid of a private home in Queens, New York, in 1996 discovered more than 85,000 pirated cassettes. The operation was copying a Mariah Carey tape with the confiscated value of $82,000 in cassettes and $30 million for 3 million labels.

According to the Recording Industry Association of America (RIAA), this one operation alone cost the recording industry more than $300 million in 1995. Overall, U.S. industry loses $200 billion from counterfeiting, according to the Better Business Bureau.[21] This is up from $60 billion in 1988. In 1982 the loss was only $5.5 billion. Advances in technology have made possible high-speed, high-quality duplication by pirates. Compact disks (CDs), either audio or video, are the medium most often copied. Even home computer owners have the ability to download and copy their own audio (CD) and video (DVD).

In a statement made in November 2002, the RIAA chairman and CEO pointed out the growing problem of piracy of CDs in Mexico. The Mexican Supreme Court recently relocated to a quieter area in an effort to get away from the loud music being played by street vendors who were selling pirated CDs.[22] Russia and China top the U.S. Trade Representatives list of piracy hotspots in 2007. Russia has pledged to take action against CD and physical piracy as it is seeking admission to the World Trade Organization.[23]

In related events, Kazaa, an Australian computer file-trading firm, was charged with U.S. copyright violations through the use of the Internet. The company has to date avoided the fate of parallel company Napster. The use of international offices to continue offering its product upset the International Federation of the Phonographic Industry, which represents global music industry interests. The World Intellectual Property Organization (WIPO) tried to eliminate nation hopping when it enacted the WIPO Copyright Treaty, which outlines copyright legislation that all countries should adopt. The problem is that many European Union nations including Italy did not sign the agreement.[24]

Piracy refers to the illegal duplication including distribution of recordings. It takes three specific and often confused forms:

- *Counterfeiting*. The unauthorized recording of prerecorded sound as well as the unauthorized duplication of original artwork, label, trademark, and packaging.
- *Pirating*. The unauthorized duplication of sound or images only from a legitimate recording.
- *Bootlegging*. The unauthorized recording of a musical broadcast on radio, television, or a live concert. Bootlegs are also known as *underground recordings*.

With the growth in this type of criminal activity, security measures are a must for any company involved in the production of audio and visual products for sale. The U.S. Customs Office seized $100 million in counterfeit products in 2003, almost double the figure seized in 2001.[25]

Besides the high-publicity piracy, other violations of copyrights and patent laws are less known to the public. In fact, many individuals who use the Internet and download documents may be unwittingly committing violations of the copyright and patent laws. There have been guidelines in the copying and distribution of copyrighted materials for years, but recent use of materials from the Internet has prompted the federal government to take a closer look at electronic media and the potential abuse of copyright laws.

Of interest and some recognition, however, is the production of illegal copies of computer software. Much as with the battle to control music file swapping, production and sale of illegal copies of operating systems and computer games is big business. Microsoft sells its Microsoft Office CD-ROM for approximately $800, but pirated copies sell for much less—as little as $10. The problem costs Microsoft an estimated $300 million each year.[26]

In the past several years, counterfeiting of products has also come to represent a number of health and safety risks. Counterfeit pharmaceuticals have caused physical harm. An alert on the drug Cialis, sold on several Websites, was issued in March 2006 by the Danish Medicines Agency when counterfeit products were advertised on the Internet.[27] The pet industry is also plagued by counterfeit pet health-care products. And most recently counterfeit auto parts have been making their way into the system. Brake pads that look like the real thing are made from compressed grass. It has been reported that there are enough counterfeit parts to assemble a complete car. In still another area, a shipment of counterfeit extension cords were seized by U.S. Customs. Not so lucky were Verizon customers who purchased new batteries that later overheated. And in China, 60 infants were reportedly killed by fake baby formula.[28]

The worst violators of copyright law are China and Russia, according to a recent report by the International Intellectual Property Alliance (IIPA). The IIPA reported losses from industry members that topped $15.25 billion in 2006 from only the top 60 worst pirating nations. If the United States and the rest of the world were included, the figure could be as much as $35 billion annually. The only recourse available to the IIPA is through the U.S. Trade Representative, which could take action against countries by taking away certain duty-free trade privileges.[29]

Summary

Although the security concerns we have covered are not present in every business, they are of significant interest to private individuals where the impact of the crime is often felt in increased costs for merchandise and services. With the growing use of the Internet and associated technology, many of these crimes are changing direction to use the reach of the Internet or exploit computer technology. To combat these crimes, security and law enforcement will need to enhance their tools by becoming proficient at monitoring and investigating crimes using computers and related technology.

□ □ □ ▬▬▬▬▬▬▬▬▬▬▬▬▬▬▬▬▬▬▬▬▬▬▬▬▬▬▬

Critical Thinking

Why should we as individuals have any concern over the illegal copying of products, particularly DVDs and CDs? After all, the only one hurt is the large corporation, and they lose only small amounts compared to their total profits. Discuss this statement.

▬▬▬▬▬▬▬▬▬▬▬▬▬▬▬▬▬▬▬▬▬▬▬▬▬▬▬ □ □ □

Review Questions

1. What distinguishes robbery from burglary?
2. What is target hardening? List several target-hardening techniques.
3. Describe the concept of robbery prevention.
4. List some of the measures that should be taken prior to a labor strike.
5. What is the latest problem associated with espionage?
6. What is the difference between piracy and bootlegging in the recording industry?

References

1. U.S. Department of Justice, Federal Bureau of Investigation, *White Collar Crime: A Report to the Public* (Washington, D.C.: U.S. Department of Justice, 1989).
2. Leaf, Clifton, "White-Collar Criminals: Enough Is Enough," downloaded 1/17/03, www.doublestandards.org/leaf1.html.
3. Ibid.
4. "The New White Collar Crime: Enemy Within?," SC *Magazine*, downloaded 1/17/03, www.scmagazine.com/scmagazine/enemy.
5. Edelhertz, as quoted in Gary S. Green, *Occupational Crime* (Chicago: Nelson Hall, 1990), p. 11.
6. Geis, Gilbert, as quoted in Green, p. 16.
7. Cunningham, William, Strauchs, John J., and Van Meter, Clifford W., *The Hallcrest Report II: Private Security Trends 1970–2000* (Boston: Butterworth-Heinemann, 1990), p. 28.
8. www.fbi.gov/ucr/04cius/documents/burglarymain.doc.
9. Bureau of Justice Statistics, *National Crime Victimization Survey: Violent Crime Trends*, 1973-2001, downloaded 1/17/03, www.ojp.usdoj.gov/bjs/glance/tables/viortrdtab.htm.
10. "The Corporate Spy," *The Integrity News*, Vol. x, No. 28, November 26, 2001.
11. "Economic Espionage Plots Loom," *Security* (August 1996): 14–15.
12. As quoted in "The Changing Rules of Corporate Spy Games," www.csmonitor.com/2006/0925/p02s01-usec.htm.
13. Maynard, Micheline, "Execs Indicted in Theft of GM Secrets," *USA Today* (December 11, 1996): 1.
14. "Industrial Security," *Security* (October 1996): 31.
15. Wallace, William Alvin, "Industrial Espionage Experts," downloaded 4/5/03, www.newhaven.edu/california/CJ625/p6.html.

16. Bernstein, David, "Pilfering Trade Secrets," *Infosecurity News* (May/June 1996): 23–25.

17. "Industrial Security," *Security* (October 1996): 31.

18. http://en.widipedia.org/wiki/Chi_Mak.

19. http://en.widipedia.org/wiki/Arms_Export_Control_Act.

20. www.fbi.gov/pressrel/speeches/gebhardt011204.htm, downloaded 7/15/2007.

21. Better Business Bureau.

22. Glasner, Joanna, "No More Music Piracy, *Por Favor*," *Wired News* (November 22, 2002), downloaded 4/5/03, www.wired.com/news/digiwood/0,1412,56522.00.html.

23. "Russia, China Once Again Top USTR List of Piracy Hot Spots," www.riaa.com/newsitem.php?news_year, downloaded 7/16/2007.

24. King, Brad, "Kazaa Taunts Record Biz: Catch Us," *Wired News* (September 25, 2002), downloaded 4/5/03, www.wired.com/news/mp3/0,1285,55356.00.html.

25. www.bosbbb.org/counterfeit/index/html, downloaded 7/16/2007.

26. Kamber, Mike, "Street Scene: Mexico's CD Pirates," *Wired News* (July 22, 2000), downloaded 4/5/03, www.wired.com/news/culture/0,1284,37482.00.html.

27. "Warning: Illegal copy of the medicinal product Cialis sold on the Internet," www.dkma.dk/visUKLSArtikel.asp?artike1ID=8728, downloaded 7/16/07.

28. "Hazardous Counterfeit Products," www.cbsnews.com/stories/2004/06/25/eveningnews/consumer/main626211.shtml.

29. Nystedt, Dan, "China and Russia Top List of Worst Copyright Violators," *InfoWorld*, www.infoworld.com/archives/article/07/02/12/HNwortcopyrightv, 2/13/2007.

Security: The Future

OBJECTIVES

The study of this chapter will enable you to:

1. Consider the future and what problems will dominate security.
2. Know what resources might be available to security operations over the next decade.
3. Discuss the relationship between public and private operations for the near future.
4. Understand the need for pandemic planning.

1 Introduction

As we enter the 21st century, most of the world is concerned about terrorism. In particular the United States and other developed nations have focused resources to wage war against terrorist organizations. While the federal government focuses on homeland security with the cooperation of state and local government, local communities must still contend with crime.

Despite the efforts of law enforcement agencies, community programs, and private security, the crime problem continues to be a major concern for most U.S. citizens. Today few would deny that the criminal justice system alone has not been effective in reducing crime. In addition, declining funding for public law enforcement, as funds are diverted to the war on terrorism, has forced most law enforcement administrators to cut back on services even in a time when the federal government is asking for more. Many such policies forbid law enforcement personnel from responding to or investigating certain types of crime. To fill this void, criminal justice administrators and scholars have called for greater involvement from the private sector. The "coproduction" of security resources by public law enforcement, private security, and citizens is necessary to reduce the fear of terrorism and crime. The private sector has responded willingly.

The overall perceptions of the terrorist threat and crime are important, but the economic impact on businesses is of greater significance to security management in the long run. Part of the problem stems from the nation's inability to find a set of accurate measures of criminal behavior. Not only has the problem of economic crime continued to grow in volume, but it has also become increasingly sophisticated, aided by the use of computers and electronic communications and transfer of funds. The recent insider trading and savings and loan scandals and major corporate failures as well as the growth of identity theft are indicators of problems yet to come.

2   The Aftermath of September 11, 2001

In January 2003 *Security Management* asked security managers, senior business executives, Wall Street analysts, and others for their perspective on how the events of September 11, 2001, had impacted security. In general, their report shows that security has become more visible in the business world. This is true not only in the corporate view of security but also in the security technology and services sector. According to a market report by Lehman Brothers, the global security industry "has moved from a peripheral activity to center stage."[1]

In a parallel study, conducted for the American Society for Industrial Security (ASIS) International by Westat, Inc., ASIS found that almost 75 percent of the security executives surveyed reported no changes in the structure of security within their companies. However, almost half reported an increase in budgets. The increased budgets did not result in additional staff in 66 percent of the organizations. Some of the increased budgets went to enhance security through new technologies, but most respondents did not place equipment at the top of their lists.[2]

Where was the money spent? For most companies, funds were used to either update or create security policies that addressed issues raised in the events of 9/11. Those firms with policies spent time dusting them off and reviewing them for currency. For others, policies were nonexistent and had to be created. Policy concerns focused on suspicious packages, bioterrorism scares, and access control issues, followed by technology.[3]

3   Private Security Resources

Growth in private security is shown by increases in expenditure, employment numbers, and value of equipment. In addition, many new firms have entered the business, established firms are showing strong growth, and some Fortune 500 companies as well as foreign firms are buying security firms.

In a time when public law enforcement is experiencing little or no growth, private security directors are experiencing greater demands on their resources. More than half of local and central station alarm firms reported annual budget increases. The private security industry will continue to grow.

To fill the gap left by public law enforcement and to help alleviate some of the public's fears, private sector security has offered its services in a variety of areas, including private patrols of residential areas, security for courtrooms and correctional facilities, traffic control, and so on.

The private sector has a tremendous impact on crime and the criminal justice system. Therefore, it is absolutely necessary to completely understand the private sector system. In the future the private sector will bear more of the burden for crime prevention and assets protection, while law enforcement will narrow the focus of police services to crime control. Most of the security managers surveyed by the researchers were willing to accept this growing role.

4 Interaction and Cooperation

Although *Hallcrest II,* in 1990, rated interaction and cooperation between the public and private sector as good, it also noted (as did the RAND report and the Private Security Advisory Council [PSAC]) that certain impediments to interaction and cooperation still existed. These impediments included role conflict, negative stereotypes, lack of mutual respect, and minimal knowledge on the part of law enforcement about private security. As we noted when these topics were discussed in earlier chapters, both private and public sector administrators are cooperating to try to overcome these problems.

We presented some discussion of these areas earlier in this text. The trend by the public sector to contract services or develop hybrid security operations, with greater cooperation between the public and private sectors, continues in the 21st century. According to the late Robert Trojanowicz:

> One question that need not be asked is whether the trend will persist. We are already too far down the road to turn back. Therefore, the ultimate question is not whether this change is good or bad, but whether these changes will occur piecemeal and poorly or thoughtfully and well.[4]

5 Limitations of Security

A great burden has been placed on the private sector, and some of the expectations will very likely not be met. It is impossible to be everything to everyone, especially in an area that is changing so rapidly.

Consider, for example, the changes in technology. Security's main purpose is to prevent losses, whether traditional, such as burglary; New Age, such as hacking and identity theft; or military, as in reduction of vulnerabilities to terrorist attacks. Historically, losses were reduced through the use of various physical security devices that served as delaying devices to would-be intruders. As the targets for theft changed, security modified its strategies and adopted new security technologies.

Today security in many companies is truly a full loss prevention operation, and within such operations, state-of-the-art security systems are coupled with traditional security methods. Integration of security systems with data processing and other company operations will become commonplace. As discussed earlier, the relationship between the chief security officer (CSO) and the chief information officer (CIO) will need to be reinforced and clearly defined.

How effective are security devices today? Security managers would be wise to remember that no system is completely effective. A determined person can find ingenious methods of defeating any system. For example, consider the progressive development of lock technology. It began with a simple doorknob lock with a spring latch. As we know today, this combination offers virtually no protection from a person who wants to gain entry. The simplest and least destructive method of gaining access would be to card the lock. If this option is removed by installing a dead latch, the intruder will have to choose another means of access. Since the latch does not extend more than half an inch into the doorframe, a burglar could spring the door or twist the doorknob off to gain access to the locking mechanism. Installing a good dead bolt lock may solve this problem.

Each step that security takes requires a burglar to use more time, but the burglar is still not stopped. The burglar chooses to either cut the dead bolt or twist the collar mechanism off the dead bolt lock. Security then responds by installing a dead bolt with a slip collar (or recessed system) and a dead bolt with a case-hardened core.

In most cases, if the door and frame are of solid construction (that is, metal), burglars will not attack them. But some might want company assets enough to find another method of entry. The keying device then becomes a target; key cores can be drilled or popped. Security managers who have been thinking ahead will purchase locks with case-hardened drill plates, which will foil both drilling and popping. However, there is still the chance of picking the lock. But security can anticipate this possibility and install a pick-resistant lock.

Has security now stopped the potential intruder? In reality most thieves would not bother to assault this level of protection; but if the target is sufficiently valuable, other alternatives exist. The thief's imagination is the only limiting factor.

With today's high-tech security devices and reliance on computers, a security manager can virtually eliminate any target's probability of being attacked. The modern age has brought Star Wars devices such as computer access-control systems based on fingerprints or voice identification, laser beam alarm systems and communication devices, and sophisticated listening devices and their counterparts, sweeping devices. Lighting technology has made it possible to illuminate areas to daylight levels with reduced costs. The list goes on, but the question remains: Why does crime continue to plague us?

The answer could lie in the fact that when thieves are sufficiently motivated, they will find a way. Or it may be because a security manager has failed to convince executives to pay for a security operation that appears to them to be an added expenditure that will not add to the profit margin. Return on investment (ROI) must become part of the vocabulary for the CSO.

High technology has made the operation of most businesses much easier. The photocopier, the fax, the computer, and 21st century communication devices make information transfer simpler and more efficient. This convenience has at the same time created new problems for security in the areas of increased information and physical security risks, as discussed in Chapter 18.

6   Trends

Although the security field is now composed of more than 1.1 million personnel, with the majority employed in contract security, the trend will continue toward fewer and smaller proprietary security operations. Firms will hire contract security or security consultants for special-purpose projects. Contract firms will continue to merge. As noted in earlier discussions, Securitas is now the largest contractor in the United States and continues to grow by buying other firms. Hybrid security operations will become commonplace.

The testing industry, geared to pre-employment, drug, and psychological testing, will continue to offer services sought after by the private sector. Advocates of privacy standards will continue to restrict the use of these types of tests.

The use of outside investigators and security specialists will increase. The trend will be toward a manager of security services using security consultants for special projects. More firms will follow the lead of Barton Protective Services in providing training for guards on the use of technology.

Liability costs, though remaining relatively high, will continue in the downward trend that began in 1986. The downward trend may be attributable to better prepared security managers who are learning the value of risk management.

Drug testing will continue to be a major issue for corporations. Until the nation is able to control the drug problem, this issue will remain an ethical as well as a legal problem for many firms. The cost associated with screening can be prohibitive, and though the public relations aspect of the EAP cannot be disputed, there are those who are now asking whether the company can afford to spend thousands of dollars on each employee who needs rehabilitation.

In addition to its role in fighting the increase of economic crime in general, security will continue to face an increase in computer and information related crime. As noted earlier in this text, estimates of the cost of computer crime range from $1 billion to $200 billion annually. On the international scale, there is more concern about security issues. The Common Market has mandated that security laws be reviewed and upgraded to bring commonality to the European Union.

Terrorism is currently the most talked about problem, especially for companies operating on an international scale. The terror of 9/11 made it clear that terrorism is truly global. The continuing attacks, such as the Madrid train bombing and the London bombings, keep terrorism in the news. The 1991 Gulf War caused a growth in concern among most multinational companies. Since 2003 the war with Iraq has also had its impact on money markets around the world. Companies can protect their assets from terrorists but have little control over the impact of nations' decisions in their efforts to control terrorist states. The key in planning antiterrorist security operations for the 21st century will be providing adequate protection without spending money for unnecessary security.

6.1 Integration Technology

Technology will continue to stress integration of computers and biometrics with CCTV and access controls. Telephone and wireless systems will be used increasingly to connect security systems and safety devices. Microprocessing chips dedicated to security purposes will be embedded in equipment, resulting in smart cameras and smart cards. The field of robotics will continue to grow, particularly in the area of corrections and guard operations within confined areas. Miniaturization is a trend. CCTV cameras the size of cigarette packages are already on the market. Electronic article surveillance (EAS) will continue to grow as prepared packaging becomes more prominent.

Still, integration of security technology is an evolutionary process rather than an event. Though the industry has come a long way from the independent systems of the early 1990s, consultants and other security practitioners continue to argue over the true extent that integration has arrived. Elliot Boxerbaum, CPP, president of Security/Risk Management Consultants, recently stated that "security [will become] just another piece of the puzzle, but at the same time its importance to the whole is increased."[5]

True integration creates a myriad of issues. First among these is the process of giving computer techies control over systems that were once the domain of security professionals. The real end result should be cooperation between the CIO and CSO. We'll have to wait for the results on this one!

7   The Future

A number of years ago, Ira Somerson, president of Loss Management Consultants, provided an excellent overview of the future in his article "The Next Generation." Security professionals must be futurists and ready to initiate and adapt to change based on the larger forces shaping the future. The following are the trends that Mr. Somerson noted. With the exception of downsizing, they are still true in 2008:

- Expansion of global markets and production will continue 24 hours per day across the globe.
- Multinational and multicultural workforces will be the norm.
- Downsizing will continue.
- Technology will move us into a "telehumanic age."
- Qualified workers will be difficult to find.
- Religious extremists will become more prevalent.
- Biotechnology will become a powerful force.
- Employee loyalty will continue to erode.[6]

The future for the security field is very positive. Professionalization is being pursued; large sums of money are being spent to improve security and loss prevention operations. For the first time since World War II, security has found its place in business. In addition, limitations of the criminal justice system have been identified, and the resultant void is being filled with some success by the private sector. The future in private security is exceptionally bright for the talented person who wants to do something special, especially if that person has had sound educational preparation.

7.1   Technology

The future for technological advances in security is also bright. In just 45 years, the security business has seen the arrival of CCTV, microwave detection systems, small portable radios and cameras, magnetic sensors, laser technology, and truly integrated computer and security systems. Security has taken advantage of these technological improvements through necessity—the realization that for every new piece of security equipment there is a person who, given the challenge, will find a way to subvert, bypass, or defeat it. Today's battles with criminals are far more often battles of intellect than they are of muscle. We may eventually see security measures such as force fields, holographic security officers, and laser pistols. The future is limited only by the security technician's imagination.

Combinations of biometric, electronic, and computer technologies will allow security and other management personnel to follow employees from the time they enter the facility until the time they leave it. Global positioning systems (GPS) are now available that will allow monitors to track vehicle position within yards on a geographic earth grid. The satellite technology that has made this possible also allows people with access to monitor activities across the globe.

By combining GPS and radio frequency identification (RFID) technologies, it is now possible for retailers to track merchandise in real time. Where is that shipment of Viagra? We can find out relatively easily. A "geofence" may also be created that would signal an alarm should a load deviate from a chosen route.

In the area of intellectual technology, the field continued its rocketlike growth from a $17 billion industry in 2001 to more than $45 billion in 2006. The strongest market will likely continue to be in security hardware and then software, with a 16 percent growth rate.[7] The demand for technology is the result of increased interest in integration of all security operating systems to include access control, surveillance, databases, GPS, and RFID technologies.

Guards equipped with wireless handheld terminals will be able to monitor surveillance cameras from remote locations, submit reports over WLANs, and access email and other data in real time. It is also likely that GPS technology will allow control centers to monitor guard locations for enhanced safety and accountability.

Managers equipped with similar technology will be able to provide real-time updates or alerts to officers in the field without radio broadcasts.[8] "Smart cameras" will replace traditional fixed CCTV and even today's state-of-the art integrated systems. These almost stand-alone cameras will not rely on hardwire systems or computer support to make adjustments. Rather, wireless technology coupled with memory chips will allow these cameras to make decisions based on preprogrammed scenarios and send information back to the central station or to remote computer receivers carried by security officers.

The issues associated with identity theft may remain, but with the increased use of "smart cards" in place of traditional credit/debit cards, credit card operations may no longer need to retain database information on customers. Removing critical information from customer databases will mean less critical information will be available to identity thieves.

WLANs may be improved through "mesh-networking." Both Microsoft and Intel are looking at ways to make the WLAN individual systems a coherent network. Issues include ways to provide proper security to wireless systems.[9] The introduction of the iPhone is just a first step in this process.

The future will also bring increased use of biometrics. Frost and Sullivan predict nonfingerprint biometric applications will increase from $66 million in 2000 to $900 million by 2006.[10]

7.2 Management

As Tom Peters notes in his writings, the manager of the future must be able to predict and manage change.[11] In fact, Peters would probably prefer the word "leader" to "manager." The security leader of the 21st century will need to be flexible. As Thomas Sege, chairman and CEO of Varian Research, notes, "You have to approach things much more flexibly. Change can come from all directions. You can't chart one course and hold to it. Course corrections are going to have to be made."[12]

All businesses will continue to stress the benefits of cost containment management. Profit margins must be improved, and security will be expected to offer its fair share (ROI). The security manager will thus become a security program educator and salesperson. Security managers must learn to sell security as though it were any other product. Because CEOs think in terms of profit, a good security manager must find ways of selling security as a cost-effective investment.

For example, perhaps better lighting is needed in a particular workplace. All the CEO sees is the cost for new lighting, but the security manager suggests it might reduce theft, vandalism, and accidents. Will possible savings in these areas offset the cost?

Probably not in the first year! But why not project the cost of the project over five or more years? Also consider the savings in electricity costs from installing more efficient fixtures and the possible reduction in insurance rates. Now the CEO is interested. All of a sudden the investment is at worst breaking even—and it might even save the company money. The bottom line will be more important than ever.

Security managers will find that safety, architecture, consulting and engineering, human resources, compliance, transportation, telecommunications, information processing, and marketing will demand more from the security operation and that to develop future-oriented security programs, they must take an interest in these areas.

The security manager of the future must carefully consider terms such as *integration, rightsizing, interfacing, hybrid security systems, ROI*, and *reengineering*. The current trend is toward downsizing and the increasing use of technology to replace or at least augment existing operations, but the future may go beyond this trend. Even as this book is being completed, more and more professional employees are completing their work assignments using technology from their home offices. From a security point of view these trends offer new opportunities as well as challenges.

7.3   Theft

The greatest threat for security managers will continue to be employee theft. Worker loyalty will decrease. Ethical issues will become important for security managers as they struggle to protect company information as well as physical property. Employee theft will continue to cost businesses about $40 billion annually. Worker gangs will conspire to steal and use company facilities and time to conduct their outside drug, money laundering, and mail fraud businesses.

7.4   Education and Professionalization

Experts predict that by the year 2020 the majority of new jobs will require postsecondary education. Yet today, 20 percent of the U.S. workforce reads at no better than an eighth-grade level. This means that unless something changes, the U.S. workers of the future will not be able to read basic materials necessary to perform at the required level. The staff at *Security* predicts that in the future, professional organizations representing security will approach colleges, universities, and community colleges and ask for help with programs that train security officers and security professionals.[13] ASIS has already moved in this direction with the development of master's level education through Webster University.

7.5   Renewed Emphasis on Counterfeiting

A 2007 study estimates that 30 out of every million $100 bills is a fake. The National Research Council believes that within the next 10 years, even low-skilled amateurs will be able to duplicate our current currency. They are recommending that the government incorporate complex starburst patterns that copies cannot duplicate. Other suggestions include inks that change color as they're exposed to various temperatures.[14] As noted in the previous chapter, counterfeiting of all types of products is big business. It is predicted that this illegal enterprise will continue to grow because it is generally much more profitable than dealing in drugs and much less risky.

7.6 Certification and Standards

The discussions presented earlier in this text point toward the need for some type of mandated minimum standards for the security industry. Recent developments led by ASIS point the way for some type of industry-imposed regulations similar to the British system. If security is to continue to take the place of law enforcement, the field must present a professional image. The image can exist only when outsiders can view the field with the respect that comes from established standards. The proliferation of certifications, if properly controlled, is a move in the right direction. Federal legislation mandating standards will hopefully lead to base-level standards for the security industry.

☐ ☐ ☐ ━━━━━━━━━━━━━━━━━━━━━━━━━━

Critical Thinking

Who should have the responsibility of maintaining an individual's security, the individual or the government? What are the consequences of deciding in favor of either option?

━━━━━━━━━━━━━━━━━━━━━━━━━━ ☐ ☐ ☐

Summary

As was stated in the seventh edition of this text, the future for security is bright. The more that education and training become a regular part of the security occupation, the greater the professional development of that occupation. It is obvious that the public cannot afford to pay for all the protection needed in our modern world. The only means of providing security as defined in Chapter 1 is through the use of private resources that keep the costs of products down and provide an environment wherein our free-enterprise system can prosper.

Current events have definitely changed the security landscape, but as we focus on the war on terrorism, the question that needs to be answered is, "How far will the American public let the federal government go in mandating security measures for the public's own good?" Years of private initiative in protecting one's own property are at stake. Only time will tell where the line will be drawn. As noted in Chapter 1, there are efforts to create federal identification databases on each person. Whether this goal will be accomplished is questionable. If it is achieved, how will it be controlled?

Review Questions

1. List several major trends for security in the 21st century. Explain their significance from a management perspective.
2. Explain the need for security managers to develop into educators and salespeople for security programs. Give an example of how you might present a security program to your CEO.
3. What role should security play in the prevention of terrorism in the 21st century?
4. What is the future of public/private cooperation in the 21st century?

References

1. Harowitz, Sherry, "The New Centurions," *Security Management* (January 2003): 52.
2. Ibid.
3. Anderson, Teresa, "A Year of Reassessment," *Security Management* (January 2003): 61–65.
4. Trojanowicz, Robert, "Public and Private Justice: Preparing for the 21st Century," *Criminal Justice Alumni Newsletter*, V(1) (Fall/Winter 1989): 2. Michigan State University.
5. Lasky, Steven, "The Age of Convergence," *Security Technology & Design* (March 2003): 6.
6. Somerson, Ira, "The Next Generation," *Security Management* (January 1995): 27–30.
7. "IT Security Market to Hit $45 Billion by 2006," *Security Beat* (February 25, 2003).
8. "Technology Training Boosts Level of Service for Barton," *Access Control & Security Systems* (January 2003): 18.
9. Jones, Mark, "Wireless Meshes with its Future," *Infoworld* (March 2003): 10.
10. Lasky, Steven, "... And the Winner Is," *Security Technology & Design* (November 2001): 4.
11. Peters, Tom, *Thriving on Chaos: A Handbook for a Management Revolution* (New York: Harper & Row Publishers, 1987).
12. "Exploring Security Trends," special report, *Security* (1989): 2.
13. Ibid., pp. 5–6.
14. www.whbf.com/Global/story.asp?S=6143306.

Appendix A
Security Journals, Magazines, and Newsletters

Access Control and Security Systems (monthly): www.securitysolutions.com
Beyond Computing (monthly)
Campus Law Enforcement Journal (bimonthly)
CIO: www.cio.com
CSO: www.csoonline.com
Economist: www.economist.com
Eweek: www.eweek.com
Federal Computer Week: www.fcw.com
Information Security Magazine
InfoWorld: www.infoworld.com
ISecurity: www.security.com.au/business
Journal of Economic Management: www.jecm.org
Journal of Healthcare Protection Management (three issues annually)
Library and Archival Security (quarterly)
Lipman Report (monthly)
LocksmithLedger (monthly): www.locksmithledger.com
Polygraph Journal (quarterly)
Protection of Assets Manual (monthly)
SCMagazine: www.scmagazine.com
Security Journal (quarterly)
Security Management: www.securitymanagement.com
Security Management Weekly
Security: www.securitymagazine.com
Security Products: www.secprodonline.com
Security Technology and Design: www.simon-net.com

Appendix B
World Wide Web Resources for Security Response

The following World Wide Web sites are useful resources for security professionals. The list is certainly not comprehensive, but it contains resources that the author has used on a regular basis. The list does not include online journals (see Appendix A). If readers believe there are other valuable sites, please contact the author via email at rjfish@macomb.com or via fax to Assets Protection Associates, Inc., (309) 837–4305.

www.aais.org	American Association of Insurance Services
www.abbott-langer.com	Abbot-Langer & Associates, Inc.
www.trucklinr.com	American Trucking Association
www.aic.gov.au	Australian Institute of Criminology
www.asisonline.org	American Society for Industrial Security
www.bls.gov	U.S. Department of Labor, Bureau of Labor Statistics
www.brookings.edu	Brookings Institution
www.cfenet.com	Association of Certified Fraud Examiners
www.fbi.gov	Federal Bureau of Investigation
www.iasir.org	International Association of Security & Investigative Regulators
www.theiacp.org	International Association of Chiefs of Police
www.ilj.org	Institute of Law and Justice
www.imra.org	International Mass Retail Association
janweb.icdi.wvu.edu	Jan, Office of Disability Employment Policy, U.S. Department of Labor
www.josephsoninstitute.org	Josephson Institute of Ethics
www.lexis-nexis.com	Lexis-Nexis
www.ojp.usdoj.gov/nij	National Institute of Justice
www.naaa.org	National Alarm Association of America
www.ncjrs.org	National Criminal Justice Reference Service
www.newslibrary.com	News Library
www.policefoundation.org	Police Foundation
www.state.gov	U.S. Department of State
www.usdoj.gov	U.S. Department of Justice
www.westpub.com	ThomsonWest Group

Appendix C
Security Licensing and Regulation Resources by State

The following is based on information from the International Association of Security and Investigative Regulators and the Detective Training Institute. Addresses and phone numbers for most states may be found on the International Association of Security Investigative Regulators Website at www.iasir.org/licensing.htm#.

Alabama	www.ador.state.al.us/licenses/sec093.html
Alaska	www.labor.state.ak.us/research/dio/fprvdet.htm
Arizona	www.dps.state.az.us/cjsd/licensingbureau/licensingbureau.htm
Arkansas	www.asp.state.ar.us/
California	www.dca.ca.gov/bsis/
Colorado	www.ppiac.org
Connecticut	www.state.ct.us/dps/SLFU/PrivateDetectivesHome.htm
Delaware	www.state.de.us/dsp/
District of Columbia	www.dc.gov/
Florida	http://licgweb.doacs.state.fl.us/
Georgia	www.sos.state.ga.us/plb/detective/default.htm
Hawaii	www.state.hi.us/dcca/pvi/areas_private_detective.html
Idaho	
Illinois	www.dpr.state.il.us/WH/dtct.asp
Indiana	www.in.gov/legislative/ic/code/title25/ar30/
Iowa	www.state.ia.us/government/dps/asd/piind.htm
Kansas	www.accesskansas.org/
Kentucky	www.state.ky.us/agencies/finance/occupations/privateinvestigators/
Louisiana	www.isbpie.com/
Maine	http://janus.state.me.us/legis/statutes/30/title32ch89sec0.html
Maryland	www.mdsp.maryland.gov/
Massachusetts	www.state.ma.us/MSP/Massachu.htm
Michigan	www.michigan.gov/cis/
Minnesota	www.dps.state.mn.us/pdb/

(*Continued*)

Mississippi	
Missouri	
Montana	www.discoveringmontana.com/dli/bsd/license/bsd_boards/psp_board/statutes.htm
Nebraska	www.sos.state.ne.us?Privatedetectives/pd.htm
Nevada	www.leg.state.nv.us/NAC/NAC-648.html
New Hampshire	www.state.nh.us/safety/nhsp/pluda.html
New Jersey	www.state.nj.us/lps/njsp/about/srb.html#pdu
New Mexico	www.rid.state.nm.us/b&c/pipolograph/index.htm
New York	www.dos.state.ny.us/lcns/pimain.html
North Carolina	www.jus.state.nc.us/pps/pps.htm
North Dakota	www.state.nd.us/pisb/index.html
Ohio	www.com.state.oh.us/odoc/real/pisgmain.htm
Oklahoma	www.cleet.state.ok.us/Private_Security.htm
Oregon	www.obi.state.or.us/
Pennsylvania	http://members.aol.com/Judiciary/22.html
Rhode Island	www.rilin.state.ri.us/Statutes/Title5/5-5/INDEX.HTM
South Carolina	www.sled.state.sc.us/SLED/default.asp?
South Dakota	
Tennessee	www.state.tn.us/commerce/sec-indust/PI&Poly/pi.htm
Texas	www.tcps.state.tx.us
Utah	www.le.state.ut.us/~code/TITLE53/53_09.htm
Vermont	http://vtprofessionals.org/opr1/investigators/
Virginia	www.dcjs.state.va.us/privatesecurity/
Washington	www.dol.wa.gov/ppu/pifront.htm
West Virginia	www.wvsos.com/licensing/piguard/main.htm
Wisconsin	www.dri.state.si.us/Regulation/applicant_information/dod124.htm
Wyoming	

Appendix D
Security surveys

Table D.1   Security Vulnerability Survey

Facility _____   Survey date _____

Address _____   Facility manager _____

                                             Telephone no. _____

1. GENERAL FUNCTION   Leased
                            Owned

_____

No. employees assnd. _____

Operating   Weekdays   Saturday   Sunday
Hours:

          Opens ____ Opens ___ Opens ____

          Closes ____ Closes ___ Closes ____

Address & phone of police jurisdiction: _____

Area evaluation:

_____

II. BUILDING & PERIMETER

_____ 1. Type of construction?

_____ 2. Door construction (hinges, hinge pins, solid core, etc.)?

_____ 3. Total number of perimeter entrances?

_____ 4. Are all exits & entrances supervised? If not, how controlled?

_____ 5. Are there perimeter fences?

        Type?

        Height?

        Distance from bldg.?

        Cleared areas?

        Barbed wire top?

        Roof or wall areas close to fence?

_____ 6. Are there any overpasses or subterranean passageways?

_____ 7. Height of windows from ground? Adequately protected?

_____ 8. Any roof openings or entries?

_____ 9. Any floor grates, ventilation openings?

_____ 10. Any materials stored outside bldg.? How controlled?

_____ 11. Adjacent occupancy?

        Comments:

III. VEHICULAR MOVEMENT

_____ 1. Is employee parking within perimeter fence?

_____ 2. Are cars parked abutting interior fences?

_____ 3. Are cars parked adjacent to loading docks, bldg. entrances, etc.?

_____ 4. Do employees have access to cars during work hours?

_____ 5. Vehicle passes or decals?

_____ 6. Are guards involved in traffic control?

        Comments:

IV. LIGHTING

_____ 1. Is perimeter lighting provided? Adequate?

_____ 2. Is there an emergency lighting system?

_____ 3. Are all doorways sufficiently lighted?

(Continued on next page.)

Table D.1   *(cont.)*

____ 4. Is lighting in use during all night hours?

____ 5. Is lighting directed toward perimeter?

____ 6. Is lighting adequate for parking area?

____ 7. How is lighting checked?

____ 8. Is interior night lighting adequate for surveillance by night guards (or by municipal law enforcement agents)?

____ 9. Are guard posts properly illuminated?

Comments:

V. LOCKING CONTROLS

____ 1. Does the facility have adequate control and records for all keys?

____ 2. Is a master key system in use?

____ 3. How many master keys are issued?

____ 4. Are all extra keys secured in a locked container?

____ 5. Total number of safes?

____ 6. Last time combination(s) changed?

____ 7. If combination is recorded, where is it stored?

____ 8. Total number of employees processing combination?

____ 9. Review procedures for securing sensitive items (i.e., monies, precious metals, high dollar value items, narcotics, etc.)?

____ 10. Who performs locksmithing function for the facility?

____ 11. Is a key inventory periodically taken?

____ 12. Are locks changed when keys are lost?

Comments:

VI. ALARMS

____ 1. Does the facility utilize any alarm devices?
Total number of alarms?

<u>Type</u> <u>Location</u> <u>Manufacturer</u> <u>Remarks</u>

____ 2. Are alarms of central station type connected to police department or outside guard service?

____ 3. Is authorization list or personnel authorized to "open & close" alarmed premise up to date?

____ 4. Are local alarms used on exit doors?

____ 5. Review procedure established on receipt of alarm?

____ 6. Is closed-circuit TV utilized?

Comments:

VII. GUARDS/SECURITY CONTROLS

____ 1. Is a guard service employed to protect this facility?
If yes. Name:____ No. of guards____
No. of posts____

____ 2. Are after hours security checks conducted to assure proper storage of classified reports, key controls, monies, checks, etc.?

____ 3. Is a property pass system utilized?

____ 4. Are items of company property clearly identified with a distinguishing mark that cannot be removed?

____ 5. Review guard patrols & frequency?

____ 6. Are yard areas and perimeter areas included in guard coverage?

____ 7. Are all guard tours recorded?

____ 8. Are package controls exercised re packages brought on or off premises?

____ 9. Does facility have written instructions for guards?

____ 10. What type of training do guards receive?

____ 11. Are personnel last leaving building charged with checking doors, windows, cabinets, etc.? Record or identity:

____ 12. Are adequate security procedures followed during lunch hours?
Comments:

VIII. EMPLOYEE AND VISITOR CONTROLS

____ 1. Is a daily visitors register maintained?

____ 2. Is there a control to prevent visitors from wandering in the plant?

____ 3. Do employees use identification badge?

____ 4. Are visitors issued identification passes?

____ 5. What type of visitors are on premises during down hours and weekends?

Table D.1 *(cont.)*

_____ 6. Does any company's employees other than _____ have access to facility?

<u>List Company Names</u>   <u>Type Service Performed</u>

_____ 7. Are controls over temporary help adequate?

Comments:

IX. PRODUCT CONTROLS (Skipping and Receiving)

_____ 1. Are all thefts or shortages or other possible problems (i.e., anonymous letters, crank calls, etc.) reported immediately?

_____ 2. Inspect and review controls for shipping area.

_____ 3. Inspect and review controls for receiving area.

_____ 4. Supervision in attendance at all times?

_____ 5. Are truck drivers allowed to wander about the area?

      Is there a waiting area segregrated from product area?
      Are there toilet facilities nearby?
      Water cooler?
      Pay telephone?

_____ 6. Are shipping or receiving doors used by employees to enter or leave facility?

_____ 7. What protection is afforded loaded trucks awaiting shipment?

_____ 8. Are all trailers secured by seals?

_____ 9. Are seal numbers checked for correctness against shipping papers? "In" and "Out"

_____ 10. Are kingpin locks utilized on trailers?

_____ 11. Is a separate storage location utilized for overages, shortages, damages?

_____ 12. Is parking (employees and visitor vehicles) prohibited from areas adjacent to loading docks or emergency exit doors?

_____ 13. Is any material stored in exterior of building? If so how protected?

_____ 14. Are trailers or shipments received after closing hours? If so how protected?

_____ 15. Are all loaded trucks or trailers parked within fenced area?

_____ 16. Review facility's product inventory control.

                 <u>Loss</u>   <u>Breakage</u>   <u>Returns</u>
Average
Monthly

_____ 17. Review controls over breakage.

Comments:

X. MONEY CONTROLS

_____ 1. How much cash is maintained on the premises?

_____ 2. What is the location and type of repository?

_____ 3. Review cashier function.

_____ 4. What protective measures are taken for money deliveries to facility?
        To bank?

_____ 5. If armored car service utilized, list name and address.

_____

_____ 6. Does facility have procedure to control cashing of personal checks?

_____ 7. Are checks immediately stamped with restricted endorsement?

_____ 8. Are employee payroll checks properly accounted for and stored in a locked container (including lunch hours) until distributed to the employee or his supervisor?

Comments:

XI. PROPRIETARY INFORMATION

_____ 1. What type of proprietary information is possessed at this facility?

_____ 2. How is it protected?

_____ 3. Is "_____Restricted" marking used?

_____ 4. Are safeguards followed for paper waste, its collection and destruction?

_____ 5. Are desk and cabinet tops cleared at end of day?

_____ 6. Is management aware of need for protecting proprietary information?

Comments:

(Continued on next page.)

Table D.1   *(cont.)*

XII. OTHER VULNERABILITIES

_____ 1. Trash pickups (hours of pickups, control of contractor, physical controls)?

_____ 2. Scrap operations (physical controls of material and area, control over scrap pickups, etc.)?

_____ 3. Other?

Comments:

XIII. PERSONNEL SECURITY

_____ 1. Are background investigations conducted on employees handling products?

Handling cash?

Engaged in other sensitive duties?

Supervisory position?

All employees?

_____ 2. If so, who conducts background investigation?

_____ 3. Are new employees given any security or other type of orientation?

_____ 4. Do newly hired employees execute a corporate briefing form for inclusion in their personnel file?

_____ 5. Are exit interviews conducted of terminating employees?

_____ 6. Is a program followed to ensure return of keys, credit cards, ID cards, manuals and other company property?

GENERAL COMMENTS

Source: Charles A. Sennewald, *Effective Security Management* (Los Angeles: Security World Publishing, 1978).

Table D.2   Small Store Security Survey

To illustrate how even small facilities can be big when it comes to loss prevention, the following store survey is a comprehensive example. It is formatted in a question and answer style.

SMALL BUSINESS SECURITY SURVEY
Name of Business:
Street Address of Business:
Manager's Name:
Business Phone:
Type of Goods and Services:

MANAGEMENT SECURITY

Employee Screening

	Yes No N/A	Comments
1. Previous employers		
a. Write them?	Yes No N/A	
b. Call on phone?	Yes No N/A	
c. Personal inquiry?	Yes No N/A	
2. Education		
a. Write them?	Yes No N/A	
b. Call on phone?	Yes No N/A	
c. Personal inquiry?	Yes No N/A	
3. Criminal history check (state and region)		
a. Is there a felony conviction record?	Yes No N/A	
4. Are personal references checked?	Yes No N/A	
5. Are Department of Motor Vehicles records checked?	Yes No N/A	

Table D.2   *(cont.)*

	Yes No N/A	Comments

Employee Awareness

6. Shoplifting
   a. Is there a shoplifting prevention program in place?   Yes No N/A
   b. Do employees know what to observe for?   Yes No N/A
   c. Do employees know what to do and what not to do around suspected shoplifters?   Yes No N/A
   d. Do you know if there are any community-sponsored programs relating to shoplifting?   Yes No N/A

7. Robbery
   a. Is a robbery prevention plan in place?   Yes No N/A
   b. Are employees trained if a robbery occurs?   Yes No N/A

8. Credit cards
   a. Are employees familiar with the different types of credit cards?   Yes No N/A
   b. Do employees know the proper identification needed for the use of credit cards?   Yes No N/A
   c. Do employees know what to do if confronted with fraudulent, altered, or stolen cards?   Yes No N/A

9. Are personal check procedures in place for cashing checks and verifying identification?   Yes No N/A

Employee Access Control

10. Is a key log maintained and are keys audited periodically?   Yes No N/A
11. Are keys turned in during extended absences?   Yes No N/A
12. Are keys retrieved when employees separate or are transferred?   Yes No N/A
13. When security is breached, are locks rekeyed?   Yes No N/A
14. Are locks rekeyed every 3 to 5 years regardless of known security violations?   Yes No N/A
15. Are keys marked "Do not duplicate?"   Yes No N/A
16. Is someone responsible for locking up premises and ensuring no security risks exist (open doors, windows, stay behinds)?   Yes No N/A

Cash and Deposit Controls

17. Is cash in registers kept to a minimum at all times?   Yes No N/A
18. Are robbery alarm actuators hidden from view?   Yes No N/A
19. When handling large sums of money, is more than one employee present at all times?   Yes No N/A
20. Are all checks, money orders, and traveler's checks stamped "for deposit only" immediately upon receipt?   Yes No N/A
21. Are all cash receipts deposited daily?   Yes No N/A
22. Is there an established routine for transportation of cash receipts to the bank to help deter a robbery?   Yes No N/A

Internal Controls

23. Are surprise audits or physical inventories conducted periodically?   Yes No N/A
24. Is valuable equipment marked with the store identification?   Yes No N/A
25. Is a record kept of serial numbers on valuable equipment?   Yes No N/A
26. Are cash registers emptied and left open after closing?   Yes No N/A
27. Are relations with the local police department maintained?   Yes No N/A

(Continued on next page.)

Table D.2   *(cont.)*

	Yes No N/A	Comments

Perimeter Doors

28. Are all unused doors secured? — Yes No N/A
29. Are doors of high quality and securely fastened in place? — Yes No N/A
30. If doors contain glass, do wire or bars protect them? — Yes No N/A
31. Are hinge pins protected so they cannot be pulled? — Yes No N/A
32. Is the latch bolt protected with a latch guard so that it cannot be pushed back, opened with a thin instrument, and/or pried? — Yes No N/A
33. Is the lock a double cylinder type? — Yes No N/A
34. Are the locks and door hardware in good working condition? — Yes No N/A
35. Are padlock hasps installed so that the screws cannot be removed? — Yes No N/A
36. Are the padlock hasps heavy duty enough? — Yes No N/A

Windows

37. Do heavy screens or bars protect easily accessible windows? — Yes No N/A
38. Are unused windows permanently closed? — Yes No N/A
39. Are bars or screens mounted securely? — Yes No N/A
40. Are window locks designed or located so they cannot be opened by just breaking the glass? — Yes No N/A
41. Are window displays avoided so as to not obstruct view into the store? — Yes No N/A
42. Are metal window grates padlocked across window displays used as protection? — Yes No N/A
43. Is all valuable merchandise removed from unprotected window displays at night? — Yes No N/A

Other Openings

44. Is there a lock on manholes, skylights, and roof hatches that give direct access to the building? — Yes No N/A
45. Are the sidewalk doors or grates securely in place so that the entire frame cannot be pried off? — Yes No N/A
46. Are accessible skylights protected by bars, screens, or intrusion alarm? — Yes No N/A
47. Are the roof doors in good condition and securely locked? — Yes No N/A
48. Are all air conditioning ducts, ventilation shafts, and fan openings protected against unauthorized entrance? — Yes No N/A
49. Are transoms properly locked or protected by bars or screens? — Yes No N/A
50. Do fire exits meet fire code for egress? — Yes No N/A

Safes

51. Is the safe designed for burglary protection as well as fire protection? — Yes No N/A
52. Is the safe located and well-lighted so that the police can view it from outside at night? — Yes No N/A
53. If there is a built-in vault, are the walls as well as the door secure? — Yes No N/A
54. Has the combination been changed if persons have separated and no longer need it? — Yes No N/A

Table D.2   *(cont.)*

	Yes No N/A	Comments

Lighting

55. Are all areas where an intrusion might occur lighted by street lights or the store's lights? — Yes No N/A

56. Are blind alleys, where a burglar might work unobserved, protected with adequate illumination? — Yes No N/A

57. Is the interior of the store lighted from rear to silhouette an intruder? — Yes No N/A

58. Are low-mounted lights free of being compromised by easily unscrewing a bulb, vandalism, etc.? — Yes No N/A

59. Is lighting adequate to allow a policeman, security officer, or passerby to readily detect an intruder attempting unauthorized entry? — Yes No N/A

60. Are lights controlled by automatic timer or manually operated? — Yes No N/A

61. If one exterior light goes out, will other existing lights compensate? — Yes No N/A

Alarms

62. Is there a protective alarm system for the premises? — Yes No N/A

63. To detect intrusion, is there an off-premises central station that sends an alarm to the police department? — Yes No N/A

64. To prevent burglary, is there a local alarm that rings into the premises to ward off intruders? — Yes No N/A

65. Is there a hold up alarm for robberies? — Yes No N/A

66. Are access points into the building (doors, windows, vents) protected by an alarm? — Yes No N/A

67. Is the alarm system maintained regularly to verify operating condition? — Yes No N/A

Fire Safety

68. Do local firefighters visit annually for inspections? — Yes No N/A

69. Are the type and number of fire extinguishers adequate? — Yes No N/A

70. Are extinguishers inspected monthly to verify they are in good working order? — Yes No N/A

71. Are all fire exits correctly marked? — Yes No N/A

72. Are all fire exits and extinguishers unobstructed? — Yes No N/A

73. If a sprinkler system is used, is it tested annually for effectiveness? — Yes No N/A

Source: Robert J. Fischer and Richard Janoski, Loss Prevention and Security Procedures (Boston: Butterworth-Heinemann, 2000).

Index